Principled Programming

Principled Programming

Introduction to Coding in Any Imperative Language

Tim Teitelbaum
Professor Emeritus
Department of Computer Science
Cornell University

DateTree Press
Ithaca

Principled Programming
Introduction to Coding in Any Imperative Language

DateTree Press / Ithaca, New York

First edition, 3/23/2023. Most recent revision, 11/19/2023.
Please send comments and corrections to Tim.Principled.Programming@gmail.com

ISBN: 979-8-9877441-0-9
Library of Congress Control Number: 2023902044

Photo Credits

Cover (front), Pascaline, https://en.wikipedia.org/wiki/Pascal%27s_calculator#/media/File:Pascaline-CnAM_823-1-IMG_1506-black.jpg, CC BY-SA 3.0 FR (by Rama).

Cover (back), Motorola MC68HC000LC8, https://commons.wikimedia.org/wiki/File:Motorola_MC68HC000LC8-2413.jpg, CC BY-SA 4.0 (by Raimond Spekking).

Page 57, *Puzzle,* https://freesvg.org, CC0 1.0.

Page 57, *Turtles,* https://en.wikipedia.org/wiki/Turtles_all_the_way_down#/media/File:River_terrapin.jpg, public domain.

Page 58, *Mona Lisa,* https://en.wikipedia.org/wiki/File:Mona_Lisa,_by_Leonardo_da_Vinci,_from_C2RMF_retouched.jpg, public domain.

Page 82, *Sierpiński Triangle,* https://en.wikipedia.org/wiki/Sierpi%C5%84ski_triangle#/media/File:Sierpinski_triangle.svg, CC BY-SA 3.0 (by Beojan Stanislaus).

Page 82, *Bracken Fern,* https://en.wikipedia.org/wiki/Fern#/media/File:Fern-leaf-oliv.jpg, CC BY-SA 3.0, (by Olegivvit).

Page 88, *Notes,* https://freesvg.org/, CC0 1.0.

Page 123, *Torus,* https://commons.wikimedia.org/wiki/File:Simple_torus_with_cycles.svg, CC BY-SA 3.0 (by Yassine Mrabet).

Page 153, *Playing Cards,* https://upload.wikimedia.org/wikipedia/commons/d/d5/Playing_card_heart_2.svg, and others, CC BY-SA 3.0 (by Cburnett).

Page 153, *Box,* https://freesvg.org/, CC0 1.0.

Page 361, *Daisies,* https://en.wikipedia.org/wiki/Leucanthemum, public domain.

Page 390, *USA,* https://freesvg.org/, CC0 1.0.

Preface

This book is an introduction to computer programming aimed at the level of a first college course. It is also suitable as a monograph for people beyond the introductory level who are unfamiliar with its methodological content.

A typical introductory programming textbook begins with the notions of *algorithm, program, computer, program execution, memory, input,* and *output.* The rest of the book presents a *programming language.* Each language feature is defined by its *syntax,* i.e., how to punctuate it, and its *semantics,* i.e., what the feature does during program execution. Small programs or program segments illustrate each feature and its utility. Because modern programming languages are large, such books are typically also large. Their organization tends toward completeness; they are broad, e.g., cover many features, and detailed, e.g., address many fine points of features. These books are intimidating in their length, but not in their depth.

Where in such *language-oriented* books are students explicitly instructed in how to program? Guidance and suggestions are scattered throughout the text, but are usually subordinate to the main chapter structure, e.g., the assignment statement, the **if**-statement, the output statement, etc. Illustrative examples are critical, but are usually presented as completed programs. The text typically explains how code works, but not how it was derived. *Programming,* the dynamic and synthetic activity of creating a program, often gets short shrift, as if you are supposed to learn how to do it by osmosis from staring at code samples. You can know a programming language thoroughly, but still not know how to program. Confronted with a programming problem, you may have no idea where to begin. Or worse, you may head off in the wrong direction, and soon find yourself mired in a morass from which the best path forward may be to back up and start all over again.

In contrast, this book is a *methodology-oriented* introduction to computer programming. Its subject is programming principles, not language features. To keep focus and avoid distraction, I limit myself to a minimal programming language, one so small that it can be said to be universal. Programming skill is measured by the ease with which you can turn a problem statement into a working program, not by the number of language features you know. The methodology presented is not specific to a particular language; rather, it applies to programming, in general.

The notation I use is essentially a small subset of Java, but I hasten to repeat: The book is about programming, not programming in Java. Appendix III Language Similarities provides mappings between this Java language subset and Python, C/C++, and JavaScript. For our purposes, these languages share a common core. In elementary physics, one doesn't start learning mechanics by studying one or another brand of springs and pulleys; rather, one learns Newton's Laws and how to apply them in arbitrary situations. Similarly, in this book, I eschew the study of any particular brand of programming language, opting instead to focus on fundamental laws formulated as rules of program composition.

The approach is distinctive in that it presents content to beginners that is often considered advanced. In particular, the following concepts are covered early, and are incorporated into the methodology: *States* described by diagrams or Boolean expressions, *specifications* written in terms of *preconditions* and *postconditions, loop invariants, data-structure invariants, loop variants,* and programming by *stepwise refinement.* Notwithstanding the subtlety of these ideas, I aim to retain the introductory character of the book—by avoiding formalism, offering intuitive analogies, and providing elementary explanations.

Any introduction to programming must deal with disparate student backgrounds. Those with significant prior exposure may be easily bored by a treatment that belabors what they already know. Such students are well-served by my focus on principles, and my deemphasis on programming-language details. Specifically, the programming notation I use (up until Chapter 18) is so limited that it is readily summarized, *in toto,* in Chapter 2 Prerequisites. For students with a modicum of background, this chapter will be a succinct refresher that firms up prior knowledge, provides standard vocabulary, and establishes a common baseline for the rest of the book. Students with no background whatsoever can learn the material from the chapter, but may wish to supplement it, e.g., with one of the many excellent and free resources on the Internet. Instructors may wish to offer a lecture, or a few recitation sections, to bring everyone up to speed.

A premise of this book is that much of programming can be reduced to a set of rules you can follow in cookbook fashion. The conceit is that programming can (almost) be algorithmic. You, the programmer, follow the rules, and out will pop a program. And not just any program, but a reasonably good program, at that. You play the role of a computer, and follow the *programming precepts* taught in the book. Your input data is a description of the problem for which a solution is desired, and your output is a program that solves the problem. The book chapters teach the precepts, and illustrate how they are applied. Some take a paragraph to explain; others whole chapters. The precepts are introduced and illustrated throughout the book; they are also listed in Appendix I as a convenient reference, and as a way to summarize one aspect of the book's contents.

Precepts are written as imperatives, albeit they are couched in equivocating phrases such as "seek", "consider", "if possible", "prefer", etc. to allow for the possibility that other (perhaps contradictory) precepts take precedence. Thus, I straddle the gap between the fiction that coding can be deterministic (just follow the rules) and the fiction that coding is pure design (inexplicable creativity).

One of my themes is the use of *programming patterns,* short fragments of code that perform frequently needed tasks. These patterns arise so often that they are best mastered as if they were primitives of the programming language. Patterns are introduced and discussed throughout the book. You are encouraged to learn each pattern so well that it becomes an atomic notion in your programming vocabulary. When, in the course of programming, you see the need to do something for which there is an established pattern, you should be able to recognize the pattern's applicability, and then immediately blast it into your program in one indivisible action. In the parlance of cognitive psychology, you should have *chunked* the pattern, and should no longer think of it in terms of its constituent parts. The programming patterns are listed in Appendix II.

The book's focus is synthesis, not analysis. Thus, no substantial code is presented as a *fait accompli* for interpretation. Rather, the essential content of the book is the stepwise development of solutions rather than the solutions *per se*. In cases where more than one approach comes to mind, each will be considered, explored, and evaluated. A few examples are consequential *algorithms*. My purpose, however, is instruction in programming, not algorithms. As such, although an example may have a well-deserved reputation and a noteworthy asymptotic running-time complexity, these will be incidental to its use in illustrating how you might develop the program yourself.

Code is presented in incremental steps displayed in numbered "movie" frames. That way, you are shown a recommended order of development, and not just the final program. Each coding "movie" starts with a specification in frame one, and ends with the finished product. Some motivating examples are sufficiently substantial to warrant chapters of their own. One of these, Running a Maze, serves in multiple chapters throughout the book. The final versions of three examples with long piecewise developments are presented whole in Appendices IV-VI.

The notions *encapsulation*, *information hiding*, and *modularity* are typically taught as an aspect of object-oriented programming, but can be addressed well before *objects*. They are introduced first at the level of statement-level specifications and implementations, and are subsequently reiterated using the easily-understood concept of a class's lexical scope—without reference to objects. In contrast, essentially all discussion of objects *per se* is deferred until the end of the book. This approach lets us focus on core programming skills, and avoids a plethora of distracting details (such as *object instantiation*, the *class hierarchy*, *inheritance*, *polymorphism*, and *dynamic method dispatch*) until they are finally introduced in the penultimate chapter. A benefit of this delay is that most of the book is truly language independent, even if Chapter 18 is not.

Much of the power of a modern programming language comes from libraries. If you plan to do any serious programming in a given language, you will surely want to master its libraries, and use them rather than "reinventing the wheel". Despite this important fact, for pedagogical purposes I focus on how to program in the base programming language, and largely ignore libraries. Although their use is minimized, libraries are far from forgotten. In fact, the text foreshadows the need for generic collections, and then implements the library class `ArrayList` as a motivating example in Chapter 18 Classes and Objects. Thus, you are led right to the pearly gates of libraries, armed with the ability to read and understand library interface specifications, and to use them to advantage.

I advocate a cautious approach to programming throughout the book, but mistakes are inevitable. Debugging code is like trying to find "a needle in a haystack", and the topic is not realistically discussed in the context of short program segments. Accordingly, the subject is deferred until the final chapter, where I deliberately introduce bugs into the largest program example of the book, and then discuss how to find them.

Language-oriented introductions to programming tend toward being encyclopedic tomes; in contrast, I have aimed for a comparatively short, coherent, and digestible book. I have aspired to tell a compelling story, knitted together by interesting, nontrivial examples that are woven throughout—a book that invites cover-to-cover reading.

The text is supplemented by Exercises in Appendix VII that give you the opportunity to test your knowledge. It is one thing to follow along and convince yourself (passively) that you understand material; it's quite another matter to confirm (actively) that you have really absorbed the message. Toward that end, you are encouraged to do as many exercises as possible. They are organized by chapter, so a reasonable approach is to turn to them after reading each chapter. Some exercises are direct applications of ideas presented in the text; others push the envelope on related topics, and in effect incorporate new material.

Many exercises call for writing programs. You are encouraged to not only solve these "on paper", but to test out your solutions on a computer. The BlueJ programming environment is recommended for this purpose [1], but any programming environment will do.

Keep in mind that the exercises are your opportunity to apply the book's principles. Don't just come up with correct solutions; rather, do so with conscious attention to the guidance being offered. One way to reinforce the material is to articulate explicitly the precept or pattern number you are applying on each coding step. My hope is that the methodology I'm advocating will eventually be second nature to you.

The Internet is an amazing resource that you can and should use to augment the text. You can find relevant articles on virtually every concept discussed in the book, and you are encouraged to Google for such supplemental material. Most of the book's literature citations refer to convenient online web pages rather than original primary sources; thus, they are only a click away. Enjoy the background provided by Wikipedia, but be sure to stop reading before its details overwhelm and discourage you.

The book's Index is rather thorough, and can be used in a manner akin to flashcards, e.g., if you have read the text up through page k, then you should understand each term in the index that refers to a page between 1 and k.

My aim in writing this book is your proficiency in programming. I wish you well.

Tim Teitelbaum
Ithaca, New York

Chapter Guide

The book is not long, and is intended to be read end-to-end and in order. Its apparent length is somewhat exaggerated by use of "movie frames" to make coding order explicit. This guide is offered for readers or instructors who wish to be selective.

Chapter 1 introduces the book and its pedagogical elements; Chapter 2 defines the programming notation used; and Chapters 3-5 present and illustrate the main methodological material. Key examples in Chapter 4 are mainly limited to scalar **int** variables, or to the use of abstract operations without their (array) implementations. Examples of Chapter 5 process linear sequences of input data on the fly, and therefore have no need for arrays (with one exception, the histogramming of values).

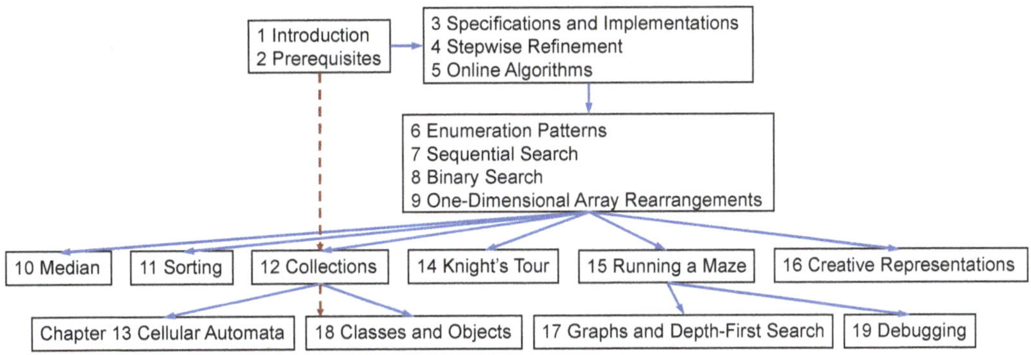

Chapter 6 discusses enumerations of integers and integer pairs; only one small example in the chapter uses a 2-D array. Chapters 7 through 9 focus on one-dimensional arrays, and illustrate their manipulations. The emphasis remains on the methodology of Chapters 3 and 4.

Each of Chapters 10-12 and 14-16 can stand on its own, or be omitted. The second half of Chapter 10 is advanced and may be skipped, but follows so naturally from earlier material that it has been included as a tasty treat.

Chapters 14 and 15 solve non-trivial applications from start to finish. The problem of Running a Maze is addressed in Chapters 1, 4, 15, 17, and 19, and thus those chapters make a coherent sequence.

Readers with sufficient background who are eager to get to object-oriented programming can make a bee-line directly from Chapter 2 to Chapters 12 and 18, and defer or skip all others. When back references are encountered, digress to the examples (in Chapter 6) that were bypassed.

Contents

CHAPTER 1

Introduction

You want to code, and toward that end have learned a bit of a programming language. But it is insufficient to only know the language; you need to know how to use it. Think of the language as a toolbox of constructs. You have a saw, screwdriver, and screws, and understand in principle what each does. But until you learn how to use the tools effectively, you are far from being a skilled carpenter. This book is about how to write programs once you know a programming language. We aim to replace *ad hoc* groping with principled methodology.

This chapter introduces key aspects of the methodology, which involves use of precepts, patterns, analysis, and a deliberative process. These generic concepts are illustrated by specific instances that are important in their own right, and reappear throughout the book. In the exposition, we use constructs of a near-universal programming language, which will serve as an initial introduction to the notation for some, and as a reminder for others. All are then combined in coding the complete solution to a simple programming problem.

Precepts

Programming precepts are rules for programming. A precept is "a command or principle intended especially as a general rule of action" [2], and this is what we want: A guide.

The first precept is self-referential:

☞ **Follow programming precepts.**

We aim for precepts that tell you what to do—rules that you can follow. This first rule is framed as an unequivocal statement, and suggests that the precepts are consistent and unambiguous.

The second precept dashes hope that precepts can be followed mechanically:

☞ **Ignore precepts, when appropriate.**

Thus, you should attempt to follow precepts, if at all possible, but may on occasion have considered reason not to do so. You will have to exercise judgment. Precepts are teachings, not ironclad diktats.

Regardless of whether you are following the first or second precept, you should program in a controlled manner:

☞ **Code with deliberation. Be mindful.**

At each step, aspire to knowing exactly what you are doing, and why you are doing it. This practice may take the form of a reference to the precept you are following, or one that you are choosing to ignore in favor of some other precept. The idea is not so much that precepts tell you unambiguously what to do, as that they provide a framework for addressing competing choices, and being self-aware.

Precepts will often come in contradictory pairs, as with the first two above. Ralph Waldo Emerson wrote: "A foolish consistency is the hobgoblin of little minds" [3]. Thus, though we may hope for rules that can be followed in cookbook style, we do not preclude giving conflicting advice.

For example, consider the standard coding practice concerning the choice of names. You learn early on that program variables have names, and that it is helpful for a name to be suggestive of the variable's purpose:

☞ **Aspire to making code self-documenting by choosing descriptive names.**

Using names like `price`, `quantity`, and `amount` is quite helpful for making a line of code like:

```
amount = price * quantity;
```

understandable and self-explanatory. The practice is strongly encouraged. But the precept has its limitations, and can easily lead to verbosity.

Consider, for example, a program that implements some board game. The program will be replete with references to the board and its coordinates. You don't really need long names for such frequently occurring variables. A line like:

```
piece = board[row+deltaRow[direction]][column+deltaColumn[direction]];
```

will be difficult to read and comprehend by virtue of the sheer number of characters in the text. Contrast its readability with:

```
piece = B[r+deltaR[d]][c+deltaC[d]];
```

in which you elect to use the first letters of some names, and prefixes of others. You trade the mnemonic value of full names for the benefit of brevity and succinctness. Repeated local reminders of purpose (the full names) are obviated by program-wide conventions (the abbreviated names).

The contravening precept is:

☞ **Use single-letter variable names when it makes code more understandable.**

This rule extends to other variables like `r`, `c`, and `d` the standard practice of using `i`, `j`, and `k` for indices. The choice of letters provides a hint of a mnemonic, which is enough to keep track of meaning.

It falls to you to decide which rule to follow in any given situation. In the face of competing precepts, the choice may not be cut and dried. There will be tradeoffs, and there will be room for personal taste. The important point is that you should make the choice with caution and deliberation:

> ☞ **Resolve contradictory precepts with care.**

A cautious approach to programming, one in which you follow precepts that advocate mindfulness and self-awareness, is reinforced by acceptance of the challenge facing you:

> ☞ **Be humble. Programming is hard and error prone. Respect it.**

You need all the help you can get, and precepts are offered in that vein.[1]

Notwithstanding the humility we advocate, you can and should still aim for perfection. Upon graduation from medical school, new doctors swear by the Hippocratic oath to "do no harm". You, too, can aspire to make no mistakes.

One form of harm in coding is premature commitment to a line of code or a data representation that you will later regret:

> ☞ **Aspire to coding it right the first time. Do no harm. Avoid writing code that must be redone.**

We shall call this careful approach "*Hippocratic coding*".

As you make your decisions, in an effort to avoid venturing in the wrong direction, consider the likelihood that what you are about to write might have to be undone. If the risk seems too great, seek an alternative.

The perfection you should aim for is not only in the quality of the finished product, but in the process that you follow in obtaining it, as well.

Patterns

One way to avoid mistakes and missteps is to choose a tried-and-true approach that you have learned from experience, or from a book. Many of these are framed as programming patterns, and form a companion to the precepts:

> ☞ **Master stylized code patterns, and use them.**

Patterns help guide your thoughts as you consider your way forward.[2]

Some patterns are architectural. They provide a framework with few constraints, and may subsume the very step you are considering. But rather than taking that step directly, the pattern provides a general characterization of an approach you can follow.

Imagine that you are confronted with a coding task that seems daunting, and you don't know where to begin. The *compute-use* pattern is often suggestive:[3]

```
/* Compute. */
/* Use. */
```

1. The precepts are listed in Appendix I, and are introduced throughout the book.
2. The patterns are listed in Appendix II, and are introduced throughout the book.
3. Patterns contain italicized placeholders e.g., `Compute` and `Use`, that are intended to be replaced by your application's specifics.

Rather than viewing what you were hoping to accomplish as a monolithic, indivisible goal, this pattern reminds you that you can structure your code as (first) the computation of some values in one or more variables, and (second) the use of those variables to accomplish your task.

This is a tiny suggestion, and may seem hardly worth writing explicitly. But for a novice, it may be the needed suggestion that breaks a seemingly-intractable challenge into more-manageable parts.

With experience, such architectural patterns become second nature, and you will find yourself using them without explicit mention. For example, you may immediately write:[4]

```
/* Let k be thus and such. */
if ( /* k has some desired property */ ) /* Do this and that. */
```

which is an instance of the compute-use pattern. Until an architectural pattern has been internalized, you may employ it explicitly as a crutch. This practice is an application of humility in programming, and recognition that you can benefit from such a device.[5]

Code patterns are useful compositions of programming primitives you already know in your programming language. You could, of course, re-derive a pattern by reconstructing it from its constituent parts, one-by-one. But it is far better to have mastered and internalized the pattern as a single conceptual unit.

Consider the pattern known as *one-dimensional indeterminate enumeration*:[6]

```
/* Enumerate from start. */
   int k = start;
   while ( condition ) k++;
```

which basically says: Using variable k, count up from *start* until *condition* is no longer **true**. If you recognize that a coding task fits this mold, you can blast this pattern into your program in one fell swoop. It is relevant whenever you need the smallest integer (greater than or equal to *start*) for which some property does not hold. Clearly, *condition* is a computation that depends on k. The *condition* is said to be "parametric in k", i.e., its value depends on the contents of variable k.

Patterns provide vocabulary that supports higher-level thinking. Consider any favorite verb or noun in English, and imagine it has been banned from your speech. You could, of course, do without the word, replacing each desired use with its definition. But you still know and think in terms of the banned word. This effect is what we wish to achieve with patterns. Pattern names, e.g., "compute-use" or "one-dimensional indeterminate enumeration", provide convenient handles for concepts. You may or may not remember the pattern's name. What's important is mastering the concept that it embodies, and having it available both mentally, and at your fingertips.

---

4. The first line of this code segment is called a "statement comment", and should not be viewed as commentary about the second line, but rather as an executable statement in its own right. Thus, the two lines are aligned one underneath the other. If a comment specifies subsequent code, that code will be indented beneath it. This indenting convention is discussed in Chapter 3 Specifications and Implementations.

5. The Compute-Use pattern is introduced here as an approach to overcoming a coding hurdle. In Chapter 4, however, we will see that it is a 2-step instance of a Sequential Refinement, one of the fundamental ways in which code is structured.

6. Patterns may contain specific variables, e.g., k, which you are free to replace with other variables.

Some patterns are specialized versions of more general patterns. Learn patterns in both their general form, and in their specialized instances. For example, the indeterminate-enumeration pattern can be seen as a restricted form of the fundamental *iterative-computation* pattern:

```
/* Initialize. */
while ( /* not finished */ ) {
   /* Compute. */
   /* Go on to next. */
   }
```

which basically says: To do something iteratively, first get ready (*Initialize*), and then (until *finished*) repeatedly do it (*Compute*) and get ready for the next time (*Go on to next*).

The general iterative-computation pattern is so important that a dedicated shorthand is defined for it:

```
for ( initialize; condition; go-on-to-next ) compute
```

But this is an abbreviation, and is essentially equivalent to the iterative-computation pattern that defines it.

Notwithstanding the generality of **for**-statements, they are typically reserved for *determinate-enumeration*, i.e., a pattern such as one of these:

```
for (int k=start; k<limit; k++) compute
for (int k=start; k<=limit; k++) compute
for (int k=start; k>limit; k--) compute
for (int k=start; k>=limit; k--) compute
```

We use such a pattern when we know the number of times a *compute* step must be executed: We count up (or down) in a variable, and perform the computation that many times.

The use of **for**-statements for only determinate enumeration is a convention of the programming community, and is one that we will follow, i.e., one could write the indeterminate-enumeration pattern as:

```
for (int k = start; condition; k++);
```

but we will never do so. Rather, we choose to let the keyword **for** be a signpost that indicates the presence of a determinate enumeration.

Analysis

Use of patterns is but one way to do Hippocratic coding; another is *analysis*. In short, don't be too quick to write code:

☞ **Analyze first.**

Given a program to write, where should you begin, and how might you structure your thinking? What issues matter, and which are inessential details? What are strategic considerations, and which are tactical matters for later consideration? What about the problem is required, and what is left unsaid, and is therefore discretionary and can be decided later?

Problem

Surely, the first step is to:

☞ **Make sure you understand the problem.**

Arguably, you don't fully understand a problem until you are finished writing the program, but early in-depth engagement with the problem's requirements will help you to avoid rework later.

The problem of Running a Maze, which is used throughout the text, is introduced here as an example:

> **Background.** Define a maze to be a square two-dimensional grid of cells separated (or not) from adjacent cells by walls. One can move between adjacent cells if and only if no wall divides them. A solid wall surrounds the entire grid of cells, so there is no escape from the maze.
>
> **Problem Statement.** Write a program that inputs a maze, and outputs a direct path from the upper-left cell to the lower-right cell if such a path exists, or outputs "Unreachable" otherwise. A path is direct if it never visits any cell more than once.

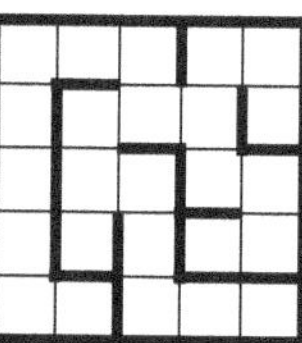

Although the problem statement is reasonably well specified, an early probing of the setup is still in order. Here are some questions you might ask yourself:

- Do I understand the nouns: *maze, grid, cell, wall, path,* and *direct path*?
- Do I understand the verbs: Specifically, how does one *move* between cells?
- How is a maze represented in the input?
- Is there any upper limit on the size of a maze? Is there a lower limit?
- What is the expected program behavior if the input is not well-formed?
- Is a *direct* path the same as a *shortest* path?
- What if there is more than one direct path?
- How is a path to be displayed in the output?

Posing such questions, and answering them, is a worthy first step.

Problem descriptions can be volatile, and one little word can make all the difference. For example, suppose the requirement were to output a *most* direct path? A correct choice of algorithm will depend on whether "most direct" means "shortest", and neglecting to consider that question initially risks setting off in an entirely wrong direction.

One way to test your understanding of the problem is to make up sample input, and solve it by hand. You can often come up with an answer intuitively even though you may never have seen the description of a systematic method for doing so. As you work the problem by hand, you are effectively following the steps of a program that you somehow already know, perhaps only subconsciously. The exercise both firms up your understanding and begins the process of programming:

☞ **Seek algorithmic inspiration from experience. Hand-simulate an algorithm that is in your "wetware". Be introspective. Ask yourself: What am I doing?**

Architecture

The analyze-first precept advocates that you defer writing code while digesting the problem. Nonetheless, an early idea of the likely architecture of the entire program is useful for framing your subsequent analysis. What are some possibilities for the top-level program structure?

- *Online computation* performs on-the-fly processing of input data items. A sample problem whose solution has this form is: Read an unbounded list of integers, and say whether each is prime or composite. A maze is a list of cells, but there isn't much that can be done with a single cell other than store it in a program variable for later processing. This pattern isn't a good fit.
- *Offline computation* (first) inputs data into program variables, (second) performs a computation, and (third) outputs an answer. This pattern seems perfect.

We can decide up front to adopt the offline-computation architecture without fear of doing harm because it is unlikely to need undoing.

The *offline-computation* pattern is:

```
/* Input. */
/* Compute. */
/* Output. */
```

which can be used as a scaffolding for restating and fleshing out the problem specification:[7]

```
/* Input a maze of arbitrary size, or output "malformed input" and stop if the
   input is improper. Input format: TBD. */
/* Compute a direct path through the maze, if one exists. */
/* Output the direct path found, or "unreachable" if there is none. Output
   format: TBD. */
```

The elaborated pattern is essentially a structured reiteration of the problem statement, with some additional details spelled out, and some explicit indications of what decisions are being deferred.

The architecture gives us the overall form of the program we will write.

Data

Programs are instructions for manipulating values, where *instructions* are code, and *values* are data. Analysis of a problem must address both code and data, and neither consideration should get very far ahead of the other. You should:

☞ Dovetail thinking about code and data.

We alternate between the two consideration because each informs the other. We have articulated an architecture, which has slightly advanced our thinking about the structure of the code; we balance that now by reflecting on the data.

The top-level architecture has brought into focus three principal computational steps that will need to work in concert: Input, Compute and Output. It is critical to:

☞ Specify how individual program steps will cooperate with one another.

The data are the glue that binds the steps together, and allows them to achieve their

7. We introduce here the presentation device of using red to highlight a change from a previous version of code.

common goal. It is important to have this *data flow* in mind as we proceed through our analysis.

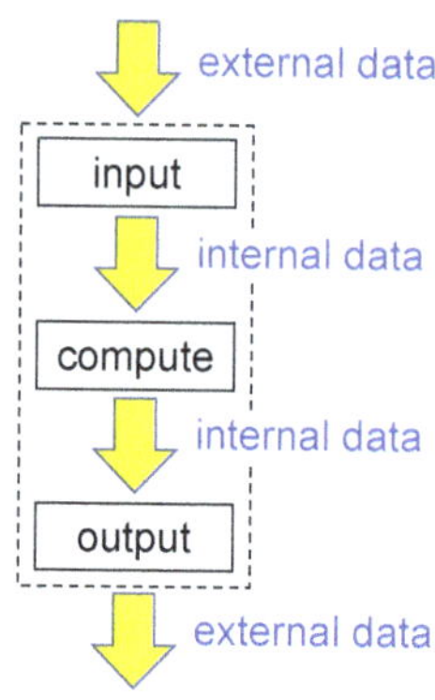

One distinguishes between *external* data, i.e., the values a program inhales and exhales as input and output, and *internal* data, i.e., the values of program variables that flow between programs steps. Clearly, a maze flows into the program, and a path (and possible error indications) flow out from the program. Similarly, a maze flows from Input to Compute, and a path flows from Compute to Output.

Typically, the critical part of a program is its Compute step, and the Input and Output steps are of secondary importance. If a problem statement leaves the external data representations unspecified, as in the present case, we will have latitude to design it to fit our convenience after the internal representation has been established.

In contrast with the external data representation, the internal data representation is of primary importance because it is the critical fabric that connects program parts:

☞ **A program's internal data representation is central to the code; consider it early.**

Finding a good internal data representation can simplify code; conversely, selecting a poor representation can introduce needless obstacles.

To begin an analysis aimed at choosing an internal data representation, start by asking: What will the algorithm need that must be represented in program variables? The answer typically includes nouns of the problem statement. In this case, we must represent the maze and its constituent parts (cells and walls), and a path (and its constituent steps). The nouns of a problem description usually name *passive* entities. In contrast, the verbs of a problem description name *active* aspects. They name procedures that modify the representation dynamically, and functions that query its current state after such modifications. For example, whereas the maze is an unchanging value, movement in the maze is a dynamic notion that modifies the path.

Components

You can't decide what operations to provide in a vacuum. Rather, you need to understand the interplay between the operations and the application that will use them. This mutual dependence is why we advocate dovetailing consideration of code and data. The precise choice of queries and actions is not rigidly fixed, and is up for negotiation. Ask: What is *needed* by the maze-running algorithm, and what can be *offered* by the data representation? Think of the data representation as a *service*, and the algorithm as a *client*. Together, they are going to interact, but each must accommodate the other: The data must offer operations to the client that are sufficient for the client to navigate the maze, but the client must limit its demands to operations the service can reasonably provide. You, the programmer, play both client and server in this negotiation.

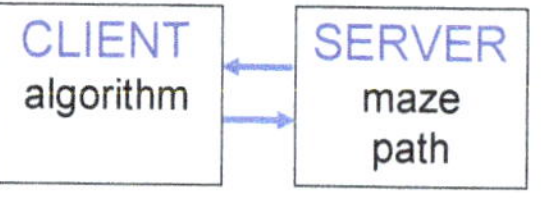

A data representation that changes in response to client actions encodes *state*. The maze-running algorithm is an *actor* that computes its way toward a solution, and records its progress by invoking operations that update the state. You can think of the last cell of a path as the location of the actor that is attempting to extend the path (if possible) or retract it (if necessary).

The idea of an algorithm as actor is a bit abstract. You may find it helpful to introduce (for conceptual purposes) an animate actor, say, a *rat* sniffing its way through the maze. With a rat in hand, our task becomes more concrete: We are coding the rat's algorithm.

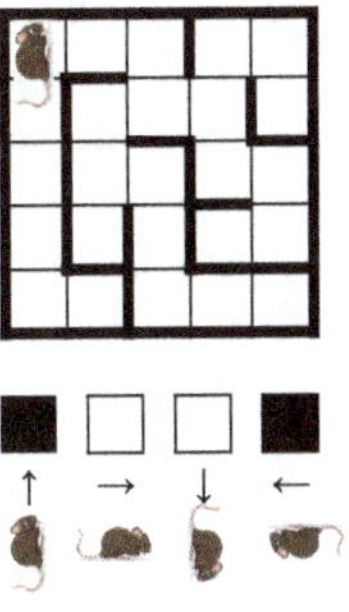

It is noteworthy that introducing a rat changes the nature of the client/server interface. Whereas an abstract maze-running algorithm might have embraced an omniscient point of view, looking down on the maze from the sky above, with the client a rat, the algorithm can adopt a rodent's more limited perspective. The rat doesn't really know where it is, or in what absolute direction it is facing. When the rat is in the upper-left cell of the given maze, it only sees a wall (when it faces up or left) or a non-wall (when it faces right or down).

An algorithm articulated from the rat's point of view can be localized and oblivious to coordinates that describe the rat's absolute position and absolute orientation in space. These can then be hidden inside the service that is being provided by the data component, which strongly influences the nature of the queries and actions flowing between the client and server. This is known as *data* and *information hiding*, which practice strongly influences the *modularity* of code.

Our purpose is not to solve the entire problem here; rather, our goal has been to illustrate the use of precepts and patterns, and the role of program analysis early on in development. Thus, we leave off further discussion of mazes, for now.[8]

Problem Transformation and Reduction

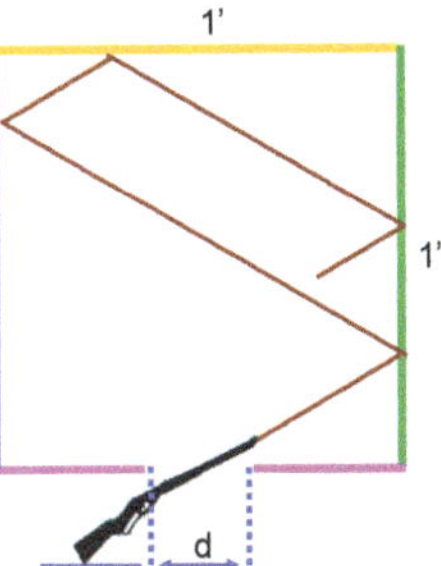

Our next example, the Ricocheting Bee-Bee problem, illustrates the potential of analysis at a higher level than code and data. It involves the representation of the problem itself.

> **Background.** A square tin box measuring one foot on each side has a slit of size d centered on one side. Insert a bee-bee gun at the center of the slit at angle Θ, and shoot. The bee-bee ricochets off sides, one after another. On each ricochet, the angle of reflection is equal to the angle of incidence.
>
> **Problem Statement.** Write a program that inputs d and Θ, and outputs the total distance the bee-bee travels before it exits.

A direct iterative solution that simulates the successive legs of the bee-bee's trajectory may be excruciating to write, and you may regret starting to code too hastily. So, take a deep breath, and think hard. Might the problem be amenable to simplification? Rather than a frontal attack:

> ☞ **Consider problem transformation or problem reduction: Solve a different problem, and use that solution to solve the original problem.**

This rule calls for innovation, invention, and even inspiration. But to ignore the possibility of problem reduction risks consigning yourself to a potentially laborious and painful coding effort.

A common way to simplify a problem is to reduce it to a known problem (and its solution) in Mathematics:

> ☞ **Sometimes iteration is unnecessary because a closed-form solution is available.**

Said another way: Don't let a problem statement that suggests iteration lead you down the garden path toward an avoidable, brute-force approach.

---

8. We return to the maze-running problem in Chapter 4 Stepwise Refinement, again in Chapter 15 Running a Maze, again in Chapter 17 Graphs and Depth-First Search, and finally in Chapter 19 Debugging.

Consider this problem:

```
/* Output the sum of 1 through n. */
```

with its knee-jerk, brute-force coding solution:

```
/* Output the sum of 1 through n. */
   int sum = 0;
   for (int k=1; k<=n; k++) sum = sum + k;
   System.out.println( sum );
```

In the famous anecdote about attempting to discipline schoolboy Carl Frederich Gauss, a teacher assigned Carl the time-consuming task of adding the integers from 1 to 100. But to the teacher's surprise, the future Prince of Mathematicians immediately answered 5050 because he analyzed the problem [4].

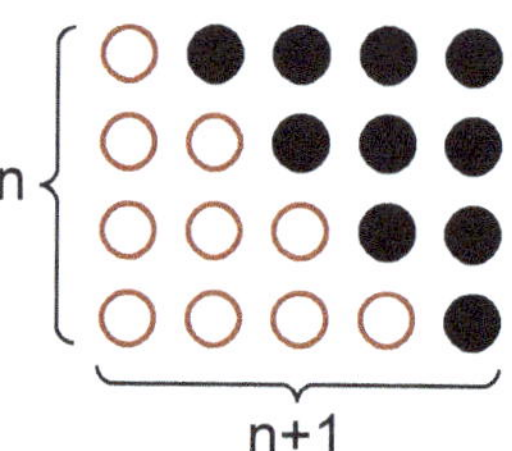

You, too, can perform the analysis and write the one-liner:

```
/* Output the sum of 1 through n. */
   System.out.println( n*(n+1)/2 );
```

The Gauss story serves as a reminder to look for simplifications before you code.

An important source of inspiration is analogy. The Ricocheting Bee-Bee problem calls for summing the lengths of a list of line segments, so we ask: What other problem is framed similarly? Answer: Computing *arc length* in calculus.[9]

Say you are given a function $y=f(x)$, and seek s, the length of the path along f between $x=a$ to $x=b$. You can slice f between a and b into n pieces, and approximate s as the sum of the lengths of the chords. The n chords are akin to the n separate zig-zag legs of the bee-bee's trajectory, and the goal is the same, the sum of the lengths of the segments, a process known as *numerical integration*. The similarity between the two problems seems auspicious.

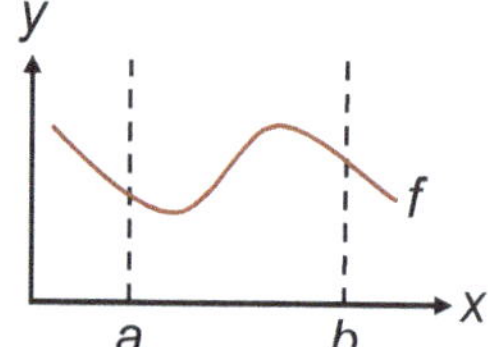

In calculus, you learn that as n gets bigger the approximation to s gets better. In the limit, as n gets arbitrarily large, the arc length along f from a to b is given by the integral shown at the right.

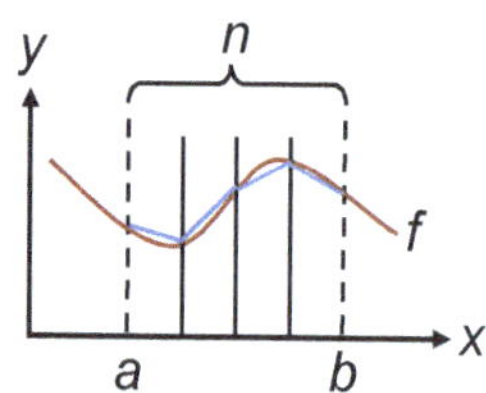

You also learn that for some f this integral can be solved in closed form, i.e., rather than computing s iteratively by numerical integration, you can obtain it by plugging the values of a and b into some formula. The possibility of a closed-form solution for the integral depends on the idea that as n gets larger, the line segments get shorter, and the piecewise-linear approximation to f improves. If f is a smooth function, we can then hope that the sum of the segment path lengths will converge to some simple formula.

$$s = \int_a^b \sqrt{1 + \left(\frac{dy}{dx}\right)^2}\, dx$$

Wouldn't that be wonderful: A single formula that expresses the total path length of the bee-bee in terms of d and Θ instead of the contortions involved in determining the lengths of each trajectory segment, and summing them up.

Analogies are inexact; in fact, that's what makes them analogies and not the problem itself. The value of an analogy is that it may suggest a fresh way to look at a problem. So, let's compare the calculus and Bee-Bee problems, and see if we gain insight from the analogy:

- In the calculus problem, the curve whose length we want to compute is given by a fixed function f, and is defined as the limit of piecewise-linear approximations to that length as the number of pieces grows without bound. A closed-form

9. In calculus, one typically first learns about determining the area under a curve, and later learns about determining the arc length of the curve itself [5].

solution can (in some cases) be determined by manipulating the formula for the curve *f*.

- In the Bee-Bee problem, the length we want to compute is the end-to-end length of a fixed sequence of connected line segments that are determined by d and Θ. No specific function *f* is given, but the segments can be thought of as chords of many such functions.

How can we reconcile these disparate points of view? By finding a related problem, one whose solution is the same as that of the Bee-Bee problem, but where the two points of view are not different. That transformed problem would be one that would be easier to solve. In seeking such a transformation, we notice that if *f* were a straight line, the zig-zag line segments would necessarily align with *f* exactly.

We have seen that one resource for problem reduction is mathematics; another is physics. Sometimes, problem analysis leads to an analogous physical apparatus, and to a question in that transformed domain whose answer is applicable. The analogy with integration in calculus suggests that we might benefit from a changed point of view in which a zig-zag trajectory becomes a straight line. In the physical domain, we can ask a related question: What if the box were made of paper, not tin?[10]

As with Running a Maze, it is not our purpose to solve the entire Ricocheting Bee-Bee problem here, so we move on to other considerations.[11]

Process

The goal of Hippocratic coding is aspirational: Get it right the first time. But we should be realistic: We will sometimes get it wrong, and require undoing work. Such realism is expressed by:

> ☞ **Don't be wedded to code. Revise and rewrite when you discover a better way.**

In fact, the only thing worse than having beaten a path in the wrong direction is soldiering on in that ill-advised direction, digging yourself deeper and deeper into a hole. Chalk it up as an exploration from which you have learned something, and start over.

Writers of prose are sometimes advised to compose a first draft, which is a tacit acceptance of the inevitability of writing a second draft. This practice is not recommended for programs, which have an exacting correctness requirement, not to mention a tool for validating solutions, i.e., a computer with which code can be tested.

Littering your program with inaccuracies leads to debugging, i.e., the need to track down errors, but you should:

> ☞ **Avoid debugging like the plague.**

It can be very painful and demoralizing. Furthermore, it tends to reduce you to a worm's-eye way of thinking about programming, as you trace execution one step at a time, inspecting the values of variables in a computer-like manner, with your nose pressed to the screen.

---

10. Examples of problem reduction appear in Chapter 4 Stepwise Refinement (p. 69), Chapter 16 Creative Representations (p. 282), and Chapter 17 Graphs and Depth-First Search.
11. It is solved in Chapter 16 Creative Representations (p. 282).

Rather than giving in to the idea of first and second drafts, it is better to:

☞ **Never be (very) lost. Don't stray far from a correct (albeit, partial) program.**

There are effective techniques that allow you to write and test small amounts of code at a time, and these are recommended. To state the precept differently: Maintain end-to-end correctness. This development approach involves finding ways to relax the notion of a full solution so that partial (albeit, end-to-end) solutions are testable. To do so, you identify a series of testable versions that converge to the final program.

One approach to staying in control omits whole steps, working on one component at a time, e.g., in Running a Maze, skip the Input and Output steps, and focus on the Compute step, manually hard coding the internal data representation of test cases, as needed.

Another approach omits a program requirement, e.g., in Running a Maze, find *any* path, and don't require that it be *direct*. But simplification will only be helpful if you have reason to believe that you will be able to add back the omitted requirement later, building on the partial solution you develop. You need to acquire a nose for sensing when omitting a requirement introduces a discontinuity that renders a solution for the simplified problem irrelevant, e.g., if the maze problem were to require finding a *shortest* path, then a solution that only finds paths connected to the perimeter of the maze is likely to be useless.

A key objective in the programming process is to be able to:

☞ **Test programs incrementally.**

That way, if and when something goes wrong, you will not have far to look for the cause because little will have changed in your code since the last time nothing was wrong. You may wish to retain the infrastructure written during incremental development for possible future use, or may wish to discard it when the program is complete.

Incremental testing does not mean that you should give in to the temptation to test half-baked work. First, keep your trigger finger off the "execute button", and think deeply about your work product. Then, experience the delight of finally running your code, and having it work correctly the first time.

Example

To recap the chapter, and illustrate some of the espoused principles, we develop code to compute the integer part of the square root of a given integer:[12]

```
/* Given n≥0, output the Integer Square Root of n. */
```
1

Although an implementation of Integer Square Root is only a few lines long, it is sufficiently subtle to benefit from a principled process. Of course, we could present the code, and explain how it works. But that would be antithetical to our goal: Teaching how to program.

12. Code developments are presented as a series of numbered snapshots. They are a "movie" that shows the literal, recommended coding order. Do not view the sequence of frames as a mere expository textbook convention for explaining code. Rather, the sequence is the order in which we suggest that the code should be written.

Similarly, we forgo a solution that uses the Math library:

```
/* Given n≥0, output the Integer Square Root of n. */
   System.out.println( Math.floor( Math.sqrt(n) ) );
```

because it would trivialize the problem, and deprive us of a useful example that demonstrates principles.

First, we make sure we understand the problem. The phrase "Given integer n≥0" means that a variable named n already contains the nonnegative integer in question. No input statement is required. It is not our concern where n came from, and how it got there. It is not our concern what n represents. The problem statement requires that we compute a value in terms of n, and output it. The code should work in any context in which a variable n exists and contains a value.

Because it is unlikely that without the aid of library functions the integer part of the square root of n can be described in a single expression whose value we can output, we will need to first compute it in a separate step, and then output it. Accordingly, we adopt the compute-use pattern:

```
/* Compute. */
/* Use. */
```

where Compute figures out what to print, and Use prints it.

The two steps must communicate with one another, and can do so via a variable. The name "r", suggestive of "root", is chosen for that variable. Thus, we refine the top-level specification of the Integer Square Root problem as two sub-steps:

2

```
/* Given n≥0, output the Integer Square Root of n. */
   /* Let r be the integer part of the square root of n≥0. */
   System.out.println( r );
```

where the second sub-step prints whatever value the first sub-step stores in r.

We now zoom in on the first sub-step:

```
/* Let r be the integer part of the square root of n≥0. */
```

and work on it in isolation. When working on a subproblem, we disregard the surrounding context, as if we were wearing blinders. It is not our concern that some other part of the code, e.g., the very next line, intends to print the contents of variable r. We only need to focus on setting the variable appropriately, i.e., as per the subproblem specification.

We may not yet know exactly how to compute r, but one thing is clear: Because n is not bounded, if we are not using a library routine or powerful arithmetic operation that subsumes an unbounded number of computational operations, our own code will need to perform those steps.

One mechanism for expressing an unbounded number of computation steps in a small, finite number of lines of code is iteration. The highfalutin precept might be: When you sense the opportunity for iteration, give it serious consideration. We prefer the more down to earth:

☞ **If you "smell a loop", write it down.**

Merely writing down a template for iteration makes consequential progress because it establishes a framework for thinking about what, exactly, needs to be done repetitively, and for how long.

The opportunity for iteration is often obvious. However, there are two forms of iteration, and before blasting in code you should think carefully about which form is appropriate for the case in hand:

> ☞ **Decide first whether an iteration is indeterminate (use while) or determinate (use for).**

The number of times an *indeterminate iteration* repeats is not knowable in advance; it will be discovered in the course of the computation. In contrast, the number of times a *determinate iteration* repeats is knowable from the get-go, either as some constant, or as the value of an arithmetic expression that can be written in terms of program variables.

Adhere to the admonition:

> ☞ **Beware of for-loop abuse; if in doubt, err in favor of while.**

and be cautious, systematic, and analytical in your choice of iteration construct. Specifically, don't be too quick to write the iteration using a **for**-statement, which deceptively seems all-powerful:

```
/* Let r be the integer part of the square root of n≥0. */
   for (int r=0; r<=n; r++) _______
```

The **for**-statement shown, on its face, announces your intention to consider *all* integers between 0 and n. The idea of iterating through the integers one-by-one has merit. However, we don't want to consider each and every one of them up through n. Rather, we are looking for the *smallest* integer with a certain property, and want to stop when we find it. This requirement is best provided by the one-dimensional indeterminate-enumeration pattern:

```
int r = 0;
while ( condition ) r++;
```

which is a search for the smallest nonnegative r for which *condition* is **false**. We don't yet know what that *condition* should be, but this pattern fits the bill. We drop it into place:

```
/* Given n≥0, output the Integer Square Root of n. */                3
   /* Let r be the integer part of the square root of n≥0. */
      int r = 0;
      while ( condition ) r++;
   System.out.println( r );
```

We haven't committed ourselves to a specific limit on r, and thus can be reasonably sure we have done no harm.[13]

We now focus on the *condition*, and again put on blinders. We ask: What property

13. However, it could be argued that we have committed to considering integers, one at a time in sequence, and that by doing so may have precluded a faster, less granular approach for converging on the r we seek. We note this possibility, in passing, but move on. See Exercise 52.

of r guarantees that r is *not* the integer part of the square root of n? Why do we ask this? Because when that property holds, we want to advance to the next r.

As phrased, we are asking an abstract question, but not everyone is equally good at abstract reasoning. If you are going to practice Hippocratic coding, you need to develop a sense of when you are "on thin ice", i.e., when you have reached the limit of your own ability to reason abstractly.

It is important to avoid overestimating your ability, and then "shooting from the hip". For example, here are some wild guesses you might be tempted to try for the *condition*:

```
r*r != n
r*r < n
r*r <= n
```

But such a "hit and miss" approach, in which you generate plausible *conditions* and then try them out, is discouraged. Remember: Avoid debugging like the plague.

Accept the principle:

☞ There is no shame in reasoning with concrete examples.

Even Ph.D. mathematicians count on their fingers some of the time.

Here is a systematic itemization of concrete examples in which, on each row, we list the values of n for which the given r is the correct answer:

r	r * r	n
0	0	0
1	1	1, 2, 3
2	4	4, 5, 6, 7, 8
3	9	9, 10, 11, 12, 13, 14, 15

Creating such a table is part of gaining familiarity with the requirements of the problem in hand:

☞ Elaborate the expected input/output mapping explicitly.

The examples provide a target to aim for.

Now pick a row to think about carefully, and in detail. Say you pick the row where r is equal to 2:

- Ask: For which n would 2 be the integer part of the square root of n?
  - Answer: 4, 5, 6, 7, or 8. In each of those cases, we want the condition to be **false** because r is the correct answer, and we need to stop iterating. Conversely, if n is 9, 10, 11, or more, we want the condition to be **true** because we need to keep iterating. Why? Because 2 is not the correct answer.
- Ask: What is special about 9?
  - Answer: It is the square of 3.
- Ask: But what is special about 3?
  - Answer: It is one more than 2, the current value of r. So, when n is the square of one more than 2, or more, we need the *condition* to be **true** so that r will advance to 3.

Such concrete reasoning informs the generalization that we must now make, because the code we write must work for arbitrary `r` and `n`. The phrase "when `n` is the square of one more than 2, or more" brings us right to the threshold of what we are looking for, which we must now express in terms of arbitrary `r`:

☞ Alternate between concrete reasoning and abstract reasoning.

Eureka: What we are seeking is a property of `r+1`, not a property of `r` itself. The *condition* is some binary relationship between `r+1` and `n`. We can drop a template for the comparison into the code:

4

```
/* Given n≥0, output the Integer Square Root of n. */
   /* Let r be the integer part of the square root of n≥0. */
      int r = 0;
      while ( (r+1)*(r+1) ____ n ) r++;
   System.out.println( r );
```

Note that we only take a baby step, lest we err. Specifically, we delay writing the relational operator, leaving a blank in its stead.

We are ready to choose the relational operator, but need to realize, in all humility, that our situation is precarious. We are juggling multiple binary considerations, any one of which could trip us up if we misconstrue it backwards:

- The *condition* must express when to keep iterating, not when to stop.
- The relation concerns `r+1`, not `r`.
- We have chosen to compare `(r+1)*(r+1)` with `n`, not `r*r` with `n-1`.
- We have chosen to write `(r+1)*(r+1)`___`n` rather than `n`___`(r+1)*(r+1)`.

Be careful and systematic because you are on the edge of being mentally overloaded.

We know that there are only six comparison operators (==, != , >, >=, <, <=), and can proceed to eliminate all but one of them, in turn. The two operands around the blank provide visual context for reasoning about each operator. We can use that context to help keep our head screwed on straight, and avoid the pitfalls we listed.

The comparison operator:

- Can't be == or != because the *condition* must be **true** for an unbounded number of possible values of `n`, and **false** for an unbounded number of values of `n`. Neither "==" nor "!=" can do that.
- Can't be > or >= because we need to stop for big `r` and little `n`, not the other way around.
- Can't be < because we need to keep going, not stop, when `r` is 2 and `n` is 9.

So, the correct comparison operator is "<=":

5

```
/* Given n≥0, output the Integer Square Root of n. */
   /* Let r be the integer part of the square root of n≥0. */
      int r = 0;
      while ( (r+1)*(r+1) <= n ) r++;
   System.out.println( r );
```

This completes the code for computing and printing the Integer Square Root of any integer n≥0.

Pragmatics

One of the happy rewards of programming is the opportunity to run code on a computer, and have it dance for us. But before we can have that pleasure, we need to complete the program.

First, we need code to obtain as input the n whose root we wish to compute. The input doesn't miraculously appear in the computer; rather, the program must ask for it:

6
```
/* Output the Integer Square Root of an integer input. */
   /* Obtain an integer n≥0 from the user. */
   /* Given n≥0, output the integer part of the square root of n. */
      /* Let r be the integer part of the square root of n≥0. */
         int r = 0;
         while ( (r+1)*(r+1) <= n ) r++;
      System.out.println( r );
```

Next, this code must be embedded in certain gobbledygook:

7
```
import java.util.Scanner;
class boilerplate {
   static Scanner in = new Scanner(System.in);
   static void main() {
      /* Output the Integer Square Root of an integer input. */
         /* Obtain an integer n≥0 from the user. */
         /* Given n≥0, output the Integer Square Root of n. */
            /* Let r be the integer part of the square root of n≥0. */
               int r = 0;
               while ( (r+1)*(r+1) <= n ) r++;
            System.out.println( r );
      } /* main */
   } /* boilerplate */
```

You do not need to understand the gobbledygook in detail at this juncture; that will come later. Suffice it to say that its purpose is to provide a receptacle for our code (`boilerplate`), extend our base programming language with a library mechanism that supports input (`Scanner`), and define a named operation for activating the code (`main`).

Finally, the remaining step is to use this framework to obtain the input n:

8
```
import java.util.Scanner;
class boilerplate {
   static Scanner in = new Scanner(System.in);
   static void main() {
      /* Output the Integer Square Root of an integer input. */
         /* Obtain an integer n≥0 from the user. */
            int n = in.nextInt();
         /* Given n≥0, output the Integer Square Root of n. */
            /* Let r be the integer part of the square root of n≥0. */
               int r = 0;
               while ( (r+1)*(r+1) <= n ) r++;
            System.out.println( r );
      } /* main */
   } /* boilerplate */
```

This completes the program. You can now invoke `main`, provide input (say, 7), and get the output (say, 2).

We have omitted pragmatic steps that are required for running a completed program on your computer. This is a task that is specific to your programming environment, and is not described here because there is too much variety. Integrated Development Environments (IDEs) are tools that hide many such details, and provide a standard programming environment that works for multiple setups, but there are many of them, too. Compounding the issue, readers may elect different languages, for example choosing one from those listed in Appendix III Language Similarities, and mentally make the small needed mappings from the book's notation to the selected programming language.

Seek supplemental documentation or instruction for the programming language and environment you plan to use.

CHAPTER 2

Prerequisites

Familiarity with computers and computer applications is ubiquitous, and so too is an understanding of basic notions of computation gained from using software. You are assumed to already know that software is implemented as programs whose code controls the behavior of the computer, and that authoring software is called *programming* or *coding*. The goal of the first section of this chapter, Programming Concepts, is to firm up your intuitive grasp of these concepts with precise definitions, and to arm you with standard vocabulary.

Familiarity with the basics of coding is also common, and you may well already know some of a programming language. The goal of the second section of this chapter, Programming Language Constructs, is to present systematically the programming notation used in the book.

Languages differ in appearance, but at the level with which we are concerned, there are few substantive distinctions. For example, you may have already learned about conditional statements, and depending on the programming language to which you have been exposed may have seen them as:

```
if condition then statement1 else statement2
```

or

```
if ( condition ) statement1 else statement2
```

or

```
if condition: statement1
else: statement2
```

Syntax (punctuation) varies from language to language, but the *semantics* (meaning) of conditional statements is essentially always the same: If the value of the *condition* is **true**, execute $statement_1$, otherwise execute $statement_2$. Don't get too hung up about syntax; the semantics is what is important.

The notation we adopt is a subset of the Java programming language, but no claim is made that it is exactly Java, or even that our language is completely or precisely defined. Our subject is how to program, and not the exact details of a language. No attempt is made to define constructs in their full (possible) generality; rather, we only define what is needed for the book.[14]

14. The correspondences between this subset of Java [6] and similar subsets of Python [7],

The language is presented in staccato fashion to facilitate use as a checklist. As with the first section, you may find that the material helps to make your prior knowledge more precise, and reinforces effective use of vocabulary. If you find the section too challenging, you may need to consult supplemental material, e.g., on the Internet, or attend appropriate recitation sessions of your class, if offered.

The third section of this chapter, English Conventions, lists the abbreviations we use when writing code specifications in English. This should be readily accessible.

The final section, Hardware and Operating System Concepts, delves a bit into details of how computers represent data, and how operating systems execute programs. It can be treated as optional, or consulted, on demand.

Programming Concepts

The following concepts are standard for most imperative programming languages, i.e., languages that describe computation by a sequence of commands.

algorithm. An algorithm is a method for solving a problem, or performing a task.

program. A program is an algorithm written down in a programming language.

programming language. A programming language is a system of notation for programs that can be executed by a computer.

computer. A computer is a device for executing programs written in a programming language. A computer has a processor and a memory.

processor. A processor is a device that can obey the instructions of a machine-code program.

memory. A memory is a device that stores both machine code and values.

machine code. Machine code is a low-level programming language specific to a particular brand of processor.

execution. To execute a program is to perform the steps it dictates. Execution is also known as **running** the program. Execution of a machine-code program follows the **fetch-execute cycle**, whereby the processor performs two steps repeatedly:

- Fetch the next machine-code instruction from the memory.
- Execute that instruction.

Analogously, execution of a program written in a high-level language repeatedly performs two steps:

- Fetch the next *statement*.[15]
- Execute that *statement*.

environment. A program is executed by a computer in an environment that includes its external data, i.e., its input data and its output data:

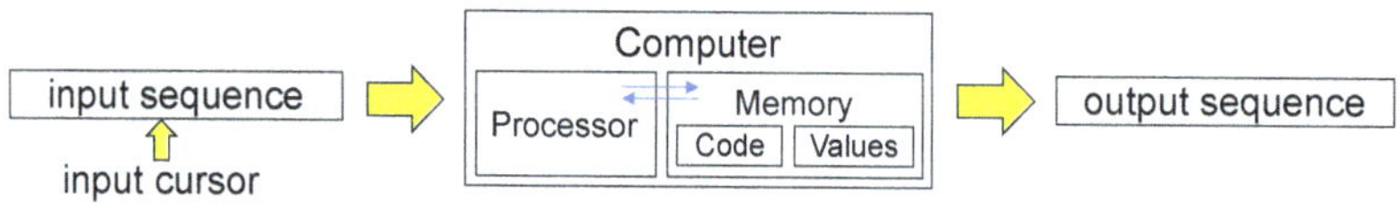

C/C++ [52], and JavaScript [53] are summarized in Appendix III. As you can see, they are not very different. In the text, we will occasionally venture beyond the given Java subset, e.g., using an extended language feature, or a Java library routine, but this will be kept to a minimum.

15. **Statements** are a generic concept defined later in this section; they also a specific syntactic category of programming-language construct, as defined in the next section. Syntactic categories are signified by italics; beside *statements*, these include *expressions*, *conditions*, *operations*, *operands*, *variables*, *types*, *names*, *declarations*, and *definitions*.

external data. External data include **input data,** which are a linear sequence of characters, with a distinguished point in the sequence denoted by the **input cursor** that indicates the next character to be input. External data also include **output data,** which are a linear sequence of characters, to which the program can append at the end.

compiler. A compiler is a program that can translate a program written in a high-level programming language, e.g., Java, into an equivalent program written in a low-level programming language, e.g., machine code for the Intel x86 family of processors.

interpreter. An interpreter is a program that can execute a program written in a high-level language without first using a compiler to translate it to machine code.

value. A value is an entity that is manipulated by a program. Values have *types*.

type. The *type* of a value is a categorization that determines how the value can be used in computation.

variable. A *variable* is a named memory location that can contain a value of a particular *type*. A *variable* is depicted by a box, prefixed by its *name*, and that contains its value.

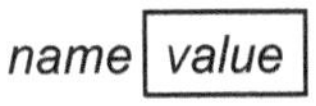

name | *value* |

assignment. Assignment is the act of storing a value in a *variable*, thereby overwriting its previous contents.

statement. A *statement* is a programming language construct whose execution has an effect on the state of execution.

state. The state of a program's execution consists of a location in its code, the values of its *variables*, the text in its input and output data, and the position of its input cursor.

effect. An effect is a change in the state of a program's execution. The program is said to transition from one state to another.

location. A location in code is the *statement* being executed, and the ordered list of method call sites whose invocations are not yet completed.

expression. An *expression* is a programming language construct whose evaluation yields a value. An **arithmetic expression** is an *expression* whose value has a numeric *type*.

condition. A *condition* is an *expression* whose value is logical rather than numeric, i.e., either **true** or **false**. Such values are also known as type `boolean`.[16]

evaluation. To evaluate an *expression* is to perform its *operations* on its *operands*, where these are specific to the given programming-language, e.g., in the *expression* "1+2", the *operands* are "1" and "2", and the *operation* is "+".

declaration. A *declaration* is a programming language construct whose execution has the effect of creating a *variable* with a *name*, and containing a value. The *name* has a scope, and the *variable* has a lifetime.

scope. The scope of a *name* is the portion of a program's text where the *name* is meaningful.

lifetime. The lifetime of a *variable* is the time interval within a program's execution during which the *variable* exists.

1-D array. A one-dimensional array is a named linear sequence of *variables* indexed

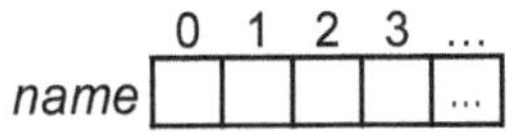

	0	1	2	3	…
name					…

16. George Boole (1815-1864) was an English mathematician, and author of The Laws of Thought. The mathematical treatment of logic is known as Boolean Algebra, with a capital "B", in his honor. The datatype is named `boolean`, in his honor, but with a lower-case "b" [44].

by consecutive integers, starting at 0. In diagrams, by convention, the *name* appears to the left of the sequence, and the indices appear above the *variables*. Each *variable* in the sequence is called an *element* of the array.

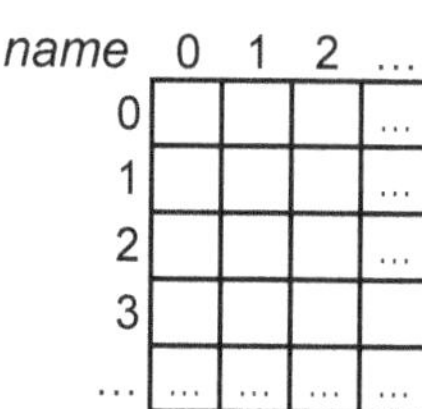

2-D array. A two-dimensional array is a named rectangular arrangement of *variables* indexed by pairs of integers, the row and column, each of which starts at 0. In diagrams, by convention, the *name* appears to the upper-left of the arrangement, and the indices appear to the left of the rows and above the columns. Each *variable* in the arrangement is called an *element* of the array.

scalar. A scalar is a *variable* that is not an array.

definition. A *definition* is a programming language construct that creates a method or a class.

method / procedure / function. A method has a *name*, and is a parameterized sequence of *declarations* and *statements* that can be executed by **invoking** (or **calling**) it from a *statement* or *expression*. Methods have **return-types**. If the return-type is `void`, the invocation only has effect, and can only appear in a *statement*. If the return-type is non-`void`, the method is known as a *function*, its invocation yields a value of the given *type*, and the invocation can appear in an *expression* or *statement*. The return value of a function that is invoked as a *statement* is discarded. Methods are also known as *procedures*.

class. A class is a group of related *declarations* and *definitions*.

Programming Language Constructs

The following constructs are standard across most imperative programming languages. There are minor syntactic differences, and there are some fine-grained distinctions, but these need not concern us.

Statements are executed for their effect; *declarations* are executed to create variables; *expressions* are evaluated to obtain their values.

Statements and *declarations* are grouped into method *definitions*, which are grouped with other *declarations* into classes.

A *program* is a distinguished method in a distinguished class. By convention, that method is often named `main`, and the class name is descriptive of the application.

Statements

`variable = expression;`

Meaning: Assign the value of *expression* to the *variable*.[17]

`variable++;`

Meaning: Shorthand for *variable=variable+*1; and called an *auto-increment* statement.

`variable--;`

Meaning: Shorthand for *variable=variable-*1; and called an *auto-decrement* statement.

`if` (*condition*) *statement*$_1$ **`else`** *statement*$_2$

Meaning: Execute *statement*$_1$ if the value of the *condition* is **true**, otherwise execute *statement*$_2$.

17. The type of *expression* must be "compatible" with the type of *variable*, i.e., the value of *expression* can be appropriately converted to a value of the type of *variable*. However, we do not define when that conversion is possible, as the subject is more technical than we wish to discuss.

`if ( condition ) statement`

Meaning: Execute *statement* if the value of the *condition* is **true**.

`while ( condition ) statement`

Meaning: Repeatedly execute *statement* provided the *condition* is **true** before each execution. A **while**-statement is called a *loop*, and its constituent *statement* is called its *body*. Executing the *body* zero or more times is called *iterating*.

`for ( initialize; condition; update ) statement`

Meaning: Equivalent to the general iterative-computation pattern:[18]

```
initialize;
while ( condition ) {
   statement
   update
   }
```

where *initialize* is one of the following:

`type name = expression`

Meaning: Declare scalar variable *name*, and initialize it with the value of *expression*. The scope of *name* is the given **for**-statement.

`name = expression`

Meaning: Assign the value of *expression* to the already-declared, *named* variable.

Update is one of the following:

`name = expression`

Meaning: Assign the value of *expression* to the *named* variable.

`name++`

Meaning: Auto-increment the *named* variable.

`name--`

Meaning: Auto-decrement the *named* variable.

`block`

Meaning: Execute the *block*, which groups *declarations* and *statements*, and permits them to be used in a syntactic context where only a single statement is otherwise allowed, e.g., in an **if**-statement, a **while**-statement, or a **for**-statement.

`System.out.println( expression );`

Meaning: Convert the value of *expression* to a `String` (if necessary), append it to the output data, and advance to the beginning of the next line in the output data. The `String` representation of an arithmetic value is base 10.

`System.out.print( expression );`

Meaning: Convert the value of *expression* to a `String` (if necessary), append it to the output data, and remain on the same line in the output data.

`System.out.println( );`

Meaning: Advance to the beginning of the next line in the output data.

`name( arguments );`

Meaning: Invoke the named method with the values of *arguments*, which is

---

18. More accurately, the defining pattern should be treated as the body of a *block* because (a) the **for**-statement is syntactically a single *statement*, and (b) the scope of the control variable (if it is declared) is just the given **for**-statement, and not the surrounding code.

a comma-separated list of *expressions*. Invoking a method with a list of *arguments* has the effect of:

(a) evaluating each *argument expression*,
(b) declaring new variables for the method's *parameters*,
(c) assigning the *argument* values to the corresponding *parameters*,
(d) evaluating the *block* of the method, and
(e) returning to the invocation site, either by execution of a **`return`** statement, or by completing execution of the method's *body*. If the method has non-**`void`** type, but was invoked as a *statement*, the computed return value is discarded.

`return;`

Meaning: Return to the method invocation site. This form of **return**-statement is only permitted in a method of type `void`.

`return` *`expression;`*

Meaning: Return to the method invocation site with the value of *expression*. If the method has non-**`void`** type *t*, *expression* must have a type that is compatible with *t*. This form of **return**-statement is not permitted in a method of type `void`.

Blocks

`{` *`declarations-and-statements`* `}`

Meaning: *Declarations-and-statements* is a list of intermixed *declaration* and *statement* constructs. A *block* is executed by executing each *declaration* and/or *statement*, in sequence. Variables declared in a *block* go out of existence each time execution of the *block* completes.

Variables

`name`

Meaning: The *variable* with the given *name*.

`class-name.name`

Meaning: The named *variable* (or *method*) that is declared in class *class-name*, e.g., `Integer.MAX_VALUE` (or `Math.sqrt`).

`name``[` *`expression`* `]`

Meaning: The value of *expression* is known as an *index*, and the named one-dimensional array is a sequence of *subscripted variables*. Let *k* be the value of *expression*. The *variable* denoted by *name*[*expression*] is the kth variable of the sequence, starting at the 0th variable. If *k* is negative, or is not less than the length of the array, a runtime "subscript-out-of-bounds" error is triggered. The time needed to access an array element is approximately the same as the time needed to access a non-subscripted variable, and is independent of the value of the index.

`name``[` $expression_1$ `][` $expression_2$ `]`

Meaning: The *named variable* is a two-dimensional array, and the meaning is similar to the one-dimensional case. $Expression_1$ and $expression_2$, known as the *row* and *column* indices, are required to be less than the height and width of the *named* array, respectively. See the one-dimensional case, above.

Expressions

Constants

`0, 1, 2, ..., -1, -2, ...`	(type **int**)
`0L, 1L, 2L, ..., -1L, -2L, ...`	(type **long**)
`6.0221409f+23, ...`	(type **float**)
`0.0, 3.14159, 6.0221409e+23, ...`	(type **double**)
`true, false`	(type **boolean**)
`'a', 'b', 'c', ..., '\u0000'`	(type **char**)
`"characters"`	(type String)

Primitives

variable

Meaning: The value contained in the *variable*.

`in.nextInt()`

Meaning: The **int** value returned by invoking the method `in.nextInt()`. The value returned is the binary fixed-point representation of the base-10 integer that is in the input data at the position of the input cursor. Invocation has the effect of advancing the input cursor beyond the integer that has been read. Variable `in` is assumed to have been initialized by:

```
Scanner in = new Scanner(System.in);
```

earlier in the code.

name(*arguments*)

Meaning: The value returned by an invocation of the *named* non-**void** method with the values of the given *arguments*. The last statement executed by the method must be a **return**-statement, which provides the value for the method invocation. (See method invocation under *statements*.)

new *type*[*expression*]

Meaning: Create a 1-dimensional array of variables of the given *type*, whose length is given by the value of *expression*. The variables of the array are known as its *elements*, and are indexed by nonnegative integers starting at 0. Array elements are initialized with the *type*'s default value.

new *type*[$expression_1$][$expression_2$]

Meaning: Create a 2-dimensional array of variables of the given *type*, whose height and width are given by the values of $expression_1$ and $expression_2$, respectively. The variables of the array are known as its *elements*, and are *indexed* by pairs of nonnegative integers starting at 0. Array elements are initialized with the *type*'s default value.

Binary Operations

$operand_1$ *binary-operator* $operand_2$

where the *operands* are *expressions*, and the *binary-operators* are:

+, -, *, /, %	(arithmetic)
<, <=, >, >=, ==, !=	(relational)
&&, ||	(**boolean**)
+	(concatenation)

The binary arithmetic operators +, -, *, /, and % are addition, subtraction, multiplication, division, and modulus (i.e., remainder after integer division). The type of the result is integer if both operands are integer; and is floating point if either operand is floating point.

The arithmetic binary relational operators `<`, `<=`, `>`, `>=`, `==`, and `!=` are less-than, less-than-or-equal, greater-than, greater-than-or-equal, equal, and not equal.

Operators `==` and `!=` should not be applied to non-arithmetic values, e.g., strings and arrays, until certain subtleties are explained in Chapters 12 and 18.

The binary operator `+` when at least one operand has type `String` is string concatenation. A common use of this is to construct output for `System.out.println(...)` that consists of an arithmetic value, e.g., an **`int`**, concatenated with the value of a `String` constant, e.g., a single space character `" "`. The non-`String` argument, e.g., the value contained in the **`int`**, is converted to a `String`, e.g., its base-10 representation, and then the two strings are concatenated. Without the space character being appended to the output, consecutive integers would run into one another.

Unary Operations

`unary-operator operand`

where the *operand* is an *expression*, and the *unary-operators* are:

`-`	(arithmetic)
`!`	(**`boolean`**)

The unary arithmetic operator "`-`" is negation. The unary Boolean operator "`!`" is **not**.

Grouping

`(` *`expression`* `)`

Meaning: The value of the *expression*.

Types

`int`

Meaning: A value of type **`int`** is a 32-bit, two's-complement, fixed-point binary integer. Default value: `0`.

`long`

Meaning: A value of type **`long`** is a 64-bit, two's-complement, fixed-point binary integer. Default value: `0L`.

`float`

Meaning: A value of type **`float`** is a signed, 32-bit, floating-point number. Default value: `0.0f0`.

`double`

Meaning: A value of type **`double`** is a signed, 64-bit, floating-point number. Default value: `0.0e0`.

`boolean`

Meaning: A value of type **`boolean`** is either **true** or **false**. Default value: **`false`**.

`char`

Meaning: A single Unicode character [8]. Default value: `'\u0000'`.

`String`

Meaning: A value of type `String` is a linear sequence of 0 or more Unicode characters Default value: **`null`**.

`void`

Meaning: There are no values or variables of type **`void`**. A method defined with **`void`** return type returns no value, and can only be invoked as a *statement* for its effect.

`type``[]`

Meaning: A value of type *type*`[]` signifies a one-dimensional array of variables, each of which has type *type*. Default value: **`null`**.

`type``[][]`

Meaning: A value of type *type*`[][]` signifies a two-dimensional array of variables, each of which has type *type*. Default value: **`null`**.

Declarations[19]

`type name;`

Meaning: Create a variable *name* of the given *type*. There are two kinds of declared variables: *class variables* and *method variables*.

A *class variable* is declared in a class. Its declaration appears outside any method, and is always prefixed by the modifier **`static`**, i.e.,[20]

```
static type name;
```

Its scope begins at the declaration, and extends to the end of the class definition within which its declaration appears. The lifetime of a class variable begins when its declaration is executed, and lasts thereafter for the rest of program execution. If it is not explicitly initialized, a class variable is initialized with the *type*'s default value.

A *method variable* is declared in a method. Its *scope* begins at the *declaration*, and extends to the end of the *block* within which its *declaration* appears. The scope is either the whole method (if that *block* is the defining *block* of the method), or an inner *block* within the method. The lifetime of (each dynamic instance of) a method variable begins when the declaration is executed (in a new dynamic instance of the *declaration*), and ends when (that instance of) the *block* completes. The compiler must be able to reason that a method variable is necessarily initialized before it can be used.

If *type* ends with brackets, i.e., `[]` or `[][]`, the brackets can be moved to the right of *name*. For example, the declaration "**`int`**`[] A;`" can be written as "**`int`** `A[];`", and means the same thing.

`type name`` = `*`expression`*`;`

Meaning: Create a variable *name* of the given *type*, and initialize it with the value of *expression*.

`type name``[] = { `*`list-of-expressions`*` };`

Meaning: Create a variable *name*, which signifies a 1-D array of *type* elements, and initialize it with the values in the comma-separated *list-of-expressions*.

19. Declarations (this section) and method definitions (next section) can be prefixed by *modifiers*, which are explained in the text later, when introduced. These include: **`static`**, **`public`**, **`private`**, **`protected`**, and **`final`**.

20. Chapter 18 introduces variables whose declarations in a class are not prefixed by the modifier **`static`**. Such variables are known as *instance variables*.

Definitions

`static` *`type name( parameters ) block`*

Meaning: Define a method with the given *name* and *parameters*. If *type* is **`void`**, the method can only be invoked as a statement for its effect. If *type* is non-**`void`**, the method can only be invoked as an expression that computes a value. The *block* is called the *body* of the method. Methods of **`void`** *type* are referred to as *procedures*, and methods of non-**`void`** type are referred to as *functions*.[21]

`class` *`name { declarations-and-methods }`*

Meaning: *Declarations-and-methods* is a list of intermixed *declaration* and *method definition* constructs. A class is a scope within which *names* of variables and methods are made accessible to the code therein. Outside the class, the names of variables, e.g., `v`, and methods, e.g., `m`, must be qualified by the class name, e.g., *name*`.v` and *name*`.m`.

Arguments and Parameters

`arguments` `is 0 or more` *`expressions`* `separated by commas`

Meaning: Before entry to the method being invoked, each *argument* is evaluated.

`parameters` `is 0 or more` *`type-name`* `pairs separated by commas`

Meaning: On entry to the method being invoked, a variable is declared for each *type-name* pair. Each such variable, known as a *parameter*, has the given *type* and *name*, and is initialized with the value of the corresponding *argument* given in the method invocation. The scope of a *parameter* is the method definition in which it appears. The lifetime of (each dynamic instance of) a *parameter* begins on the invocation of (a new dynamic instance of) the method, and ends when (that instance of) the method returns.

Comments

`/* any-text */`

Meaning: Ignored.

`// any-text-to-end-of-line`

Meaning: Ignored.

Libraries

Libraries are predefined classes. One such library is `Math`, which contains methods such as `Math.abs` (for absolute value), `Math.sqrt` (for square root), `Math.pow` (for exponentiation), `Math.min` (for minimum), `Math.max` (for maximum), etc.

English Conventions

Comments are written in English, but abbreviations are important for keeping them succinct. Because comments play a key role in the methodology advocated in this book, it is worthwhile to summarize our conventions. Formal *specification languages*

21. Chapter 18 introduces methods whose definitions are not prefixed by the modifier **`static`**. Such methods are known as *instance methods*.

have been devised for what we write in comments, but we stop short of embracing one. Rather, we use English, with the quasi-formal locutions, below. The notations of this section cannot be used in code outside of comments.

`Let variable be text`
: Meaning: Set the *variable* (or *variables*) equal to the value(s) described by *text*. Synonymous with "`Set` *variable* `equal to` *text*".

`Given text₁, text₂`
: Meaning: Provided that the state is as described by $text_1$, establish $text_2$.

`name`
: Meaning: The *name* is either a local indeterminate used in the comment as a pronoun, or it is an actual program *variable*, in which case it either already exists, or is to be declared.

`variable[expression₁..expression₂]`
: Meaning: The consecutive elements of the array *variable* with indices in the range $expression_1$ to $expression_2$, inclusive. When $expression_2$ is less than $expression_1$, the sub-array referred to is empty, i.e., contains no elements.

`⟨expression₁, expression₂⟩`
: Meaning: A pair of values, considered as a single entity, consisting of the value of $expression_1$ and the value of $expression_2$.

`s.t. text`
: Meaning: Such that *text*.

`i.e., text`
: Meaning: That is, *text*.

`e.g., text`
: Meaning: For example, *text*.

`iff text`
: Meaning: if and only if *text*.

`resp. text`
: Meaning: Respectively, *text*.

`in situ`
: Meaning: In place, e.g., without copying values to an extra array of variables.

`variable^expression`
: Meaning: *Variable* raised to the power given by the value of *expression*.

Example

```
/* Given A[0..n-1] in non-decreasing order, let A[0..n-1]
   be rearranged in situ s.t. A is in non-increasing order,
   e.g., in the reverse order. */
```

Meaning: Provided the code is executed in a state in which:

- There is an integer variable named `n` that contains a value (say, *n*), or alternatively that `n` is an arithmetic expression that evaluates to the integer *n*;
- There is a numerical array named `A` whose length is at least *n*, i.e., `A` has elements `A[0]` through `A[`*n*`-1]`;
- The array elements `A[0]` through `A[`*n*`-1]` contain values that are arranged in numerical order, but that may contain duplicates;

rearrange the values in those array elements to have the opposite order. That is, after execution of the code, the values in the consecutive array elements `A[0]` through `A[`n`-1]` never increase. Do not use an extra array.

Hardware and Operating System Concepts

This (optional) section peeks under the hood, and provides a few concrete details about how computation on a computer works.

bit. A bit is the smallest unit of information in a computer. The word "bit" is both descriptive (as in, "a small quantity") and an acronym (**b**inary dig**it**). A bit can be stored in a 2-state physical device, i.e., a switch that is either "on" or "off", "up" or "down", etc. By convention, the two possible states of a bit are known as 0 and 1.

byte. A byte is eight bits. Because each bit in a byte can independently be 0 or 1, a byte has 2^8=256 possible values.

byte-addressable memory. A byte-addressable memory consists of an ordered sequence of bytes (depicted by gray boxes) each of which has an individual numerical address.

address. An address is the name by which a byte in a memory is known. A memory's set of addresses is known as its **address space**.

word. A word is the unit of information conveyed to or from a memory in a single operation. Modern computers typically have 8-byte (64-bit) words. The locus of a memory-transfer operation is specified by the address of a single byte, but the transfer involves a whole word in the vicinity of that byte.

access time. The access time of a memory reference is the time required to convey a word of information to or from the memory.

RAM. A RAM is a physical device that implements a byte-addressable memory for which the access time is uniform and independent of the address. "RAM" is an acronym for Random Access Memory, so called because any of its bytes can be accessed, in an arbitrary order, in the same amount of time.

memory hierarchy. A stratification of computer memories by size, access time, and price. Typically, large memories have slower access times, and are less expensive per byte. Conversely, smaller memories can have faster access times, but are more expensive per byte. We consider three strata of the memory hierarchy: virtual, physical, and cache. Memory hierarchies achieve efficiency by exploiting locality of memory accesses.

locality. Locality is a measure of the confinement of memory accesses to limited regions of an address space for extended periods of time. Locality allows bytes to temporarily reside in a smaller but faster stratum of the memory hierarchy.

address translation. When a byte at address b in a given stratum s of the memory hierarchy temporarily resides at address b' in another stratum s' of the hierarchy, references to b in s must be mapped to b' in s'. That mapping is known as address translation.

process. A process is a machine-code program in the midst of being executed. A computer may have multiple active processes at any given moment. Processes reference locations in virtual memory, where a **virtual address** typically corresponds to an offset in a region of disk memory reserved for the process. A disk may be an actual rotating device, or a solid-state facsimile of one. Disks have a large address space, and are inexpensive per byte.

virtual memory. Processes run in an address space of virtual memory, but processors execute programs in physical memory, where the correspondence between virtual and physical addresses is maintained dynamically by address translation. Let b be the virtual address of a byte referenced by a process. If byte b (in virtual memory) currently resides at address b' (in physical memory), the reference to b is translated to a reference to b', and that byte is accessed accordingly.

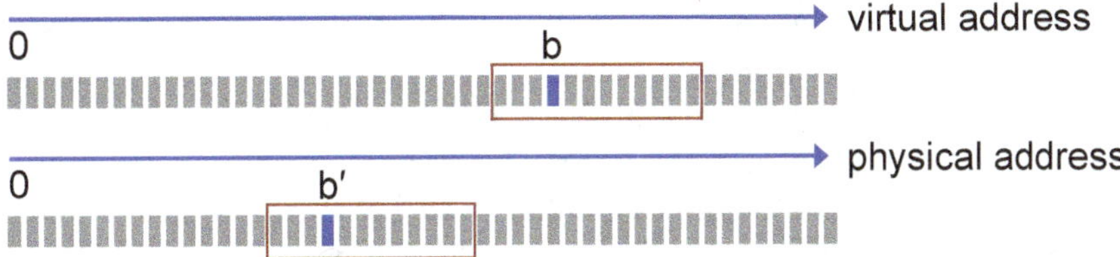

If byte b does not currently reside in physical memory, then a location b' (in physical memory) must be found for it, the value currently in b' must be copied back to whatever byte (in virtual memory) that physical location is currently being used for, and b can then be copied into b'. Ideally, a byte in physical memory will be referenced many times before it needs to be expelled. For practical reasons, bytes are grouped into *pages*, e.g., blocks of 512 or 1024 bytes, and the expulsion mechanism (known as **paging**) is performed on whole pages at a time. A typical paging policy expels the least-recently-used (LRU) page.

physical memory. The physical memory of a computer is a RAM that is shared by all active processes of the computer. Computers typically accommodate incremental installation of additional RAM, with the benefit of increasing the amount of virtual memory that can be mapped into physical memory at the same time, thereby reducing paging, and speeding execution.

cache memory. A cache is a small but very fast memory that temporarily represents bytes of physical memory. Abstractly, address mapping from physical to cache memory is similar to address mapping from virtual memory to physical memory. However, the two mechanisms are distinct, and their implementations in hardware are quite different.

array layout. One-dimensional arrays of length n of m-byte elements are typically laid out in n consecutive m-byte groups, starting at some base address in virtual memory:

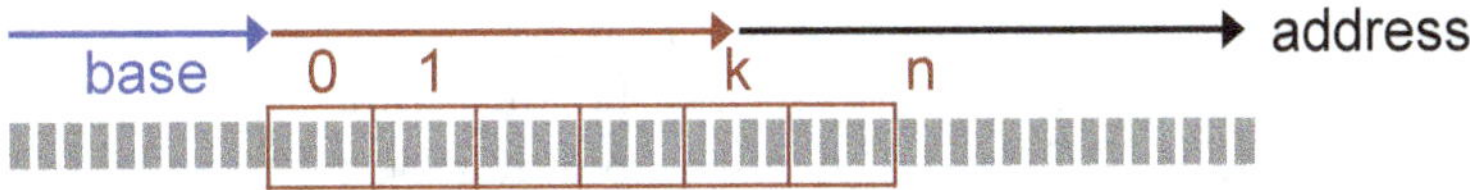

Access to the kth array element requires computing its virtual address as $base+m\cdot k$, and then using an operation that either loads or stores values at that location, where the corresponding physical-memory location is obtained by address mapping. The simple model whereby the time to access an array element `A[k]` is constant, and is independent of the value of k, assumes that entire array already resides in physical memory, and ignores the time involved in paging regions of the array into physical memory.

numerical representation. A numerical representation is a convention whereby a sequence of bits is interpreted as the representation of a number. There are two principal forms of numerical representation: fixed point and floating point. Each form has two varieties: 32-bit and 64-bit.

fixed-point binary integer. A fixed-point binary integer is a sequence of bits interpreted positionally as powers of 2. Thus, just as the decimal fixed-point integer 101 represents $(1 \cdot 10^2)+(0 \cdot 10^1)+(1 \cdot 10^0)$, i.e., a hundred and one, so the binary fixed-point integer 101 represents $(1 \cdot 2^2)+(0 \cdot 2^1)+(1 \cdot 2^0)$, i.e., five. When N-bits are interpreted as an unsigned integer, they can represent 0 through 2^N-1 The types **`int`** and **`long`** are 32-bit and 64-bit two's-complement fixed-point integers, respectively.

two's-complement integer. A convention for representing signed integers in N bits. A leading 0 bit followed by the remaining N-1 bits is interpreted as a positive (N-1)-bit binary integer, and a leading 1 bit followed by the remaining N-1 bits is interpreted as a negative binary integer. In this case, instead of the next number after 2^{N-1}-1 being interpreted as the positive number, 2^{N-1}, it is interpreted as the most negative negative number, -2^{N-1}. Continuing "up", we eventually reach all 1s, which as an unsigned integer would be the largest value, but in two's complement, is interpreted as -1.

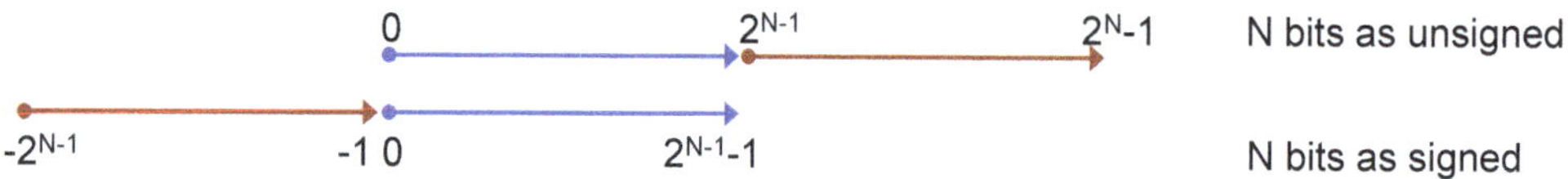

To make this concrete, here is the case for N=3:

bits	as unsigned	as signed
0 0 0	0	0
0 0 1	1	1
0 1 0	2	2
0 1 1	3	3
1 0 0	4	-4
1 0 1	5	-3
1 1 0	6	-2
1 1 1	7	-1

floating-point number. A floating-point number is a number in scientific notation. It consists of a signed **mantissa**, and a signed **exponent**. In base-2, if the value of the mantissa is m, and the value of the exponent is e, then the number represented is $m \cdot 2^e$. The **`float`** type has 32 bits, and the **`double`** type has 64 bits. The exact interpretation of bits need not be understood. Suffice it to say that **`double`** has more bits than **`float`** for both mantissa and exponent. The correspondence between binary (base-2) floating-point numbers (used internally) and decimal (base-10) floating-point numbers (used externally for input and output) is approximate.

character set. A character set is an encoding of symbols as sequences of bits.

Unicode. The international *Unicode* standard is a character set intended to represent almost every known symbol on Earth, including many emojis [8]. The most common 65,536 symbols are representable as a **`char`**, and are encoded in two bytes. The remaining symbols are encoded as two **`char`** values.

CHAPTER 3

Specifications and Implementations

Programs serve a purpose: They satisfy a *requirement*. Some requirements are minuscule, e.g., square a number; others are grandiose, e.g., control a rocket to the moon. Ours is not to reason why. We accept a requirement as the goal of our client, and design a program to meet the challenge.

In large and complicated projects, an extensive dialogue between client and programmer may be needed to elicit exactly what is wanted, but once the goals have been identified, a specification is written to serve as a contract. The programmer then writes the code that implements the specification, and delivers the completed system. These roles and activities are at play regardless of whether you are working for an actual client, e.g., your teacher or boss, or for yourself (in which case you are playing two roles, and it can be important to keep in mind which role you are fulfilling at any given moment).

Your program will be a composition of various kinds of programming-language constructs:

- Statements, which define effects.
- Declarations, which create program variables.
- Methods, which group statements and declarations into meaningful operations.
- Classes, which aggregate methods and declarations into coherent modules.

The contribution of each component in your program design can itself be specified. This chapter discusses such component specifications, and explains how they work together to define and implement a program specification.

Statement Specifications

A *specification* is a precise articulation of a requirement. A specification says *what* is required, not *how* it is to be accomplished. Writing specifications for code is an essential aspect of programming.

Specifications are written in a language other than the programming language. Formal specification languages have been devised, but we shall use English.

Specifications are written in the program as comments, which allow escape from the constrained syntax of the programming language's other constructs:

```
/* Specification. */
```

Here is a simple example:

```
/* Output the square of an integer that is provided as input data. */
```

This specification is an instance of what is known as an *input-output specification*, or *I/O spec*, for short. It says what is in the input data: An integer. It says what must happen: The square of that integer must be output. It does not say how to make this happen.

A specification may serve as the contract for an entire program. For the example given, the program's complete input consists of one integer, and the program's complete output consists of one output, its square.

Alternatively, a specification may define only a small requirement within a larger context. The specification is understood relative to what has happened so far during program execution. For the example given, the program's input data may consist of many things. Some initial input may already have been read into the program, but the input cursor now resides immediately before an integer that has not yet been read. Similarly, during program execution up to this point, much may have already been output. The specification requires that the square of the next input integer now be appended to that output. A specification that is a part of the program is called a *fragment* or *segment*.[22]

Implementations

An *implementation* is a precise statement of *how* a requirement is to be met. A specification is a desire, whereas its implementation is a description of how that desire is to be fulfilled. In general, there are many possible implementations for a given specification. Selecting and writing an implementation for a specification is an essential aspect of programming.

The implementation of a specification is written indented beneath it using this pattern:

```
/* Specification. */
   Implementation
```

For example,

```
/* Output the square of an integer that is provided as input data. */
   int n = in.nextInt(); System.out.println( n*n );
```

This implementation is written as two consecutive executable statements in the programming language. Specifications are typically easier to understand than code: They are English.

22. The text contains many examples that are fragments. If you wish to run them on a computer, you must provide them with the context of a full program, e.g., the boilerplate that is presented in section Pragmatics of Chapter 1. Additionally, if the fragment assumes the existence of certain variables, they should be declared and initialized ahead of the fragment.

The implementation is called a *refinement* of the specification. The refinement states the same thing as the specification, but in greater detail. In the squaring example, the detail is total because the refinement provides complete code that implements the specification.

In contrast, a refinement may provide only partial additional detail. For example, the following refinement introduces variable s, and specifies that it be set to the square of n, but leaves open the question of how that square is to be computed:

```
/* Output the square of an integer that is provided as input data. */
   int n = in.nextInt();
   /* Let s be the square of n. */
   System.out.println( s );
```

Further refinement may use multiplication to compute s:

```
/* Output the square of an integer that is provided as input data. */
   int n = in.nextInt();
   /* Let s be the square of n. */
      int s = n*n;
   System.out.println( s );
```

Alternatively, we can compute s in some different way, e.g., if the multiplication operation "*" were disallowed, we could compute s by repeated addition of the absolute value of n:

```
/* Output the square of an integer that is provided as input data. */
   int n = in.nextInt();
   /* Let s be the square of n. */
      int m = Math.abs(n);
      int s = 0;
      for (int k=0; k<m; k++) s = s + m;
   System.out.println( s );
```

Authors of essays are often urged to write hierarchical outlines, which use indentation to indicate subordination. In an outline, the idea expressed on a given line is elaborated by ideas expressed in lines indented below it. We have the same intent with refinements.

The implementation is secondary to the specification in the sense that it is not needed for a human reader who wishes to understand the relationship between the specification and the rest of the program. Of course, the implementation is essential for the program because the specification is written in a language that is beyond the capacity of the programming language to understand (not to mention that it is a comment, and is therefore completely ignored).

Specification Style

Write specifications as *imperatives*, i.e., authoritative commands to do something. Focus on action words, i.e., verbs. Specifications are not literature. They should be precise, staccato, and to the point. Avoid meandering descriptions.

Succinctness in specifications is beneficial. One way to achieve this is by eliminating needless words. Here is a small step in that direction in which the words "that is" are omitted:

```
/* Output the square of an integer that is provided as input. */
   int n = in.nextInt(); System.out.println( n*n );
```

Stylized forms are also helpful. One such convention is to describe input before output:

```
/* Input an integer, and output the square of that integer. */
   int n = in.nextInt(); System.out.println( n*n );
```

Returning to the goal of succinctness, and the technique of eliminating needless words, we may use a pronoun:

```
/* Input an integer, and output its square. */
   int n = in.nextInt(); System.out.println( n*n );
```

Pronouns (like "its") work well when they are unambiguous, but are often confusing when you cannot tell which of two or more things is intended.

A useful convention is to introduce names in place of anonymous pronouns. Typically, single letters are used for such names. For example:

```
/* Input integer k, and output k squared. */
   int n = in.nextInt(); System.out.println( n*n );
```

When a specification must refer to more than one thing, you can use different letters to distinguish between them.

Although a name such as "k" is often called a "variable", this risks confusion with program variables. In the specification, k is a named pronoun, not a memory location that contains a value. A name such as "k" is used within the specification for brevity and disambiguation. It has no meaning outside the specification. Its *scope* is said to be local to the specification, and it has no relationship with any other uses of the same name elsewhere in the program.

Any letter can serve as a name. For example, the following specification uses "j" instead of "k", and says the same thing:

```
/* Input integer j, and output j squared. */
   int n = in.nextInt(); System.out.println( n*n );
```

You can use the name "n", as in:

```
/* Input integer n, and output n squared. */
   int n = in.nextInt(); System.out.println( n*n );
```

in which case you can consider it as serendipitous that the pronoun and variable happen to have the same name, or you can consider the specification to be speaking of the variable "n". However, a different implementation of the same specification, one that doesn't even have a variable, drives home the point that in the specification "n" is not necessarily speaking of a variable:[23]

23. This implementation outputs n squared as a **double**, e.g., 4.0, whereas the previous implementations output it as an **int**, e.g., 4. The specification does not require a particular format, so we are free to choose.

```
/* Input integer n, and output n squared. */
   System.out.println( Math.pow(in.nextInt(),2) );
```

A final step results in an even more succinct specification:

```
/* Input integer n, and output n*n. */
   int n = in.nextInt(); System.out.println( n*n );
```

Here, we use the programming notation "n*n" in the specification. This is common and permissible. It could be argued that in using an arithmetic expression, we are losing some of the benefit of the English specification because comprehension now requires knowing that "*" means "multiply". Specifications have an audience, and you should adopt a style for specifications that is appropriate for the literacy of your audience. If you are your own audience, feel free to adopt conventions that suit yourself.

When you use an arithmetic expression like n*n in a specification, you are not requiring the implementation to compute n squared, say, using that expression. Rather, you are merely referring to the expression's value for whatever purpose you may have. You may not even need to compute it, as in the following specification and refinement for printing the square root of whatever number is input:

```
/* Input integer x, and output the number n such that n*n=x. */
   System.out.println( Math.sqrt(in.nextInt()) );
```

Specifications as Higher-Level Code

Suppose you need to exchange the contents of two variables, (say) x and y. The specification:

```
/* Swap x and y. */
```

can be read as an unambiguous statement in a higher-level language than your programming language. In this case, the names "x" and "y" are not pronouns; rather, they are the names of actual program variables.

If the programming language had included a form of statement such as:

```
swap x with y;
```

you would have written it that way, but alas there is no such construct, so you write it as a specification that you will implement later using actual statements of the programming language. The specification is referred to as a *statement-comment*. It is precise, unambiguous, and as good as a real statement for expressing a desired effect.

Having written the specification, you can carry on coding whatever broader problem you were working on, and not get distracted by implementing the swap now. You are following a process suggested by the precept:

☞ **Write comments as an integral part of the coding process, not as afterthoughts.**

Statement-comments let you stay focused on your higher-level goals, and not get mired in details. Of course, if you forget to implement a statement-comment, the program won't run correctly, but that is the least of your problems. Concentrate on what you were trying to accomplish in the first place when you wrote the statement-comment.

When an implementation is so standard that you can blast it in, and not lose your train of thought, you may prefer to do so, and get it over with:

```
/* Swap x and y. */
   int temp = x;
   x = y;
   y = temp;
```

Regardless of whether you write the implementation now or later, the specification still serves the useful purpose of stating a desired net effect. Thus, write specifications even when you intend to immediately write the code that implements them. Don't write code whose purpose must be discerned by deciphering low-level statements; rather, provide the summary in a high-level specification.

When you read code, ignore indented implementations as if they had been folded into an ellipsis. For example, think of the code above as:

```
/* Swap x and y. */
   ...
```

If your code editor actually supported such folding as a feature, you might use it to hide the implementation, which would then allow you to better see the relationship between the specification and the rest of the program. The indentation convention supports something similar: It helps you to visually skip over the implementation, and better interpret the specification in its context.

Each specification relates to the rest of the program in two distinct directions. In the *inward* direction, the relationship is between the specification and its implementation. In the *outward* direction, the specification is part of an implementation for an encompassing specification.

To illustrate how a specification faces two ways, like the Roman god Janus, consider this implementation of swap, in which we introduce a completely superfluous specification for pedagogical purposes:

```
/* Swap x and y. */
   /* Declare int variable temp, and initialize it to x. */
      int temp = x;
   x = y;
   y = temp;
```

The specification (in red) relates inward to its implementation:

```
int temp = x;
```

and outward to the encompassing specification:

```
/* Swap x and y. */
```

for which it provides an element of an implementation. Note that the actual declaration and initialization code is indented still further because it is now the refinement of the (red) specification.

As before, you can think of eliding the implementation, and viewing a specification as if it were executable:

```
/* Swap x and y. */
   /* Declare int variable temp, and initialize it to x. */
      ...
   x = y;
   y = temp;
```

The three lines (not counting the ellipsis) indented beneath the swap specification are its implementation, and are a hybrid mixture of code and specification. You don't need to see the elided code to understand that the implementation of swap is correct because you read the statement-comment not as commentary but as if it were an executable statement.

It can be confusing that indentation is used for a second purpose in code: Compound programming-language constructs are frequently formatted using indentation to indicate the relationship between the whole construct and its constituent subparts. For example,

```
if ( expression ) statement1 else statement2
```

and

```
while ( expression ) statement
```

are frequently formatted as

```
if ( expression )
   statement1
else
   statement2
```

and

```
while ( expression )
   statement
```

Similarly, indentation is often used for the body of a block, as in:

```
if ( expression ) {
   List-of-statements1
   }
else {
   List-of-statements2
   }
```

and

```
while ( expression ) {
   List-of-statements
   }
```

These uses of indentation are distinct from use to show subordination of an implementation to its specification. Indentation is said to be *overloaded*. Indentation in code signifies two different things: The specification-implementation hierarchy, and the whole-part hierarchy.

It is unfortunate that the construct we use for specifications is called a "comment" because this suggests that they are inessential window dressing. Yes, from the point of view of the programming language, comments are inessential. They are frequently omitted, and are sometimes only added to code later as an afterthought, perhaps to avoid having points deducted by the homework grader. But that attitude is entirely the reverse of what is being advocated here. You are trying to learn how to program, both easily and well. There is no point in writing code before you know what that code is supposed to accomplish. Write a specification (in a comment) that defines the task required *before* writing code that performs the task.

Because specifications are written in comments, they are totally ignored by the programming language, as if they were not there. Thus, what we are describing is a mere convention, and the programming language couldn't care less whether the specifications are there or not. But it is the premise of this book that specifications, and the conventions described here for writing them, are essential for programming. It is up to you, however, to exercise the required self-discipline for following the convention we advocate.

What? Not How?

When we write a specification, we follow the precept that:

☞ **A statement-comment says exactly what code must accomplish, not how it does so.**

Sometimes the distinction between *what* and *how* is abundantly clear because the specification states only the net effect required, and is completely mute on the subject of how to achieve that effect. For example, the specification:[24]

```
/* Rearrange the values of array A[0..n-1] into non-decreasing order. */
```

in no way constrains the algorithm used to do the rearrangement.

The notion of specifications as higher-level code somewhat muddies the waters. A statement comment says "do this", or "do that". It is an imperative, and its verbs can come close to commands in a programming language in which the specification strongly resembles executable code, e.g., "`swap x with y;`". In fact, that's the whole point: *What* for a low-level language is *how* for a higher-level language, with its higher-level abstractions. Programming, in a large measure, involves inventing new conceptual frameworks, and then using them.

Internalizing the distinction between *what* and *how* takes time and practice. There is a natural tendency to describe *processes* and not *requirements*, and this leads people to write specifications in operational terms. The tendency is acute when the likely implementation is iterative.

For example, suppose (at some place in your program) you need to know whether a value `v` occurs in the one-dimensional array `A`. You may be inclined to write:

---

24. This is the first mention of arrays outside of Chapter 2 Prerequisites. If your understanding of arrays and subscripting is shaky, you may wish to review the relevant material there. The notation "`A[`*j*`..`*k*`]`" in a specification refers to the region of array `A` consisting of elements `A[`*j*`]` through `A[`*k*`]`.

```
/* Scan through array A from left to right, inspect each element of A,
   and stop if and when you find v. */
```

This specification describes a *process* the computer can follow to determine whether v is in A. But it is far better to write the specification as something like:

```
/* Determine whether v is in A. */
```

which, although not great, at least says what you want to know, and not how to find out.

Why is this approach better? You might reason: I'm going to have to write code eventually, so why not write a process-oriented description of it in the comment, and be a step ahead? But consider the wider context in which this specification arose: The client of the specification doesn't care a whit how you go about making the determination; it only wants to know whether v is in A. Don't tell the client how you will go about the task; that's your problem. Of course, you are also the client, and take turns considering each perspective.

Writing a specification before rushing headlong into an implementation gives you a chance to ruminate on what it is that you really want. Do you want to know whether v is in A, or do you need to know how many times v occurs in A? Would it be helpful to know exactly where in the array v occurs? In that case, do you want the location of the left-most occurrence, the right-most occurrence, or doesn't it matter. If you will provide the location of v in A, what if it's absent? How then will you convey that fact to the rest of your program? Asking such questions is akin to a requirements elicitation.

Alternation between first specifying and then implementing is a salutary rhythm that supports the recommendation:

☞ **Code with deliberation. Be mindful.**

Even the most experienced coders are sometimes in a bit of a fog as they grope their way toward a solution. Early mindfulness will save you time in the long run, and writing the specification is a good place to start.

A specification provides a forgiving framework in which to sharpen written expression of your ideas. The familiar setting of English, rather than the temperamental setting of code, lets you:

☞ **Repeatedly improve comments by relentless copy editing.**

You are presumably more comfortable in English than in your programming language. Perfecting the specification in a natural language allows you to focus, and avoid distractions.[25]

As you work on the specification, one touchstone is human readability and comprehensibility, and not arcane syntax and other rules of your programming language. Which human? You, for starters. It is helpful to have a conversation with yourself while writing the comment, as your thoughts clarify. Second, you should assume that others will read your code; comments provide the only explicit way in code to record your intent, and your readers will appreciate a record of your thinking.[26] And finally,

25. However, be on the lookout for ambiguities that can arise in English, and are one of its shortcomings.

26. We have emphasized the distinction between What? (the specification), and How? (the

you again. While writing code, you are immersed in it, and your ideas are readily at hand. But step away, and return a few days later, and your code will "look like Greek" to you. You will no longer remember your own rationale, and you will appreciate having left behind a record of your intent—for yourself.

A specification articulates what a piece of code provides to the rest of the program. It is a *contract* (double line) between the implementation (gray), and the rest of the program (green). It says, in effect, "My implementation will provide you with such and such so that you can do whatever is necessary to get the rest of the program to work". But a specification is not a blanket promise. The contract has a proviso: "My promise is contingent on the rest of the program providing me with this and that, which is what I need to do my thing".

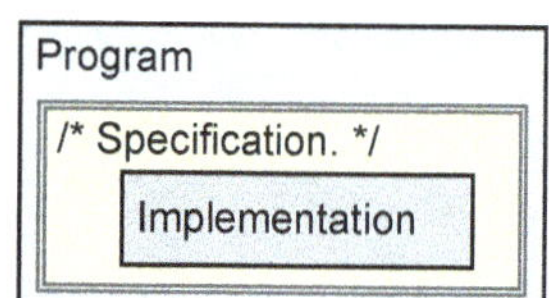

Specifications introduce *modularity* in code. The *interface* (double line) subdivides a program into two parts: a surrounding context (green), and an implementation (gray). Modularity in code is essential. It is a fundamental notion that allows coders to

☞ **Control complexity.**

It works all scales: Between thousand-line modules, and within one-page methods. Today's toy exercise is tomorrow's critical infrastructure on which someone's life, or some organization's well-being, will depend. Writing specifications from the get-go prepares for that inevitable mission creep.

A specification is at once both liberating (the implementation *can* be *any* code that delivers on the contract), and constraining (the implementation *must* deliver *what* the contract promises). Specifications enhance code pliability, and code comprehensibility.

Pliability derives from the specification's limited domain of discourse: Implementation details that are not described in the specification are off limits to the rest of the program. This principle, known as *information hiding*, lubricates the code, and allows the implementation to change without affecting the surrounding program. Note, however, that no programming-language feature prevents access to the implementation details; rather, you must voluntarily enforce information hiding to preserve your code's pliability.[27]

The specification's restricted focus also promotes comprehensibility: To understand the code, a client only needs to absorb what the specification says, and can ignore what it doesn't say.

Once you adopt the mindset that a specification is a contract, you realize that text like:

```
/* Determine whether v is in A. */
```

is hopelessly vague: What exactly is it that will be determined, and under what circumstances? And it is with such concerns in mind that a specification ends up as the more precise:

---

implementation). One might argue that Why? (the intent) is a third and distinct aspect deserving separate memorialization in code. However, we will let What? stand in for Why? rather than invent a new kind of comment or comment convention. In effect, What? explains why you wrote the code you did.

27. The programming language has support for information-hiding at the level of methods and classes. The convention whereby fine-grained specifications are treated as abstraction barriers between statements adopts the client-server encapsulation model of methods and classes.

```
/* Given array A[0..n-1], n≥0, and value v, let k be smallest nonnegative
   integer s.t. A[k]==v, or let k==n if there are no occurrences of v in A. */
```

Notice how this specification addresses and answers all the open questions we previously had with the vague specification.

Although the more precise specification is rather detailed, it still harbors subtle, unstated and understated assumptions:

- The type of array elements is left unsaid. Absent such a mention, the contract does not restrict the type of array elements.
- On the other hand, the specification mentions `A[k]==v`, and thus implies that (this kind of) equality must be defined for the types of `v` and array elements of `A`.
- The bound `n≥0` allows `n` to equal 0. Thus, the contract subtly requires the implementation to work in the degenerate case of an array of no variables.

The implementation must work correctly whenever the specification occurs in a context in which `A`, `n`, and `v` exist and satisfy the requirements.

One can legitimately ask whether very precise specifications are comprehensible. Detail, even if essential, can adversely impact understandability. With this in mind, it is helpful to allow for a modicum of informal text to set the stage:

☞ Consider including a brief descriptive prefix in a statement-comment.

This could lead us to the following specification:

```
/* Find v in A[0..n-1]. Given array A[0..n-1], n≥0, and value v, let k be
   the smallest nonnegative integer s.t. A[k]==v, or let k==n if there are no
   occurrences of v in A. */
```

The specification prefix provides helpful context, but is insufficiently precise by itself.

Additional implementation notes that annotate statements in an implementation can also be helpful. These are inward-facing documentation that is not meant for the specification's client. We illustrate such annotations in a refinement of our sample specification, albeit one might hope that such clarifying comments would not be needed. They are explanatory, and are more of the *how* than the *what* variety:

```
/* Find v in A[0..n-1]. Given array A[0..n-1], n≥0, and value v, let k be
   smallest nonnegative integer s.t. A[k]==v, or let k==n if there are no
   occurrences of v in A. */
   int k = 0;             // Start k at the left end of array A.
   while ( k<n &&         // Stop as soon as k runs off the right end of A, or
           A[k]!=v )      //    as soon as A[k]==v.
      k++;                // Step one place to the right.
```

Our guidelines aim for the advantages of a blend of both precision and informality.

Finally, observe that a specification can be totally redundant and counterproductive, e.g., the following two lines say exactly the same thing:

```
/* Declare int variable temp, and initialize it to x. */
   int temp = x;
```

The precept that rules out such wasteful nonsense is:

☞ **Omit specifications whose implementations are at least as brief and clear as the specification itself.**

Of course, your reading literacy for code will influence whether you consider any given specification duplicative.

States and Effects

The input-output specification

```
/* Input integer n, and output n*n. */
```

defines the behavior of a program in terms of its external input data and its external output data. In the specification, "input" is the verb meaning "read external input data", and "output" is the verb meaning "write the value to external output data".

The term "I/O spec" is also used more generally to define required behavior of a code fragment with respect to certain program variables. For example, in the specification:

```
/* Given array A[0..n-1], n≥0, and value v, let k be smallest nonnegative
   integer s.t. A[k]==v, or let k==n if there are no occurrences of v in A. */
```

the "inputs" are the values in variables `A[0..n-1]`, `n`, and `v`, and the "output" is the value in variable `k`.

Similarly, in the specification

```
/* Swap x and y. */
```

the "inputs" are the values in variables `x` and `y` beforehand, and the "outputs" are the values in variables `x` and `y` afterwards.

In general, a specification defines outputs in terms of inputs, be they external inputs and outputs, or variables of the program.

We frequently write specifications using the *precondition-postcondition* pattern:

```
/* Given precondition, establish postcondition. */
```

where *precondition* is what can be assumed, and *postcondition* is what must be accomplished. A variable whose value is used in the *precondition* is an input, and a variable whose value must (or can) be modified to establish the postcondition is an output.

For example, in

```
/* Given x≥0, let y be the square root of x. */
```

`x` is an input (variable) and `y` is an output (variable). The value of input variable `x` is also used in the postcondition to define how `y` must be changed.

When a variable is both an input and output, it is important to distinguish between the value in the variable beforehand, and the value afterwards. For example, were we to write:

```
/* Swap x and y. */
```

in the precondition-postcondition form, it might read:

```
/* Given x==X and y==Y, establish x==Y and y==X. */
```

where we have introduced the local pronouns "X" and "Y" to refer to the values in x and y beforehand.

The values of a program's variables, and the status of its external input and output data streams, change as the program executes. In fact, each execution of a program statement causes such a change, and that can be said to be its purpose. The values of variables, and the status of the external input and output streams, are collectively part of the program's *execution state*, or *state* for short, and a change in state is known as an *effect*.

The set of states about which a specification says anything is proscribed by its precondition. The specification says nothing about what may or must happen if the code is executed in any other state. Behavior in such cases is *undefined*, and can be anything.

For example, the specification:

```
/* Given x≥0, let y be the square root of x. */
```

says nothing about what *must* happen if x is negative. It only says: Provided the state beforehand is as described, then the state afterwards must be as described. The implementation may apply to other states, but that would be serendipitous because it is only required to work for states that are characterized by the precondition. Thus,

```
/* Given x≥0, let y be the square root of x. */
   y = Math.sqrt( Math.abs( x ) );
```

happens to execute without error for *any* possible x. But such self-protection is totally unnecessary because the precondition effectively says: Don't worry about the case of negative x. In fact, silently accepting unexpected values can be counterproductive because the practice may delay the discovery of program errors.[28]

Strictly speaking, it is not an error for a program to reach a specification in a state that does not satisfy the specification's precondition—it is just rare and undesirable because programs are intended to do something specific and not arbitrary.

We aim for specifications that are both precise and complete, but in practice there are practical limits on how much detail to include in a specification. Accordingly, we adopt conventions that govern what is taken for granted, and therefore can be omitted from explicit mention in a specification. These include:

- *Input variable declarations and initializations.* All input variables have been declared, and contain values.[29]
- *Output variable declarations.* All output variables have either been declared, or are to be declared afresh.
- *No declaration conflicts.* Fresh variable declarations will not interfere with already-existing variables with the same name.
- *Memory sufficiency.* The computer memory has space for any new variables required.

28. See the further discussion on this point in section Assertions (p. 49).

29. In the language defined in Chapter 2, if a variable is not otherwise initialized by an explicit expression, it is initialized with the default value of the variable's type. Nonetheless, because in some languages, e.g., C/C++, declared variables are not necessarily initialized with specific values, the text will allow for the possibility that a variable is *uninitialized*.

- *I/O effect.* If input is required, the input-cursor will be advanced beyond whatever is input.
- *No side effects.* Unmentioned preexisting variables must not be changed, and no input or output operations occur other than what is mentioned.
- *Numerical representations.* Numerical input and output data are base-10 numerals, possibly in scientific notation, optionally signed.
- *Numerical magnitudes.* Numerical input data fit in whatever type of program variables the program chooses to use for them.
- *Numerical precision.* Requirements stated as if values were infinite precision reals may hold only approximately when implemented as floating-point values.
- *No arithmetic overflows.* Either no overflows occur, or their effects are considered benign.
- *Termination.* Execution completes unless an unending process is explicitly specified.
- *Time sufficiency.* Execution is not time constrained unless a performance guarantee is explicitly specified.
- *Defensive programming optional.* It is not necessary to detect badly-formed input data; the program can fail gracelessly when given such inputs unless detection of bad input is explicitly specified.
- *Syntactic adequacy.* The implementation must have appropriate syntax for the context in which it occurs. For example, in a setting that requires a single *statement*, the implementation will be a single *statement*.

Thus, for example, the implementation we have written in:

```
/* Input integer n, and output n*n. */
   int n=in.nextInt(); System.out.println( n*n );
```

is acceptable even though:

- The magnitude of the input could exceed the square root of the largest integer that can be represented in 32 bits, in which case the computation of `n*n` would cause an arithmetic overflow.
- The input could be text that is not a base-10 numeral, in which case `nextInt()` will fail.
- The code fragment could be executed in a state in which there is no room left in the computer memory for even one more variable, e.g., `n`, in which case the program will stop running with a message about being "Out of memory".
- The given implementation will not be acceptable in a context where only a single *statement* is allowed. However, it could be fixed by writing the implementation as a *block*:

```
if ( condition )
   /* Input integer n, and output n*n. */
      { int n=in.nextInt(); System.out.println( n*n ); }
```

Many real-world programs are required to account for exceptional cases such as those that are assumed by convention to not arise. These requirements are so pervasive that they are usually described in an overarching document rather than in each and every specification. We typically ignore such considerations in this book, and assume they are not at issue. We note, however, that "exceptions are the rule", and much of the difficulty of writing good code involves proper handling of exceptional cases.

Conditions and Sets of States

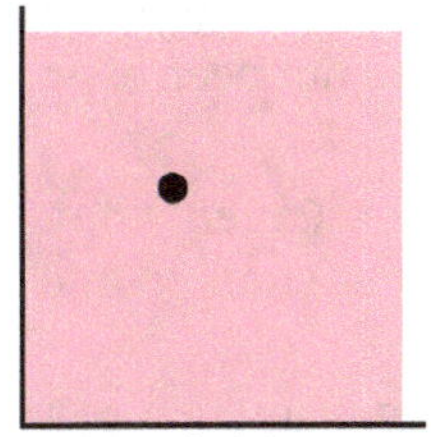

state and state space

Interrupt a program's execution, and inspect the contents of each of its *n* variables. The *n* values you find in the snapshot can be thought of as the coordinates of a point in an *n*-dimensional space, where there is one dimension for each variable. We have called such a point a *state* of the program's execution, and we call the set of all such states that may arise the program's *state space.*

A program's state space differs in a number of ways from the Euclidean space one is accustomed to in mathematics or physics. For one thing, the values contained in the numerical variables of a digital computer are discrete, not continuous. Also, some variables have non-numerical values, like characters, strings, and Booleans. In addition to variables, the status of the input and output streams is also relevant, so add two more dimensions for those aspects of the state. Furthermore, variables come and go during execution, so the number of dimensions is dynamic, and changes over the course of a program's execution. Finally, the location in the program of the next statement to be executed is also part of the state. Notwithstanding these distinctions, thinking of the snapshot as a point in a higher-dimensional space is a compelling abstraction.

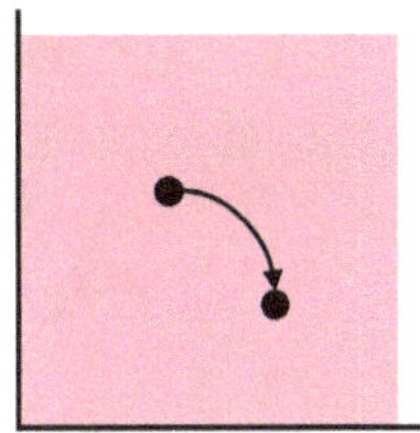

state transition

Programs execute by transitioning in the state space from state to state.

Armed with the notions of state and state space, we can restate the meaning of the specification:

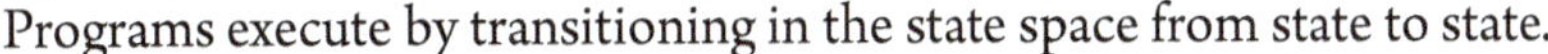

```
/* Given precondition, establish postcondition. */
```

more precisely. It means:

```
/* Provided the program is in a state that is described by the precondition,
   transition to a state that is described by the postcondition. */
```

which can be depicted by the Venn diagram to the right.

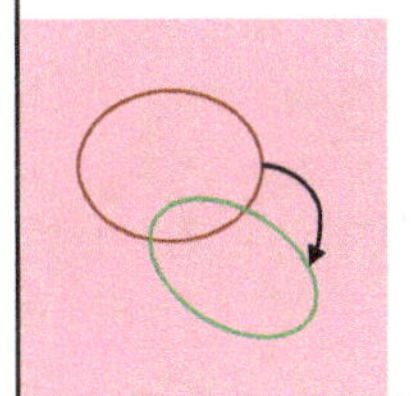

precondition to postcondition

This begs the question: How are states described? Before addressing this question, let's consider two specifications for which no obvious preconditions are at play.

The first example has no precondition whatsoever, and thus its implementation must work correctly in every conceivable state of the state space:

```
/* Output "Hello World." */
```

The postcondition requires that the text "Hello World." be appended to the output, and the implicit "no side effects" convention requires that no variables be changed. This refinement does the trick:

```
/* Output "Hello World." */
   System.out.println( "Hello World." );
```

The second sample specification is:

```
/* Swap x and y. */
```

Like the first example, this also appears to have no precondition, but that is not quite true. It has an unstated, implicit precondition: Variables x and y must exist, and must have been assigned values. The implementation of this specification is not required to do anything meaningful when it occurs in a context where there are no such variables; it is not even required to compile. Nor is it required to do anything meaningful if values have not been assigned to both x and y. Thus, the swap specification is really:

```
/* Given that variables x and y have been declared and have assigned values,
   swap x and y. */
```

This can be refined either by the standard implementation:

```
/* Swap x and y. */
   int temp = x;
   x = y;
   y = temp;
```

or by this alternative implementation:

```
/* Swap x and y. */
   x = x+y;
   y = x-y;
   x = x-y;
```

The two refinements are equivalent, and are therefore both technically correct. They are equivalent in the sense that their net effect is the same for all possible values of x and y.[30]

Returning to the original question, we ask: How does a precondition (or postcondition) describe a set of states? One answer is that in a specification, you are free to use the descriptive power of English to define the set; we have been doing so all along. A second answer is that you can use the descriptive power of your programming language's Boolean expressions, i.e., *conditions*.

You are already familiar with the notion of a *condition*, e.g., in **if**-statements, **while**-statements, and **for**-statements. For example, in the code:

```
/* Set y to the square root of x if x is not negative, and 0 otherwise. */
   if ( x>=0 ) y = Math.sqrt(x); else y = 0;
```

the *condition* x>=0 is evaluated during program execution, and determines the next statement to be executed depending on whether it evaluates to **true** or **false**.

In contrast, in a specification, the same *condition* is *not* code; rather, it defines a set of states, i.e., the set of states for which the Boolean expression is **true**. In the specification:

```
/* Given x≥0, let y be the square root of x. */
```

the *condition* x≥0 is the precondition, i.e., it is a definition of the set of states for which

30. Notwithstanding their equivalence, the second implementation offends as "too cute by a half", and should be avoided. You can readily understand the standard code for swap, whereas you need to study the second implementation to be convinced that is also correct. Equivalence of the two implementations follows from arithmetic properties of infinite-precision integers (if we ignore the possibility of arithmetic overflow), or from arithmetic properties of two's-complement, finite-precision integers (if we don't ignore the possibility of arithmetic overflow). This property is not obvious at first glance. It is a curiosity that is not worth the bother. Precept: Avoid obscurity.

the implementation is required to establish the postcondition. That set consists of all states for which x is greater than or equal to 0, and no others. Specifically, all states for which x is less than 0 are eliminated from consideration, and can be ignored. The values of all the other variables are unconstrained, i.e., they are free to be anything.

In the given specification, "let y be the square root of x" is the postcondition, i.e., a description of the set of states one of which the program is required to reach. A Boolean expression that describes that set is "y*y==x", which constrains the x and y components of the state, and leaves all other components unconstrained.[31] Notice that the specification is *nondeterministic*, i.e., it admits both of the following two implementations:

```
/* Given x≥0, let y be the square root of x. */
   y = Math.sqrt(x);
```

and

```
/* Given x≥0, let y be the square root of x. */
   y = -Math.sqrt(x);
```

A good rule of thumb is:

☞ **Don't make postconditions any more specific than needed.**

For example, writing the postcondition as the Boolean expression "y==Math.sqrt(x)" would exclude the second implementation. If there is no reason to exclude an implementation, don't.

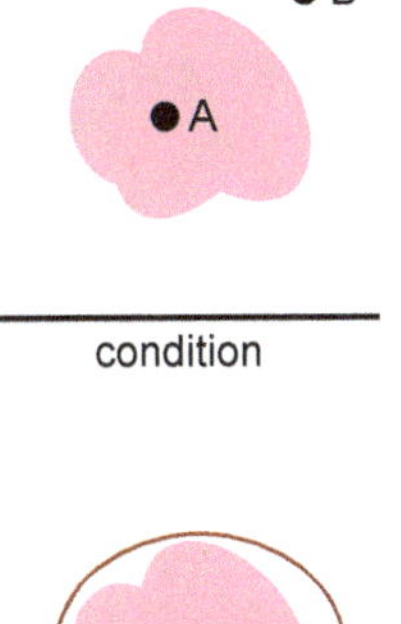

condition

Consider an arbitrary *condition*, say, one that defines the blob-like set of states depicted. Each point in the region of the state space defined by the *condition* is said to *satisfy* the *condition*, e.g., state A. Conversely, each point outside the region is said to not satisfy the *condition*, e.g., state B.

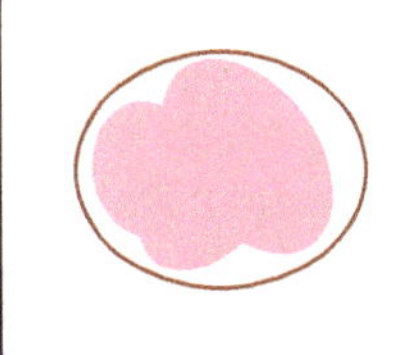
weakened condition

The *condition* can be *weakened* to define a superset of the blob's states, e.g., all those inside the red oval, or *strengthened* to define a subset of the blob's states, e.g., only those inside the green oval. A weakened *condition* is *weaker* in the sense that it is *less* constraining. Similarly, a strengthened *condition* is *stronger* in the sense that it is *more* constraining.

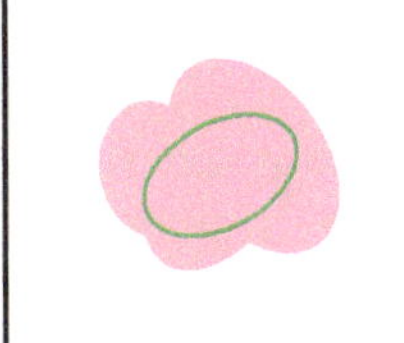
strengthened condition

To be specific, suppose the blob is defined by the *condition* "point in NYC". Then the red oval might be the weakened *condition* "point in NY state", and the green oval might be the strengthened *condition* "point in Manhattan". We return to this example in the next chapter.[32]

Assertions

Methods can protect themselves from misuse by their clients by explicitly checking the validity of their arguments, and aborting execution if any are invalid. Alternatively, a protection may derive from a builtin check. For example, because **int** division by

31. The requirement that this action be done without changing x is implicit in the locution "let y be", i.e., in the absence of an indication that x can be changed, it can't.

32. Strangers to the United States need to know that NYC is New York City, which is situated in the state of New York. NYC consists of five boroughs, one of which is Manhattan. Note the two uses of "state": One for points in the state space, and the other for one of the fifty regions that are united in the USA.

zero is not defined, the method nth (below) will abort program execution if it is ever invoked with a zero argument for n:

```
/* Given n!=0, return x/n. */
static int nth(int x, int n) { return x/n; }
```

The rationale for self-protection is that it is far better for the program to stop and warn than it would be for it to exhibit undefined behavior, e.g., return an arbitrary result.

This example illustrates the benefit:

```
/* Compute n!=0 such that blah blah. */
   ...
/* Given n!=0, let y be the nth part of x. */
   y = nth(x,n);
/* Whatever. */
   ...
```

When we wrote "blah blah", we fully believed that it would never produce an n that was zero, but we may have erred. Were it not for nth aborting execution when n is zero, we might have executed Whatever with unpredictable consequences.

Now consider this analogous code:

```
/* Compute n!=0 such that blah blah. */
   ...
/* Given n!=0, do Whatever. */
   ...
```

It has no invocation of nth to protect it, but is just as vulnerable to the mistake in "blah blah". Specifically, Whatever might do nonsensical computations based on the false assumption that n could never be zero, and eventually the program crashes or produces garbage output. You would then have to understand why, and after a laborious debugging process, would discover that "blah blah" could (and did) produce a zero n, perhaps way earlier in the program's execution.

You would have saved yourself a lot of grief if you had written:

```
/* Compute n!=0 such that blah blah. */
   ...
/* Given n!=0, do Whatever. */
   assert n!=0: "blah blah computed a zero n";
   ...
```

where the **assert**-statement prints the given error message and stops program execution if the *condition* n!=0 is not **true**. Alternatively, rather than placing the **assert** ahead of Whatever (to guarantee its precondition) you could have placed it at the end of "blah blah" (to guarantee its postcondition):

```
/* Compute n!=0 such that blah blah. */
   ...
   assert n!=0: "blah blah computed a zero n";
/* Given n!=0, do Whatever. */
   ...
```

It is clearly overkill to begin or end the implementation of every specification with an explicit **assert**. But when programs are complicated, and there is a significant risk of error, judicious placement of **assert**-statements can pay off. When the *condition* is complicated, it is common to write a **boolean** method to do the check, and invoke that method from the **assert**.[33]

It is worth noting that floating-point division by 0 is different from **int** division by 0: Rather than aborting execution, the result of floating-point division by zero is `Infinity`. Other extended floating-point values include `-Infinity` and `NaN` (Not a Number). For example, `Math.sqrt(x)` of a negative `x` is `NaN`. Such values propagate through computations without causing exceptions, but are at least distinguishable from normal numbers, which is a clue that something has gone awry.

Declaration Specifications

We have focused on specifying how code affects the values of variables; thus, we adopted a code-centric perspective. We now switch orientation, and embrace a data-centric perspective. Specifically, we ask: What values do the variables contain during program execution, and what do those values represent? The answers are articulated in the variables' declarations and their specifications.

The specification of a single variable has the form:

```
Declaration-of-one-variable // Specification.
```

and for a group of variables has the form:

```
/* Specification. */
   Declarations-of-related-variables
```

A declaration associates a type with a variable, which provides an initial constraint on the set of values the variable can contain. Such a restriction is helpful, but it is a very weak form of specification.[34]

A full declaration specification provides what is known as a *representation invariant*, a constraint on the permissible values of the variable(s) according to their purpose in the program. The specification states that at all times during the execution of the program (other than during brief moments before initialization, and prior to completion of updating) the variable(s) have the properties and relationships ascribed to them by the representation invariant.

---

33. If your programming language doesn't support **assert** statements, you can write the similar code:

```
if ( n==0 ) {
   System.out.println("blah blah computed a zero n");
   System.exit(1);
   }
```

where calling `System.exit` with a non-zero argument terminates execution with an error code. The advantages of **assert** statements include:

- They are succinct and distinctive documentation of required conditions.
- They pinpoint their location when they fail to hold.
- Automated software analysis tools can use them as a point of departure for reasoning about program correctness.
- Their runtime overhead can be eliminated in one fell swoop with a compiler directive to ignore them if you choose to live dangerously in "production mode".

34. A major difference between Java and C/C++ (on the one hand) and Python and JavaScript (on the other) concerns typed variables. Python and JavaScript variables are untyped, and can be assigned values of any type. Java and C/C++ variables can only be assigned values whose type is compatible with the variable's declared type.

For a single variable that stands on its own, we typically write the representation invariant to the right of the declaration. The more precise you are about a variable's representation invariant, the easier it will be to write code that maintains and uses it. In effect, the representation invariant becomes a glossary entry that states the variable's precise meaning.

For example, suppose each value in the external input data is first "read" and is subsequently "processed". Then this specification ascribes one meaning to variable `count`:

```
int count; // # of input values read so far.
```

while this specification ascribes a different meaning to variable `count`:

```
int count; // # of input values processed so far.
```

The distinction may be important (during the period between inputting the value and processing it), and you will benefit from having stated the representation invariant clearly and explicitly.

When an action by the program makes a variable's representation invariant no longer hold, the variable should be updated as soon as practical. For example, say `count` is the number of values processed so far. Then it should be incremented immediately after processing in order to minimize the period during which its invariant doesn't hold.

A *data structure* is a group of variables that work together in a coordinated fashion. We typically write a data structure's representation invariant in a comment that introduces the declarations of the variables. Additional comments on individual declarations can be used to further clarify the invariant.

For example, suppose we wish to specify how the array `A`, and variables `size` and `maxSize` work together to store a list of at most `maxSize` integers, where `size` is the current number of items in the list. We write:

```
/* A[0..size-1] are the current items in A[0..maxSize-1], 0≤size≤maxSize. */
   int A[];       // receptacle for items in a list.
   int size;      // current # of elements in list, 0≤size≤maxSize.
   int maxSize;   // maximum # of elements storable in the list.
```

to specify the representation invariant of the list.

We mentioned earlier that what a specification doesn't say is (in a sense) as important as what it does say. In this regard, note how the representation invariant above does not in any way constrain the values in `A[size..maxSize-1]`. Specifically, the implementation is free to use that region however it wishes, e.g., it can leave detritus there when the number of elements in the list is reduced.[35]

Updating a data structure often requires multiple steps, and until those steps have been completed, the collection of variables that make up the structure are in a bit of disarray. During that time, the data structure's representation invariant does not hold; it should be restored in its entirety as soon as possible.

With the exception of the brief periods before it can be fully restored, a representation invariant serves as a precondition for every statement in its scope—provided, of course, that we take care to maintain it as circumstances unfold.

---

35. This data structure is discussed at length in Chapter 12 Collections, and again in Chapter 18 Classes and Objects.

Method Specifications

A method's specification describes the effects (if any) and the return value (if any) of the method in terms of its parameters, and in terms of the (static) variables of the class in which the method is declared. It takes the form:

```
/* Specification. */
Method definition
```

The method's specification is known as its *header-comment.* In contrast with the implementation of a statement comment, we do not indent the method definition under its header-comment.[36]

For example:

```
/* Return the larger of the values x and y. */
int max(int x, int y) { if ( x<y ) return y; else return x; }
```

The list of parameter types is implicitly part of the method's specification, i.e., invocation of `max` requires two arguments of type **`int`**.[37]

In contrast with `max`, which must work correctly for any two argument values of type **`int`**, some methods impose additional requirements on their argument values. For example, method `find`:

```
/* Given int array A[0..n-1] sorted in non-decreasing order, and int v, return
   an index where A[k]==v, or return n if v does not occur in A. */
int find( int A[], int n, int v) { ⟨body of find⟩ }
```

requires that in any invocation of `find` the first argument must be an array that is sorted in non-decreasing order, and the second argument must be an **`int`** that is no greater than the length of that array. These requirements are parts of the *precondition* that constrains input parameters `A` and `n`.

The specification of a method that depends on (or that modifies) a class variable should state so explicitly. For example:

```
class C {
   static int v;         // Current input value.
   static int count;     // # of input values processed so far.
   ...
   /* Process the current input value v, and increment count. */
   static void process() {
      ⟨Code to process v.⟩
      count++;
      }
   }
```

Alternatively, you can implicitly rely on the variable's representation invariant as part of the method specification's precondition and postcondition, and omit mention of it, e.g., by leaving out the red phrase above.

---

36. This layout convention saves horizontal space, and we choose to forgo explicit acknowledgment of the hierarchical relation between a method's header and its definition.

37. We assume here that there is only one definition of method `max`. Some programming languages, e.g., full Java, support multiple definitions of methods with a given name but different parameter types. This feature is known as *method overloading.*

It is the client's obligation to only invoke a method with input arguments that satisfy the preconditions of the method's corresponding parameters. The method may choose to protect itself by asserting that the conditions hold, and thereby abort execution if they don't. Alternatively, the method may choose to trust its clients, and let them suffer the consequences of misuse.

Methods with return type **void** do not return a value; rather, they are invoked for their side effects. For example, method sort:

```
/* Rearrange array A[0..n-1] to be in non-decreasing order. */
void sort( int A[], int n) { ⟨body of sort⟩ }
```

requires that when sort returns, the values in the first argument of the invocation (an **int** array) must have been rearranged to be in non-decreasing order. This requirement is the *postcondition* that constrains output parameter A.

We have seen that the implementation of a statement specification of the form:

```
/* Given precondition, establish postcondition. */
```

is required to establish the postcondition whenever it is executed in a state that satisfies the precondition. Similarly, the body of a method is required to establish the postcondition(s) of its output arguments (and/or return value) whenever it is invoked with input arguments that satisfy their preconditions.

Class Specifications

The specification of a class has the form

```
/* Specification. */
Class definition
```

As for methods, the class's specification is known as its *header-comment*, and we do not indent the definition under the header-comment.

A class consists of its methods and declarations, each of which already has its own specification. It is pointless to repeat all of that in the class's header comment, so we consider it to be incorporated "by reference".[38]

Because class specifications can rely on the specifications of the class's variables and methods for their technical aspects, they are often more descriptive and historical than the other forms of specification. For example:

```
/* Rational. A module for the manipulation of rationals, including operations
   for +, -, *, /, conversion to String, and equality.
   Author: Joe Blow.
   Created: 12/25/2022.
   Revision History: Converted to use unbounded integers, 12/25/2023. */
class Rational {
   ...
   } /* Rational */
```

38. We will learn later that methods and declarations can be **private**, which means that they are not part of the exported interface of the class. Thus, only the non-**private** methods and declarations are incorporated by reference into the class's specification.

CHAPTER 4

Stepwise Refinement

We have defined a *refinement* to be the implementation of a specification. Some refinements consist entirely of code:

```
/* Swap x and y. */
   int temp = x;
   x = y;
   y = temp;
```

while other refinements consist entirely of further specifications:

```
/* Swap A[0..n-1] and B[0..n-1]. */
   /* Declare temp[0..n-1], and let temp[0..n-1] be A[0..n-1]. */
   /* Let A[0..n-1] be B[0..n-1]. */
   /* Let B[0..n-1] be temp[0..n-1]. */
```

In general, the refinement of a specification is a mixture of code and other specifications that must themselves be further refined in order to complete the program segment.

The process of refining specifications until they have all been elaborated in code is known as Stepwise Refinement. It is an example of the general problem-solving technique called Divide and Conquer.

Divide and Conquer

Solving a problem by dividing it into constituent parts, and then solving those subparts, is known as *Divide and Conquer*. The technique is said to have been invented by Julius Caesar, who used it in warfare, and may have declared:

> All Gaul is divided into three parts. To conquer Gaul:
> - First, conquer the first part.
> - Then, conquer the second part.
> - Finally, conquer the third part.

Writing a computer program is a task that is amenable to Divide and Conquer. In a proclamation parallel to Caesar's, we say:

> To write a program:
> - First, break it into subprograms.
> - Then, write each subprogram separately.

Divide and Conquer, when used as a methodology for programming, is called *Stepwise Refinement.*

Stepwise Refinement is a *top-down* approach to programming. You begin at the *top*, which is an all-encompassing specification of what your program must do, and you work your way *down* to the minutest details of how it will do so:

☞ **Program top-down, outside-in.**

The sub-specifications defined by refinements on the way down form a hierarchy, like subsections in the outline of an essay.

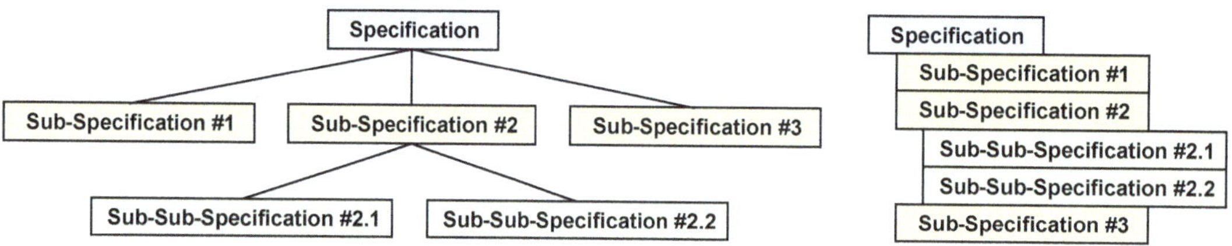

You may view the refinement hierarchy as either a tree or an outline; it's the same, regardless.

Stepwise Refinement can be viewed as a program for coding: To write a program *P*, you follow these instructions:

```
if ( P is simple to write ) Write it;
else {
    Refine P into simpler subprograms;
    Write each subprogram;
    }
```

Understand that this is not a template for the code that you are writing. Rather, it is a rule for you to follow as you program, as if you were a computer, and it is the program you are executing.

In the description of Stepwise Refinement, **Refine** means "divide into parts". For our purposes, there are only five ways to do so:

Sequential steps
Do one thing after another.
Case analysis
Do one thing or another.
Iteration
Do one thing repeatedly.
Recursion
Do something based on self-similarity.
Selection from a library of patterns
Do some complex pattern of the previous four kinds of refinement, selected from a library of known techniques.

This limited pallet of possibilities allows you to ask at each stage of Stepwise Refinement the simple question: Which of the five choices do I make? We discuss the five types of refinement, and the requirements on their constituent subparts, in separate sections below.[39]

39. We omit discussion of a sixth possibility, parallel programming, which allows the additional form of refinement:
Concurrency: Do multiple things simultaneously.

Stepwise Refinement is *recursive* because it uses itself in its own definition: The way you "Write each subprogram" is to use the very Divide-and-Conquer method being described.

If you are new to recursion, you may worry that the process may never stop. The first two lines of the poem *Siphonaptera* by the 19th-century mathematician Augustus De Morgan suggest this possibility [9]:

> Great fleas have little fleas upon their backs to bite 'em,
> And little fleas have lesser fleas, and so ad infinitum.
> And the great fleas themselves, in turn, have greater fleas to go on;
> While these again have greater still, and greater still, and so on.

However, if we are careful to require that the refinements are progressively simpler to write, the recursion will eventually stop at the so-called *base case*:

if (*P* is simple to write) Write it;

The base case in programming is a specification that you don't have to think about because you instinctively know how to code it. Accordingly, provided that the subproblems into which you refine *P* in fact get simpler, you don't have to worry about an infinite regress.[40]

When you refine a specification, you may sometimes deceive yourself into thinking that a proposed sub-specification will be simpler to code, only to discover that the opposite is true. Be alert to the possibility that you are inadvertently "digging yourself into a hole", and be ready to stop digging.

You may occasionally have a considered reason to refine a specification into something that is decidedly more difficult to code. For example, you may care more about the efficiency of the program you are developing than your own efficiency in completing the programming task. The tradeoff between "quick and dirty" and "if it's worth doing, it's worth doing right" is yours to balance. Be aware that perfectionism risks a regress in the direction of piling greater fleas upon great fleas, *ad infinitum*.

Refining a program into subprograms must be done with care. Yes, "the whole is the sum of its parts", but the parts have to fit together like pieces of a jigsaw puzzle. Each part offers tabs to other parts, which must have matching sockets. A challenge of dividing a program into subprograms is finding interlocking parts that fit together appropriately. Each form of refinement has its own rules for interconnecting its subparts.

Sequential Refinement

A Sequential Refinement implements a specification P with a sequence of steps P_1 through P_n to be executed one after the other:

```
/* Specification P. */
   /* Specification P1. */
   /* Specification P2. */
   ...
   /* Specification Pn. */
```

40. A cosmological version of *Siphonaptera* concerns what supports the Earth? The answer, a giant turtle, inevitably begs the questions: And what supports the turtle? Etc. The ultimate answer: It's turtles all the way down [46].

In general, each step P_k accomplishes something that enables the subsequent steps $P_{k+1},\ldots,P_n$ to contribute to the implementation. Although we have written each step as a specification in a comment, each specification can be a code-level *statement*. Sequential Refinement is so natural that one almost doesn't think of it as refinement. Nonetheless, it is the essence of Divide and Conquer, and the bedrock of Stepwise Refinement.

In the following examples, think of programs as "driving itineraries" or "plans" that describe the route of a trip, say, for a self-driving car. For each plan, we write a specification, and then consider ways to refine it.

Example 1

We wish to drive from LA to NYC, so our top-level specification is:

```
/* Drive from LA to NYC. */
```

If we think of our location as a point in a (geographical) state space, the desired plan is a program that will get us from (somewhere in) LA to (anywhere in) NYC:

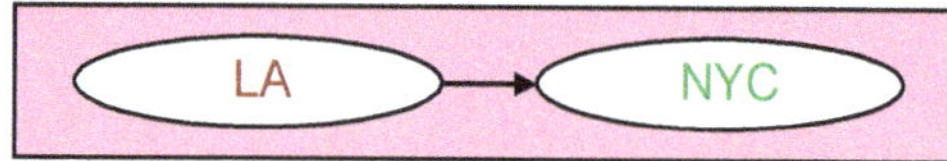

We decide to use Sequential Refinement, and break the journey into two sub-trips:

```
/* Drive from LA to NYC. */
   /* Drive from LA to Chicago. */
   /* Drive from Chicago to NYC. */
```

In the state-space view, we see that the plan will accomplish its goal in two steps, and will take us through the intermediate city of Chicago:

If we think of the two sub-specifications as pieces of a jigsaw puzzle, then the first has a tab, *get to Chicago*, and the second has a matching socket, *starting in Chicago*. The two fit together and interlock. The first leg of the trip enables the second:

Once coupled, the two pieces form a compound piece that offers only a "starting in LA" socket, and a "get to NYC" tab. It is as if the Chicago socket and tab weren't there; they are internal details of no importance to the user of the "Drive from LA to NYC" itinerary. The exposed LA socket and NYC tab of the compound piece are called its *interface*.

Example 2

There is nothing magical about Chicago. We could have chosen St. Louis as the intermediate city:

```
/* Drive from LA to NYC. */
   /* Drive from LA to St. Louis. */
   /* Drive from St. Louis to NYC. */
```

Different roads and scenery, but the same net effect: We get from LA to NYC. Repeating the jigsaw analogy, this compound piece has a different internal structure, but offers other pieces the identical external interface: A socket ("I can leave from LA"), and a tab ("I will arrive in NYC").

Example 3

The following is an incorrect refinement:

```
/* Drive from LA to NYC. */
   /* Drive from LA to Chicago. */
   /* Drive from St. Louis to NYC. */
```

You can't force the mismatched subparts together to achieve your goal. The accomplishment of the first step (getting to Chicago) is irrelevant to the requirement of the second step (being in St. Louis). This is a bug in your plan. Of course, you could create a correct three-part Sequential Refinement by interposing the journey:

```
/* Drive from Chicago to St. Louis. */
```

between the two mismatched subparts.

Example 4

The efficiency of your plan depends on your choice of intermediate city. For example, this route would be inefficient:

```
/* Drive from LA to NYC. */
   /* Drive from LA to Tokyo. */
   /* Drive from Tokyo to NYC. */
```

But even worse, it is not effective: You can't drive from LA to Tokyo because there is a small ocean in the way. Just because you write a specification doesn't mean that it can be achieved.

Example 1, continued

Program execution, like an actual drive, will require reading the plan from top to bottom, and performing those steps, in turn. But Stepwise Refinement is a method for *writing* code, not for *executing* it. Accordingly, we can further refine the subparts in any order:

```
/* Drive from LA to NYC. */
   /* Drive from LA to Chicago. */
   /* Drive from Chicago to NYC. */
      /* Drive from Chicago to Pittsburgh. */
      /* Drive from Pittsburgh to NYC. */
```

Programming can be like painting, where you are free to fill in the details of a sketch in any order:

> ☞ **Refine specifications and placeholders in an order that makes sense for development, without regard to execution order.**

Example 4, continued

If in the course of attempting a refinement you run into difficulty, you can *backtrack*, i.e., undo the refinement that led you to the problematic specification, and try another. Perhaps you only discover the Pacific Ocean when you go to refine:

```
/* Drive from LA to Tokyo. */
```

Then this is the time to undo the Sequential Refinement:

```
/* Drive from LA to NYC. */
   /* Drive from LA to Tokyo. */
   /* Drive from Tokyo to NYC. */
```

and find another:

> ☞ **Don't be wedded to code. Revise and rewrite when you discover a better way.**

Hippocratic coding (introduced earlier) aimed to avoid this, but it happens. You're only human.

Example 5

Consider refining the specification:

```
/* Drive from LA to NYC and buy a new car (in any order). */
```

Sequentiality is so intrinsic to natural language that the parenthetical is needed to avoid the implication that "and" means "and then". Two distinct refinements come to mind:

```
/* Drive from LA to NYC and buy a new car (in any order). */
   /* Drive from LA to NYC. */
   /* Buy a new car. */
```

and

```
/* Drive from LA to NYC and buy a new car (in any order). */
   /* Buy a new car. */
   /* Drive from LA to NYC. */
```

Yet another sequential decomposition would be to buy the car in Chicago. We can imagine the conceivable benefits of each order, but these are beyond the scope of what the specification requires. Its two requirements are independent, and each order is admissible.

From the point of view of program states, there are two dimensions, "location of car" and "age of car", and the specification is oblivious to any possible interdependence. Viewed as such, the specification and its (first) refinement are really:

```
/* Get from ⟨LA,OLD⟩ to ⟨NYC,NEW⟩. */
   /* Get from ⟨LA,OLD⟩ to ⟨NYC,OLD⟩. */
   /* Get from ⟨NYC,OLD⟩ to ⟨NYC,NEW⟩. */
```

Note that in reading the informal step:

```
/* Drive from LA to NYC. */
```

you assumed implicitly that the car's status didn't change during that leg of the journey, as per our implicit *no-side-effects* rule that unmentioned state components remain unchanged (p. 46), whereas a full description of the step as a mapping in a two-dimensional state space makes this requirement explicit:

```
/* Get from ⟨LA,OLD⟩ to ⟨NYC,OLD⟩. */
```

as does the Sequential Refinement of this step that passes through Chicago:

```
/* Get from ⟨LA,OLD⟩ to ⟨NYC,NEW⟩. */
   /* Get from ⟨LA,OLD⟩ to ⟨NYC,OLD⟩. */
      /* Get from ⟨LA,OLD⟩ to ⟨Chicago,OLD⟩. */
      /* Get from ⟨Chicago,OLD⟩ to ⟨NYC,OLD⟩. */
   /* Get from ⟨NYC,OLD⟩ to ⟨NYC,NEW⟩. */
```

Generalization

Our sample itineraries have set the stage for defining the general principle of Sequential Refinement. We will generalize in several ways. First, we move beyond geographic locations to arbitrary conditions. Second, we loosen the ways in which the parts of a Sequential Refinement couple.

From Locations to Arbitrary Conditions

First, let's generalize specifications like:

```
/* Drive from LA to NYC. */
```

to:

```
/* Get from PRE to POST. */
```

where PRE and POST could be any cities. We have also switched from "drive" to "get" to allow for different means of conveyance.

But why restrict PRE and POST to cities, and why restrict "get" to modes of transportation? Why not allow them to be anything:

```
/* Get from RAGS to RICHES. */
/* Get from MISERY to HAPPINESS. */
/* Get from THEOREM to PROOF. */
/* Get from x≥0 to y is a number that when squared equals x. */
```

In each case, we start in a before-state, and wish to arrive at an after-state.

Thus, PRE and POST are arbitrary preconditions and postconditions, and the specification:

```
/* Get from PRE to POST. */
```

is shorthand for:

```
/* Given that the program is in a state that satisfies condition PRE,
   get to a state that satisfies condition POST. */
```

As with driving, the simplest form of Sequential Refinement is a two-part division, with a specific midpoint MID:

```
/* Get from PRE to POST. */
   /* Get from PRE to MID. */
   /* Get from MID to POST. */
```

This pattern is a direct articulation of the general principle of Divide and Conquer.

Loosening the Coupling

Returning to our trip from LA to NYC, we consider various alternatives to direct application of the above rule. First, consider this refinement:

```
/* Get from LA to NYC. */
   /* Get from LA to Chicago. */
   /* Get from Illinois to NYC. */
```

Because Chicago is in the (USA) state of Illinois, getting to Chicago automatically gets you to Illinois, so this decomposition is valid. But the match between the postcondition of the first leg of the journey and the precondition of the second leg is inexact: Chicago and Illinois.

In the analogy with jigsaw-puzzle pieces, it is as if the socket of the right piece were reamed out to accommodate other kinds of tabs, not only Chicago:

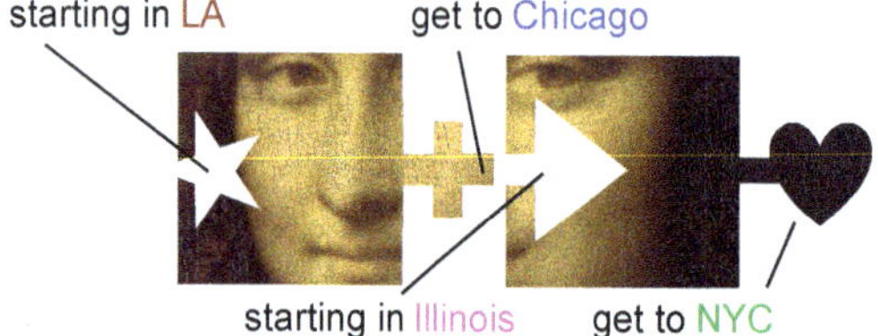

Technically, we have weakened the piece's precondition, from "starting in Chicago" to "starting in Illinois".

The situation is similar for the first leg of the journey. For example, another valid refinement would be:

```
/* Get from LA to NYC. */
   /* Get from California to Chicago. */
   /* Get from Chicago to NYC. */
```

If we know how to get from (anywhere in) California to Chicago, we can get from LA to Chicago.

Again, making the connection with jigsaw-puzzle pieces, it is as if the socket of the left piece were reamed out to admit tabs bigger than "get to LA":

The precondition of the left piece has been weakened.

As we have illustrated, we can use a solution method that is more general than is strictly necessary. Similarly, we can use a method of solution that achieves a more specific goal than is strictly required. For example, consider this refinement:

```
/* Get from LA to NYC. */
   /* Get from LA to Chicago. */
   /* Get from Chicago to Manhattan. */
```

We only need to get to NYC, so a plan that gets us to a particular borough of NYC will do. Rather than reaming out a socket, we shave down a tab:

The "get to Manhattan" tab has been trimmed compared to the original "get to NYC" tab, but still fits in any "starting in NYC" socket. Technically, we have strengthened the piece's postcondition.

Putting all three loosenings together, we obtain the Sequential Refinement:

```
/* Get from LA to NYC. */
   /* Get from California to Chicago. */
   /* Get from Illinois to Manhattan. */
```

In the state-space view, we see that this plan will accomplish its goal in two steps:

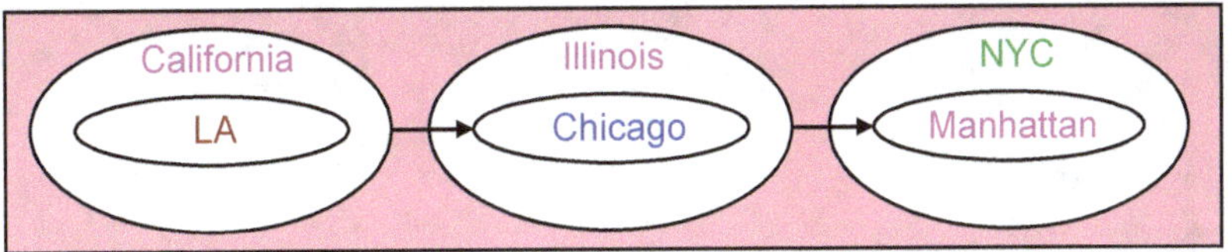

The first step will transition us from anywhere in California (which includes LA) to somewhere in Chicago, and the second step will transition us from anywhere in Illinois (which includes Chicago) to somewhere in Manhattan (which is within NYC).

Although it is self-evident that such a refinement is valid, you may wonder why from the point of view of program development we would call for a more general plan than is needed? At first glance, this refinement is counterintuitive because it would seem to require more ingenuity to get from an arbitrary location in Illinois to NYC than only from Chicago. Aren't we making life more difficult for ourselves? Similarly, you may wonder why we would impose on ourselves the additional burden of getting to Manhattan, a specific borough of NYC, when any borough would do?

The answer is: Methods that are more general-purpose than needed, and methods that achieve more specific goals than needed, are frequently available. Weakening preconditions and strengthening postconditions creates additional valid ways for parts to couple, and anticipates use of such methods. The next section illustrates that this situation occurs frequently, and is standard practice. In fact, doing otherwise is simply not feasible.

Summarizing, the general pattern of a two-part Sequential Refinement is:

```
/* Get from PRE to POST. */
   /* Get from A1 to B1. */
   /* Get from A2 to B2. */
```

where satisfying PRE automatically satisfies A_1, satisfying B_1 automatically satisfies A_2, and satisfying B_2 automatically satisfies POST.

The general pattern of an n-way Sequential Refinement of specification P is:

```
/* Specification P: Get from PRE to POST. */
   /* Get from A1 to B1. */
   /* Get from A2 to B2. */
   ...
   /* Get from An to Bn. */
```

where if PRE is satisfied then A_1 is automatically satisfied, if B_k is satisfied then A_{k+1} is automatically satisfied (for $1 \le k < n$), and if B_n is satisfied then POST is automatically satisfied.

Weakening and Strengthening in Practice

The previous section focused on the internal boundaries of a Sequential Refinement. An alternative and equivalent viewpoint takes the perspective of an individual specification:

```
/* Get from PRE to POST. */
```

in the context of the surrounding program:

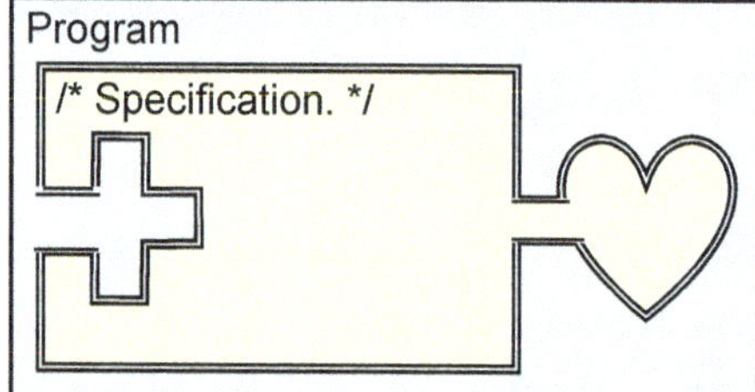

We observe that this specification can be implemented by any code that satisfies the specification:

```
/* Get from PRE' to POST'. */
```

where PRE' is any weakening of PRE, and POST' is any strengthening of POST. Said set theoretically, the set of states assumed to be possible by PRE' can be any superset of the set of states that could have been assumed by PRE. Similarly, the set of states required to be reached by POST' can be any subset of the set of states that would have been required by POST.

We adopt this viewpoint in the following examples, and consider what weakening of the precondition (if any) and strengthening of the postcondition (if any) have been adopted by each implementation.

Example 1. In some settings, the given precondition is absolutely essential, and cannot be weakened:

```
/* Get from x≥0 to y is a number that when squared equals x. */
   y = Math.sqrt(x);
```

The implementation must accept the constraint of the given precondition because the concept of (real) square root is not defined without it, i.e., any weakening of the precondition would result in a specification for which there is no implementation. On the other hand, the implementation choses to compute the positive root of x and ignore the negative root. In effect, it strengthens the postcondition to produce only positive roots. The specification did not say which root was required, so we were free to select one.

Example 2. In some settings, the given precondition is useful, although it is not essential:

```
/* Get from x≥0 to y is |x|. */
   y = x;
```

Given that x is not negative, we can just set y to x, and know that y thereby becomes the absolute value of x. Any weakening of the precondition x≥0 would be counterproductive because it would require the implementation to use a more general method of computing the absolute value of x.

Example 3. In some settings, the given precondition is completely superfluous:

```
/* Get from x≥0 to y is x squared. */
   y = x*x;
```

That x is nonnegative is irrelevant to our ability to compute its square using multiplication. In fact, we are hard pressed to think of a squaring method that relies on x's non-negativity.[41] A precondition is made available to a specification by the context in which it occurs, but there is no requirement on the implementation that it must work *only* in such states. The implementation of x squared as x*x effectively weakens the precondition x≥0 to one that only requires variable x to exist and contain a value.

Example 4. In some settings, it is conceivable that the given precondition might be useful, but the norm is to ignore it:

41. Perhaps, adding x to itself x times could be said to rely on x being nonnegative.

```
/* Get from array A's elements are unique to A's elements are numerically
   ordered. */
```

Chapter 11 Sorting presents four algorithms for rearranging elements of an array into numerical order. Each algorithm allows for duplicate values in the array. In effect, use of any of those sorting methods weakens the precondition "A's elements are unique" to "A's elements are arbitrary", and is indifferent to uniqueness.

Example 5. Recall this specification of the Integer Square Root problem from Chapter 1:

```
/* Given n≥0, output the integer part of the square root of n. */
```

Blind adherence to the Divide and Conquer pattern:

```
/* Get from PRE to POST. */
   /* Get from PRE to MID. */
   /* Get from MID to POST. */
```

would have led us to write:

```
/* Given n≥0, output the integer part of the square root of n. */
   /* Given n≥0, let r be the integer part of the square root of n≥0. */
   /* Given that r is the integer part of the square root of n≥0, output the
      integer part of the square root of n. */
```

but what we actually wrote was:

```
/* Given n≥0, output the integer part of the square root of n. */
   /* Given n≥0, let r be the integer part of the square root of n≥0. */
   System.out.println( r );
```

Let's reflect carefully about this shortcut to understand exactly why it worked.

First, we omitted an explicit specification for the output step because the code itself sufficed. In doing so, we followed the recommendation to avoid writing superfluous specifications.

But more germane to the present discussion, we weakened its precondition, and used a general-purpose way to output r. Consider the output statement, in isolation:

```
System.out.println( r );
```

and show it as a mapping between two regions of the state space:

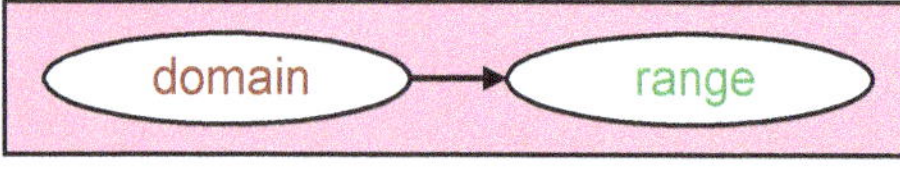

What exactly are the domain and range of this mapping?

The domain is the set of all states in which variable r exists and has been assigned some value. The range is the set of all states in which the output component of state ends with a String representation of the r component of state, for every possible value of r. The domain includes, as a proper subset, the set of states in which r is the integer part of the square root of n≥0. Call that set *d*. In choosing to implement the second step with the general-purpose output statement, we implicitly understood that it is permissible to weaken a step's precondition, even though only states in *d* can arise in the given context.

Conjunctive Normal Form

Strengthening and weakening conditions are important aspects of program refinement. We have discussed them in numerous equivalent ways, but have avoided reliance on formal logic. Instead, we have assumed that informal intuition will be adequate for reasoning about them.

The following small step toward formalization is easily grasped, yet provides a useful framework for thinking about weakening and strengthening.

A condition C is said to be in *Conjunctive Normal Form* when it is expressed as the *conjunction* of *conjuncts* C_1, C_2, ..., and C_n, i.e.,

C_1 **and** C_2 **and** ... **and** C_n

For example, the precondition "x≥0" can be thought of as the conjunction of these three conjuncts:

x is declared **and** x contains a value **and** x is greater than or equal to 0

Similarly, the precondition "in Chicago" can be thought of as:

state is Illinois **and** city is Chicago

A condition presented in Conjunctive Normal Form can be weakened by deleting a conjunct. For example, strike "city is Chicago" from the above, and you are left with "state is Illinois". Similarly, a condition can be strengthened by appending an additional conjunct. For example, the condition

state is NY **and** city is NYC

can be strengthened by appending the conjunct "borough is Manhattan", yielding:

state is NY **and** city is NYC **and** borough is Manhattan

Although the process of expressing a condition in Conjunctive Normal Form remains informal, deleting and adding conjuncts is a simple and mechanical way to think about weakening and strengthening.

Implicit Preconditions

Life is too short to require that every specification explicitly state its full precondition and postcondition. Instead, we abbreviate specifications, and leave the details to be inferred by the reader, resorting if necessary to the underlying theory of Sequential Refinements to understand the required coupling of constituent parts. Thus, the theory recedes into the background, but is available when needed as a basis for comprehension.

An example will make this point clear:

```
/* Get from LA to NYC. */
   /* Get to Chicago. */
   /* Get to St. Louis. */
   /* Get to NYC. */
```

A reader of this abbreviated Sequential Refinement assumes and understands the implicit preconditions of each part:

```
/* Get from LA to NYC. */
   /* (Given that we are in LA) Get to Chicago. */
   /* (Given that we are in Chicago) Get to St. Louis. */
   /* (Given that we are in St. Louis) Get to NYC. */
```

It was not necessary to state the preconditions explicitly, and we chose to omit them on the assumption that a reader attempting to reconstruct why the plan works can infer them from context, and can validate that they were established prior to their being needed.

The reader also understands that postconditions established by early steps can be invalidated by subsequent steps. For example, although the first sub-step established our location as Chicago, the second sub-step caused that to no longer be true: Once you are in St. Louis, you're not in Chicago. In general, learning what preconditions hold requires a backward scan to see what postconditions, once established, have survived. In general, such a scan may need to reach arbitrarily far back in the code, which is undesirable.

We are "caught between a rock and a hard place". On the one hand, we don't want to require explicit (and repeated) re-articulation of conditions in order to propagate useful information to a locality in code; on the other hand, we don't want to impose an unbounded search on a reader who is attempting to confirm what can be assumed at a given point in the code.

A partial remedy is to structure the program so that the textual distance between code that establishes a given postcondition, and code that relies on it as a necessary precondition, is reduced. For example, you should aim to avoid gratuitous gaps between the initialization of a variable, and use of that initialization. Of course, there is a world of difference between looking at the top of the page for information, and looking ten pages back.

One of the motivations behind the claim that:

☞ **Many short procedures are better than large blocks of code.**

relates to this issue. In particular, consider the difference between:

```
int k = 0;
/* 10 pages of code to do whatever. */
   ...
k++;
```

and code where those ten pages have been factored into a method named `whatever`:

```
int k = 0;
whatever();
k++;
```

The advantage is not only that in the second example, the initialization is only two lines earlier. It is that the definition of method `whatever` can be positioned in the program where variable `k` is not even visible, i.e., in scope. Thus, a scan of the ten-page body of `whatever` to confirm that it doesn't overwrite the initialization of `k` would be obviated because its access to `k` is an impossibility.

If all else fails for making the program understandable, you can cross reference relevant code:

```
/* Given PRE (established at point p in the code), get to POST. */
```

Problem Reduction

Chapter 1 introduced the notion of problem reduction: To solve problem *P*, solve a different but related problem, *P′*, and then use that solution to solve the original problem *P*. Problem reduction is a special case of Sequential Refinement.

We illustrated a simplistic form of problem reduction in the example above:

```
/* Get from LA to NYC. */
   /* Get from LA to Chicago. */
   /* Get from Illinois to NYC. */
```

Here, we reduced a specific problem instance (Get from Chicago to NYC) to a more general problem (Get from Illinois to NYC). Each time we weaken a specification's precondition, we are effectively performing a problem reduction. However, by "problem reduction", we typically mean something more substantial.

For example, consider this problem:

How many distinct values occur in an **int** array `A[0..n-1]`?

A	14	7	14	34	7

A direct attack on this problem would tally each first instance of a value i.e., each `A[k]` for which that value does not occur in `A[0..k-1]`, for `k` from 0 through `n-1` (e.g., the number of blue circles in the example).

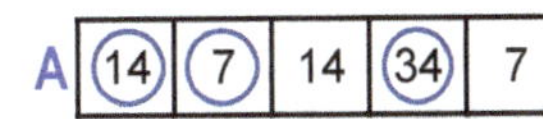

However, we observe that the number in question is precisely one more than the number of adjacent pairs of unequal elements in `A'`, a version of `A` that has been rearranged to be in numerical order (e.g., one more than the number of red bars in the example).

A'	7	7	14	14	34

Accordingly, we can refine the specification:

```
/* Let u = #unique values in A[0..n-1]. */
```

by the problem reduction:

```
/* Let u = #unique values in A[0..n-1]. */
   /* Let v = #unequal adjacent elements in a version of A[0..n-1]
      that has been rearranged into non-decreasing order. */
   u = v+1;
```

and then further refine the subproblem by:

```
/* Let u = #unique values in A[0..n-1]. */
   /* Let v = #unequal adjacent elements in a version of A[0..n-1]
      that has been rearranged into non-decreasing order. */
      /* Let A'[0..n-1] be a version of A[0..n-1] that can be modified. */
      /* Rearrange A'[0..n-1] to be in non-decreasing order. */
      /* Let v = #unequal adjacent elements in A'[0..n-1]. */
   u = v+1;
```

This problem reduction will be advantageous if we use an efficient method for rearranging the values of an array into numerical order, e.g., QuickSort (p. 185) or MergeSort (p. 188). In the worst-case, where all values in A are unique, the number of steps taken by the naive brute-force solution is quadratic in n.[42] But sorting can be done in n log n steps,[43] so sorting followed by a scan through the array to count the number of unequal adjacent element pairs is fundamentally faster.

Sometimes problem reduction is merely convenient—because you happen to have useful code "on the shelf" that may or may not result in a faster program.

In general, Sequential Refinement by problem reduction takes this form:

```
/* Specification P: Get from PRE to POST. */
   /* Get from PRE to A. */
      /* Define problem P' based on PRE. */
      /* Solve problem P'. */
      /* Establish A from the solution to problem P'. */
   /* Get from B to POST. */
```

where satisfying A satisfies B.

We note that *P* and *P'* may, in general, be problems in different domains. For example, the Ricocheting Bee-Bee problem (p. 9) concerns matter (a metal pellet in a tin box), but may be reducible to a problem in optics (a ray of light in a glass box). In this case, what is needed is appropriate mappings from one domain to the other.

Case Analysis

Case Analysis implements a specification *P* as a choice of one step to execute from among $P_1, \dots, P_n$:

```
/* Specification P. */
   if ( condition_1 ) /* Specification P_1. */
   else if ( condition_2 ) /* Specification P_2. */
   ...
   else if ( condition_n-1 ) /* Specification P_n-1. */
   else /* Specification P_n. */
```

Case Analysis is appropriate when a specification requires distinct program behaviors in different situations. For example:

- A program that manipulates representations of real-world objects may need to distinguish between animal, vegetable, and mineral. A three-way Case Analysis would be in order if there is no commonality in the three cases.

42. For each k between 0 and n-1, the k values in A[0..k-1] are inspected, so the total number of steps is 0+1+...+(n-1), which Gauss could tell you is proportional to n squared (p. 10).
43. n log n *on average* for QuickSort, or n log n *in the worst case* for MergeSort.

- You are simulating a rat running in a maze. At each step, the rat can either step into a neighboring cell in a given direction, or it can't because there is a wall in the way. The rat's behaviors in the two cases are different.
- After a search, you either found what you were looking for, or you didn't. You need to do one thing or another depending on the outcome of the search.

Case Analysis is an essential method of refinement. It can be done explicitly in **if**-statements, or implicitly when subsumed within a procedure, operator, or table lookup.

Examples

Absolute value. Suppose that you want to set variable `y` to be the absolute value of variable `x`. Then an explicit Case Analysis can be used:

```
/* Let y be |x|. */
   if ( x>=0 ) y = x;
   else y = -x;
```

When `x>=0`, the absolute value of `x` is `x`, so that is what should be assigned to `y`. When `x` is negative, the absolute value of `x` is `-x`, so that is what should be assigned to `y`.

Case Analysis subsumed in a procedure. You should always be on the lookout for a *uniform* way to accomplish your goal rather than an explicit Case Analysis, i.e., a way to perform the task without making unnecessary distinctions in **if**-statements. For example, the `Math` library function `abs` subsumes the sign test, and lets you write the assignment to `y` in a uniform way:

```
/* Let y be |x|. */
   y = Math.abs(x);
```

Of course, the case analysis that has been obviated in your code probably still occurs in the library implementation of `abs`. But *your* code is cleaner, and less bloated. More importantly, it is expressed at a higher level of abstraction: It embraces the concept and vocabulary of *absolute value*. In general, it is an advantage to push Case Analyses down into methods, and you should bear this in mind when you start to design your own methods.

Case Analysis subsumed in an operator. It is instructive to reflect on how an operator like "+" spares you from Case Analysis. Put yourself back in grade school, and recall learning about signed numbers after you had already learned about subtraction. You were probably presented with a three-way Case Analysis something like this:

> The sum of a positive `x` and a signed `y` is:
> - `x`, if `y` is 0
> - `x+y`, if `y` is positive
> - `x-|y|`, if `y` is negative

But once you learned the concept *addition of signed numbers*, a case split became completely unnecessary because these distinctions are built into the very definition of "+". You write "`x+y`", and the signed values are taken care of uniformly. This example is perhaps obvious and belabored, but the following direct analogue of it isn't.

Consider arithmetic **mod** N, in which numbers start at 0, and after N-1, wrap around to 0 again. If you don't know how to use the modulus operator (%), you will end up writing explicit case analyses that detect crossing over the wraparound point (in either the positive or negative direction), e.g.,

```
/* Increment k mod N. */
   if ( k==N-1 ) k = 0; else k++;
```

or

```
/* Decrement k mod N. */
   if ( k==0 ) k = N-1; else k--;
```

But if you have mastered the modulus operator, you can write

```
/* Increment k mod N. */
   k = (k+1)%N;
```

or

```
/* Decrement k mod N. */
   k = (k+N-1)%N;
```

Detections of the wraparound points are subsumed by the modulus operator. Mastering this extended form of arithmetic can simplify your code. Of course, simplicity (like beauty) is in the eye of the beholder, and use of the modulus operator will be more complex for some people.[44]

Case Analysis subsumed in a table lookup. Selecting the `k`-th element of an array `A` by writing `A[k]` is, in effect, a Case Analysis on the value of `k`.[45]

Thus far, we have given only examples where explicit Case Analysis is not needed. But computation typically requires making distinctions that cannot be reduced to uniform operations. Each such case split uses a *condition* to discriminate among choices. Recognize this as a point of vulnerability:

☞ **Be alert to high-risk coding steps associated with binary choices: "==" or "!=", "<" or "<=", "x" or "x-1", *condition* or !*condition*, positive or negative, 0-origin or 1-origin, "even integers are divisible by 2, but array segments of odd length have middle elements".**

Reflect on each *condition* you write, and ask: Did I get it backwards? Did I miss a corner case?

Here are some sample specifications where essential distinctions must be drawn. Are the implementations correct?

Parity. Every integer `n` is either odd or even, and reflects the exact divisibility of `n` by 2. This is true, but it is not what the following code segment implements:

```
/* Output whether n is odd or even. */
   if ( (n%2)==1 ) System.out.println( "odd" );
   else System.out.println( "even" );
```

When `n` is odd and negative (which the specification does not rule out), `n%2` is -1, not +1. Accordingly, the code will label negative odd numbers "even", and is incorrect. The following code is correct:

```
/* Output whether n is odd or even. */
   if ( (n%2)==0 ) System.out.println( "even" );
   else System.out.println( "odd" );
```

---

44. See section Enumeration Mod N of Chapter 6 (p. 118) for a further discussion of modular arithmetic.

45. Replacing a Case Analysis that is implemented in code using explicit **if**-statements by an indexed lookup in an array is called *table-driven programming*, and is used to good effect in Chapter 14 Knight's Tour (p. 232) and Chapter 15 Running a Maze (p. 255).

Our mistake was a simple misunderstanding about the modulus operator.

Roots. Suppose we are writing code to output the roots of the quadratic equation $Ax^2+Bx+C=0$. In high-school Algebra, we learned the mantra: "Minus B plus or minus the square root of B squared minus four A C, all over two A". The output format will depend on whether the roots are real or imaginary:

```
/* Let im be true iff the roots of quadratic Ax²+Bx+C=0 are imaginary. */
   boolean im;  // Roots are imaginary.
   if ( B*B-4*A*C < 0 ) im = true;
   else im = false;
```

When `B*B-4*A*C` is negative the roots are imaginary, and when it is positive the roots are real. The case of a `B*B-4*A*C` being exactly zero deserves separate care, lest we put it in the wrong case, but upon reflection we conclude that the code is correct, as written.

Because a Boolean expression can appear on the right side of an assignment statement to a **boolean** variable, or in the initialization of a declaration of a **boolean** variable, the **if**-statement is not actually required:

```
/* Let im be true iff the roots of quadratic Ax²+Bx+C=0 are imaginary. */
   boolean im = B*B-4*A*C < 0;   // Roots are imaginary.
```

This is yet another example where a Case Analysis can be replaced by a uniform expression, albeit one that uses a relational operator to do the discrimination.

Parallel lines. We are given two straight lines, and wish to report whether they are parallel or intersect:

```
/* Output whether lines y=m1·x+b1 and y=m2·x+b2 are parallel or intersect. */
   if ( (m1==m2) && (b1!=b2) ) System.out.println( "parallel" );
   else System.out.println( "intersect" );
```

When the slopes of two distinct lines are equal, the lines are parallel. That's certainly true when the slopes are given as infinite-precision real numbers, but what about when they are given as finite-precision floating-point numbers?

For example, consider two lines, one with slope 0.0e0, and the other with slope equal to the smallest positive double-precision floating point number (2.2250738585072014E-308). A test for equality of these two slopes will be **false**, but do we really want to say that such lines intersect?

Similarly, suppose two lines have identical slopes (i.e., `m1==m2` is true), and have near-equal but unequal intercepts (e.g., `b1` and `b2` could be the above two unequal values). Would we want to say that such lines are not identical (and are therefore parallel) or identical (and therefore intersect infinitely often)?

Our immediate goal here is to alert you to risks, and advocate for caution. Rather than get sidetracked on how to code this segment correctly, we will state a simple rule relevant to the example, and move on:

☞ **Never test two floating-point numbers for equality or inequality.**

Rather, explicitly compare the magnitude of their difference to a specific tolerance.

Generalization

The refinement of specification *P* by Case Analysis is:

```
/* Specification P: Get from PRE to POST. */
   if ( condition )
      /* Specification P1: Get from PRE && condition to A1. */
   else
      /* Specification P2: Get from PRE && !condition to A2. */
```

where if A_k is satisfied then POST is necessarily satisfied, for k either 1 or 2.

The code for each of P_1 and P_2 can be simpler than P itself because they benefit from the more limited before-states from which they must get to POST.

The analogous n-way version is:

```
/* Specification P: Get from PRE to POST. */
   if ( condition1 )
      /* Get from PRE && condition1 to A1. */
   else if ( condition2 )
      /* Get from PRE && !condition1 && condition2 to A2. */
   ...
   else
      /* Get from PRE && !condition1 && !condition2 && … && !conditionn-1
         to An. */
```

where if A_k is satisfied then POST is necessarily satisfied (for $1 \le k \le n$).

The implementation of each P_k is simpler than P itself because it benefits from the falsehood of *condition*$_1$ through *condition*$_{k-1}$, and the truth of *condition*$_k$.

Iterative Refinement

An Iterative Refinement implements specification P by repeatedly executing step P':

```
/* Specification P. */
   /* Setup for P′. */
   while ( condition )
      /* Specification P′. */
```

You may ask how repeatedly doing the same thing, P', can make progress? Isn't doing the same thing over and over again, and expecting a different outcome, the definition of insanity?

The answer is that although the static *text* of P' can be said to "do the same thing", each dynamic execution of P' (typically) occurs in a different state, so the *effect* each time is *not* the same. The meaning of P' is parametric with respect to state, and therefore P' (typically) does something different each time. If P' ever fails to change the state, the program has entered an infinite loop from which there is no escape.

For every iteration, there are two essential considerations: *Termination* and *correctness*. Does the loop stop iterating, and if it does, will it have produced the desired outcome?[46]

Termination is addressed by the *loop variant:* Something must change in a manner

46. Although we focus on loop termination as a desirable property, we sometimes deliberately write loops that are nonterminating. This can be because we wish to produce an unbounded amount of output, and are prepared to interrupt execution when we have seen enough. It also arises in the setting of *reactive systems*, where programs interact with one another and the real world for an indefinite period of time.

whereby progress is made. The maximal number of iterations remaining must be some nonnegative integer that counts down by at least one on each execution of the loop body. Typically, the loop variant is not an explicit program variable; rather, it is an implicit expression that can be written in terms of the program variables.

Correctness is addressed by the *loop invariant:* Something must stay the same, so the loop body *P′* continues to apply each time. That property must be established by the setup code so that *P′* applies the first time. Given that the invariant has been established by the setup, and is maintained on each iteration, it is guaranteed to hold if and when the loop terminates. The negation of the *condition*, taken together with the invariant, must entail what you were trying to accomplish with the loop.

Iteration in the Real World

Consider this analogy: To drive a nail into a block of wood, repeatedly hit the nail with a hammer:

```
/* P: Drive a nail vertically into a block of wood. */
   /* Setup: Stabilize the nail vertically, with height≥0. */
   while ( /* any of the nail sticks out */ )
      /* P′: Hit the nail with the hammer squarely. */
```

The loop variant is the height of the nail head above the block of wood. The loop invariant is the fact that the nail is vertical, and the height of the nail head is non-negative.

Let's restate the hammering program, annotated with further remarks about the variant and invariant:

```
/* Drive a nail vertically into a block of wood. */
   /* Setup: Stabilize the nail vertically, with height≥0. */
                  // Establish invariant: Nail vertical, and height≥0.
                  // Initial variant: Height of nail.
   while ( /* any of the nail sticks out */ ) {
      /* Hit the nail with the hammer squarely. */
                    // Maintain the invariant:
                       // Hit the nail vertically, but not so hard
                       // that its height becomes negative.
                    // Reduce the variant:
                       // Hit the nail hard enough to reduce the
                       // height such that a finite # of hits suffices.
      }
                 // Invariant still holds: Nail vertical, and height≥0.
                 // Variant reduced to zero: height==0.
```

What can go wrong with this code?

- You may fail to adequately establish the initial verticality of the nail, and the very first blow of the hammer flattens it. This may occur even if the hammer hits the nail squarely. Thus, the loop body may be perfectly correct, but its precondition is not met.
- You may fail to hit the nail squarely, and it bends over. The body of the loop must maintain the invariant that the nail is vertical, and hitting the nail at an angle is a bug. You manage to reduce the height to zero, but the nail ends up being sideways.

- You may hit the nail too hard, and the height goes negative. The body of the loop must maintain the invariant's requirement that height≥0, and hitting the nail too hard is a bug. Your hammering must not be so forceful that you split the wood, and drive the nail into the tabletop.
- You may hit a knot, and the nail stops going in fast enough, if at all. The body of the loop must make enough progress so that the variant gets smaller with each blow. And not just smaller, but smaller in a way that guarantees termination. Hammering that reduces the nail height by a half each time is a bug: In calculus, the infinite series 1, ½, ¼, etc. "approaches 0 in the limit", but in programming we require loops to terminate in a finite number of steps. The value of the loop variant should be some *necessarily* nonnegative *integer* quantity that is reduced by at least one on each iteration. You can only do that a finite number of times before you reach 0.

Why, after the iteration, have you achieved your goal? Because negation of the *condition* (the loop terminated, with the head flush with the surface of the wood), and the invariant (the body of the loop maintained the nail's verticality) entail what you wished to accomplish: The nail is vertical and the head is flush with the wood's surface.

Nontermination

There are three ways in which an iteration may fail to terminate, and it is worth distinguishing them.

First, at some point progress may cease. For example, replace the hammer with a feather, and the nail may not budge from the get-go. Even if you use a serious hammer, you may come on a circumstance where your blows are insufficient to make a difference. This is the case of getting trapped at a *stuck state.* If ever a pass through the loop body fails to change the state, going around the loop another time won't help because it too will make no change.

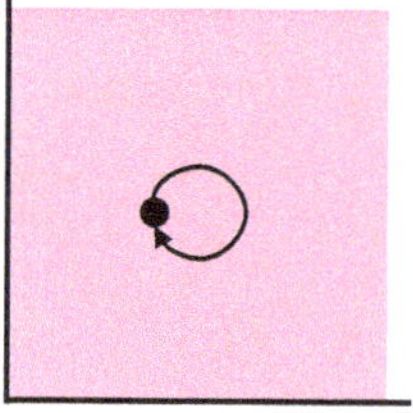
stuck state

Second, although each time around the loop may change the state, no progress is really being made because you are destined to return to the state of some previous iteration. The loop appears to be doing something, but it is all for naught. You are caught in an endless cycle in state space, which is known as an *orbit.*

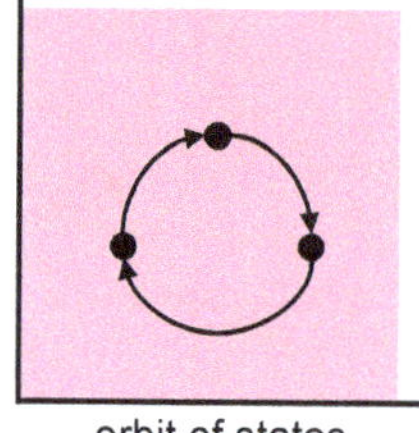
orbit of states

Consider this example: You are given a triangle that points up, and wish to rotate it in place (say, clockwise) so that it points down. You decide to use Iterative Refinement, rotating the triangle some computed angle on each iteration. However, suppose that angle turns out to be 120° every time:

```
/* Given a triangle pointing up, rotate it in place so that it points down. */
   while ( /* triangle is not pointing down */ )
      /* Rotate some computed angle. */
```

The triangle's orientation goes from 0° to 120° to 240°, and then back to 0° again. Note that we are dealing with two different kinds of unending cycle: One is among states in state space, i.e., an orbit; the other is among the statements in the body of the loop.

The third way in which an iteration may fail to terminate is that it transitions through an infinite sequence of states. If you repeatedly halve the nail height in the real world, you don't reach a height of zero in a finite number of iterations, i.e., the loop doesn't terminate. What about in code?

Consider this loop:

```
h = 10;
while ( h!=0 ) h = h/2;
```

in which variable h is directly analogous to nail height. We have not indicated the type of h, and will consider several possibilities.

Suppose the type of h is **int** or **long**. The loop would terminate after h takes on the values 10, 5, 2, 1, 0.

Suppose the type of h is float or double. The value of h would eventually reach a value close to the smallest positive (nonzero) floating-point number of type float or double, and that divided by 2 is zero. So, the loop would terminate in that case, too.

Finally, suppose the type of h is an infinite-precision real (or rational) number. Are there really such variables in our language, or is this just a theoretical fiction? The base language of Chapter 2 Prerequisites has only finite-precision arithmetic types (which we dispatched in the first two cases, above), but we shall learn in Chapter 18 Classes and Objects how to define new datatypes such as Rational. If we were to declare h to have type Rational, then in our halving loop it would take on the values of the infinite series 10, 5, 5/2, 5/4, 5/8, etc., and the loop would never terminate.[47]

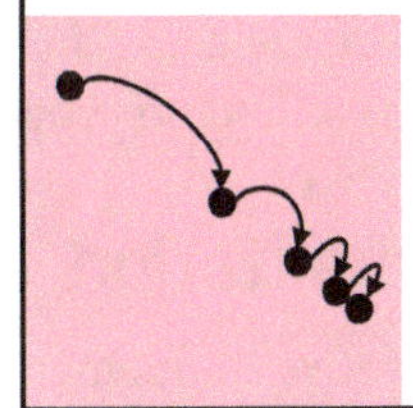
sequence of states

Actually, we don't need the complexity of an infinite arithmetic series to illustrate code that transitions through an infinite number of different states because the following trivial program does so:

```
while ( true ) System.out.println( "Hello World." );
```

The program's output, which we have taken to be one of the dimensions of the state space, is in effect a textual value of unbounded size. Thus, each time the loop appends yet another greeting to the output, the program transitions to yet another state.

Finding Loop Invariants

POST

When you decide to use Iterative Refinement to implement a specification:

```
/* Get from PRE to POST. */
```

you must discover and articulate a loop INVARIANT. How do you do that? Answer: Start with POST, and weaken it.

INVARIANT

Recall that weakening a condition means generalizing it. In our hammering example, POST is "the nail is vertical **and** the height of the nail head is equal to 0". This can be generalized by weakening it to become the INVARIANT "the nail is vertical **and** the height of the nail head is greater than or equal to 0". Speaking set-theoretically, the states that satisfy INVARIANT are a superset of the states that satisfy POST.

Each successive iteration improves the fit, i.e., shrinks the set. When the loop stops, the goal is established because the fit is either exactly POST, or a subset of it.

Think of the loop INVARIANT as a *parametric* description of *approximations* to POST, and the role of the loop is to modify the parameters so that the approximation becomes either exactly POST, or some strengthening of POST.

improving approximations

In the hammering example, the parameter of the INVARIANT is the height of the nail above the surface of the wood. We attain our goal, POST, when that parameter is 0 (and the nail remains vertical). The set of states that satisfy the INVARIANT

47. If the type of variable h were Rational, the code would need to be different:

```
Rational h = new Rational(10);
while ( !Rational.isZero(h) )
   h = Rational.divide( h, new Rational(2) );
```

but this is a small technicality.

include many with nonnegative heights. Some of these (those with height zero) are contained in POST.[48]

Each blow of the hammer eliminates many of the states that satisfy the INVARIANT, but with height greater than zero. The precise number of such eliminated states will depend on the forcefulness of the blows.

The loop terminates when the nail height is equal to zero, i.e., when the only states that continue to satisfy the INVARIANT are those with height zero.

In our triangle example, the INVARIANT must include POST (the goal state, 180°), as well as all states the triangle may take on before reaching the goal state, i.e., 0°, 120°, and 240°. Unfortunately, the set of states described by the INVARIANT never gets any smaller because the body of the loop is inadequate. We are caught in an orbit in state space, and no progress is being made.

Generalization

The Iterative Refinement of specification *P* is:

```
/* Specification P: Get from PRE to POST. */
   /* Setup: Get from PRE to INVARIANT. */
   while ( condition ) {
      /* Get from condition && INVARIANT to INVARIANT. */
      }

where !condition && INVARIANT entails POST.
```

Termination requires the existence of an integer variant expression that is necessarily nonnegative, and that is necessarily reduced by at least one on each iteration. This can only go on a finite number of times, and therefore the loop is guaranteed to terminate.

We illustrate Iterative Refinement with three famous integer algorithms: Integer Division, Euclid's Algorithm for the greatest common divisor, and the mysterious Collatz Conjecture.

Integer Division

We introduced important concepts associated with Iterative Refinement in the setting of carpentry rather than program development. It is time to write some real code. Our goal now is to illustrate those concepts without getting distracted, so the example is deliberately simple: We implement unsigned integer division (/) and modulus (%) on the assumption that those built-in operators are not available:

```
/* Given int x≥0 and int y>0, set int q to x/y, and int r to x%y. */    1
```

The arithmetic expressions x/y and x%y in the specification's postcondition are shorthand that we must flesh out using their definitions. The following diagram depicts POST, a characterization of the set of desired after-states:

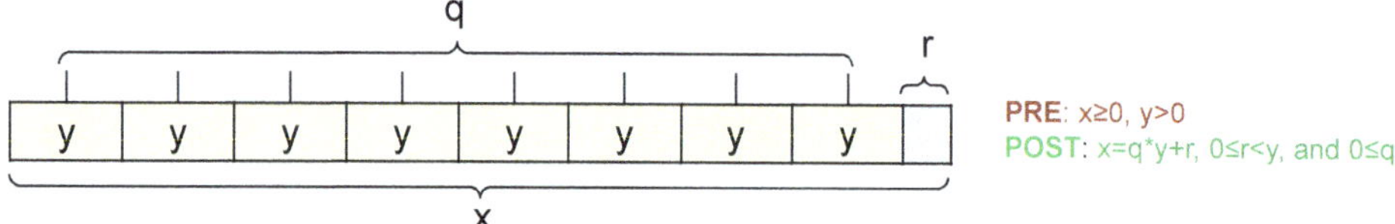

48. Why plural? Is there not only one state with height zero? You are forgetting all the other dimensions of the state space, e.g., the type of wood, the kind of nail, etc.

The quotient q is the whole number of times y occurs in x; the remainder r is what would be left over if those instances of y were to be removed from x. Thus, POST is the set of states ⟨r,q⟩ that satisfy the condition: x=q·y+r, where 0≤r<y and 0≤q.

Clearly, we require an iteration. For the purpose of this exercise, we ignore the possibility of a clever algorithm, and just use repeated subtraction, i.e., we cast instances of y out of (a copy of) x one at a time until no more whole instances of y remain. Whatever is left over is r.

The iteration is indeterminate because the number of repetitions is unknown; in fact, it is the very quotient q that we are seeking:

```
/* Given int x≥0 and int y>0, set int q to x/y, and int r to x%y. */     2
______
while ( ___ ) ______
```

To find the loop INVARIANT, we ask: What would the diagram look like at an intermediate stage, after an arbitrary number of iterations? We do this by weakening POST, e.g., by eliminating the constraint that r<y:

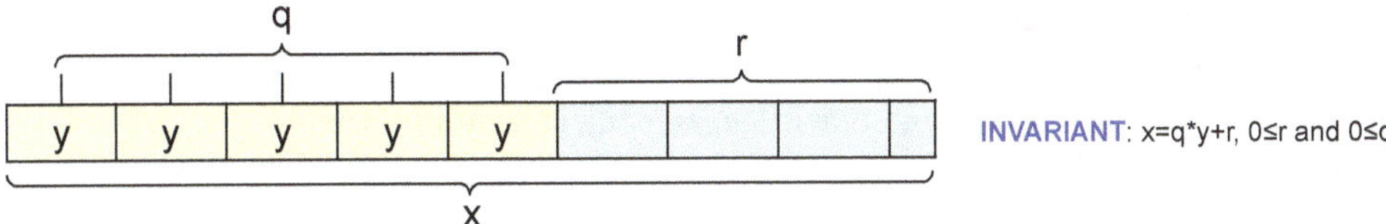

Think of r, the green portion of the diagram, as the protruding portion of a nail. With each blow of our hammer, we drive the nail further into the wood by an amount y. With each reduction of r by y, we increment q to maintain the INVARIANT:

```
/* Given int x≥0 and int y>0, set int q to x/y, and int r to x%y. */     3
______
while ( ___ ) { r = r-y; q++; }
```

In carpentry, the goal is to drive the nail so that the head becomes flush with the surface of the wood, but without splitting it. We didn't elaborate on the exact mechanism that accomplishes this, but it presumably has something to do with the counterforce of the wood surface eventually blunting the force of the hammer, allowing us to drive the last bit of nail into the wood without splitting it. But in Integer Division, our hammer is primitive: It can only reduce the nail height by a fixed integer amount y, and as a result a portion of the nail (some remainder r less than y) may remain exposed:

```
/* Given int x≥0 and int y>0, set int q to x/y, and int r to x%y. */     4
______
while ( r>=y ) { r = r-y; q++; }
```

Initially, when we haven't yet cast any instances of y out from r, the setup code must establish the INVARIANT. The diagram looks like this:

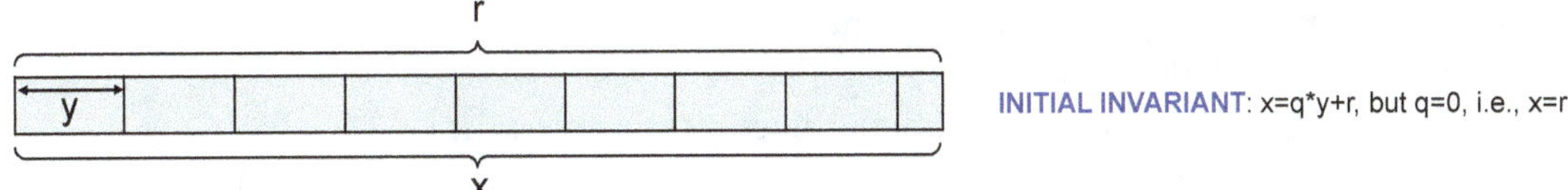

Think of x as the full length of the nail. In the same way that a carpenter must stabilize a nail vertically before beginning to hammer, we must initialize r to x and q to 0:

```
/* Given int x≥0 and int y>0, set int q to x/y, and int r to x%y. */    5
   int r = x; int q = 0;
   while ( r>=y ) { r = r-y; q++; }
```

The loop variant is some necessarily nonnegative quantity that is reduced by at least 1 on each iteration, and therefore must reach 0. Think of this as an upper bound on the number of iterations remaining. One such quantity is x/y-q. Another is r-x%y. The first expression is reduced by one on each iteration; the second expression is reduced by y.

There are numerous algorithms for division, and even a schoolchild doesn't use repeated subtraction. Each such algorithm has its own INVARIANT, and its own kind of hammer [10].

Euclid's Algorithm

Loop invariants and loop variants are intrinsic to iterative computation, and have been known to mathematicians since Euclid more than 2000 years ago [11].

The *greatest common divisor* (*GCD*) of two positive integers is the largest integer that divides them both exactly, i.e., without a remainder. For example, 6 is the GCD of 18 and 24 because it divides both 18 and 24 exactly, and no larger integer does.

Euclid's Algorithm is:

```
/* Given x>0 and y>0, return the greatest common divisor of x and y. */
static int gcd(int x, int y) {
   while ( x!=y )
      if ( x>y ) x = x-y;
      else y = y-x;
   return x;
   }
```

What are the loop invariant and loop variant, and how do they contribute to the correctness and termination arguments?

Let GCD be the mathematical function (not the code) for the greatest common divisor, and let X and Y be the initial argument values in a call to gcd (the code). The loop invariant is quite simply that x>0 **and** y>0 **and** GCD(X,Y)=GCD(x,y). Clearly, this equality holds immediately after method invocation, when x and y are initialized to X and Y, respectively. So, the invariant is established from the start.

Why does the invariant continue to remain **true** upon execution of the body of the loop when x≠y? The **if**-statement discriminates among the two remaining cases: x>y and y>x.

Assume, without loss of generality, that x>y, and suppose that x and y have a greatest common divisor of d, i.e., x=$x'{\cdot}d$ and y=$y'{\cdot}d$, for some x' and y'. Then x-y has that same factor d in common with x and y because x-y= $x'{\cdot}d-y'{\cdot}d = (x'-y'){\cdot}d$. Thus, replacing x with x-y preserves the property that x and y have d as a greatest common divisor, and because x>y both x and y remain positive.

The symmetric argument holds if y>x.

Accordingly, replacing the larger of x and y with the difference preserves the GCD, and the property that x and y are positive.

Arguments x and y start out positive, and on each iteration the larger is replaced by the difference of the two, which is also positive. A trivial upper bound on the total number of iterations before x and y become equal is thus x+y. Therefore, the iteration necessarily terminates.

Finally, since the GCD of any number and itself is that number, and when the iteration stops, x and y are equal, the invariant reads: GCD(X,Y)=GCD(x,y)= GCD(x,x)=x. So, returning x returns GCD(X,Y), as required.

Collatz Conjecture

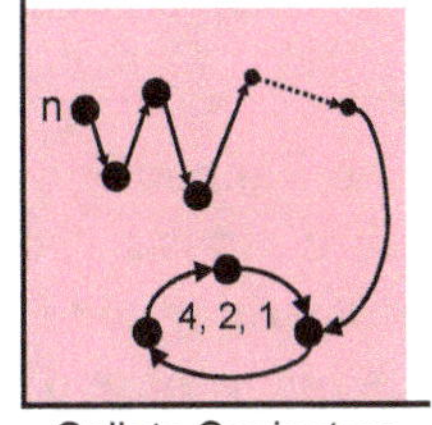

Collatz Conjecture

Start with any positive integer. If it is even, divide it by 2; otherwise, multiply it by 3 and add 1. Repeat the process until reaching 1. The Collatz Conjecture [12] is that no matter what positive integer *n* you start with, the sequence will reach 1, e.g., 3, 10, 5, 16, 8, 4, 2, 1.

Consider the following two program segments that purport to implement the same specification:

```
/* Given input n>0, output "done". */
   int n = in.nextInt();
   System.out.println( "done" );
```

and

```
/* Given input n>0, output "done". */
   int n = in.nextInt();
   while ( n!=1 )
      if ( (n%2)==0 ) n = n/2;
      else n = 3*n+1;
   System.out.println( "done" );
```

The first segment is clearly correct: It reads an integer, ignores it, and prints "done". The second segment is more convoluted, but is it equivalent, i.e., does it have the same net effect as the first when executed?

One difference is that the second program will certainly take longer. But we are only asking about net effect, and so, speed is of no concern. Another difference is that the second program may lead to values of n that are so large that they exceed the capacity of an **int** variable to store them. For the purpose of this exercise, however, please ignore this issue, and assume that there is no upper bound on the size of integers that can be stored in **int** variables.

With these caveats in mind, we ask again: Does the second program segment necessarily print "done"? The answer turns on whether its loop necessarily terminates. The Collatz Conjecture is that the loop necessarily terminates. But the Collatz Conjecture is an open problem in Mathematics, i.e., it is not known whether it is true or not.[49]

The example points out that although you may write a loop, and have its invariant correct, you may have difficulty proving that it will always terminate with the answer. Said more technically: It's not always so easy to find a loop variant. In fact, the situation is far worse than merely difficult: There are loops for which it is not logically possible to know whether or not they terminate. It is not only unknown; it is unknowable.[50]

49. Paul Erdős, the prominent 20th-century mathematician, said this about the Collatz Conjecture: "Mathematics may not be ready for such problems" [42].

50. Exercise 29.

Recursive Refinement

A Recursive Refinement implements specification *P* by identifying smaller instances of the same problem within a given problem, and then using the very refinement being defined to solve those subproblems, as well:

```
/* Specification P. */
   if ( base case ) /* P0. */
   else
      /* Identify smaller instance(s) of P within P itself, apply this
         approach to each such instance, and combine the results. */
```

Recursive Refinement resembles Stepwise Refinement in its use of Divide and Conquer, but it is a structure for the code we are writing, not an approach to the process of writing code.

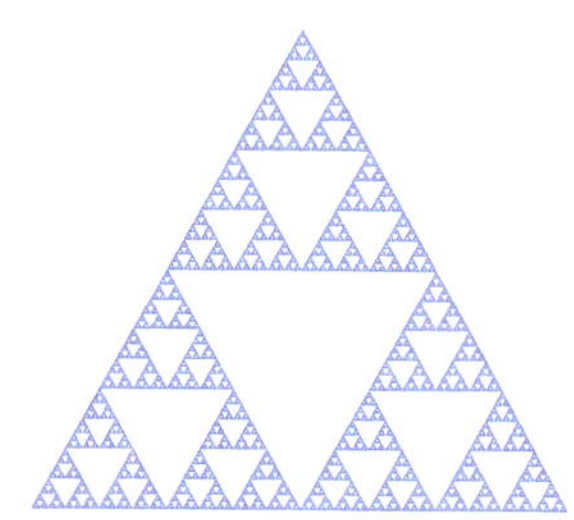

Something whose parts resemble the whole has *self-similarity*. A problem with self-similarity looks the same at all scales. When you zoom in for a closer look, you see the same, or a very similar, structure. Another term for such an object is *fractal*.

The Sierpiński Triangle shown is an excellent geometric example of a fractal, but once you have been introduced to the idea of self-similarity, you begin to see fractals everywhere, especially in Nature.

Fractals such as the Sierpiński Triangle go on forever (in principle), but others, like the branches of an actual tree or the fronds of a fern, stop after a finite number of self-embeddings.

Even the lowly integers can be seen as a fractal, for example, at rocket bases, where 0 is usually pronounced as "BLASTOFF". To count down from 5, you just say 5, and then count down from 4, etc. More generally, the backwards sequence of integers that starts at $n>0$ contains the self-similar backwards subsequence of integers that starts at n-1.

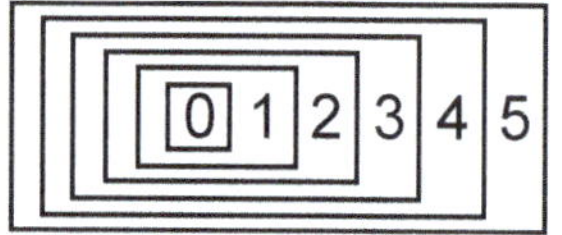

Recursive Refinement works by identifying the fractal structure of a problem, and by applying the very refinement we are defining to those self-similar parts. To do so requires that it have a name so we can refer to it. Accordingly, we write the refinement as the body of a method, and then use the method's name (within its own body, and from elsewhere) to invoke it.

For example, consider the specification to count down from five. It can be implemented recursively as:

```
/* Count down from 5, and say "BLASTOFF" at 0. */
   countdown(5);
```

where method `countdown` is defined by:[51]

```
/* Count down from n, and say "BLASTOFF" at zero. */
static void countdown(int n) {
   if ( n==0 ) System.out.println( "BLASTOFF" );
   else {
      System.out.println( n );
      countdown(n-1);
      }
   }
```

51. This is the first time in the text where we define a method. All method definitions will be prefixed by the modifier **`static`** until Chapter 18 Classes and Objects, when absence of **`static`** is explained. You may safely ignore the modifier until then.

As illustrated, a recursive method has parameters; it can also have a return value. For example, the specification given Carl Friedrich Gauss to sum the integers from 1 to 100 could have been implemented recursively as:

```
/* Output the sum of 1 through 100. */
   System.out.println( sum(100) );
```

where method sum is defined by:

```
/* Return the sum of 0 through n. */
static int sum(int n) {
   if ( n==0 ) return 0;
   else return sum(n-1)+n;
   }
```

This is a direct application of the fractal structure of the integers given earlier. The additions proceed from left to right as the recursion emerges *from* the base case e.g., (...(((0+1)+2)+3)+...+n). It is analogous to the iterative code introduced in Chapter 1:

```
/* Let sum be the sum of 0 through n. */
   int sum = 0;
   for (int k=1; k<=n; k++) sum = sum+k;
```

An alternative definition of sum performs the additions from right to left, on the way *to* the base case. This approach, which is known as *accumulation*, leverages the associativity of addition, and defines sum as:

```
/* Return the sum of 0 through n. */
static int sum(int n) { return sumAux(n,0); }
```

where the auxiliary method sumAux is defined by:

```
/* Return the sum of 0 through n, and acc. */
static int sumAux(int n, int acc) {
   if ( n==0 ) return acc;
   else return sumAux(n-1, n+acc);
   }
```

The sum computed this way is (1+(2+(3+...+(n+0)...))). It is analogous to the iteration:

```
/* Let sum be the sum of 0 through n. */
   int sum = n;
   for (int k=n-1; k>0; k--) sum = k+sum;
```

The examples we have given here were selected to show the resemblance of recursion to iteration when a problem has only one instance of self-similarity. The full power of recursion is best illustrated with problems whose fractal nature consists of two or more instances of self-similarity. We defer such examples until later in the text.[52]

---

52. Recursive Refinement is used by Print in reverse order (p 102), Worst-Case Linear-Time Median (p. 180), QuickSort (p. 185), MergeSort (p. 188), and Depth-First Search (p. 286).

Library of Patterns

Patterns are parameterized compositions of program constructs that have proven to be useful in practice. The more patterns you know, the less you have to reinvent. As you gain experience in programming, master new patterns and add them to your personal library. The patterns presented in the text and deemed essential are collected in Appendix II.

For the purpose of Stepwise Refinement, a pattern offers a more efficient development step because some details of the internal coupling of a pattern's subparts have been established once and for all, and do not have to be rethought.

Choosing a Refinement

Programming is not deterministic, and there are multiple programs that may emerge to solve any given problem. From where, exactly, does the variety derive?

The first opportunity for variety arises when we are programming by top-down Stepwise Refinement, and select the form of refinement. The overall shape of an algorithm is often determined by that choice because code structured as a fixed number of steps in a Sequential Refinement is likely to encode a different approach from code that is structured as a Case Analysis, which is likely a different approach from code that is structured as an Iterative Refinement.

Recall, from Chapter 1, the two different implementations for outputting the sum of the integers from 1 through n. The brute-force solution was a Sequential Refinement, consisting of three steps, the second of which was an Iterative Refinement:

```
/* Output the sum of 1 through n. */
   int sum = 0;
   for (int k=1; k<=n; k++) sum = sum + k;
   System.out.println( sum );
```

The alternative solution consisted of only one statement that was deemed "simple to write", and did not involve any refinement at all:

```
/* Output the sum of 1 through n. */
   System.out.println( n*(n+1)/2 );
```

These are two different algorithms.

A second opportunity for variety arises when defining the specific constituents that make up a given refinement. Recall the two different implementations of swap presented in Chapter 3:

```
/* Swap x and y. */           /* Swap x and y. */
   int temp = x;                 x = x+y;
   x = y;                        y = x-y;
   y = temp;                     x = x-y;
```

Both implementations are three-step Sequential Refinements, but the individual steps are completely different. The first involves only data movement, whereas the second involves specific properties of arithmetic operators. These are two different algorithms for swap. The point here is not that the second implementation is good.[53] Rather, the point is only to illustrate two distinct ways in which a three-step Sequential Refinement can implement the same specification.

53. In fact, we denigrated it in Chapter 3.

There is still plenty of room for originality despite the limited number of refinement forms. This potential is particularly true given that Sequential Refinement subsumes problem reduction. The choice of the loop invariant in Iterative Refinement is another vital source of variety because two invariants for the same problem is likely to lead to very different algorithms, as demonstrated in Chapter 11 Sorting.

Extended Example: Running a Maze

Recall from Chapter 1 that we had started to develop a solution for this problem:

Background. Define a *maze* to be a square two-dimensional grid of cells separated (or not) from adjacent cells by *walls*. One can move between adjacent cells if and only if no wall divides them. A solid wall surrounds the entire grid of cells, so there is no escape from the maze.

Problem Statement. Write a program that inputs a maze, and outputs a *direct path* from the upper-left cell to the lower-right cell if such a path exists, or outputs "Unreachable" otherwise. A path is direct if it never visits any cell more than once.

We now replay that development in the context of Stepwise Refinement, and then extend the code as a further illustration of the methodology:

> ☞ **Use Stepwise Refinement. Write simple code immediately, otherwise refine the problem statement using: (a) Sequential Refinement, (b) Case Analysis, (c) Iterative Refinement, (d) a known pattern.**

The specification of the problem statement:

1

```
/* Find path in maze from upper-left to lower-right, if one exists. */
```

was first refined using a known architectural pattern:

2

```
/* Find path in maze from upper-left to lower-right, if one exists. */
   /* Input. */
   /* Compute. */
   /* Output. */
```

Then, following several precepts:

> ☞ **Write comments as an integral part of the coding process, not as afterthoughts.**
> ☞ **Repeatedly improve comments by relentless copy editing.**

we arrived at a more robust elaboration of the three steps. In essence, we used the pattern as a scaffolding on which to hang different aspects of the problem requirements:

3

```
/* Find path in maze from upper-left to lower-right, if one exists. */
   /* Input a maze of arbitrary size, or output "malformed input" and
      stop if the input is improper. Input format: TBD. */
   /* Compute a direct path through the maze, if one exists. */
   /* Output the direct path found, or "unreachable" if there is none.
      Output format: TBD. */
```

This decomposition of the problem is where we left off in Chapter 1.

The next steps are analysis, not coding. We telescope the relevant rules here:

- ☞ **Analyze first.**
- ☞ **Confirm your understanding of a programming problem with concrete examples. Elaborate the expected input/output mapping explicitly.**
- ☞ **There is no shame in reasoning with concrete examples.**
- ☞ **Simple examples may be as good (or better) than complicated ones for guiding you toward a solution.**
- ☞ **Seek algorithmic inspiration from experience. Hand-simulate an algorithm that is in your "wetware". Be introspective. Ask yourself: What am I doing?**

Let's assume that the outcome of our analysis is the following set of five graduated examples. The examples suggest an algorithm that performs a systematic clockwise exploration that hugs walls and effectively works its way out of cul-de-sacs, as necessary, until reaching the lower-right cell, or discovering that it is unreachable.

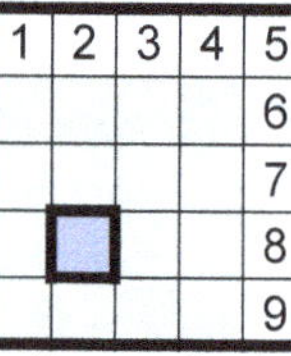

Example 1

In Example 1, we found a path from the upper-left to the lower-right cell by merely traversing cells along the outer perimeter. Green cells were unvisited, as was the unreachable (blue) cell.

Example 2

In Example 2, we interposed a protruding wall that blocked the move that in Example 1 was from 6 to 7. We found a path by traversing cells as in Example 1, but when blocked, continued along the protruding wall. On reaching the end of the protruding wall, we pirouetted around to its other side, and continued to the lower-right cell.

Example 3

In Example 3, we interposed a second protruding wall that blocked the move that in Example 2 was from 11 to 12. The path hugged the top of the second protruding wall until it emerged from the cul-de-sac, at which point we pirouetted around to the other side of the second wall, and continued to the lower-right cell. Yellow cells are part of the abortive side excursion.

Example 4

In Example 4, we interposed a third wall that blocked the move that in Example 3 was from 12 to 13. The path hugged the top (and left side) of this third wall, and finally pirouetted to its other side at cell 1, at which point it hugged the wall's other side until reaching the lower-right cell. The yellow cells are all visited but are not part of the final direct-path solution.

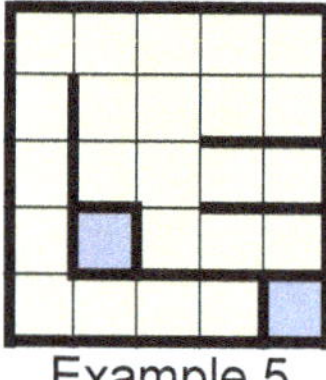
Example 5

In Example 5, we added a wall that makes the lower-right cell unreachable. The exploration proceeded exactly as it did in Example 4, but on failing to enter the lower-right cell, continued along the bottom and left outer walls until reaching the upper-left cell once again. We visited every reachable cell, after which we concluded that the lower-right cell is unreachable.

The full maze explorations are not "direct", but we conjecture that they may form the core of a solution. We decide to defer the "direct" requirement for now, and focus on doing a systematic exploration that includes cul-de-sacs. We assume that we will be able to find a way to trim off side excursions later:

```
/* Find path in maze from upper-left to lower-right, if one exists. */     4
   /* Input a maze of arbitrary size, or output "malformed input" and
      stop if the input is improper. Input format: TBD. */
   /* Compute a direct path through the maze, if one exists. */
   /* Output the direct path found, or "unreachable" if there is none.
      Output format: TBD. */
```

We are now ready to code.

Mazes have unbounded size, yet programs are finite. Therefore, we need a way to express the computation using a construct that can perform an unbounded number of steps. There are only two choices: Iteration and recursion.

An exploration that ignores the issue of side excursions and cul-de-sacs is linear: It just keeps plowing ahead. This observation suggests iteration rather than recursion. We may have a momentary twinge of concern on realizing that big cul-de-sacs can have little cul-de-sacs (just as great fleas can have little fleas), and thereby explorations can have a fractal nature. If this issue turns out to matter later, we may want to replace iteration with recursion, but having made our decision for now to ignore the question of direct paths, the choice of iteration over recursion smells right:

> ☞ **If you "smell a loop", write it down.**

This application of Stepwise Refinement requires little thought, and is close to being what we call a "no-brainer":

```
/* Find path in maze from upper-left to lower-right, if one exists. */    5
   /* Input a maze of arbitrary size, or output "malformed input" and
      stop if the input is improper. Input format: TBD. */
   /* Compute a direct path through the maze, if one exists. */
      _________
      while ( _________ ) _________
      _________
   /* Output the direct path found, or "unreachable" if there is none.
      Output format: TBD. */
```

Even though the refinement may be a no-brainer, it accomplishes a great deal in terms of Divide and Conquer: One problem is partitioned into four:

> ☞ **Benefit from the fact that a while-loop divides a region of code into four subregions.**

This coding step can't do harm, or be very wrong. Of course, the devil will be in the details.

We name the four subregions of an Iterative Refinement thus:

```
initialization
while ( !termination ) body
finalization
```

and suggest, cookbook style, that coding should follow this order of attack:

> ☞ **Code iterations in the following order: (1) body, (2) termination, (3) initialization, (4) finalization, (5) boundary conditions.**

We proceed in the suggested order, below.

When working on the body, we aim for code that avoids consideration of special cases, like the first or last iteration. In the course of coding the body, if you find yourself worrying about those cases, you are breaking the rule. You are supposed to be working on part (1), the body, but are getting distracted by part (2), (3), and (4) considerations, which will come soon enough.

Here is a recipe for coding a loop body:

> ☞ **Body. Do 1st. Play "musical chairs" and "stop the music". Characterize the "program state" when the music stops, i.e., at the instant the loop-body is about to execute yet again. If you had stopped one iteration later, what would have looked the same (the "loop invariant"), and what would have changed (the "loop variant")?**

Readers unfamiliar with the game of musical chairs only need to know that n children dance around n-1 chairs until the music stops, at which point they scramble for a chair. The child who doesn't get a chair is ejected, a chair is removed, and the music resumes. The salient part of the game for us is not the chair part; it is the uncertainty about when the music will stop. Think of the music as program execution. The purpose of the analogy is to force you to consider program state after an *arbitrary* number of iterations, when the music suddenly stops.

Where are you when the music stops? In the maze world, you are in some cell, ready to make your next move. In the program, you are at the beginning of the loop body ready to perform an arbitrary next step of the iteration.[54]

In musical chairs, when the music stops, you have to size up the situation, and then decide what to do. In the loop body, that is also what must happen. The loop body must deal with every situation that might arise.

> ☞ **A Case Analysis in the loop body is often needed for characterizing different ways in which to decrease the loop variant while maintaining the loop invariant.**

We can review the five Examples from our analysis, and tease out four distinct cases.

In Example 1, most of the transitions are similar, e.g., from 1 to 2, from 2 to 3, ..., and from 8 to 9. Imagine that you are in one of the peripheral non-corner cells of the maze, facing the wall with your outstretched left arm touching the surface in front of you. In each such case, you sidestep to the right. If we represent your orientation by a black arrow, we can depict the rule you are following in a before-and-after diagram:

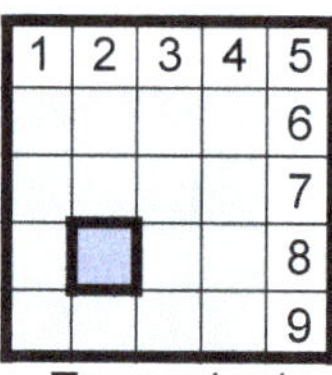

Example 1

- *Normal wall.* Step sideways to the right.

The same rule applies to the vertical movements as well as the horizontal movements, i.e., it depends on the way you are facing. At the corner, 5, a second rule applies:

- *Wall at convex corner.* Turn the corner 90° clockwise.

Both rules transition to an adjacent wall without your needing to remove your hand from the surface; the convex-corner rule also changes your orientation.

In Example 2, the same two rules apply, and include some additional cases, i.e., normal-wall transitions from 6 to 7, from 10 to 11, from 11 to 12, and from 12 to 13, and convex-corner transitions at 6 and at 11. An additional rule is needed, however, to transition from 7 through 8 and 9 to 10:

Example 2

- *Wall at hairpin turn.* Turn the hairpin 180° counterclockwise, passing through

54. We only consider stopping when we are at the beginning of each complete execution of the body, a slight difference from musical chairs, for which the music may stop at any time.

two "corner" cells in an instant, and pirouetting to the other side of the wall, touching the opposite surface.

As in the first two rules, you do not need to take your left hand off the wall as you slither around the hairpin turn, and end up touching the obverse surface of the wall.

In Example 3, the current three rules cover all situations, although additional reflection is needed to understand exactly how. The difference between Examples 2 and 3 only arises at 11 (in Example 2) when the interposed second wall prevents the sidestep from 11 to 12. Backing out of the cul-de-sac (shown as **a** and **b** in Example 3) is accomplished by an additional application of the convex-corner rule at **a** (leading you to face down), followed by a sidestep from **a** to **b**, followed by a hairpin turn from **b** through 9 and 10 to 11.

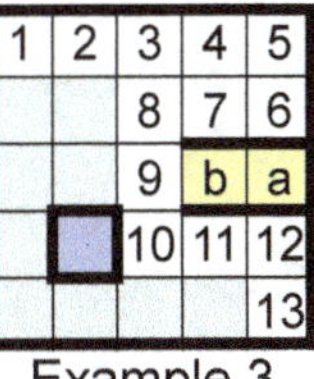

Example 3

In Example 4, you need a fourth rule to move from **a** through **b** to **c**, on your way out of the giant cul-de-sac (yellow):

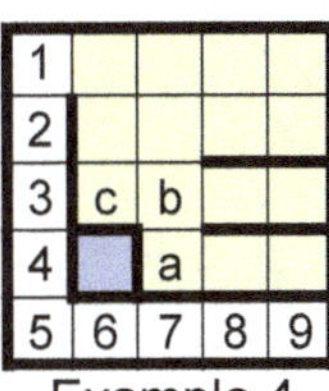

Example 4

- *Wall at concave corner.* Turn the corner 90° counterclockwise, passing through the corner cell in an instant.

Once again, you are able to move from wall to wall without removing your hand.

For each of the four cases, you are following the so-called "left-hand rule":

- *Invariant 1*: Your left hand is on the interior surface of a peripheral wall.

If you keep your left hand on the interior surface of a peripheral wall and advance clockwise, you will eventually reach every reachable cell that is connected to it. In Example 1, it is clear that the given surface runs along the inside of the outer maze wall, and is connected to the lower-right cell. In other examples, the notion of "peripheral wall" is less clear. In these cases, imagine that the interior wall surface is made of a flexible rubber sheet. To make an additional peripheral-wall segment, pinch the rubber between two fingers, and pull it inward to make the new segment. Provided that in doing so you don't subdivide the interior space, this operation preserves any valid path (red), albeit the path would then be stretched out along the additional interior wall segment. If the wall-stretching operation subdivides the interior space, there are two cases: (a) the path endpoints end up in the same subdivision, in which case the path between them is shortened (in one subdivision, and the other subdivision becomes unreachable), or (b) the endpoints end up in opposite subdivisions, in which case there is no valid path between them.

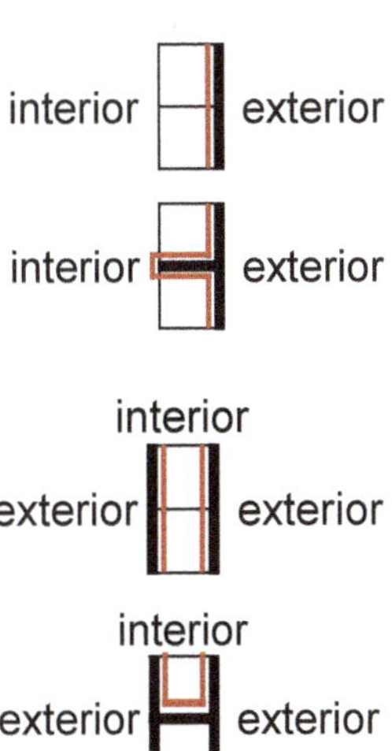

Reflecting on the progress you make whenever you apply one of the four rules, we see that you get closer to the lower-right cell (if it is reachable) one wall-segment-surface at a time. Thus, the "distance" from the goal that is being reduced each time is not Euclidean,[55] or the so-called Manhattan metric,[56] or the number of cells away. Rather, it is the number of wall-segment surfaces away:

- *Variant 1*: The number of **wall-segment-surfaces** away from either the lower-right cell or from the surface at which you discover that the lower-right cell is unreachable.

55. $\sqrt{(row - row')^2 + (col - col')^2}$

56. $|row - row'| + |col - col'|$

Example 5

The variant includes the possibility that the goal is unreachable (as in Example 5).

All we have to do now is to refine the loop body with a four-way Case Analysis:

```
if ( ____ ) ____
else if ( ____ ) ____
else if ( ____ ) ____
else ____
```

We would then code the *conditions* (to recognize the wall topologies for the different rules), and code the *statements* (to perform the corresponding maneuvers). This is certainly doable, but the topologies and maneuvers are complex, which would result in considerable code complexity. For example, the *condition* that discovers the possibility of sidestepping (the first rule) would have to detect two collinear adjacent walls that are not separated by a perpendicular third wall.

It will be good to avoid such complexity, which we can do by implementing each of the four rules by a sequence of micro-steps. In designing the micro-steps, our goal is fewer cases to consider, with simpler conditions to test, and simpler maneuvers to execute. We shall allow only one condition to test:

- Facing a wall or not

and three maneuvers to execute:

- Turn 90° clockwise in place
- Turn 90° counterclockwise in place
- Step forward one cell

The four rules are implemented by micro-steps, as follows:

- *Normal wall.* Turn 90° clockwise, then step forward and turn 90° counterclockwise to restore our original direction. This sequence of actions effectively sidesteps one cell to the right:

- *Wall at convex corner.* Turn 90° clockwise, which leads us to again face a wall:

- *Wall at hairpin turn.* Turn 90° clockwise, and then pirouette to the other side of the wall by thrice stepping forward and turning 90° counterclockwise:

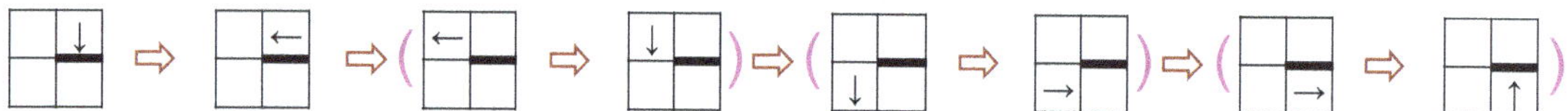

- *Wall at concave corner.* Turn 90° clockwise, then make our way around the corner by twice stepping forward and turning 90° counterclockwise:

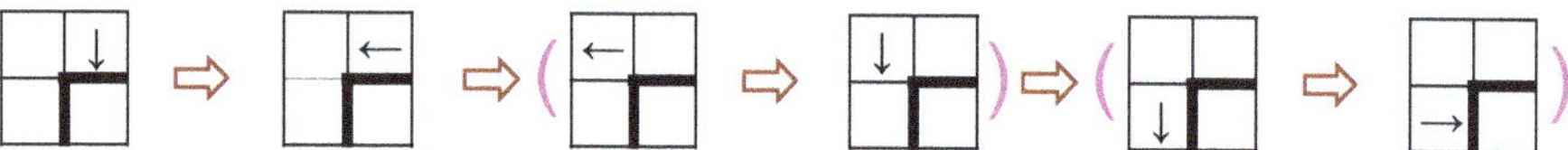

Notice that in all but the convex-corner case, we begin by taking our left hand off the wall temporarily until the macro-step is complete.

If the micro-steps are to be spread across multiple iterations of our loop, the loop invariant can no longer be that our hand is on a **wall-segment-surface** because this is manifestly not the case. Where then is our hand after each micro-step? When our hand is not on a **wall-segment-surface**, we can distinguish two cases: It is at a **door** (a non-wall through which we must pass), or it is at an **other** (a position about which we currently know nothing).

In the diagrams, we have grouped state-pairs with parentheses, and note that the first state of each pair is an **other** case, whereas the second state is a **door** case. We must always step through a door, but would have no idea what to do if we had to confront an **other** situation. Accordingly, we resolve to require that the operations "Step forward" and "Turn 90° counterclockwise" be performed as an indivisible pair within the same loop iteration, thereby making **other** states transitory.

With the vocabulary of **door** in hand, we can now state a new invariant and variant:

- *Invariant 2:* Your left hand is on the interior surface of a peripheral wall, or at a **door**.
- *Variant 2:* The number of **wall-segment-surfaces-or-doors** away from either the lower-right cell or from the surface-or-door at which you discover that the lower-right cell is unreachable.

We have replaced Invariant 1 (face a **wall-segment-surface**) with one that holds in more situations (e.g., face a **wall-segment-surface-or-door**), which is an example of a technique that often proves effective in simplifying code: Weakening the (original) invariant. We are now ready to refine the loop body with a two-way Case Analysis:

6

```
/* Find path in maze from upper-left to lower-right, if one exists. */
   /* Input a maze of arbitrary size, or output "malformed input" and
      stop if the input is improper. Input format: TBD. */
   /* Compute a direct path through the maze, if one exists. */
      _________
      while ( _________ )
         if ( /* facing-wall */ )
            ___________
         else ___________
      _________
   /* Output the direct path found, or "unreachable" if there is none.
      Output format: TBD. */
```

and specify actions for the two cases:

7

```
/* Find path in maze from upper-left to lower-right, if one exists. */
   /* Input a maze of arbitrary size, or output "malformed input" and
      stop if the input is improper. Input format: TBD. */
   /* Compute a direct path through the maze, if one exists. */
      _________
      while ( _________ )
         if ( /* facing-wall */ )
            /* Turn 90° clockwise. */
         else {
            /* Step forward. */
            /* Turn 90° counterclockwise. */
            }
      _________
   /* Output the direct path found, or "unreachable" if there is none.
      Output format: TBD. */
```

Having now completed the Case Analysis, and therefore the loop body, we turn to

(2) termination. What is needed is the *condition* for continuing, i.e., negation of the *condition* for stopping. The exploration must continue as long as we haven't reached either the lower-right cell, or the upper-left cell about to cycle around again:

```
/* Find path in maze from upper-left to lower-right, if one exists. */     8
   /* Input a maze of arbitrary size, or output "malformed input" and
      stop if the input is improper. Input format: TBD. */
   /* Compute a direct path through the maze, if one exists. */
      _________
      while ( /* !in-lower-right && !in-upper-left-about-to-cycle. */ )
         if ( /* facing-wall */ )
            /* Turn 90° clockwise. */
         else {
            /* Step forward. */
            /* Turn 90° counterclockwise. */
            }
      _________
   /* Output the direct path found, or "unreachable" if there is none.
      Output format: TBD. */
```

Having now completed the loop body and its termination, we turn to (3) initialization. The problem statement dictates that we start in the upper-left cell. We establish the loop invariant (facing a **wall-segment-surface-or-door**) by facing up:

```
/* Find path in maze from upper-left to lower-right, if one exists. */     9
   /* Input a maze of arbitrary size, or output "malformed input" and
      stop if the input is improper. Input format: TBD. */
   /* Compute a direct path through the maze, if one exists. */
      /* Start in upper-left cell, facing up. */
      while ( /* !in-lower-right && !in-upper-left-about-to-cycle */ )
         if ( /* facing-wall */ )
            /* Turn 90° clockwise. */
         else {
            /* Step forward. */
            /* Turn 90° counterclockwise. */
            }
      _________
   /* Output the direct path found, or "unreachable" if there is none.
      Output format: TBD. */
```

1	8	7		
2		6		
3	4	5		

To see that starting out facing an outside wall is a critical requirement for the algorithm to work, consider starting in the upper-left cell facing down in the maze shown. We would go around and around the unreachable (blue) cell counterclockwise. Starting out by facing up establishes the invariant that we face an outer wall.

It is interesting to note that the sufficiency of the invariant that we face a **wall-segment-surface-or-door** relies critically on a restriction given in the problem statement: A solid wall surrounds the entire grid of cells. Consider what would happen if we were to start, facing up, in a maze that has two exterior walls removed. We would go round and round counterclockwise, sometimes in the maze, and sometimes outside it. In a sense, the distinction between inside and outside has been destroyed, and we are trapped on an island of walls, not unlike the previous example. Our algorithm wouldn't work at all.

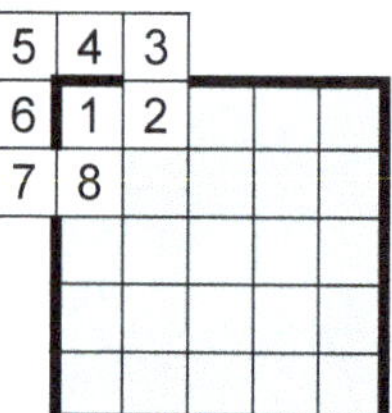

Thinking a little more deeply, we realize that an essential aspect of our invariant is that the **wall-segment-surface-or-door** we face must be "connected" to an interior surface of the lower-right cell (if it is reachable). In particular, we must never switch our orientation to a "disconnected island" because doing so would strand us. Of course, a consequence of remaining in touch with the peripheral wall (even if via a door) is that we will never reach disconnected goal cells, were the problem setup changed to allow them (see the placement of the cheese in the figure).

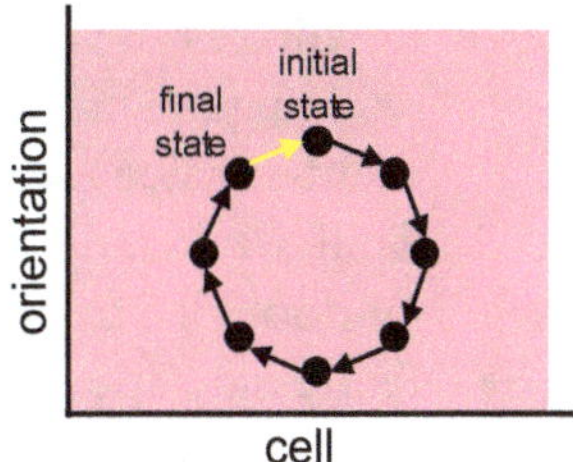

There is a little more to say about termination when the lower-right cell is unreachable. Specifically, what do we mean by "in-upper-left-about-to-cycle"? As we have seen, Example 4 requires passing through the upper-left cell in the *middle* of a systematic exploration along the way to finding a solution, so this condition is not merely that you have returned to the upper-left cell.[57] Correct treatment of termination requires understanding that states in the exploration state space include both the identity of the cell you are in, and your orientation. The initial state is ⟨upper-left,up⟩, and the final state is ⟨upper-left,left⟩, and failure to prevent transition from the final state back to the initial state (yellow) would result in an unending orbit in state space, and an infinite loop in the code, i.e., nontermination.

There is nothing to do for (4) finalization, which turns on a somewhat subtle point: At the given level of detail, the loop body only computes the next cell state of a path. Suppose, however, that an additional computation were required at each state reached, e.g., say, we wanted to output some state information before moving on. Because the final state (be it in the lower-right cell or the upper-left cell) does not get to be processed in the loop body, such processing would have to be done for the final state in the finalization code.

There is nothing to do for (5) boundary conditions. We may review the degenerate case of a 1-by-1 maze, but find nothing special about it.

We have introduced three primitive actions (Turn 90° clockwise, Turn 90° counterclockwise, and Step Forward), and three primitive queries (facing-wall, in-lower-right, and in-upper-left-about-to-cycle), and defined the algorithm in terms of them. We are far from finished, but are well on our way toward a solution.

Original variant and invariant, reconsidered

Suppose that we had insisted on sticking with the original invariant in which we never take our left hand off a **wall-segment-surface**, and the original variant, in which we get one **wall-segment-surface** closer on each iteration. We could still have used micro-steps. In particular, the body of the (outer) loop could have been implemented with an inner loop, as follows:

```
while ( condition ) {
   /* Get one wall-segment-surface closer. */
      /* Turn 90° clockwise. */
      /* Advance to facing a wall, if necessary. */
         while ( /* !facing-wall */ ) {
            /* Step forward. */
            /* Turn 90° counterclockwise. */
            }
   }
```

57. Another reason this would be incorrect is that we start in the upper-left cell, so such a condition would prevent us from getting started in the first place.

In other words, *within* the body of the (outer) loop, we are permitted to temporarily break its invariant, provided the invariant is reestablished by completion of the body of that (outer) loop.[58]

This contrasting, more complicated, code illustrates several worthwhile principles:

- Choice of variant and invariant influence code complexity. Be on the lookout for choices of variant and invariant that simplify your code. In this example, retaining the first invariant that came to mind (keep your hand on a **wall-segment-surface**) would have led to more complicated code with nested loops, while weakening the invariant (keep your hand on a **wall-segment-surface-or-door**) led to simpler code with only one loop.
- Expressing special-purpose composite operations (e.g., sidestep) in terms of a sequence of general-purpose micro-operations (e.g., Turn 90° clockwise, Step forward, and Turn 90° counterclockwise) may be advantageous. Micro-operations can be simpler to write, and may have multiple applications. Definition and use of micro-operations goes hand in hand with simpler *conditions* (e.g., facing-wall), as opposed to composite conditions (e.g., facing-normal-wall) that may be cumbersome to write (i.e., a wall that is collinear with another wall, with no perpendicular wall between them).

We return to complete the maze problem in Chapter 15.

58. An astute reader will recognize that even in the one-loop version of the code, the invariant (hand on **wall-segment-surface-or-door**) may be temporarily broken when we step forward, but is then immediately restored by turning counterclockwise.

CHAPTER 5

Online Algorithms

Suppose you have an unbounded amount of input data and wish to process it. One possible strategy would be to follow the offline-computation pattern, which suggests that you read all data into program variables before you start processing them:

```
/* Input. */
/* Compute. */
/* Output. */
```

This may work well for small files, but for a massive amount of data the approach runs the risk that there is insufficient computer memory to store all data in program variables. The key word in the problem statement is "unbounded", and this requirement rules out the offline-computation pattern.[59]

Some problems lend themselves to *online computation* in which each input value is read, processed, and discarded. A pattern for this is:

```
v = /* first input value */;
/* Initialize. */
while ( v != /* stoppingValue */ ) {
   /* Process v. */
   v = /* next input value */;
   }
/* Finalize. */
```

where *stoppingValue* is some distinguished input value that signals the end of meaningful data. The pattern handles the case of no meaningful data, i.e., the degenerate case where the only value in the input is the *stoppingValue*.[60]

---

59. In modern computer systems, programs run in *virtual memory* (p. 31), which is essentially unlimited. Thus, the issue isn't really limited memory; rather, it is the efficiency of the paging mechanism that implements virtual memory.

60. The online-computation pattern can be seen as an instance of the general iterative-computation pattern:

```
/* Initialize. */
while ( /* not finished */ ) {
   /* Compute. */
   /* Go on to next. */
   }
```

where /* not finished */ is a check for not having reached the input *stoppingValue*, and /* Go on to next. */ reads the next input value. This is then followed by finalization.

The key to online computation is that whatever is important about each input value can somehow be taken into account in summary program variables or output before the value is discarded. A problem that lends itself to online computation can perform a computation *incrementally* as the data are read in, and then compute a final result (if any) from those incrementally-maintained summary variables after all data have been individually processed.

An online algorithm nicely illustrates loop-invariants because the state of the program variables after some (but perhaps not all) of the values have been read in and processed must reflect an invariant, and processing each subsequent input value must maintain that invariant. Online computation is possible *precisely* because there is sufficient information in intermediate program variables for the needed final result to be computed and output. The nature of that information is what the invariant is all about.

The examples in this chapter assume that the data to be processed are nonnegative integers, and the *stoppingValue* is -1. Thus, the online-computation pattern specializes to:

```
int v = in.nextInt();  // Next integer to be processed, or -1.
/* Initialize. */
while ( v != -1 ) {
   /* Process v. */
   v = in.nextInt();
   }
/* Finalize. */
```

The pattern is parametric in three aspects: initialization, per-datum processing, and finalization. As a device in the text for emphasizing this viewpoint, we label the parameters α, β, and γ, and subsequently define those parameters for each example:

```
int v = in.nextInt();  // Next integer to be processed, or -1.
/* α: Initialize. */
while ( v != -1 ) {
   /* β: Process v. */
   v = in.nextInt();
   }
/* γ: Finalize. */
```

Note that because initialization at α follows input of the first value, it can depend on that value.

Data Processing

Consider the application of processing exam grades. Each grade is an integer in the range 0-100, but the number of grades is unbounded. There may be no grades, or there may be a million grades. We further specialize the pattern for the application at hand:

```
int grade = in.nextInt();  // Next grade to be processed, or -1.
/* α: Initialize. */
while ( grade != -1 ) {
   /* β: Process grade. */
   grade = in.nextInt();
   }
/* γ: Finalize. */
```

We consider five grade-processing applications: print, count, average, highest, and grade distribution, which provide simple settings in which to gain experience in thinking about invariants.

Print

The simplest application is to print all grades in the input. There is no need for initialization, finalization, or intermediate computed values. We just print the value contained in variable `grade`:

```
β: System.out.println( grade );
```

The loop invariant states that on reaching β all grades previously input (except for the current one) have been output, and the most recent value input (either a grade or -1) is in variable `grade`:

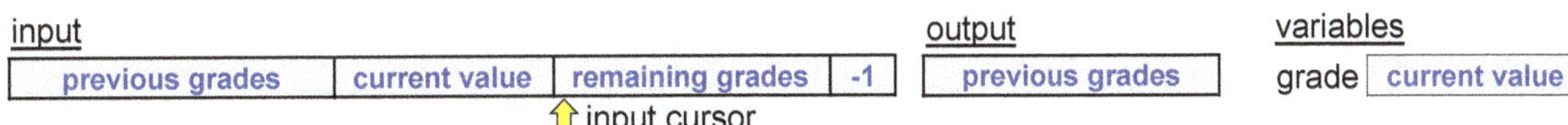

If the current value in variable `grade` is an actual grade (i.e., not -1), the loop body executes: It maintains the invariant by printing `grade`, and then reading the next input value. The online-computation pattern guarantees termination because execution of the loop body reduces the loop variant by 1 (i.e., the number of values remaining in the input before the stopping signal).

The diagrammatic depiction of the loop invariant shows the general case, but it is important to realize that various labeled sections may, in general, be empty. For example, the regions labeled "previous grades" may be "all grades", in which case: (a) the input cursor is really beyond the -1, (b) the "current value" is really one and the same as the -1, and (c) the region labeled "remaining grades" is empty:

This is the loop invariant at the moment that the loop terminates, i.e., on reaching γ. You can read the correctness of the program right off the diagram.

At the opposite extreme, the region labeled "previous grades" is empty, in which case: (a) the value in `grade` is the first value of the input, (b) all grades except that initial value lie ahead of the input cursor, and (c) nothing has been output yet:

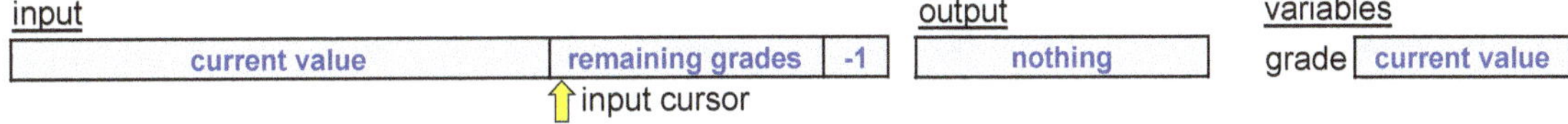

This is the loop invariant immediately after initialization at α, before any grades have been processed.

And finally, the degenerate case where "previous grades" is empty, and "current value" is the -1:

This is the loop invariant immediately after initialization at α, and also immediately prior to finalization at γ, when there are no grades in the input at all.

Count

Let's say you want to output how many people took the exam. Begin a mental exercise of determining the program output for sample input data, and observe what you are keeping track of in your head as you scan the input from left to right: The number of grades counted so far. Following the precept:

> ☞ **Introduce program variables whose values describe "state".**

it is clear that you need a declaration akin to:

```
int count; // The number of grades processed so far.
```

The comment is a simple example of a representation invariant, i.e., an assertion that precisely characterizes the value in the variable `count` at all times.

> ☞ **Write the representation invariant of an individual variable as an end-of-line comment.**

Next, ask yourself: What does it mean to process a grade for this particular application, because this is what you must do at β? Clearly, you must count it:

```
β: count++;
```

At α, how many grades have been processed so far? Yes, you have already *read in* the first input value, which may be a grade or may be the -1, but you haven't *processed* it yet. That is what happens at β. So, at α you haven't processed any grades yet:

```
α: int count = 0; // The number of grades processed so far.
```

Execution doesn't reach γ until `grade` is equal to -1, i.e., until we have processed all grades. Thus, at γ, the value of variable `count` (the number of grades processed so far) is the total number of grades in the input:

```
γ: System.out.println( count );
```

You probably could have written this code in your sleep without all the methodological verbiage. However, our purpose has been to illustrate the methodology and show careful thought processes in an exceedingly simple setting.

The overarching precept that has controlled the order of coding is:

> ☞ **Code iterations in the following order: (1) body, (2) termination, (3) initialization, (4) finalization, (5) boundary conditions.**

The online-computation pattern takes care of termination from the get-go, and no boundary condition arose that needed to be addressed. Thus, steps (2) and (5) were obviated, and we first coded β (body), then α (initialization), and then γ (finalization), in that order.

In each case, we used the representation invariants (first for `grade`, and then for `count`) to reason about what code to write, and why it is correct. That's why we wrote the representation invariants in the first place.

We are developing code for pattern parameters α, β, and γ in isolation rather than in place (in the pattern instance itself) to emphasize the importance of thinking about them in terms of their roles in the parametric, general-purpose scheme: initialize, process, finalize. Typically, you would develop such code in place, but mentally zoom in to each of β, α, and γ, in turn, as if you were wearing blinders.

Average

We want the program to output the average grade. Imagine scanning the input data yourself so you can output the average. If you are thinking about writing down the grades on a sheet of paper so that you can then add up the full list and divide that sum by the count, you are missing the point. You are inadvertently slipping into an *offline* algorithm that requires access to each and every grade, potentially millions of them, before doing the addition. What is needed for the *online* algorithm is a *running sum* of the grades seen so far. That way you can discard the grades themselves as you read through them. This suggests the declarations:

```
int count;    // The number of grades processed so far.
int sum;      // The sum of the grades processed so far.
```

At β, where we process each `grade` in preparation for reading in the next one, we must maintain the representation invariants:

```
β: count++; sum = sum + grade;
```

At α, before any grades have been processed, the sum of the grades processed so far is 0. Why 0? So that when we process the first grade, `sum` will be replaced by `sum+grade`, i.e., `0+grade`, which will be the first `grade` itself.[61]

```
α: int count = 0; // The number of grades processed so far.
   int sum = 0;   // The sum of the grades processed so far.
```

At γ, we can print the average:[62]

```
γ: System.out.println( sum/count );
```

The five-step coding order for loops that we advocate defers consideration of boundary conditions until last, but that time has now come:

☞ Boundary conditions. Dead last, but don't forget them.

What are they, where do you find them, how do you deal with them, and why do we defer them until last?

What are they? Boundary conditions are situations in which general-purpose code does not apply, and special handling is required.

61. Technically, 0 is called the *identity* with respect to "+", i.e., a value *e* with the property that for any *x*, *e*+*x* is *x*.

62. When both operands of division (/) are **int**, the quotient is **int**, and any fractional part is truncated. Thus, this code prints the integer part of the average. If the average with a fractional part is wanted, the expression can be written as `(float)sum/count`, which converts `sum` to a **float**, and then divides it by `count`. This produces a **float** quotient.

Where are they found?

☞ **Find boundary conditions at extrema, and at singularities, e.g., biggest, smallest, 0, edges, etc.**

First, let's consider the extrema of possible grades: 0 and 100. All that we are doing is adding `grade` to `sum`, and nothing about a grade of 0 or 100 is special. An unbounded number of grades in the input raises the possibility of an *arithmetic overflow*, i.e., the magnitude of sum could get too large to be contained in 32-bits, but this is typically considered an exception rather than a boundary condition. So, we ignore the possibility of a trillion grades in the input.[63] But what about the other extreme of input-file size: no grades at all. This is a problem because 0/0 is not defined, and if this computation occurs, it will cause the program execution to crash.

How do you deal with them? Typically, a Case Analysis is performed to detect a boundary condition by inspection of the values of variables. The present situation is straightforward:

```
γ': if ( count==0 ) System.out.println( "no grades" );
    else System.out.println( sum/count );
```

Why deferred? We defined a boundary condition as a situation in which general-purpose code does not apply. We may identify a *potential* special case early, but in advance of actually coding the general case, it is not possible to know whether or not the special case is an actual boundary condition requiring special handling. Often, the code for the general case happens to handle the special case. Another possibility is that the code for the general case can be slightly modified so that it handles the special case gracefully, i.e., without special attention. Because of these possibilities, there is no point in worrying about boundary conditions early.

Highest grade

Computing the highest grade offers only one small additional idea. Nonetheless, we shall run through the development in the correct methodological order.

The online algorithm requires a variable to keep track of the highest grade processed so far:

```
int highest;    // The highest grade processed so far.
```

Processing the current grade requires updating `highest` before we discard the grade and read the next input value:

```
β: if ( grade>highest ) highest = grade;
```

or alternatively:

```
β': highest = Math.max(highest, grade);
```

Before any grade has been processed, what is the highest grade that has been processed so far? The correct answer is not 0 because we must distinguish this situation

63. If we are concerned, we could buy ourselves some headroom by changing the type of `sum` from **`int`** to **`long`**.

(no grades processed so far) from the one in which every single grade (input so far) is 0, and therefore the highest grade (so far) is 0.

What is needed for an initial value of `highest` is some value that is guaranteed to be *smaller* than the first grade processed. That way, after processing the first grade, `highest` will be that grade. Any negative value will do (since grades are in the range 0-100):

```
α: int highest = -1;  // The highest grade processed so far, or -1 if no
                      // grades processed yet.
```

We can then use the value of `highest` to test the boundary condition, i.e., if there were no grades:

```
γ: if ( highest==-1 ) System.out.println( "no grades" );
   else System.out.println( highest );
```

Suppose grades could be any (signed) integer that can be represented as an **`int`**, including negative numbers.[64] How then would we initialize `highest`? We need a number that is smaller than any possible grade, but there is no such **`int`**. Given that initialization follows the reading (but not the processing) of the first grade, we can use it to initialize `highest`:

```
α': int highest = grade;  // The highest grade processed so far, or first
                          // value in input if no grades processed yet.
```

but then the test for no grades in the input must be changed to use some other method of detection, e.g., an explicit count.[65]

Grade Distribution

We want the program output to be the grade distribution, i.e., for each grade between 0 and 100, we want to know the number of people who obtained that grade. The problem is like counting the total number of grades, but instead of one variable, `count`, we need 101 counters, `freq[0..100]`. We can declare these counters all in one fell swoop as the array `freq`, together with their representation invariant:

	0	1	2	···	99	100
freq				···		

```
α: /* For 0≤k≤100, freq[k] is the number of grades of k processed so far. */
   int freq[] = new int[101];
```

Since each element of the array is initialized to zero, the default value for **`int`** variables, the representation invariant for `freq` is satisfied from the get-go, i.e., before any grades have been processed.

The array `freq` is known as a *histogram*, and the individual elements of the array are known as *bins*. Creating a histogram for a collection of values is often very useful, not just for statistical analysis, but as a general programming technique.[66]

---

64. We shall ignore the issue that the `stoppingValue` of -1 would now be a legal grade.

65. What is needed is an *identity* with respect to "**max**", i.e., a value *e* with the property that for any *x*, *e* **max** *x* is *x*. That value is -∞, but there is no such value in a computer. One can't use -2^{31}, the most negative **`int`**, because that still doesn't allow us to distinguish between no input and the maximal grade being -2^{31}. One could declare `highest` to be a **`long`** variable, and initialize it with -2^{63}, which is effectively -∞ with respect to grades of type **`int`**.

66. Chapter 12 Collections uses histograms to represent a multiset that consists of natural

The coding step at β must maintain the representation invariant of `freq` as each grade is processed:

```
β: freq[grade]++;
```

That is, we increment the counter associated with the value of `grade`. If any input is outside the range 0 through 100, this statement will crash with a "subscript-out-of-bounds" error, but we assume for simplicity that the input data are well formed.

Clearly, we can only output the grade distribution when we reach finalization:

```
γ: System.out.println( "grade frequency" );
   for (int g=0; g<101; g++) System.out.println( g + "      " + freq[g]);
```

Said more technically (and a bit pedantically): On reaching γ, the representation invariant for `freq` effectively states that it contains the grade distribution because at γ all grades have been processed.

Print in reverse order

The prototypical application that is *not* amenable to online computation is: Print the grades in *reverse order*. What can we possibly do with the first value other than save it for printing last? And similarly, we have to save the second value read so we can print it second to last. Etc. All we can do at β is save `grade` in a program variable so it can be printed later after all grades have been read in. The entire collection of such variables is a data structure. Because there is no upper bound on the number of grades in the input, the number of variables in the data structure must also be unbounded. In effect, our online-computation pattern degenerates into the Input-Compute-Output steps of the offline pattern:

```
/* Input. Read all grades and enter them into a data structure. */
   int grade = in.nextInt();  // Next grade to be processed, or -1.
   /* α: Initialize a data structure for saving all grades. */
   while ( grade != -1 ) {
      /* β: Process grade by saving it in the data structure. */
      grade = in.nextInt();
      }
   /* γ: Finalize the data structure. */
/* Compute. Empty. */
/* Output the grades stored in the data structure in reverse order. */
```

A recursive method offers an attractive alternative to the three-part offline-computation pattern for this problem because each recursive invocation of a method creates a new instance of each of the method's local variables, e.g., `grade`:

```
/* Read grades up to -1, and then print them in reverse order. */
static void readRest() {
   int grade = in.nextInt();  // Next grade read in, or -1.
   if ( grade != -1 ) {
      readRest();
      System.out.println( grade );
      }
   }
```

numbers in a limited range of values. It then generalizes them to implement hash tables, which can represent a multiset of arbitrary values.

Data Compression

Data compression is an important data-processing application that is amenable to online computation: Given an arbitrary file, we wish to make it shorter (by encoding it) in such a way that we can recover the original file perfectly (by decoding it). Data compression leverages redundancies in the input file to find a more succinct representation of the sequence of values. For example, compression of a digital image might leverage the common occurrence that neighboring pixels in an image are highly likely to have the same color.

General purpose compression algorithms can find many forms of redundancy automatically. One of the simplest examples of data compression is *run encoding.*

Background. Consider a sequence consisting of any number of nonnegative integers, followed by a stopping value of -1. For example:

```
10 10 10 10 10 10 1 1 1 1 1 1 1 1 7 7 7 8 9 10 10 10 -1
```

A maximally-long subsequence of repeated values is called a *run*. For example, the sequence above consists of runs of:

6 tens, 8 ones, 3 sevens, 1 eight, 1 nine, and 3 tens.

When a sequence is known to consist of many long runs, it may be more efficient to represent each run by two integers: The value and the number of repetitions of that value. This representation is called a *run encoding* of the sequence. For example, the run encoding of the sample sequence is:

```
10 6 1 8 7 3 8 1 9 1 10 3 -1 -1
```

We duplicate the stopping value of -1 at the end of the run-encoded sequence, as shown above, for the convenience of the *decoder*, which reads pairs if integers, and converts them back to a normal sequence of integers, terminated by a single -1.

Problem Statement. Write a program segment that does online run encoding of an input sequence of integers, as described. Write another program segment that does online run decoding, i.e., takes a run-encoded input, and converts it back to the original.

Encoding

Begin a solution with its specification:

```
/* Given 0 or more nonnegative inputs followed by a stopping signal of -1,
   output the equivalent run-encoded sequence followed by -1 -1. */
```
1

After making sure you understand the problem and the sample output provided, the first thing to do is recognize that the problem requires online computation because no upper bound has been given for the length of the input:

☞ **Decide between an on-line vs off-line algorithm, e.g., processing data incrementally as it is input vs inputting all data, storing it in variables, and processing it thereafter..**

Having completely mastered the online-computation pattern, you blast it in, leaving space for α, β, and γ, and choosing v as the name of the variable holding the input:

```
/* Given 0 or more nonnegative inputs followed by a stopping signal of -1,
   output the equivalent run-encoded sequence followed by -1 -1. */
   int v = in.nextInt();  // Next integer to be processed, or -1.
   α
   while ( v != -1 ) {
      β
      v = in.nextInt();
      }
   γ
```
2

Explicit placeholders α, β, and γ are shown in the development snapshot above, but in practice you might leave blank lines in the code.

The online-computation pattern contains a loop, and as with any loop there are two things to consider: termination (using the loop variant), and correctness (using the loop invariant).

- *Variant.* This is clearly the number of input values (other than -1) that remain to be processed. The online-computation pattern guarantees this will be reduced by one on each iteration. Accordingly, there is nothing further to say about it, provided we don't inadvertently write code at β that somehow breaks termination.
- *Invariant.* This remains for us to discover. It will be established by initialization at α, and will be maintained by the combination of code at β, and the statement

  ```
  v = in.nextInt();
  ```

  that is built into the body of the loop of the online-computation pattern.

As with any iteration, the order of coding is given by the precept:

☞ **Code iterations in the following order: (1) body, (2) termination, (3) initialization, (4) finalization, (5) boundary conditions.**

Accordingly, we start thinking about the body of the loop first. But there is no point in starting to code before we know what the invariant is because the whole objective of β (followed by the input statement) is to maintain that invariant.

As we have seen previously, a systematic way to discover loop invariants is to follow this rule:

☞ **Body. Do 1st. Play "musical chairs" and "stop the music". Characterize the "program state" when the music stops, i.e., at the instant the loop-body is about to execute yet again. If you had stopped one iteration later, what would have looked the same (the "loop invariant"), and what would have changed (the "loop variant")?**

"A diagram is worth a thousand words", so begin with sample input data, and augment it with diagrammatic details. A good place to start is with a red line at an arbitrary location to indicate how far the program had gotten in processing input before the music stopped:

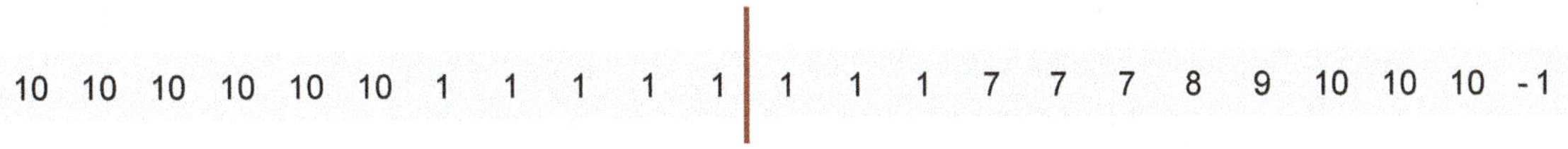

10 10 10 10 10 10 1 1 1 1 1 | 1 1 1 7 7 7 8 9 10 10 10 -1

Although the line position is described as "arbitrary", it is actually far from it; rather, it was chosen with considerable care, and not at all randomly. We deliberately chose to not pick a place in the middle of either run of 10s, reasoning that there may be something special about being the first or last run that is best to avoid for now. We could have picked the runs of 8s or 9s, but as runs of length one, they seem more like special cases to be checked later; they are not the "normal case". The run of 7s might have been fine, but seemed a tad too short to represent the general case. So, we picked the run of 1s for the red line. But where in that run? Surely, not at the beginning or end because these are again potential special cases. We picked somewhere in the middle, sufficiently far from the first or last 1. As we have illustrated, there is some skill in picking an "arbitrary" point at which to "stop the music", but it is not difficult to develop.

The red line is a boundary between what has been considered in the *past*, and what will be considered in the *future*. Such a boundary is (almost) always associated with a variable that records an essential aspect of the state of the computation:

☞ **Introduce program variables whose values describe "state".**

In this case, the boundary is immediately in front of the next input value to be processed. In association with the online-computation pattern, we had already chosen variable v to hold that value, so we add an indication of it to the diagram. The standard depiction of a variable is a box with an adjacent name, so, the diagram is modified, thus:

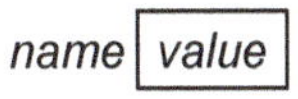

name | *value*

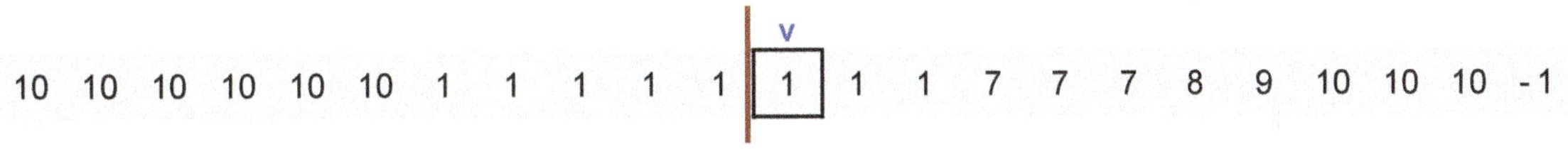

10 10 10 10 10 10 1 1 1 1 1 | v: [1] 1 1 7 7 7 8 9 10 10 10 -1

Reflecting on what other boundaries may be important, we consider the first and last 1 in the current run. The last 1 is in the future, so we have no basis for recording anything about it, but the first 1 is a different matter. We have seen it, and can know that it is the first value in a run. Accordingly, we draw in another boundary there, and invent a variable, r, to hold that value:

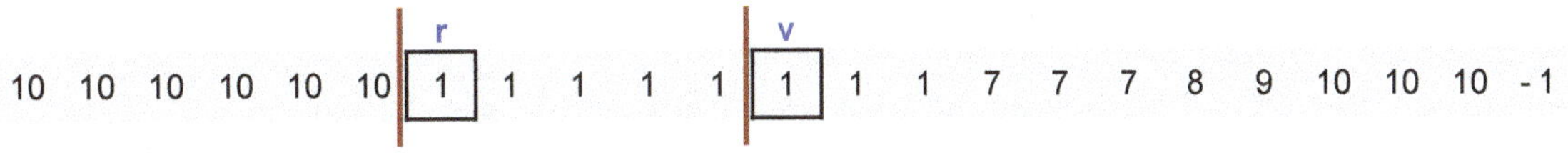

10 10 10 10 10 10 | r: [1] 1 1 1 1 | v: [1] 1 1 7 7 7 8 9 10 10 10 -1

A run is defined as a "maximally-long subsequence of repeated values", and the *full run* is not known at this time. We do, however, know that it is a run of r values.

You may never have thought about runs before, and will benefit from defining concepts to help you think about them. Language is a powerful aid to understanding, and words matter:

☞ **Invent (or learn) vocabulary for concepts that arise in a problem.**

We have only seen an initial subsequence of a full run. A word for that idea might help. How about the noun "prefix"? A prefix is something that comes first, and that is what we have between the two red lines: A *prefix* of a run. It could be the whole run, or it could be a *proper prefix*, i.e., not the full run. We don't know which, and won't know until seeing a subsequent input that is not the same as r. It is useful to learn and use established words for concepts, and Google Search is a powerful tool for discovering them. However, it is far more important that you identify relevant concepts, and name them (in words of your own invention, if necessary) so that you can think and talk about them.

Introduce another variable, n, for the *length* of the prefix currently in hand. Add n to the diagram, omitting the box for the variable, i.e., write n over a double-arrow that indicates the length of the prefix, and adopt the convention that merely writing it there signifies that there is such a variable, and that its contents is the length. In this case, n would contain 5:

n
r v
10 10 10 10 10 10 1 1 1 1 1 1 1 1 7 7 7 8 9 10 10 10 -1

Visual language is also a powerful aid to understanding, and pictures matter:

☞ **Invent (or learn) diagrammatic ways to express concepts.**

As with vocabulary, there are established pictorial conventions, but invent your own, if necessary.

Now ask yourself: What would have happened if the music had stopped one iteration later? Variable r would be the same, n would be one larger, and the right boundary would still be to the right of a 1 in the run, one 1 later:

n
r v
10 10 10 10 10 10 1 1 1 1 1 1 1 1 7 7 7 8 9 10 10 10 -1

The two diagrams are essentially the same, except for the minor detail that the scanned prefix of 1s is now one longer. This observation is a clue that we are close to identifying the loop invariant.

What would the diagram have looked like if the music had stopped a few iterations later?

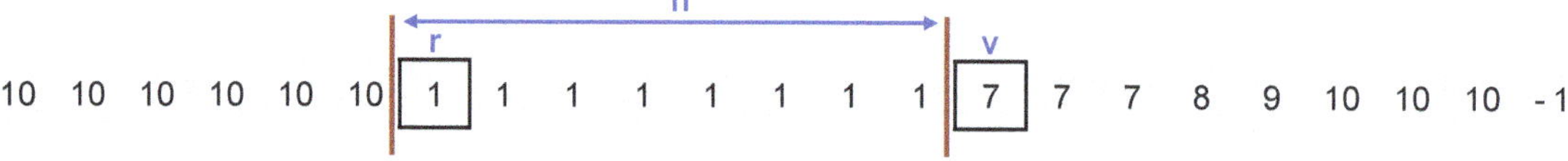

Again, similar. Variable r would remain the same, n would be even larger, and the right boundary would still be to the right of a 1. But this case is quite different. This time, the contents of v is 7, not 1. This is the precise moment when the end of a run is detected.

The loop invariant is implicit in these diagrams, but is obscured by their concreteness, i.e., they show too many specific details. The invariant must be stated for the general case, and therefore it is better to draw abstract, schematic diagrams that omit details. The details of the concrete diagrams devised so far were useful for teasing out aspects of the invariant, but we now switch to a schematic diagram that pictorially characterizes *regions of interest* between boundary lines:

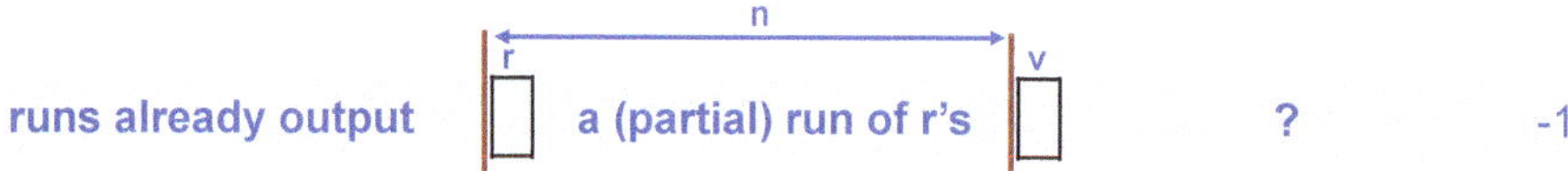

The diagram states that the input consists of three regions: The runs that have already been output, the prefix of a run currently being processed, and an unknown region. In interpreting the diagram, you must understand the convention that any of the identified regions may be empty. Specifically, in this case:

- No runs may have been output, i.e., r could be the very first value in the input.
- The value in v could equal or not equal r, i.e., we could be in the middle of a run, or beyond the right end of a complete run of r's.
- There may be no unknown and unprocessed values (labeled "?"), i.e., the run of r's could be the very last run, and the "?" region could be empty. In this case, v would be -1.
- There may be no runs at all, in which case both r and v would be -1, and there would be no values other than the -1.

The diagram states the invariant pictorially, and can be read in words as:

> Zero or more runs have been output. We have scanned a run prefix of r's of length n≥0, and have read v, the next input integer after that prefix.

This paragraph is the textual form of the loop invariant.

We can now write declarations for the variables mentioned in the invariant. End-of-line comments are used to express the role each variable plays, but the initializations are deferred until later:

3

```
/* Given 0 or more nonnegative inputs followed by a stopping signal of -1,
   output the equivalent run-encoded sequence followed by -1 -1. */
   int v = in.nextInt();  // Next integer to be processed, or -1.
   int r = ____;  // The run prefix is of r values.
   int n = ____;  // The processed prefix has length n.
   while ( v != -1 ) {
      β
      v = in.nextInt();
      }
   γ
```

Armed with the explicit picture (or statement) of the loop invariant, we now approach the question: How is the invariant to be maintained while making progress through the input?

Our analysis revealed a key distinction between two situations: The middle of a run, and the end of a run. Accordingly, we refine the body of the loop with a Case Analysis:

4

```
/* Given 0 or more nonnegative inputs followed by a stopping signal of -1,
   output the equivalent run-encoded sequence followed by -1 -1. */
   int v = in.nextInt();  // Next integer to be processed, or -1.
   int r = ____;  // The run prefix is of r values.
   int n = ____;  // The processed prefix has length n.
   while ( v != -1 ) {
      if ( ______ ) ______________
      else ______________
      v = in.nextInt();
      }
   γ
```

What exactly is it that distinguishes the two cases? A comparison between r and v. In the first case, they are the same, and in the second they are different:

```
/* Given 0 or more nonnegative inputs followed by a stopping signal of -1,     5
   output the equivalent run-encoded sequence followed by -1 -1. */
   int v = in.nextInt();  // Next integer to be processed, or -1.
   int r = ____;  // The run prefix is of r values.
   int n = ____;  // The processed prefix has length n.
   while ( v != -1 ) {
      if ( v==r ) ______________
      else ______________
      v = in.nextInt();
      }
   γ
```

The first case corresponds to having "stopped the music" in the *middle* of a run. The value in v must be incorporated logically into the run prefix, which we can do by incrementing n by 1 (and then subsequently reading the next input integer):

```
/* Given 0 or more nonnegative inputs followed by a stopping signal of -1,     6
   output the equivalent run-encoded sequence followed by -1 -1. */
   int v = in.nextInt();  // Next integer to be processed, or -1.
   int r = ____;  // The run prefix is of r values.
   int n = ____;  // The processed prefix has length n.
   while ( v != -1 ) {
      if ( v==r ) n++;
      else ______________
      v = in.nextInt();
      }
   γ
```

You can confirm that in the case v equal to r, the loop invariant is maintained.

In the second case, at the end of the run, we can emit the output pair because we now know that its length is n:

```
/* Given 0 or more nonnegative inputs followed by a stopping signal of -1,     7
   output the equivalent run-encoded sequence followed by -1 -1. */
   int v = in.nextInt();  // Next integer to be processed, or -1.
   int r = ____;  // The run prefix is of r values.
   int n = ____;  // The processed prefix has length n.
   while ( v != -1 ) {
      if ( v==r ) n++;
      else {
         System.out.print( r + " " + n + " " );
         }
      v = in.nextInt();
      }
   γ
```

Outputting the run effectively incorporates it into the region of already-output runs (to the left of the left boundary), which we can reflect by moving the left boundary line to the right of that run, i.e., by setting r to v. The input statement built into the online-computation pattern will then advance the right boundary line (and v) to the right of r, effectively incorporating it as the sole value in a new prefix of length 1:

8

```
/* Given 0 or more nonnegative inputs followed by a stopping signal of -1,
   output the equivalent run-encoded sequence followed by -1 -1. */
   int v = in.nextInt();  // Next integer to be processed, or -1.
   int r = ____;  // The run prefix is of r values.
   int n = ____;  // The processed prefix has length n.
   while ( v != -1 ) {
      if ( v==r ) n++;
      else {
         System.out.print( r + " " + n + " " );
         r = v; n = 1;
         }
      v = in.nextInt();
      }
   γ
```

You can confirm that in the case of v not equal to r, the loop invariant is preserved.

This step completes the coding of the loop body. We have established that in both cases, it preserves the invariant.

Coding the loop *condition* would normally come next, but it has already been coded as part of the online-computation pattern. Accordingly, we move on to the initialization:

☞ **Initialization. Do 3rd. Initialize variables so that the loop invariant is established prior to the first iteration. Substitute those initial values into the invariant, and bench check the first iteration with respect to that initial instantiation of the invariant.**

Clearly, the first run is a run of whatever value is in v, so set r to v. But what is the length of the run prefix? Specifically, should we set n to 0 or to 1? The value in v has *not* yet been processed (the body of the loop does that), so the run is initially a run of zero r's. We are in a degenerate situation: The run prefix is a run of a known value (r), but none have been processed so far. The first time the loop body executes, it will observe that v is equal to r, and increment n to be 1:

9

```
/* Given 0 or more nonnegative inputs followed by a stopping signal of -1,
   output the equivalent run-encoded sequence followed by -1 -1. */
   int v = in.nextInt();  // Next integer to be processed, or -1.
   int r = v;  // The run prefix is of r values.
   int n = 0;  // The processed prefix has length n.
   while ( v != -1 ) {
      if ( v==r ) n++;
      else {
         System.out.print( r + " " + n + " " );
         r = v; n = 1;
         }
      v = in.nextInt();
      }
   γ
```

Thinking about degenerate situations like the above can make your head hurt. It was well worth deferring initialization until *after* the loop body was completed, and *after* the loop invariant was fully expressed and understood. Furthermore, the code of the loop-body supports *bench checking* the initialization: After the first iteration, the following diagram holds:

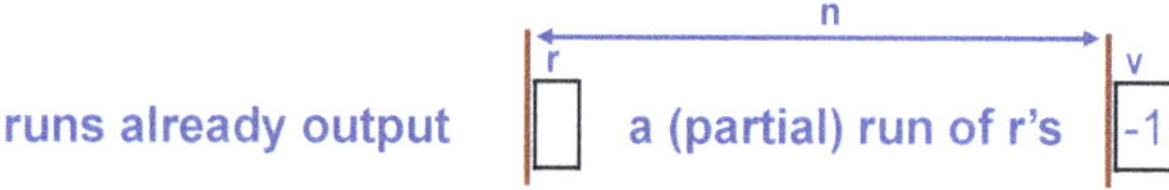

which is readily seen as a special case of the general loop invariant. Were we to have initialized n to 1, the first iteration would have made it 2, which would have violated the invariant. This step completes the coding of the initialization.

We turn, now, to finalization. Referring to the schematic diagram, consider the case where the "?" region is empty, and v is -1:

runs already output | r | a (partial) run of r's | v -1 (n spans the run)

Consider how this state arose, and realize that the previous iteration must have advanced the right boundary line to the right of the last run, which has not yet been output. Accordingly, it must be output now, in the finalization, together with the -1s:

```
/* Given 0 or more nonnegative inputs followed by a stopping signal of -1,
   output the equivalent run-encoded sequence followed by -1 -1. */
   int v = in.nextInt();  // Next integer to be processed, or -1.
   int r = v;  // The run prefix is of r values.
   int n = 0;  // The processed prefix has length n.
   while ( v != -1 ) {
      if ( v==r ) n++;
      else {
         System.out.print( r + " " + n + " " );
         r = v; n = 1;
         }
      v = in.nextInt();
      }
   System.out.print( r + " " + n + " " );
   System.out.println( "-1 -1" );
```
10

This step completes coding of the finalization.

We turn, now, to boundary conditions. The problem statement said the code must run correctly even when the only input is "-1", i.e., no runs at all. Here you see clearly the advantage of having delayed consideration of the boundary condition until dead last: The structure of code for the general case has been completed, and can be used to reason about the special case: No input other than -1. Initialization will have set n to 0, and the loop will not have executed at all. The finalization code is reached, which normally outputs the last run. But the value of n indicates that there is no run. Or, if you delight in being pedantic, you could say that the "last run", in this case, is "a run of length 0", so be sure not to output it because there's nothing there:

```
/* Given 0 or more nonnegative inputs followed by a stopping signal of -1,      11
   output the equivalent run-encoded sequence followed by -1 -1. */
   int v = in.nextInt();  // Next integer to be processed, or -1.
   int r = v;  // The run prefix is of r values.
   int n = 0;  // The processed prefix has length n.
   while ( v != -1 ) {
      if ( v==r ) n++;
      else {
         System.out.print( r + " " + n + " " );
         r = v; n = 1;
         }
      v = in.nextInt();
      }
   if ( n != 0 ) System.out.print( r + " " + n + " " );
   System.out.println( "-1 -1" );
```

Are there any other boundary conditions that should be checked? Thinking back to the original game of musical chairs, when we chose an "arbitrary" place to stop the music, we were skittish about picking either the run of one 8 or one 9, thinking that these might be special cases. Perhaps our anxiety was warranted; perhaps it wasn't. Best to bench-check the code for these cases. The run of 7s was output after the 8 was seen in v. We then set r to 8, n to 1, and read the next integer input, advancing v to 9:

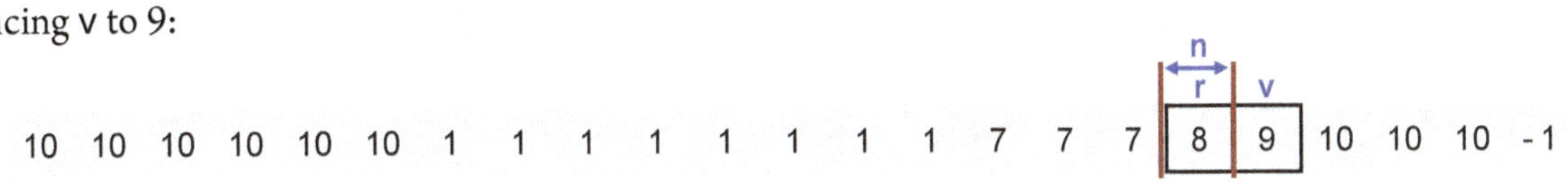

10 10 10 10 10 10 1 1 1 1 1 1 1 1 7 7 7 8 9 10 10 10 -1

On the very next iteration, the Case Analysis will detect the end of a run (of 8s) because v is not equal to r. So, the run of 8s (all one of them) is output, r is set to 9, n is set to 1 (which it already was), and we read the next integer input, advancing v to 10:

10 10 10 10 10 10 1 1 1 1 1 1 1 1 7 7 7 8 9 10 10 10 -1

Once again, the very next iteration immediately outputs the run of one 9, and advances to the run of 10s. So, there is no problem. Runs of length one turn out to not be a special case.

This completes the code for the encoder.

Decoding

The code for online run *decoding* is considerably simpler. It is presented for completeness, but presents only one small new idea: Reading input values in pairs:

```
/* Given zero or more pairs of integers ⟨r,n⟩, each pair representing a        1
   run encoding of n r's, followed by the pair ⟨-1,-1⟩, output the
   decoding, followed by -1. */
```

Clearly this is again an opportunity to use the online-computation pattern, but only after modifying it to read pairs of values each time:

```
/* Given zero or more pairs of integers ⟨r,n⟩, each pair representing a
   run encoding of n r's, followed by the pair ⟨-1,-1⟩, output the
   decoding, followed by -1. */
   int r = in.nextInt();  // The run value currently being processed.
   int n = in.nextInt();  // The length of the current run.
   α
   while ( r != -1 ) {
      β
      r = in.nextInt();
      n = in.nextInt();
      }
   γ
```
2

Some might prefer to test both r and n for -1, but the code above suffices, and the extra test would be redundant, albeit arguably useful for detecting possible input format errors.

Write the body of the loop, blasting out the printing of n instance of r:

```
/* Given zero or more pairs of integers ⟨r,n⟩, each pair representing a
   run encoding of n r's, followed by the pair ⟨-1,-1⟩, output the
   decoding, followed by -1. */
   int r = in.nextInt();  // The run value currently being processed.
   int n = in.nextInt();  // The length of the current run.
   α
   while ( r != -1 ) {
      for (int k=0; k<n; k++) System.out.print( r + " " );
      r = in.nextInt();
      n = in.nextInt();
      }
   γ
```
3

There is no initialization. Finalization prints -1, which completes implementation of the decoder:

```
/* Given zero or more pairs of integers ⟨r,n⟩, each pair representing a
   run encoding of n r's, followed by the pair ⟨-1,-1⟩, output the
   decoding, followed by -1. */
   int r = in.nextInt();  // The run value currently being processed.
   int n = in.nextInt();  // The length of the current run.
   while ( r != -1 ) {
      for (int k=0; k<n; k++) System.out.print( r + " " );
      r = in.nextInt();
      n = in.nextInt();
      }
   System.out.println( -1 );
```
4

CHAPTER 6

Enumeration Patterns

To *enumerate* is to list off, one by one. In application software, there are many things to enumerate: People, planets, toasters, etc. In the absence of any particular application, we can focus on enumerating numbers and tuples of numbers, e.g., pairs, triples, etc., and thereby gain generality.

There are many forms of enumeration. For example, we may count forwards or backwards, by ones or by twos. Objects arranged two dimensionally can be listed in left-to-right reading order (English), in right-to-left reading order (Hebrew), or in top-to-bottom reading order (Chinese).

Complete familiarity with various enumeration patterns, and with the code patterns that implement them, is highly advantageous. First, enumeration patterns provide conceptual vocabulary for addressing problems. Second, once a needed enumeration has been identified, the corresponding code pattern can be blasted into a program by reflex, and without detailed thought.

For example, suppose you need to fill a 4-by-4 array with integers, as shown. You should aspire to responding instantly: I need to enumerate array cells in left-to-right reading order, and drop consecutive integers into place as I go. The code pattern known as row-major-order enumeration is perfect. Pow! I know how to count up from 1. Pow! Done.

1	2	3	4
5	6	7	8
9	10	11	12
13	14	15	16

This chapter covers a range of standard enumerations, and illustrates their use with appropriate examples.

Counting

Children learn to count: 1, 2, 3, etc. Computers can count, too:

```
int k = 1;
while ( true ) k++;
```

Counting is one of the simplest examples of iteration. Here, we enumerate the *positive integers*, using variable k.

Before long, children learn the concept of 0 and, with a certain sense of pride, can start counting from there:

```
int k = 0;
while ( true ) k++;
```

Here, k runs through the *natural numbers*.

So-called *0-origin* counting immediately creates linguistic confusion. Ask 0-origin counters what number they enumerated *first,* and the answer is 0, what number they enumerated *second,* and the answer is 1, etc. The good news is that some questions have more felicitous answers for 0-origin counters. Ask them how many times they *incremented* their counter, and the answer is k, i.e., whatever value is in the variable k. The shoe is on the other foot for 1-origin counters: Ask them how many times they incremented their counter, and the answer is k-1.

Clearly, the counting pattern can be generalized:

```
int k = start;
while ( true ) k++;
```

whereupon the linguistic issues get a bit more complicated. Suppose *s* is the value of the expression *start,* and call such people "*s*-counters". Assume *s* is nonnegative. Then the first number for an *s*-counter is *s*, and the number of times k has been incremented is k-s.

The subtle difference between "what's first?" questions and "how many?" questions is the source of much confusion, and contributes to notorious *off-by-1 errors* in programming. Associate natural numbers with the N elements of an ordered collection of objects, and ask what number is associated with the last object? Answer: N-1.

Questions about "how many between?" and "distance between?" are another source of confusion and off-by-one errors. For example, how many integers are there inclusively between p and q? Answer: q-p+1. Ask what is the distance between x and x' on the real number line? Answer: $|x-x'|$.

Keep in mind that such questions are fraught, and error rates are high even after decades of experience. Until you notice yourself rarely making off-by-one errors, it is best to be humble and always check yourself when you write expressions for such quantities. It is your choice whether to reason abstractly (with arbitrary variables), or concretely (with specific values for the variables). There's no shame in doing the check because everyone makes mistakes. The appropriate aphorism is: An ounce of prevention is worth a pound of cure, where the cure is debugging.

Children learn the concept of infinity from counting. They learn that a google is a 1 followed by a hundred 0s, and after that, there are still more numbers to count.

Alas, computers have only finite-precision numbers built in, and there is a largest positive integer that can be stored in an **int** variable. So, what happens when the variable k in our counting code has reached that largest integer, and we attempt to increment it yet another time? It continues enumerating *negative* numbers backwards. What? That's right!

The largest positive number that can be stored in an **int** variable is 2^{31}-1, and the next number after that is a representation of the most-negative negative number: -2^{31}. Signed numbers are represented in *two's-complement* form, where half are nonnegative, and the other half are negative. Our loops are indeed infinite, but k does not get arbitrarily large. Rather, k cycles clockwise through the ring of numbers depicted. The phenomenon whereby 2^{31}-1 is followed by -2^{31} is called *arithmetic overflow,* and occurs silently on most computers, i.e., without any error indication.

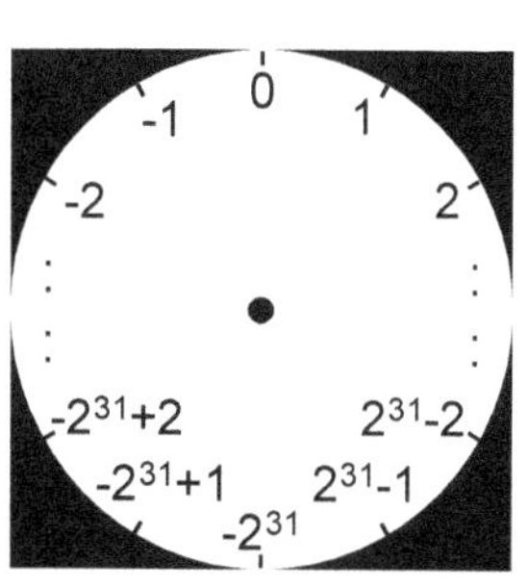

Normally, we don't worry about arithmetic overflow. If you are worried about it for your application, use **long** instead of **int**. The largest positive **long** value is 2^{63}-1, which is not quite a google, but is getting closer.[67]

67. If 2^{63}-1 isn't big enough, you can always use a *bignum* package, which represents a number's digits in an array of **int** (or **long**) values. Addition of two integers (say, of *A* and *B*) is

All good things must come to an end, and we must replace our infinite loops with finite ones:

```
int k = start;
while ( condition ) k++;
```

where *condition* determines how long to keep counting. Herein lies another pitfall: Confusion between "when to stop?" questions and "when to continue?" questions. Confuse the two, and you will easily say the opposite of what you intended. There is no common term for such mistakes (akin to "off-by-one" errors); perhaps we could call them "get it backwards" errors.

There are two forms of bounded counting: Indeterminate and determinate. In the first, you don't know ahead of time how long you are going to keep counting; in the second, you do.

1-D Indeterminate Enumeration

Counting until you find an integer with a given property is called the *1-D indeterminate-enumeration* pattern:

```
/* Enumerate from start until !condition. */
   int k = start;
   while ( condition ) k++;
```

where *condition* is the negation of the property sought.

In the case where the existence of an integer with the desired property is not guaranteed, but where it is known that no integer beyond a *maximum* has the property, the bound can be added to the *condition*:

```
/* Enumerate from start until !condition, but no further than maximum. */
   int k = start;
   while ( k<=maximum && condition ) k++;
```

which will terminate either having found a `k` with the property sought, or with `k` equal to *maximum*+1. Subsequent code can use the value of `k` to easily distinguish between the two cases by checking whether `k>maximum`:

```
/* Enumerate from start until !condition, but no further than maximum. */
   int k = start;
   while ( k<=maximum && condition ) k++;
if ( k>maximum ) /* condition was true for all k in [start..maximum]. */
else /* k is smallest in [start..maximum] for which condition is false. */
```

Here is the reasoning: Upon termination of the iteration, if `k` is greater than *maximum*, it must have been incremented in the final iteration, and so, the *condition* when `k` was equal to *maximum* must have been **true**. Furthermore, it must have been **true** for

---

performed by iterating over the elements of the arrays for the two operands (say, `A[0..n-1]` and `B[0..n-1]`) from right to left, as you learned in grade school. The difference is that each "digit" of a bignum can be one of the unsigned values between 0 and 2^{32}-1 (or 2^{64}-1). Now we're getting close to infinity! Implementing bignum is a nice exercise, if you are looking for practice. Bignum is available in Java as `BigInteger`. Python's integer variables are bignums by default.

every previous iteration. Thus, the property sought, which is the negation of the *condition*, didn't hold for any integer between *start* and *maximum*, inclusive. Conversely, if k is not greater than *maximum*, the reason the iteration terminated must have been because the *condition* was **false** for some integer not greater than *maximum*. The value of k is that integer, and because we are iterating in order of increasing values, that k is the smallest integer greater than or equal to *start* with the desired property.

As given, the patterns enumerate ever *larger* integers. Clearly the direction of the enumeration can be reversed, and you can enumerate ever *smaller* integers:

```
/* Enumerate from start in the negative direction. */
   int k = start;
   while ( condition ) k--;
```

1-D Determinate Enumeration

Counting until you have enumerated some given number of integers is called the *1-D determinate-enumeration* pattern:

```
/* Do whatever n times. */
   int k = 0;
   while ( k<n ) {
      /* whatever */
      k++;
      }
```

In determinate enumeration, the enumeration range is known in advance. In some situations, it is already known when you are writing the program, even before it runs, e.g., if you write a constant instead of the variable n:

```
/* Do whatever 10 times. */
   int k = 0;
   while ( k<10 ) {
      /* whatever */
      k++;
      }
```

In other situations, the number of values enumerated is *not* known until the program runs and control reaches the code with some particular value in n. In this case, we still say the enumeration is determinate rather than indeterminate. In fact, *each* time control reaches this iteration statement, n may contain a different value, and the enumeration range will be different, but we still call it determinate because the number of iterations is established before iteration commences.

As described in Chapters 1 and 2, determinate iteration is so common that programming languages have an abbreviation for it:

```
/* Do whatever n times. */
   for (int k=0; k<n; k++)
      /* whatever */
```

This code pattern does exactly the same thing as the determinate-iteration pattern using a **while**-statement. Determinacy is a property of an enumeration that is independent of how you express it, i.e., using a **for**-statement, or using the **while** pattern. The property is: The extent of the enumeration is known (each time) before it begins. Use of a **for**-statement makes it a little easier to identify determinativeness in code because you don't need to look for the telltale **while** pattern.

Nothing (other than self-discipline) prevents you from altering the extent of a determinate iteration while it is executing. For example, you can write:

```
for (int k=0; k<n; k++) {
   /* whatever */
   if ( condition ) k = n;
   }
```

and thereby terminate the enumeration prematurely. Some programming languages even provide a special construct for "breaking out of a **for**-loop". This practice is *strongly discouraged.* Specifically, if there is any reason why you must allow for the possibility that an enumeration may stop "in mid-stream", you should use the indeterminate-iteration pattern, and express the exceptional circumstance up front:

```
k = 0;
while ( k<n && !condition ) {
   /* whatever */
   k++;
   }
```

Don't use a **for**-statement that says up front "Count from 0 through k-1" and then, buried deep in the body of the loop, say "Oops, I changed my mind. Stop!". Make the indeterminacy explicit.[68]

Beware of being bewitched by **for**-statements. They are like the Sirens of Homer's Odyssey who enticed sailors to their destruction with their irresistible appeal. Only use a **for**-statement for determinate enumeration. Each time you are tempted to use one, ask yourself: Is this really a determinate case? If not, deny yourself its questionable utility, and stick with the lowly **while**-statement:

☞ **Beware of for-loop abuse; if in doubt, err in favor of while.**

Read problem specifications carefully to distinguish between the two kinds of iteration. Here are some examples:

```
/* Print all divisors of p. */
```

This calls for *determinate* enumeration because you need to check every integer between 2 and p, and print only those integers that are divisors of p. With a little thought, you may deduce a smaller upper bound for the number of iterations.

```
/* Print the smallest divisor of p. */
```

This calls for *indeterminate* enumeration because you want to stop as soon as you find a divisor of p.

68. There is a subtle difference between the two examples: In the first case, *condition* is tested after each iteration; in the second case, condition is tested before each *iteration*.

```
/* Print the smallest value in a list of n values. */
```

This calls for *determinate* enumeration because you can't know which value in the list is smallest unless you consider each and every one of them.

```
/* Print a value (among a list of n values) that is smaller than p. */
```

This calls for *indeterminate* enumeration because you want to stop as soon as you find a value smaller than p.

```
/* Print how many values (in a list of n values) are smaller than p. */
```

This calls for *determinate* enumeration because you need to inspect each value.

Enumeration Mod N

The modulus operation can be thought of as providing the remainder after an integer division. If `k` is a nonnegative **`int`**, the expression `k/N` is the integer *quotient*, whereas `k%N` is the *remainder* after that integer division. If you find this difficult, perhaps that is because third grade (before you learned about decimals) was so long ago.

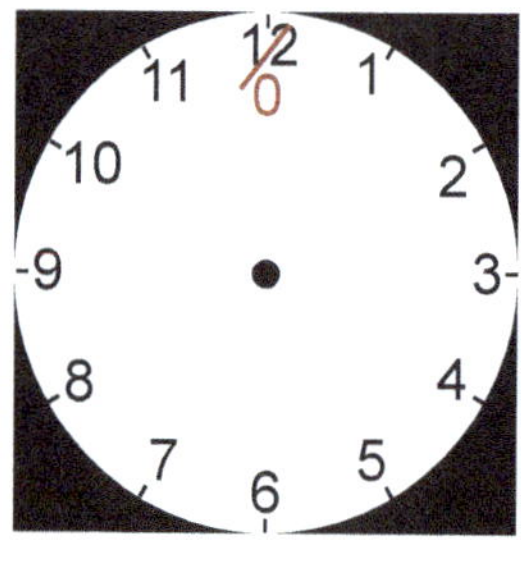

Arithmetic in a finite domain of integers, where the next number after the last integer is the first integer, is called *modular arithmetic*. We have all learned to do this with the hours on a clock, where the hour after 12 o'clock is 1 o'clock. Life would have been easier (or at least more mathematical) if noon at been called 0 o'clock. Arithmetic **mod** N for the case N=12 is easily understood as addition of hours on this 0-origin clock. Let `h` be an hour. Then the next hour is `(h+1)%12`, and the previous hour is `(h+11)%12`.

For example, the next hour after 11 is `(11+1)%12`, or 0. The hour preceding 1 is found by going 11 hours forward from 1: `(1+11)%12`, or `12%12`, which is 0.

Why, you might ask, isn't the previous hour `(h-1)%12`? Because the modulus operator (`%`) yields negative results for negative left operands. For example, `(0-1)%12`, which is `-1%12`, evaluates to -1. Winning the battle to call noon 0 o'clock will be hard enough; let's not take on trying to call 11 o'clock "-1 o'clock"! So, instead of going backward 1 hour, go all the way around by 11 hours, and then use the modulus operation to map the result into 0 through 11.

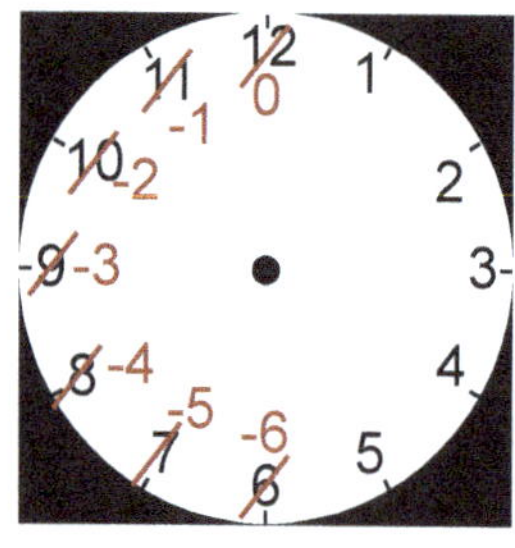

In point of fact, calling 11 o'clock "-1 o'clock" is exactly what is done in computers. And not only that: 10 o'clock is "-2 o'clock", 9 o'clock is "-3 o'clock", etc., all the way to 6 o'clock, which is "-6 o'clock". By adopting this convention, the arithmetic of signed numbers is implemented as addition **mod** N. Check it out:[69]

- (-1)+(-2) ~ (11+10) **mod** 12 = 21 **mod** 12 = 9 ~ -3
- 1+2 ~ (1+2) **mod** 12 = 3 **mod** 12 = 3 ~ 3
- (+1)+(-2) ~ (1+10) **mod** 12 = 11 **mod** 12 = 11 ~ -1

Of course, for type **`int`**, N is not 12, but 2^{32}.

Indeterminate enumeration of integers **mod** N, beginning with *start*, takes the form:

```
int k = start;
while ( condition ) k = (k+1)%N;
```

69. We indicate regions where the convention regarding the representation of signed numbers is at play in red.

This is fine when it is known that the *condition* will be **false** for at least one of the N integers in the cycle. But to handle the possibility that *condition* is **true** for all k in the range [0..N-1], it is infeasible to bound the number of iterations by testing k. Specifically, you will not find a satisfactory expression for *bound-check* in:

```
int k = start;
while ( bound-check && condition ) k = (k+1)%N;
```

The problem is that the value of k after an exhaustive enumeration of the integers **mod** N that begins at *start* is *start*. Any *bound-check* that would terminate execution at that point would also prevent execution of the first iteration. Accordingly, it is best to control the iteration with a normal integer k, and replace k with k%N in the *condition*:

```
int k = start;
while ( k<=(start+N-1) && condition-with-k-replaced-by-k%N ) k++;
```

Sieve of Eratosthenes

This example illustrates enumeration of one-dimensional-array indices.

Background. An integer greater than or equal to 2 whose only divisors are 1 and itself is called a *prime* number; otherwise, it is called *composite*. We observe, as did Eratosthenes [14], that if the integers from 2 through *n* are written out in order, then each integer we come to in left-to-right reading order that has not yet been crossed out is prime, at which point we can cross out all its multiples. For example, say *n* is 15:

2 3 4 5 6 7 8 9 10 11 12 13 14 15

First, we come to 2, which is prime. We cross out all its multiples:

(2) 3 4 5 6 7 8 9 10 11 12 13 14 15

Next, we come to 3, which is prime. We cross out all its multiples. Note that 6 and 12 were already crossed out (2 is a factor) but this is of no concern. We cross them out again:

2 (3) 4 5 6 7 8 9 10 11 12 13 14 15

Then, we come to 4, but it has been crossed out because it is composite, so we skip it. Five is next, and it is prime. We cross out its multiples (10 and 15) again:

2 3 4 (5) 6 7 8 9 10 11 12 13 14 15

And so on, picking up 7, 11, and 13 as primes.

Problem Statement. List all prime numbers that are not larger than some given integer n.

Solution. The first step is to recognize that the code for finding primes:

```
/* Print primes up to n. */                                    1
```

using the Sieve of Eratosthenes has the structure of the initialize-compute pattern:

```
/* Print primes up to n. */                                                2
   /* Initialize sieve to all prime. */
   /* Print each prime in sieve, and cross out its multiples. */
```

Mastery of one-dimensional determinate enumerations allows you to refine the specifications in short order. The initialization can run through the integers using a standard 1-D determinate enumeration:

```
/* Print primes up to n. */                                                3
   /* Initialize sieve to all prime. */
      for (int j=2; j<=n; j++) __________
   /* Print each prime in sieve, and cross out its multiples. */
```

Each of those integers must then be considered, but this can be done using exactly the same enumeration:

```
/* Print primes up to n. */                                                4
   /* Initialize sieve to all prime. */
      for (int j=2; j<=n; j++) __________
   /* Print each prime in sieve, and cross out its multiples. */
      for (int j=2; j<=n; j++) __________
```

If an integer has not been crossed out, it's prime: Print it and cross out all its multiples:

```
/* Print primes up to n. */                                                5
   /* Initialize sieve to all prime. */
      for (int j=2; j<=n; j++) __________
   /* Print each prime in sieve, and cross out its multiples. */
      for (int j=2; j<=n; j++)
         if ( ______ ) {
            System.out.println(j);
            for (int k=2*j; k<=n; k=k+j) __________
            }
```

This completes the code outline. Now, we consider how to represent the sieve, and choose a one-dimensional **`boolean`** array named `prime` of the appropriate size:

```
/* Print primes up to n. */                                                6
   boolean prime[] = new boolean[ ____ ];  // prime[k] true iff k is prime.
   /* Initialize sieve to all prime. */
      for (int j=2; j<=n; j++) prime[j] = true;
   /* Print each prime in sieve, and cross out its multiples. */
      for (int j=2; j<=n; j++)
         if ( prime[j] ) {
            System.out.println(j);
            for (int k=2*j; k<=n; k=k+j) prime[k] = false;
            }
```

Getting the size of the array right is a bit of a fussy detail that we have saved for last. We are using subscripts between 2 and `n` (inclusive), but need to allow for the unused indices 0 and 1. So, a size of `n+2` seems plausible. However, we are ever-alert to the pitfalls of off-by-one errors, and are mindful of our limitations, so we check

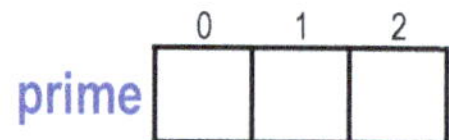

our hunch with a degenerate example: n equal to 2, for which we only require the array shown. Oops. We only need the array to be of size n+1, i.e., 3.

☞ **Beware of off-by-one errors.**

We can now complete the code:

```
/* Print primes up to n. */
   boolean prime[] = new boolean[n+1];  // prime[k] true iff k is prime.
   /* Initialize sieve to all prime. */
      for (int j=2; j<=n; j++) prime[j] = true;
   /* Print each prime in sieve, and cross out its multiples. */
      for (int j=2; j<=n; j++)
         if ( prime[j] ) {
            System.out.println(j);
            for (int k=2*j; k<=n; k=k+j) prime[k] = false;
            }
```
7

The essential lesson of this example is: Master one-dimensional determinate iterations. One can easily imagine that sufficient proficiency would allow you to complete this code in only a few minutes.

An important proviso is to avoid distractions. For example, suppose you had gotten hung up over duplicate cross outs, and had tried to avoid them. Then your code for crossing out multiples of prime j might have been:

```
for (int k=2*j; k<=n; k=k+j)
   if ( prime[k] ) prime[k] = false;
```

But why bother? Operations whose net effect is no change at all are harmless, and if it takes as long to detect an immanent superfluous operation as it would take to just do it, then just do it.

Similarly, if you had gotten hung up over the fact that the sieve contains no multiples of primes greater than n/2, then you might have fretted about avoiding iterations that iterate zero times, writing the cross-out code as:

```
if ( j<=(n/2) )
   for (int k=2*j; k<=n; k=k+j) prime[k] = false;
```

But again, it takes roughly as long to test that you are passed the halfway point as it takes for the **for**-loop to determine that 2*j is already greater than n, so just allow the loop to repeatedly do nothing.

Avoid special-case code by following the precept:

☞ **Code the general case first. Then attempt to make the boundary case fit the general case, if possible, making as slight a change to the code as possible.**

Don't litter you program with unneeded code. As in architecture: Less is more.

Yet another hang up might have arisen when you went to implement the sieve with the array prime. Had you fretted about the unused array elements prime[0] and prime[1], you might have been tempted to offset the subscripts by -2. In general:

☞ **Avoid index arithmetic, if possible and convenient.**

In this case, the cost of two superfluous array elements in the sieve is negligible, and identifying the sieve subscript with the integer whose primality is being represented simplifies the code.

The decision to represent the sieve as a **boolean** array `prime` rather than as an **int** array `sieve` containing the integers (crossed out or not) deserves some review and comment. Specifically, what split-second thoughts took place at the moment we chose this representation?

On its face, a sieve contains integers, so the choice of an **int** array would have been tempting. But then, we would still have had to represent whether an integer was crossed out or not. It is common, but inelegant, to represent a binary property (like "crossed out") by negating an otherwise positive integer. This encoding squeezes one more bit of information into a value, while still allowing the original (positive) integer to be recovered, if necessary, by negating it. While such tricks may seem clever, they are "too smart by a half", and should be avoided. It is best to:

☞ **Avoid obscurity. Be as direct as possible.**

Instinctive aversion to obscure encodings led us to consider a second array, say, `crossedOut`, to represent the state of the corresponding integer in `sieve`, i.e., `crossedOut[j]` would indicate whether or not `sieve[j]` had been crossed out. Clearly, `crossedOut` could be a **boolean** array. But the next insight was that because the value in `sieve[j]` is `j` itself, `sieve` is really quite superfluous. We only need the **boolean** array.

Finally, rather than calling the array `crossedOut`, we recognized that a number is crossed out precisely when we discover that it is composite, so we considered renaming the array `composite`. But noticing that the conditional tests primality rather than compositeness, we flipped the sense of the array (thereby avoiding the need for negation), and called it `prime`.

2-D Enumerations

Enumeration of integer pairs ⟨`r`,`c`⟩ through a range of values can be done in various orders. We call the two integers `r` and `c` (for row and column) for geometric intuition, even though a two-dimensional array is not (necessarily) involved.

We restrict our attention here to two dimensions, although there is nothing special about two. In fact, in Chapter 13 Cellular Automata, we will find ourselves doing five-dimensional enumerations, with loops nested five deep. For introductory purposes, two will do.

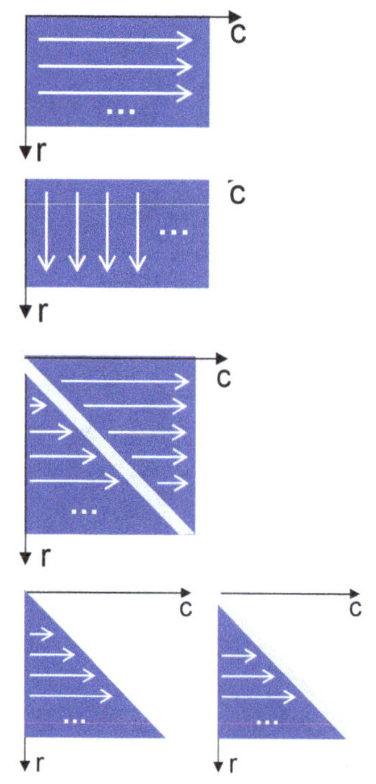

Orders

Row-major order enumeration proceeds by rows, and within each row, by columns. Conversely, *column-major order* proceeds by columns, and within each column, by rows. Both enumerations consider every combination of integer values ⟨`r`,`c`⟩ in a rectangular region.

Sometimes one wishes to enumerate pairs ⟨`r`,`c`⟩ in a square region, (say) in row-major order, but without duplicates. In this case, the pairs on the diagonal are omitted. You can think of the range of values as a set from which we select two distinct values in an *ordered* fashion given by the pair, i.e., `r` is the first value selected, and `c` is the second.

We may wish to select a pair of values from a set, but in an *unordered* fashion, i.e., we wish to consider ⟨`r`,`c`⟩ and ⟨`c`,`r`⟩ as indistinct. In this case, we only consider a *lower-triangular region*. One can distinguish between a *closed* triangle (which includes the diagonal), and an *open* triangle (which excludes it). For example, if one wanted to enumerate all two-element sets of distinct natural numbers {r,c} in some range, one could enumerate an open lower-triangular region.

Diagonal order is useful when no *a priori* bound is known for either value of a pair. In diagonal order, we enumerate pairs ⟨r,c⟩ in order of r+c, and for a given value of r+c, from left to right, i.e., ⟨0,0⟩ ⟨1,0⟩, ⟨0,1⟩, ⟨2,0⟩, ⟨1,1⟩, ⟨0,2⟩, etc. In contrast with the other enumerations, diagonal-order enumeration is unbounded.

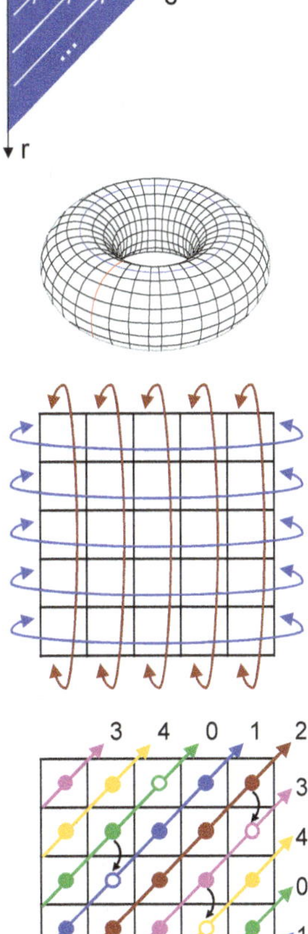

Toroidal-enumerations occur on the surface of a *torus*, i.e., a donut. You can think of a torus as a two-dimensional clock, for which modular arithmetic applies in both the horizontal and vertical dimensions. It is as if the top and bottom edges of a rectangle are one and the same, and the right and left edges are one and the same. Exiting at the top (resp. bottom) reenters at the bottom (resp., top); exiting at the right (resp. left) reenters at the left (resp. right).[70]

Diagonal order enumeration on the surface of a torus is also of interest. In general, which diagonal to start on, where to start on it, and the skew in selecting the start position on the next diagonal are parameters of the ordering. The order illustrated runs along diagonals numbered starting at 0, starts in the middle of the top row, and uses a skew ⟨Δ*r*,Δ*c*⟩ of ⟨+1,0⟩, i.e., ⟨down 1, no horizontal change⟩ from the *last* position on the previous diagonal to the *first* position on the next diagonal. We term this order "magical".[71]

Nested Loops.

Two-dimensional enumerations are typically implemented by nested loops. For example, a 3-by-4 row-major-order enumeration:

```
/* Enumerate ⟨r,c⟩ in [0..2][0..3] in row-major order. */
   for (int r=0; r<3; r++)
      for (int c=0; c<4; c++)
         /* whatever */
```

It is conventional to explain such code by means of a temporal *trace* that shows the moment of each variable assignment. For the example, the trace would be:

r	0						1						2						3				→ time
c		0	1	2	3	4		0	1	2	3	4		0	1	2	3	4					

Traces are a mechanical way to understand nested loops: In terms of the memory operations taken by the computer. Now that you have seen a trace once, wean yourself of this habit. Rather, adopt a linguistic viewpoint, and leverage the power of English to express nested iteration conceptually:

> For each natural number r between 0 and 2 (inclusive), consider each natural number c between 0 and 3 (inclusive), and do whatever.

Avoid the worms-eye view, if at all possible. Train yourself to reason in a natural language and in terms of loop invariants. For example, the invariant for a row-major-order enumeration is:

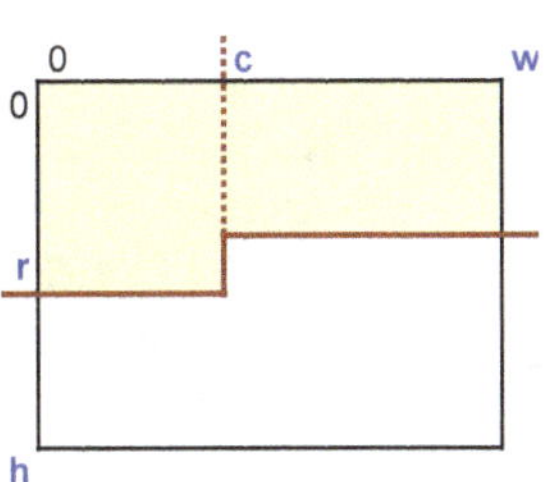

> r of h complete rows of width w, and c columns of the next row have been enumerated.

70. A torus is used to model a finite Universe in Chapter 13 Cellular Automata.
71. Toroidal Diagonal Order enumeration is used to construct Magic Squares (p. 128).

Code Patterns for Two-Dimensional Enumerations

We provide code patterns for each enumeration order above without further discussion. For row-major order, we provide both determinate and indeterminate patterns of enumeration. Diagonal-order enumerations are typically indeterminate.

Row-Major Order

Determinate, 0-origin:

```
/* Enumerate ⟨r,c⟩ in [0..height-1][0..width-1] in row-major order. */
   for (int r=0; r<height; r++)
      for (int c=0; c<width; c++)
         /* whatever */
```

Determinate, 1-origin:

```
/* Enumerate ⟨r,c⟩ in [1..height][1..width] in row-major order. */
   for (int r=1; r<=height; r++)
      for (int c=1; c<=width; c++)
         /* whatever */
```

Indeterminate, 0-origin:
The pattern of two nested **for**-loops for determinate row-major-order enumeration is ingrained and knee jerk. Accordingly, there is a strong temptation to adapt it for the indeterminate case. Notwithstanding this, we still advocate using a **while** for indeterminate iteration, as follows:

```
/* Enumerate ⟨r,c⟩ in [0..height-1][0..width-1] in row-major order
   until condition, and do whatever for each. */
   int r = 0; int c = 0;
   while ( r<height && !condition ) {
      /* whatever */
      if ( c<width-1 ) c++; // Not the end of a row; go to next column.
      else { c = 0; r++; }  // The end of a row; go to start of next row.
      }
if ( r==height ) /* fail */ else /* succeed */
```

Column-Major Order

```
/* Enumerate ⟨r,c⟩ in [0..height-1][0..width-1] in column-major order. */
   for (int c=0; c<width; c++)
      for (int r=0; r<height; r++)
         /* whatever */
```

Triangular Order

Closed:

```
/* Enumerate ⟨r,c⟩ in a closed lower-triangular region of
   [0..size-1][0..size-1] in row-major order.*/
   for (int r=0; r<size; r++)
      for (int c=0; c<=r; c++)
         /* whatever */
```

Open:

```
/* Enumerate ⟨r,c⟩ through an open lower-triangular region
   of [0..size-1][0..size-1] in row-major order.*/
   for (int r=1; r<size; r++)
      for (int c=0; c<r; c++)
         /* whatever */
```

Diagonal Order

```
/* Unbounded enumeration of ⟨r,c⟩ starting at ⟨0,0⟩ until condition. */
   int d = 0;
   while ( !condition ) {
      int r = d;
      for (int c=0; c<=d; c++) {
         /* whatever */
         r--;
         }
      d++;
      }
```

Toroidal diagonal order

The code for toroidal-order enumeration uses modular arithmetic to handle wrap-around indexing.

```
/* n-by-n toroidal-diagonal enumeration in "magical order". */
   int r = 0; int c = n/2;
   for (int d=0; d<n; d++) {
      for (int k=0; k<n; k++) {
         /* whatever */
         r = (r+n-1)%n; c = (c+1)%n; // up 1 and right 1.
         }
      r = (r+2)%n; c = (c+n-1)%n;    // down 2 and left 1.
      }
```

Ramanujan Cubes

This example illustrates two-dimensional iteration outside the context of two-dimensional arrays.

Background. Srinivasa Ramanujan startled British Mathematician G. H. Hardy by knowing off the top of his head that the number 1729 is the smallest integer that can be expressed as the sum of two positive cubes in two different ways [15].

Problem Statement. Write a program to verify Ramanujan's claim.

Enumeration. The cube root of 1729 is approximately 12.0023, so we can enumerate all sets of distinct values {r,c} selected from the domain 1 through 12, and look for duplicates in a histogram of the values r^3+c^3. Think of r as the larger of the two values, c as the smaller of the two, and the loops as an open triangular-order enumeration:

```
/* Record the values of r^3+c^3 that arise for all sets {r,c} of distinct      1
   positive integers that are no larger than 12. */
   for (int r=2; r<13; r++)
      for (int c=1; c<r; c++)
         /* Keep track of having seen r^3+c^3. */
/* Confirm that 1729 is the smallest integer that arose twice. */
```

Manual inspection of the values that arose will confirm that 1729 is the only one that occurs more than once. The development of this code is continued in Chapter 12 (p. 206), after we have discussed the use of a histogram for keeping track of a collection of values.

Rational Numbers

This example is used in the text for many purposes, both here and in subsequent chapters. It is based on simple grade-school arithmetic, yet introduces many substantive issues. First, it draws a distinction between an abstract value, e.g., a rational number, and the multiple representations of that value, e.g., as different unreduced fractions. Second, it illustrates an unbounded enumeration (in diagonal order), i.e., code that deliberately contains an infinite loop, and discusses the related concept of the size of an infinite set. Third, it presents an application in which one can maintain a dynamically-growing data structure in the course of a computation, e.g., a set of values. We turn to such data structures in Chapter 12 Collections. Fourth, it germinates the idea of user-defined datatypes that would allow new kinds of values to be manipulated with ease. We invent such types in the specifications used here, but without addressing the technical details needed to make them a reality. The need to do so motivates Chapter 18 Classes and Objects, and the whole subject of object-oriented programming.

Background. A *rational number* is any number that can be expressed as a fraction p/q, where *numerator* p and non-zero *denominator* q are integers. Each rational has multiple representations, e.g., 2/3, 4/6, 10/15, etc. A representation p/q for which p and q have no common factors is called *reduced*, e.g., 2/3. One obtains the reduced version of a fraction by dividing both the numerator and the denominator by their greatest common divisor g, where g can be computed by Euclid's Algorithm (p. 80).[72]

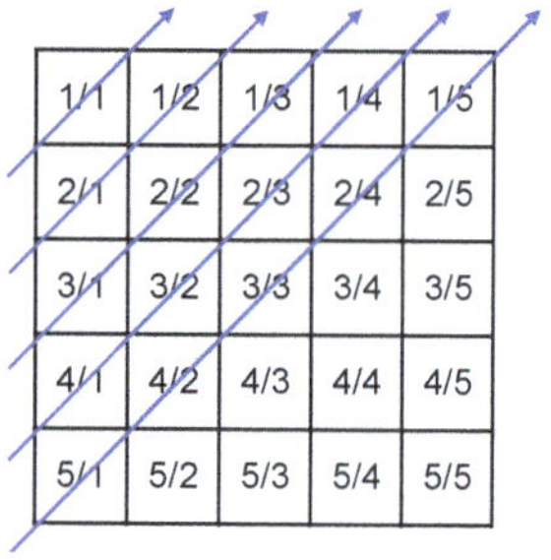

1/1	1/2	1/3	1/4	1/5
2/1	2/2	2/3	2/4	2/5
3/1	3/2	3/3	3/4	3/5
4/1	4/2	4/3	4/4	4/5
5/1	5/2	5/3	5/4	5/5

Although it would seem that there are *more* rationals than integers, this is not the case: One can enumerate the fractions in diagonal-order as an infinitely long list, one per line, as shown in output A.[73] We then observe that for each line number (an integer) there is a fraction, and for each fraction there is a line number.

```
1/1                                  A
2/1
1/2
3/1
2/2
1/3
4/1
3/2
2/3
1/4
5/1
4/2
3/3
2/4
1/5
etc.
```

This itemization demonstrates that the number of unreduced positive fractions is the same as the number of positive integers. The notion of "number" can thus be extended to include the size of the infinite set. That number is called "aleph null", and is written as $\aleph_0$. The size of any infinite set that can be listed, one item per integer, is said to be $\aleph_0$, and the set is called *countable*.

To show that the set of rationals is countable, we must restrict the enumeration of fractions to *reduced* fractions. We can easily do so by omitting from our list any fraction that represents an already-listed rational, e.g., we skip 2/2 because we have

72. To avoid confusion with division, we could have written the fraction p/q as $\frac{p}{q}$. However, we won't bother to do so.

73. In the following discussion, we ignore negative numbers, and zero (in all its different manifestations as a fraction), e.g., 0/1, 0/2, 0/3, etc.

already listed 1/1. In this more discriminating enumeration, there are still just as many rationals as there are integers, and thus its size is $\aleph_0$. The diagram shows the omitted fractions shaded in gray.

Problem Statement. Enumerate each positive rational, one per line.

Enumeration. We start with code to enumerate all positive unreduced fractions using the diagonal-order enumeration:[74]

```
/* Output positive fractions, including those equivalent as rationals. */
   int d = 0;
   while ( true ) {
      int r = d;
      for (int c=0; c<=d; c++) {
         System.out.println( (r+1) + "/" + (c+1) );
         r--;
         }
      d++;
      }
```
1

We then modify this code to avoid listing any rational more than once.

We choose to maintain a list of the reduced fractions as they are output. Each fraction in the diagonal-order enumeration is looked up in this list to see if its reduced form has already been output, and if it has, we skip it:[75]

```
/* Output reduced positive fractions, i.e., positive rationals. */
   int d = 0;
   /* set reduced = { }; */
   while ( true ) {
      int r = d;
      for (int c=0; c<=d; c++) {
         /* Let z be the reduced form of the fraction r/(c+1). */
            int g = gcd(r+1, c+1);
            /* rational z = ⟨(r+1)/g,(c+1)/g⟩; */
         if ( /* z is not an element of reduced */ ) {
            System.out.println( /* z */ );
            /* reduced = reduced ∪ {z}; */
            }
         r--;
         }
      d++;
      }
```
2

The code in red suggest the possibility of defining new types of values, e.g., `rational` and `set`, declaring variables that have such types, e.g., `z` and `reduced`, and programming in terms of operations on such values, e.g., pairing two **`int`** values to make a `rational`, or testing whether a particular value `z` occurs in the set `reduced`, or updating the set `reduced` to contain an additional value `z`.

Clearly, the ability to define new datatypes would be a highly-desirable

74. We use the diagonal-order enumeration pattern exactly as presented on page 124, but add 1 to both `r` and `c` so that pairs of positive (rather than nonnegative) integers are printed.

75. This is one of those places in the book where, for pedagogical purposes, we deliberately overlook something. Perhaps you have detected it. It will be revealed and resolved in Chapter 18 (p. 317), but only after we have learned a great deal about how to maintain a set of values in a data structure.

generalization. Rest assured that modern programming languages support the notion being foreshadowed here. However, it involves numerous rather technical language features that are well-beyond the minimal language subset assumed in Chapter 2 Prerequisites. Accordingly, we defer completing this example until Chapter 18 Classes and Objects (p. 302), where the needed features will be presented, motivated (in part) by this example. Until then, we continue to focus on programming using only the primitive datatype **int**, and arrays of **int** variables.

Magic Squares

This example illustrates toroidal-order enumeration, and its use of modular arithmetic.

Background. An N-by-N array containing distinct integers such that the sum of any row, column, or diagonal is the same is called a *Magic Square.* A sample 3-by-3 Magic Square is shown, where each row, column, and diagonal sums to 15.

			15
8	1	6	15
3	5	7	15
4	9	2	15
15	15	15	15

A Magic Square (for odd N) can be constructed, as follows: Start at 1 in the middle of the top row, and proceed diagonally up and to the right, filling in consecutive integers. Whenever you leave the array, re-enter at the opposite side, i.e., as if the top and bottom edges were one and the same, and as if the right and left edges were also one and the same. Whenever you come to an array element that is already filled, drop down to the next row in the same column. Stop when you return to 1.

Problem Statement. Create an N-by-N Magic Square in **int** array M, for odd N.

Enumeration. A determinate enumeration of the integers from 1 through N*N controls the iteration, and is synchronized with a toroidal-diagonal-order enumeration of array coordinates ⟨r,c⟩, as described on page 123:

1

```
/* Let M be an N-by-N Magic Square, for odd N≥1. */
   int M[][] = new int[N][N];  // Initialized to zeros.
   int r = 0; int c = N/2;
   for (int k=1; k<=N*N; k++) {
      M[r][c] = k;
      /* Advance ⟨r,c⟩ in toroidal-diagonal order. */
      }
```

We use a simplification of the toroidal-order-enumeration code pattern given on page 125 that advances to the next diagonal when an already-filled array element is detected:

2

```
/* Let M be an N-by-N Magic Square, for odd N≥1. */
   int M[][] = new int[N][N];  // Initialized to zeros.
   int r = 0; int c = N/2;
   for (int k=1; k<=N*N; k++) {
      M[r][c] = k;
      /* Advance ⟨r,c⟩ in toroidal-diagonal order. */
         if ( M[(r+N-1)%N][(c+1)%N]!=0 ) r = (r+1)%N;
         else { r = (r+N-1)%N; c = (c+1)%N; }
      }
```

Why the process described results in a Magic Square is beyond the scope of this book.[76]

76. A delightful application of the sample 3-by-3 Magic Square appears in a program to play the game of Tic-Tac-Toe (p. 275).

CHAPTER 7
Sequential Search

To *search* is to look for something systematically. Code that uses a search result is called its *client*, and we assume for convenience that the client code immediately follows the search. Thus, the compute-use pattern specializes to the *search-and-use* pattern:

```
/* Search. */
/* Use the search result. */
```

Search is ubiquitous in computing, and should be mastered.

In general, we search *for* a given item *in* a collection of items. The set of items searched in may have *unbounded* size, e,g., we may search for some value in a program's input data, or for an integer with a given property. Alternatively, the set may be *bounded*, e.g., the elements of an array, or the characters of a text fragment.

A bounded search can *succeed* or *fail*, which fact must be conveyed to the client. A successful search typically provides additional information to the client beyond only success or failure. For example, a search for an item in an array may indicate the subscript of the element where the item was found. An unbounded search can succeed (if given enough time) or run forever (if the value sought doesn't exist).

When each item of the collection searched is logically associated with another value, we may think of the collection as a table of ordered ⟨*key*, *value*⟩ pairs. In this case, the item searched for is a particular key, and a successful search conveys to the client the value that is associated with that key in the table. If no key occurs in the table with more than one associated value, the search is effectively the evaluation of a function, where the domain of the function is the set of keys in the table, and the range of the function is the set of associated values. Search failure occurs when the key sought is not in the table, i.e., when the key is outside the domain of the function. If a key occurs in the table with more than one associated value, it cannot be thought of as a single-valued function. In this case, some additional criterion must be invoked to select from among multiple entries with the same key.

A search that considers one item at a time is called *Sequential Search*. It takes no shortcuts, and in the worst case, when the item sought isn't found, inspects each and every possibility. Sequential Search is also known as *Linear Search*.[77]

---

77. Binary Search (p. 143) and Hash Tables (p. 207) are techniques that are able to consider more than one item at a time.

The mother of all Sequential Searches is the 1-D indeterminate-enumeration pattern:

```
int k = 0;
while ( condition ) k++;
```

which is a search for the smallest nonnegative k for which *condition* is **false**. The value found by this search is conveyed in variable k to the client, which can do whatever it wants with it:

```
int k = 0;
while ( condition ) k++;
/* Use k. */
```

Although this code appears to be an unbounded search, a bound can be built into the *condition*. Specifically, if we seek an integer k for which *condition* is **false**, but where k is no larger than some *maximum* value, the code can take this form:

```
int k = 0;
while ( k<=maximum && condition ) k++;
if ( k<=maximum ) /* Found. */
else /* Not found */
```

The section Search in an Unordered Array (below) illustrates this case, where k ranges over array subscripts, and *maximum* is a largest subscript of the array.

When the set of items being searched is complex, a single integer k may not be sufficient for keeping track of progress. For example, we may search in a 2-D array (using row and column indices), or in some complex data structure. If we introduce the notion of an abstract locator p into an abstract collection of items, then the general *search-and-use* pattern is:

```
/* Let p be the location of what you are looking for, or an indication that
   no such thing exists. */
   p = the-first-place-look;
   while ( p is-not-beyond-the-last-place-to-look &&
           p is-not-what-you-are-looking-for )
      p = the-next-place-to-look;
if ( p is-not-beyond-the-last-place-to-look ) /* Found. */
else /* Not found. */
```

The first four subsections of this chapter illustrate Sequential Search in various settings. The fifth subsection illustrates a search of a very different character: Finding a minimal value in an array. Doing so is a "search", in a sense, but one that requires looking at each and every value.

Primality Testing

An integer greater than or equal to 2 whose only divisors are 1 and itself is called a *prime* number, and is otherwise called *composite*. Consider implementing the specification:

```
/* Given p≥2, output whether p is prime or composite. */                1
```

The first step is to recognize that Primality Testing is a search problem, and that the specification can be implemented by Sequential Search. The Search step looks through possible divisors of p until finding one. The Use step uses whatever you learned from the Search to output whether p is prime or composite.

If this algorithm is not obvious to you, follow the recommendation:

> ☞ **Seek algorithmic inspiration from experience. Hand-simulate an algorithm that is in your "wetware". Be introspective. Ask yourself: What am I doing?**

The precept advocates that you should quite literally choose specific numbers, and figure out whether they are prime or composite.

> ☞ **There is no shame in reasoning with concrete examples.**

Pick one prime and one composite so that you cover the gamut. Force yourself to be systematic. Use pencil and paper, or a computer file and editor.

Don't just eyeball the problem and announce an answer. In psychology, a *gestalt* is something that is perceived as a "unified whole", but if you gestalt Primality Testing,[78] or otherwise intuit the answer, you defeat the purpose of the exercise. Your program is going to have to be systematic, so you should be systematic, too.

One way to force yourself to be systematic is to pick a big enough number so that you can't immediately know or sense the answer, and you have no alternative to being systematic. Another tactic is to write out (in advance) the list of things you plan to consider, cover them up with a card so that you can't just eyeball them, and force yourself to decide when and why you should move the card (ever so slightly) to reveal the next thing to consider.

Let's say that you write out the sequence of possible divisors:

2 3 4 5 6 7 8 9 10 11 12 13 14 15 16...

Then cover them up. Pick a number to test for primality. Say, 7. Now, reveal one possible divisor at a time, and ask (in turn):

- Is 2 a divisor of 7? No.
- Is 3 a divisor of 7? No.
- Is 4 a divisor of 7? No.
- Is 5 a divisor of 7? No.
- Is 6 a divisor of 7? No.
- Is 7 a divisor of 7? Yes.

Use a diagram that helps you to visualize what you are doing:

> ☞ **Invent (or learn) diagrammatic ways to express concepts.**

For example, underline the numbers you check before declaring a number (in red) "prime":

78. In English, every noun can be verbed!

2 3 4 5 6 7 8 9 10 11 12 13 14 15

Try another number, say, 15, for which you only check 2 and 3 before declaring "composite":

2 3 4 5 6 7 8 9 10 11 12 13 14 15

Label your diagrams with the variable p, and invent another variable to indicate your progress as you work your way through the numbers from left to right. Say you pick d for that variable. Your diagrams would then be:

```
          p
2 3 4 5 6 7 8 9 10 11 12 13 14 15
          d
```

and

```
                                p
2 3 4 5 6 7 8 9 10 11 12 13 14 15
  d
```

Review your activity. Describe what you were doing: You are enumerating possible divisors: 2, 3, 4, etc. You stop as soon as you find one. You start your search for a divisor at 2.

From this exercise, you should recognize that you are using Sequential Search. You should also realize that Search can convey its findings to its client via d, the divisor of p that it finds:

```
/* Given p≥2, output whether p is prime or composite. */
   /* Search: Let d≥2 be the smallest divisor of p. */
   if ( condition ) System.out.println( "prime" );
   else System.out.println( "composite" );
```
2

Note that the refinement is a Sequential Refinement into two "statements": The first is a statement-comment, and the second is a conditional statement. The refinement is half comment, half actual code, and that is fine.

Since the effect of the search is fully specified, there is sufficient information to complete the *condition* in the client code:

```
/* Given p≥2, output whether p is prime or composite. */
   /* Search: Let d≥2 be the smallest divisor of p. */
   if ( d==p ) System.out.println( "prime" );
   else System.out.println( "composite" );
```
3

You can now check the (partially developed) program for correctness because you can:

☞ **Interpret a statement-comment as executable code.**

In fact, the code reads like the very definition of what it means to be a prime number.

Continuing to code, you recognize that the search can be implemented with the 1-D indeterminate-enumeration pattern starting at 2, which you blast in:

```
/* Given p≥2, output whether p is prime or composite. */
   /* Search: Let d≥2 be the smallest divisor of p. */
      int d = 2;
      while ( condition ) d++;
   if ( d==p ) System.out.println( "prime" );
   else System.out.println( "composite" );
```
4

Now you can see that the list of questions you were asking when you worked the problem by hand,

- Is 2 a divisor of 7? No.
- Is 3 a divisor of 7? No.
- Is 4 a divisor of 7? No.
- Etc.

was essentially a trace of the execution of a 1-D indeterminate enumeration. All that remains is to determine the *condition*, which we have deliberately deferred until last.

When you code, it is important to know when you can coast vs when you must pay careful attention because you are at a delicate moment. Writing the loop *condition* is one of those delicate moments. Why?

One reason is that *condition* is the condition for *continuing* to loop rather than the condition for *terminating* the iteration. If you are not careful, you will be thinking "when should I stop", and implement the *condition* backwards.

A second reason is that you must think about whether a remainder of zero when p is divided by d indicates *divisibility* or indicates *non-divisibility*. This isn't rocket science, but the two issues together are enough of a mental overload to lead to a non-zero error rate.

Recognizing the potential for error, we type the operands first, and delay writing the operation. Our methodology deliberately aims to provide as much visual context as possible for the delicate step of writing the comparison operation:

```
/* Given p≥2, output whether p is prime or composite. */
   /* Search: Let d≥2 be the smallest divisor of p. */
      int d = 2;
      while ( (p%d) __ 0 ) d++;
   if ( d==p ) System.out.println( "prime" );
   else System.out.println( "composite" );
```
5

Now we can reason it out: When d divides p, the remainder is 0, i.e., p%d is equal to 0. In this case, we should stop. But *condition* must be the condition for *not* stopping, so we need the opposite test, i.e., *not equal* to 0:

```
/* Given p≥2, output whether p is prime or composite. */
   /* Search: Let d≥2 be the smallest divisor of p. */
      int d = 2;
      while ( (p%d)!=0 ) d++;
   if ( d==p ) System.out.println( "prime" );
   else System.out.println( "composite" );
```
6

Primality Testing is an example of a search for which you are guaranteed to find what you are looking for, and thus the search loop need not check to see whether it has gone "passed the last place to look". Why? Because every integer p divides itself, and we started enumerating at 2, an integer that is less than or equal to any p that we are required to consider. Were you to have started d at 3, the loop wouldn't have terminated for the case of p equal to 2.

It is also critical that we started the search at 2 and not 1. Were we to have started at 1, we would have identified 1 as a divisor of p, and then declared every p≥2 to be composite.

Search in an Unordered Array

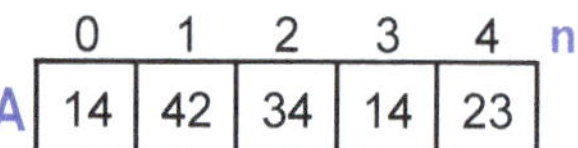

Consider data contained in an **int** array named A. For example, the sample array shown contains five elements, in an arbitrary order, and has one duplicate (14). The diagram shows the indices of A, the subscripts, *above* the array. They start at 0. Because we depict arrays as shown, we sometimes refer to the *left end* (resp., *right end*) of the array, meaning the element with lowest (resp., highest) subscript, even though there is nothing left-like about 0.

By convention, we usually refer to the number of items in the array as n. There are several ways to think of n. It may be:

- A constant, e.g., 5 in the above example.
- An **int** variable that contains the number of items.
- An expression that evaluates to the number of items.
- The expression A.length.[79]

The last element of the array has subscript n-1.

Consider the problem of finding whether a given value v occurs in array A[0..n-1]. As with n, v could be a constant, or a variable containing the value of interest, or an expression whose value is sought. More generally, v could be a description of a property for the value sought, e.g., "an even number". If v is a property, there is uncertainty about exactly what value in the array was found, which will be up for the client to resolve.

A loose specification of the search problem is:

```
/* Find v in A[0..n-1], or indicate it's not there. */
```

which begs three questions:

- How will what is found be conveyed to a client?
- What value will indicate that nothing was found?
- What is conveyed when duplicates of v occur in A[0..n-1]?

Surely, the most straightforward way to convey a finding is by its subscript, i.e., where v was found. In the case where v is a property, the client can then inspect the array element to determine which of multiple possibilities satisfying the property were found.

"Not found" can be signified by any value other than an integer in the range 0 through n-1. Which such value should be used? Even a tiny-little question such as this deserves careful consideration:

> ☞ **Code with deliberation. Be mindful.**

79. Arrays in Java are objects, a topic introduced in Chapter 12 Collections. Technically, expression A.length accesses the length field of the object referred to by A.

We could choose a negative number, which has some appeal because its very negativity conveys that it could not possibly be the location of an array element. But if we are going to look through the array from left to right (0 to `n-1`), a negative number (say, -1) is an unwelcome discontinuity. It is always nice when special cases in code can be eliminated, which can often be accomplished by following the precept:

> ☞ **Choose data representations that are uniform, if possible.**

The uniform choice for "not found" is `n`, the very next place *after* the last place we need to look. A uniform data representation creates the felicitous prospect that the special case will "come for free" as a result of uniform code that handles the general case. We shall see how this arises, below.

If a specification does not say what should happen when there are multiple possibilities, its implementation is free to choose. The phrase "Find `v` in `A[0..n-1]`" doesn't say which, so *any* occurrence of `v` will do, e.g., the leftmost. If the choice is important, the specification must say so. Proper use of articles is important. For example, "**an** occurrence" suggests the possibility of duplicates and makes clear that the choice is arbitrary, whereas "**the** occurrence" makes explicit a claim that there is only one occurrence.

> ☞ **Use article "the" for a unique instance; use articles "a" or "an" for an arbitrary instance.**

With this discussion behind us, it is time to re-state the specification more precisely:

```
/* Given array A[0..n-1], n≥0, and value v, let k be the smallest non-
   negative integer s.t. A[k]==v, or let k==n if there are no
   occurrences of v in A. */
```
1

Although this specification does not explicitly constrain the search order, it surely suggests a left-to-right search.

The following Sequential Search is straightforward, and finds the leftmost occurrence of `v`, if any. The standard 1-D indeterminate iteration is sufficient:

```
/* Given array A[0..n-1], n≥0, and value v, let k be the smallest non-
   negative integer s.t. A[k]==v, or let k==n if there are no
   occurrences of v in A. */
   int k = start;
   while ( condition ) k++;
```
2

Although `k` is a run-of-the-mill **`int`** variable, we are thinking of its value as a subscript of array `A`, which is depicted diagrammatically, thus:

The red line dissects the elements of the array into two disjoint regions, and the value of variable `k` identifies the location of the boundary. More specifically, `k` is the subscript of the first element of the region to the right of the boundary.

Imagine that the loop has been iterating for a while. How would we characterize the two regions at the precise moment depicted, above? Assuming that it is our intention to stop searching as soon as we find what we are looking for, we would know that value v does not occur in the left region. And we would know nothing whatsoever about the right region because those values have not yet been inspected:

This is the loop invariant that must be preserved while we make progress by advancing k. If A[k] is equal to v, then incrementing k would break the invariant. Thus, the loop *condition* must not allow k to be incremented when A[k] is equal to v:

```
/* Given array A[0..n-1], n≥0, and value v, let k be the smallest non-      3
   negative integer s.t. A[k]==v, or let k==n if there are no
   occurrences of v in A. */
   int k = start;
   while ( A[k]!=v ) k++;
```

In other words, we must keep searching as long as we *haven't* found what we are looking for.

In the case where v does not occur anywhere in A[0..n-1], k will reach n, which is beyond right end of the array. We only want to keep searching if there are more places to look:

```
/* Given array A[0..n-1], n≥0, and value v, let k be the smallest non-      4
   negative integer s.t. A[k]==v, or let k==n if there are no
   occurrences of v in A. */
   int k = start;
   while ( k<n && A[k]!=v ) k++;
```

In other words, we only keep going if we *haven't* passed the right end of the array.

Clearly, we should start the search at the left end, with k equal to zero:

```
/* Given array A[0..n-1], n≥0, and value v, let k be the smallest non-      5
   negative integer s.t. A[k]==v, or let k==n if there are no
   occurrences of v in A. */
   int k = 0;
   while ( k<n && A[k]!=v ) k++;
```

This establishes the loop invariant, with the "v not in here" region empty, and the unknown region "?" the entire array.

When the iteration stops, the **while** *condition* is **false**. Said the other way around, when the iteration stops, the negation of the *condition* is **true**. In reasoning about loop *conditions*, it is useful to know de Morgan's Laws,[80] and be able to use them with ease:

☞ **Reason about conditions using de Morgan's Law(s):**
not (P and Q) ≡ (not P) or (not Q)
not (P or Q) ≡ (not P) and (not Q)

---

80. The very same de Morgan who wrote *Siphonaptera*, (p. 57).

where the symbol ≡ should be read as "is equivalent to", or "is interchangeable with".

In the present example, we can use the first law to derive the *stopping condition* by negating the loop's *condition* for continuing to iterate:

not (*condition*)
≡ **not** (`k<n && A[k]!=v`)
≡ (**not** `k<n`) **or** (**not** `A[k]!=v`)
≡ (`k>=n`) **or** (`A[k]==v`)

The stopping condition that results can be read as: Either we have gone passed the right end of the array (i.e., `v` wasn't there), or `A[k]` equals `v` (i.e., `v` was there).

The order of operands for "&&" is critical. Specifically, you must *first* check to see if you have gone passed the end of the array, and *then* check to see if you have found what you are looking for. If you were to write the operands in the reverse order, then when `v` is not in `A[0..n-1]`, i.e., when `k` equals `n`, your program will crash with a "subscript-out-of-bounds" error when it attempts to index the nonexistent element `A[n]`. The reason this error does *not* occur when the operands are written as shown is that "&&" is a so-called *short-circuit* operator that doesn't evaluate its right operand if the left operand evaluates to **false**.[81]

The final code for Sequential Search in an array is clearly a special case of the general search pattern presented at the beginning of the chapter. It is fundamental, however, and should be mastered. You will have frequent opportunities to use it.

Although the symbol `v` denoting the value sought is typically a variable or constant, we have allowed that it might be might be a property. We can make this generalization explicit by presenting Sequential Search in terms of an arbitrary *predicate* $P(x)$, i.e., a Boolean expression that is parameterized by x:

```
/* Given P(x), a boolean-valued expression parameterized by x, with domain
   0..n-1, let k be the smallest int s.t. P(k) is true, or n if there is no
   such k. */
   int k = 0;
   while ( k<n && !P(k) ) k++;
```

Expression $P(x)$ can be either an explicit invocation of a **`boolean`**-valued method `P(int x)`, or an expression that is parameterized by the metavariable x. For example, $P(x)$ could be the expression `(A[x]%2)==0`, which evaluates to **true** if and only if *x* is even:

```
/* Let k be the smallest index in A[0..n-1] s.t. A[k] is even, or n if all
   A[0..n-1] are odd. */
   int k = 0;
   while ( k<n && (A[k]%2)!=0 ) k++;
```

In this example, `!`*P*`(k)` is `!(A[k]%2)==0)`, which simplifies to `(A[k]%2)!=0`. As we have illustrated, your ability to manipulate expressions according to algebraic laws is an important skill to have.

There are many occasions when we need to find something in an array, and Sequential Search will do it for you.

---

81. The other short-circuit operator, "||" doesn't evaluate it right operand if the left operand evaluates to **true**.

Array Equality

Suppose you have two arrays, A and B, of equal length. How might you determine whether they are equal, i.e., contain exactly the same elements?[82]

```
/* Given arrays A[0..n-1] and B[0..n-1], set e to true if A equals B,
   else set e to false. */
```
1

Your first step is to recognize that testing equality of two arrays is searching for corresponding elements of the arrays that are *not equal:*

```
/* Given arrays A[0..n-1] and B[0..n-1], set e to true if A equals B,
   else set e to false. */
   /* Let k≥0 be smallest s.t. A[k]!=B[k], or n if A equals B. */
   boolean e = (k==n);
```
2

There are two ways in which the development may proceed. The first way re-derives the code: Drop in the 1-D indeterminate-enumeration pattern:

```
/* Given arrays A[0..n-1] and B[0..n-1], set e to true if A equals B,
   else set e to false. */
   /* Let k≥0 be smallest s.t. A[k]!=B[k], or n if A equals B. */
      int k = 0;
      while ( condition ) k++;
   boolean e = (k==n);
```
3

and instantiate *condition* with searching for unequal elements:

```
/* Given arrays A[0..n-1] and B[0..n-1], set e to true if A equals B,
   else set e to false. */
   /* Let k≥0 be smallest s.t. A[k]!=B[k], or n if A equals B. */
      int k = 0;
      while ( k<n && A[k]==B[k] ) k++;
   boolean e = (k==n);
```
4

A better way in which the development may proceed comes from having fully internalized the pattern:

```
/* Given P(x), a boolean-valued expression parameterized by x, with domain
   0..n-1, let k be smallest int s.t. P(k) is true, or n if there is no
   such k. */
   int k = 0;
   while ( k<n && !P(k) ) k++;
```

in which case, thinking of the property $P(x)$ as `A[x]!=B[x]` leads the same code, but in one fell swoop.

Learning Patterns

This is a good moment to reflect on what it means to learn a pattern, and be able to use it with facility. The premise of this book is that patterns are so fundamental to coding performance that they should be *fully internalized.* How you reach such a state is not

82. Java has a standard method for testing array equality, but we shall ignore that.

unique to programming: *Study* the pattern, *understand* it, *memorize* it, put it under your pillow at night or make flash cards or whatever, and *use* it over and over again.

One day, you will find yourself blasting the pattern into code in one indivisible step without thinking of its constituent parts. Furthermore, you will have internalized exactly what the pattern's parameters are. For example, in the search pattern above, `A` can be *any* array of *any* length, `k` can be *any* **`int`** variable, `n` can be *any* way of expressing the length of `A`, and $P(x)$ can be *any* Boolean property. As you blast a pattern into code, you will find yourself substituting for its parameters "without thinking". Aspire to having patterns in your typing fingers' muscle memory.

Quite apart from *how* to go about learning patterns is your *will* to learn them. If you were learning a natural language, you would understand the need to learn vocabulary:

- Le, la, les
- Der, das, dem
- Uno, dos, tres
- Etc.

Patterns are the vocabulary of programming. They are essential, and should be mastered.

Sentinel Search

The general pattern for search checks when to stop. There are two cases: When you find what you are looking for, and when there are no more places to look. *Sentinel Search* merges these two cases into one by making sure that you will always find what you are looking for. The sentinel is a guard that prevents you from going too far. It does so by being an example of what you are looking for, so that you stop.

The benefit of Sentinel Search is that it only performs one test rather than two on each iteration. Thus, it is a code *optimization*.[83] Typically, optimization come at the expense of code simplicity, and you should adhere to this precept:

☞ **Don't optimize code prematurely.**

Nonetheless, the technique so important that we introduce it here. We start with the standard sequential-search pattern in an array:

```
/* Let k be an index in A[0..n-1] containing v, or n if no v in A. */
   int k = 0;
   while ( k<n && A[k]!=v ) k++;
```

and transform it into Sentinel Search.

First, we make a useful observation: Recall the search for smallest divisor in the code for Primality Testing (p. 130), and ask: Why, in that case, was there no test to prevent `d` from going too far?

```
/* Search: Let d≥2 be the smallest divisor of p. */
   int d = 2;
   while ( (p%d)!=0 ) d++;
```

83. The term "optimization" in programming is a misnomer. By convention, in programming, optimization means "improvement", not "making optimal".

The answer is that p always divides itself: If p is prime, the loop will stop with d equal to p (and if p is composite, the loop will have stopped earlier). The "divisibility of p by itself" stood guard, like a sentinel, preventing d from going too far.

Suppose the array is actually one larger than n, i.e., there is an extra array element at A[n] that is otherwise unused, e.g., the array was actually allocated to have size n+1, or larger. Then that extra location can be used for the sentinel, a copy of v itself:

```
/* Let k be an index in A[0..n-1] containing v, or n if no v in A.
   Assume an A[n] exists. */
   A[n] = v;
   int k = 0;
   while ( k<n && A[k]!=v ) k++;
```

The sentinel at A[n] stands guard, and stops k from going passed n:

and because the check k<n is now superfluous, it can be eliminated:

```
/* Let k be an index in A[0..n-1] containing v, or n if no v in A.
   Assume an A[n] exists. */
   A[n] = v;
   int k = 0;
   while ( A[k]!=v ) k++;
```

Requiring that an array be allocated one larger than n is sometimes onerous. As an alternative, you can use A[n-1] for the sentinel provided the value there is first saved in a temporary variable; you can then put it back when you are done with the search:

```
/* Let k be an index in A[0..n-1] containing v, or n if no v in A.
   Assume n>0. */
   int temp = A[n-1]; A[n-1] = v;  // Save A[n-1]. Replace it with v.
   int k = 0;
   while ( A[k]!=v ) k++;
   A[n-1] = temp;                  // Restore A[n-1].
   if ( k==n-1 && A[n-1]!=v ) k=n; // Test A[n-1] when sentinel found.
```

This code works provided the array has at least one element.

Sentinels are a general technique for dealing with boundary conditions. In the case of Sequential Search, the boundary condition is "falling off the end of the array".[84]

Find Minimal

Finding a *minimal* element in an array is a search problem, but differs from all previous examples in this chapter.[85]

---

84. Other examples of boundary conditions where sentinels are used to good effect appear in Chapter 14 Knight's Tour, and Chapter 15 Running a Maze

85. We say "minimal" rather than "minimum" to allow for the possibility that there is more than one occurrence of a smallest value in A[0..n-1]. Similarly, we would say "maximal" rather than "maximum" to indicate the possibility of duplicate largest values.

```
/* Given A[0..n-1], find k s.t. A[k] is minimal in A[0..n-1]. */
```
1

Earlier examples used an indeterminate enumeration because it made sense to terminate the search as soon as the value sought was found. In contrast, finding a minimal value in an array requires inspecting each and every value. Accordingly, a determinate iteration that enumerates each possible index in a range is appropriate, and we can use a **for**-statement:

```
/* Given A[0..n-1], find k s.t. A[k] is minimal in A[0..n-1]. */
   ________
   for (int j= ____; ____; ____ ) ___________
```
2

As with any other iteration, develop the body of the loop first, and defer termination, initialization, finalization, and boundary conditions until later. One way to obtain an INVARIANT for the loop is to start with the desired postcondition (call it POST):

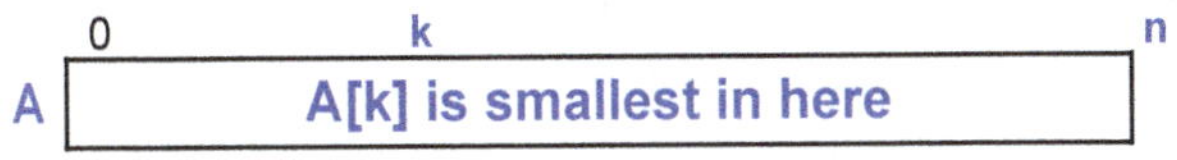

and (as per p. 77) apply the precept:

☞ **To get to POST iteratively, choose a weakened POST as an INVARIANT.**

leading to the INVARIANT:

Alternatively, we could play musical chairs, stop the music, and reflect on what has been accomplished after an arbitrary number of iterations.

Our goal now is to maintain INVARIANT while increasing j by 1. A Case Analysis on A[j] is in order. We must consider the case where k must be updated to j:

```
/* Given A[0..n-1], find k s.t. A[k] is minimal in A[0..n-1]. */
   int k = ____;  // Index of the minimal element of A[0..j-1].
   for (int j= ____; ____; ____ )
      if ( condition ) k = j;
```
3

which surely depends on a comparison between A[j] and A[k]. As in previous examples, we establish a visual context for thinking carefully about the correct comparison operation:

```
/* Given A[0..n-1], find k s.t. A[k] is minimal in A[0..n-1]. */
   int k = ____;  // Index of the minimal element of A[0..j-1].
   for (int j= ____; ____; ____ )
      if ( A[j] ____ A[k] ) k = j;
```
4

We update k to j when A[j] is strictly less than A[k]. Using "<=" instead of "<" wouldn't be wrong; it would just change whether the code finds the leftmost or rightmost instance of a minimal value. Because the specification didn't say which, we are free to choose:

```
/* Given A[0..n-1], find k s.t. A[k] is minimal in A[0..n-1]. */      5
   int k = ____;  // Index of the minimal element of A[0..j-1].
   for (int j= ____; ____; ____ )
      if ( A[j]<A[k] ) k = j;
```

The *increment* and *limit* condition are straightforward:

```
/* Given A[0..n-1], find k s.t. A[k] is minimal in A[0..n-1]. */      6
   int k = ____;  // Index of the minimal element of A[0..j-1].
   for (int j= ____; j<n; j++ )
      if ( A[j]<A[k] ) k = j;
```

Assuming `A[0..n-1]` has at least one element, we can establish the loop invariant by setting k to 0, and starting `j` at 1:

```
/* Given A[0..n-1], find k s.t. A[k] is minimal in A[0..n-1]. */      7
   int k = 0;     // Index of the minimal element of A[0..j-1].
   for (int j=1; j<n; j++ )
      if ( A[j]<A[k] ) k = j;
```

Why does this initialization establish the loop invariant, which asserts that `A[k]` is the minimal element in `A[0..j-1]`? Because when `j` is 1, `j-1` is 0, so the range of elements of A considered by the invariant is `A[0..0]`, i.e., `A[0]`. In that set, `A[0]` is a minimal value. Of course, it is also the only value.

If n can be 0, i.e., if the array can be empty, a Case Analysis is needed to convey an appropriate value for k. We note that the specification is inadequate in that case because it doesn't say what the value of k should be. One possibility would be to return k as -1:

```
/* Given A[0..n-1], find k s.t. A[k] is minimal in A[0..n-1].          7a
   k is -1 if n=0. */
   int k = -1;  // Index of the minimal element of A[0..j-1], or -1.
   if ( n!=0 ) {
      k = 0;
      for (int j=1; j<n; j++ )
         if ( A[j]<A[k] ) k = j;
      }
```

The code for finding a minimal value in an array should be seen as a specialization of a general pattern that is not specific to arrays. Let $S(j)$ be any scoring function on a non-empty domain of **int** values `j` in the range *first* through *last*. We seek a k for which $S(j)$ is minimal:

```
/* Given int-valued function S(j) defined on non-empty int domain
   first through last, let k in that domain be s.t. S(k) is minimal. */
   int k = first;
   int minS = S(first);
   for (int j=first+1; j<=last; j++) {
      int s = S(j);
      if ( s<minS ) { minS = s; k = j; }
      }
```

CHAPTER 8

Binary Search

Chapter 7 discussed how to use Sequential Search to find a value `v` in an array `A[0..n-1]` when the elements of the array occur in an arbitrary order. When the elements are known to be in numerical order, there is a far-faster way to search. The inspiration for this method comes from the everyday experience of looking up a word in a dictionary.[86]

> ☞ **Seek algorithmic inspiration from experience. Hand-simulate an algorithm that is in your "wetware". Be introspective. Ask yourself: What am I doing?**

Say you wanted to find the definition of the word **proboscis** in a 512-page dictionary. You wouldn't use Sequential Search starting on the first page, say, with **aardvark**. You would start roughly in the middle. From there, you would:

- Repeatedly halve the portion of the dictionary that remains under consideration, doing so by looking at the middle page of the region in hand, and discarding whichever half is revealed thereby to not contain **proboscis**.
- Once the search has been narrowed to a single page, you would look on that page to see if **proboscis** is there.[87]
- If it is, you found its definition; otherwise, it isn't in the dictionary.

The method is called *Binary Search*, and is an example of a Divide and Conquer algorithm. Binary Search is astoundingly fast.

An Application of Divide and Conquer

The specification for Binary Search is similar to that of Sequential Search, but with the added qualification that the elements of the array are ordered:

```
/* Assume A[0..n-1] is arranged in non-decreasing order. Let k be an
   index of A where A[k]==v, or n if no v in A. */
```

86. Everyday experience? Well, sort of. Before Google and the Internet, there were things called "books" that contained sheets of paper called "pages". One looked up words in a book by searching for a page that contained the word, and then found the word's definition on that page.

87. The fact that a dictionary page contains more than one word is an irrelevant artifact of the example that somewhat confuses the analogy. To make it fit better, imagine that each page contains only one word, so once you have found the page, you have found the word (or not).

Why the awkward phrase "non-decreasing"? Why not say "increasing"? Because when there are duplicates, the sequence of values does not (strictly speaking) increase, e.g., they could be all the same.

The implementation of Binary Search presents an excellent opportunity to demonstrate of our methodology. It is straightforward, but requires careful analysis in a number of spots.

How do we begin? Surely, with the loop:

☞ **If you "smell a loop", write it down.**

We sense the presence of an iteration, and hasten to insert a looping construct into our code. But before doing so, it is essential to:

☞ **Decide first whether an iteration is indeterminate (use a while) or determinate (use a for).**

An iteration is determinate when it is possible to know, in advance, the number of times the loop will repeat. While technically, our loop is determinate, the calculation is far from simple because it must apply even when n, the number of elements in the array, is not a power of 2.

Aware of the precept:

☞ **Beware of for-loop abuse; if in doubt, err in favor of while.**

we decide that the calculation it is not worth the effort, and we just use a **while**-statement:

```
/* Assume A[0..n-1] is arranged in non-decreasing order. Let k be an
   index of A where A[k]==v, or n if no v in A. */
   while ( condition ) { ________ }
```
2

You can never get in trouble when you choose a **while** because it subsumes the determinate case. Recall that the **for**-loop:

```
for ( initialize; condition; update ) statement
```

is really shorthand for:

```
initialize;
while ( condition ) {
   statement
   update
   }
```

so, if it turns out that a determinate iteration is in order, your code will reflect that in the pattern of statements that emerges, and (if you feel the need) you will be able to retrofit a **for** in place of the **while** afterwards.

Strictly speaking, the code we have written is a pure Iterative Refinement (one **while**-statement); however, to allow for initialization prior to the loop, and finalization after the loop, it is advantageous to consider the code as a three-statement Sequential Refinement, with placeholders for the first and third parts:

```
/* Assume A[0..n-1] is arranged in non-decreasing order. Let k be an
   index of A where A[k]==v, or n if no v in A. */
   _________
   while ( condition ) { _________ }
   _________
```
2b

We will elide these placeholders rather than indicating them explicitly, but will feel free to insert code before and/or after the **while** if the need arises:

> ☞ **Benefit from the fact that a while-loop divides a region of code into four subregions; a for-loop divides it into six.**

This step is a painless (and somewhat mindless) application of Divide and Conquer. All we did was smell a loop, write it down, and we divided Gaul into four parts!

We must now decide in what order to fill in the blanks. We find guidance in:

> ☞ **Code iterations in the following order: (1) body, (2) termination, (3) initialization, (4) finalization, (5) boundary conditions.**

Accordingly, we start with the body of the loop.

Surely, you now smell a Case Analysis because we must choose between the left and right halves of the array. Write it down:

```
/* Assume A[0..n-1] is arranged in non-decreasing order. Let k be an
   index of A where A[k]==v, or n if no v in A. */
   while ( condition ) {
      if ( condition ) __________; else __________;
      }
```
3

As with the **while**-statement, you can think of there being invisible placeholders before and after the **if**-statement, and can insert code there, if necessary.

The virtue of developing the body of a loop first is that it forces you to consider the general case first, and not get mired in specific details of the first and last time around the loop:

> ☞ **Body. Do 1st. Play "musical chairs" and "stop the music". Characterize the "program state" when the music stops, i.e., at the instant the loop-body is about to execute yet again. If you had stopped one iteration later, what would have looked the same (the "loop invariant"), and what would have changed (the "loop variant")?**

To develop the loop invariant for array problems, it is very helpful to have a diagram:

> ☞ **If the problem lends itself to diagrammatic reasoning, draw diagrams that characterize the invariant, and label key boundaries with program variables.**

After an **arbitrary** number of iterations, the region of interest will have been reduced to some portion of the array. We can identify the boundaries of the region by two red lines.

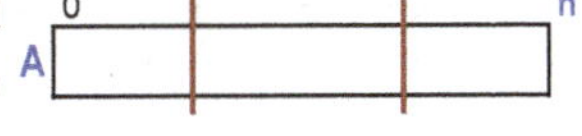

Next, we label the boundaries with variables, i.e., variables that will contain the subscripts of the left and right elements of the region between them. Think of L and R as your left and right hands bracketing the set of pages in the dictionary that are still under consideration. They are somewhere, but we don't know exactly where.

You may look at the given diagrams and object that the region A[L..R] seems to straddle the midpoint. This situation can never arise after the first iteration, you say, because Binary Search halves regions, going from the whole, to a half, to a quarter, etc.

If this is your thinking, you misunderstand how to read a schematic diagram. Specifically, what it means for a diagram to be "schematic" is that it makes no claims about the specific locations of indices like L and R. We choose to depict them arbitrarily, and for visual convenience. You must not infer anything from the proportional distance of A[L] from A[0], or of A[R] from A[n-1] in a schematic diagram.

The convention as to exactly what A[L] and A[R] denote is, in a measure, arbitrary. As implied by the diagram, we have chosen to consider them to be the first and last elements of the region still under consideration. We could have chosen otherwise, say letting R be the subscript of the first element beyond that region, but the symmetry of our selection seems propitious.

The diagram visually specifies the equivalent of the textual form of the representation invariant:

```
int L; // Leftmost index of the region of A still under consideration.
int R; // Rightmost index of the region of A still under consideration.
```

but does so very succinctly.

What must the loop invariant be? That the value we are looking for has not slipped through our hands. Specifically, that if v is in A[0..n-1], then it is in A[L..R]. The invariant can be depicted diagrammatically:

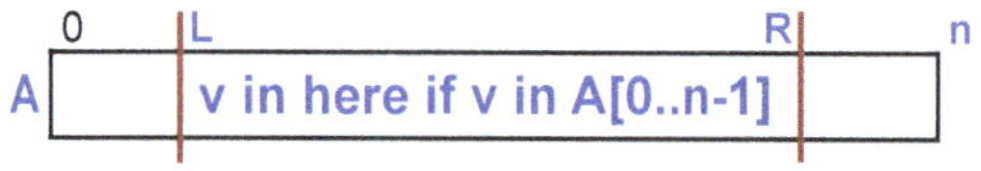

v in here if v in A[0..n-1]

To reduce clutter, we omit this annotation from our subsequent diagrams, but the invariant is far from "clutter"—it's the essence of what makes Binary Search work!

What must the loop variant be? That the number of array elements in A[L..R] is reduced by at least 1 on each iteration. However, we will (usually) do far better than that.

How will we decrease the loop variant while maintaining the loop invariant? By dividing A[L..R] roughly in half, and choosing the appropriate half, ever so carefully. What we mean by "ever so carefully" is that we will take care to maintain the invariant. What we mean by "roughly" is that if the number of elements in A[L..R] is even, then we will divide it exactly into halves; otherwise, one of the "halves" will be one element larger than the other.

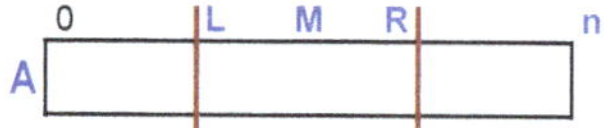

We introduce the variable M for the midpoint, and add it to our diagram. What subscript for M is roughly in the middle? The integer part of the average of L and R. We slip a declaration of M initialized to (L+R)/2 into the code,[88] as well as initialized declarations for L and R.[89]

88. When both operands of division (/) are **int**, the quotient is **int**, and any fractional part is truncated.

89. If the array is very large, the expression (L+R)/2 may cause an arithmetic overflow,

4

```
/* Assume A[0..n-1] is arranged in non-decreasing order. Let k be an
   index of A where A[k]==v, or n if no v in A. */
   int L = ____; int R = ____;
   while ( condition ) {
      int M = (L+R)/2;
      if ( condition ) __________; else __________;
      }
```

Thinking about what it means to choose the left (resp., right) half of `A[L..R]`, we see that it requires changing `R` (resp., `L`), but exactly how, we are not yet sure:

5

```
/* Assume A[0..n-1] is arranged in non-decreasing order. Let k be an
   index of A where A[k]==v, or n if no v in A. */
   int L = ____; int R = ____;
   while ( condition ) {
      int M = (L+R)/2;
      if ( condition ) R = ____; else L = ____;
      }
```

We have now arrived at a program with six blanks. We are sketching the program a little bit at a time, and in deciding on a coding order are following the guidance to:

☞ **Defer challenging code for later; do the easy parts first.**

Along the same lines, we can sketch in the **if**-*condition* following the suggestion that:

☞ **When refining a condition placeholder, establish the operands first, then the relational operation.**

The test will clearly have something to do with comparing `v`, the value we are looking for, and `A[M]`, the array element at the midpoint. That's the easy part:

6

```
/* Assume A[0..n-1] is arranged in non-decreasing order. Let k be an
   index of A where A[k]==v, or n if no v in A. */
   int L = ____; int R = ____;
   while ( condition ) {
      int M = (L+R)/2;
      if ( v ___ A[M] ) R = ____; else L = ____;
      }
```

We have been putting off the hard and risky work for as long as possible, as per:

☞ **Procrastinate: Never code today what you can defer until tomorrow.**

But tomorrow has now arrived.

---

especially if the value sought is at the right end of the array. Specifically, if `L` is at least half the largest **`int`** value, then `L+R` is guaranteed to overflow. The risk of overflow is eliminated if the average is computed by the expression `L+(R-L)/2`, which is mathematically equivalent for infinite-precision integers, but is not equivalent for finite-precision, 32-bit integers. We continue to use the expression `(L+R)/2` in the code presented because it is more intuitive, but would adopt the safer expression in the end.

It is time to figure out expressions for setting new values of R and L. Different people have different abilities to reason abstractly, but this seems like a fine occasion to embrace concrete examples, and reason from them:

> ☞ **Alternate between concrete reasoning and abstract reasoning.**

We obtain several concrete examples by annotating the previous schematic diagram with specific subscripts, so that it is no longer schematic. In doing so, we observe that it may be worthwhile to distinguish between the cases of an even number and an odd number of elements in `A[L..R]`.

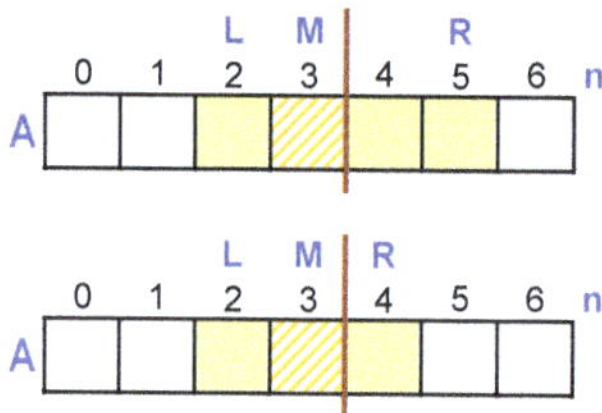

We determine M by simple arithmetic: After truncating the fractional part in quotients, (2+5)/2 equals 3, and (2+4)/2 equals 3. There is a bit of an art to picking concrete examples. Clearly, the primary touchstones are *generality* and recognition of appropriate *cases*. In the present examples, our choices included the *cases* for even and odd sizes, *where* in the array to position the `A[L..R]` region, and the *size* of the region.

For *where*, the sample regions can be translated left or right in the array without effect; try it (mentally) in the diagram, and validate the property that `A[M]` is the rightmost element of the left "half" regardless of where it is positioned.

For *size*, the length of the regions doesn't matter; try (mentally) growing (resp., shrinking) the sample regions by successively appending (resp., truncating) cells pairwise on the left and right ends of the region, and validate the property that `A[M]` is the rightmost element of the left "half" regardless of its size. In the case of even-length regions, M remains 3 regardless of whether the region is `A[2..5]`, `A[3..4]`, or `A[1:6]`. Similarly, in the case of odd-length regions, M remains 3 regardless of whether the region is `A[2..4]`, `A[1..5]`, or `A[0..6]`.

We conclude from the diagrams that we can *uniformly* use M as the subscript of the right end of the left "half", and can use M+1 as the subscript of the left end of the right "half", independent of whether the region size is even or odd.

With this observation in hand, we can update L and R appropriately:

```
/* Assume A[0..n-1] is arranged in non-decreasing order. Let k be an
   index of A where A[k]==v, or n if no v in A. */
   int L = ____; int R = ____;
   while ( condition ) {
      int M = (L+R)/2;
      if ( v ___ A[M] ) R = M; else L = M+1;
      }
```
7

You may have been tempted to use M for both expressions. It is clear that there is nothing wrong with the choice we have adopted. The effect of using M for both expressions is less clear, and will be discussed later.

It's time to reason about the relational operator in the **if**-*condition*. The choice between "less" rather than "more" should be clear by abstract reasoning: When v is smaller than `A[M]`, what we are looking for must be to the left.

We note, in passing, that we are skirting an easy mistake to make: To choose the left half, we must move R (not L), and to choose the right half, we must move L (not R). It is easy to imagine "having a screw loose", and getting this code backwards.

To make the choice between "<" or "<=", we consider the case when `A[M]` is v. Clearly, in the equal case, we should choose the left half because otherwise we risk letting v slip through our fingers, thereby breaking the invariant:

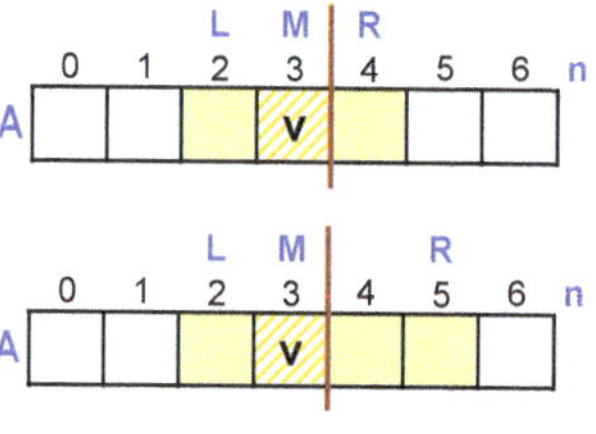

8

```
/* Assume A[0..n-1] is arranged in non-decreasing order. Let k be an
   index of A where A[k]==v, or n if no v in A. */
   int L = ____; int R = ____;
   while ( condition ) {
      int M = (L+R)/2;
      if ( v<=A[M] ) R = M; else L = M+1;
      }
```

When we choose the left half, we do so in full recognition that when v occurs more than once in A[L..R], it may also appear in the right half, as well. The loop invariant requires that we must be sure to keep *an* instance of the value v in A[L..R] as we shrink the region. The invariant does not require that we bracket *all* instances.

This step completes development of the loop body, so we move on to loop termination. We must continue to subdivide regions until they have been shrunk to a size of 1:

9

```
/* Assume A[0..n-1] is arranged in non-decreasing order. Let k be an
   index of A where A[k]==v, or n if no v in A. */
   int L = ____; int R = ____;
   while ( L!=R ) {
      int M = (L+R)/2;
      if ( v<=A[M] ) R = M; else L = M+1;
      }
```

For termination, we must argue that the loop variant is reduced on each iteration, i.e., that the size of A[L..R] necessarily gets smaller each time around the loop, and therefore must eventually reach size 1. If ever the region stops getting smaller, we will never reach the *condition* that L==R, and as a result, the loop will not terminate.

Let's consider what we hope will be the penultimate iteration, where the size of the region under consideration is 2. Then the size of the next region must be 1 regardless of which half is chosen. But here we see the difficulty were we to have chosen the right half by (incorrectly) setting L to M rather than (correctly) to M+1. Specifically, consider the case where A[M] is not v. In this case, we must select the right half, but by setting L to M, would be selecting A[3..4] for the right half, and would continue to do so *ad infinitum*. The loop would never terminate.

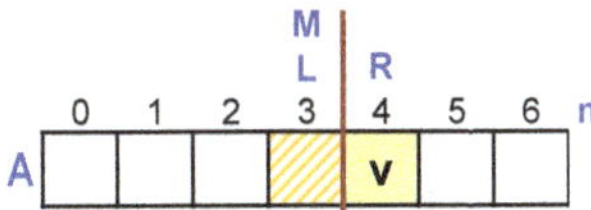

The next step is the initialization of L and R, which is straightforward:

10

```
/* Assume A[0..n-1] is arranged in non-decreasing order. Let k be an
   index of A where A[k]==v, or n if no v in A. */
   int L = 0; int R = n-1;
   while ( L!=R ) {
      int M = (L+R)/2;
      if ( v<=A[M] ) R = M; else L = M+1;
      }
```

After initialization comes finalization: The result must be conveyed as the value of variable k, as per the specification.

```
/* Assume A[0..n-1] is arranged in non-decreasing order. Let k be an
   index of A where A[k]==v, or n if no v in A. */
   int L = 0; int R = n-1;
   while ( L != R ) {
      int M = (L+R)/2;
      if ( v<=A[M] ) R = M; else L = M+1;
      }
   if ( A[L]==v ) k = L; else k = n;
```
11

The final step in the code development is checking boundary conditions:

☞ **Boundary conditions. Dead last, but don't forget them.**

The boundary condition for this code is the situation where the array `A` is empty, i.e., where `n` equals zero.

We inspect the code we have developed for the general case to see what would happen. Conceivably, we would luck out, and all would be well. Unfortunately, this is not the case:

- `R` will have been set to -1, and therefore will not be equal to `L`. Thus, the loop *condition* will be **true**, and the loop body will execute. Midpoint `M` will be computed as 0, and the non-existent array element `A[0]` will be accessed, resulting in a runtime error.
- Even if we were to arrange for the loop *condition* to be **false** in this case, the test "`A[L]==v`" would also access the non-existent array element `A[0]`.

Our choice is to attempt a surgical adjustment of the existing code, or to treat the case of `n` equal to zero as special. The latter is the easier path:

```
/* Assume A[0..n-1] is arranged in non-decreasing order. Let k be an
   index of A where A[k]==v, or n if no v in A. */
   if ( n==0 ) k = 0;
   else {
      int L = 0; int R = n-1;
      while ( L != R ) {
         int M = (L+R)/2;
         if ( v<=A[M] ) R = M; else L = M+1;
         }
      if ( A[L]==v ) k = L; else k = n;
      }
```
12

Boundary conditions often involve considering degenerate cases, e.g., empty arrays, which can be confusing to reason about. The present example is no exception. Our fix has avoided subscripting a non-existent array element, and we have followed the specification exactly, setting `k` to `n`, i.e., 0. But this would seem to suggest that we found `v` in `A[0]`, which may engender a momentary panic.

What is the difference, we think, between an array of length 1 containing `v` in `A[0]` (in which case `k` must be set to 0), and an empty array (in which case we set `k` to 0)?

Something seems very wrong here: As a general principle, two very different cases (one where we found `v`, and the other where we didn't) shouldn't yield the same result! Could it be that there is something inadequate about our convention that a failed search for `v` in `A[0..n-1]` should be indicated by a result location of `n`?

We relax when we consider the proper use of a search result by its client, and realize that the correct test for whether a value has been found is:

```
if ( k<n ) /* Found. */ else /* Not found. */
```

When both k and n are zero, the *condition* evaluates to **false**, which indicates that the value sought was *not* found. All is well!

We have argued that the loop invariant and variant are critical both during code development, and for understanding the correctness of the code afterwards. Yet they are nowhere to be seen *in* the code. This is partly a consequence of our extensive use of graphical diagrams, which don't lend themselves to placement in code. Incorporating textual versions of the invariant and variant into the code is a good idea, although we don't urge that this always be done:

13

```
/* Assume A[0..n-1] is arranged in non-decreasing order. Let k be an
   index of A where A[k]==v, or n if no v in A. */
   if ( n==0 ) k = 0;
   else {
      int L = 0; int R = n-1;
      /* Invariant: v is in A[L..R] if v is in A[0..n-1]. */
      /* Variant: R-L. */
      while ( L!=R ) {
         int M = (L+R)/2;
         if ( v<=A[M] ) R = M; else L = M+1;
         }
      if ( A[L]==v ) k = L; else k = n;
      }
```

Running time and space

The performance of Binary Search is truly wonderful. For example, searching an array of size 512 requires only 9 times around the loop! Count the region sizes: 512, 256, 128, 64, 32, 16, 8, 4, 2, 1. Far superior to Sequential Search, and the code isn't that complicated. A constant amount of work must be performed by the body of the loop on each iteration, and the size of the regions are (approximately) halved on each iteration. Thus, the total number of iterations will be (approximately) $1+\log_2$ n. We say that the running time is proportional to log n.[90]

No extra space is required.

There is no better illustration of the power of Divide and Conquer than Binary Search.

90. Typically, additive constants and logarithm bases are not mentioned in describing the order of a running time because they only effect the constant of proportionality.

CHAPTER 9

One-Dimensional Array Rearrangements

The need to rearrange values in a one-dimensional array is commonplace. For example, you may need to reverse the order of the values, or move the first value to the right end, shifting all remaining values to the left one cell. It is important to be able to write such code easily.

Everyday experience can often suggest how to approach a problem. For many tasks, you know how to do it; you just need to learn how to code what your brain already understands:

☞ **Seek algorithmic inspiration from experience. Hand-simulate an algorithm that is in your "wetware". Be introspective. Ask yourself: What am I doing?**

Because values in a one-dimensional array resemble a hand of playing cards, you can hope to draw on your experience playing card games for inspiration in dealing with arrays. For example, Sequential Search for a value in an array is essentially the same as left-to-right search for a particular card in a hand.

The analogy is helpful up to a point, but is flawed when cards are removed, inserted, or rearranged: Cards shift to fill removals, and shift to make room for insertions, without your even thinking about it, let alone dong anything to make it happen. But this is not how arrays work.

A closer analogy to an array is an ordered sequence of boxes containing the cards. When you pull a card from a box (e.g., 2♥), you leave an empty box, and when you (try to) insert a card (e.g., 5♠), nothing moves over automagically to make room.[91]

The shifts come for free in cards, but require effort in an array. Notwithstanding this important difference, you can still draw on your experience for algorithmic inspiration, e.g., when we come to Sorting in Chapter 11, we will encounter two algorithms commonly used by card players: Selection Sort and Insertion Sort. But

91. Even this analogy is flawed because, in programming, values are *copied* from variables, not *pulled* from them, as with cards from boxes.

keep in mind that there is "no free lunch": If your algorithm requires shifting values in an array, you must code it yourself.[92]

This chapter addresses several important array manipulations, including reversing, shifting, rotating, partitioning, and collating. It is also an excellent setting in which to master iteration, and improve your ability to think in terms of loop invariants.

Reverse

We wish to reverse the order of values in a subregion of an array:

```
/* Given int array A[0..n-1], reverse the order of the subsequence
   A[L..R] in situ without affecting the rest of A. */
static void Reverse( int A[], int L, int R ) {
   } /* Reverse */
```
1

The Latin term *in situ* means "in place", and in this context means "without use of another array". We define a method, `Reverse`, so that we may use it later.

Clearly, an enumeration of subscripts is needed, but is it determinate or indeterminate? Asked another way, can we predict before the iteration begins how many times to loop, say in terms of the values of parameters `L` and `R`? The answer is "yes", but perhaps with some difficulty. So, rather than fussing with what might be a delicate and error-prone expression for the limit of a determinate enumeration, we treat the problem as indeterminate, and see how that works out:

```
/* Given int array A[0..n-1], reverse the order of the subsequence
   A[L..R] in situ without affecting the rest of A. */
static void Reverse( int A[], int L, int R ) {
   while ( condition ) {
      }
   } /* Reverse */
```
2

Working an example by hand, say, 1,2,3,4,5,6, we hit on the idea of swapping the first and last elements (getting 6,2,3,4,5,1), swapping the second and second to last elements (getting 6,5,3,4,2,1), etc.

Following the rule to develop the loop body first, and the rule to draft a schematic diagram for the general case (after an arbitrary number of iterations), we draw:

0	L			R	n
A	already swapped	not swapped yet	already swapped		

The blue boundaries define the original region of the array to be reversed (as given by method parameters), and the red boundaries delimit the subregion that has not yet been swapped. But now we see a recursive aspect of the problem: Reversing the remaining subregion is the same problem as we started with, just smaller.[93] We realize

92. The need to do these shifts relates directly to the way in which arrays are laid out in a computer memory (p. 31). The `list` datatype of some languages, e.g., Python, is a generalization of arrays that supports such insertions and deletions as built-in operations. You may wonder whether the language implementation is doing the shifts for you "under the hood", or whether it has a completely different way to represent arrays in memory.

93. The term "recursive" is being used here to describe an aspect of the *problem*, not a *coding* technique. We could have implemented `Reverse` as a recursive method, but have chosen to use iteration, instead. That choice doesn't change the fact that the problem itself is recursive.

that we can avoid introducing new variables for the red boundaries by moving the parameters L and R after each swap:

which leads to the code:[94]

3

```
/* Given int array A[0..n-1], reverse the order of the subsequence
   A[L..R] in situ without affecting the rest of A. */
static void Reverse( int[] A, int L, int R ) {
   while ( condition ) {
      /* Swap A[L] and A[R]. */
         int temp = A[L]; A[L] = A[R]; A[R] = temp;
      L++; R--;
      }
   } /* Reverse */
```

All that remains is to consider termination. Clearly, as long as L is strictly less than R, we still have more swapping to do:

4

```
/* Given int array A[0..n-1], reverse the order of the subsequence
   A[L..R] in situ without affecting the rest of A. */
static void Reverse( int[] A, int L, int R ) {
   while ( L<R ) {
     /* Swap A[L] and A[R]. */
         int temp = A[L]; A[L] = A[R]; A[R] = temp;
      L++; R--;
      }
   } /* Reverse */
```

This code is very straightforward; it is easy to understand that it is correct.

This is a good opportunity to reflect on the precept:

☞ **Beware of for-loop abuse; if in doubt, err in favor of while.**

and consider some of the disagreeable possible consequences that might have arisen were we to have ignored it.

The knee-jerk instinct for many would have been to write:

94. A subtle distinction between scalar and array parameters is at play in this example. As described in Chapter 2 (p. 28), scalar parameters are local variables of the method that are initialized with the values of corresponding argument expressions. Thus, we are free to change L and R within Reverse without concern that we are thereby changing variables of the caller. In contrast, when Reverse modifies elements of array A (where A is an array parameter), the elements that are being changed are in the corresponding argument array that is provided by the caller of Reverse. The mechanism that effects this is explained in a footnote on page 203.

```
/* Given int array A[0..n-1], reverse the order of the subsequence         2a
   A[L..R] in situ without affecting the rest of A. */
static void Reverse( int[] A, int L, int R ) {
   for (initialize; condition; go-on-to-next)
      /* Swap A[___] and A[___]. */
   } /* Reverse */
```

which we term a "seduction". How might we have proceeded from there?

A key aspect of a **for**-statement is its use of a single control variable. We would have had two choices: Either introduce a new variable, say, k:

```
for (int k=___; condition; go-on-to-next)
   /* Swap A[___] and A[___]. */
```

or use L itself (or R) as the control variable, say:

```
for (L=___; condition; go-on-to-next)
   /* Swap A[___] and A[___]. */
```

Let's explore each possibility.

If we introduce a new variable k to control the **for**, we have two choices: Either it is an offset from L that starts at zero, and counts up:

```
for (int k=0; condition; k++)
   /* Swap A[L+k] and A[R-k]. */
```

or it is an index that starts at L, and marches to the right:

```
for (int k=L; condition; k++)
   /* Swap A[k] and A[___]. */
```

In the first case, we have only to write a *condition* that compares k with an appropriate *limit*. For the *limit*, we might inadvertently write R-L+1 (the number of array elements in A[L..R]), forgetting to divide by 2, and thereby re-reversing the array back to where it started. Assuming we do remember to divide by 2, we would have to fret about the distinction between an even and an odd number of elements in A[L..R], what happens when integer division truncates a fractional part, and the like.

Yes, the midpoint is still of concern in our solution, but not in the stressful context of attempting to write a correct arithmetic expression for the *limit*. It was far easier to code: Continue swapping provided L is strictly less than R. For an odd number of elements, L and R will end up being equal, and by terminating in that case, we avoid the useless swap of the midpoint with itself.[95] For an even number of elements, L and R pass each other, and L ends up being R+1. But this is nothing to worry about, at least if we wrote the *condition* for continuing the iteration as L<R. Of course, had we written it as L!=R, then we would have had a bug!

Treating control variable k as an offset (in the positive direction from L, and in the negative direction from R) offers a pleasing symmetry that is often advantageous. It

95. Not that this would be a problem because swapping A[*j*] and A[*k*] when *j* happens to equal *k* works fine. When this occurs, A[*j*] and A[*k*] are called *aliases*, i.e., two ways to refer to the same thing.

shares this with our solution. But it introduces an extra conceptual level that is absent from our solution: Index arithmetic. Specifically, the indices of the array elements to be swapped must be understood as the results of calculations, rather than just as the values of L and R themselves.

In general, it is best to:

☞ **Avoid index arithmetic, if possible and convenient.**

The approach where the control variable k starts at L and marches to the right aims to avoid index arithmetic (for the left participant in the swap), but does so at the expense of introducing nontrivial expressions for the *limit*, and for the *subscript* of the right participant in the swap:

```
for (int k=L; k<limit; k++)
   /* Swap A[k] and A[subscript]. */
```

You might try writing the *limit* and *subscript* as an exercise, but then revel in the simplicity of our **while**-loop solution.

For completeness, we return to the final possibility mentioned for the control variable, using L itself:

```
for (L=___; L<=midpoint; L++)
   /* Swap A[L] and A[subscript]. */
```

This has computational difficulties that are similar to those of the previous approach, as well as the obscurity of having to replace the initialization of L (shown in blue) with empty.

We trust that the advantages of our **while**-loop solution are manifest.

Left-Shift-k

We want to shift the elements of an array left some number, k, of positions:

```
/* Given array A[0..n-1], and 0≤k, shift elements of A left k places.      1
   Values shifted off the left end of the array are lost. Values not
   overwritten remain as they were originally. */
static void LeftShiftK( int A[], int n, int k ) {
   } /* LeftShiftK */
```

We define a method, LeftShiftK, so that we may use it later.

Clearly, an iteration is called for, and because we can compute the number of repetitions beforehand, a **for**-loop can be used:

```
/* Given array A[0..n-1], and 0≤k, shift elements of A left k places.      2
   Values shifted off the left end of the array are lost. Values not
   overwritten remain as they were originally. */
static void LeftShiftK( int A[], int n, int k ) {
   for (int j= ____; condition; j++) ___________
   } /* LeftShiftK */
```

Our loop-coding-order precept calls for working on the body first.

A template for assigning one element of the array into another is immediate, and can be dropped into the body:

```
/* Given array A[0..n-1], and 0≤k, shift elements of A left k places.     3
   Values shifted off the left end of the array are lost. Values not
   overwritten remain as they were originally. */
static void LeftShiftK( int[] A, int n, int k ) {
   for (int j= ____; condition; j++) A[destination] = A[source];
   } /* LeftShiftK */
```

It is somewhat arbitrary whether the control variable of the loop, j, should be used as the subscript of the *destination* variable, or the *source* variable. We choose *destination* arbitrarily:

```
/* Given array A[0..n-1], and 0≤k, shift elements of A left k places.     4
   Values shifted off the left end of the array are lost. Values not
   overwritten remain as they were originally. */
static void LeftShiftK( int[] A, int n, int k ) {
   for (int j= ____; condition; j++) A[j] = A[source];
   } /* LeftShiftK */
```

A diagram is helpful for visualizing the expression for the *source* subscript:

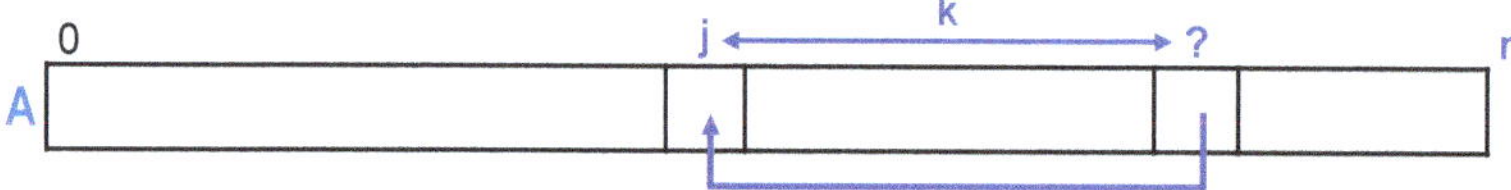

We can guess that *source* is j+k, but are on the alert for the possibility that an adjustment by ±1 may be required. However, when we consider case where k is 0, we know that the *source* and *destination* must be the same, so it is clear that no such adjustment is needed or appropriate:

```
/* Given array A[0..n-1], and 0≤k, shift elements of A left k places.     5
   Values shifted off the left end of the array are lost. Values not
   overwritten remain as they were originally. */
static void LeftShiftK( int[] A, int n, int k ) {
   for (int j= ____; condition; j++) A[j] = A[j+k];
   } /* LeftShiftK */
```

This completes the code for the loop body. Next, we tackle termination of the loop.

Deriving a *limit* expression is a common programming challenge for which it is useful to have a repeatable technique. We can either attempt it with a general, schematic diagram like the above, for arbitrary k and n, or reason about it for some specific value of n, say, 4, and then generalize. Either way, we should first choose a relational operator, "<" or "<=", for the *limit* comparison. This is somewhat a matter of personal taste, but "<" is recommended, especially for 0-origin enumerations. Accordingly, *condition* will take the form "j<*limit*".

Let's try reasoning about the general case directly, and consider the last array element to be shifted:

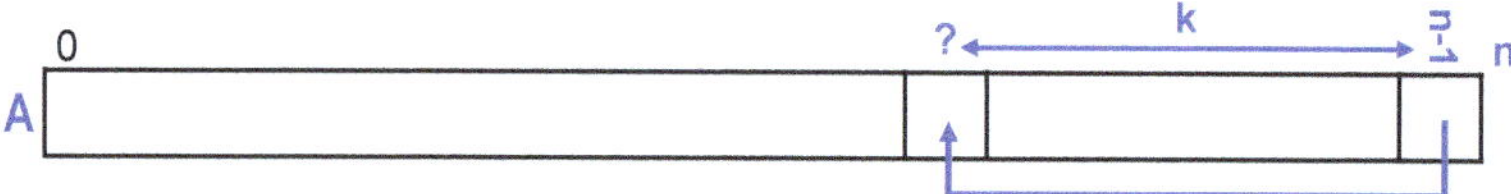

The last *source* variable is `A[n-1]`, and in terms of variables n and k, the last *destination* variable would be `A[(n-1)-k]`. The last value of j, for which the *condition* "j<*limit*", must be **true**, is when j is (n-1)-k, so *limit* must be one larger, i.e., (n-1)-k+1. Thus, simplifying, *limit* is n-k.

Here's how the derivation might go if we were to reason somewhat more algebraically. Each variable that occurs in the *limit* will appear linearly, i.e., not raised to a power, and with a coefficient of ±1. For each such variable, we can tease out the sign of the coefficient. The bound clearly depends on n in a *positive* sense because the bigger n, the more array elements must be shifted. Equally clearly, the bound depends on k in a *negative* sense because the bigger k, the fewer array elements must be shifted. Thus, we tentatively choose the *limit* "n-k+*constant*", where the *constant* is likely to be 0, but may be ±1. With humility, we are allowing for the possibility of an off-by-one error in our reasoning.

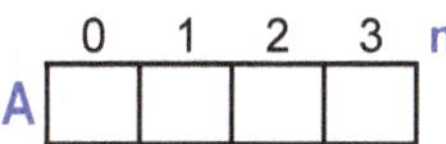

Now, let's consider a concrete example, say n is 4, and make a table showing desired values of "n-k+*constant*" for different values of k:

n	k	last assignment	last j	last j+1	n-k+constant
4	1	A[2]=A[3];	2	3	4-1+*constant*
4	2	A[1]=A[3];	1	2	4-2+*constant*
4	3	A[0]=A[3];	0	1	4-3+*constant*

We can see that the *constant* is 0, the *limit* is n-k, and the code must be:

```
/* Given array A[0..n-1], and 0≤k, shift elements of A left k places.     6
   Values shifted off the left end of the array are lost. Values not
   overwritten remain as they were originally. */
static void LeftShiftK( int[] A, int n, int k ) {
   for (int j= ____; j<n-k; j++) A[j] = A[j+k];
   } /* LeftShiftK */
```

It is time to code the initialization, which (baring some obscure boundary condition) is trivial:

```
/* Given array A[0..n-1], and 0≤k, shift elements of A left k places.     7
   Values shifted off the left end of the array are lost. Values not
   overwritten remain as they were originally. */
static void LeftShiftK( int[] A, int n, int k ) {
   for (int j=0; j<n-k; j++) A[j] = A[j+k];
   } /* LeftShiftK */
```

Finally, we turn our attention to the boundary conditions. The two that come to mind are k≥n, and k==0.

In the first case, because k≥n, the expression n-k is negative or 0; thus, when j is initialized to 0, the *condition* j<n-k is immediately **false**, and the **for**-statement doesn't iterate at all. Good.

The second case, where k is 0, is somewhat surprising: The loop for a left shift of 0 iterates n times, assigning `A[j]` to `A[j]`, for every j between 0 and n-1. The code is correct, but it is mildly offensive that in the case where there is nothing to do, we do the most work. We special-case this boundary condition, and bypass the loop:

```
/* Given array A[0..n-1], and 0≤k, shift elements of A left k places.    8
   Values shifted off the left end of the array are lost. Values not
   overwritten remain as they were originally. */
static void LeftShiftK( int[] A, int n, int k ) {
   if ( k>0 )
      for (int j=0; j<n-k; j++) A[j] = A[j+k];
   } /* LeftShiftK */
```

Given this check, we could now relax the requirement that k not be negative, if we wish.

The chain of reasoning for deriving LeftShiftK has been surprisingly difficult. Why? Because we have had to consider three variables (n, k, and j), 0-origin subscripts, a 0-origin enumeration of j, and a strictly-less-than relation in the *condition*, all at once. This stretches the limit of our ability to juggle. Don't lose heart; it's hard for everyone.

Left-Rotate-1

Method LeftShiftK preserved the k elements at the right end of the original array. We could have called for it to zero-fill, i.e., to replace those values with 0, but chose not to. We now seek to rotate all of the values of an array one place to the left, filling A[n-1] from A[0]:

```
/* Given int array A[0..n-1], shift A[1..n-1] 1 place left, with the    1
   value originally in A[0] reentering at right in A[n-1]. */
static void LeftRotateOne(int A[], int n) {
   } /* LeftRotateOne */
```

We define a method, LeftRotateOne, so that we may use it later.

The value A[0], which will be overwritten by the left shift, is first saved, so that it is available to fill A[n-1]:

```
/* Given int array A[0..n-1], shift A[1..n-1] 1 place left, with the    2
   value originally in A[0] reentering at right in A[n-1]. */
static void LeftRotateOne(int A[], int n) {
   int temp = A[0];
   LeftShiftK(A, n);
   A[n-1] = temp;
   } /* LeftRotateOne */
```

Although copying the value in A[0] to temp leaves the original value unaltered, it is helpful to think of the operation as having *moved* that value, leaving behind a "hole". Similarly, we can think of shifting A[1..n-1] into A[0..n-2] as creating a "hole" in A[n-1]. Finally, we fill the "hole" in A[n-1] by "moving" the value in temp to A[n-1]. This is not, of course, the way things actually work, but is a worthwhile conceptualization, nonetheless.

Left-Rotate-k

Generalizing Left-Rotate-1 to Left-Rotate-k offers a pleasantly rich opportunity to consider multiple algorithms for the same problem:

```
/* Given int array A[0..n-1], and integer k, 0≤k<n, left shift A[k..n-1]
   k places, with values originally in A[0..k-1] reentering at right. */
```
1

We present four distinct ways to implement Left-Rotate-k, followed by a discussion about their relative merits. Interestingly, two are Sequential Refinements (Swap Generalization and Three Flips), and two are Iterative Refinements (Repeated Left-Rotate-1 and Juggle in Cycles). Who said Stepwise Refinement was deterministic?

Repeated Left-Rotate-1

This is straightforward, especially given that we defined LeftRotateOne as a method. We just call it k times:

```
/* Given int array A[0..n-1], and integer k, 0≤k<n, left shift A[k..n-1]
   k places, with values originally in A[0..k-1] reentering at right. */
   for (int j=0; j<k; j++) LeftRotateOne(A, n, 1);
```
2a

Swap Generalization

This solution to Left-Rotate-k is akin to the standard 3-statement code pattern for swapping two scalar variables:

```
/* Swap x and y. */
   int temp = x;
   x = y;
   y = temp;
```

We introduce a temporary *array* into which to copy the initial k elements of A, thereby creating a "hole" that is k elements wide. Then, we shift the remaining elements left k places, thereby creating a k-wide "hole" at the right. Then, we fill that hole from the temporary:

```
/* Given int array A[0..n-1], and integer k, 0≤k<n, left shift A[k..n-1]
   k places, with values originally in A[0..k-1] reentering at right. */
   int temp[] = new int[k];
   /* temp[0..k-1] = A[0..k-1]; */
   LeftShiftK(A, n, k);
   /* A[___..n-1] = temp[0..k-1]; */
```
2b

While some programming languages support aggregate assignments of sub-arrays (as suggested by our statement comments), ours does not. Nonetheless, we can use such assignments in our specifications to advantage. Note that, for now, we have omitted a potentially vexing subscript calculation.

The code implementing the copy of the first k elements into temp benefits from two things: the data manipulations are left-aligned, i.e., begin at 0, and indexing in A and temp are aligned, so subscripting takes place in lock step. Only the *limit* condition j<k requires thought. How many values need to be copied to temp? Answer: k values. We can use the standard pattern for doing something k times:

```
/* Given int array A[0..n-1], and integer k, 0≤k<n, left shift A[k..n-1]
   k places, with values originally in A[0..k-1] reentering at right. */
   int temp[] = new int[k];
   /* temp[0..k-1] = A[0..k-1]; */
      for (int j=0; j<k; j++) temp[j] = A[j];
   LeftShiftK(A, n, k);
   /* A[___..n-1] = temp[0..k-1]; */
```
3b

The code for copying temp back to the right end of array A will require a bit of care. Our first step is to select the enumeration pattern for the iteration, and we have two choices: Enumerate subscripts of the source array, i.e., temp, or subscripts of the target array, i.e., A. We follow the precept:

☞ **Avoid gratuitous differences in code. Reuse code patterns, if possible.**

and deploy exactly the same enumeration pattern as we just used:

```
/* Given int array A[0..n-1], and integer k, 0≤k<n, left shift A[k..n-1]
   k places, with values originally in A[0..k-1] reentering at right. */
   int temp[] = new int[k];
   /* temp[0..k-1] = A[0..k-1]; */
      for (int j=0; j<k; j++) temp[j] = A[j];
   LeftShiftK(A, n, k);
   /* A[___..n-1] = temp[0..k-1]; */
      for (int j=0; j<k; j++) A[___] = temp[j];
```
4b

The parallel structure of the two **for**-loops gives us less to think about. Specifically, it is easy to see that the very same values that were copied *into* temp are then copied *from* temp.

All that remains is the target subscript expression, for which we must be alert to a possible off-by-one error. The difficulty is similar to that experienced in writing Left-Shift-k.

The subscript expression must depend on j in a positive sense because this is the control variable stepping through the elements of temp, from left to right, copying them back. It must depend on n in a positive sense because the bigger n, the further to the right the values in temp must go. It must depend on k in a negative sense because the bigger k, the more values there are in temp, and thus the copying back must start at smaller subscripts. Thus, we tentatively choose the subscript expression n-k+j+*constant*, where the constant is likely to be 0, 1, or -1. Now we can reason about where the last element to be copied back goes, A[n-1]. Since this will happen when j equals k-1, our subscript expression simplifies to n-k+(k-1)+*constant*, which simplifies to n-1+*constant*, which must be n-1, so the *constant* is 0:

```
/* Given int array A[0..n-1], and integer k, 0≤k<n, left shift A[k..n-1]
   k places, with values originally in A[0..k-1] reentering at right. */
   int temp[] = new int[k];
   /* temp[0..k-1] = A[0..k-1]; */
      for (int j=0; j<k; j++) temp[j] = A[j];
   LeftShiftK(A, n, k);
   /* A[n-k..n-1] = temp[0..k-1]; */
      for (int j=0; j<k; j++) A[n-k+j] = temp[j];
```
5b

Three Flips

A simple and elegant implementation of Left-Rotate-k comes from thinking about order reversal as a geometric operation, i.e., reflection, rather than a result of concentric swaps. For example, the reverse of 1, 2, 3, 4, 5, 6 is ə,ƨ,ߤ,Ɛ,Ƨ,ɿ .

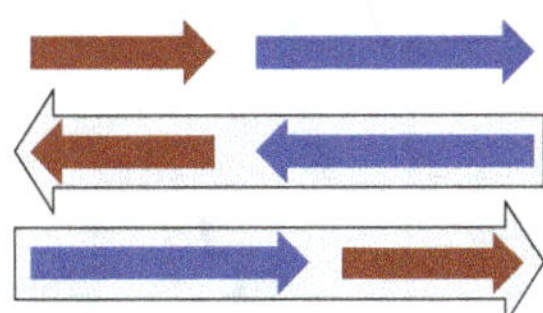

Representing ordered sequences as arrows, we draw `A[0..k-1]` as a red arrow, `A[k..n-1]` as a blue arrow, and then observe that three reflections effect a rotation: Reverse the red arrow, then reverse the blue arrow, then reverse the gray arrow, i.e., the pair of red and blue arrows, as one. Beautiful and efficient:

```
/* Given int array A[0..n-1], and integer k, 0≤k<n, left shift A[k..n-1]
   k places, with values originally in A[0..k-1] reentering at right. */
   Reverse(A, 0, k-1);
   Reverse(A, k, n-1);
   Reverse(A, 0, n-1);
```
2c

Notice that the implementation of the problem specification is a Sequential Refinement, not an Iterative Refinement, and turns on a property of the algebra of arrow transformations.[96]

Juggle in Cycles

A tempting approach that you may easily fall into is to start moving elements, one at a time, into their correct target location in the array. We can start by moving `A[k]` to `A[0]`, but before doing so, must create a "hole" at `A[0]` by first saving `A[0]` in a temporary variable. Copying `A[k]` into that "hole" fills it, but creates a new "hole" at `A[k]`. Now you can fill that hole, etc. You are effectively swapping "holes" with the values that belong in them, pushing the "holes" forward along a chain of array elements, in a fashion akin to juggling:

```
/* Given int array A[0..n-1], and integer k, 0≤k<n, left shift A[k..n-1]
   k places, with values originally in A[0..k-1] reentering at right. */
   int p = 0;                        // Start at A[0]
   int temp = A[0];                  //   and make a hole there.
   while ( condition ) {
      A[p] = A[____];                // Fill hole at p, making a new hole.
      p = ____;                      // Advance to the new hole.
      }
   A[p] = temp;                      // Fill the last hole from temp.
```
2d

It is easy to see that for large `n` and small `k`, a "hole" at subscript `p` gets filled with the value at `A[p+k]`, and the "hole" then works its way to the right `k` elements at a time. When we reach beyond the right end of array `A`, we must wrap around, as if the elements of `A` were arranged in a circle. We do this by using modular arithmetic (p. 118), i.e., by considering `(p+k)%n` rather than `p+k`. It is as if we were advancing the hand on an `n`-hour clock (with hours 0 through `n-1`) at a rate of `k` hours each step:

96. The reflection of x is its inverse x^{-1}, i.e., the transformation that composed with x is the identity transformation. Our code leverages $(x^{-1} \circ y^{-1})^{-1} = y \circ x$.

```
/* Given int array A[0..n-1], and integer k, 0≤k<n, left shift A[k..n-1]      3d
   k places, with values originally in A[0..k-1] reentering at right. */
   int p = 0;                    // Start at A[0]
   int temp = A[0];              //   and make a hole there.
   while ( condition ) {
      A[p] = A[(p+k)%n];         // Fill hole at p, making a new hole.
      p = (p+k)%n;               // Advance to the new hole.
      }
   A[p] = temp;                  // Fill the last hole from temp.
```

We keep going until we would be about to start undoing what we had accomplished: The loop continuation *condition* looks ahead to the next value of p (on the n-hour clock), and assures that the loop will stop before it would set p back to 0 again:

```
/* Given int array A[0..n-1], and integer k, 0≤k<n, left shift A[k..n-1]      4d
   k places, with values originally in A[0..k-1] reentering at right. */
   int p = 0;                    // Start at A[0]
   int temp = A[0];              //   and make a hole there.
   while ( (p+k)%n!=0 ) {        // Stop if p is about to be 0 again.
      A[p] = A[(p+k)%n];         // Fill hole at p, making a new hole.
      p = (p+k)%n;               // Advance to the new hole.
      }
   A[p] = temp;                  // Fill the last hole from temp.
```

Bench-checking this code provides evidence that it works for various values of n and k, e.g., for n of 8, and k equal to 1, 3, 5, and 7. However:

☞ **Beware of premature self-satisfaction.**

Unfortunately, the code does not work correctly for k of 2, 4, or 6, and for a rather interesting reason.

Consider the case of n equal to 8, and k equal to 2. The cycle of values moved would be those from A[2], A[4], A[6], and then temp, which was holding A[0]. But what about the rest? They would be left unmoved:

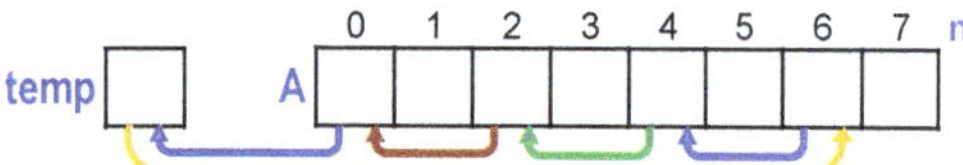

Similarly, consider the case of n equal to 8, and k equal to 6. The cycle of values moved would be those from A[6], A[4], A[2], and then temp, which was holding A[0]. The same set of (gray) values are moved, albeit to different locations. Again, the rest of the values are unmoved:

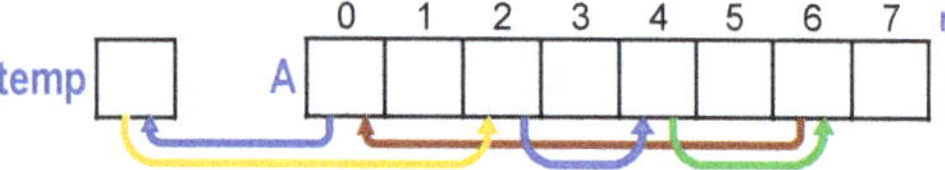

Finally, consider the case of n equal to 8, and k equal to 4. This time, only A[4] and A[0] are moved, and the rest of the values are ignored:

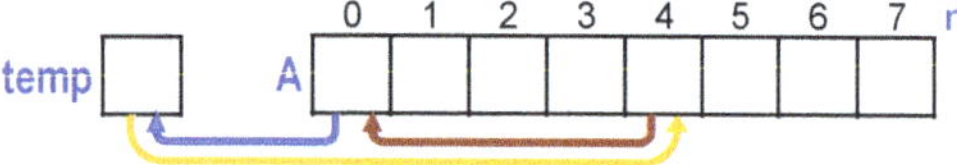

Clearly, we have stumbled into unexpected complexity. The code only works correctly when n and k are relatively prime, i.e., have no common divisors other than 1.

We have deliberately spun out this yarn to illustrate how misfortune can befall you. Starting with promising but flawed intuition, we envisioned the code as a generalization of Left-Rotate-1, in which the array is fashioned into a circle, and "left shifting" is performed in a stride of `k` array elements per step. With the diagrams above so clearly illustrating that the code is inadequate, it is difficult in hindsight to recall why we ever thought it would work. Perhaps we were snookered by so many cases that did work. This is a lesson in what can happen in the absence of a sound, top-down approach: Derivation of a code fragment of uncertain utility.

We now have two choices: Attempt to rescue the approach, or abandon it. We have inadvertently run headlong into some mathematics that may be beyond our ability, so it may be best to back out. However, for closure here, we state the relevant mathematics [16], without proof, and use it to complete the code:

- Left-Rotate-k of an array of length n can be decomposed into GCD(n,k) disjoint cycles that advance k elements at a time, where GCD(n,k) is the greatest common divisor of n and k (p. 80).
- The elements `A[0..`GCD(n,k)-1`]` appear in distinct cycles.

This knowledge allows us to embed our code fragment in a loop that considers all cycles:

```
/* Given int array A[0..n-1], and integer k, 0≤k<n, left shift A[k..n-1]
   k places, with values originally in A[0..k-1] reentering at right. */
   int g = gcd(n,k);
   for (int j=0; j<g; j++) {
      int p = j;                     // Start at A[j]
      int temp = A[p];               //   and make a hole there.
      while ( (p+k)%n!=j ) {         // Stop if p is about to be j again.
         A[p] = A[(p+k)%n];          // Fill hole at p, making a new hole.
         p = (p+k)%n;                // Advance to the new hole.
         }
      A[p] = temp;                   // Fill the last hole from temp.
      }
```

Discussion

The efficiency of the four algorithms for Left-Rotate-k can be compared in terms of the total number of array-element moves:

Version of Left-Rotate-1	#moves	Explanation
Repeated Left-Rotate-1	$k \cdot n$	Each Left-Rotate-1 moves all n elements. Done k times.
Swap Generalization	$n+k$	The copies into and out from `temp` do $2 \cdot k$ moves, and the shift does n-k moves.
Three Flips	$2 \cdot n$	Each element moves during the 1st two reverses, and then again for the 3rd reverse.
Juggle in Cycles	n+gcd(n,k)	Each element moves once, plus the first element of each of the gcd(n,k) cycles must first be saved in `temp`.

Juggle in Cycles is best in terms of move counts, but has poor locality because it repeatedly does only one update before moving on to the next region of the array.

The other methods do more work in a region (or two regions) at a time before moving on. Locality can be critical in virtual-memory environments.

Repeated Left-Rotate-1 is worst in terms of move counts, but is probably the conceptually easiest to understand.

Swap Generalization appears to do fewer moves than Three Flips, but the count shown ignores the fact that initialization of `temp` as part of its allocation (e.g., as is built into some programming languages), would add another `k` operations. This overhead can be rendered unimportant by allocating `temp` once, and not every time Swap Generalization is run. Even if this were done, the total number of moves approaches `2·n` (the bound for Three Flips) when `k` approaches `n`. The main disadvantage of Swap Generalization is that it is not *in situ*, and therefore requires extra memory space.

Three Flips is conceptually easy to understand, has a bound on the number of values moved that is independent of `k`, is *in situ* (and therefore needs only one extra scalar variable for the swaps in Reverse), has good locality, and is easy to code correctly. The favorite.

Dutch National Flag

Given array `A[0..n-1]` consisting of three different values, (say) red, white, and blue, we want to rearrange `A` so all reds precede all whites, which precede all blues. The problem takes its name from the Dutch National Flag, which consists of three stripes—red, white, and blue. We say "rearrange" to preclude counting the number of each color, and then overwriting `A` with the corresponding number of each color. For motivation, imagine that each element of `A` has additional information that must be moved together with the element.

The problem was used by Edsger Dijkstra—a Dutchman—to illustrate the power of thinking about programming in terms of invariants and variants. It may be viewed as a degenerate form of sorting, for the case where there are only three different values. It is a fundamental manipulation of general applicability:

```
/* Given array A[0..n-1] consisting of only three values (red, white,
   and blue), rearrange A into all red, then white, then blue. */
```
1

Clearly, there is an iteration. We could jump to the conclusion that it is a determinate iteration, and write a **for**-statement, but it is better to defer judgment on that until seeing what the invariant might be. We can always replace a **while** with a **for** if its familiar pattern emerges:

```
/* Given array A[0..n-1] consisting of only three values (red, white,
   and blue), rearrange A into all red, then white, then blue. */
   while ( condition ) ____________
```
2

We have often advocated working sample data by hand, and inferring an invariant by introspection. However, one can easily list four obvious (possible) invariants for this problem, and consider their relative merits—in the abstract. Interestingly, we ignore experience, and drive algorithm discovery via the candidate invariants:

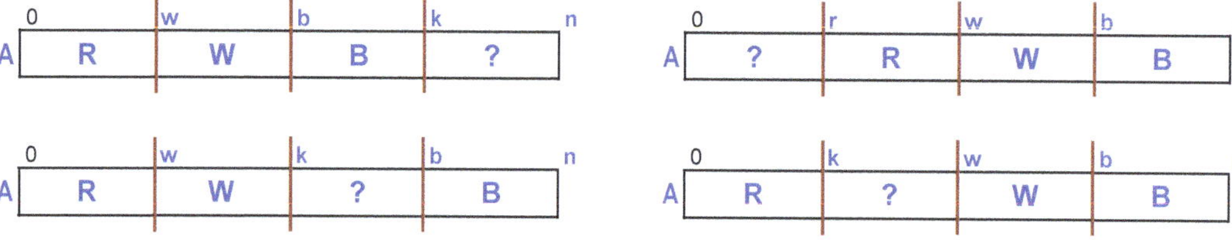

Let's call the four possible invariants NW, NE, SW, and SE, respectively.

NW and NE are symmetric in the sense that they both have the red, white, and blue regions (R, W, B) abutting one another, with the unknown region (?) to either their right or left. The intuition of NW is that the next item to consider is `A[k]`, which will be moved appropriately based on whether it is red, white, or blue. Then `k` will be incremented, and the unknown region will get one smaller. We will be done when `k` reaches `n`. This sounds quite like a determinate iteration, with `k` as the control variable, leaving R, W, and B regions behind it as it marches from left to right over the array. Anyone smell a **for**-loop?

Interestingly, despite its symmetry with the NW version, the NE version seems harder to fathom. The processing would seem to be best done from right to left on items of the unknown region, which is atypical. Also, labeling the left boundary of the red region `k` seems unnatural, so we chose to label it `r` instead. But then, what is the control variable stepping through the unknown region? Perhaps it would be more natural if the right-most cells of regions were the ones labeled, as in:

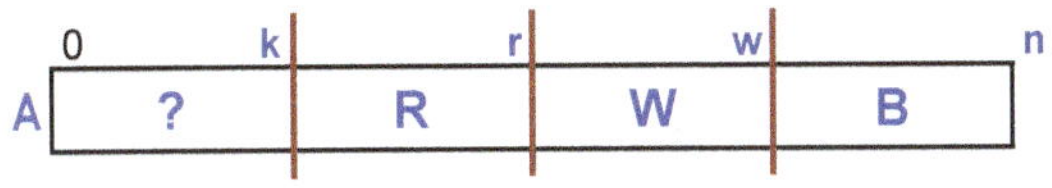

```
  0      k|      r|      w|      n
A|   ?    |   R   |   W   |   B   |
```

But we have grown accustomed to labeling that is done the other way, and if we switch now, `n` will seem at odds with the others. Since NW and NE should, in principle, offer the same algorithmic advantages and disadvantages, we abandon NE in favor of its symmetric NW cousin.

SW and SE both seem intuitive and should be algorithmically equivalent. In either case, the unknown region can be processed from left to right, deciding on each iteration what to do with `A[k]`. But now, `k` doesn't march all the way from 0 through `n-1`. Rather, the unknown region will shrink, and we will stop when it has been reduced to nothing. Smells more like a **while**-loop. Because the choice between SW and SE seems arbitrary, we pick at random: SW.

Which invariant should we choose between NW and SW, and on what basis? How, in fact, do they differ? The answer lies in their topologies. In NW, the right boundary of the unknown region (?) is rigidly tied to the right boundary of `A[0..n-1]` itself, and can't move. In contrast, either the left or the right boundary of the unknown region in SW can shift. Our code can take advantage of the greater freedom of action offered by the SW invariant. Accordingly, we select it:

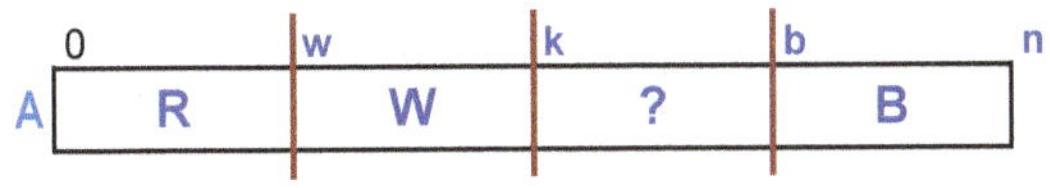

```
  0      |w      |k      |b      n
A|   R    |   W   |   ?   |   B   |
```

In words, the invariant is:

> `A[0..w-1]` red, `A[w..k-1]` white, `A[b..n-1]` blue, for `0≤w≤k≤b≤n`.

The textual representation makes explicit in the inequalities "`0≤w≤k≤b≤n`" the implicit diagrammatic rule that "any region can be empty". Specifically, when `w` is 0 (resp., `k` is `w`, or `b` is `n`), region `A[0..w-1]` (resp., `A[w..k-1]` or `A[b..n-1]`) is empty, i.e., contains no array elements at all.

We introduce declarations for the three variables, together with representation invariants for those variables, but leave the initializations for last:

3
```
/* Given array A[0..n-1] consisting of only three values (red, white,
   and blue), rearrange A into all red, then white, then blue. */
   /* A[0..w-1] red, A[w..k-1] white, A[b..n-1] blue, for 0≤w≤k≤b≤n. */
      int k = ____; int w = ____; int b = ____;
   while ( condition ) ______________
```

Clearly, there is a three-way Case Analysis on the value in A[k]. Assume that R, W, and B are variables whose values are whatever we mean by red, white, and blue:

4
```
/* Given array A[0..n-1] consisting of only three values (red, white,
   and blue), rearrange A into all red, then white, then blue. */
  /* A[0..w-1] red, A[w..k-1] white, A[b..n-1] blue, for 0≤w≤k≤b≤n. */
      int k = ____; int w = ____; int b = ____;
   while ( condition )
      if ( A[k]==B ) _________
      else if ( A[k]==R ) _________
      else /* A[k]==W */ _________
```

The easiest case is when A[k] is white because merely incrementing k incorporates A[k] into the white region, and makes progress by shrinking the size of A[k..b-1]:

5
```
/* Given array A[0..n-1] consisting of only three values (red, white,
   and blue), rearrange A into all red, then white, then blue. */
  /* A[0..w-1] red, A[w..k-1] white, A[b..n-1] blue, for 0≤w≤k≤b≤n. */
      int k = ____; int w = ____; int b = ____;
   while ( condition )
      if ( A[k]==B ) _________
      else if ( A[k]==R ) _________
      else /* A[k]==W */ k++;
```

Suppose A[k] is blue. Then swapping A[k] and A[b-1] moves A[k] to the beginning of the blue region, and moves A[b-1] (an unknown value) to the beginning of the unknown region. The boundaries must be updated appropriately to reestablish the invariant, and shrink the size of A[k..b-1]. We do this by decrementing b, but leave k unchanged because the value we just placed in A[k] is still of unknown color:

6
```
/* Given array A[0..n-1] consisting of only three values (red, white,
   and blue), rearrange A into all red, then white, then blue. */
  /* A[0..w-1] red, A[w..k-1] white, A[b..n-1] blue, for 0≤w≤k≤b≤n. */
      int k = ____; int w = ____; int b = ____;
   while ( condition )
      if ( A[k]==B ) {
         /* Swap A[b-1] and A[k]. */
            int temp = A[b-1]; A[b-1] = A[k]; A[k] = temp;
         b--;
         }
      else if ( A[k]==R ) _________
      else /* A[k]==W */ k++;
```

In the remaining case, A[k] is red. Then swapping A[w] and A[k] moves A[k] to the end of the red region, and moves A[w] (a white value) to the end of the white region.

The boundaries must be updated appropriately to reestablish the invariant, and shrink the size of `A[k..b-1]`. This update is done by incrementing both `w` and `k`:

7

```
/* Given array A[0..n-1] consisting of only three values (red, white,
   and blue), rearrange A into all red, then white, then blue. */
  /* A[0..w-1] red, A[w..k-1] white, A[b..n-1] blue, for 0≤w≤k≤b≤n. */
      int k = ____; int w = ____; int b = ____;
   while ( condition )
      if ( A[k]==B ) {
         /* Swap A[b-1] and A[k]. */
            int temp = A[b-1]; A[b-1] = A[k]; A[k] = temp;
         b--;
         }
      else if ( A[k]==R ) {
         /* Swap A[w] and A[k]. */
            int temp = A[k]; A[k] = A[w]; A[w] = temp;
         k++; w++;
         }
      else /* A[k]==W */ k++;
```

This step completes the coding of the body. In each of the three cases, we make progress (reducing the variant expression `b-k`) while maintaining the invariant.

The *condition* for continuing to iterate is that the unknown region is not (yet) empty:

8

```
/* Given array A[0..n-1] consisting of only three values (red, white,
   and blue), rearrange A into all red, then white, then blue. */
  /* A[0..w-1] red, A[w..k-1] white, A[b..n-1] blue, for 0≤w≤k≤b≤n. */
      int k = ____; int w = ____; int b = ____;
   while ( k!=b )
      if ( A[k]==B ) {
         /* Swap A[b-1] and A[k]. */
            int temp = A[b-1]; A[b-1] = A[k]; A[k] = temp;
         b--;
         }
      else if ( A[k]==R ) {
         /* Swap A[w] and A[k]. */
            int temp = A[k]; A[k] = A[w]; A[w] = temp;
         k++; w++;
         }
      else /* A[k]==W */ k++;
```

Finally, we are ready to code the initializations such that the initial unknown region is the entire array `A[0..n-1]`, and the other regions are empty. Surely, the left boundary of the unknown region is at the left end of the array, so we should set `k` to 0. The other two boundaries are somewhat more difficult to think about, and you should sense danger:

☞ **Be alert to high-risk coding steps associated with binary choices: "==" or "!=", "<" or "<=", "x" or "x-1", *condition* or !*condition*, positive or negative, 0-origin or 1-origin, "even integers are divisible by 2, but array segments of odd length have middle elements".**

We are dealing with extrema such as empty regions, and these are inherently less comprehensible. The left boundary of the blue region is easiest to think about, so let's do it first. If we were (incorrectly) to set `b` to `n-1`, then the blue region would contain all variables between `A[n-1]` (i.e., `A[b]`) and `A[n-1]` (i.e., the right end of the array). How many such variables are there? One, i.e., `A[n-1]`. So, we are off by 1. We need to initialize `b` to `n` so that the left and right boundaries of the blue region are `A[n]` and `A[n-1]`, respectively. How many variables are there between those two boundaries? None!

Now consider the empty white region `A[w..k-1]` immediately to the left of the unknown region. The idea of nothing being somewhere may make your head hurt. We have already decided that `k` will be initialized to 0, so the initial white region is `A[w..-1]`. So, do we initialize `w` to -1 or to 0? Consider initializing `w` to -1. Then the white region would contain only one element, `A[-1]`. Yes, yes, we know that there are no negative subscripts. But that is not the point. If there were, then initializing `w` to -1 would give us a region of one variable, and that would be wrong. Consider initializing `w` to 0 so that the region is `A[0..-1]`. That's the empty region we want. All nothing of it.

This reasoning is sufficiently subtle that it is probably best to bench check it on a concrete example, one in which `A[0]` is white. In this situation, the last case of the body of the loop increments `k` to 1. The white region is all variables between `A[w]` and `A[k-1]`, inclusive, i.e., all between `A[0]` and `A[0]`. That the very white cell we identified. Bingo!

```
/* Given array A[0..n-1] consisting of only three values (red, white,      9
   and blue), rearrange A into all red, then white, then blue. */
  /* A[0..w-1] red, A[w..k-1] white, A[b..n-1] blue, for 0≤w≤k≤b≤n. */
     int k = 0; int w = 0; int b = n;
   while ( k!=b )
     if ( A[k]==B ) {
        /* Swap A[b-1] and A[k]. */
           int temp = A[b-1]; A[b-1] = A[k]; A[k] = temp;
        b--;
        }
     else if ( A[k]==R ) {
        /* Swap A[w] and A[k]. */
           int temp = A[k]; A[k] = A[w]; A[w] = temp;
        k++; w++;
        }
     else /* A[k]==W */ k++;
```

We developed this code with considerable care, and there can be little concern that we got it wrong (other than typos, and other such carelessness). But what is the algorithm? Interestingly, it is essentially:

> Here's the invariant (see above). Here's the variant expression: `b-k`. Reduce the variant to zero while maintaining the invariant, doing the obvious things.

The "algorithm design" consisted of inventing the invariant, and maintaining it.

It is worth reflecting on the adverse consequences, were you to have been seduced by a **for**-loop as coding began. Nothing too terrible, but a bit of extra and unnecessary work. We noted above that the choice of determinate iteration would have pushed you into the NW invariant, with its more constrained choices:

The case of A[k] being blue is handled by the **for**-loop's built-in increment of k, and the case of A[k] being white is handled by swapping it with B[b] and incrementing b. The case of A[k] being red is now more complicated: It can be done with two swaps, first B[b] with A[k], and then B[b] with A[w], followed by incrementing w and b.

Running time and space

There is a constant upper bound on the number of steps performed on each iteration of the loop, and the total number of iterations is n. Thus, the running time of the Dutch National Flag code is linear in n. The work is done *in situ*, and therefore no extra space is required for the values of the array (other than the temp used by swap).

Partitioning

Suppose the three colors of the Dutch National Flag algorithm were properties rather than values. In particular, let the tests for red, white, and blue array elements be numerical comparisons with a value p known as the *pivot*. Then the Dutch National Flag code is readily modified to implement an algorithm for *partitioning* array A[0..n-1] into three disjoint regions:

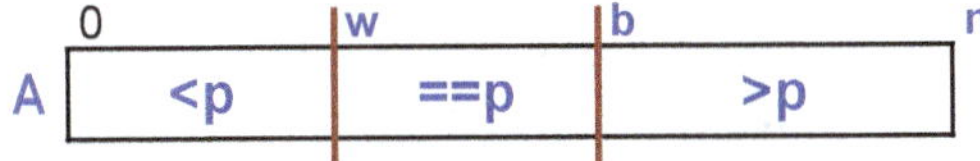

Think of all values that are strictly less than p as red, all occurrences of p as white, and all values that are strictly greater than p as blue.

We can also generalize the code to work for an arbitrary sub-array A[L..R-1] of A[0..n-1]:

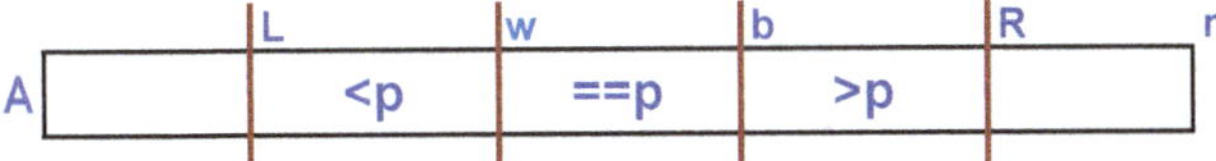

And finally, we can package the code as a general-purpose method:

```
/* Rearrange A[L..R-1] into all <p, then all ==p, then all >p. */
static void Partition( int A[], int L, int R, int p ) {
   /* A[L..w-1]<p, A[w..k-1]==p, A[b..R-1]>p, for L≤w≤k≤b≤R. */
      int w = L; int k = L; int b = R;
   while ( k!=b )
      if ( A[k]>p ) {
         /* Swap A[b-1] and A[k]. */
            int temp = A[b-1]; A[b-1] = A[k]; A[k] = temp;
         b--;
         }
      else if ( A[k]<p ) {
         /* Swap A[w] and A[k]. */
            int temp = A[k]; A[k] = A[w]; A[w] = temp;
         k++; w++;
         }
      else /* A[k]==p */ k++;
   } /* Partition */
```

where we have made the following substitutions in the Dutch National Flag code: "L" for "0", "R" for "n", ">p" for "==B", "<p" for "==R", and "==p" for "==W". Rather than inventing new variable names for the subscripts of the left ends of the "==p" and ">" regions, we retain "w" and "b" from the **w**hite and **b**lue of the Dutch National Flag problem.

Choice of pivot

Clients of Partition are free to choose the pivot parameter, and typically do so with the goal of often obtaining "<p" and ">p" regions of similar size.[97] How, then, do the resulting region sizes depend on the choice of pivot?

In certain cases, Partition doesn't subdivide A[L..R-1] whatsoever. Specifically, if pivot p is smaller than the smallest (resp., larger than the largest) value in A[L..R-1], then Partition will create just one ">p" (resp., "<p") region containing all values. Similarly, if all of the values in A[L..R-1] are equal to p, Partition will create just one "==p" region containing all occurrences of p. Partitioning is pointless for such pivots.

Suppose the pivot, p, is a value selected from A[L..R-1]. Then either all values are equal to p, or there is some other value, q, that is not equal to p. If q<p then Partition creates at least two non-empty regions, "<p" and "==p". On the other hand, if q>p then Partition creates at least two non-empty regions "==p" and ">p". So, if we chose as pivot a value in the array, either we discover that all values are equal to the pivot, or we have achieved a partitioning into at least two regions.

How might one choose as pivot a value from A[L..R-1] that is likely to partition the array into "<p" and ">p" regions that both have a substantial number of elements? If the array consists of randomly ordered values, we can pick an arbitrary element, say, A[L]. Sometimes this choice will work out well, and sometimes it won't. But if the values are randomly ordered, we can do no better.

But it is unwise to assume that the values in sub-array given as arguments to Partition are uniformly distributed among the (R-L)! possible orderings.[98] In fact, it is often the case that the argument happens to be sorted, (say) in non-decreasing order. In this case, A[L] would be far from a "random" value. In fact, it would be a minimal value, and as such the "<p" region produced by Partition will be empty. If the array has no duplicates, the "==p" region would then contain only A[L], and the ">p" region will contain all the rest of the values. The symmetric problem would arise if the array is ordered, and we were to choose A[R-1] as the pivot.

To deal with the possibility that the array will often be ordered, one can choose the average of the first and last values, i.e., (A[L]+A[R-1])/2. It does not matter that this value is likely not a value that occurs in the array because partitioning will still work fine: The "==p" region will be empty, but there will be no harm when that occurs.

Running time and space

Partitioning is a repackaging of the Dutch National Flag problem. Thus, its performance is the same: Running time linear in n, the size of the array. No extra space is required (other than the temp variable used for swap).

---

97. Three clients of Partition in the text are QuickSelect (p. 176), Linear-Time Median (p. 180), and QuickSort (p. 185).

98. The number of permutations, i.e., rearrangements, of n things is *n factorial*, written $n!$, where $n! = n \times (n\text{-}1) \times \ldots \times 3 \times 2 \times 1$.

Collation

Suppose you are given two ordered arrays, and wish to create a third ordered array containing the elements of both:

```
/* Given ordered arrays A and B of lengths na and nb, create ordered
   array C of length na+nb consisting of those values. */
```
1

The analogy with playing cards helpful. Let A and B be two ordered piles of face-up cards. You wish to create a hand of all cards that is ordered. You repeatedly draw the smallest card, be it from pile A or pile B, and append it to the accumulated cards in your hand (C). Removing a card from a pile reveals the next card in that pile. You break ties arbitrarily in the event of duplicates.

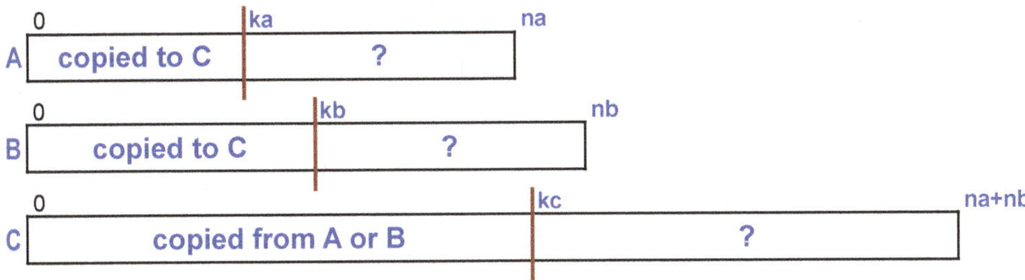

When one of the piles is exhausted, you move the remaining cards from the unexhausted pile to your hand, one at a time.

A trigger-happy coder enthralled with **for**-loops will immediately jump to the refinement:

```
/* Given ordered arrays A and B of lengths na and nb, create ordered
   array C of length na+nb consisting of those values. */
   for (int kc=0; kc<na+nb; kc++)
      /* Let C[kc] be the appropriate value from A or B. */
```

pushing all of the complexity of the problem into the body of the one loop. The subtleties will involve an interplay between deciding which array to draw from, A or B, and dealing with a fully-processed array, be it A or B. However, multiple shallow loops are usually easier to understand than single intricate loops. Hence, the following initial Sequential Refinement is preferred:

```
/* Given ordered arrays A and B of lengths na and nb, create ordered
   array C of length na+nb consisting of those values. */
   int C[] = new int[na+nb];          // C[0..kc-1] is collation of
                                      // A[0..ka-1] and B[0..kb-1].
   int ka = 0; int kb = 0; int kc = 0;  // Indices in A, B, and C.
   /* Copy values from A or B into C until one array is exhausted. */
   /* Copy remaining values into C from the unexhausted array. */
```
2

Each sequential step is then simple to code because there is less to think about at once:

```
/* Given ordered arrays A and B of lengths na and nb, create ordered    3
   array C of length na+nb consisting of those values. */
   int C[] = new int[na+nb];          // C[0..kc-1] is collation of
                                      // A[0..ka-1] and B[0..kb-1].
   int ka = 0; int kb = 0; int kc = 0; // Indices in A, B, and C.
   /* Copy values from A or B into C until one array is exhausted. */
      while ( ka<na && kb<nb )
         if ( A[ka]<B[kb] ) { C[kc] = A[ka]; ka++; kc++; }
         else { C[kc] = B[kb]; kb++; kc++; }
  /* Copy remaining values into C from the unexhausted array. */
```

Specifically, the *condition* `ka<na && kb<nb` guarantees that both `A[ka]` and `B[kb]` exist.

Refinement of the second step need not explicitly identify which array is not exhausted:

```
/* Given ordered arrays A and B of lengths na and nb, create ordered    4
   array C of length na+nb consisting of those values. */
   int C[] = new int[na+nb];          // C[0..kc-1] is collation of
                                      // A[0..ka-1] and B[0..kb-1].
   int ka = 0; int kb = 0; int kc = 0; // Indices in A, B, and C.
   /* Copy values from A or B into C until one array is exhausted. */
      while ( ka<na && kb<nb )
         if ( A[ka]<B[kb] ) { C[kc] = A[ka]; ka++; kc++; }
         else { C[kc] = B[kb]; kb++; kc++; }
   /* Copy remaining values into C from the unexhausted array, A or B. */
      while ( ka<na ) { C[kc] = A[ka]; ka++; kc++; }
      while ( kb<nb ) { C[kc] = B[kb]; kb++; kc++; }
```

Collation is a key part of MergeSort (p. 188).

CHAPTER 10

Median

The *median* of a set of ordered data is the "middle value", i.e., the value *m* for which half the data are less than or equal to *m*, and half are greater than or equal to *m*. Given an array `A[0..n-1]` that is ordered, it is trivial to use indexing to find the median: `A[n/2]`.[99]

But what if the array A is not ordered? We could, of course, do a problem reduction: Sort `A[0..n-1]`, and then select `A[n/2]`. But sorting is intrinsically more complex than finding the median, and we are averse to the idea of "reducing" a problem to a more difficult one.[100]

We seek a way to find the median of `A[0..n-1]` that has a *worst-case running time* that is linear in n. Specifically, what this means is that there is a fixed integer *k* (independent of n) such that it is possible to find the median of `A[0..n-1]` using no more than *k*·n comparisons (for arbitrarily large n). It is a minor miracle that this is possible.[101]

To get a feel for the challenge involved, stop reading now, and work at trying this problem before reading on. The worst-case linear-time median finding algorithm is *not* a method that you already know. Accordingly, the following precept is useless:

> ☞ **Seek algorithmic inspiration from experience. Hand-simulate an algorithm that is in your "wetware". Be introspective. Ask yourself: What am I doing?**

Be alert to the possibility that everyday experience is not always a useful guide:

> ☞ **Consider the possibility that your manual approach may be suboptimal, and a different approach may be better.**

But from where can you hope to find inspiration?

99. When n is even, we select the first value of the greater half rather than the average of the two middle values, which is more standard. We choose to omit this fussy detail.

100. It can be shown that if you only have the ability to ask of two values x and y in `A[0..n-1]` whether x is less than or equal to y, i.e., to compare them, then sorting requires a minimum of $n \log_2 n$ comparisons.

101. Constant *k* turns out to be about 3.33, so this means that if n is a thousand, only 3.33 thousand comparisons are needed, and if n is a million, only 3.33 million comparisons are needed. Whether or not this compares favorably with using an $n \log_2 n$ sorting algorithm, followed by direct access to `A[n/2]`, depends on the size of n, and the additional bookkeeping overhead of the algorithm we will come up with.

One general-purpose approach that often leads to insight is to seek a fast way to divide the problem in half:

☞ **Consider Divide and Conquer when designing an algorithm.**

For example, Binary Search (p. 143) uses Divide and Conquer to good effect, but relies on an array being ordered. Partitioning (p. 171) divides the elements of an unordered array into three subsets relative to some pivot value, and may provide the linear-time behavior we seek.

A second general-purpose approach is to use an algorithm that is already in hand. Accordingly, you can mentally scan known algorithms for relevance, a sort of brute force approach to inspiration. The very algorithm we are working on will be in hand as soon as we complete it, so it should also be considered available, provided you only use it for a proper subset of the data:

☞ **Consider recursion when designing an algorithm.**

Recursion, when it works, often seems creative and inspired.

A third general-purpose approach to algorithm design is generalization:

☞ **Consider generalizing a problem when designing an algorithm.**

It is sometimes easier to solve a more general problem, and then specialize it to the restricted case of interest than it is to work only on the special case. This is particularly true in conjunction with recursion because the subproblems obtained by Divide and Conquer often require the more general version of an algorithm for their solution.

We shall present a derivation of the worst-case linear-time median algorithm in a way that is designed to suggest how you might have been able to go about inventing it yourself by following the general-purpose principles described.

Average-Case Linear-Time Algorithm

The generalization of finding the median of a set of values is known as *selection*: Given a set of `n` rank-ordered values, we wish to select the `j`th smallest value of the set. For example, the minimal value would be the 0th smallest value, the maximal value would be the `n-1`th smallest value, and the median value would be the `n/2`th smallest value. We assume that the values are given in an unordered array `A[0..n-1]`, and that we are free to rearrange `A`.

Recall the Partitioning algorithm (p. 171), which was based on the Dutch National Flag problem (p. 166): Given a value known as the pivot, `p`, partitioning rearranges array `A[0..n-1]` into three disjoint regions indicated by boundaries `w` and `b`:

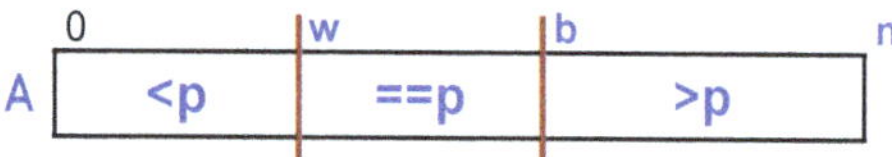

Suppose `A[0..n-1]` has been so partitioned, for some pivot `p`. Then there are three possible places where the `j`th smallest value may occur:

`0≤j<w`. The `j`th smallest value is the `j`th smallest value of `A[0..w-1]`.
`w≤j<b`. The `j`th smallest value is the pivot, `p`.
`b≤j<n`. The `j`th smallest value is the `(j-b)`th smallest value in `A[b..n-1]`.

If the jth value is the pivot, we are done. If not, we have only to decide whether to focus on the "<p" or the ">p" region of A, and then repeat the process.

You may be thinking of this as an opportunity for recursion, but given that we only need to refocus on *one* of the three regions, recursion is unnecessary. Thus, it is not difficult to implement the algorithm iteratively. We start with the code for `Partition`:

```
/* Rearrange A[L..R-1] into all <p, then all ==p, then all >p. */    1
static void Partition( int A[], int L, int R, int p ) {
   ⟨body of Partition⟩
   } /* Partition */
```

and modify it to be `QuickSelect` by making the following straightforward textual changes:

- Change the name of the method from `Partition` to `QuickSelect`.
- Change the return type of the method from **`void`** to **`int`**.
- Introduce a parameter n for the size of the array A.
- Introduce a parameter `j` to signify the rank order of the value to be selected and returned.
- Change parameters L and R be to be local variables of the method rather than parameters. Initialize L to 0, and R to n. Note that ⟨body of Partition⟩ remains parametric in L and R, which we intend to change with each iteration.
- Change the pivot parameter p to be a local variable of the method rather than a parameter, so that it can be computed internally on each iteration.
- Introduce a **return**-statement to return the jth smallest value of `A[0..n-1]`.

This yields the code:

```
/* Given int 0≤j<n, return j-th smallest in A[0..n-1]. */    2
static int QuickSelect( int A[], int n, int j ) {
   int L = 0; int R = n;
   int p = /* value of pivot */ ;
   ⟨body of Partition⟩
   return ____;
   } /* QuickSelect */
```

We are now ready to replace the code that implements a single partitioning step:

```
int p = /* value of pivot */ ;
⟨body of Partition⟩
```

with code that iterates through a number of partitioning steps while maintaining the invariant:

The replacement code is an instance of the general iterative-computation pattern:

```
/* Initialize. */
while ( /* not finished */ ) {
   /* Compute. */
   /* Go on to next. */
   }
```

where

- /* Initialize. */ is already coded as the initialization of L and R.
- /* Compute. */ is the single partitioning step.
- /* Go on to next. */ is the code to select the appropriate next region of A.

This yields the code:

```
/* Given int 0≤j<n, return j-th smallest in A[0..n-1]. */          3
static int QuickSelect( int A[], int n, int j ) {
   int L = 0; int R = n;
   while ( condition ) {
      int p = /* value of pivot */ ;
      ⟨body of Partition⟩
      /* Go on to “<p” or “>p” region if j-th smallest is there;
         else return p. */
      }
   return ____;
   } /* QuickSelect */
```

If the jth smallest value falls into the "<p" region, focus on that region. If the jth smallest value is p, then return p. If the jth smallest value falls into the ">p" region, focus on that region.

Recall that the body of Partition sets variables w and b to establish the boundaries of the three regions. Accordingly, we can select the next region, as follows:

```
/* Given int 0≤j<n, return j-th smallest in A[0..n-1]. */          4
static int QuickSelect( int A[], int n, int j ) {
   int L = 0; int R = n;
   while ( condition ) {
      int p = /* value of pivot */ ;
      ⟨body of Partition⟩
     /* Go on to “<p” or “>p” region if j-th smallest is there;
        else return p. */
         if ( j<w ) R = w;
         else if ( j<b ) return p;
         else L = b;
      }
   return ____;
   } /* QuickSelect */
```

When we focus on the ">p" region, you may be thinking that some manipulation of j is in order because we need to select the (b-j)th element of A[b..n-1]. But we are not *copying* the region over to a new array (with 0-origin). Rather, we are focusing on the ">p" region *in situ*. Thus, we leave j as a subscript in the region whose origin *in situ* begins with the subscript b. In fact, the value of j never changes during the execution of the algorithm. Rather, the algorithm merely guides partition selection so that, in the end, the last partition selected is A[j..j], and the value we seek has been moved into A[j].

When the size of the region containing A[j] is less than 2, we stop, and the jth smallest value is A[j]:

```
/* Given int 0≤j<n, return j-th smallest in A[0..n-1]. */          5
static int QuickSelect( int A[], int n, int j ) {
   int L = 0; int R = n;
   while ( R-L>1 ) {
      int p = /* value of pivot */ ;
      ⟨body of Partition⟩
      /* Go on to "<p" or ">p" region if j-th smallest is there;
        else return p. */
        if ( j<w ) R = w;
        else if ( j<b ) return p;
        else L = b;
      }
   return A[j];
   } /* QuickSelect */
```

Choice of pivot

Correctness follows from maintenance of the invariant, regardless of how the pivot is computed, but termination depends on regions shrinking, which depends in turn on the choice of pivot. Section Partitioning (p. 172) discussed the choice of pivot, and suggests that (A[L]+A[R-1])/2 be used:

```
/* Given int 0≤j<n, return j-th smallest in A[0..n-1]. */          6
static int QuickSelect( int A[], int n, int j ) {
   int L = 0; int R = n;
   while ( R-L>1 ) {
      int p = (A[L]+A[R-1])/2;
      ⟨body of Partition⟩
      /* Go on to "<p" or ">p" region if j-th smallest is there;
        else return p. */
        if ( j<w ) R = w;
        else if ( j<b ) return p;
        else L = b;
      }
   return A[j];
   } /* QuickSelect */
```

Running time and space

Consider the best case: On each iteration, we happen to select as pivot the median of A[L..R-1]. Then the successive regions of QuickSelect will be (approximately) halved, and the running time will be proportional to n+(n/2)+(n/4)+ … = 2·n, i.e., linear in n.

Consider the worst case: One each iteration, we happen to select as pivot an extremum, say, a minimal value of A[L..R-1]. Then the successive regions of QuickSelect will be (approximately) only one smaller, and the running time will be proportional to n+(n-1)+(n-2)+...+3+2+1 = n·(n-1)/2. In other words, the behavior of QuickSelect in the worst case is quadratic in n.

On average, QuickSelect runs in time proportional to n. A careful derivation of this property is beyond the scope of the text. Suffice it to say that assuming each of the n! permutations of values in the array is equally likely results in an expected runtime that is proportional to n. In other words, cases where super-linear performance arise are sufficiently infrequent and unweighty as to not blow up the linear average.

QuickSelect is *in situ*, and therefore requires no extra space for the array values (other than the `temp` used by swap).

Worst-Case Linear-Time Algorithm

We have, in hand, a way to compute the median whose running time is, on *average*, linear in n: We just call `QuickSelect(A,n,n/2)`. However, we seek a way to compute the median that is guaranteed to have linear runtime performance in the *worst-case*.

Before delving into algorithmic details, it is worthwhile to consider why we might care. Specifically, isn't QuickSelect good enough? A practical answer is "yes, it is almost always good enough". But the worst-case behavior, when on each iteration QuickSelect happens to pick as pivot an absolute pessimal value, is not pleasant: Execution time that is quadratic in n. The gnawing fear that we might stumble into a situation where the worst case arises motivates us to find an algorithm with a better worst-case time bound. We might be willing to pay a little more on average (a higher constant of proportionality) to have the assurance that we will never encounter quadratic behavior.

A setting where the distinction between average-case and worst-case performance might matter is a life-critical *real-time application* in which an algorithm's user is painfully aware of runtime disparities from one execution to another. It is little consolation to tell the widow: Yes, Mrs. Smith, but on average the code would have been fast enough to have saved the life of your husband.

A second reason to study the worst-case linear-time median finding algorithm is to see what we might learn from it about programming and innovation. How much is pure creativity, and how much is just the application of acquired expertise? Let's see what we can learn.

The key insight is that on each iteration of `QuickSelect` it might be possible to choose a pivot value that *guarantees* that whichever region contains the jth smallest value (and is therefore the next region to be considered) shrinks in size by at least some specific ratio, r. If such an r exists, we would be *guaranteed* that the running time *not counting the time to compute the pivot* would be no worse than proportional to $n+n{\cdot}r+n{\cdot}r^2+n{\cdot}r^3+\ldots = n/(1-r)$, for some $|r|<1$.[102] Thus, for example, if r were (say) 70%, then the sum of lengths of successive regions inspected would be no worse than $n + n{\cdot}(7/10) + n{\cdot}(7/10)^2 + n{\cdot}(7/10)^3 + \ldots = (10/3){\cdot}n$, i.e., linear in n.

Up until now, the pivot has been computed in a *constant* amount of time, e.g., we have used `(A[L]+A[R-1])/2`, and so this time cost could be ignored. But we are now prepared to expend a non-constant effort to come up with a good pivot, provided the payoff from doing so is sufficient: We want the efforts to partition regions *plus* the efforts to compute pivots to remain worst-case linear in n.

A second intuition derives from considering the best-case choice for pivots: The

102. This sum is a *geometric series*. See [43] for a derivation of the closed-form solution, if you don't recall it.

medians themselves. That is, suppose by happenstance we were to always select as the pivot the median of `A[L..R-1]` itself. Then the size of the successive regions would be (approximately) halved on each iteration, and the running time would be proportional to $n + n\cdot(1/2) + n\cdot(1/4) + n\cdot(1/8) + \ldots = 2\cdot n$, i.e., linear in n. But happenstance is not sufficient; we seek some way to *guarantee* that the sizes of the regions shrink by a constant ratio.

A third intuition is that there might be a way to pick as pivot a value that is "sufficiently close" to the median, i.e., close enough to the median so that the worst-case behavior of the algorithm is still linear, as if we had happened on the median itself. Specifically, perhaps there is an appropriate subset of *representative values* of `A[L..R-1]` such that their median is guaranteed to be close to the median of the whole. If it doesn't take too long to determine that representative subset of values, and if there aren't too many of them, then we can use the median algorithm itself (recursively) to find the median of the representative subset, and hope that the total time remains linear in n. The key issue will be the balance between the magnitude of the reduction ratio achieved (using the median of the representative subset as pivot), and the time required to compute that median.

The fourth and key intuition is that one can group values of `A[L..R-1]` into fixed-size chunks, and use the set of their medians as the representative subset of values. This scheme is termed the "median of medians" algorithm.

For example, suppose the chunks were groups of three. Then the following code can be used to compute each chunk's median in constant time:

```
static int MedianOfThree(int a, int b, int c) {
   if ((a <= b) && (b <= c)) return b;  // a b c
   if ((a <= c) && (c <= b)) return c;  // a c b
   if ((b <= a) && (a <= c)) return a;  // b a c
   if ((b <= c) && (c <= a)) return c;  // b c a
   if ((c <= a) && (a <= b)) return a;  // c a b
   return b;                            // c b a
   } /* MedianOfThree */
```

Using groups of three, there will be (approximately) $n/3$ such medians. We can (recursively) use our median finding algorithm on them, and use their median as the pivot for the sub-array `A[L..R-1]`.

Why might we hope that the median of medians will be a good pivot, e.g., yield a guaranteed constant worst-case reduction ratio for the sizes of regions produced by partitioning? Let us reason with the aid of a specific example, where the median we seek is the emboldened **61**:

	0	1	2	3	4	5	6	7	8	9	10	11	12	13	14	15	16	17	18	19	20
A	51	60	73	92	57	54	75	59	91	58	71	62	67	66	59	52	**61**	72	55	60	79

51	60	73	92	57	54	75
59	91	58	71	62	67	66
59	52	**61**	72	55	60	79

Now imagine that these values were laid out in a two-dimensional array of height 3 in row-major order, where we have colored the median of each column red. We are conducting a "thought experiment", and do not intend to suggest that the algorithm would actually copy the values into a two-dimensional array, or actually perform any of the operations we now describe. We are merely imagining the manipulation.

51	52	58	71	55	54	66
59	60	**61**	72	57	60	75
59	91	73	92	62	67	79

Next, imagine each column of three values were sorted, which would bring the individual column medians to the middle row.

55	51	52	54	58	66	71
57	59	60	60	**61**	75	72
62	59	91	67	73	79	92

Continuing with the thought experiment, imagine rearranging the columns horizontally to be ordered left-to-right by their medians, which would put the median of medians, 60, in the central column (green background).

55	51	52	54	58	66	71
57	59	60	60	**61**	75	72
62	59	91	67	73	79	92

Now color code all cells in the left half of the columns according to whether their values are less than or equal to their respective medians (pink), and all cells in the right half of the columns according to whether their values are greater than or equal to their respective medians (blue). Then all pink-background values are necessarily no bigger than the median of medians (green background), and all blue-background values are no smaller than the median of medians (green background).[103] The remaining values (yellow background) may be smaller, larger, or equal to the median of medians, as illustrated.

Therein lies the power of choosing the median of medians as `p`, the pivot for partitioning: Either the median we seek turns out to fall in the "`==p`" region (and we are done because, in that case, the median is `p`), or it falls in either the "`<p`" or "`>p`" regions, which are each guaranteed to contain no more than 2/3 of the values. Thus, the median of medians as pivot guarantees that the next region to be considered shrinks in size by a constant reduction ratio.

Why 2/3? Without loss of generality, say the median falls in the "`<p`" region. Then the blue-background values are all in the other region ("`>p`"), and are excluded. The blue values are 2/3 of half of the columns in our thought experiment, i.e., 1/3 of all values. Thus, the "`<p`" region can be no larger than 2/3 of the whole. The symmetric argument holds if the median falls in the "`>p`" region, in which case 1/3 of the values are pink background, and are excluded from further consideration.

To make this argument very concrete, here are the values of `A[L..R-1]` before partitioning, showing their color coding according to the thought experiment:

	0	1	2	3	4	5	6	7	8	9	10	11	12	13	14	15	16	17	18	19	20
A	51	60	73	92	57	54	75	59	91	58	71	62	67	66	59	52	**61**	72	55	60	79

and here they are after partitioning with a median of medians pivot of 60:

	0	1	2	3	4	5	6	7	8	9	10	11	12	13	14	15	16	17	18	19	20
A	51	55	57	54	52	59	59	58	60	60	62	67	66	71	91	**61**	72	75	92	79	73

To find the median, QuickSelect would have been called with a rank parameter `j` equal to 21/2=10, i.e., we seek the 10th smallest value (0 origin). After partitioning with a pivot value of p=60, the 10th smallest value falls in the "`>p`" region (`A[10..20]`), so we select that region, leaving behind all values in the "`<p`" region (and all values in the "`==p`" region). By the argument above, the values excluded necessarily include all pink ones, which are at least a third of them all.

So, we have achieved half of what we set out to achieve: Using the median of medians of groups of three as pivot guarantees a constant reduction ratio. We can code up this approach, and it will work fine, i.e., it will find the median by looking in consecutive sub-arrays that are each no larger than 2/3 the size of the previous one.

Alas, there is one hitch: There are too many groups of three. Specifically, there are fully $n/3$ such groups, and the recursive call to QuickSelect to find the median of their medians dominates the cost, and renders the overall algorithm super-linear. Imagine the heart break when it was first realized that the cost of computing the

103. This property follows by transitivity. In each column, each (pink) value is less than or equal to its respective median, which is necessarily also less than or equal to the median of medians. The argument for the blue values is symmetric.

pivots (using the median of medians of groups of three) outweighs the benefit of the constant reduction ratio achieved.

But don't lose heart. What about groups of 5 elements? The guaranteed reduction will be slightly smaller, 30% instead of 33.3%. Why 30%? Because 3/5 of half of the columns are guaranteed to be in the "opposite partition region", and half of 3/5 is 3/10. But the cost to compute the pivot as the median of medians is significantly reduced because there are only n/5 (rather than n/3) such groups. One way to think of this tradeoff is: The change from 33.3% to 30% is relatively small, but the change from 1/3 to a 1/5 is relatively large. There is just enough of a marginal advantage to render the overall algorithm linear.[104] Bingo!

To complete the code, the pivot computation in QuickSelect must be replaced by a recursive call to find the median of the medians of groups of five. Partitioning is *in situ*, but one must also find a way to put all the medians of the groups of five in contiguous elements of an array so that the algorithm can be used on them recursively. This data manipulation can also be done *in situ* in the same array without destroying the integrity of the partition for which the median-of-medians will serve as a pivot in the next round of partitioning. Writing this code it is left as an exercise.[105]

Now that you have seen full development of the guaranteed worst-case linear-time median finding algorithm, you can judge: Is the invention genius, or workman-like expertise?

Running time and space

Some empirical evidence indicates that the cost of guaranteeing linear-time worst case selection is about 3x, i.e., the median-of-medians algorithm is on average three times slower than QuickSelect [17]. However, there are other claims that it can be made competitive, i.e., without penalty [18].

---

104. Exercise 58.
105. Exercise 57.

CHAPTER 11
Sorting

To *sort* is to arrange values in some designated order. The order may be numerical, or lexicographic, or something else you define with your own comparison operation.

In this chapter, we continue to focus on values in an **int** array A[0..n-1], and use the built-in order associated with integers. Sorting arrays of other types of values would be similar, and would require no special consideration.

We present four sorting algorithms: QuickSort, MergeSort, Selection Sort, and Insertion Sort. Why present four; isn't one good enough? Actually, none is truly needed since every programming language comes equipped with a library implementation for sorting.

Our motivation for presenting sorting is pedagogical. The derivations illustrate principles:

- Creativity in code development can be inspired by starting with an invariant.
- Different invariants lead to different algorithms, some better than others.
- Algorithms based on Divide and Conquer can have superior performance.
- Algorithms based on everyday experience can have inferior performance.
- Divide-and-Conquer approaches are naturally implemented by recursive procedures.
- Fast algorithms are not necessarily harder to code than slow algorithms.
- Implementations often draw on established code patterns.
- Precise specifications support careful reasoning during implementation.

Sorting is important in its own right because many problems can be reduced to sorting, followed by further processing that is relatively easy once the sequence of values in question has been ordered.

The chapter ends with a brief discussion of a property of sorting algorithms called *stability*.

The description of each sorting algorithm is augmented with a link to an entertaining online video that shows numbered folk-dancers rearranging themselves according to the given method.

QuickSort

Recall the Partitioning algorithm (p. 171) that emerged as an application of the Dutch National Flag problem (p. 166): Given a value known as the pivot, p, partitioning rearranges an array A[0..n-1] into three disjoint regions consisting of all

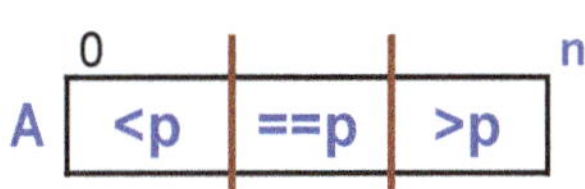

values of the array that are less than, equal to, and greater than `p`, respectively. Think of `A[0..n-1]` as Gaul having been divided by Caesar into three parts. The three parts, as aggregates, are in numerical order, but within each part the values are in a jumble.

Suppose Caesar's conquest goal were to rearrange the entire array `A[0..n-1]` into non-decreasing order. How would the father of Divide and Conquer have dealt with the fact that the left and right regions of the partition are themselves not yet internally ordered? By applying the Partition algorithm to them individually, of course. And so on, and so forth, recursively, until reaching partitions of length 1 or 0, which perforce are (trivially) ordered. This is QuickSort.

The code for `Partition` is in hand:

```
/* Rearrange A[L..R-1] into all <p, then all ==p, then all >p. */       1
static void Partition( int A[], int L, int R, int p ) {
   〈body of Partition〉
   } /* Partition */
```

We can start with this code, and edit it to become `QuickSortAux`, an auxiliary method that sorts an arbitrary array region `A[L..R-1]`:

☞ **Don't type if you can avoid it; clone. Cut and paste, then adapt.**

First, we change the name Partition to QuickSortAux, and move the pivot parameter into the body of QuickSortAux, where it will be computed internally rather than being passed in as a parameter:

```
/* Choose a pivot p and rearrange A[L..R-1] into all <p, then all ==p,   2
   then all >p. */
static void QuickSortAux( int A[], int L, int R ) {
   int p = /* value of pivot */ ;
   〈body of Partition〉
   } /* QuickSortAux */
```

Second, we know that a region `A[L..R-1]` of length 1 or 0 is already sorted, so we return immediately in those cases:

```
/* Choose a pivot p and rearrange A[L..R-1] into all <p, then all ==p,   3
   then all >p. */
static void QuickSortAux( int A[], int L, int R ) {
   if ( R-L>1 ) {
      int p = /* value of pivot */ ;
      〈body of Partition〉
      }
   } /* QuickSortAux */
```

Third, we recurse on the "<p" and ">p" subregions individually. In doing so, we use variables `w` and `b` established by the 〈body of Partition〉 as the subscripts of the leftmost elements of the "==p" and ">p" regions, respectively.

0 w b n
A | <p | ==p | >p |

4

```
/* Choose a pivot p and rearrange A[L..R-1] into all <p, then all ==p,
   then all >p. */
static void QuickSortAux( int A[], int L, int R ) {
   if ( R-L>1 ) {
      int p = /* value of pivot */ ;
      ⟨body of Partition⟩
      QuickSortAux(A, L, w);
      QuickSortAux(A, b, R);
      }
   } /* QuickSortAux */
```

Fourth, method `QuickSort` invokes `QuickSortAux` on the entire array:

5

```
/* Rearrange values of A[0..n-1] into non-decreasing order. */
static void QuickSort(int A[], int n) { QuickSortAux( A, 0, n ); }
```

Finally, we need to compute the pivot appropriately. The same considerations discussed in Partition (p. 171) and QuickSelect (p. 176) hold. Correctness follows from the correctness of Partition. Termination follows from an argument about the reduction in the lengths of the partitions, which turns on the computed value of the pivot. As discussed on pages 172 and 179, an appropriate pivot is `(A[L]+A[R-1])/2`:

6

```
/* Choose a pivot p and rearrange A[L..R-1] into all <p, then all ==p,
   then all >p. */
static void QuickSortAux( int A[], int L, int R ) {
   if ( R-L>1 ) {
      int p = (A[L]+A[R-1])/2;
      ⟨body of Partition⟩
      QuickSortAux(A, L, w);
      QuickSortAux(A, b, R);
      }
   } /* QuickSortAux */
```

This completes the code.

Enjoy the QuickSort dance performance on the web [19]. Can you discern how the dancers are choosing the pivot?

Running time and space

On average, the regions produced by partitioning have balanced sizes, and therefore grow smaller geometrically. Accordingly, the depth of recursion will on average be $\log_2 n$. Unlike QuickSelect, sorting requires that we recurse on *both* partitions, so at each level of recursion, the sum of all partitioning will require order n operations. Accordingly, the average running time of QuickSort will be proportional to $n \log_2 n$.

QuickSort works *in situ*, and therefore requires no extra space for the values of the array (other than the `temp` used by swap in the ⟨body of Partition⟩). It does, however, require extra storage associated with the recursion.

On average, the deepest recursion will be on the order of $\log_2 n$, and therefore the amount of extra space required will be proportional to $\log_2 n$. However, in the worst case, when one of the "<p" or ">p" regions repeatedly contains only a single value, the recursion may reach a depth of order n.

To reduce this space overhead, rather than recursing on both regions, we can recurse only on the smaller of the two, and perform the partitioning of the larger of the two regions within the current activation of the procedure, much as is done in QuickSelect. This optimization technique, whereby a recursive invocation is replaced by a local iteration, is known as *tail-recursion*.[106]

MergeSort

QuickSort first partitions the array based on a pivot p, and then recurses on the "<p" and ">p" regions, individually. The lengths of the regions depend on the specific values in the array and the choices of pivots. Although it has excellent performance on average, in the worst case, the region sizes turn out to be disadvantageous, and the running time becomes quadratic in n, i.e., proportional to n^2.

MergeSort, like QuickSort, is a Divide and Conquer algorithm. However, rather than taking its chances on the sizes of subdivisions, MergeSort guarantees balance by recursively dividing the array `A[0..n-1]` into halves, quarters, eighths, etc. independent of the values in the array. Subdividing stops at the base case, which is a region of size 1 or 0 that is perforce ordered.[107]

On the way out of the recursions, with a pair of ordered adjacent regions in hand, MergeSort uses Collation (p. 173) to interleave values appropriately, and make a single ordered region from the pair.

First, we define `MergeSortAux` following the plan outlined:[108]

```
/* Rearrange values of A[L..R] into non-decreasing order. */
static void MergeSortAux(int A[], int L, int R) {
   if ( R>L ) {
      int m = (L+R)/2;
      MergeSortAux(A, L, m);    // Sort left half.
      MergeSortAux(A, m+1, R);  // Sort right half.
      /* Given A[L..m] and A[m+1..R], both already in non-decreasing
         order, collate them so A[L..R] is in non-decreasing order. */
      }
   } /* MergeSortAux */
```
1

Second, we provide a main routine, `MergeSort`, that invokes `MergeSortAux`:

```
/* Rearrange values of A[0..n-1] into non-decreasing order. */
static void MergeSort(int A[], int n) { MergeSortAux(A, 0, n-1); }
```
2

Recall the specification of Collation given in Chapter 9 (p. 173):

```
/* Given ordered arrays A and B of lengths na and nb, create ordered array C
   of length na+nb consisting of those values. */
```

106. Exercise 64.

107. As with Binary Search, one of the two "halves" of a region with odd length is one longer than the other.

108. Note that we embrace the convention that R is the subscript of the last element of the region, as in Binary Search, whereas in QuickSort, it was convenient for R to be the subscript of the next element beyond the last, as in Partition.

There are several mismatches between our present need and what Collation offers:

First, it assumes that the two sources of values to be collated are separate arrays, `A[0..na-1]` and `B[0..nb-1]`. In contrast, MergeSort needs those source to be two regions of one array, `A[L..m]` and `A[m+1..R]`. Inspection of the code for Collation reveals that this is a trifling difficulty, and the code is easily modified to draw values from `A[L..m]` and `A[m+1..R]`.[109]

Second, it assumes that the result is to be placed in a third array `C[0..na+nb-1]`. In contrast, MergeSort needs the result to placed back in the array region `A[L..R]`. This is not easily done *in situ*, so MergeSort typically uses a second array, and the coding challenge revolves around minimizing effort associated with the use of two arrays.[110]

Enjoy the dance of Merge Sort [20]. It is quite easy to follow the algorithm, and also to see that it is not *in situ*.

Running time and space

MergeSort resembles Binary Search in its recursive halving of regions until reaching length one or zero. For a region of length n, halving can only be done at most $1+\log_2 n$ times. Think of the subdivisions in strata. Collating two subregions of length (approximately) n/2 takes effort proportional to n. Similarly, collating each pair of subregions of length n/4 takes efforts proportional to n/2. Since there are two such pairs, the total is again n. Similarly, the total collation effort on each stratum requires order n effort. Therefore, the total effort is proportional to $n \log_2 n$, worst case, average case, and every case.

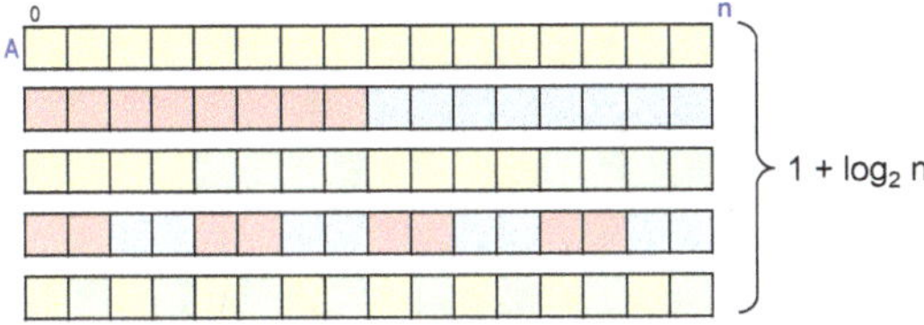

The fact that the running time of MergeSort is guaranteed to always be proportional to $n \log_2 n$ is a distinct advantage over QuickSort. The need for a second array is a distinct disadvantage.

Selection Sort

The key algorithmic idea of Selection Sort is to repeatedly *select* a smallest of the remaining unordered elements, extract it, and put it next in an emerging region of correctly-positioned elements. Many people sort this way when ordering a hand of playing cards:

```
/* Rearrange values of A[0..n-1] into non-decreasing order. */      1
```

Clearly there is an iteration, and some control variable (say, `j`) marching across the subscripts of the array. Equally clearly, `j` will start at the left end of `A` (more or less), and will stop at the right end (more or less), so a determinate enumeration seems safe:

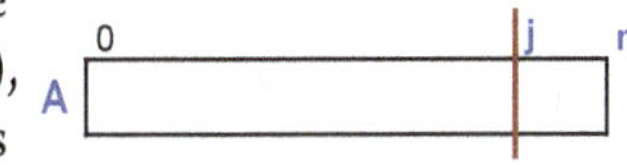

109. Exercise 65.
110. Exercise 66.

```
/* Rearrange values of A[0..n-1] into non-decreasing order. */
   for (int j = ____; ____; j++) ____________
```
2

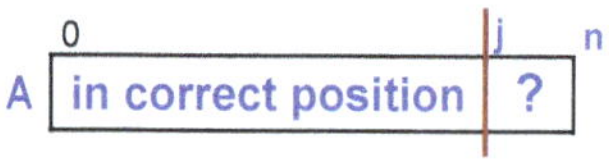

From the top-level description of the algorithm, we understand that we will have selected the smallest values of the array, and put them in their correct, final positions. The diagram expresses the loop invariant.

We seek to increase the size of the left region while maintaining the invariant, and to do so, will need to place the correct value in A[j] before j is incremented. The value to be placed in A[j] must be a minimal value of A[j..n-1], say, one found at element A[k]:

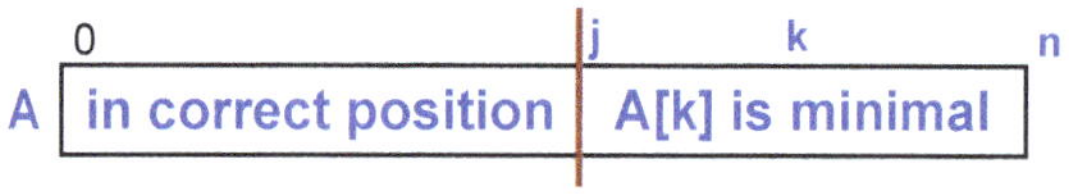

We can then swap A[j] and A[k]:

```
/* Rearrange values of A[0..n-1] into non-decreasing order. */
   for (int j = ____; ____; j++) {
      /* Let k be s.t. A[k] is a minimal value in A[j..n-1]. */
      /* Swap A[j] and A[k]. */
      }
```
3

Because the loop body is fully specified, we can pronounce it (temporarily) done, and proceed to code its termination and initialization. Alternatively, we could delay doing so until the loop body is fully coded. It shouldn't really make any difference because the statements (actually, statement comments) are complete. Even if we were to wait, we would still want to reason with those specifications rather than their implementations.

As per the precept on the order of developing loops, the next step is to code termination. We observe that there is no need to consider a rightmost region of size one, e.g., A[n-1..n-1], since it will contain only the last remaining value of the array, which perforce must be in its correct, final position. The value in A[n-1..n-1] at this point has failed every comparison for minimality, and as a result of (perhaps) multiple swaps has been propagated into that position. It is maximal:

```
/* Rearrange values of A[0..n-1] into non-decreasing order. */
   for (int j = ____; j<(n-1); j++) {
      /* Let k be s.t. A[k] is a minimal value in A[j..n-1]. */
      /* Swap A[j] and A[k]. */
      }
```
4

Were you to have missed this minor optimization, there would have been no harm: You would compute that a minimal value of A[n-1..n-1] is (duh?) A[n-1], which you would then swap with A[j], where j happens to be one and the same as n-1, thereby causing no net effect. This is fine because it is exactly where it belongs.

It is noteworthy that the fail-safe aspect of this code, whereby no harm comes from executing a last (superfluous) step, derives in part from making sure that all code always handles boundary conditions gracefully and correctly. Specifically, when implementing the code for

```
/* Let k be s.t. A[k] is a minimal value in A[j..n-1]. */
```

you might say: Who would be stupid enough to invoke this code when `j` is `n-1`; do I really need to code this case, and do so correctly? The answer is "yes", because that person may very well be you.

Moving on to initialization of the control variable `j`, we observe that there is nothing special about the left boundary of the array, and accordingly `j` should start at 0:

5

```
/* Rearrange values of A[0..n-1] into non-decreasing order. */
   for (int j=0; j<(n-1); j++) {
      /* Let k be s.t. A[k] is a minimal value in A[j..n-1]. */
      /* Swap A[j] and A[k]. */
      }
```

Swap is standard:

6

```
/* Rearrange values of A[0..n-1] into non-decreasing order. */
   for (int j=0; j<(n-1); j++) {
      /* Let k be s.t. A[k] is a minimal value in A[j..n-1]. */
      /* Swap A[j] and A[k]. */
         int temp = A[j]; A[j] = A[k]; A[k] = temp;
      }
```

The code for finding the minimal element of a region of an array is essentially the same as given in Chapter 9, (p. 140), except that instead of the left boundary of the region having index 0, it has index `j` (shown in blue):[111]

7

```
/* Rearrange values of A[0..n-1] into non-decreasing order. */
   for (int j = 0; j<(n-1); j++) {
      /* Let k be s.t. A[k] is a minimal value in A[j..n-1]. */
         int k = j;
         for (int i=j+1; i<n; i++) if ( A[i]<A[k] ) k = j;
      /* Swap A[j] and A[k]. */
         int temp = A[j]; A[j] = A[k]; A[k] = temp;
      }
```

This completes the code for Selection Sort.

Enjoy the Selection Sort dance [21], which conveys the tediousness of a quadratic algorithm excellently. If you watch until the end, you will see that `A[n-1]` swaps with herself, i.e., the dancers run their outer loop one time more than needed.

Running time and space

The running time of Selection Sort is dominated by its inner loop, which (in successive iteration of the outer loop) iterates (`n-1`) times, then (`n-2`) times, ..., then 2 times, then 1 time. As Gauss could have told you, the total number of iterations of the inner loop is thus `n`·(`n-1`)/2, so the running time of Selection Sort is quadratic in `n`.

Selection Sort works *in situ*, so it requires no extra space (other than `temp`).

111. There is one other small change in the code: Because we are already using variable `j` for a different purpose, the control variable needs to change from `j` to `i`.

Insertion Sort

The key algorithmic idea of Insertion Sort is to repeatedly *insert* a next array element into its proper place in an emerging region of ordered elements. Many people (the ones who don't use Selection Sort) use this algorithm when ordering a hand of playing cards:

```
/* Rearrange values of A[0..n-1] into non-decreasing order. */      1
```

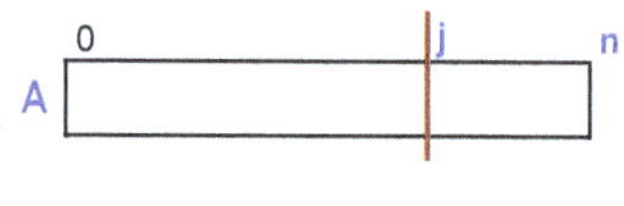

Clearly, we need iteration, and some control variable (say, j) marching across the subscripts of the array. Equally clearly, j will start at the left end of A (more or less), and will be stop at the right end (more or less), so a determinate enumeration is appropriate:

```
/* Rearrange values of A[0..n-1] into non-decreasing order. */      2
   for (int j= ____; ____; j++) ____________
```

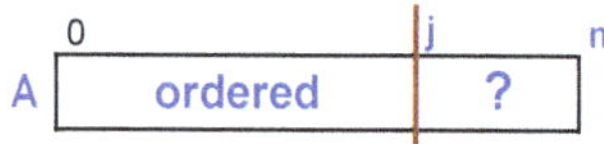

From the top-level description of the algorithm, we understand that the left region will be ordered, albeit (unlike Selection Sort) the values are not (yet) necessarily in their final positions. The diagram depicts the loop invariant.

We seek to increase the size of the left region while maintaining the invariant, and to do so, need to place A[j] in its correct place within the ordered region A[0..j] before j is incremented.

You may be uncomfortable about the phrase "within A[0..j]", and wonder whether it should have been "within A[0..j-1]"? No, because A[j] may be larger than all values in A[0..j-1], in which case it belongs exactly where it is:

```
/* Rearrange values of A[0..n-1] into non-decreasing order. */      3
   for (int j= ____; ____; j++) {
      /* Given A[0..j-1] ordered in non-decreasing order, rearrange
         values of A[0..j] so it is ordered. */
      }
```

Because the loop body is fully specified, we can pronounce it (temporarily) done, and proceed to code the loop termination and loop initialization.

Termination: Unless the last element of the array, A[n-1] is maximal, it must be inserted somewhere to its left, so the last element cannot be skipped:

```
/* Rearrange values of A[0..n-1] into non-decreasing order. */      4
   for (int j= ____; j<n; j++) {
      /* Given A[0..j-1] ordered in non-decreasing order, rearrange
         values of A[0..j] so it is ordered. */
      }
```

Initialization: A prefix of the array of length one, i.e., A[0..0], is clearly ordered, so j can start at 1:

```
/* Rearrange values of A[0..n-1] into non-decreasing order. */          5
   for (int j=1; j<n; j++) {
      /* Given A[0..j-1] ordered in non-decreasing order, rearrange
         values of A[0..j] so it is ordered. */
   }
```

This complete the code, except of course that the loop body must be refined.

You may be excited to spot your first opportunity to use Binary Search in an application: The prefix `A[0..j-1]` is ordered, and we need to find where within it `A[j]` belongs. Binary Search is a fast way to figure that out.

But alas, knowing where `A[j]` belongs, say, at `A[k]`, is only half the battle. The other half is shifting array elements to the right to make room to insert `A[j]`. The fast (logarithmic-time) search will be overshadowed by the slow (linear-time) right shift, so it's not worth bothering with.

0 k j n
A | ordered, all ≤ A[j] | ordered, all > A[j] | ? |

To insert `A[j]` where it belongs, we first create a "hole" at `A[j]` by copying it to a temporary variable. We then shift `A[k..j-1]` right one place thereby moving the "hole" to `A[k]`. Finally, we plug that hole with the value from the temporary variable:

```
/* Rearrange values of A[0..n-1] into non-decreasing order. */          6
   for (int j=1; j<n; j++) {
      /* Given A[0..j-1] ordered in non-decreasing order, rearrange
         values of A[0..j] so it is ordered. */
         int temp = A[j];
         /* Shift A[k..j-1] right one place, where k is the largest
            integer s.t. A[k-1]≤temp, or 0 if temp is smallest. */
         A[k] = temp;
   }
```

A boundary condition for this code is that `A[0..j]` is already ordered, i.e., `A[j]` doesn't have to move because it is maximal in `A[0..j]`. In this case, the shift right will have no effect, and the action of the loop body as a whole will be to copy `A[j]` to `temp`, and then to copy it right back again to `A[j]`. Is it worth singling out this case for special treatment? No. Quite fortuitously, it takes care of itself. Without even thinking about it, we have complied with this precept:

> ☞ **Code the general case first. Then attempt to make the boundary case fit the general case, if possible, making as slight a change to the code as possible.**

We turn now to implementing the shift. The following are intuitive: (a) there is an iteration; (b) the iteration is indeterminate because we don't know when it will stop; (c) within the iteration, variable `k` will be moving from right to left as we seek the location at which to insert the value that was originally in `A[j]`; (d) within the body of the loop, there must be an assignment statement that effects the shift of one element of the array; and (e) within the body of the loop, variable `k` must be decremented.

We sketch the code with the part we intuit, and leave blanks for the parts that will require care:

```
/* Rearrange values of A[0..n-1] into non-decreasing order. */
   for (int j=1; j<n; j++) {
      /* Given A[0..j-1] ordered in non-decreasing order, rearrange
         values of A[0..j] so it is ordered. */
         int temp = A[j];
         /* Shift A[k..j-1] right one place, where k is the largest
            integer s.t. A[k-1]≤temp, or 0 if temp is smallest. */
            int k = ____;
            while ( ______ ) {
               A[ _____ ] = A[ ____ ];
               k--;
               }
         A[k] = temp;
      }
```
7

The sketching technique is in keeping with the safe-coding precept: Only write down what you are confident about.

We now have a choice. If we were to follow the precept to code the body of a loop first, we would now concentrate on the assignment statement "`A[____] = A[____];`".

Alternatively, we may recognize that we have sketched a backwards sequential search for the largest `k` with a certain property, and a freeloading shifting assignment slipped into the search for the ride. From that perspective, we could complete the search first, ignoring the shift, and then deal with the shift afterwords.

We favor the latter coding order because this is a case where getting the body right intimately depends on the search-loop variable `k`, and the range of values it takes on. And it is even a case where early reasoning about boundary conditions is helpful.

Recall that one of the boundary conditions is that `A[j]`, which we have copied to variable `temp`, may not need to move at all. In other words, in the case where the shifting loop iterates 0 times, `k` must remain at `j` so that the assignment statement "`A[k]=temp;`" will just put `temp` back in `A[j]`. This observation nails the initialization:

```
/* Rearrange values of A[0..n-1] into non-decreasing order. */
   for (int j=1; j<n; j++) {
      /* Given A[0..j-1] ordered in non-decreasing order, rearrange
         values of A[0..j] so it is ordered. */
         int temp = A[j];
         /* Shift A[k..j-1] right one place, where k is the largest
            integer s.t. A[k-1]≤temp, or 0 if temp is smallest. */
            int k = j;
            while ( ______ ) {
               A[ _____ ] = A[ ____ ];
               k--;
               }
         A[k] = temp;
      }
```
8

We are searching (backwards) for a value in the array that is in some relationship to `temp`, the value for which we seek the insertion point. The first such value to compare with `temp` is `A[j-1]`, and in general, as we decrement `k`, must be `A[k-1]`:

```
/* Rearrange values of A[0..n-1] into non-decreasing order. */    9
   for (int j=1; j<n; j++) {
      /* Given A[0..j-1] ordered in non-decreasing order, rearrange
         values of A[0..j] so it is ordered. */
         int temp = A[j];
         /* Shift A[k..j-1] right one place, where k is the largest
            integer s.t. A[k-1]≤temp, or 0 if temp is smallest. */
            int k = j;
            while ( A[k-1] ____ temp ) {
               A[ ____ ] = A[ ____ ];
               k--;
               }
         A[k] = temp;
      }
```

If we first clarify for ourselves that we are writing the *condition* for iterating, we will be clear that the comparison must be either "`>`" or "`>=`". This can be confirmed by reflection on the schematic diagram: If the value in `A[k-1]` is bigger than `temp`, we need to keep searching because `temp` belongs to the left of that `A[k-1]`.

The equal case is also clarified by reflecting on the diagram: We can stop searching if we find (another) instance of `temp` because we can insert it last in a run of values equal to `temp`. So the *condition* should be **false** if `A[k-1]` is equal to `temp`:

```
/* Rearrange values of A[0..n-1] into non-decreasing order. */    10
   for (int j=1; j<n; j++) {
      /* Given A[0..j-1] ordered in non-decreasing order, rearrange
         values of A[0..j] so it is ordered. */
         int temp = A[j];
         /* Shift A[k..j-1] right one place, where k is the largest
            integer s.t. A[k-1]≤temp, or 0 if temp is smallest. */
            int k = j;
            while ( A[k-1]>temp ) {
               A[ ____ ] = A[ ____ ];
               k--;
               }
         A[k] = temp;
      }
```

Last but not least is the boundary condition for the search: In the case where `temp` must be inserted at `A[0]`, i.e., when `temp` is smaller than all values in `A[0..j-1]`, the search must stop with `k` equal to 0. In this case, the final comparison "`A[k-1]>temp`" would be between `A[-1]` and `temp`. Of course, there is no such variable as `A[-1]`, and so this comparison must be avoided by an explicit test on `k`. Colloquially, we must prevent falling off the left end of the array:

```
/* Rearrange values of A[0..n-1] into non-decreasing order. */
   for (int j=1; j<n; j++) {
      /* Given A[0..j-1] ordered in non-decreasing order, rearrange
         values of A[0..j] so it is ordered. */
         int temp = A[j];
         /* Shift A[k..j-1] right one place, where k is the largest
            integer s.t. A[k-1]≤temp, or 0 if temp is smallest. */
            int k = j;
            while ( k>0 && A[k-1]>temp ) {
               A[ ____ ] = A[ ____ ];
               k--;
               }
         A[k] = temp;
      }
```
11

This completes the search, and we are ready to code the shift.

It is convenient to reason from the example of the very first iteration, where it is `A[j]` that must be filled from `A[j-1]`. Since `k` has been initialized as `j`, a shift that fills `A[k]` from `A[k-1]` will accomplish that:

```
/* Rearrange values of A[0..n-1] into non-decreasing order. */
   for (int j=1; j<n; j++) {
      /* Given A[0..j-1] ordered in non-decreasing order, rearrange
         values of A[0..j] so it is ordered. */
         int temp = A[j];
         /* Shift A[k..j-1] right one place, where k is the largest
            integer s.t. A[k-1]≤temp, or 0 if temp is smallest. */
            int k = j;
            while ( k>0 && A[k-1]>temp ) {
               A[k] = A[k-1];
               k--;
               }
         A[k] = temp;
      }
```
12

This completes the code.

It is worth reflecting on the coding order we presented, which was the exact opposite of what is called for by:

> ☞ **Code iterations in the following order: (1) body, (2) termination, (3) initialization, (4) finalization, (5) boundary conditions.**

From a boundary condition (5), we reasoned out where the search should start (3). Then, from another boundary condition, we reasoned out where the search should stop (2). Finally, we completed the shift-loop body (1), again leveraging a boundary condition to get the subscripts right.

By what rationale did we choose this contrarian order? In a sense, what we really did was think of the implementation as a modified instance of the *search-and-use* pattern:

```
/* Search. */
/* Use the search result. */
```

The search discovers the location `k` where `A[j]` needs to be inserted. The search-client code could have been written as a separate loop, but we performed a code optimization known as *loop fusion,* whereby two consecutive loops with the same range can be merged into one.

Enjoy the Insertion Sort dance [22]. If you study the dancers, you will see that the code presented in the text is marginally more efficient. The dancers don't have the concept of initially copying `A[j]` to `temp`. Rather, they perform insertion by successive swaps of neighbors.

Running time and space

The running time of Insertion Sort is dominated by its inner loop. In the worst case (given values in decreasing order), it iterates 1+2+...+ (n-1) times, which is quadratic in n. In the best case (given values already in non-decreasing order), the inner loop does no work, so the running time of the algorithm is linear in n. In the average case, Insertion Sort is quadratic in n.[112]

Insertion Sort is *in situ,* so it requires no extra space (other than `temp`).

Stability

A sort algorithm is *stable* if it preserves the order of subsequences of equal values. You might well ask: What difference does it make? Specifically: How can you tell the difference between a stable and an unstable sort? Isn't one instance of a number indistinguishable from another. You are quite right, and are asking a legitimate question. Here's why stability matters.

Sort algorithms, as presented, rearrange values of an **`int`** array `A[0..n-1]`. Let's call these values *keys.* It is atypical for keys to stand alone. Rather, keys are more often paired with associated *values.* When a sort algorithm sees two equal keys, the corresponding associated values may not be equal. A stable sort algorithm preserves the order of a subsequence of key-value pairs with equal keys, and thereby avoids gratuitous changes in the order of the associated values in that subsequence.

Chapter 18 presents the needed programming language construct used for representing key-value pairs. Until then imagine that keys and values are stored in parallel arrays, and that whenever the key array is rearranged, so, too, is the parallel value array.

Let's review each sort algorithm and decide whether it is stable or not:

- **QuickSort.** Not stable. The Dutch National Flag partitioning algorithm swaps values without regard to the effect on stability. For example, the first step in rearranging the sequence ⟨B, B', R⟩ is to swap B and R, resulting in the sequence ⟨R, B', B⟩. We have reversed the order of equal values B and B'. Game over.
- **MergeSort.** The stability of MergeSort follows quite simply from the stability of Collation.
- **Selection Sort.** Not stable. The first key-value pair in the unsorted region is swapped with the key-value pair with the minimal key. If there are multiple key-value pairs with equal keys, we can be careful to select the leftmost such pair. But this doesn't matter because the swap destroys the order we wish to preserve. For example, consider applying Selection Sort to the sequence ⟨3, 3, 2⟩. When 2 (the smallest value) is swapped with the first 3, it destroys the order of the two 3s.
- **Insertion Sort.** Stable. Each value in the unsorted region of the array is

---

112. Offered here without proof.

considered in left-to-right order, and each such value is then slotted into the appropriate place in the emerging sorted region. When there is a run of keys in the sorted region that are equal to the key being moved, we just have to be careful to move it to the right end of the sequence.

CHAPTER 12

Collections

Many examples in the text consider entire **int** arrays:

Why might you have such a thing? It could be a list of grades, or ages, or even just integers of mathematical interest. The integers contained in A[0..n-1] are relevant for some reason, but we need not really be concerned with why.

We have heretofore considered all n elements of an array A[0..n-1] as fixed and not changing over the course of program execution, but in a typical program this is not the case. Rather, the number of relevant items often varies dynamically. For example, an array of grades may initially contain none, and as the grades are read from the input, starts to fill. Subsequently, the number of grades in the array may shrink, e.g., if we were to remove duplicates.

A group of values that changes dynamically during program execution is called a *collection*. This chapter presents three different ways to represent collections: Lists, Histograms, and Hash Tables. It ends by discussing Two-Dimensional Arrays.

Lists

The *list* representation of a collection stores the relevant values in an initial *prefix* of an array, where the length of the prefix is kept in a variable like size:

The currently meaningful elements of A are the prefix A[0..size-1], and the unused elements of A are the *suffix* A[size..n-1]. Whereas up until now, n was considered to be the number of meaningful values in A, now size plays that role, and n is the maximum number of meaningful values that can be stored in A. The slots of the suffix are available for the prefix to grow into as values are added to the collection.

In Chapter 3, we called a grouping of variables like A, n, and size a data structure, and we provided it with a representation invariant:[113]

113. The variable maxSize, which we used in Chapter 3, is replaced here by n, to which we have become accustomed.

```
/* A[0..size-1] are the current items in A[0..n-1], 0≤size≤n. */
   int A[];    // receptacle for items in a list.
   int size;   // current # of elements in list, 0≤size≤n.
   int n;      // maximum # of elements storable in the list.
```

This is the specification we must maintain as items in a collection come and go.

Abstractly, what does such a structure represent? It is not a *set* because sets do not have repetitions, whereas the list does. It is what is called a *multiset*, i.e., a set with *multiplicity*. Another word for multiplicity is *frequency*. Any rearrangement of the values in the prefix of A represents the same multiset.[114]

Given a multiset **M** and a value *v*, we would like to be able to invoke various operations on **M**, including:[115]

- Add an instance of *v* into **M**, i.e., increase its multiplicity.
- Remove an instance of *v* from **M** if it is in **M**, i.e., decrease its multiplicity.
- Test membership of *v* in **M**, i.e., ask if its multiplicity is greater than zero.
- Obtain the multiplicity of *v* in **M**.
- Enumerate the elements of **M** in an arbitrary order, i.e., list them off, repeating *m* times an element with multiplicity *m*.

Let **A** be the multiset represented by `A[0..size-1]`, a prefix of `A[0..n-1]`. We can code the various multiset operations as follows, where in each case we are careful to maintain the representation invariant stated above:

Add. To add a value v to A, append v to the prefix of A that stores the elements of the multiset, and increase `size`:

```
/* Add v to A. */
   /* Ensure that A has the capacity for another element. */
      if ( size==n ) /* Make room for more values, or sound an alarm. */
   A[size] = v;
   size++;
```

The capacity issue is addressed later in the chapter.

Remove. To delete a value v from **A**, first find it (say, in `A[k]`), and then eliminate it from the prefix. The auxiliary method `indexOf` performs a Sequential Search to find v:

```
/* Return k, a location of v in A, or return size if no v in A. */
static int indexOf(int v; int A[], int size) {
   int k = 0;
   while ( k<size && A[k]!=v ) k++;
   return k;
   }
```

Since the elements of a multiset are not ordered, there is no need to maintain the order of values in the prefix of A by shifting `A[k+1..size-1]` left one slot to fill the "hole" made by deleting v. Instead, we can just move the *last* element into the hole. Thus, rather than using a shift operation that in the worst case would take `size-1`

114. The situation is quite analogous to fractions and rationals, in which many different fractions, e.g., 1/3, 2/6, 3/9, etc., all represent the same rational.

115. We are working towards implementation in Chapter 18 of a built-in notion in Java known as an ArrayList (p. 303), but for now the similarity should be considered coincidental and not exact.

steps (when the value in `A[0]` is deleted), the operation takes only one step. Note, however, that because the value `v` must first be found, the total number of steps is `size` (in the worst case) anyway. In some cases, the index of the value to be deleted will be known, and the `indexOf` search for it will not be needed. When this is the case, just plugging the hole with the last value in the list is advantageous:

```
/* Remove v from A. */
   int k = indexOf(v, A, size);
   if ( k==size ) /* v is not in A. */
   else { size--; A[k] = A[size]; }
```

What to do when `v` is not in `A` will depend on the application.

When a value (say, at position `k`) is removed from the collection, and the prefix is kept compact by filling the hole at `A[k]` with the value from the last array element of the prefix, that element is no longer part of the collection, and when we decrement `size` that slot effectively moves into the unused suffix. A newly unused slot need not be zeroed out, i.e., it can continue holding whatever value it had. We don't care because only elements in `A[0..size-1]` are considered meaningful at any given moment. Thus, when the collection shrinks, detritus is left behind in `A[size..n-1]`, but this is of no concern.[116]

Membership. To test membership of `v` in **A**, find (any occurrence of) `v` in the array prefix, if any:

```
/* Set b to true if v is in A, and false otherwise. */
   int k = indexOf(v, A, size);
   boolean b = (k<size);
```

Multiplicity. To find the multiplicity of `v` in **A**, run through the entire prefix `A[0..size-1]` and count the number of occurrences of elements equal to `v`:

```
/* Set m to the multiplicity of v in A. */
   int m = 0;
   for (int k=0; k<size; k++) if ( A[k]==v ) m++;
```

Enumeration. To enumerate the elements of **A**, list off `A[0..size-1]`:

```
/* Enumerate elements of A. */
   for (int k=0; k<size; k++) /* Enumerate A[k]. */
```

The number of steps required for each of these operations is as follows:

Operation	Steps
add	constant
remove	worst case linear in `size`
membership	worst case linear in `size`
multiplicity	linear in `size`
enumeration	linear in `size`

116. Such detritus is not a problem for a collection of primitive values of type **`int`**, but for a collection of references to objects (which are introduced in Chapter 18), the unused suffix of the array is best maintained as **null** values. See section Garbage Collection (p. 313).

Ordered Lists

In the foregoing section, the order of values in the array prefix `A[0..size-1]` was treated as irrelevant because the list was considered to represent a multiset. An alternative point of view is to consider the list to represent an *ordered collection*. This requires introducing a new operation to insert a value `v` at a given location in the ordered collection, and revising the implementation of **Remove** to maintain order.

Add. It is useful to retain the previous notion of appending a value to the end of the list, but then introduce an additional operation for inserting a value `v` at a specific index `k`. To guard against out-of-bounds indices, we first require that `k` be legitimate. As with adding a value at the end, we must also ensure that there is sufficient capacity in `A`. Then, we shift values in `A[k..size-1]` right one place to preserve their order, and drop `v` into the hole thereby created. Finally, we increment `size` to preserve the invariant that the elements in the ordered collection are `A[0..size-1]`:

```
/* Add v at position k of A. */
   /* Check index. */
      if (k>size) /* Alert: Bad index. */
   /* Ensure that A has capacity for another element. */
      if ( size==n ) /* Make room for more values. */
   /* Shift A[k..size-1] right one place.*/
      for (int j=size-1; j>=k; j--) A[j+1] = A[j];
   A[k] = v;
   size++;
```

An astute reader may complain that the code shown does not confirm that `k` is not negative. We deliberately omit this check, and allow the underlying subscript bounds check to detect that violation. The same astute reader may be concerned that the test for a bad index should be `k>=size` rather than `k>size`. We are allowing `k` to equal `size`, with the interpretation that in this case the item `v` is being appended to the end of the list.

Remove. Given that we now wish to maintain order, it is no longer legitimate to merely overwrite the `k`-th element with the last element. Rather, we must shift all values in the prefix `A[k+1..size-1]` left one place:

```
/* Remove value in position k of A. */
   /* Check index. */
      if (k>=size) /* Alert: Bad index. */
   size--;
   /* Shift A[k+1..size] left one place. */
      for (int j=k; j<size; j++) A[j] = A[j+1];
```

Array Overflow

One loose end remains about the representation of a collection in an array: What to do when the multiset has grown to the point at which there is no more room for another element to be added? This case arises when `size` becomes equal to `n`, the size of array `A`.

The case is easily handled, but first we must let go of a fiction we have been perpetrating. Specifically, we have consistently depicted arrays by writing the array name immediately to the left of the row of variables `int[0..n-1]`, as if it were the name of the array itself. In this sense, we depicted an array in the same way that we have depicted a scalar (i.e., non-array) variable. But this model is not accurate.

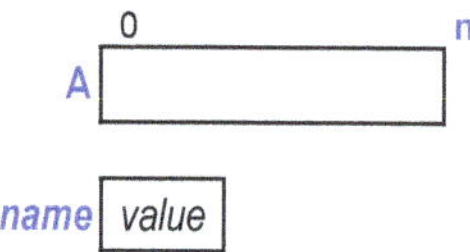

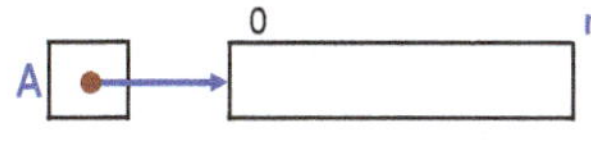

In reality, A is the name of a *scalar* variable whose value is a reference to a separate object that is a linear sequence of **int** variables. The correct picture should have been drawn all along as shown at the right. The reference is depicted as a red dot (•) at the tail of an arrow that points to the array object **int**[0..n-1]. It is the array object that can be subscripted, not the array reference. When we denote an element of an array A by writing A[*expression*], we really mean:

> The variable that is obtained by evaluating *expression*, and then using that integer to index in the array object that is referred to by the value in A.

This point is clarified if we ask: What is the effect of executing this initialized declaration?

```
int B[] = A;
```

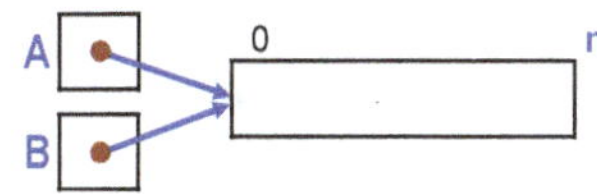

The answer is *not* that B become a *copy* of the entire array referred to by A. Rather, only the scalar reference to the array object **int**[0..n-1] is used to initialize B. The state after execution of the declaration really looks as shown to the right. In other words, A and B refer to one and the same object **int**[0..n-1]. The variables A and B are said to be *aliases* of one another, i.e., the names (or more accurately, the contents of the scalar variables with names A and B) both refer to the same "array".[117]

The point is driven home by a little puzzle:

```
int A[] = new int[10];
int B[] = A;
A[0] = 7;
B[0] = 8;
System.out.println( A[0] ); // What does this line print?
```

If you think it prints 7, then you have not understood; reread the text to understand why it prints 8.

With these preliminaries behind us, we complete the implementation of multiset add as:

```
/* Add v to A. */
   /* Ensure the capacity of A for another element. */
      if ( size==n ) { A = ensureCapacity(A); n = A.length; }
   A[size] = v;
   size++;
```

where ensureCapacity(A) returns a reference to a new array object that contains the same values as the array argument A, but is twice as long. The new array object provides headroom for more values to be added. The value returned is used to update

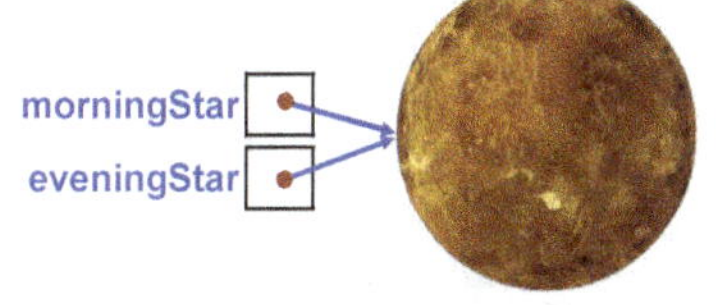

117. The situation is analogous to the planet Venus, which has been known as both the Morning Star and the Evening Star because it shines brightly at both times [47]. There is only one planet, with two aliases.

The fact that the value of an array variable (say, A) is really a reference (•) to an array object explains a mystery about how a method with an array parameter (say, B[]) can change elements in the corresponding array argument (say, A): On method invocation, parameter B is initialized with the (scalar) reference value (•) contained in A, whereupon A and B become aliases for the same array object. Array elements accessed in the method by subscripting B are thereby really one and the same as elements of A. Furthermore, the cost of providing an array argument to a method is minimal and independent of the size of the array object because the only value copied is the reference to the array object, not the array elements themselves.

A (to point to the new array object), and n is updated with A.length, the length of the new array object.

The code for add points out a drawback of a convention we have been following: That the length of the array is stored in a separate variable, say, n. This convention has been a convenient simplification in our presentations, but now means that we must update n separately. We could have been using A.length instead of n all along.

Here is the code for ensureCapacity:

```
/* Return a reference to a copy of A in an object that is twice as long. */
static int[] ensureCapacity( int A[] ) {
   /* Make B refer to an object that is twice as long as A. */
      int B[] = new int[2*A.length];
   /* Copy the values from A (the old object) to B (the new object). */
      for (int k=0; k<A.length; k++) B[k] = A[k];
   return B;
   } /* ensureCapacity */
```

When the array representing a multiset is doubled in length, the cost of doing so is proportional to the length of the array. The values in the old array must be copied into the new array, but the new array (in Java) is first initialized to all 0s. So, the number of steps required for doubling is proportional to the length of the new array. One way to think about this cost is to amortize it across all of the insert operations that led to the need to double the array in the first place. Think of it as if each insert operation that didn't require an immediate array doubling took a little longer, but only a constant time longer.[118]

Critique

We have presented code for maintaining a collection in an array, but something very important is missing: The notion of such a collection as a first-class value with which to compute. In particular, there is no way to treat the data structure as a single entity. Rather, it is made up of an array (A), a current size (size), and a maximum size (n). In short, it consists of dribs and drabs, and there is no way to talk about it as one thing.

Furthermore, there is no way to enforce maintenance of the collection's representation invariant; rather, we have to rely on the uncertain skill and self-discipline of the collection's clients.

What is needed is a linguistic mechanism that hides the implementation details behind an abstraction barrier (where the separate components of the data structure will be inaccessible to the clients), and that also provides a mechanism to access the data structure as a single entity.

The needed notions are deferred until Chapter 18 Classes and Objects. Until then, we can make do with self-discipline, and suffer the awkwardness caused by the inability to refer to a data structure as a whole.

---

118. The amortization-of-effort argument does not consider the possible requirements of a *real-time* or *interactive* application. Specifically, the cost of making the copy occurs in a burst, and places a short-term demand on the computer that may prevent it from meeting an obligation to be highly responsive at all times. You may have noticed momentary delays in interactive programs, which can be caused by a phenomenon such as array doubling. Two consecutive operations that each require a list insertion seem similar and innocuous; the first is instantaneous, but the second must double the array size, and thereby causes a hiccup in responsiveness.

Histograms

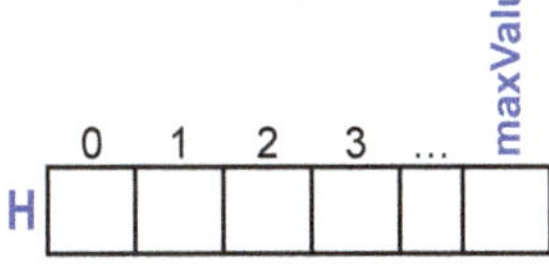

Suppose the values of a multiset **M** are known to be integers in a restricted range 0 to `maxValue`. Then **M** can be represented in array `H[0..maxvalue]`, where `H[k]` is the frequency of `k` in **M**. Such a representation is called a *histogram*.

We previously used histograms for statistical analysis (p. 101), but they are also a perfectly fine way to represent a multiset of integers (in a given range). Whereas the list representation of multisets only consumes space for the maximum number of items **in** the multiset, the histogram representation consumes space for each value **in the range** of possible values, and then consumes no additional space as the multiset grows.

We can now re-implement the unordered collection operations using the histogram representation. Call the multiset so represented **H**:

Add. To add a value `v` to **H**, increment its multiplicity:

```
/* Add v to H. */
   H[v]++;
```

Remove. To delete a value `v` from **H**, first confirm that its current multiplicity is positive, and then decrement it:

```
/* Remove v from H. */
   if ( H[k]==0 ) /* Alarm: attempt to remove a value not in H. */
   else H[k]--;
```

Membership. To test membership of `v` in **H**, evaluate the *condition* `H[v]>0`, i.e., no search is required whatsoever.

```
/* b = true iff v is in H. */
   boolean b = (H[v]>0);
```

Multiplicity. The multiplicity of `v` in **H** is exactly what `H` is all about:

```
/* m = Multiplicity of v in H. */
   int m = H[v];
```

Enumeration. To enumerate the elements of **H**, the entire range must be scanned, and for each element `k` with positive multiplicity `H[k]`, `k` must be enumerated that many times:

```
/* Enumerate elements of H. */
   for (int k=0; k<=maxValue; k++)
      for (int j=1; j<=H[k]; j++)
         /* Enumerate k */
```

The number of steps required for each of the operations is as follows:

Operation	Steps
add	constant
remove	constant
membership	constant
multiplicity	constant
enumeration	linear in `maxValue` + number of elements in the multiset

The first four operations are each implemented in a constant number of steps, independent of the size of the multiset.[119] This efficiency is achieved at the expense of (potentially) a lot more storage, and a (potentially) slower enumeration.

Not all multisets can be represented by histograms because there are limitations on their use:

- *Integer items.* Elements of the multiset must be integers. In contrast, lists can be used to store any type of value, and Sequential Search can be used to find values of any type in a list, provided an equality operation is provided for that type.
- *Limited range.* The integer elements of the multiset must lie in a limited range of values, a range for which there is enough memory for the histogram, `H[0..maxValue]`. Note, however, that a range that doesn't begin at 0 can be translated to such a range. The *size* of the range is what matters, not its origin.
- *Slow enumeration.* Operations for inserting, deleting, testing membership, and reporting multiplicity are fast, but at the cost of making the enumeration operation (possibly) very slow. Think of a *short* list of values in a very *large* range, and you will appreciate the (possible) downside of the histogram representation.
- *Associated values.* The histogram representation of a multiset does not provide an obvious way to represent the associated value components of ⟨key,value⟩ pairs. In contrast, to represent a multiset of ⟨key,value⟩ pairs in the list representation, not just integer keys, one can store the keys in one array, say, `A[0..n-1]`, and the values in a parallel array, say, `B[0..n-1]`. Alternatively, array `A` can contain references to ⟨key,value⟩-pair objects, and the implementation of the multiset operations can be adapted to inspect the key fields of those objects.[120]

The restrictions listed are certainly not fatal because there are many settings in which the limitations and tradeoffs of the histogram representation are unimportant, and the benefits are compelling. The limitations of histograms are all addressed by Hash Tables, which are described later in this chapter.

Bit Vectors

A Boolean-valued histogram can be used to represent a set, in which case the histogram is known as a *bit vector*. The histogram array `H` is initialized to all **false**, representing the empty set, and operations `add` and `remove` maintain the invariant "`k` in set **H** iff `H[k]` is **true**", i.e., "add `k`" is implemented by the assignment "`H[k]=true;`" and "remove k" is implemented by the assignment "`H[k]=false;`".

Example: Ramanujan Cubes, continued

Recall the problem of confirming the claim by Ramanujan that 1729 is the smallest integer that can be expressed as the sum of two positive cubes in two different ways. The program we began (p. 125) was:

119. The constant-time performance of these histogram operations is a direct consequence of the histogram's implementation as an array, e.g., consecutive bytes in a Random Access Memory (p. 30), and the constant-time access to the bytes of such a memory. Which bytes are accessed for the kth element of the histogram is determined by *address arithmetic* in which the base address of the array is added to $4*k$, where 4 is the number of bytes in an **`int`**.

120. You don't yet know about how such pair objects can be made. This is covered in Chapter 18 Classes and Objects.

```
/* Confirm Ramanujan's claim that 1729 is the smallest number that is the      1
   sum of two positive cubes in two different ways. */
   /* Record the values of r^3+c^3 that arise for all sets {r,c} of
      distinct positive integers that are no larger than 12. */
      [0..12][0..12] in row-major order.*/
      for (int r=2; r<13; r++)
         for (int c=1; c<r; c++)
            /* Keep track of having seen r^3+c^3. */
   /* Confirm that 1729 is the smallest integer that arose twice. */
```

and was used to illustrate a row-major-order enumeration of integer pairs. However, now armed with the technique of using a histogram to represent a multiset, we can complete the code:

```
int N = 12*12*12+11*11*11+1;  // (Max r)^3+(max c)^3+1, for r!=c in [0..12].  2
int H[] = new int[N];         // H[k] = # of {r,c}, r!=c, s.t. k=r^3+c^3.
/* Confirm Ramanujan's claim that 1729 is the smallest number that is the
   sum of two positive cubes in two different ways. */
      /* Let H be a histogram of r^3+c^3, for each set {r,c} of distinct
         positive integers that are no larger than 12. */
         for (int r=2; r<13; r++)
            for (int c=1; c<r; c++)
               H[r*r*r+c*c*c]++;
   /* Output non-zero bins of histogram H. */
      for (int k=0; k<N; k++)
         if ( H[k]>0 ) System.out.println(k + " " + H[k]);
```

Manual inspection of the program output confirms that the smallest k for which H[k]>1 is H[1729]. Alternatively, we can automate the inspection by finding the smallest k for which H[k]>1, and confirming that H[k]==2 and k==1729:

```
int N = 12*12*12+11*11*11+1;  // (Max r)^3+(max c)^3+1, for r!=c in [0..12].  3
int H[] = new int[N];         // H[k] = # of {r,c}, r!=c, s.t. k=r^3+c^3.
/* Confirm Ramanujan's claim that 1729 is the smallest number that is the
   sum of two positive cubes in two different ways. */
   /* Let H be a histogram of r^3+c^3, for each set {r,c} of distinct
      positive integers that are no larger than 12. */
      for (int r=2; r<13; r++)
         for (int c=1; c<r; c++)
            H[r*r*r+c*c*c]++;
   /* Let k be smallest index s.t. H[k]>1. */
      int k=0;
      while ( H[k]<2 ) k++;
   if ( H[k]==2 && k==1729 ) System.out.println( "confirmed" );
   else System.out.println( "not confirmed" );
```

Hash Tables

A *hash table,* sometimes referred to as a *hash set,* can be viewed as a representation of a collection with the benefit of direct, indexed access (like histograms), and the ability to store values of arbitrary type (e.g., as in a list). All the limitations of histograms are resolved with hash tables.

We present hash tables starting with histograms, and then make five changes:[121]

First, we replace the frequency count stored in each element of the histogram, H[k], with a reference to an individual array that lists the items of the multiset with a given key value k. In general, the size of each array, n_k, and the number of elements in the array prefix, s_k, will differ. Each H[k] is called a *bucket*.

Second, we relax the requirement that the integer elements of the multiset are limited to the range 0 through maxValue; rather, we allow any positive values of type **int**. We don't want array H to be that big, so rather than indexing H by key k, we index it by hash(k) **mod** hSize, where hash is a function that maps any possible key value into the range 0 through 2^{31}-1. This many-to-one mapping frees us to make H whatever size we want.

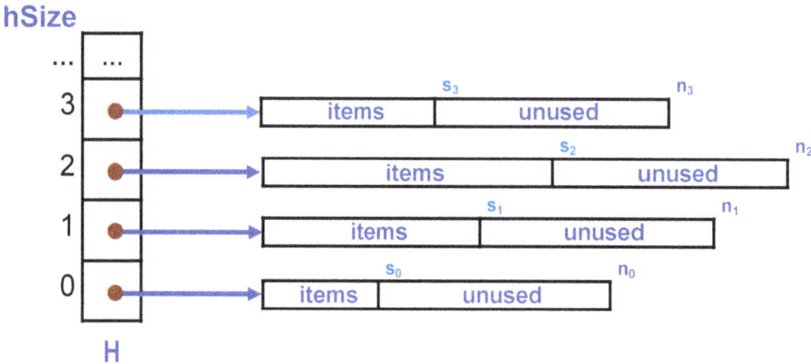

A good hash function thoroughly scrambles keys, and results in a high likelihood that the number of items in each bucket will be (nearly) uniformly distributed. Because items with different keys may map to the same bucket, which is known as a *collision*, a Sequential Search in the bucket's array will be needed to find items with a given key k within a given bucket.

Third, we observe that with the introduction of a hash function, there is no longer any reason to restrict attention to **int** keys. The domain of function hash can be any datatype, e.g., pairs of integers, or strings of characters. As long as function hash maps such keys into integers, we get the benefit of direct access via H.

Fourth, we note that after identifying the array of items for a bucket, processing reverts to Sequential Search. However, because the arrays are far shorter, the average time to search the array is drastically reduced—provided we set an appropriate size for H. If H is too short, the individual arrays will be too long. In the limit (when H is way too short), the benefit of direct access via H is totally lost, and we revert to maintaining the multiset in a single array. If H is too long, it will be too sparsely populated, with many empty buckets and much wasted space in H. We seek a happy medium, which can be accomplished by dynamically keeping track of the total number of items in the table, and adjusting the length of H so that the lengths of the bucket arrays remain, on average, no worse than some given constant. Typically, when the threshold is crossed, we double the length of H. Because changing hSize scrambles hash values, the doubling requires that individual items be redistributed to different buckets. The cost of doubling H as a hash table grows can be amortized across all insertions that caused it to grow. This accounting device results in a constant-time cost per item lookup, the same as with the original histogram.

Finally, we observe that something must be done whenever an individual array,

121. This section presents the principles underlying hash tables. In Chapter 18, we present the built-in notion in Java known as a HashSet (p. 315), but for now the similarity should be considered inexact.

say, bucket b, uses up its available space, i.e., when s_b reaches n_b. Array doubling, as described earlier in the chapter, could be used. Typically, however, the items in a bucket are not stored in arrays. Rather, each item is stored in a separate block of dynamically allocated storage, and the items of the bucket are chained together in a linearly-linked fashion:

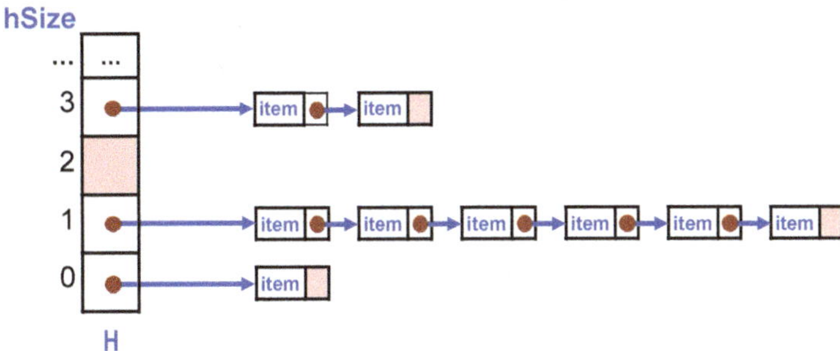

This linked representation of buckets obviates the need for array doublings for individual buckets.

Two-Dimensional Arrays

Now that it has been revealed that a one-dimensional array is really a reference (•) to an array object, and we have seen in Hash Tables an example of an array each of whose elements is an array, it is time to fess up to the fact that a two-dimensional array is really a reference to a one-dimensional array object whose elements are references to one-dimensional array objects.

Thus, the two-dimensional array declaration:

```
int A[][] = new int[3][3];
```

really creates this structure:

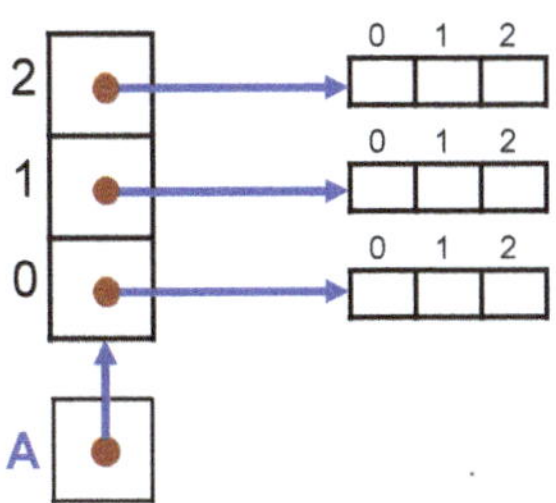

which is strikingly similar to the (initial) structure of a Hash Table (developed above).

As illustrated by Hash Tables, the lengths of each one-dimensional "column array object" need not be the same. When this occurs, the array is known as *ragged*.

For example, the following code creates a 3-by-3 triangular array:

```
int A[][] = new int[3][];
for (int r=0; r<3; r++) A[r] = new int[r+1];
```

Chapter 2 (p. 31) described the layout of a one-dimensional array in a byte-addressable memory as looking like this:

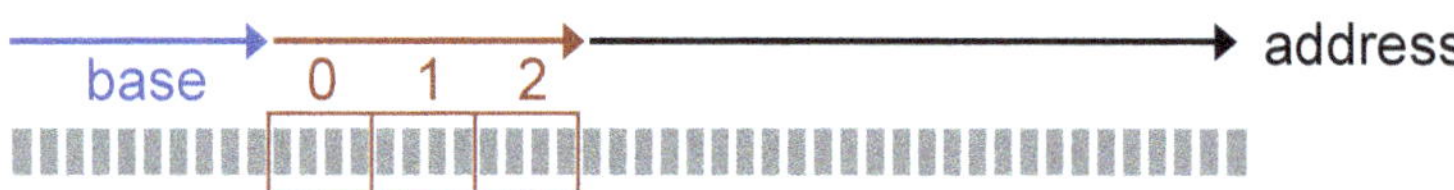

where a "reference to an array object" can be understood as the base address of the array in memory. Similarly, the triangular array created by the above code can be understood as this memory layout:

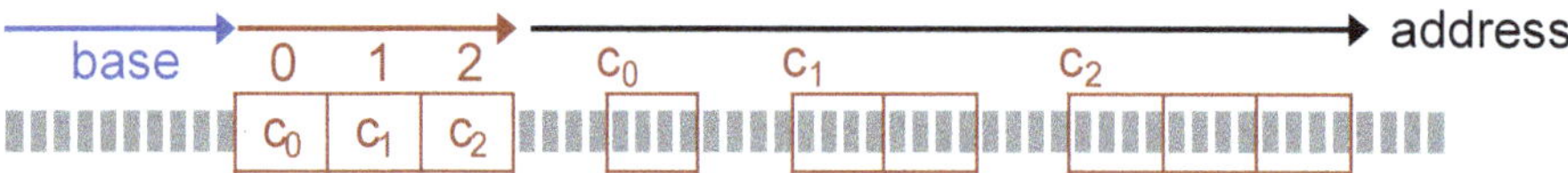

where c_0, c_1, and c_2 are the base addresses of the three column arrays of lengths 1, 2, and 3 (respectively), which can be located anywhere in the memory, and in any order.[122]

---

122. A ragged 2-D array is used to advantage in Chapter 17 Graphs and Depth-First Search. A graph is a collection of *nodes* with *edges* between them. In the *edge-list* representation of a graph, nodes are integers, *n*, and the list of edges from each node *n* is stored as a one-dimensional "column" array that is referred to in element *n* of the one-dimensional "row" array. The elements of the graph, viewed as a 2-D array, are integers, i.e., the target nodes of edges.

In contrast to the edge-list representation of a graph, an *adjacency matrix* represents a graph in a square 2-D **boolean** array G, where G[*n*][*m*] is **true** if and only if there is an edge from node *n* to node *m*.

CHAPTER 13

Cellular Automata

In the 1940s, von Neumann[123] and Ulam conceived of a two-dimensional model of space known as a *cellular automaton* [23]. In this model, the *Universe* consists of a rectangular grid of *cells*, each in a given *state*. *Time* advances in discrete steps, with each cell deciding synchronously what state it will enter at the next clock tick based on its current state and the current states of its neighbors. Each cell makes its decision independently, but all cells follow the same rules in doing so.

This chapter presents cellular automata for the purpose of illustrating the manipulation of two-dimensional arrays. It is also chock full of **for**-statements, their constant companions. It is important that you be totally comfortable with nested iteration, and the sample code herein (with **for**-statements nested five deep!) should help in this.

Cellular automata are an interesting concept in modern physics because some believe that space in the Universe (the real one) is effectively a cellular automaton, and that the model is a viable candidate for how the Universe works [24].

An issue that concerned von Neumann was whether a local configuration within a cellular automaton could reproduce. More precisely, the question was whether there exists an initial configuration of cells in various states, and rules whereby those cells transmogrify, such that after some finite period of time, two copies of that same configuration would exist side by side. And similarly, after still more time, there would be four copies of the configuration, then eight, and so on. von Neuman succeeded in devising such a machine with 29 states [25]. Only a few years later, Watson and Crick discovered DNA, with its similar ability to self-replicate.

In 1970, John Conway devised a 2-state cellular automaton that is more biological than physical. The two states are called *alive* and *dead*, and Conway's rules determine which cells live, die, and are born in each generation [26].

The code developed in this chapter first establishes a general framework for simulating any cellular automaton, and then focuses on Conway's Game of Life as a specific example. The development illustrates the top-down programming style advocated in the text.

---

123. John von Neumann [45] was a towering figure of the 20th century who played vital roles in Mathematics, Logic, Physics, the Manhattan Project (which created the first atomic bomb), Game Theory (he invented it), and development of the earliest computers built in the United States [48].

Top-level Code Structure

In general, a program is a collection of classes, but the program we will write is simple enough to require only one:

```
/* A cellular automaton. */
class CellularAutomaton {
   } /* CellularAutomaton */
```
1

Method `main` of this class will contain the automaton simulator:

```
/* A cellular automaton. */
class CellularAutomaton {
   /* Simulate a cellular automaton. */
   static void main() {
      } /* main */
   } /* CellularAutomaton */
```
2

The empty template for method `main` is where we begin.

The fundamental pattern for iterative computation:

```
/* Initialize. */
while ( /* not finished */ ) {
   /* Compute. */
   /* Go on to next. */
   }
```

would be appropriate if we want to simulate an indefinite number of generations. We could use the *condition* **true** if we want to run until manually interrupting execution.

We choose instead to iterate a fixed number of generations:

```
/* Initialize. */
for (int generation=1; generation<=LAST_GEN; generation++)
   /* Compute. */
```

This pattern provides the top-level structure for method `main`.

Following the precept:

☞ **Many short procedures are better than large blocks of code.**

we introduce three methods: One for creating the initial Universe, one for displaying it, and a third for updating it to be the next generation. We assume that `generation` will be declared at the level of the class so that it can be accessed for display purposes:

3

```
/* A cellular automaton. */
class CellularAutomaton {
   static int generation;                         // Generation number.
   /* Simulate a cellular automaton. */
   static void main() {
      /* Create the initial Universe and display it. */
         Initialize();
         Display();
      /* Simulate and display remaining generations. */
         for (generation=1; generation<=LAST_GEN; generation++) {
            /* Update Universe to next generation and display it. */
               NextGeneration();
               Display();
            }
      } /* main */
   } /* CellularAutomaton */
```

Having conceived of three methods, we immediately write their stubs to get that out of the way:

4

```
/* A cellular automaton. */
class CellularAutomaton {
   ...
   /* Create the initial Universe. */
      static void Initialize() { } /* Initialize */
   /* Display the Universe. */
      static void Display() { } /* Display */
   /* Update Universe to be the next generation. */
      static void NextGeneration() { } /* NextGeneration */
   ...
   } /* CellularAutomaton */
```

We are proceeding in a strictly top-down fashion, which also happens to follow the precept:

☞ **Defer challenging code for later; do the easy parts first.**

Entering boilerplate stubs for methods is mindless, and we might as well get it out of the way while warming up.

Data Representation

The Universe of the automaton is unbounded, but we are going to want to watch a finite piece of it evolve within the (finite) output console. Accordingly, we declare an `M`-by-`N` array `old[][]` to represent the region of the Universe being modeled, where `M` and `N` are defined constants of the program.

Each cell determines its next state synchronously, so it will not be possible to update `old[][]` *in situ*. Said differently, the simulation must proceed as if all cells determine their next state simultaneously and in parallel, but because our simulation is sequential, we cannot update cells *in situ* because doing so would interfere with the decision of neighboring cells yet to be simulated. Accordingly, we declare `next[][]`, a parallel Universe in which to compute the next generation:

5

```
/* A cellular automaton. */
class CellularAutomaton {
   static final int M = 6;                      // Height of Universe.
   static final int N = 20;                     // Width of Universe.
   static int old[][] = new int[M][N];          // old Universe.
   static int next[][] = new int[M][N];         // next Universe.
   static final int LAST_GEN = 50;              // Last generation.
   static int generation;                       // Generation number.
   ...
   } /* CellularAutomaton */
```

These variables are declared within the same class as the methods we are writing, and accordingly are accessible to them.[124]

Display

To output a two-dimensional array, it is commonplace to use a row-major order enumeration, which pattern should be absolutely second nature to any programmer. It is convenient to provide a header that separates one generation from the next:

6

```
/* Display Universe old[][] as an M-by-N grid. */
static void Display() {
   System.out.println( "Generation: " + generation );
   for (int r=0; r<M; r++) {
      for (int c=0; c<N; c++) System.out.print( old[r][c] + " " );
      System.out.println();
      }
   } /* Display */
```

With `Display` in hand, we can execute the code. We have an empty Universe, and no rules that update cells. Only outer space. But the simulation runs without error.

Update

In general, the rules for updating the state of a cellular automaton can be defined in a function `F` that maps the cell's current state, `old[r][c]`, and that state's neighbors, to its new state, `next[r][c]`. It is common to consider eight neighbors, i.e., to include diagonal neighbors, in which case `F` is a function of nine arguments. Restricted notions of neighborhood could be considered, e.g., only four:

7

```
/* Update old[][] to be the next generation of the Universe. */
static void NextGeneration() {
   /* Determine each state of next[][] as F(old[][] states). */
      for (int r=0; r<M; r++)
         for (int c=0; c<N; c++)
            /* next[r][c] = F( old[r][c] and its neighbors ); */
   /* Swap old[][] and next[][] Universes. */
      int temp[][] = old; old=next; next=temp;
   } /* NextGeneration */
```

124. The modifier **`final`** on a declaration signifies that the variable has its final value, i.e., it is a constant. The convention in Java, as in many other programming languages, is that the names of such constants are all capital letters.

It is very pleasant to see the application of arrays as references, whereby the swap of the references `old` and `next` supports adopting a new Universe in a constant-time operation. The two `M`-by-`N` arrays are allocated once and for all when class `CellularAutomaton` is instantiated (at the beginning of the program's execution), and thereafter each generation switches back and forth between use of one or the other of them. See Chapter 12 (p. 202) if this code is mysterious to you.

We are deferring, for now, the question about how to handle the neighbors of cells at the edge of our finite portion of an infinite Universe.

This step completes the framework for arbitrary cellular automata with integer states. You may wish to experiment with various functions `F`, but we will move on to the Game of Life.

Game of Life

As mentioned in the chapter introduction, the Game of Life is a set of rules for a cellular automaton with only two states: alive and dead. The rules are as follows:

- Live cells with two or three live neighbors survive, other live cells die.
- Dead cells with three live neighbors come alive; other dead cells stay dead.

Because there are only two states, the general framework is specialized to model a Universe of **`boolean`** rather than **`int`** cells. We use **false** to represent dead, and **true** to represent alive. By virtue of the default initialization of **`boolean`** variables to **false**, we automatically start out with two Universes of dead cells:

8

```
/* A cellular automaton. */
class CellularAutomaton {
   static final int M = 6;                          // Height of Universe.
   static final int N = 20;                         // Width of Universe.
   static boolean old[][] = new boolean[M][N];      // cell true iff alive.
   static boolean next[][] = new boolean[M][N];     // cell true iff alive.
   static final int LAST_GEN = 50;                  // Last generation.
   static int generation;                           // Generation number.
   ...
   } /* CellularAutomaton */
```

Rather than printing each cell as **true** or **false**, we also modify method `Display` so that it uses "X" for alive, and "_" for dead:

9

```
/* Display Universe old[][] as an M-by-N grid. */
static void Display() {
   System.out.println( "Generation: " + generation );
   for (int r=0; r<M; r++) {
      for (int c=0; c<N; c++)
         if ( old[r][c] ) System.out.print( "X" );
         else System.out.print( "_" );
      System.out.println();
      }
   } /* Display */
```

The obvious two-step Sequential Refinement of the code to compute `next[r][c]` for each `old[r][c]` is an instance of the compute-use pattern:

```
/* Compute. */
/* Use. */
```

Specifically:

10

```
/* Update old[][] to be the next generation of the Universe. */
static void NextGeneration() {
   /* Determine each state of next[][] as Life(old[][] states). */
      for (int r=0; r<M; r++)
         for (int c=0; c<N; c++) {
            /* Let liveNeighbors be number alive around old[r][c]. */
            /* Set next[r][c] according to the birth and death rules. */
            }
   /* Swap old[][] and next[][] Universes. */
      int temp[][] = old; old=next; next=temp;
   } /* NextGeneration */
```

The easiest way to examine the eight neighbors of `old[r][c]` is to inspect the 3-by-3 region centered there, and ignore the cell in the middle. We will increment the `liveNeighbors` counter for each such cell that is alive. Take pride in the fact that the statement that will perform that increment is five **for**-loops deep (counting the loop that steps through generations), and you are not at all troubled. You are learning to comprehend computational structures hierarchically, and are taking it in your stride.

The code to compute `next[r][c]` is a straightforward four-way Case Analysis that follows the rules.

11

```
/* Update old[][] to be the next generation of the Universe. */
static void NextGeneration() {
   /* Determine each state of next[][] as Life(old[][] states). */
      for (int r=0; r<M; r++)
         for (int c=0; c<N; c++) {
            /* Let liveNeighbors be number alive around old[r][c]. */
               int liveNeighbors = 0;
               for (int dr=-1; dr<=+1; dr++)
                  for (int dc=-1; dc<=+1; dc++)
                     if ( (dr!=0||dc!=0) && old[r+dr][c+dc] )
                        liveNeighbors++;
            /* Set next[r][c] according to the birth and death rules. */
               if ( old[r][c] ) /* Currently live. */
                  if ( liveNeighbors==2 || liveNeighbors==3 )
                     next[r][c] = true;
                  else next[r][c] = false;
               else /* Currently dead. */
                  if ( liveNeighbors==3 ) next[r][c] = true;
                  else next[r][c] = false;
            }
   /* Swap old[][] and next[][] Universes. */
      int temp[][] = old; old=next; next=temp;
   } /* NextGeneration */
```

If your trigger finger hits the "execute button", you will be sorely disappointed: We have followed the admonition to defer boundary conditions until dead last, and have not yet taken them into account. What is the problem? The upper-leftmost neighbor of `old[0][0]` is cell `old[-1][-1]`, which causes a "subscript-out-of-bounds" exception. In fact, the entire outside boundary of our finite portion of the Universe is surrounded by such out-of-bounds cells!

The motivation for deferring consideration of boundary conditions is the hope that once the code for the general case is in place, it will be possible to slip something in "surgically". The offending code is the expression that is colored blue, above. Those are the subscripts with potential to go out of bounds.

A common technique for a simulation of an infinite space within a limited observation window is to do the simulation on the finite surface of a torus. This mapping deals with boundary-conditions by eliminating them, i.e., a torus has no boundaries. We only need to index neighbors using modular arithmetic (as described on page 118):

12

```
/* Update old[][] to be the next generation of the Universe. */
static void NextGeneration() {
   /* Determine each state of next[][] as Life(old[][] states). */
      for (int r=0; r<M; r++)
         for (int c=0; c<N; c++) {
            /* Let liveNeighbors be number alive around old[r][c]. */
               int liveNeighbors = 0;
               for (int dr=-1; dr<=+1; dr++)
                  for (int dc=-1; dc<=+1; dc++)
                     if ( (dr!=0||dc!=0) && old[(r+dr)%M][(c+dc)%N] )
                        liveNeighbors++;
            /* Set next[r][c] according to the birth and death rules. */
               if ( old[r][c] ) /* Currently live. */
                  if ( liveNeighbors==2 || liveNeighbors==3 )
                     next[r][c]= true;
                  else next[r][c] = false;
               else /* Currently dead. */
                  if ( liveNeighbors==3 ) next[r][c]=true;
                  else next[r][c]=false;
            }
   /* Swap old[][] and next[][] Universes. */
      int temp[][] = old; old=next; next=temp;
   } /* NextGeneration */
```

The program now works like a charm, with a minor problem: We are still in outer space with no existing life. Specifically, method `Initialize` is still a stub.

We now define a bit of life known as a glider:[125]

13

```
/* Establish original configuration in old. */
static void Initialize() {
   /* Glider */
      old[0][1] = old[1][2] = old[2][3] = old[2][1] = old[2][2] = true;
   } /* Initialize */
```

and watch it transform in the output, coasting diagonally down and across the screen every fourth generation. (A).

125. We use a slight generalization of assignment statements that permits more than one target *variable* to be listed.

As a final step, we arrange for the generations to overwrite one another (by putting a form-feed character at the beginning of the header), and introduce a timing delay of 300 milliseconds to allow each generation to be viewed before it is overwritten:

```
/* Display Universe old[][] as an M-by-N grid. */
static void Display() {
   System.out.println( "\u000CGeneration: " + generation );
   for (int r=0; r<M; r++) {
      for (int c=0; c<N; c++)
         if ( old[r][c] ) System.out.print( "X" );
         else System.out.print( "_" );
      System.out.println();
      }
   /* Sleep for 300 milliseconds. */
      try { Thread.sleep(300); } catch (InterruptedException ie) { }
   } /* Display */
```
14

This step completes the implementation of the Game of Life.

You are now all set to try out different versions of Initialize, perhaps selected from the literature.

A

```
Generation: 0
_X__________________
__X_________________
XXX_________________
____________________
____________________
____________________
Generation: 1
____________________
X_X_________________
_XX_________________
_X__________________
____________________
____________________
Generation: 2
____________________
__X_________________
X_X_________________
_XX_________________
____________________
____________________
Generation: 3
____________________
_X__________________
__XX________________
_XX_________________
____________________
____________________
Generation: 4
____________________
__X_________________
___X________________
_XXX________________
____________________
____________________
etc.
```

CHAPTER 14

Knight's Tour

This chapter presents a solution to an ancient puzzle. The development of a program that solves the puzzle is traced from start to finish, and illustrates the process of a complete coding project. Each step along the way is explained in terms of the precept being followed at that juncture. Many precepts will be familiar from earlier chapters; others will be new. The essential content of the chapter is the overall process of writing a program, from beginning to end, and the rationale for proceeding in the order presented.

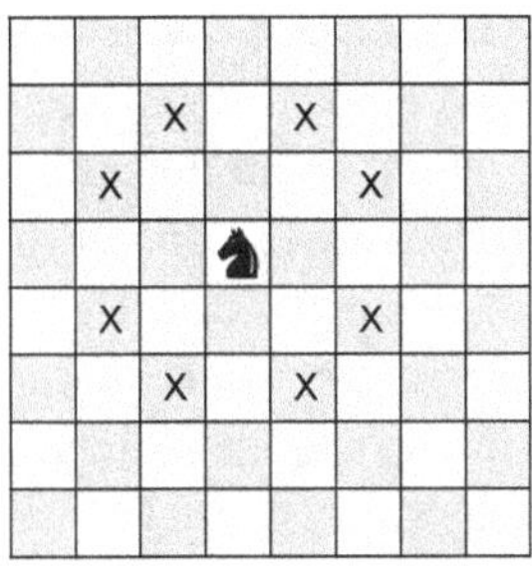

Background. Chess is played by moving pieces on a board that consists of an 8-by-8 two-dimensional grid of squares. Pieces can move from square to square in only proscribed ways. A Knight is a piece that is permitted to travel two squares in one direction (horizontal or vertical), and one square in a perpendicular direction (vertical or horizontal) on each move. Thus, as shown in the figure, if a Knight is placed in the square signified by ♞, then in one move it can travel to any of the squares marked "X", and to no other square. Note that a Knight that is too close to the edge of the board may not be able to move to as many as eight other squares. Suppose a Knight is placed on the upper-left square of the board. We may ask: Is it possible for the Knight to move successively such that it visits all sixty-four squares of the board without ever visiting any square more than once? Such a sequence of squares is called a *Knight's Tour.*[126]

1	10	23	42	7	4	13	18
24	41	8	3	12	17	6	15
9	2	11	22	5	14	19	32
0	25	40	35	20	31	16	0
0	36	21	0	39	0	33	30
26	0	38	0	34	29	0	0
37	0	0	28	0	0	0	0
0	27	0	0	0	0	0	0

Problem Statement. Write a program that attempts to find a Knight's Tour. The output should be an 8-by-8 grid showing the order in which each square is visited, or the numeral 0 if the square is unvisited. Thus, for example, the output of a program that fails to complete a Knight's Tour might be as shown in the figure. Ideally, the program will find a complete Knight's Tour, but this is not required. The partial tour shown stopped at the square numbered 42 because the Knight got stuck in a *cul-de-sac,* i.e., a square from which there is no way out. Your program should not give up unless the Knight gets stuck in a cul-de-sac, but it need not complete a tour.

Understanding the Problem

The given problem statement is rather complete, but a bit of exploration is still recommended:

126. Some formulations of the problem require that the Knight return to the original square. We shall ignore this constraint.

☞ **Make sure you understand the problem.**

You can read and reread the description, and study the sample tour presented, but it is important to test your understanding by working a solution by hand:

☞ **Confirm your understanding of a programming problem with concrete examples.**

There is really nothing special about the fact that the board is 8-by-8, so it occurs to us to simplify our task by considering a smaller board, which will have the benefit of eliminating the tedious detail of the 8-by-8 case. Considering multiple examples often reveals aspects of a problem that might not have been initially apparent. Accordingly, we generalize the problem to an *n*-by-*n* board, and then gain a better understanding by instantiating *n* with different specific values.

For *n*=1, the tour is complete from the get-go, so in general, a complete tour is possible.

For *n*=2, no complete tour is possible because the Knight is stuck in the upper left square with nowhere to go. From these two examples, we have learned that for some *n* there is a solution, and for others there isn't. This may be useful to know.

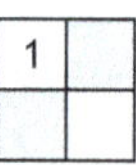

For *n*=3, we can wander around the perimeter of the board, but can never reach the center square, so no complete tour is possible in this case either. In fact, only two distinct maximal-length tours are possible because after the first move (for which there are two choices, as shown), there is only one unvisited square to which the Knight can move at each subsequent step. The example illustrates a second case for which no complete tour is possible, but we learn two additional things, as well.

1	4	7
6		2
3	8	5

1	6	3
4		8
7	2	5

First, sometimes the Knight has choices, e.g., on the first move, and sometimes moves are forced, e.g., after the first move, there are no choices.

Second, we notice that the two tours are really one and the same, in the sense that they are symmetric images of one another. Specifically, flip the board around the major diagonal, and you get the other tour. Leveraging the problem's symmetries may (or may not) prove to be a useful technique as we go forward.

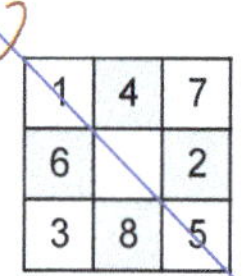

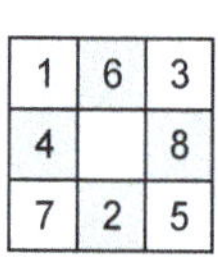

Notice that we have picked up on the style of pictorial images introduced in the problem statement, and are using it to advantage. Although we did this instinctively, it is worth stating the precept explicitly:

☞ **Invent (or learn) diagrammatic ways to express concepts.**

For *n*=4, we encounter the full complexity of the problem. In this case, the Knight has numerous choices available to it along the way. Trial and error may be inconclusive, and we may give up in frustration before finding a solution. In fact, there is none, but this may not be obvious.

It may cross our mind that perhaps only the trivial case of *n*=1 has a complete solution, but we really have no basis for concluding this. We could think deeply at this point, following the precept:

☞ **Analyze first.**

and attempt to derive an algorithm that would be guaranteed to find a complete tour whenever one exists. However, the problem statement invites us to output a partial (i.e., incomplete) tour, so we opt to proceed without a deeper understanding. There's no point in trying to solve a harder problem than we have been asked to solve.

Top-level Code Structure

It is our intention to test our code frequently during development. Accordingly, we begin with a template for the entire program, which will be needed before the code will even compile. This template is sometimes referred to as *boilerplate*:

1

```
/* Knight's Tour: See problem statement in Chapter 14. */
class KnightsTour {
   /* Output a (possibly partial) Knight's Tour. */
   static void main() { } /* main */
   } /* KnightsTour */
```

Class and method definitions each have header comments:

☞ **A class header-comment is descriptive, and omits the details of the methods and variables of the class. Reference available auxiliary documentation.**

A class header will often contain information such as who wrote the class, when it was written, revision history, and the like.

The method header for `main` states its effect, and nothing else:

☞ **A method header-comment specifies the effect of invoking it, and (if the method has non-void type) the value returned. If the method has parameters, the specification is written in terms of those parameters.**

The practice of repeating a class or method name after its definition can be very helpful for keeping track of your location in program text, and for keeping braces matched and appropriately indented:

☞ **Label the end of a long class or method definition with its name in a comment.**

The program has no input, and it cannot output anything until the Knight has either completed a tour, or is stuck in a cul-de-sac. Accordingly, the code can be structured as an instance of the *initialize-compute-output* architectural pattern:

```
/* Initialize. */
/* Compute. */
/* Output. */
```

We drop this pattern into the body of method `main` as scaffolding for the program:

2

```
/* Knight's Tour: See problem statement in Chapter 14. */
class KnightsTour {
   /* Output a (possibly partial) Knight's Tour. */
   static void main() {
      /* Initialize. */
      /* Compute. */
      /* Output. */
      } /* main */
   } /* KnightsTour */
```

This has largely been busywork, but we might as well get it over with early. More importantly, we have established that the top-level structure for the program has three major parts, which will inform our subsequent considerations.

Having advanced the code a bit, it's time to work on the data representation:

☞ **Dovetail thinking about code and data.**

lest one consideration get too far ahead of the other.

Data Representation

Data representation is central to a program. "Data" refers not to "input data" but to the values in internal program variables that the program manipulates. You may have been ruminating on this already, but frontal consideration of the issue is now upon us:

☞ **A program's internal data representation is central to the code; consider it early.**

The obvious things that must be represented are the board, and the partial tours being computed.

Board Representation 1

We begin by choosing an initial representation of the Chess board, keeping in mind that it may prove desirable to modify it later.

A straightforward representation of the board is as a two-dimensional array. In deciding on this, we instinctively model a physical object, the 2-D board, with a corresponding data structure, a 2-D array. Such parallel structure has appeal, but we note that mere resemblance to the physical system being modeled is not a sufficient justification for a representation:

☞ **The touchstone of a data representation is its utility in performing the needed operations.**

It remains to seen whether there might be a better alternative.

The default rule for naming variables is:

☞ **Aspire to making code self-documenting by choosing descriptive names.**

but in this case the board is so central to our program that we are not in danger of needing the help of a full name. The seemingly-countervailing rule may be more apt:

☞ **Use single-letter variable names when it makes code more understandable.**

Accordingly, we choose the letter `B` for the two-dimensional array representing the board. Even if your personal taste inclines you to spell it out as `board`, you may wish to use `B` during development, and then rename it later, (say) using a rename feature of your program editor.

We hinted at the possibility that we might discover a good reason to change the board representation during development of the program. It is important to anticipate such changes so that they are not too disruptive, if and when they arise.

One approach to minimizing future disruptions is:

☞ **Minimize use of literal numerals in code; define and use symbolic constants.**

The use of symbolic constants makes code more understandable because the name is mnemonic, whereas a constant is just a bare numeral. But more importantly, the use of a symbolic constant reduces the number of places that will need to be changed if we wish to alter the value.

An ultimate goal is one place in the code to change, if need be:

☞ **Aim for single-point-of-definition.**

Accordingly, we introduce the symbolic constant `N` for the size of the array, and `lo` and `hi` for the low and high ranges of its indices. We also introduce `BLANK` as the symbolic name of the value representing a currently-unvisited square, thereby avoiding explicit and cryptic uses of `0` in the code.

The need to change the value of a constant may arise for various reasons. First, the problem specification itself might change. For example, we can anticipate that as soon as we get the code working for the 8-by-8 case, someone will ask: How about a 6-by-6 board? How nice it would be to be able to change the definition of `N`, in one place, and have the program immediately work correctly for the revised board size.

A second and somewhat more subtle reason the value of a constant may change is that we may discover, in the course of writing the code, a good reason to pad `B` with extra cells, e.g., we may want to model an 8-by-8 Chess board in a 12-by-12 array, allowing for a double-cell border around a central 8-by-8 region.

The definitions of `N`, `lo` and `hi` can be written in various ways. Here are three, in order of increasing utility:

- `int N=8; int lo=0; int hi=7;` This achieves the first-order benefit of replacing these uses of 8, 0, and 7 in the program with names that render the code self-documenting. This is a major step toward providing single-points-of-definition.
- `int N=8; int lo=0; int hi=lo+7;` This anticipates that `lo` may change, and if it does, allows the value of `hi` to be adjusted automatically.
- `int N=8; int lo=0; int hi=lo+N-1;` This also allows `N` to change, and lets `hi` take on the correct value automatically.

Clearly, the last choice is best.

Declarations for the variables and constants we have been discussing are written at the beginning of class `KnightsTour`, and are provided with *representation invariants*:

☞ **A representation invariant describes the value(s) of one or more program variables, and their relationships to one another as the program runs. The invariant is typically written as a comment associated with the declaration(s) of the relevant variable(s).**

Here's the code:

```
/* Knight's Tour: See problem statement in Chapter 14. */                3
class KnightsTour {
   /* Chess board B is an N-by-N int array, for N==8. Unvisited squares
      are BLANK, and row and column indices range from lo to hi. */
      static final int N = 8;              // Size of B.
      static int B[][] = new int[N][N];    // Chess board, initially 0s.
      static final int BLANK = 0;          // Unvisited square in board.
      static final int lo = 0;             // First row or column index.
      static final int hi = lo+N-1;        // Last row or column index.
      ...
   } /* KnightsTour */
```

Variables N, BLANK, lo, and hi are each given the additional modifier **final**, which states that these variables, as initialized in their declarations, are not permitted to change subsequently, i.e., they are truly constant, and are not allowed on the left side of assignment statements. It would be okay to omit **final**, and have the self-discipline to never change the values of these variables, but you should instead:

☞ **Leverage features of the programming language and its compiler that protect you from mistakes.**

Why take on the burden of self-discipline when the compiler can be your enforcer?

Along those lines, now would be a good time to compile the program, and discover any typos and syntax errors that may have crept in. Nip problems in the bud:

☞ **Never be (very) lost. Don't stray far from a correct (albeit, partial) program.**

You could even run the program. Of course, it doesn't do anything interesting, but at least you can confirm that it doesn't crash with a runtime error exception (as it would if N were inadvertently defined as a negative number).

Our use of symbolic constants is aimed at keeping code limber, following the precept:

☞ **Avoid rigid code. Anticipate change. Parameterize.**

It is worth mentioning, however, that endless different changes may arise, and it is impossible to anticipate them all. The degree of parameterization adopted may be a matter of personal taste, or may reflect your circumstances. For example, it would not have been difficult to allow for the possibility of boards that aren't square. We chose to not do so, but you might have chosen otherwise. Note that too much parameterization can easily make code more difficult to understand.

We have defined the size, shape, and type of the board representation as the **int** array B, but have not yet said what it contains.

We turn now to the representation of tours.

Tour Representation 1

The obvious representation for a (partial) tour corresponds directly to the images we have been using, above: Store the visit-sequence number of a square in the corresponding element of array B, and store BLANK in the other array elements that correspond to squares not currently on the tour. Defining BLANK to be 0 guarantees that it cannot be confused with a square that is currently on a tour.

We test the utility of this representation by considering the operations that will need to performed on it, and with it.

Clearly, the Initialize and Output steps will be straightforward: Initialize can store a 1 in square `B[0][0]`, and Output can print out array `B`.

What operations must the Compute step perform, and is the proposed representation sufficient and convenient for them? The key operation will be to extend a partial tour by one square. This will entail finding a `BLANK` element in array `B` that is reachable in one legal move from the last square of the present tour, and storing the next visit-sequence number there. To do this, we will need to know the location and visit-sequence number of that last square, which is the Knight's present location, as it were. How will we know where that is?

Refer to the example given in the problem statement, and ask: Where is the last square of the partial tour shown? It turns out to be in row 0, column 3; the array element containing 42. And how did you deduce that? You had to search the entire array to find the maximum visit-sequence number. This could be done, so the representation would be sufficient, but it is certainly not convenient. Surely, we don't want to have to repeatedly search for the Knight's location in the present tour, especially since we just decided to move there in the previous iteration.

The key precept is:

> ☞ **Introduce redundant variables in a representation to simplify code, or make it more efficient.**

Clearly, we can and should maintain the row and column indices of the Knight's present position in redundant variables. Let's use `r` and `c` for those variables. The visit-sequence number of the Knight's present location is knowable as `B[r][c]`, but it will also be useful to introduce another redundant variable, `move`, for that.

As with the board representation, we declare the variables that represent the present tour at the beginning of class `KnightsTour`, (say) after the variables for the board, and provide a representation invariant for them:

```
/* Knight's Tour: See problem statement in Chapter 14. */
class KnightsTour {
   /* Chess board B is an N-by-N int array, for N==8. Unvisited squares
      are BLANK, and row and column indices range from lo to hi. */
      ...
   /* A Tour of length move is given by elements of B numbered 1
      to move. Squares numbered consecutively go from ⟨0,0⟩ to
      ⟨r,c⟩, and correspond to legal moves for a Knight. */
      static int move;      // Length of Tour.
      static int r, c;      // Position of Knight.
   ...
   } /* KnightsTour */
```
4

The diagram in the margin illustrates the representation invariant at a moment when the path has reached move 5. The path is shown with a gray background.

Our goal in the Compute step will be to maintain this representation invariant while increasing the length of the tour as much as we can.

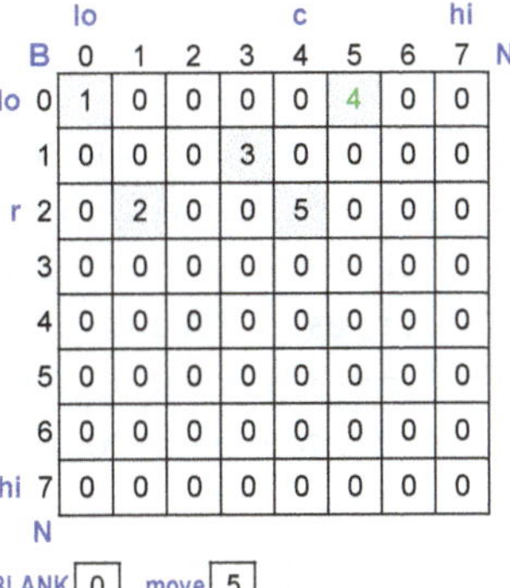

Alternative Board and Tour Representations

We have readily embraced the "obvious" representations of board and tour (above), but a bit a care and reflection are called for before we plow ahead. Might there be an alternative representation that is equally good, or perhaps even better?

When we considered the operations that the Compute step must perform, we focused on *extending* a tour one move at a time in the forward direction. Although we haven't yet devised an algorithm, we are aware of a technique known as *backtracking* in which, having reached a cul-de-sac, we would wish to *retract* the last move of the tour in order to explore the possible advantages of alternative, earlier moves.

Accordingly, we ask: Does our representation conveniently support backing out of the last move? Specifically, we would need to replace the present ⟨`r`,`c`⟩ with the coordinates of the next-to-last square of the tour. But where is that square? Our representation would seem to require that we search among the (up to) eight places from which the Knight might have come for the element of `B` that is numbered `move-1`. Such a search is doable, but is unfortunate.

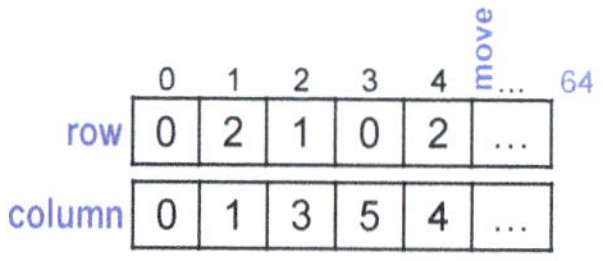

There is a completely different representation of a tour that would simplify retraction: We could use lists, as discussed in Chapter 12 Collections. Specifically, instead of storing visit-sequence numbers in elements of array `B`, we could store the coordinates of the consecutive squares of a tour in two 1-dimensional arrays, `row` and `column`. For example, the tour of length 5 that is shown on the previous page, which visits squares ⟨0,0⟩, ⟨2,1⟩, ⟨1,3⟩, ⟨0,5⟩, and ⟨2,4⟩, would be represented as shown.

	0	1	2	3	4	move ... 64
row	0	2	1	0	2	...
column	0	1	3	5	4	...

The coordinates of the Knight's current position would be given by `row[move-1]` and `column[move-1]`, i.e., 2 and 4. Extending the tour, (say) to square ⟨1,2⟩ would be effected by appending 1 and 2, respectively, to the ends of the `row` and `column` lists, i.e., set `row[move]` to 1, `column[move]` to 2, and incrementing `move`. Retracting the last square from the tour would be effected by decrementing `move`, with no need to search for the next-to-last square. By decrementing `move`, the Knight effectively returns to the previous square of the tour, as if by magic.

The list representation of a tour simplifies retraction, but how well does it support extension? Specifically, how will the Compute step locate an unvisited square to which the Knight might move? Given that the Knight is currently at ⟨`row[move-1]`,`column[move-1]`⟩ it is easy enough to determine coordinates of squares reachable in one legal move, but how will we know that such a square is currently unvisited? If ⟨`r`,`c`⟩ are the coordinates of a candidate square, one could search the current tour (represented in lists `row` and `column`) for the absence of ⟨`r`,`c`⟩, in which case the square is unvisited:

```
/* = true if square at ⟨r,c⟩ is not on current tour, and false otherwise. */
static boolean isUnvisited(int r, int c) {
   int k = 0;
   while ( k<move && !(row[k]==r && column[k]==c) ) k++;
   return (k==move);
   }
```

Notice that the list representation of a tour completely obviates the need for an explicit representation of the board, i.e., `B` is not needed at all, at least not for the Compute step. However, recall that we disliked having to locate the next-to-last square using a search in `B`. Surely, having to use a search in lists `row` and `column` to determine whether a given square ⟨`r`,`c`⟩ is unvisited is as bad, or worse. Thus, the list representation of a tour, while sufficient, is unsatisfactory by itself.

What would be useful would be a redundant representation that would eliminate the need for search to determine whether square ⟨r,c⟩ is unvisited. How about a 2-D **boolean** array B, where B[r][c] is **true** if and only if the square with coordinates ⟨r,c⟩ is unvisited? Instead of searching for ⟨r,c⟩ in the lists row and column, we would then test B[r][c].

Amusingly, we've come almost full circle back to our original representation of a board. Only now, array B is **boolean** rather than **int**, and it serves only as an auxiliary data structure in support of the list representation of tours.

So, which representation do we prefer: The 2-D **int** array B containing visit-sequence numbers, or lists row and column containing the coordinates of visited squares on the tour?

Reflecting on the Output step, we realize that to produce a 2-D display requires having the visit-sequence numbers in a 2-D **int** array, anyway. This suggests that we might as well use the original representation. If it turns out that our algorithm uses backtracking, we can consider introducing lists row and column, not as a complete tour representation, but as redundant variables that serve only to facilitate retraction.

Note that the problem statement might have required that the program's output be presented as the linear sequence of tour squares identified by their coordinates, rather than in a 2-D display. Perhaps this would have tipped the balance in favor of the list representation of tours. In fact, if the tour were stored only in the 2-D array B, it would be a bit of a chore to output it as an itemization of the coordinates of the squares visited.

We have illustrated a situation that arises often: Competing representations, each with respective advantages and disadvantages. In weighing the tradeoffs between them, we have tried to anticipate future needs. But there is a limit to our ability to foresee shifting requirements.

☞ **Don't let the "perfect" be the enemy of the "good". Be prepared to compromise because there may be no perfect representation. Don't freeze.**

Accordingly, we will choose one representation, and move on. We note, however, a looming risk: The code we write is likely to be highly dependent on whichever representation we choose. We have advocated techniques, such as the use of symbolic constants, to help in keeping code limber. Coding now with respect to a specific data representation is an unfortunate step toward code ossification because a later change of representation may require major surgery on that code. We note the need for a technique that would ease this pain, but defer introducing it until Chapter 15 Running a Maze.[127]

Top-level Procedures

With the initial data representation settled (for now), it is time to return to the definition of main, and elaborate its subtasks. It is not necessary to describe them in terms of the program variables because the representation invariant spells that all out globally:

127. Exercise 76 asks you to revise the code for KnightsTour using data encapsulation, the technique introduced in Chapter 15 for isolating a data representation from the algorithm that is its client.

```
/* Knight's Tour: See problem statement in Chapter 14. */
class KnightsTour {
      ...
      /* Output a (possibly partial) Knight's Tour. */
      static void main() {
         /* Initialize: Establish invariant for a tour of length 1. */
         /* Compute: Extend the tour, if possible. */
         /* Output: Print tour as numbered cells in N-by-N grid of 0s. */
         } /* main */
   } /* KnightsTour */
```
5

Following the precept:

☞ **Many short procedures are better than large blocks of code.**

we introduce methods `Initialize`, `Solve`, and `Display` for the three subtasks:

```
/* Knight's Tour: See problem statement in Chapter 14. */
class KnightsTour {
      ...
      /* Output a (possibly partial) Knight's Tour. */
      static void main() {
         /* Initialize: Establish invariant for a tour of length 1. */
            Initialize();
         /* Compute: Extend the tour, if possible. */
            Solve();
         /* Output: Print tour as numbered cells in N-by-N grid of 0s. */
            Display();
         } /* main */
   } /* KnightsTour */
```
6

Method `Initialize` requires only a few lines because it benefits from built-in initialization of array `B` to 0, the very representation chosen for a `BLANK` board:

```
/* Knight's Tour: See problem statement in Chapter 14. */
class KnightsTour {
   ...
   /* Initialize: Establish invariant for a tour of length 1. */
   static void Initialize() {
      r = lo; c = lo;
      move = 1; B[r][c] = move;
      } /* Initialize */
   ...
   } /* KnightsTour */
```
7

For now, we only provide an empty *stub* for Method `Solve`:

```
/* Knight's Tour: See problem statement in Chapter 14. */
class KnightsTour {
   ...
   /* Compute: Extend the tour, if possible. */
   static void Solve() { } /* Solve */
   ...
   } /* KnightsTour */
```
8

This will eventually be the heart of the program, but for now, we follow what we shall call the "procrastination rule":

> ☞ **Defer challenging code for later; do the easy parts first.**

One rationale for this rule is that doing easy stuff first often establishes a framework, and offers familiarity with the problem space that can help when tackling harder stuff. The rule can backfire if you later discover you were thinking about the problem all wrong, in which case you may have wasted effort knocking off easy code that turns out to be irrelevant. But in this case, it is clear we are moving in a good direction. Initially, we only write a stub for method `Solve` so that the program as a whole is complete and testable.

Method `Display` requires a standard row-major-order enumeration of array indices, and can be knocked off easily:

9

```
/* Knight's Tour: See problem statement in Chapter 14. */
class KnightsTour {
   ...
   /* Output: Print tour as numbered cells in N-by-N grid of 0s. */
   static void Display() {
      for (int r=lo; r<=hi; r++) {
         for (int c=lo; c<=hi; c++)
            System.out.print(B[r][c] + " ");
         System.out.println();
         }
      } /* Display */
   ...
   } /* KnightsTour */
```

Initial Test

We are in a good position to test our code. Admittedly, a tour that stops when not in a cul-de-sac does not satisfy the problem description. But, validating the code now is worthwhile, nonetheless. First, accidental typos and bad syntax can be discovered and fixed in this very simple setting. Second, if for some reason the code doesn't manage to print an 8-by-8 display with a 1 in the upper-left square, and the rest all 0, we won't have far to look for the cause. Specifically, various combinations of `print` and `println` statements incorrectly placed in the **for**-loops of method `Output` will produce ill-formatted output, e.g., all values on one line, or each value on its own line, etc., and we might as well get this right.

We strongly advocate the rule:

> ☞ **Test programs incrementally.**

Incremental testing, coupled with procrastination (deferring hard stuff for later), supports the general admonition to:

> ☞ **Control complexity.**

Knowing that the code in hand works as expected engenders a warm feeling of well-being.

Method Solve

All that now remains is to flesh out method `Solve`. Recall its specification:

```
/* Compute: Extend the tour, if possible. */
```

The first step, which is not difficult, is to recognize that an iterative process is involved:

> ☞ **If you "smell a loop", write it down.**

We are clearly not going to be able to accomplish what is required in one fell swoop. We need iteration, and insert a **while**-loop template:

```
/* Knight's Tour: See problem statement in Chapter 14. */        10
class KnightsTour {
   ...
   / * Compute: Extend the tour, if possible. */
      static void Solve() {
         _________
         while ( _________ ) _________
         _________
         } /* Solve */
   ...
   } /* KnightsTour */
```

We can paraphrase the pattern of general iterative computation as:

```
/* Start at "the beginning". */
   while ( /* not "beyond the end" */ ) {
      /* Process the current "place". */
      /* Advance to "the next place" (or to "beyond the end"). */
      }
```

where, in general, the notion of "place" is abstract, and not specifically a "location in 3-D space". For example, in an indeterminate-enumeration pattern, "place" is a point in the sequence of integers being counted off, and in the online-computation pattern, "place" is a point in the input sequence.

In the present problem, "place" is a square on the chess board, or more precisely, a point in the array `B` that represents the square of the Chess board at the end of a partial tour.

In the refinement of the general iterative pattern, we can:

- Omit where to start, because method `Initialize` has already placed the Knight in the upper-left corner of the board, and has established the representation invariant.
- Combine "Process" and "Advance" into one "Extend" operation.
- Interpret the *condition* "not beyond the end" as "not stuck in a cul-de-sac".

We obtain the code:

11

```
/* Knight's Tour: See problem statement in Chapter 14. */
class KnightsTour {
   ...
  / * Compute: Extend the tour, if possible. */
      static void Solve() {
         while ( /* not in cul-de-sac */ )
            /* Extend the tour 1 square, if possible. */
         } /* Solve */
   ...
   } /* KnightsTour */
```

How should the Extend step be refined? Given that the problem statement does not require doing particularly well, a so-called *greedy algorithm* will suffice: Find *any* legal place to go, and go there. Failure to find a legal place to go means we are in a cul-de-sac. This is an opportunity for the search-use pattern:

```
/* Search. */
/* Use what's found. */
```

First *search* for a place to go, then *use* that place to extend the tour. The search pattern is instantiated, as follows:

12

```
/* Knight's Tour: See problem statement in Chapter 14. */
class KnightsTour {
   ...
   /* Compute: Extend the tour, if possible. */
   static void Solve() {
      while ( /* not in cul-de-sac */ ) {
         /* Extend the tour 1 square, if possible. */
            /* Locate unvisited neighbor, or indicate cul-de-sac. */
            if ( /* not in cul-de-sac */ )
               /* Extend the tour to unvisited neighbor. */
            }
      } /* Solve */
   ...
   } /* KnightsTour */
```

Introduction of the term *neighbor* is an important aspect of this refinement. By neighbor, we mean "square that is reachable from the current position of the Knight by a legal move".

☞ Invent (or learn) vocabulary for concepts that arise in a problem.

Apt terms help conceptualize a problem, and articulate its solution.

Given that we are being greedy, and have no further preference (for now), we can seek the first unvisited neighbor we can find in the neighborhood, enumerating possibilities in an arbitrary order.

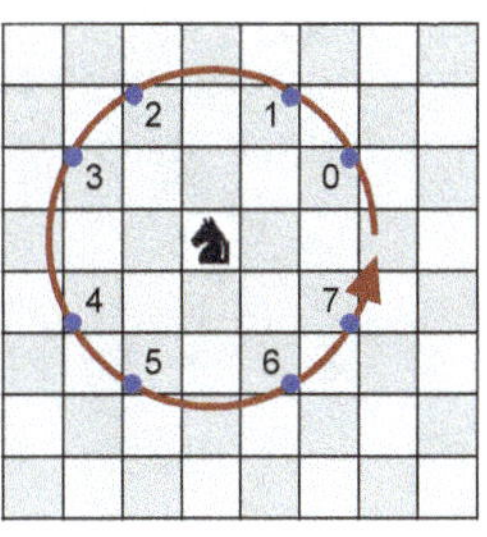

The notion of a neighborhood suggests introducing a local frame-of-reference centered on the Knight's position, and a one-dimensional coordinate system akin to the angle of polar coordinates. The eight neighbors are not spaced uniformly around the circle by angle; rather, they are just itemized in (say) counterclockwise order, starting at an arbitrary neighbor.

With this coordinate system in hand, we can think of the search for an unvisited neighbor of the Knight as a search for the index number of the neighbor (0-7), or CUL_DE_SAC, which is convenient to represent as 8:

```
/* Knight's Tour: See problem statement in Chapter 14. */
class KnightsTour {
   ...
   /* Compute: Extend the tour, if possible. */
   static void Solve() {
      while ( /* not in cul-de-sac */ ) {
         /* Extend the tour 1 square, if possible. */
            /* Let k = # of unvisited neighbor, or CUL_DE_SAC. */
            if ( k!=CUL_DE_SAC )
               /* Extend the tour to unvisited neighbor. */
            }
      } /* Solve */
   ...
   } /* KnightsTour */
```
13

We drop the standard sequential-search pattern into the code, omitting for now the detail as to how we will test whether a given neighbor is unvisited:

```
/* Knight's Tour: See problem statement in Chapter 14. */
class KnightsTour {
   ...
   /* Compute: Extend the tour, if possible. */
   static void Solve() {
      while ( /* not in cul-de-sac */ ) {
         /* Extend the tour 1 square, if possible. */
            /* Let k = # of unvisited neighbor, or CUL_DE_SAC. */
               int k = 0;
               while ( k<CUL_DE_SAC && /* neighbor k visited */ ) k++;
            if ( k!=CUL_DE_SAC )
               /* Extend the tour to unvisited neighbor. */
            }
      } /* Solve */
   ...
   } /* KnightsTour */
```
14

With faith that we will find a uniform way to compute the row and column indices in array B of neighbor k, we write a template for testing whether that neighbor has been visited:

```
/* neighbor k visited */
   B[___][___]!=BLANK
```

Notice that coding the test as a single *expression* is in sharp contrast to a possible instinct to perform an eight-way Case Analysis. We drop the *expression* into the *condition* of the **if**-statement:

```
/* Knight's Tour: See problem statement in Chapter 14. */
class KnightsTour {
   ...
   /* Compute: Extend the tour, if possible. */
   static void Solve() {
      while ( /* not in cul-de-sac */ ) {
         /* Extend the tour 1 square, if possible. */
            /* Let k = # of unvisited neighbor, or CUL_DE_SAC. */
               int k = 0;
               while ( k<CUL_DE_SAC && B[___][___]!=BLANK ) k++;
            if ( k!=CUL_DE_SAC )
               /* Extend the tour to unvisited neighbor. */
            }
      } /* Solve */
   ...
   } /* KnightsTour */
```

15

Then, we turn to the question of how to compute the neighbor's indices.

Coordinates in a neighborhood are what, in physics, is called a *local frame of reference*. It is "local" in the sense that it is oriented relative to the current position of the Knight. As we have mentioned, it is polar in nature.

We can also place a Cartesian coordinate system, ⟨Δr,Δc⟩, with origin at the Knight's location, and then define the coordinates of the Knight's eight neighbors in that local coordinate system using two arrays of constants:

```
//                             0   1   2   3   4   5   6   7
static final int deltaR[] = {-1, -2, -2, -1,  1,  2,  2,  1};
static final int deltaC[] = { 2,  1, -1, -2, -2, -1,  1,  2};
```

If a Knight is located at ⟨r,c⟩ in the global coordinate system, and has a neighbor located at ⟨Δr,Δc⟩ in the local coordinate system, then that neighbor is located at ⟨r+Δr,c+Δc⟩ in the global coordinate system. Accordingly, we can use expressions `r+deltaR[k]` and `c+deltaC[k]` for the row and column indices of neighbor k.

We are illustrating a very general technique that allows us to avoid Case Analysis in code. Specifically, we are following the precept:

☞ **Introduce auxiliary data to allow code to be uniform.**

Rather than (say) having an eight-way Case Analysis, with one case for each of the eight possible neighbors, we have effectively factored out the differences of those eight cases into the arrays of data, `deltaR` and `deltaC`, thereby allowing our index expressions to be uniform. This technique is called *table-driven programming*.

The same index expressions can be used in both the *condition* that tests an element of `B` for `BLANK`, and in the code that extends the tour to incorporate neighbor `k`:

16

```
/* Knight's Tour: See problem statement in Chapter 14. */
class KnightsTour {
   ...
   /* Compute: Extend the tour, if possible. */
   static void Solve() {
      while ( /* not in cul-de-sac */ ) {
         /* Extend the tour 1 square, if possible. */
            /* Let k = # of unvisited neighbor, or CUL_DE_SAC. */
               int k = 0;
               while ( k<CUL_DE_SAC &&
                       B[r+deltaR[k]][c+deltaC[k]]!=BLANK ) k++;
            if ( k!=CUL_DE_SAC )
               /* Extend the tour to unvisited neighbor. */
                  r = r+deltaR[k]; c = c+deltaC[k];
                  move++; B[r][c] = move;
            }
      } /* Solve */
   ...
   } /* KnightsTour */
```

This completes the code for the body of the loop, which can be read as "extend the tour, if possible, while maintaining the defined representation invariant for tours". Double checking the code with respect to the invariant is recommended as a guard against inadvertent failure to update all of the variables of the representation.

Finally, we turn to termination of the loop, and observe that failure of the search for an unvisited neighbor (in the previous iteration) supports the test we need. Variable `k` must be initialized to anything but `CUL_DE_SAC` to guarantee that the *condition* for iterating is initially **true**. We hadn't anticipated that we would use `k` for the loop condition, so we must now move its declaration out of the loop body:

17

```
/* Knight's Tour: See problem statement in Chapter 14. */
class KnightsTour {
   ...
   /* Compute: Extend the tour, if possible. */
   static void Solve() {
      int k = 0; // Neighbor number not CUL_DE_SAC.
      while ( k!=CUL_DE_SAC ) {
         /* Extend the tour 1 square, if possible. */
            /* Let k = # of unvisited neighbor, or CUL_DE_SAC. */
               k = 0;
               while ( k<CUL_DE_SAC &&
                       B[r+deltaR[k]][c+deltaC[k]]!=BLANK ) k++;
            if ( k!=CUL_DE_SAC )
               /* Extend the tour to unvisited neighbor. */
                  r = r+deltaR[k]; c = c+deltaC[k];
                  move++; B[r][c] = move;
            }
      } /* Solve */
   ...
   } /* KnightsTour */
```

Of course, suitable declarations and initializations of variables `deltaR`, `deltaC`, and `CUL_DE_SAC` are required:

18

```
/* Knight's Tour: See problem statement in Chapter 14. */
class KnightsTour {
   ...
   /* Neighbor coordinate system. */
      static final int CUL_DE_SAC = 8;    // Not a neighbor.
      /* Row and column offsets for eight neighbors. */
         //                      0   1   2   3   4   5   6   7
         static final int deltaR[] = {-1, -2, -2, -1,  1,  2,  2,  1};
         static final int deltaC[] = { 2,  1, -1, -2, -2, -1,  1,  2};
   ...
   } /* KnightsTour */
```

This completes the code for method Solve.

We are well-aware that we cannot successfully execute the program because right from the get-go, neighbor 0 of the upper-left square of the board would be off the board. If, in our enthusiasm to finish Solve, we were to attempt to run the program now, we would be sorely disappointed to receive the "subscript-out-of-bounds" run-time exception. Ideally, this would jolt us into remembering that we have not yet taken boundary conditions into account. If we are mindful, we would not start inspecting the code in detail to track down this "bug", which would be a total waste of time.

Boundary Conditions

As per the relevant precept, we delayed worrying about boundary conditions until dead last, but that consideration is finally upon us.

☞ **Boundary conditions. Dead last, but don't forget them.**

The rationale for the delay was optimism that once Solve was written, we would find a clean way to take care of the boundaries.

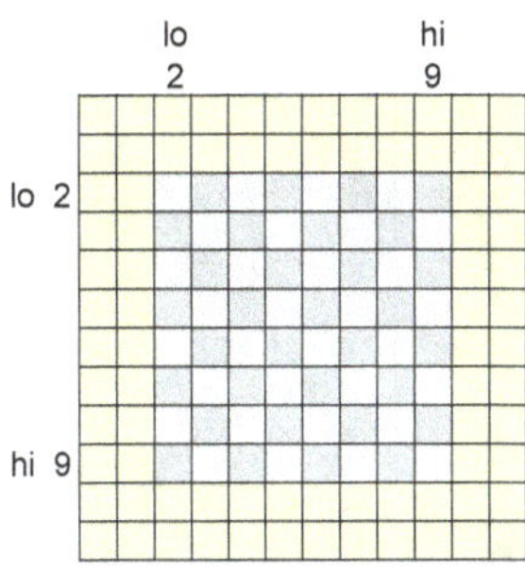

One approach would be to insert explicit range checks into Solve. This would clutter up the code, and would also take time in the most frequently executed code of the program. We prefer to use sentinels, which allow us to leave Solve completely unperturbed. We place a ring of sentinels around the board 2-squares wide, where their values can be anything other than BLANK. That way, they will never be chosen as "unvisited neighbors". By this device, the code for Solve remains uncluttered, and the boundary conditions are completely eliminated!

Returning to the representation invariant of the board, we are able to change just a few places, as a consequence of our earlier decision to use defined constants:

19

```
/* Knight's Tour: See problem statement in Chapter 14. */
class KnightsTour {
   /* Chess board B is an N-by-N int sub-array, for N==8, embedded in a
      2-cell ring of sentinel squares. Unvisited squares are BLANK, and
      row and column indices range from lo to hi. */
      static final int N = 8;              // Size of B.
      static int B[][] = new int[N+4][N+4]; // Chess board, initially 0s.
      static final int BLANK = 0;          // Unvisited square in board.
      static final int lo = 2;             // First row or column index.
      static final int hi = lo+N-1;        // Last row or column index.
      ...
   } /* KnightsTour */
```

Previously, we were able to begin with an all-zero board, as per the default initialization of **int** variables to 0, and our choice of BLANK as 0. But now we must initialize the sentinels that will keep the Knight from going off the board.

One approach to doing this would be to view the border as four 2-by-10 slabs, arranged as shown. One could then write the code as:

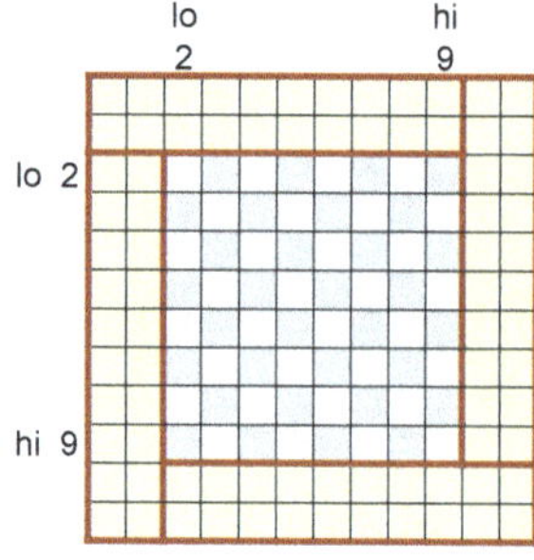


```
for (int width = 0; width<2; width++)
   for (int length = 0; length<N+2; length++) {
      B[width       ][length      ] = BLANK+1; // Top.
      B[length      ][hi+2-width ] = BLANK+1; // Right.
      B[hi+2-width ][hi+2-length] = BLANK+1; // Bottom.
      B[hi+2-length][width       ] = BLANK+1; // Left.
      }
```

We prefer the simplicity of initializing the entire board to be the sentinel value (BLANK+1), and then overwriting the central N-by-N board with BLANK. The familiarity of row-major-order traversals of rectangular regions reduces the risk of error, and the inefficiency of duplicate assignments to the central 8-by-8 square is not worth worrying about:

20

```
/* Knight's Tour: See problem statement in Chapter 14. */
class KnightsTour {
   ...
   /* Initialize: Establish invariant for a tour of length 1. */
   static void Initialize() {
      /* Set B to N-by-N board of BLANKs in 2-cell ring of non-BLANK. */
         for (int r=lo-2; r<=hi+2; r++)
            for (int c=lo-2; c<=hi+2; c++)
               B[r][c] = BLANK+1;
         for (int r=lo; r<=hi; r++)
            for (int c=lo; c<=hi; c++)
               B[r][c] = BLANK;
      r = lo; c = lo;
      move = 1; B[r][c] = move;
      } /* Initialize */
   ...
   } /* KnightsTour */
```

This step completes coding of the greedy algorithm for extending the tour.

Testing, revisited

With the changes made to address boundary conditions, the program runs without error and produces the partial tour that reaches a cul-de-sac at move 42. Since the problem statement did not require that our program find a complete tour, we may consider the program done.

We note that the output (A1) is ragged because we neglected to take care that each square is printed with a fixed number of characters. This omission was not an oversight; rather, it was an application of the precept:

A1

```
1 10 23 42 7 4 13 18
24 41 8 3 12 17 6 15
9 2 11 22 5 14 19 32
0 25 40 35 20 31 16 0
0 36 21 0 39 0 33 30
26 0 38 0 34 29 0 0
37 0 0 28 0 0 0 0
0 27 0 0 0 0 0 0
```

☞ **Ignore fussy details for as long as possible.**

It would have been a distraction to have considered output formatting early; we had far more important things to think about. Furthermore, it was only in this last test that we had output sufficiently general to reveal that we had not taken formatting into account correctly. Thus, were we to have addressed formatting earlier, we would not have had a convenient test case in hand. We can now easily perfect and test a change to method `Display`:[128]

21

```
/* Knight's Tour: See problem statement in Chapter 14. */
class KnightsTour {
   ...
   /* Output: Print tour as numbered cells in N-by-N grid of 0s. */
   static void Display() {
      for (int r=lo; r<=hi; r++) {
         for (int c=lo; c<=hi; c++)
            System.out.print( (B[r][c]+"   ").substring(0,3) );
         System.out.println();
         }
      } /* Display */
   ...
   } /* KnightsTour */
```

and confirm that it produces orderly output (A2).

A2

```
1  10 23 42 7  4  13 18
24 41 8  3  12 17 6  15
9  2  11 22 5  14 19 32
0  25 40 35 20 31 16 0
0  36 21 0  39 0  33 30
26 0  38 0  34 29 0  0
37 0  0  28 0  0  0  0
0  27 0  0  0  0  0  0
```

Heuristics

It is pleasant that the greedy algorithm gets as far as it does before boxing itself into a cul-de-sac. We note, in passing, that tour length may depend on the order of neighbors because we just take the first unvisited neighbor in the list, and go there. Conceivably, a different order of neighbors would yield a tour of length 64, or lead to a far shorter tour.

We now seek some way to do better. We wish to avoid the vagaries of the arbitrary choice of neighbor. We also hope to extend the tour further.

The code that implemented the greedy algorithm is shown in blue, below:

---

128. We obtain a `String` of length 3 that contains the left-adjusted digits of the visit number by concatenating those digits with blanks on the right, and then truncating that `String` to length 3. The code is inadequate for chess boards larger than 9-by-9, but is easily corrected to allow for bigger boards.

Although it is unnecessary to completely understand the code at this juncture, for completeness, we explain it here. The expression `B[r][c]` has type **`int`**. To concatenate an **`int`** with blanks, the **`int`** is first converted to its decimal-numeral representation, which is a value of type `String`. Decimal numerals have length 1 for integers in the range 0-9, length 2 for integers in the range 10-99, etc.

Chapter 12 Collections introduced objects (p. 202), mentioned that arrays are objects, and told that such objects have a field named `length` that can be accessed using the dot notation, e.g., `A.length`. Similarly, a value of type `String` is also an object, such an object, *o*, has a method named `substring`, and that method can be accessed using the dot notation, e.g., *o*`.substring(...)`.

Method `substring` has two parameters: The start index (inclusive), and the end index (exclusive) of the substring being copied. Thus, the expression `(B[r][c]+"   ").substring(0,3)` yields a `String` of length 3 regardless of the **`int`** value of `B[r][c]`.

```
/* Knight's Tour: See problem statement in Chapter 14. */                17
class KnightsTour {
   ...
   /* Compute: Extend the tour, if possible. */
   static void Solve() {
      int k = 0; // Neighbor number not CUL_DE_SAC.
      while ( k!=CUL_DE_SAC ) {
         /* Extend the tour 1 square, if possible. */
            /* Let k = # of unvisited neighbor, or CUL_DE_SAC. */
               k = 0;
               while ( k<CUL_DE_SAC &&
                  B[r+deltaR[k]][c+deltaC[k]]!=BLANK ) k++;
            if ( k!=CUL_DE_SAC )
               /* Extend the tour to unvisited neighbor. */
                  r = r+deltaR[k]; c = c+deltaC[k];
                  move++; B[r][c] = move;
            }
      } /* Solve */
   ...
   } /* KnightsTour */
```

Suppose that we have a scoring mechanism to evaluate the desirability of choosing a given unvisited neighbor, and we wish to go to the neighbor with the best score. We can change the blue code, as follows:

```
/* Let k = # of unvisited neighbor, or CUL_DE_SAC. */                    A1
   /* Let bestK be favored unvisited neighbor, or CUL_DE_SAC, if all
      neighbors are already visited. */
   k = bestK;
```

The interface of this code with the rest of the program need not change because we are just exchanging the greedy algorithm with one that may do better. The rest of the program need not even be aware of the switch.

Without loss of generality, assume the scoring mechanism is provided by an **int**-valued evaluation function, `Score`, where low scores are considered more desirable than high scores. The following code (adapted from p.142) picks a neighbor with a minimal score, or sets `k` to `CUL_DE_SAC` if there are no unvisited neighbors:

```
/* Let k = # of unvisited neighbor, or CUL_DE_SAC. */                    A2
   /* Let bestK be favored unvisited neighbor, or CUL_DE_SAC, if all
      neighbors are already visited. */
      int bestK = CUL_DE_SAC;  // Neighbor # of favored neighbor.
      int bestScore = Integer.MAX_VALUE;  // Score of neighbor bestK.
      for (k=0; k<8; k++)
         if ( B[r+deltaR[k]][c+deltaC[k]]==BLANK ) {
            int s = Score(r+deltaR[k],c+deltaC[k]);
            if ( s<bestScore ) { bestScore = s; bestK = k; }
            }
   k = bestK;
```

All that remains is to invent a scoring function.

A *heuristic* is a rule of thumb that (sometimes) works. There is intuition that suggests it has benefits, but no solid argument that it is guaranteed to work. The following heuristic for the Knight's Tour was given by Warnsdorff in 1823:

Go to an unvisited neighbor that has the fewest unvisited neighbors.

Let's think about why this rule may be beneficial.

Consider a Knight choosing which neighbor among 0-7 to go to next using Warnsdorff's Rule. Suppose neighbor 2 is the neighbor amongst 0-7 that has the fewest unvisited neighbors. The Knight's neighbors are depicted in blue, and the neighbors of square 2 are depicted in pink. Let square 2 have *m* unvisited neighbors, and consider the cases:

- **m=0.** Then the Knight's current square is the only way to get to square 2, and if it doesn't go there now, it will never get another chance. So, it might as well go there now. Yes, it will then be in a cul-de-sac, so, if we hope for a tour of length 64, this move better be the 64th step. If not, the Knight is effectively cutting its losses, and ending a doomed tour. If the goal were to *maximize* the tour length, it might be better *not* to go there now, unless this is move 64. Warnsdorff's Rule is "going for broke".

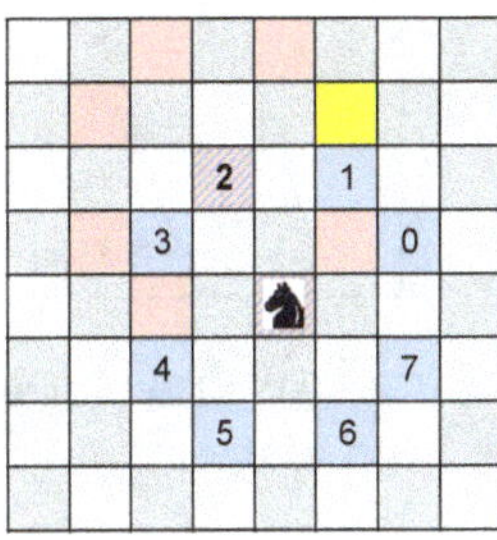

- **m=1.** There is only one way out (shown in yellow). If the Knight goes to 2 now, the next move (to yellow) removes 2 from further concern. But if it doesn't go there now, then when it eventually gets to yellow, it will be forced to go to 2, which will end the tour in a cul-de-sac. So, best to pass *through* 2 now, for otherwise it will loom as a hazard.
- **m>1.** Too hard to think about. Perhaps the above is good enough to complete a tour.

Here is method `Score` for Warnsdorff's Rule:

```
/* Return # of unvisited neighbors of <r,c>. (Warnsdorff's Rule) */
static int Score(int r, int c) {
   int count = 0;    // # unvisited neighbors among 0..k.
   for (int k=0; k<8; k++)
      if ( B[r+deltaR[k]][c+deltaC[k]]==BLANK ) count++;
   return count;
   }
```
A3

You should not be troubled by the reuse of `r`, `c`, and `k` in method `Score`; we are following the precept:

☞ **Avoid gratuitously different names for parameters and variables whose use is essentially the same. Practice conceptual economy.**

It is for precisely this reason that the creators of modern programming languages invented the notion of *scope*: So that names could be reused. In support of this precept, we have been careful to keep the scopes of variables small:

☞ **Declare variables with as small a scope as possible.**

Testing, revisited yet again

Run the program once again, and be pleasantly surprised that the Knight completes a Tour of length 64, as shown in the output (B).

```
1  22 3  18 25 30 13 16   B
4  19 24 29 14 17 34 31
23 2  21 26 35 32 15 12
20 5  56 49 28 41 36 33
57 50 27 42 61 54 11 40
6  43 60 55 48 39 64 37
51 58 45 8  53 62 47 10
44 7  52 59 46 9  38 63
```

Monte Carlo Tours

A *Monte Carlo method* for a problem uses random trials to search for a solution. Rather than our initial greedy approach, or our subsequent heuristic approach, let's explore the effectiveness of a Monte Carlo solution to the Knight's Tour. At each step we can choose an arbitrary unvisited neighbor selected at random.

The needed machinery is mostly in hand. We only need a random number generator, which is readily obtained from the Java library:

```
import java.util.*;                                                    M1
class KnightsTour {
   ...
   static Random rand = new Random();  // Random number generator.
   ...
   } /* KnightsTour */
```

The top-level program can keep trying random solutions until a Tour of length 64 has been found:

```
/* Perform random Knight's Tours until finding a solution. */          M2
static void MonteCarlo() {
   while (move != 64 ) {
      /* Initialize: Establish invariant for a tour of length 1. */
         Initialize();
      /* Compute: Extend the tour, if possible. */
         RandomSolve();
      }
   /* Output: Print tour as numbered cells in N-by-N grid. */
         Display();
   } /* MonteCarlo */
```

At each step, `RandomSolve` merely lists the unvisited neighbors, and selects one at random:

```
/* Compute: Extend the tour, if possible, making random moves. */          M3
static void RandomSolve() {
   int k = 0;  // Neighbor number.
   while ( k != CUL_DE_SAC ) {
      /* Let unvisited[0:count-1] be neighbor numbers of the count
         unvisited neighbors of ⟨r,c⟩. */
         int unvisited[] = new int[8];
         int count = 0;  // # unvisited neighbors
         for (k=0; k<8; k++)
            if ( B[r+deltaR[k]][c+deltaC[k]]==Blank ) {
               unvisited[count]=k; count++;
               }
      if ( count==0 ) k = CUL_DE_SAC;
      else {
         k = unvisited[rand.nextInt(count)];
         /* Extend the tour to neighbor k. */
            move++; r = r+deltaR[k]; c = c+deltaC[k];  B[r][c]=move;
         }
      }
   } /* RandomSolve */
```

The calculation "`rand.nextInt(count)`" provides a random integer in the range 0 through `count-1`.

If, instead of printing the solution, we wish to study the behavior of the Monte Carlo search, we can collect data in a histogram:

```
/* Perform random Knight's Tours until finding a solution. */               M4
static void MonteCarlo() {
   int freq[] = new int[N*N+1]; // Histogram of Tour lengths.
   while (move != 64 ) {
      /* Initialize: Establish invariant for a tour of length 1. */
         Initialize();
      /* Compute: Extend the tour, if possible. */
         RandomSolve();
      /* Bin the path length. */
         freq[move]++;
      }
   /* Output the histogram freq[1:64]. */
      for (int j=1; j<=64; j++ ) System.out.println( j+" "+freq[j] );
   } /* MonteCarlo */
```

The code assumes that an tour of length 64 would eventually be found, and fortunately that is the case. Dropping the output into a plotting program shows the distribution of the random tour lengths found:

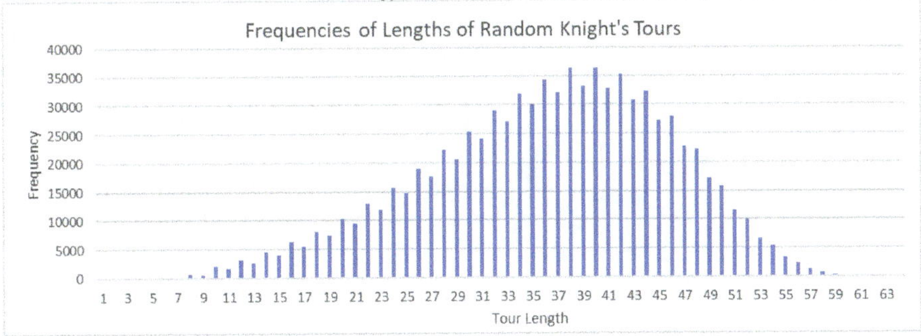

Interestingly, with a little ingenuity it is possible to work oneself into a cul-de-sac in eight moves. Who would have guessed that a Knight could be so stupid?

Reflections

Basking in our success, it is worthwhile to review the code, and observe that it primarily consists of apt uses of familiar patterns:

Method `Solve`

- The greedy algorithm to find an unvisited square is a straightforward Sequential Search (p. 129).
- The heuristic algorithm is a standard search for best (p. 142).
- The method's outer loop is a simple indeterminate iteration until stuck, using the representation invariant of maze and path as the loop invariant.

Method `Score`

- The scoring function for Warnsdorff's Rule just counts unvisited neighbors of a given square.

Methods `Initialize` and `Display`

- Straightforward 2-D determinate enumerations in row-major order.

Method `RandomSolve`

- A small revision of `Solve` that builds a list of unvisited neighbors, as per Chapter 12, and then selects one at random.

Method `MonteCarlo`

- A standard Sequential Search for a successful solution.
- Use of an array to compute a histogram, as per Chapter 12 (p. 205).

Complete Program

Because the full program is long, and the presentation has been fragmented, it is reprinted all together in Appendix IV.

CHAPTER 15

Running a Maze

This chapter presents a complete solution to the maze-running problem. We have seen the problem twice before: In Chapter 1, to illustrate use of Precepts and Patterns, and in Chapter 4, to illustrate careful reasoning about correctness and termination using loop invariants and loop variants. In an effort to make this chapter somewhat self-contained, we largely repeat the material from Chapter 1, with apologies, and incorporate the material of Chapter 4, by reference, at the appropriate point in the development.[129]

The maze-running problem has sufficient complexity to motivate introduction of techniques that support the programming of nontrivial applications. First, how to partition code into multiple *modules*. Second, how to use encapsulation and information hiding to segregate concerns and keep code limber. Third, incremental development and incremental testing as a way to control the process.

Background. We define a maze to be a square two-dimensional grid of cells separated (or not) from adjacent cells by walls. One can move between adjacent cells if and only if no wall divides them. A solid wall surrounds the entire grid of cells, so there is no escape from the maze.

If we drop a rat into the upper-left cell, it may eventually locate a wedge of cheese placed in the lower-right cell. Although a rat's initial path to the cheese will perforce be indirect and inefficient, after repeated trials it may make a beeline to the cheese, as shown in the figure.

Problem Statement. Write a program that inputs a maze, and outputs a direct path from the upper-left cell to the lower-right cell if such a path exists, or outputs "Unreachable" otherwise. A path is direct if it never visits any cell more than once. The output should show the direct path as a sequence of numbered cells, as illustrated. You must design the format in which input data defines a maze. Your program should check that the input data correspond to a well-formed maze, and output "Malformed input" if it does not. You must design the output format in which the program displays the direct path if one exists, but it need not have fancy graphics.

Top-level Code Structure

Given the blank sheet of paper before you, where do you begin?

129. The problem is used in yet two more places: In Chapter 17 Graphs and Depth-First Search, and in Chapter 19 Debugging.

☞ **Start by writing a top-level decomposition of the solution.**

A cursory reading of the problem statement suggests the top-level architecture of the program, an application of the offline-computation pattern. We can use that pattern for the initial structure of the program in method `main`[130] of class `RunMaze`:[131]

```
/* Rat running. See Chapter 15 of text. */                R1
class RunMaze {
   /* Run maze. */
   public static void main() {
      /* Input. */
      /* Compute. */
      /* Output. */
      } /* main */
   } /* RunMaze */
```

This is a start, but omits details that are readily apparent in the problem statement. A more complete reading of the problem statement leads to the following, more detailed articulation of the top-level structure of a solution:

```
/* Rat running. See Chapter 15 of text. */                R2
class RunMaze {
   /* Run a maze given as input, if possible. */
   public static void main() {
      /* Input a maze of arbitrary size, or output "malformed input"
         and stop if the input is improper. Input format: TBD.*/
      /* Compute a direct path through the maze, if one exists. */
      /* Output the direct path found, or "unreachable" if there is
         none. Output format: TBD. */
      } /* main */
   } /* RunMaze */
```

This adds the fact that the maze is given as input, adds the error condition that the input may not be well-formed, clarifies the required nature of a solution, and adds the boundary condition that no direct path may exist.

You may feel that even this more detailed top-level structure is far too obvious to be worth writing down explicitly, but consider the benefits. The decomposition helps to structure your thinking, and writing it down makes explicit what you may only sense implicitly. The written outline provides an initial program skeleton that serves as a map to help guide your subsequent work. Writing down the structure begins the introduction of vocabulary useful for expressing your thoughts, approaches, and possible solution.

A *certain* problem decomposition is one that is unlikely to be wrong and in need of rework. We follow the Hippocratic Oath to "Do no harm", which in this context means "Avoid going down a garden path in a wrong direction".

---

130. This is the first time we have used the modifier **`public`**, which indicates that a name is visible outside the class, and is therefore is available to its client, i.e., the user. The modifier is not necessary because **`public`** is the default visibility. However, we use it explicitly here and subsequently for emphasis, and in contradistinction to the modifier **`private`**, which we will soon introduce.

131. In this chapter, we develop two classes, `RunMaze` and `MRP`. The developments of each class are numbered starting at 1, and bear prefixes `R` and `M`, respectively.

☞ Code with deliberation. Be mindful.

If a decomposition is sure to be part of the eventual solution, then you have nothing to lose and much to gain by writing it down early.

The initial tripartite decomposition into three steps is safe; it is hard to imagine that it could be wrong. One small design decision warrants reflection. Specifically, the responsibility to emit the message "Unreachable", when appropriate, has been delegated to Output. You may ask: Won't Compute perforce discover that there is no direct path to the cheese, and given that, would it not be more convenient to have it emit the "Unreachable" message when it makes that discovery?

Here's an analysis. Yes, Compute is sure to discover unreachability, for otherwise it will be at risk of running forever. But while it might be convenient to emit the "Unreachable" message there, doing so does not free us from having to convey the information to Output so that it can omit the display of a path. Given this, we might as well consolidate all output within Output. Thus, our design decision, while not forced, is worthwhile nonetheless, and very likely "does no harm".[132]

We follow the precept that:

☞ Many short procedures are better than large blocks of code.

and lay in this framework at the start by invoking a method for each of the three parts:

R3

```
/* Rat running. See Chapter 15 of text. */
class RunMaze {
   /* Run a maze given as input, if possible. */
   public static void main() {
      /* Input a maze of arbitrary size, or output "malformed input"
         and stop if the input is improper. Input format: TBD.*/
         Input();
      /* Compute a direct path through the maze, if one exists. */
         Solve();
      /* Output the direct path found, or "unreachable" if there is
         none. Output format: TBD. */
         Display();
      } /* main */
   } /* RunMaze */
```

As long as we are building a scaffolding for our program, we might as well follow the precept

☞ Don't type if you can avoid it; clone. Cut and paste, then adapt.

and provide shells for the three methods, together with their header comments:

132. One could argue that upon discovering unreachability Compute could abort program execution rather continuing on, which point is taken. However, as a general rule, we prefer to retain the discipline that every code fragment has a single point of entry and single point of exit, which discipline promotes *compositionality*, i.e., the property that every fragment *of* code, and every placeholder *for* code, presents the same interface, and are therefore "plug compatible", at least from the point of view of the flow of control through code.

```
/* Rat running. See Chapter 15 of text. */                                   R4
class RunMaze {
   /* Input a maze of arbitrary size, or output "malformed input"
      and stop if the input is improper. Input format: TBD. */
   private static void Input() { } /* Input */
   /* Compute a direct path through the maze, if one exists. */
   private static void Solve() { } /* Solve */
   /* Output the direct path found, or "unreachable" if there is none.
      Output format: TBD. */
   private static void Output() { } /* Output */
   ...
   } /* RunMaze */
```

Although it looks like a lot of new text, almost none of it is because most came for free via a single cut-and-paste operation.

Introduction of the modifier **private** for the three methods, in contrast with the **public** modifier of `main`, begins articulation of the interface between this class and its client, the user: The three methods are internal implementation concerns for class `RunMaze` about which others have no need to know. Thus, we hide them from view. The user will know about `main`, and nothing else. It is useful from the get-go to:

☞ **Practice information hiding.**

The three methods are said to be *encapsulated* within `RunMaze`.

It might be said that we have only been engaged in busywork that almost offends our sense of intelligence. This looks like a fun problem, and we are eager to get on with thinking about the challenging parts. The temptation to start working on those aspects is magnetic, and clambers for our attention. But we have been proceeding in a purist, top-down fashion, and have been deferring bottom-up considerations. Admittedly, these may influence our direction, but they will come soon enough. The kind of drivel we have been writing will have to be there eventually, and so, we might as well get it over with now. The precept:

☞ **Ignore fussy details for as long as possible.**

argues for focus on substantial matters, and for delay of distracting busywork. The counterargument is that early attention to architectural matters is worthwhile, especially while we are getting acclimatized to the problem.

Algorithm

How can a rat systematically explore a maze? For that matter, what would you do? To make progress on this question, we turn to the physical system being modeled, and follow the rule:

☞ **Seek algorithmic inspiration from experience. Hand-simulate an algorithm that is in your "wetware". Be introspective. Ask yourself: What am I doing?**

"Hand-simulate" what, you may ask? Hand-simulate the unspoken program that you must have in your head if you can systematically solve the problem yourself.

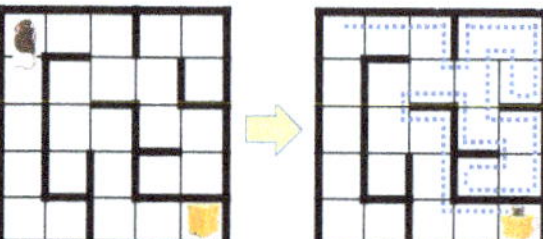

Imagine that *you* are in the upper-left cell of the maze (say) facing up. You put your left hand on the wall in front of you, and trace it all the way around as you move to the right from cell to cell. You discover that you will eventually reach the lower-right cell if there is a path to it. If you can do it, the rat can do it.

Replaying this example systematically, we draw a series of diagrams in which your left arm (or the rat's paw) is symbolized by an arrow. The run begins like this:

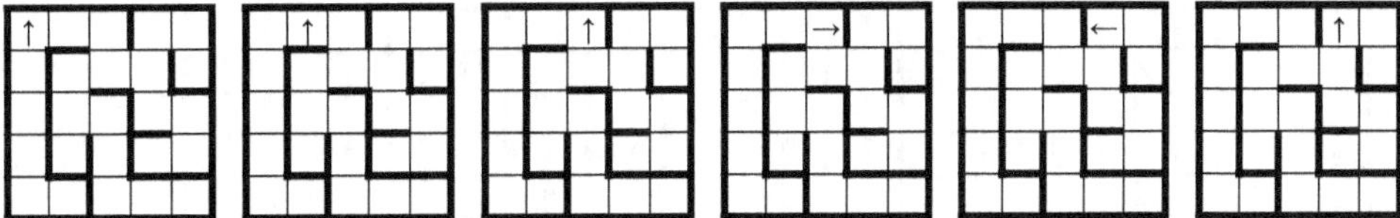

From these diagrams, which are effectively a trace of the algorithm that you are following, we can read off the sequence of operations that you performed:

- Sidestep to the right.
- Sidestep to the right.
- Turn the concave corner 90 degrees clockwise.
- Pirouette into the cell on the opposite side of the wall, making a 180-degree hairpin turn counterclockwise.
- Turn the concave corner 90 degrees clockwise.

The trace then continues:

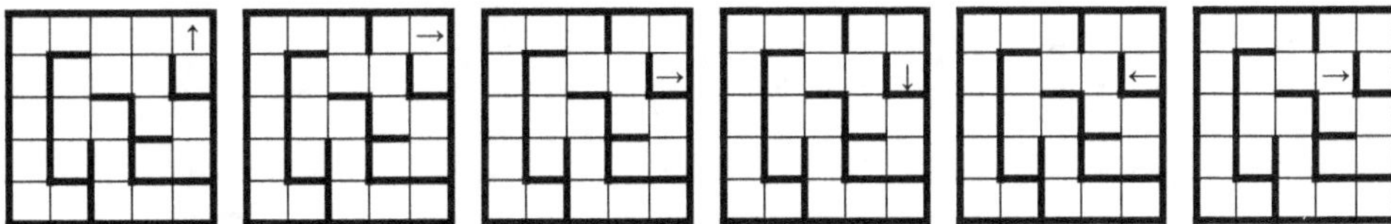

as you perform these next operations:

- Sidestep to the right.
- Turn the concave corner 90 degrees clockwise.
- Sidestep to the right.
- Turn the concave corner 90 degrees clockwise.
- Turn the concave corner 90 degrees clockwise.
- Pirouette counterclockwise into the cell on the opposite side of the wall, making a 180-degree hairpin turn counterclockwise.

Three possible operations have emerged that are candidates for implementation: Sidestep right, turn clockwise, and pirouette counterclockwise. Further inspection of the example reveals the need for a fourth operation that arises in the very next step: Turn the convex corner 90 degrees counterclockwise.

The important point being illustrated is that when you can perform an algorithm (the code for which is in your head) you can often observe a trace of what you are doing, and discover a first approximation to the operations that need to be performed.

In the section Extended Example: Running a Maze of Chapter 4, we analyzed the very four operations we just elicited, and observed that they can be advantageously replaced by three alternative fine-grained actions:

- Turn the rat (in place) 90 degrees clockwise.
- Turn the rat (in place) 90 degrees counterclockwise.
- Advance the rat one cell forward, i.e., in the direction faced.

To these, we added three fine-grained queries:

- Is the rat facing a wall?
- Is the rat at the cheese?
- Is the rat about to repeat itself?

Replaying the algorithm on the example, we obtain the following trace, now expressed in the vocabulary of the smaller steps:

Although it is tempting to call the maze-exploration algorithm derived in Chapter 4 "pseudo-code", there is no reason why it cannot be real code: We express the pseudo-operations as method calls, place the initialization in `Input`, and place the iteration in `Solve`:

R5

```
/* Rat running. See Chapter 15 of text. */
class RunMaze {
   /* Input a maze of arbitrary size, or output "malformed input"
      and stop if the input is improper. Input format: TBD. */
   private static void Input() {
      ⟨Obtain maze from input.⟩
      ⟨Establish initial state: In upper-left cell, facing up.⟩
      } /* Input */
   /* Compute a direct path through the maze, if one exists. */
   private static void Solve() {
      while ( !isAtCheese() && !isAboutToRepeat() )
         if (isFacingWall()) TurnClockwise();
         else {
            StepForward();
            TurnCounterClockwise();
            }
      } /* Solve */
   ...
   } /* RunMaze */
```

By hand simulating the code, we confirm that it generates the trace depicted above.

Taking stock, we realize that the code in hand performs a systematic exploration, but does not yet address the question of recording a path. Working through the example has clarified that converting an exhaustive exploration to a direct path will require some form of surgery on the exploration path. However, we don't engage in that now because it is past time to consider the design of the data representation:

> ☞ **Dovetail thinking about code and data.**

Data Representation

The simple act of writing down the tripartite, top-level decomposition of the program brings into focus a key question: How will method `Input` convey the maze to method `Solve`, and how will method `Solve` convey the direct path it finds to method `Output`?

These matters of internal representation are critical:

> ☞ **A program's internal data representation is central to the code; consider it early.**

Choosing a good internal representation can greatly simplify writing the code for the computation-intensive part of a program. Conversely, choosing a bad internal representation can make the program so complicated that down the road you are forced to discard your unfinished code, redesign the representation, and start all over again.

We need to represent three things:

- The *maze* with its collection of walls.
- The position and orientation of the *rat*.
- The *path* taken by the rat (so far) during its exploration.

The maze will be given as input, but once read in, will not change. In contrast, the path will be developed one step at a time. We will need a collection of variables that together represent the *state* of the aggregate maze-rat-path system as it evolves over the course of program execution. Such a collection of variables is called a *data structure*.

Designing an efficient data structure for representing the key elements of our problem is a critical aspect of the program that we will consider in detail soon enough. But, efficient for what? As we have stated before:

> ☞ **The touchstone of a data representation is its utility in performing the needed operations.**

Reflecting back on the Knight's Tour in Chapter 14, you would be hard pressed to single out the operations supported by the board-knight-tour system because they were interleaved in the code that implements the Knight's strategy. That code accesses the elements of the data structure directly; its fine-grained steps are not segregated from the Knight's Tour algorithm; the operations are not named.

In contrast, the maze-running algorithm is already expressed in a vocabulary that suggests a set of operations. Rather than accessing the maze-rat-path data structure directly, the code for the maze-running algorithm invokes named methods. In effect, we have factored the program by moving the code for each operation into the definition of a separate method, and we have replaced that code in the algorithm by an invocation of the corresponding method.

Competing designs for a data structure must be assessed in the context of the primitive computational steps that must be supported. In designing the algorithm, we first asked *what* we wanted from the representation without worrying about *how* the representation would support a reply. It is now time to design the underlying data structure that can be used to implement the operations efficiently. If this proves to be difficult, we may have to consider revising the set of operations originally proposed.

In addition to factoring the operations into methods, we take the additional step of factoring the method definitions into a separate class. The overall program will consist of two distinct *modules*: The algorithm (in class `RunMaze`) and the data representation (in class `MRP`, which we now introduce):

```
/* Maze, Rat, and Path (MRP) Representations. */                M1
class MRP {
   } /* MRP */
```

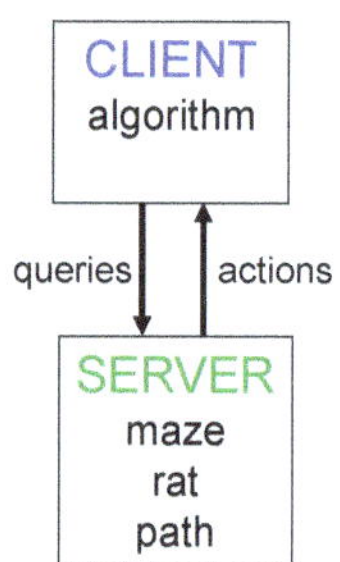

The service rendered to the algorithm by class `MRP` will consist entirely of the **`public`** features it makes available. We say that the class *publishes* or *exports* its **`public`** features, and that those features are made *visible* to clients. The visible features are known as the class's *interface*.[133]

We could allow the underlying data structure to be a visible feature of `MRP`, but it is our intention to hide it, i.e., to make it **`private`** and not part of the interface. We will require that the **`public`** methods of `MRP` constitute a sufficient vocabulary in which to express the maze-running algorithm. Whatever data structure we devise to represent maze, rat, and path will be in support of implementing these **`public`** methods, and nothing more. This technique, which is called *data encapsulation*, is designed to allow the representation to be changed later without affecting the client algorithm.

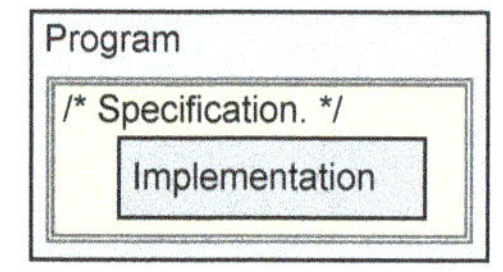

Recall that at the level of individual *statement*-level specifications and their refinements, we had to exercise self-discipline to prevent the rest of the program from relying on the details of the specification's implementation. In contrast, at the level of a class, and the implementation of methods, there is linguistic support: The compiler enforces information hiding by only allowing access to the **`public`** features of a class. The class is said to implement an *abstract data type* if its interface consists only of methods, and not its data structure.

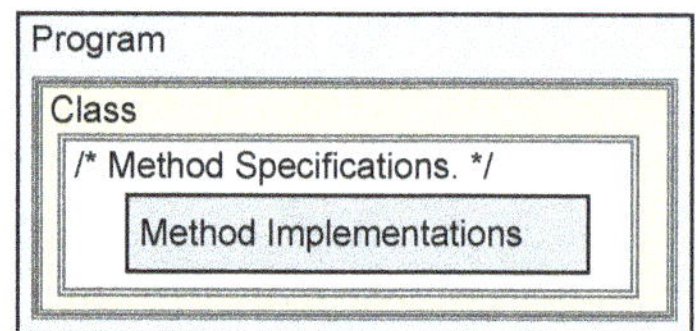

We create a stub for each of the six methods used by the algorithm, specifying the return type **`boolean`** for queries, and return type **`void`** for actions:

```
/* Maze, Rat, and Path (MRP) Representations. */                M2
class MRP {
   public static void TurnClockwise() { }
   public static void TurnCounterClockwise() { }
   public static void StepForward() { }
   public static boolean isFacingWall() { return ____; }
   public static boolean isAtCheese() { return ____; }
   public static boolean isAboutToRepeat() { return ____; }
   } /* MRP */
```

Additional operations may be needed later, but for now we focus only on these six. We are ready to consider the design of the data structure that will support their implementations.

Recall that we need to represent three things: The maze with its collection of walls, the position and orientation of the rat, and the path taken by the rat during its

133. We use the term "interface" generically, and do not refer to the Java construct **`interface`**. Similarly, we will use the term "abstract" generically, and not as Java's **`abstract class`**.

exploration so far. Together, these representations must support implementation of the abstract queries and actions used to express the exploration:

Maze Representation 1

A straightforward representation of an N-by-N maze is as an `N`-by-`N` integer array, say, `W`, where element `W[r][c]` represents the walls immediately surrounding cell ⟨`r`,`c`⟩.

In general, for each cell ⟨`r`,`c`⟩ there are 2^4=16 possible combinations of four walls and non-walls surrounding that cell. Accordingly, `W[r][c]` can encode the configuration of walls at cell ⟨`r`,`c`⟩ using the following numbering scheme:

0 1 2 3 4 5 6 7 8 9 10 11 12 13 14 15

One may interpret a number (0-15) as a 4-bit binary numeral ⟨$b_3b_2b_1b_0$⟩, where the four bits represent the absence or presence of a wall in the direction ⟨up,right,down,left⟩, respectively. Thus, for example, configuration 6 can be interpreted as:

$$6_{10}= 4_{10}+ 2_{10}= 0\cdot2^3+ 1\cdot2^2 + 1\cdot2^1+ 0\cdot2^0 = 0110_2 = \langle \texttt{NoWall,Wall,Wall,NoWall} \rangle.$$

W	0	1	2	3	4
0	9	10	12	9	12
1	5	9	2	4	7
2	5	1	12	3	12
3	5	7	5	11	6
4	3	14	3	10	14

An important advantage of this representation is the simplicity of the correspondence between the coordinates of cells in the N-by-N maze, and the indices of elements in the `N`-by-`N` array `W`. As a consequence of this correspondence, we are not likely to struggle with brittle indexing arithmetic in the code that explores the maze. In particular, when the rat is in cell ⟨`r`,`c`⟩, we will readily be able to consult `W[r][c]` to ascertain what walls exist for that cell.

What, if any, are the implications, limitations, or possible drawbacks of this representation?

First, we can anticipate the need to *decode* the representation of a cell's walls, i.e., for a cell whose encoding of walls is *w*, we will need to determine whether there is a wall on side `d` of the cell. It was for this reason that we chose a systematic rather than a chaotic encoding of walls. In our encoding, if we number the wall positions ⟨up,right,down,left⟩ as ⟨3,2,1,0⟩, respectively, we can tell whether or not a wall is present on side `d` by inspecting bit b_d in the cell's binary wall encoding w=⟨$b_3b_2b_1b_0$⟩. Mindful of the rule:

☞ **Beware of unnecessary Case Analysis; hope for code uniformity; avoid code bloat.**

we may plan to bury the bit-twiddling decoding operation in a Boolean function `isWall(r,c,d)` that returns **true** if and only if maze cell ⟨`r`,`c`⟩ has a wall on side `d`. This approach seems feasible.

It is somewhat concerning that Maze Representation 1 violates a standard rule:

☞ **Choose representations that by design do not have nonsensical configurations.**

W	0	1	2	3	4
0	9	11	12	9	12
1	5	9	2	4	7
2	5	1	12	3	12
3	5	7	5	11	6
4	3	14	3	10	14

Our representation `W` of maze walls allows inconsistencies, i.e., one cell can claim there is a wall between it and a neighbor, while the neighbor can claim there is no such wall. For example, the upper-left cell of the maze shown to the right is encoded as 9, i.e., no wall to the right, whereas the walls of the cell to its right are encoded as

11, i.e., a wall to the left. The input routine will be able to make sure that such inconsistencies never arise, but the possibility of such meaningless configurations suggests that there may be a more efficient representation where they don't arise because walls are uniquely represented.

We note, however, that there is a countervailing precept to the one above that results in exactly the sort of "nonsensical" representations the previous precept seeks to avoid:

☞ **Introduce redundant variables in a representation to simplify code, or make it more efficient.**

---

so, tradeoffs are necessarily involved. For example, in the Knight's Tour problem, we considered various representations of tours, and considered mutually-supportive redundant representations that support the full complement of operations needed (p. 224). The introduction of redundancy necessarily creates the risk of inconsistency, but in support of a worthy cause.

Path Representation 1

A direct path from the upper-left cell can be represented by integers 1, 2, 3, etc. in the elements of an N-by-N integer array, say, `P`, where `P[r][c]` represents the sequence number along the **p**ath to cell ⟨`r,c`⟩. If cell ⟨`r,c`⟩ is not along the path, then element `P[r][c]` can contain some value, say, 0, that is distinct from any legitimate path sequence number. We shall use the symbolic constant `Unvisited` to denote that value, where the name is not meant to connote that the cell has *never* been visited, only that it is *not* visited along the current path.

P	0	1	2	3	4
0	1	2	3	0	0
1	0	5	4	0	0
2	0	6	7	0	0
3	0	0	8	0	0
4	0	0	9	10	11

Maze Representation 2

A drawback of Maze Representation 1 was that each wall was represented in two different places in the data structure, and this could lead to inconsistencies. Although we observed that inconsistencies are an inevitable consequence of redundant representations, there is no point in allowing gratuitous inconsistencies. Accordingly, we may reach for a different representation of a maze without that downside.

We observe that for an N-by-N maze, **v**ertical walls can be represented by an N-by-(N+1) **`boolean`** array `V`, and **h**orizontal walls can be represented by an (N+1)-by-N **`boolean`** array `H`. In the figures in the margin, we show **true** in yellow. Were we to adopt this representation, the **`boolean`** function `isWall(r,c,d)` suggested above could consult `V[r][c]` or `V[r,c+1]` for the presence of a wall if direction `d` is left or right, and could consult `H[r][c]` or `H[r+1][c]` for the presence of a wall if direction `d` is up or down.

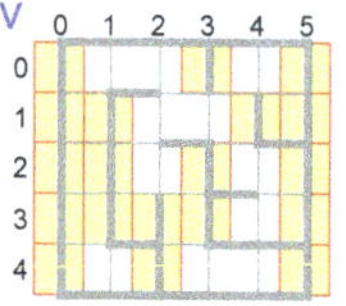

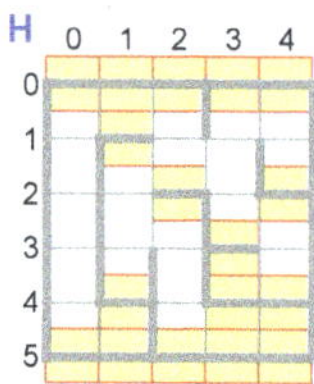

By representing each possible wall uniquely, we eliminate the possible inconsistencies of Maze Representation 1, albeit at the expense of violating a different rule:

☞ **Choose data representations that are uniform, if possible.**

Representing vertical and horizontal walls in distinct arrays is disconcerting, although as with Maze Representation 1, such details can be encapsulated in a function such as `isWall`. But the aesthetic negatives of Maze Representation 2 suggest that we continue to explore the design space of alternative wall representations.

Maze Representation 3

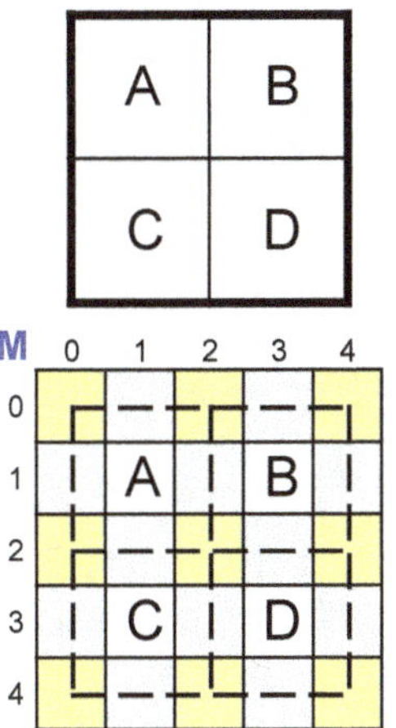

We observe that we can represent the walls of an N-by-N maze, as well as a direct path through it, in a single (2·N+1)-by-(2·N+1) array `M`. We illustrate the possibility with a sample 2-by-2 maze in which the four cells are labeled A, B, C, and D. Elements of `M` with gray background correspond to positions of possible walls, where the association of a cell and its four possible walls is implicit in array indices, i.e., the presence or absence of a wall in the ⟨up,right,down,left⟩ direction for the maze cell represented by array element `M[r][c]` is given by a value (say, `Wall` or `NoWall`) in ⟨`M[r-1][c]`, `M[r][c+1]`, `M[r+1][c]`, `M[r][c-1]`⟩, respectively. Elements of `M` with yellow background are unused. The elements of `M` labeled A, B, C, and D are used for storing sequence numbers along a direct path through that cell, or `Unvisited`.

The positives for this representation include these:

- Maze Representation 3 accommodates a representation of walls and paths in one and the same array `M`, which may be preferred to the separate arrays for walls and paths of Maze Representations 1 and 2.
- Maze Representation 3 characterizes each wall position by a unique element of `M` whose simple binary encoding (`Wall`, `NoWall`) describes the presence or absence of a wall there. It thus eliminates Maze Representation 1's need to decode an integer encoding of walls, and also eliminates the possibility of ambiguous configurations.
- We have replaced Maze Representation 2's dual array representation of vertical and horizontal walls by a uniform indexing mechanism within a single array for accessing information about a cell's possible walls.

The negatives of Maze Representation 3 are these:

- We have lost the simple correspondence between the coordinates of cells in the physical maze, and the coordinates of elements in its representation. In particular, in Maze Representation 3, the physical cell with coordinates ⟨`r`,`c`⟩ corresponds to array element `M[2*r+1][2*c+1]`. Similarly, when the rat advances to a neighboring cell, the row or column index in `M` must change by ±2, and not ±1.
- Roughly one quarter of the space in `M` is wasted, but alas this is the cost of a simplified indexing scheme that uniquely, and therefore unambiguously, relates cells and their walls.

Note that in evaluating the alternatives above, we considered only internal, and not external, data representations. That is, we did not concern ourselves with how a maze is to be represented in input, and how it will be displayed in output, along with a direct path. It could well turn out that one representation is easier than the others to translate from input or to output, but this should not be determinative at this juncture. We follow the rule:

> ☞ **Design internal data representations based on internal computational needs, ignoring input and output format considerations.**

and are prepared to let the chips fall where they may regarding input and output.

We embrace Maze Representation 3 for our solution, recognizing that its alternatives also have their merits; the choice is, to some extent, a matter of taste.

It is always a good idea to review the representation design, and to firm up its description in a *representation invariant*, i.e., a statement of relationships among a collection of variables. The representation invariant is a statement of properties that will hold if the representation constitutes a well-formed description of what is being modeled, i.e., the maze and its walls.

```
/* Maze, Rat, and Path (MRP) Representations. */                                M3
class MRP {
   /* Maze. Cells of an N-by-N maze are represented by elements of
      array M[2*N+1][2*N+1]. Maze cell ⟨r,c⟩ is represented by array
      element M[2*r+1][2*c+1]. The possible walls ⟨top, right, bottom,
      left⟩ of the maze cell corresponding to ⟨r,c⟩ are represented by
      Wall or NoWall in ⟨M[r-1][c], M[r][c+1], M[r+1][c], M[r][c-1]⟩.
      The remaining elements of M are unused. lo is 1, and hi is
      2*N-1. */
      private static int N;       // Size of maze. */
      private static int M[][];  // Maze, walls, and path.
      private static final int Wall = -1;
      private static final int NoWall = 0;
      private static int lo, hi; // Left/top and right/bottom maze indices.
   ...
   } /* MRP */
```

We work hard to perfect the statement of a representation invariant. The more precise it is, the easier it will be to write code later because you will be able to consult the invariant for guidance.

Following the rule:

> ☞ **Minimize use of literal numerals in code; define and use symbolic constants.**

we state the invariant using constants (`Wall`, `NoWall`) to provide greater readability, and to allow for easier changes later should the need arise. We have also introduced variables (`lo` and `hi`) for the indices in `M` of the left/top and right/bottom sides; these are variables rather than constants because the size of `M` will not be known until the input has been read.

Rat Representation

Given the representation of the maze that we have chosen, representation of the rat's location is straightforward; we have only to keep track of its row and column coordinates in array `M`. The orientation of the rat is easily represented by an integer from 0 to 3 representing (say) up, right, down, and left, respectively. Thus, the rat's representation invariant is:

```
/* Maze, Rat, and Path (MRP) Representations. */                                M4
class MRP {
   ...
   /* Rat. The rat is located in cell M[r][c] facing direction d, where
      d=⟨0,1,2,3⟩ represents the orientation ⟨up,right,down,left⟩,
      respectively. */
      private static int r, c, d;
   ...
   } /* MRP */
```

Note that the coordinate system for the rat's location is chosen as row and column indices in the data structure M rather than in the two-dimensional physical maze itself. Thus, when the rat is in the lower-right cell of an N-by-N maze, the location ⟨r,c⟩ will be ⟨2*N-1,2*N-1⟩, and is not ⟨N-1,N-1⟩.

Path Representation 2

Given that we have adopted Maze Representation 3, there is no need for a separate array for paths, as in Path Representation 1. There is room for the path in array M. Thus, the representation invariant for a path is:

```
/* Maze, Rat, and Path (MRP) Representations. */                    M5
class MRP {
   ...
   /* Path. When the rat has traveled to cell ⟨r,c⟩ via a given path
      through cells of the maze, the elements of M that correspond to
      those cells will be 1, 2, 3, etc., and all other elements of M
      that correspond to cells of the maze will be Unvisited. The
      number of the last step in the path is move. */
      private static final int Unvisited = 0;
      private static int move;
   ...
   } /* MRP */
```

We have taken a holistic approach to designing the internal data representation of maze, path, and rat. We strived for a harmonious design that enables different aspects to leverage one another, and have come up with an integrated representation of the path with the maze that we find pleasing.

Although our representation is economical, a tight coupling can be a mixed blessing because too much cohesion can also be a disadvantage. One of the so-called "ilities" of programming is "modifiability". Packing separate concerns into one data structure can result in a "house of cards", where a small perturbation in one part of the program risks causing the entire edifice to collapse. If you were to approach the choice of data representation with future modifiability in mind from the get-go, you might eschew packing walls and path into the same array, and make a different choice in which separate concerns are presented separately.

Interface Implementation

With the representation invariants of maze, rat, and path in hand, we can turn to coding the queries and actions we require. The six operations used in the exploration algorithm are easily coded with the aid of auxiliary constant arrays of "unit vectors" in the four directions:

```
/* Maze, Rat, and Path (MRP) Representations. */                        M6
class MRP {
   ...
   // Unit vectors in direction d =          0,     1,    2,    3
   //                                       up, right, down, left
      private static final int deltaR[] = { -1,     0,    1,    0 };
      private static final int deltaC[] = {  0,     1,    0,   -1 };
   public static void TurnClockwise()
      { d = (d+1)%4; }
   public static void TurnCounterClockwise()
      { d = (d+3)%4; }
   public static void StepForward()
      { r = r+2*deltaR[d]; c = c+2*deltaC[d]; move++; M[r][c] = move; }
   public static boolean isFacingWall()
      { return M[r+deltaR[d]][c+deltaC[d]]==Wall; }
   public static boolean isAtCheese()
      { return (r==hi)&&(c==hi); }
   public static boolean isAboutToRepeat()
      { return (r==lo)&&(c==lo)&&(d==3); }
   } /* MRP */
```

The use of modular arithmetic for `TurnClockwise` and `TurnCounterClockwise` is standard, but if you are rusty on it, you may incorrectly fall into coding counterclockwise as `(d-1)%4`, which doesn't work because when `d-1` is negative `(d-1)%4` is also negative. If you were to make this mistake, the code would index `deltaR` and/or `deltaC` with a negative number, which will cause a "subscript-out-of-bounds" error.

The code for `StepForward` is only correct when stepping into an as-yet unvisited cell. For now, we continue to ignore the looming question of how to excise a side-path exploration from an exhaustive path to make a direct-path.

Before we forget, we need to return to class `RunMaze`, the client of these six operations in class `MRP`, and provide *qualified names* for them. When code in one class uses a name defined or declared in another class, it must qualify it:

```
/* Rat running. See Chapter 15 of text. */                               R6
class RunMaze {
   ...
   /* Compute a direct path through the maze, if one exists. */
   private static void Solve() {
      while ( !MRP.isAtCheese() && !MRP.isAboutToRepeat() )
         if ( MRP.isFacingWall() ) MRP.TurnClockwise();
         else {
            MRP.StepForward();
            MRP.TurnCounterClockwise();
            }
      } /* Solve */
   ...
   } /* RunMaze */
```

I/O Methods

We have focused on the important query and action methods of class MRP, but it must also support input/output. Class RunMaze has Input and Output methods, but they are in the client application, which knows nothing about the data representation. We must implement corresponding methods in class MRP, where we have the needed access to the representation variables.

Input. Because input is often fussy, we choose at this stage to just temporarily hard-code the degenerate 1-by-1 maze:

M7

```
/* Maze, Rat, and Path (MRP) Representations. */
class MRP {
   ...
   public static void Input() {
      /* Maze. As per representation invariant. */
         N = 1;                        // Size of maze.
         M = new int[2*N+1][2*N+1];    // Maze, walls, and path.
         lo= 1; hi = 2*N-1;            // First and last indices of maze.
         M[0][1] = M[1][0] = M[1][2] = M[2][1] = Wall;
      /* Rat. Place rat in upper-left cell facing up. */
         r = lo; c = lo; d = 0;
      /* Path. Establish the rat in the upper-left cell. */
         move = 1; M[r][c] = move;
      } /* Input */
   } /* MRP */
```

In writing this code, we use the representation invariants for mazes, rats, and paths as guides and checklists for what to write. Hand-coding a simple maze rather than addressing the general case gives us confidence as we approach our first test of the algorithm that the sample maze is properly represented. It also minimizes our investment, a precaution that acknowledges the possibility of a surprise that would necessitate changing something about the representation.

The Input routine of the algorithm in client class RunMaze invokes MRP.Input in the server class MRP:

R7

```
/* Rat running. See Chapter 15 of text. */
class RunMaze {
   /* Input a maze, or reject the input as malformed. */
   private static void Input() { MRP.Input(); } /* Input */
   ...
   } /* RunMaze */
```

Output. As with input, we don't have access to representation details in RunMaze, so we must rely on an output routine provided by class MRP. Writing and debugging a general-purpose PrintMaze method now will enable us to work with more complicated examples later, secure in the knowledge that at least the output routine is working.

We have a choice: Ignore the fact that we will eventually need to deal with visit-sequence numbers with differing numbers of digits, or bite the bullet and deal with that now. We do the latter (to simplify the presentation in the text), although there are good reasons to defer it (until we have an example in hand to test it on). The code traverses the elements of the maze in row major order, and for each element creates an appropriate string representation that consists of two characters, padded on the right, if necessary, by blanks:

```
/* Maze, Rat, and Path (MRP) Representations. */                        M8
class MRP {
   ...
   /* Output N-by-N maze, with walls and path. */
   public static void PrintMaze() {
      for (int r = lo-1; r<=hi+1; r++) {
         for (int c = lo-1; c<=hi+1; c++) {
            String s;
            if (M[r][c]==Wall) s = "#";
            else if (M[r][c]==NoWall || M[r][c]==Unvisited) s = " ";
            else s = M[r][c]+"";
            System.out.print((s+"    ").substring(0,3));
            }
         System.out.println();
         }
      } /* PrintMaze */
   } /* MRP */
```

The Output method of the algorithm in client class RunMaze either prints "Unreachable", or invokes the MRP.PrintMaze method in the server class MRP:

```
/* Rat running. See Chapter 15 of text. */                              R8
class RunMaze {
   ...
   /* Output the direct path found, or "unreachable" if there is none. */
   private static void Output() {
      if (!MRP.isAtCheese()) System.out.println("Unreachable");
      else MRP.PrintMaze();
      } /* Output */
   } /* RunMaze */
```

Initial Tests

We are now ready to test the code.

It is helpful to never stray far from a correct, albeit partial, program so that when something goes wrong (as it inevitably does) we won't have far to look for the problem. In support of this approach, it is often useful to write simplified initial versions of procedures so that we may get off the ground quickly, and also control the complexity of the code under test at any one time. We hard-coded the 1-by-1 maze in MRP.Input in that spirit, but in the case of method RunMaze.Solve, have gotten a little ahead of ourselves. Accordingly, we put it aside, and temporarily replace it with an empty method.

Compiling and running the program at this juncture allows us to remove syntax errors, confirm that all variables are declared and initialized, and obtain output. In the event that we had forgotten to initialize some variables in Input, or had blundered in indexing M, we would be able to make corrections easily in this highly controlled setting. However, all is well.

Test 1. The program runs, and produces the correct output. We show the input graphically at the right, but recall that it is hard-coded.

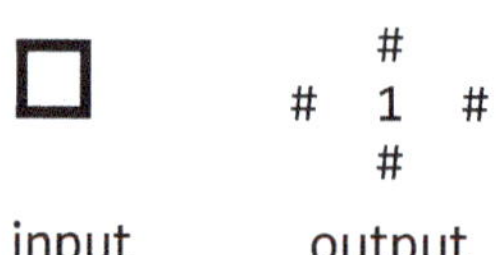

Test 2. With very little extra effort, we can change MRP.Input to hard-code the empty 2-by-2 maze. We can then confirm that we obtain the output "Unreachable". This output is wrong, of course, but that is just a reflection of the fact that Solve currently does nothing. Doing this, however, confirms that we can at least compile a version of the hard-coded empty 2-by-2 maze, test the routine isAtCheese, and exercise the conditional statement in RunMaze.Output.

```
Unreachable
```

input output

Test 3. We have gone about as far as possible with an empty Solve method, so it is time to adopt the real one. On the empty 2-by-2 maze above, we get our first substantive output. The rat runs around the outer wall clockwise, as expected.

```
  #   #
# 1   2 #

#     3 #
  #   #
```

input output

Test 4. It is a simple matter to change MRP.Input to hard code an obstacle in the maze. We run the program again, and the rat avoids the obstacle. Although it appears to be running counterclockwise around the outside perimeter of the maze, this is an illusion because it is really running clockwise around the obstacle, but stumbles into the cheese first. We are off to a good start.

```
  #   #
# 1 #   #

# 2   3 #
  #   #
```

input output

Direct Paths

So far, the code we have written for Solve assumes that the exploration path is the desired direct path. Said another way, the code assumes the rat never needs to back out of a cell it has already visited. But as we have seen in our initial motivating example, the rat can reach the end of a cul-de-sac, at which point it must retrace its steps, effectively canceling a side-excursion.

It is often effective to reason about a phenomenon using the simplest example we can devise, and we can do that in our 2-by-2 maze by orienting the obstacle so there is a cul-de-sac in the upper-right cell. The rat will then have to back out of that cell, reenter the upper-left cell (facing down), StepForward into the lower-left cell, and then proceed to the lower-right cell:

Let's see what happens in this case. We will not be surprised to get the wrong output because we know that our code is oblivious to the fact that the rat can enter a cul-de-sac. This is the advantage of testing in a controlled setting: Problems are not hard to pinpoint.

Test 5. We easily change MRP.Input to hard code the maze above, and try our code. We confirm that we obtain this disappointing output.

```
  #   #
# 3   2 #
      #
# 4   5 #
  #   #
```

input output

Method Solve ignores the fact that it is about to renter a cell that is on the current path, just keeps going, and overwrites the path.

As a first step to addressing direct paths, we need a way for Solve to detect the imminent reentry to a cell that on the current path. MRP has no such query, so we add one to its interface:

```
/* Maze, Rat, and Path (MRP) Representations. */                M9
class MRP {
   ...
   public static boolean isFacingUnvisited()
      { return M[r+2*deltaR[d]][c+2*deltaC[d]] == Unvisited; }
   ...
   } /* MRP */
```

and update `Solve` to use it:

```
/* Rat running. See Chapter 15 of text. */                          R9
class RunMaze {
   ...
   /* Compute a direct path through the maze, if one exists. */
   private static void Solve() {
      while ( !MRP.isAtCheese() && !MRP.isAboutToRepeat() )
         if ( MRP.isFacingWall() ) MRP.TurnClockwise();
         else if ( MRP.isFacingUnvisited() {
            MRP.StepForward();
            MRP.TurnCounterClockwise();
            }
         else Retract();
      } /* Solve */
   ...
   } /* RunMaze */
```

Rather than blindly reentering an already-visited cell and overwriting the path number there, we stop and pass the buck to routine `Retract` to do the right thing, whatever that may be.

Consider the simple 2-by-2 example at the exact moment when `Retract` is called: The rat is in the upper-right cell, and is about to reenter the upper-left cell. It will be convenient to introduce some terminology. We shall call the upper-left cell, which is on the current path, and to which it now is about to return, a *reentry cell.* The rat must truncate the current path by one cell, return to the reentry cell, and orient itself passed the opening from which it came.[134]

We accomplish retraction by stepping into the reentry cell using method `StepBackward`, which code can be viewed as systematically undoing the effect of method `StepForward`:

```
/* Rat running. See Chapter 15 of text. */                          R10
class RunMaze {
   ...
   /* Unwind abortive exploration. */
   private static void Retract () {
      MRP.StepBackward();
      MRP.TurnCounterClockwise();
      } /* Retract */
   ...
   } /* RunMaze */
```

First, a terminological clarification. When we say "step backward", we do not mean "step in the opposite direction from which the rat is facing". Rather, we mean step *forward* in the direction the rat is facing, but effectively moving *backward* along the current path, thereby undoing the abortive visit.

On returning to the reentry cell, the rat's orientation `d` is 180 degrees from the way it faced when it previously left that cell. Had it skipped doing so, it would have continued another 90 degrees clockwise, omitting the side excursion to the cul-de-sac.

134. We label this point in the solution development "Start of garden path", for subsequent reference. We are about to "inadvertently" make a mistake. Can you spot it?

We get that effect now by turning 90 degrees *counterclockwise* on returning to the reentry cell.

Method `StepBackward`, which depends on the data representation, is defined in class `MRP`:

```
/* Maze, Rat, and Path (MRP) Representations. */
class MRP {
   ...
   public static void StepBackward() {
      M[r][c] = Unvisited; move--;
      r = r+2*deltaR[d]; c = c+2*deltaC[d];
      }
   ...
   } /* MRP */
```
M10

This code erases the visit number from the current cell, decrements the move counter, and steps into the reentry cell.

Test 6. We run our code on the Test 5 example with the above version of `Retract`, and obtain the correct output. We are ecstatic.

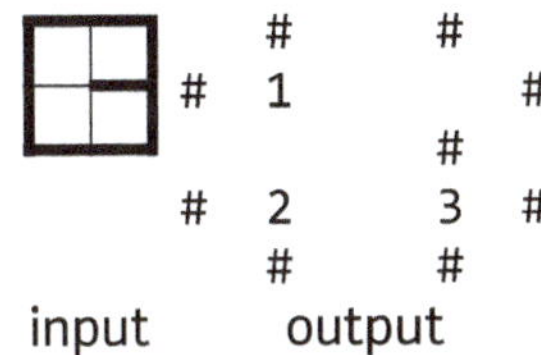

Could it be that we are done? We will surely need to test many more mazes, but we have pretty well exhausted what we can do with a 2-by-2 maze, and continuing to hard-code larger mazes will be tedious. So, it is time to bite the bullet, and write code for `MRP.Input` that handles arbitrary mazes.

Input

We start with the version of `MRP.Input` in which we hand-encoded a small maze, and turn it into a template. The principle is to change as little as possible, lest we break something that has already been tested and works. The maxim is:

☞ **Maximize code reuse.**

We already have the basic structure and variable initializations, and only need to change where the maze size and walls come from:

```
private static void Input() {
   /* Maze. */
      N = ⟨value for N⟩; M = new int[2*N+1][2*N+1];
      lo = 1; hi = 2*N-1;
      ⟨Define each element of M⟩
   /* Rat. */
       r = lo; c = lo; d = 0;
   /* Path. */
      move = 1; M[r][c] = move;
   } /* Input */
```

A straightforward input format is a line containing the integer N, followed by 2·N+1 lines, where each line consists of 2·N +1 characters. Thus, the input data is (essentially) an external image of array `M`. Each of the values in the input can be interpreted according to where it is in the (2·N+1)-by-(2·N+1) input matrix:

- In positions corresponding to maze cells, we can (forgivingly) ignore the input and hard-code the cell as Unvisited.
- In positions corresponding to walls (or no walls), a space in the input can represent "no wall", and any other character can represent a wall.
- In positions corresponding to unused elements of M, we can use any encoding because these cells will be ignored. We adopt the same encoding as is used for walls.

Here is the code:

```
/* Maze, Rat, and Path (MRP) Representations. */                          M11
class MRP {
   ...
   /* Input N, and (2N+1)-by-(2N+1) values; non-blanks are walls. */
   public static void Input() {
      /* Maze. */
         Scanner in = new Scanner(System.in);
         N = in.nextInt(); in.nextLine();
         M = new int[2*N+1][2*N+1]; // Maze, walls, and path.
         lo = 1; hi = 2*N-1;        // Left and right ends of maze.
         for (int r=lo-1; r<=hi+1; r++) {
            String line = in.nextLine();
            for (int c=lo-1; c<=hi+1; c++)
               if ((r%2==1) && (c%2==1)) M[r][c] = Unvisited;
               else if (line.substring(c,c+1).equals(" "))
                  M[r][c] = NoWall;
               else M[r][c] = Wall;
            }
      /* Rat. */
         r = lo; c = lo; d = 0;
      /* Path. */
         move = 1; M[r][c] = move;
      } /* Input */
   } /* MRP */
```

The code is a bit fussy, and may take a few runs to get the calls to `nextLine` right.

Test 7. We start with input mazes for which we have already tested the algorithm, the 1-by-1 case (A), and the 2-by-2 cases (B1, B2, B3). We confirm, by getting the same output for each case that we got before, that `MRP.Input` seems to be working correctly.[135]

```
1        A
xxx
x x
xxx
```

```
2        B1
XXXXX
X   X
X   X
X   X
XXXXX
```

```
2        B2
XXXXX
X X X
X X X
X   X
XXXXX
```

```
2        B3
XXXXX
X   X
X XXX
X   X
XXXXX
```

135. As written, routine `MRP.Input` obtains input from `System.in`, which typically corresponds to text entered interactively. It is often desirable to obtain input from a text file, e.g., it is tedious to repeatedly reenter the same, or slightly different, inputs. In lieu of files, which we do not cover in this text, a useful trick is to temporarily embed the input within the program as a `String` constant. In this string, we represent the end-of-line character with the escape sequence "\n". For example, to embed the 2-by-2 maze with only exterior walls (input B1), we can replace the line:

```
Scanner in = new Scanner(System.in);
```

with the line:

```
Scanner in = new Scanner("2\nxxxxx\nx   x\nx   x\nx   x\nxxxxx\n");
```

This allows us to repeatedly retest on the same maze without risk of making a typo in the input.

Testing, revisited

We can now test our code on a myriad of new examples. Depending on our imagination (or lack thereof), we may find that it works correctly on each example we devise, including such seemingly-robust cases as our original motivating example. However, the program may not in fact work correctly on all possible input mazes. Mere *multiplicity* of test cases does not demonstrate *generality*:

> ☞ **Beware of premature self-satisfaction.**

The euphoria of getting code to work correctly on many examples can easily lead to self-deception. If we were to stop now, we might leave behind a latent bug.

How can we go about assuring the full generality of a solution? In principle, we are not supposed to have missed any cases because we were supposed to have been following the precept:

> ☞ **Code with deliberation. Be mindful.**

But doing so requires considerable discipline and diligence, and in the excitement of getting code to work, it is all too easy to let our guard down, and forget to fully deliberate. Aware of this all-too-human shortcoming, we must:

> ☞ **Test programs thoroughly.**

But this then begs the question: How do we assure the full generality of test data?

So, where do we stand at this point in developing our solution?

We believe we have a correct program, but can't be absolutely sure. The program appears to work on many examples. We think we have been systematic and covered all cases, but we may be kidding ourselves. We have three choices: Think more deeply about *code*, think more deeply about *mazes*, or declare victory and stop (at our peril).

Let's return to program development and review key decisions.

Code Development, revisited

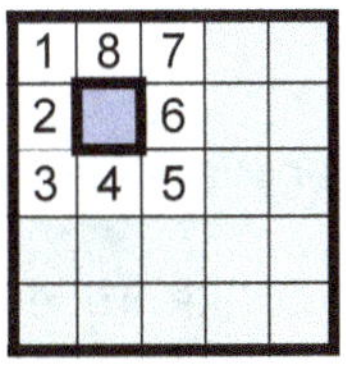

Our algorithm has three key elements: exhaustive exploration, detection of side-excursions, and retraction of side-excursions. Let us reconsider each in turn.

Exhaustive exploration. We coded a systematic maze exploration using the left-hand-on-wall rule, modified to allow us to temporarily take our paw off the wall and face a door. Is this rule correct, and if so, what exactly is the argument? Or conversely, can we spot a counterexample, i.e., a special case for which the rule is wrong?

Looking for a concrete counterexample for which the rule might fail is easier than constructing an abstract correctness argument, so let's start there. We seek a maze for which the rat would fail to get to reachable cheese.

In the section Extended Example: Running a Maze of Chapter 4 (p. 85), we already mentioned cases where the left-hand rule just squeaks by:

- The rule would have failed if the rat didn't start by facing an outside wall.
- The rule would have failed if mazes were permitted to have breaks in the outside wall.[136]
- The rule would have failed if the cheese were permitted to be in an isolated inte-

136. Why does 1 break in the wall not sink the left-hand rule?

rior cell, in which case the rat would run around the outer perimeter, and never stumble into it.

We fail to devise a counterexample, but are struck by the delicate nature of the problem. Were it not for the carefully-crafted constraints in the problem setup, the left-hand-on-wall rule would definitely not have been correct.

Our failure to find a counterexample is worthwhile, nonetheless, because the effort nets insights that may prove useful in making a solid argument that the rule is correct: (a) the rat starts facing an outside wall, (b) the maze is closed to the outside world, (c) the cheese is in a room with an outside wall. The left-hand-on-wall rule does not, in fact, perform an *exhaustive* exploration (in that it does not eventually visits every *reachable* cell of the maze), but seems adequate nonetheless.

So, what exactly is the correctness argument? Presumably, some form of mathematical induction is needed, but what exactly is the integer parameter on which one would be inducting? One possibility would be the number of additional interior peripheral-wall segments constructed by the process of pulling on a rubber sheet (red) on the interior surface of the peripheral wall, as described on page 89 and illustrated in the diagram to the right, starting from a maze with no protruding interior walls. Let us acknowledge that we don't have an airtight argument, and move on.

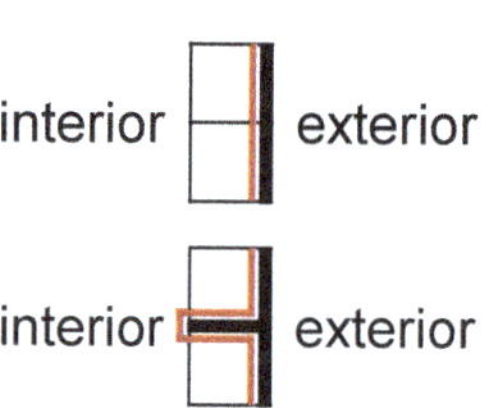

Detection of side excursions. Consider any path $c_1,c_2,\ldots,c_m$ through the cells of a maze, where c_1 is the upper-left cell, and c_m is the lower-right cell. Let c_s be the earliest repeated occurrence of a cell in this list, and let c_r be the first repeated occurrence of that cell. Then $c_{r+1},\ldots,c_s$ is an unnecessary side-excursion that can be excised from the path, leaving behind a shorter and (more) direct path to the cheese. Our code detects the earliest occurrence of a repeated cell, and calls `Retract` to excise it from the path. It does this for each and every subsequent occurrence of any repeated cell. Thus, if and when it reaches the lower-right cell, the code has at least attempted to excise every side-excursion. On the assumption that the excising code is correct, the path will be direct. This reasoning seems unassailable, but relies on the correctness of method `Retract`. Perhaps a careful argument about `Retract` would reveal an incorrect assumption that led us down a flawed garden path on page 260.

Retraction of side-excursions. When we coded `Retract`, we argued that a small example was helpful, and so, we used the simple 2-by-2 maze of **Test 6**. We detected the cul-de-sac in the upper-right corner just as the rat, facing left, was about to reenter the upper-left cell. We coded `Retract` as:

```
/* Unwind abortive exploration. */
private static void Retract() {
   MRP.StepBackward();
   MRP.TurnCounterClockwise();
   } /* Retract */
```

and validated this solution.

Looking for generality, we considered (but did not explicitly mention in the text) bigger mazes, and were pleased to see that the rat could back out deeper cul-de-sacs, and continue on to the cheese. For example, we tested the 3-by-3 maze shown below, with a trace of the rat's behavior:

Next, we considered our original motivating example, and were again pleased to see that our code could handle cul-de-sacs with arbitrary zigs and zags, as well as multiple cul-de-sacs, and continue on to the cheese.

We had started with a small and simple example, but in seeking generality, moved on to longer cul-de-sacs, and then to multiple, higgledy-piggledy cul-de-sacs. All of this built confidence in our solution. Furthermore, not only did the solution work on paper, but we were able to run the code on these very examples, and have the pleasure of getting correct output.

But this was the precise moment of danger, where overconfidence led to letting our guard down. Pleased with having generalized paths in two ways, size and straightness, we neglected a third issue: topology. Said differently, all mazes we considered consisted of cramped, 1-cell-wide corridors. But why not a maze with a wide-open space — a room, as it were?

Test 8. It is easy enough to find out what happens in this case; we just run the code on the maze shown in the figure (below, left), and get the disappointing output shown in the figure (below, right). At first, the presence of a direct path to the cheese leaves us befuddled as to where the spurious 3 and 4 came from. Then, we notice that the path to the cheese is also incorrectly numbered. It's a mess:

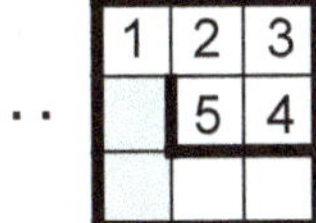

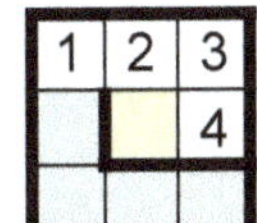

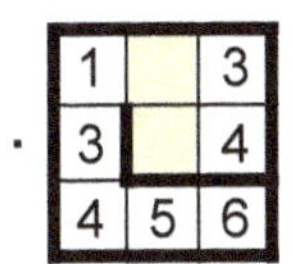

The trace shown in the four central panels of the figure reveal the mystery:

- Having made a clockwise excursion around the 2-by-2 room, and having reached the cell numbered 5, the rat discovered that it was about to enter the already-visited reentry cell numbered 2. It then stepped "backward" into that cell (erasing 5, and decrementing `move` to 4), and turned counterclockwise (to face left). The rat was programmed to treat a reentry cell as the place from which it had entered a cul-de-sac, and it acted accordingly.
- The rat again faced an already-visited cell (numbered 1). So, it again stepped (backward) into that cell (erasing 2, and decrementing `move` to 3), and turned counterclockwise (to face down).
- From there, the rat proceeded to the cheese, leaving chaos behind.

Let's call such a side-excursion a *loop*. In effect, we had only considered degenerate loops, but this is a more general case. Back to the drawing board, as they say.[137]

Direct Paths, revisited

In the general case, the rat must not *complete* the loop; rather, it should *unwind* it. The rat must repeatedly "step backward" into the cell *from which it actually came,* until finally backing into the reentry cell. In all the preceding cases, immediately stepping into the reentry cell effectively unwound a length-1 loop, but this doesn't always work, as we have now seen.

For the present example, the rat must step backward from 5 to 4, from 4 to 3, and

137. We started "leading you down the garden path" on page 260. You may find it worthwhile to reread the text at that point to review how we mistakenly convinced ourselves we were proceeding with all due care and deliberation.

from 3 to 2, while (like Hansel and Gretel) picking up the numbered breadcrumbs along the way. Then, having reached cell 1 facing down, it's on its way:

Accordingly, we replace the code

```
/* Unwind abortive exploration. */
private static void Retract () {
   MRP.StepBackward();
   MRP.TurnCounterClockwise();
   } /* Retract */
```

with the code;

```
/* Unwind abortive exploration. */
private static void Retract () {
   while ( /* not unwound */ ) {
      MRP.FacePrevious();
      MRP.StepBackward();
      }
   MRP.TurnCounterClockwise();
   } /* Retract */
```

where `FacePrevious` reorients the rat to face the cell from which it came.[138]

Our proposed code unwinds the loop, but when should it stop? Specifically, should the rat "unwind" cell 2, or just return there facing an appropriate direction? Interestingly, the example is a special case that is deceptive and misleading.

Reasoning from the example, we see that the topology *does* require the rat to *eventually* back out from 2 (as well as from 5, 4, and 3). Thus, we are sorely tempted to write the loop *condition* for this unwinding so that it (incorrectly) does exactly that. However, were we to do that, we would risk repeating our unfortunate experience of overconfidently declaring victory when we get the code working on a particular example, and fail to take into account yet another group of mazes!

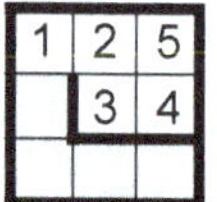

There is another seductive observation that (incorrectly) suggests that the rat should unwind cell 2 now. If it were to return to cell 2 (from the right, after unwinding from 5), and turn counterclockwise (as the present version of `Retract` does), it will be facing down. Upon returning to `Solve` from `Retract`, the rat would then step forward through the opening at the bottom, and begin traversing the loop all over again, albeit this time in the counterclockwise direction. We may (incorrectly) reason that the problem would have been caused by failing to have unwound cell 2,

138. In the Knight's Tour, section Alternative Board and Tour Representations, we considered representing a tour as a list of (row,column) pairs rather than as sequence numbers within the cells of the board. It is interesting to note that if we had used such a list representation for the Rat's Tour, we might well have not overlooked the case of general loops. Rather, to trim a side-excursion back to the reentry cell, we might have removed coordinate pairs from the list one at a time, from right to left, and in so doing would have done the proper unwinding. A list that obeys a Last In First Out (LIFO) discipline is called a *stack*. The rightmost element of the list is called the *top* of the stack, and removing it is called *popping* the stack.

and that if we had unwound cell 2, then this bizarre behavior would not have happened. But the problem is not that we didn't unwind 2 now; the problem is that on returning to cell 2, we established the wrong orientation.

What is the issue? Or rather, what question should we be asking ourselves in order to decide about the termination *condition* for the loop in `Retract`?

The question: Is the rat finished exploring the cell at the head of a loop when, after detecting the loop, the side excursion is excised? Or said another way: Is there a maze such that the direct path to the cheese must include that "loop-head" cell? Or in a third way: Call the four sides of a cell, in clockwise order, **a**, **b**, **c**, and **d**. Is there a maze such that one may enter a loop-head cell via **a**, begin a loop via **b**, discover the loop via **c**, and after trimming the **b**-**c** side excursion (backwards), continue on a direct path via **d**?

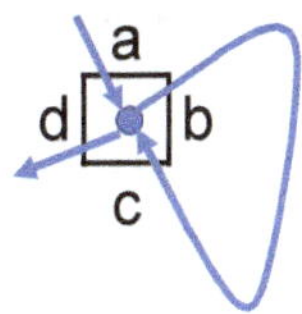

While at first it may not be obvious that there is such a maze, eventually we find one. We arrive at the loop-head cell 3 from cell 2 (via side **a**). From there, we begin a side-excursion that starts with cell 4 (via side **b**). The excursion proceeds from cell 4 to cells 5, 6, 7, 8, 9, 10, whereupon the loop-head cell 3 is detected (via side **c**). The rat must unwind 10, 9, 8, 7, 6, 5, and 4, and then proceed left from 3 to the cheese (via side **d**), resuming the numbering of the next cell as 4. If we had mistakenly unwound the loop-head cell 3 in `Retract`, we would have returned to 2, and from there to 1, at which point we would have incorrectly declared "Unreachable"!

This analysis resolves the question of how far to unwind, but leaves open the question of exactly which way to face once we return to a loop-head cell. Consider how the rat would have turned in its exhaustive exploration, back when it was not worrying about numbering (and un-numbering) of cells along the path. From the cell numbered 10 in the example, it would have stepped forward (into the cell numbered 3) and turned counterclockwise (facing left). Despite the intervening loop unwinding, the rat must now end up facing that same direction. We can accomplish this if, at the same time as we record the location of the loop-head cell (so that we know when to stop the loop unwinding), we also record the rat's orientation (so that we can restore it back to that orientation after unwinding the loop).

The way to the solution is now clear, but we are at another moment of truth: In which class should this code go? Specifically, is `Retract` a large-grained service of `MRP`, with full access to the data representation therein, or is `Retract` a client operation in `RunMaze`, which must be implemented in terms of fine-grained `MRP` services that we must now invent?

The temptation to do the former is great. In fact, here is an implementation of `Retract` that we could create inside `MRP`, and be done:

```
/* Unwind abortive exploration. */
public static void Retract() {
   int neighborNumber = M[r+2*deltaR[d]][c+2*deltaC[d]];
   int neighborDirection = d; // Save direction.
   while ( M[r][c] != neighborNumber ) {
      FacePrevious();
      StepBackward();
      }
   d = neighborDirection;      // Restore direction.
   TurnCounterClockwise();
   } /* Retract */
```

where `FacePrevious` remains to be created (also in `MRP`). By placing `Retract` inside MRP, the code highlighted in blue takes advantage of direct access to the data representation.

Encapsulation and information hiding is like a tax that we force ourselves to pay now so that we may garner (possible) benefits later. In the short run, it is undeniably a nuisance and an annoyance. But experience has shown that it is good medicine. Today's throwaway programs have a way of growing into substantial bodies of code that stick around for years to come. And who knows when we are going to decide to change the data representation?

Just as we need to be on guard against leaking data-representation details *out* from the MRP service to its client, so too we need to also guard against leaking algorithmic details *into* the MRP service. We must strive to invent appropriate algorithm-independent, fine-grained methods for MRP that are sufficient for the client to implement a maze-running algorithm that is representation independent. It is important to learn how to tease code apart so one achieves such a separation of concerns.

FacePrevious seems like a suitable algorithm-independent, micro-level operation that MRP can reasonably support. It basically says: The rat originally arrived at the present cell from some neighboring cell; aim it in that direction. Implementing this will not be hard. We just must find the neighboring cell that is numbered 1 less than the current cell. Let's add this to the MRP interface:

M12

```
/* Maze, Rat, and Path (MRP) Representations. */
class MRP {
   ...
   public static void FacePrevious() {
      int d = 0;
      while ( isFacingWall() ||
              M[r][c]-1!=M[r+2*deltaR[d]][c+2*deltaC[d]] ) d++;
      } /* FacePrevious */
   ...
   } /* MRP */
```

Retract, on the other hand, is algorithmic, and has non-local reach. It doesn't belong in MRP. But if it is to be implemented in the client class RunMaze, the parts in blue (which access the data representation) must be replaced by uses of new, general-purpose routines that we add to the MRP interface.

In effect, we must equip the rat with an arrow that it can orient and toss into the loop-head cell when it first discovers it. Then, it can use later discovery of that arrow to know both when the unwinding is complete, and the direction in which to face at that time. The needed micro-operations are:

- The rat is facing some neighboring cell in a given direction, and needs to remember this.
- As the rat retraces its steps, it would like to test whether it has arrived in that remembered cell.
- The rat then needs to restore it orientation to be as it was when it first faced that neighbor.

We can implement these operations as methods:

- RecordNeighborAndDirection
- isAtNeighbor
- RestoreDirection

with the following code:

```
/* Maze, Rat, and Path (MRP) Representations. */                  M13
class MRP {
   ...
   private static int neighborNumber;     // Recorded visit #.
   private static int neighborDirection;  // Dir. at time of recording.
   public static void RecordNeighborAndDirection () {
      neighborNumber = M[r+2*deltaR[d]][c+2*deltaC[d]];
      neighborDirection = d;
      }
   public static boolean isAtNeighbor()
      { return M[r][c]==neighborNumber; }
   public static void RestoreDirection()
      { d = neighborDirection; }
   ...
   } /* MRP */
```

Notice how the **static** variables neighborNumber and neighborDirection are used to record the location and orientation of the rat's arrow. Declaring these variables **static**, i.e., at the level of the class as a whole, and not local to a method, allows their values to be preserved between the initial call to method RecordNeighborAndDirection and subsequent calls to methods isAtNeighbor and RestoreDirection.

We can now define method Retract in the client class RunMaze, replacing the blue code with invocations of the new methods that we have added to MRP's interface:

```
/* Rat running. See Chapter 15 of text. */                          R11
class RunMaze {
   ...
   /* Unwind abortive exploration. */
   private static void Retract() {
      MRP.RecordNeighborAndDirection();
      while ( !MRP.isAtNeighbor() ) {
         MRP.FacePrevious();
         MRP.StepBackward();
         }
      MRP.RestoreDirection();
      MRP.TurnCounterClockwise();
      } /* Retract */
   ...
   } /* RunMaze */
```

We are ready for another test.

Test 9. The program with the new version of Retract runs successfully on the **Test 8** example.

Boundary Conditions

We have followed the precept:

☞ **Boundary conditions. Dead last, but don't forget them.**

None jumped out at us in the course of developing the program, but the time has come to think hard about what we might have overlooked. It is a good idea to reread the problem statement carefully, and confirm that we have considered every requirement.

Our attention is drawn to this sentence:

> Your program should check that the input data correspond to a well-formed maze, and output "Malformed input" if it does not.

How might the input have failed to correspond to a well-formed maze, or be otherwise malformed? The problem background section states:

> A solid wall surrounds the entire grid of cells, so there is no escape from the maze.

This requirement was left unchecked. Given non-compliant input, the rat would have wondered out of the maze (and caused a "subscript-out-of-bounds" exception). We can correct this in a fashion consistent with our forgiving approach, and insert any missing walls.

On reflection, it occurs to us that silent correction may not satisfy the persnickety requirement that all malformed input be reported, but we shall not dwell on this.

As second, more pernicious form of malformed input occurs when the requisite number or types of input values is not provided in the data. For example, a runtime exception will arise if the first line does not have the form of an integer. Similarly, the program will crash if one of the lines of the maze does not contain the required number of characters. All such errors can be handled in one fell swoop by enclosing the input code in a **try**-**catch** construct:[139]

139. We `try` to read the input, but if it is malformed, an error exception will be "thrown", which will be "caught" by the innermost pending `catch` for exceptions. In this case, we abort execution by invoking `System.exit`.

```
/* Maze, Rat, and Path (MRP) Representations. */
class MRP {
   ...
   /* Input N, and (2N+1)-by-(2N+1) values; non-blanks are walls. */
   public static void Input() {
      /* Maze. */
         Scanner in = new Scanner(System.in);
         try {
            N = in.nextInt(); in.nextLine();
            M = new int[2*N+1][2*N+1];
            lo = 1; hi = 2*N-1;
            for (int r=lo-1; r<=hi+1; r++) {
               String line = in.nextLine();
               for (int c=lo-1; c<=hi+1; c++)
                  if ((r%2==1) && (c%2==1)) M[r][c] = Unvisited;
                  else if (line.substring(c,c+1).equals(" "))
                     M[r][c] = NoWall;
                  else M[r][c] = Wall;
               }
            /* Insert any missing walls. */
               for (int k=lo; k<=hi; k=k+2) {
                  M[lo-1][k] = Wall; M[hi+1][k] = Wall; // top; bottom
                  M[k][lo-1] = Wall; M[k][hi+1] = Wall; // left; right
                  }
            }
         catch (Exception e) {
            System.out.println("Malformed Input");
            System.exit(1);
            }
      /* Rat. */
         r = lo; c = lo; d = 0;
      /* Path. */
         move = 1; M[r][c] = move;
      } /* Input */
   ...
   } /* MRP */
```
M14

Quite possibly, you may have inadvertently entered erroneous input while testing your program earlier. In that case, you might well have decided to write the self-protective code earlier.

Self-Checking Code

We have been humbled by the subtleties of the maze-running problem, and are now mindful of our own limitations. In particular, we almost missed the possibility of side-excursions that involve a loop. In the absence of an airtight proof of correctness, we return to the question of how to gain greater confidence in our program.

The four error cases we must consider are that for a valid input maze the program may:

- Incorrectly purport to have found a valid path to the cheese, but that is not so.
- Incorrectly report "unreachable" when there is a valid path to the cheese.
- Crash, with a runtime error.
- Get caught in an infinite loop, and run forever.

Finally, there is the small matter of the infinite number of legal mazes to consider. We address the first two issues here, and the remaining issues in the next section.

Consider visually inspecting a large maze, and notice that you cannot easily tell whether or not it has a solution: You need to perform a search, just as our program does. But suppose the image shows a claimed path, and you ask the same question: Does the maze have a solution? You can (partially) answer the question by checking the path shown. If it is indeed valid, you can answer "yes"; if it is not, you can refute the claim, but still don't know whether a solution exists.

Notice that an algorithm for checking the *validity* of a path is different from a search to *find* a path, and is far easier to perform. We can code it up, say, as the **boolean** method `MRP.isSolution`, and incorporate it into our program in an **assert**-statement, at the very end:[140]

```
assert MRP.isSolution(): "internal program error";
```

If our program contains a bug, and makes a false claim, the **assert** will detect that, and abort execution.

Importantly, self-checking can only be used to debunk a proposed path that is bad; it cannot refute a claim that no such path exists, i.e., the second issue listed above. To do so would requires a counterexample to the claim, i.e., a valid path. But finding such a path is what the program is all about in the first place!

What level of assurance is obtained from self-checking? It is certainly far better than nothing, but isn't perfect because `isValidPath` is itself code, and may contain its own bug(s). For example, an (incorrect) implementation as:

```
static boolean isSolution() { return true; }
```

would never fail. Less overt errors in `isSolution` may overlook invalid paths only on rare occasions, but cannot be ruled out—at least without a proof of correctness of the self-checking code. However, because of the (relative) simplicity of `isSolution`, such a proof is conceivable.

An implementation of `isSolution` can walk the path backward from the lower-right corner, and confirm that it started in the upper-left corner:

```
/* Return false iff rat reached lower-right cell via an invalid path.*/
public static boolean isSolution() { return isValidPath(hi,hi); }

/* Return false iff rat reached cell ⟨p,q⟩ via an invalid path.*/
public static boolean isValidPath(int r, int c) {
   if ( M[r][c]==Unvisited ) return true; // No claim if Unvisited.
   else
      while ( !((r==lo)&&(c==lo)) ) {
         /* Go to any valid predecessor; return false if there is none. */
            int d = 0;
            while ( d<4 && ( M[r+deltaR[d]][c+deltaC[d]] == Wall ||
                    M[r+2*deltaR[d]][c+2*deltaC[d]] != M[r][c]-1) ) d++;
            if (d==4) return false;
            r = r+2*deltaR[d]; c = c+2*deltaC[d];
         }
   return true; // Reached upper-left cell.
   } /* isValidPath */
```

140. The **assert**-statement was introduced in Chapter 3 on page 49, and is further discussed in Chapter 19, section Defensive Programming (p. 335).

Note that variables r, c, and d in isValidPath are all local so that it can be called without disturbing the global MRP state variables r, c, and d.[141]

Testing, revisited yet again

In the absence of a proof of correctness that holds for any possible maze, we must be resigned to the possibility that some input may cause the program to crash or loop forever. Two (partial) remedies are to exhaustively test our code on all legal mazes of size up to a given size, or to test our code on some number of random larger mazes. In each such test, we can demonstrate that the program terminates normally, and if a path is found, that it passes the self-check, as discussed above.

First, let us count how many mazes there are of any given size. The 4·N walls on the perimeter of a maze are required, but each of the N rows of cells has N-1 interior vertical wall positions, and each of the N columns of cells has N-1 interior horizontal wall positions, each of which is free to be a wall or not. Allowing for the two possibilities in each of those cases means that there are $2^{2 \cdot N \cdot (N-1)}$ mazes of size N:

N	$2^{2 \cdot N \cdot (N-1)}$
1	2^0=1
2	2^4=16
3	2^{12}=4,096
4	2^{24}=16,777,216
5	2^{90}

Based on these numbers, it is feasible to test our program exhaustively on all mazes of size up through 4, and not feasible to do so for size 5 and above. We can easily construct an N-by-N maze with interior walls given by the bits of an **int** parameter w:

```
/* Create an N-by-N maze with walls given by the bits of w. */
public static void GenerateInput(int N, int w) {
   /* Maze. */
      M = new int[2*N+1][2*N+1];
      lo = 1; hi = 2*N-1;
      /* Set boundary walls. */
         for (int i=0; i<=hi+1; i++)
            M[lo-1][i] = M[hi+1][i] = M[i][lo-1] = M[i][hi+1] = Wall;
      /* Set 2*n*(n-1) interior walls to the corresponding bits of w. */
         for (int r=lo; r<=hi; r++)
            for (int c=lo; c<=hi; c++)
               if ( (r%2==0 && c%2==1)||(r%2==1 && c%2==0) ) {
                  if ( w%2==1 ) M[r][c] = Wall; else M[r][c] = NoWall;
                  w = w/2;
                  }
   /* Rat. */
      r = lo; c = lo; d = 0;
   /* Path. */
      move = 1; M[r][c] = move;
   } /* GenerateInput */
```

We then generate and test all mazes of sizes up through 4-by-4:

141. A small flaw is that the cells off a valid path must be Unvisited, and this property is not checked by the version of method isValidPath presented. Exercise 79 asks you to correct this.

```
/* Generate/solve all mazes of sizes up through N; validate paths found. */
public static void test() {
   for (int N=1; N<=4; N++)
      for (int i=0; i<Math.pow(2,2*N*(N-1)); i++) {
         MRP.GenerateInput(N,i);
         Solve();
         assert MRP.isSolution(): "internal program error";
         }
   System.out.println( "passed" );
   } /* test */
```

If method `test` terminates normally, it outputs “passed”; otherwise, something is wrong.

For larger N-by-N mazes, we can use a random number generator to create wall configurations (represented by integers in the range 0 through $2^{2 \cdot N \cdot (N-1)-1}$ and test our solution. However, we won’t get very far because a Java **`int`** is limited to 32 bits. Note that the solver can easily handle large mazes; it is only the input generator that took its wall configurations from the bits of an **`int`**. If we really want to follow this path, we could switch the representation of wall configurations in the testing code to Java’s **`long`** or `BigInteger` integers, and proceed.

Generation and testing of random data, as described, is called *fuzz testing*.

Complete Program

Because the full program is longish, and the presentation has been fragmented, it is reprinted all together in Appendix V Running a Maze.

CHAPTER 16

Creative Representations

The representations illustrated in the text have been mostly straightforward. Typically, there has been a direct correspondence between the physical object modeled and the programming-language data structure used to model it, e.g., a 2-D maze and a 2-D array, but this need not be the case. This chapter illustrates that there is room for considerable creativity in the choice of computer representations, often to great advantage:

> ☞ **The touchstone of a data representation is its utility in performing the needed operations.**

Tic-Tac-Toe

This example illustrates the potential of a nonstandard program representation based on a careful problem analysis to eliminate dreary, brute-force code.

Background. *Tic-Tac-Toe*, known as *Noughts and Crosses* in the British Empire, is played on a 3-by-3 board consisting of 9 cells. Two players take turns marking cells with either an "X" or an "O". The objective is to obtain 3 of your marks in a row, column, or one of the two main diagonals.

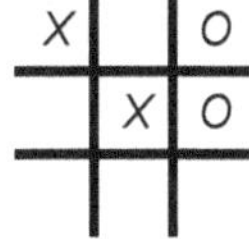

Problem Statement. Write a program that plays Tic-Tac-Toe.

Representation. The straightforward representation of the state of play is clearly a 2-D array of characters, in direct correspondence to the board:

```
char T[][] = new char[3][3];
```

T	0	1	2
0	X		O
1		X	O
2			

The sample array shows an imminent win for "X", who typically goes first.

A brute-force test for a win by "X" would be odious, requiring an exhaustive check for all nine possible winning configurations:

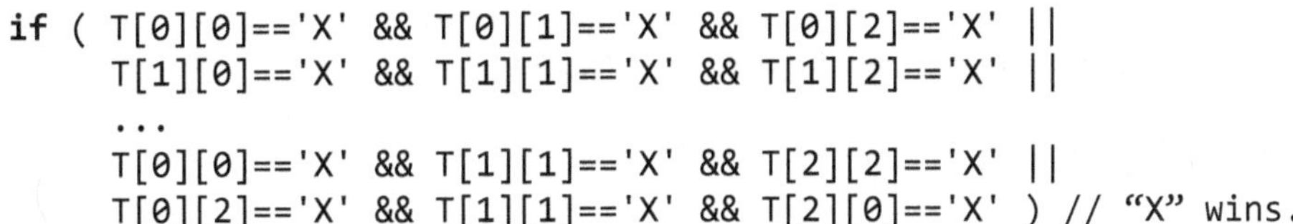

```
if ( T[0][0]=='X' && T[0][1]=='X' && T[0][2]=='X' ||
     T[1][0]=='X' && T[1][1]=='X' && T[1][2]=='X' ||
     ...
     T[0][0]=='X' && T[1][1]=='X' && T[2][2]=='X' ||
     T[0][2]=='X' && T[1][1]=='X' && T[2][0]=='X' ) // "X" wins.
```

An initial improvement occurs to us immediately: Change the datatype of elements of T from **char** to **int**, and represent "X" by +1, "O" by -1, and blank by 0:

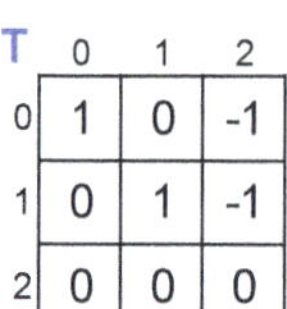

T	0	1	2
0	1	0	-1
1	0	1	-1
2	0	0	0

```
int T[][] = new int[3][3];
```

The sample board T would then be as shown.

The change to integers allows a simplified check for a win by "X" by summing the values on the rows, columns, and diagonals:

```
if ( T[0][0]+T[0][1]+T[0][1]==3 ||
     T[1][0]+T[1][1]+T[1][2]==3 ||
     ...
     T[0][0]+T[1][1]+T[2][2]==3 ||
     T[0][2]+T[1][1]+T[2][0]==3) // "X" wins.
```

This code is still fairly verbose, but at least we have made an initial creative lurch.

Tic-Tac-Toe is a trivial game, and we certainly have no reason to be concerned about the efficiency of our check for a win. But for illustrative purposes, suppose we wish to reduce the work performed to check for a win. We can:

☞ **Introduce redundant variables in a representation to simplify code, or make it more efficient.**

An additional variable that counts moves would be helpful:

```
int movesX = 0; // Number of moves made by "X".
```

where movesX would be incremented on each move by "X". The check for a win could then begin with a shortcut:

```
if ( movesX<3 ) // Not a win for "X".
else // Win for "X" possible.
```

We still have to consider the remaining cases of 3, 4, and 5 moves by "X", but have dispatched the cases of 0, 1, and 2 moves handily.

Consider the case of "X" having made 3 moves. Then "X" wins if and only if there are three +1s in the same row, column, or diagonal. We have already simplified the check for a win by counting moves, and by allowing ourselves to sum up our numerical representation of marks on each row, column, and diagonal individually, but is there anything we could sum across all moves by "X", regardless of where they are, that would indicate a win by "X". Perhaps something magical? Hint. Hint.

Recall the 3-by-3 Magic Square M (p. 128): Each row, column, and diagonal sums to 15. Conversely, any three elements of M that are **not** in the same row, column, or diagonal do **not** sum to 15.

M	0	1	2
0	8	1	6
1	3	5	7
2	4	9	2

We introduce an additional redundant variable:

```
int sumX = 0; // Sum of the elements of M corresponding to moves made by "X".
```

Each time "X" marks board position ⟨r,c⟩, the following code is executed:

```
T[r][c] = 1;                // Mark T with 1 for "X".
movesX++;                   // Increment count of "X" marks.
sumX = sumX + M[r][c];      // Add the magic value corresponding to ⟨r,c⟩.
```

The check for a win by "X" is now quite simple:

```
if ( movesX<3 ) // Not a win for "X".
else if ( movesX==3 && sumX==15 ) // "X" wins.
else // Win for "X" is still possible, but only in 4 or 5 moves.
```

Consider the case of "X" having made 4 moves. Suppose "X" wins. Then three of its four +1s will appear in the same row, column, or diagonal, and those three will contribute 15 to `sumX`. The fourth "X" will also have contributed some other magic value to `sumX`. In general, that additional value will be between 1 and 9, so the corresponding `sumX` will be between 16 and 24. Now turn the question around: Suppose four distinct integers sum to `sumX`, and "X" has **not** marked the cell that corresponds to a magic number of `sumX-15`. Then "X" does **not** win. Why not? Because the fourth move by "X" must be somewhere else, and that place will have contributed some *different* number, say, `d`, to `sumX`. But then `sumX-d` must not sum to 15, and so, the remaining three marks **cannot** be in the same row, column, or diagonal.

To implement these observations, we introduce `TT`, yet another redundant representation of the board. Whereas `T` is a 2-D array indexed by row and column, `TT` is a 1-D array indexed by magic numbers:

```
int TT[] = new int[10]; // M[m]==1 iff "X" has marked T[r][c] and M[r][c]==m.
```

For the position we have been illustrating, the value in `TT` needs to record that "X" is occupying cells that correspond to magic numbers 5 and 8.

The code executed for each move by "X" would now be:

	0	1	2	3	4	5	6	7	8	9
TT	0	0	0	0	0	1	0	0	1	0

```
T[r][c] = 1;                // Mark T with 1 for "X".
TT[M[r][c]] = 1;            // Mark TT with 1 for "X".
movesX++;                   // Increment count of "X" marks.
sumX = sumX + M[r][c];      // Add the magic value corresponding to ⟨r,c⟩.
```

and the check for a win by "X" in four moves uses the above analysis:

```
if ( movesX<3 ) // Not a win for "X".
else if ( movesX==3 && sumX==15 ) // "X" wins.
else if ( movesX==4 && 9<=sumX && sumX<=24 && TT[sumX-15]==1 ) // "X" wins.
else // Win for "X" is still possible, but only in 5 moves.
```

We shall not finish the code for the case of a win by "X" in five moves because the point has been adequately made: Analysis and redundant variables can lead to a completely novel representation that may simplify code. Of course, "simple" is in the eye of the beholder.

Checkers

This example illustrates how constraints and uniformity in a two-dimensional problem can be leveraged in a beautiful and historic, one-dimensional representation. It also provides an anecdote that shows that all is not Logic because historical accident can play an important role.

Background. *Checkers,* known as *Draughts* in the British Empire, is played by moving *pieces* diagonally on a *board* that consists of an 8-by-8 two-dimensional grid of 64 *squares.* Initially, each player has twelve pieces, arranged on dark squares, as shown. Pieces, known as *men,*[142] can only move to blank squares, diagonally forward (up) for black, and diagonally forward (down) for red. Another kind of piece, known as a *queen,* can move diagonally forward and backward. We will not further discuss the rules of the game. The salient fact of Checkers for our purpose is that although the board has 64 squares, only the dark squares matter. Specifically, because all moves are diagonal, fully half the squares (the light ones) are irrelevant.

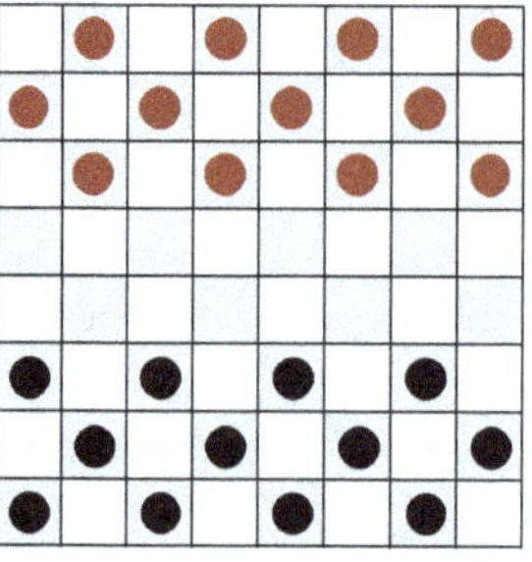

0	-1	0	-1	0	-1	0	-1
-1	0	-1	0	-1	0	-1	0
0	-1	0	-1	0	-1	0	-1
0	0	0	0	0	0	0	0
0	0	0	0	0	0	0	0
+1	0	+1	0	+1	0	+1	0
0	+1	0	+1	0	+1	0	+1
+1	0	+1	0	+1	0	+1	0

Problem Statement. Write a program that plays Checkers.

Representation. A straightforward representation of the state of play would be a two-dimensional array of **`int`** values denoting pieces, in direct correspondence to the board. We could choose to encode blank squares as 0, black men (resp., queens) as +1 (resp., +2), and red men (resp., queens) as -1 (resp., -2). However, the sparseness of this array, where fully half the array elements are unused, is unappealing.

First, we notice that if the dark squares are numbered from 0 to 31, then the 2-D representation can be replaced by a 1-D array with elements indexed by the number of the square, 0 to 31, where each element contains one of the same five possible values. This would achieve a 50% saving of memory space.

	28		29		30		31
24		25		26		27	
	20		21		22		23
16		17		18		19	
	12		13		14		15
8		9		10		11	
	4		5		6		7
0		1		2		3	

A second space efficiency stems from the observation that there are only five possible values at each of the 32 squares. Since each **`int`** variable has 32 bits, and can therefore represent 2^{32} different things, the choice of an **`int`** for each square is profligate. Replacing the one 1-D array of **`int`** elements with five 1-D arrays of **`boolean`** elements, one for each of the five things to be represented, achieves considerable savings:[143]

0	1-10	11	12-19	20	21-30	31	
+1	...	+1	0	-1	...	-1	Board

- `Blanks`. Initially **true** in elements 12-19, and **false** elsewhere.
- `BlackMen`. Initially **true** in elements 0-11, and **false** elsewhere.
- `RedMen`. Initially **true** in elements 20-31, and **false** elsewhere.
- `BlackQueens` and `RedQueens`. Initially both all **false**.

0	1-10	11	12-19	20	21-30	31	
F	...	F	T	F	...	F	Blanks

0	1-10	11	12-19	20	21-30	31	
T	...	T	F	F	...	F	BlackMen

0	1-10	11	12-19	20	21-30	31	
F	...	F	F	T	...	T	RedMen

Our representation is getting rather compact.

You may be wondering why we worry about space efficiency given that computer memories are so large? The answer lies in the fact that a checkers-playing program explores and evaluates many future moves and countermoves: If black were to move here, red could move in any of these different ways, and for each of those ways, black could reply in these different ways, etc. Depending on the depth of lookahead, the number of different boards that might be considered reaches millions, or more.

Spatial efficiency is only one consideration; another is speed:

> ☞ **The touchstone of a data representation is its utility in performing the needed operations.**

We must consider what operations are needed, and how efficient they are for the given representation. One operation is considered here as an example:

142. Apologies. It's an old game.

143. There are only two **`boolean`** values, **true** and **false**, so in principle only one bit is required for each **`boolean`** variable. Whether or not a given programming language implementation actually represents each **`boolean`** variable efficiently in one bit, or uses 8 or 32 bits, is a separate matter. For compactness in the diagrams, we denote **true** and **false** as T and F, respectively.

```
/* Compute all target squares of forward-right moves by black men. */
```

Ideally, we will be able to do this computation uniformly with two of the 1-D **`boolean`** arrays: `BlackMen` and `Blanks`.

Our spirits are lifted when we observe:

- $0 \mapsto 4;\ \ 1 \mapsto 5;\ \ 2 \mapsto 6;\ \ 3 \mapsto 7$

and realize that in each case the men advance to a square numbered 4 greater. We recall the simplicity of the Left-Shift-k operation from Chapter 9 One-Dimensional Array Rearrangements, and are excited by the prospect of using its analogue, Right-Shift-k, to compute all target squares. But alas, on the second row, we observe:

- $4 \mapsto 9;\ \ 5 \mapsto 10;\ \ 6 \mapsto 11;\ \ 7 \mapsto 12$

i.e., each forward-right diagonal move from the second row advances to a square numbered 5 greater. And then the increments alternate, with the third row adding by 4, the fourth row adding by 5, etc. Our hopes for uniformity are dashed.

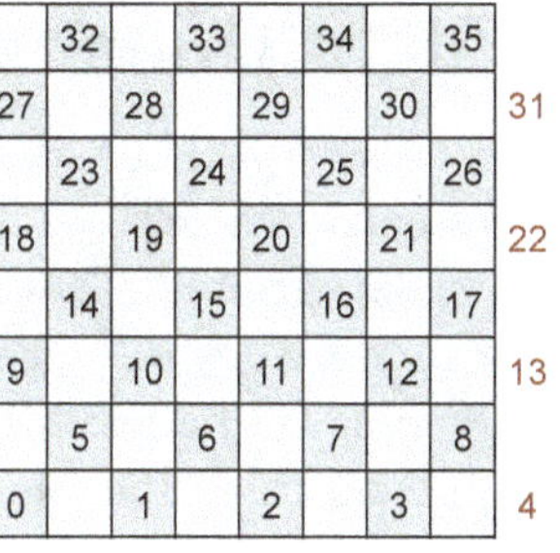

But wait! What if we were to introduce four *phantom squares* numbered 4, 13, 22, and 31, as shown? Check it out! Now, from each square numbered s anywhere on the board, the forward-right diagonal square is numbered $s+5$. Accordingly, if we record the location of black men as **true** in a **`boolean`** array of length 36, all squares reachable by a forward-right diagonal move by any of them can be computed by a single Right-Shift-5, and all squares reachable by a forward-left diagonal move can be computed by Right-Shift-4. Similarly, for the red-men, all squares reachable by a forward-right (resp., left) diagonal move can be computed by Left-Shift-5 (resp., Left-Shift-4) of the 1-D array that represents their positions.[144]

Finally, we must deal with the small issue of moves to phantom squares that incorrectly appear legal. But we needed to deal anyway with the question of whether a target square is blank or not because only moves to vacant squares are legal. Moves to phantom squares can be automatically discarded if elements 4, 13, 22, and 31 of `Blanks` are kept as **false**. In effect, these values are non-blank sentinels that disallow moves to phantom squares.

Thus, for the example of black men, the complete code to compute all legal targets of forward-right diagonal moves requires just two operations:

- Right-Shift-5 the array `BlackMen`, which identifies as `T` the squares to which black men could move, if only they were unoccupied.
- Perform elementwise logical **and** of the resulting shifted array with `Blanks`, the array that represents all blank non-phantom squares.

	0	1	2	3	4	5	6	7	8	9	10	11	12	13	14	15	16	17	…	35
BlackMen	T	T	T	T	F	T	T	T	T	T	T	T	T	F	F	F	F	F	…	F
BlackMen right shifted 5	F	F	F	F	F	T	T	T	T	F	T	T	T	T	T	T	T	T	…	F
Blanks	F	F	F	F	F	F	F	F	F	F	F	F	F	F	T	T	T	T	…	F
all targets of forward-right moves	F	F	F	F	F	F	F	F	F	F	F	F	F	F	T	T	T	T	…	F

The figures show the computation of all initial moves by black men, and color codes the values as follows: The four black men in the front row that can initially move diagonally forward right are tracked in the diagrams in green, and the **false** values that fill elements vacated by the Right-Shift-5 are displayed in blue. Legal targets are cells 14, 15, 16, and 17.

Remarkable as this representation is, the story gets even better.

The fundamental unit of data in a computer is called a *word*: Each machine-language instruction manipulates one word at a time. For example, a single instruction's execution can load a word from memory into the Central Processing Unit (CPU), or

144. The version of shifting needed has one small difference from those of Chapter 9. The k elements vacated by the shift are filled with **false** (rather than remaining as they were), reflective of the fact that no pieces move onto the board from off it.

add a word to another word, or store a resulting word back into memory. Of special interest for our purposes: Shifting the bits of a word left or right *k* places, and bitwise logical **and** of two words, can each be performed in one instruction.

Think of a word of length *n* bits as a **boolean** array of length *n*. Computers are built with enough hardware, i.e., transistors and circuits, to guarantee that each word-based machine instruction can be performed in one cycle, its smallest unit of time. Word-based manipulations are the fundamental units of work in a computer, and have maximal efficiency.

A Checkers playing program, written in the mid-1950s by Arthur Samuels, was one the earliest examples of Artificial Intelligence and Machine Learning [27]. The program was written for the IBM 701 computer, and had access to its efficient word-based instructions. The word length of the IBM 701 was serendipitously, you guessed it, 36 bits. In other words, Samuel's program could compute all forward-right diagonal moves of all black men in 2 machine cycles![145]

Eight Queens Problem

This example illustrates the principle of building problem constraints into the representation itself.

Background. Chess is played on an 8-by-8 board consisting of 64 squares. Queens can move any distance on the same row, column, or diagonal. The *Eight Queens Problem* is whether it is possible to place eight Queens on the board so that no two of them are on the same row, column, or diagonal.

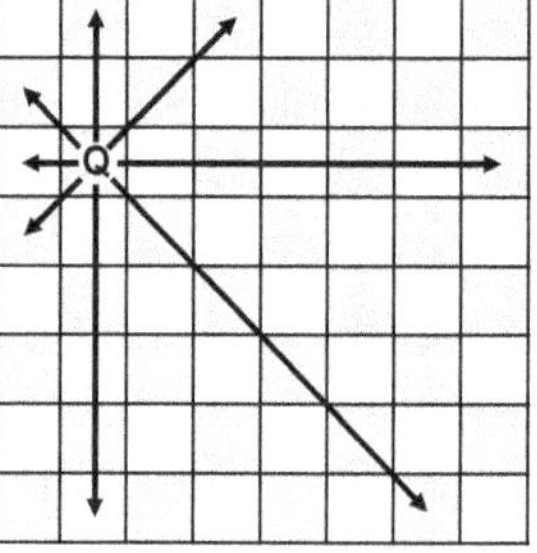

Problem Statement. Write a program that prints out a solution to the Eight Queens problem as a two-dimensional array, with the positions of the queens denoted by "Q" and blank squares denoted by "_". If there is no solution, print the message "not possible".

Representation. The Eight Queens Problem is a search: We seek a layout of eight Queens that satisfies the problem constraints. A straightforward representation of the board would be a two-dimensional 8-by-8 array of `boolean` values, in direct correspondence with the physical setup. The declaration would be

```
boolean B[ ][ ] = new boolean[8][8];
```

Each array element `B[r][c]` would denote by **true** (resp., **false**) the presence (resp., absence) of a Queen in the corresponding board square ⟨r,c⟩. There are 2^{64} different such arrays. That's a very large number [28].

A precept of data representations, especially for search problems, is:

☞ **Choose representations that by design do not have nonsensical configurations.**

Why do we allow so many manifestly failing configurations in our representation, e.g., a board filled with 64 Queens? Why not choose a data structure that only permits placement of exactly one Queen in each column? We can do this with a one-dimensional array `R` of integers, where `R[c]` is the row number of the Queen in column `c`:

145. In the 1960s, the conventional word length of computers switched from 36 bits to 32 bits. Although the 32 squares of a checker board could still be represented in the 32 bits of a word, without the 4 extra bits for phantom squares, the appeal for checkers was considerably diminished. These days, word lengths of 64 bits are common, so there is room once again for phantom squares.

```
int R[ ] = new int[8]; // R[c] is row of Queen in column c.
```

For example, the configuration of queens for the board shown would be represented by the one-dimensional array R shown. Although the configuration fails, it is not because there is a violation of the rule "No two Queens in the same column"; we can't even represent such a board in R.

But why permit duplicate values in R? Doesn't a duplicate value indicate two (or more) Queens in the same row? For example, the number 1 appears twice in R, indicating two different Queens on row 1 of our sample board.

A *permutation* of the integers 0, 1, 2, 3, 4, 5, 6, 7 is defined to be a rearrangement of those eight integers. If we only consider permutations of those eight values, then we will automatically rule out two (or more) Queens in the same row (as well two or more Queens in the same column).

It is a well-known fact of combinatorics that the number of permutations of eight things is eight factorial, i.e., 8 × 7 × 6 × 5 × 4× 3 × 2 × 1 = 40,320. This is because there are 8 choices for the first value, but then only 7 choices for the second value, but then only 6 choices for the third value, etc. All we have to do is iterate through the up to 40,320 permutations, and stop on finding one that doesn't represent two (or more) Queens on the same diagonal.

The top-level code is quite simple:

```
/* Solve the Eight Queens problem. */
static void main() {
   /* R[c] is row of Queen in column c for 0≤c<8. */
      int R[] = { 0, 1, 2, 3, 4, 5, 6, 7 };
   /* Consider each permutation of R until the first one is found that
      represents a solution. (We won't loop forever, as a solution exists.) */
      while ( hasSameDiagonal(R) ) NextPermutation(R);
   /* Output solution R. */
      ...
   } /* main */
```

Method `NextPermutation(R)` advances array R to the next permutation (in some enumeration of permutations), and method `hasSameDiagonal(R)` returns **true** if R represents a configuration of two (or more) Queens in the same diagonal, and **false** otherwise.

Positive diagonal index: row+column

To implement `hasSameDiagonal`, we first create an indexing scheme for the diagonals: The positive diagonals can be known by the value of the expression `row+column`, and the negative diagonals can be known by the value of the expression `column-row+7`.

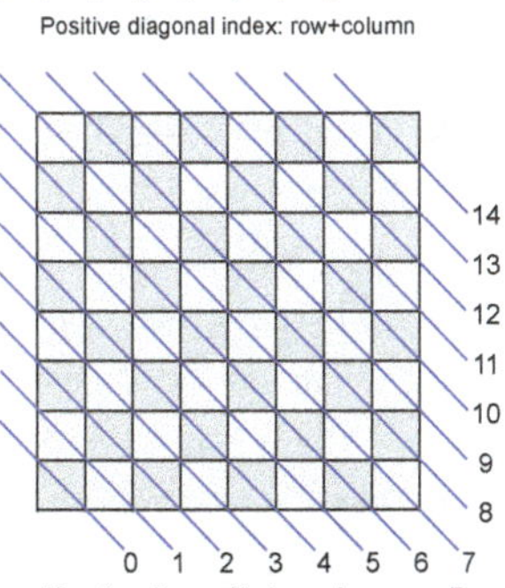

Negative diagonal index: column-row+7

The code for `hasSameDiagonal` is a search for a Queen (in the list of eight represented by a permutation) that is on a diagonal (positive or negative) that has occurred (in the list of Queens) before. We use two arrays, `PosDiag[15]` and `NegDiag[15]`, to record which diagonals have been seen before:

```
/* Return true iff R has two Queens on same diagonal. */
static boolean hasSameDiagonal( int R[] ) {
   /* PosDiag[k] (resp., NegDiag[k]) true iff a Queen in R[0..c] occurs on
      the positive (resp., negative) diagonal with index k.
      boolean PosDiag[] = new boolean[15]; // Initially false, by default.
      boolean NegDiag[] = new boolean[15]; // Initially false, by default.
   int c = 0;
   while ( c<8 && !PosDiag[R[c]+c] && !NegDiag[c-R[c]+7] ) {
      PosDiag[R[c]+c] = true; NegDiag[c-R[c]+7] = true;
      c++;
      }
   return c!=8;
   } /* hasSameDiagonal */
```

Because we have made our main point regarding data representations, we leave the implementation of `NextPermutation` as an exercise.[146] Who would have guessed that the crux of the Eight Queens Problem is enumerating permutations?

Ricocheting Bee-Bee

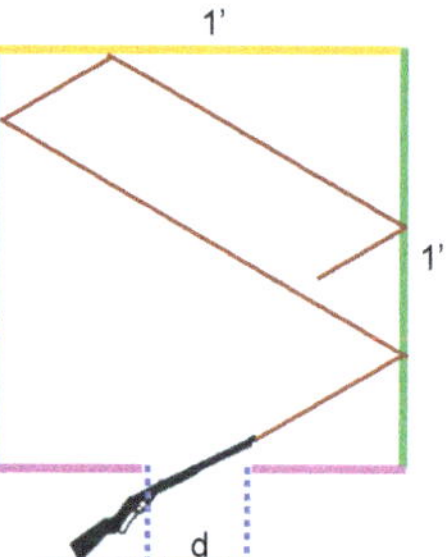

Background. A square tin *box* measuring one foot on each side has a *slit* of size *d* centered on one side. Insert a bee-bee *gun* at the center of the slit, at angle Θ, and shoot. The bee-bee ricochets off sides, one after another. On each ricochet, the angle of reflection is equal to the angle of incidence.

Problem Statement. Write a program that inputs *d* and Θ, and outputs the total distance the bee-bee travels before it exits.

Representation. The other examples in this chapter concern how to model a physical setup in program data structures. In effect, we model an aspect of the world in the computer, solve a computer problem, and then map the computer solution back to the physical world, announcing: You can perform these steps in the Real World with such and such an effect. We discovered creative ways to represent problems that still permit our computer-simulation results to say meaningful things about the original physical setup.

This problem is a bit different: We seek an alternative physical setup, and an analogous question to ask about it, such that the solution to the second problem informs our answer to the first problem. It is the second problem that we will solve in the computer. This technique, which is of fundamental importance, is called *problem reduction*, or *problem transformation*.

What makes the original problem difficult? The fact that with each ricochet, the trajectory is a different line segment. If you like to think of lines algebraically, then there is a different equation for each segment, say, $y=m{\cdot}x+b$, where m is the slope, and b is the y intercept. For sure, the slopes alternate between some m (corresponding to the original gun angle Θ) and $-m$, but the intercepts are all over the map. Are we really going to simulate each leg of the trajectory, computing which wall of the box it hits, and where it hits it? Let's hope not.

Uniformity often leads to simplicity.[147] In this problem, uniformity would follow if all line segments had the same slope and intercept, i.e., if the trajectory were

146. Exercise 86.

147. For example, introducing four phantom squares in the board for Checkers (p. 279) led to uniformity in the numbering of all board squares, which led to the simplicity of being able to use a single shift operation to compute all possible forward-right diagonal moves.

a straight line. We ask: For what similar problem would the trajectory be a straight line? In applying the rule:

> ☞ **Consider problem transformation or problem reduction: Solve a different problem, and use that solution to solve the original problem.**

and searching for an alternative problem to solve, let simplicity be your guiding star: In this case, the simplicity of a single straight line.

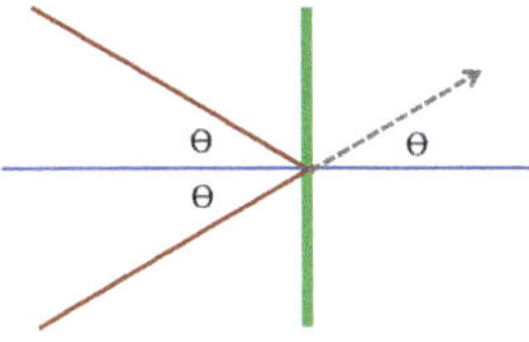

Focus on the first point of impact. Instead of ricocheting off the wall, we want the bee-bee to continue in a straight line. Wouldn't the bee-bee continue in a straight line if the box walls were paper thin? The bee-bee would pass right through the wall, and keep going. Similarly, if the bee-bee were a light ray, and the box were made of glass rather than tin, the light beam would continue indefinitely in a straight line.[148]

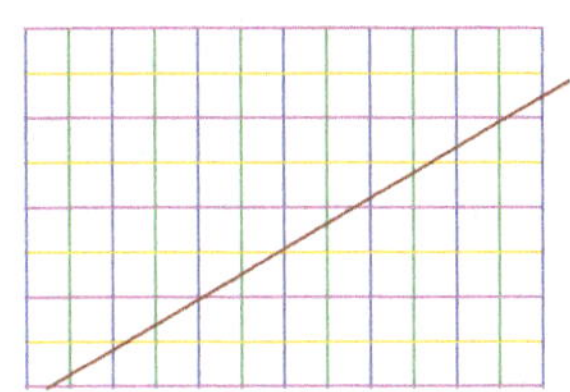

Now consider the space to the right of the box. What if this space were tessellated with images of boxes, with the trajectory continuing straight through all of them. The original box, with its ⟨right,bottom,left,top⟩ sides colored ⟨green,purple,blue,orange⟩, is the cell in the lower-left of this grid. The next cell to its right can be thought of as an image of the box, with the bee-bee traversing it to the opposite (blue) side. And the next cell to the right after that is another image of the box, with the bee-bee traversing it to the top (orange) wall. Notice that adjacent cells are mirror images of one another, not translations. When the trajectory passes through the top (orange) wall, it proceeds into an (upside-down) mirror image of the box, where the bottom (purple) wall is oriented *above* the (orange) wall.

The slits all occur on even (purple) horizontal lines for each and every column of cell images. Because the slits are symmetric on the bottom (purple) walls, they remain centered in each column despite the mirror imaging.

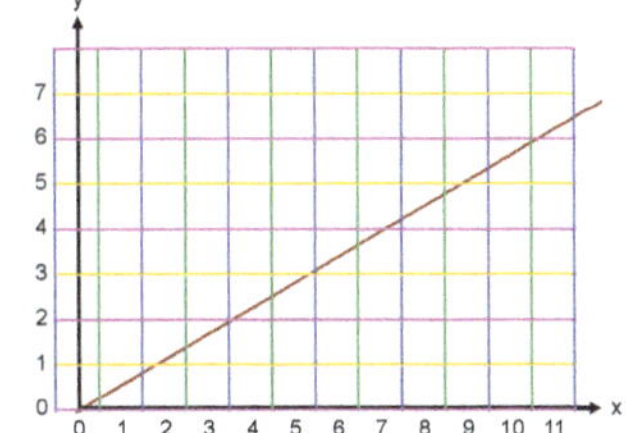

Let us sum up these observations with the aid of a Cartesian coordinate system superimposed on the tessellation, with origin in the middle of the slit, exactly at the point where the bee-bee emerges from the gun. The slit images appear on even-numbered integer y coordinates. They are centered around each integer x-coordinate k, from k-d/2 to k+d/2. We seek the smallest even integer $y \geq 2$ such that the straight line passes through a slit:

```
int y = 2;
while ( /* line does not pass through a slit at y */ ) y = y+2;
/* Output the length of the line between ⟨0,0⟩ and ⟨x,y⟩, where x is
   computed from y and theta. */
```

It's a simple search! Once the search stops at some `y` (and corresponding `x`), the distance traveled is given by the Pythagorean formula, of course:

```
/* Return length of hypotenuse of triangle with sides x and y. */
static double Hypotenuse( double x, double y ) {
   return Math.sqrt( x*x + y+y );
} /* Hypotenuse */
```

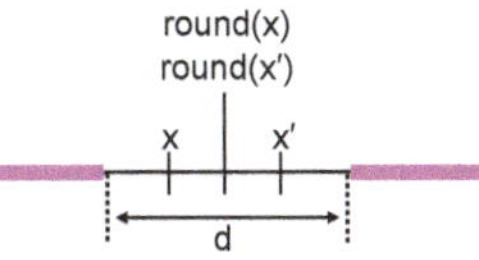

The line passes through a slit for a given `y` if its corresponding `x` value is less than `d/2` away from `round(x)`, the integer nearest to `x`. The unsigned distance between x_1 and x_2 is $|x_2 - x_1|$, so we ask that `|x-round(x)|<d/2`. Using `x(y,theta)`, an

148. Ignoring refraction.

as-yet-undefined method for computing x from y and theta, and fully qualifying the names abs and round, we obtain the *condition*:

```
/* line does not pass through a slit at y */
   Math.abs(x(y,theta)-Math.round(x(y,theta)))>=d/2
```

and the code:

```
double d = in.nextDouble();
double theta = in.nextDouble();
int y = 2;
while ( Math.abs(x(y,theta)-Math.round(x(y,theta)))>=d/2 ) y = y+2;
System.out.println( Hypotenuse( x(y,theta),y) );
```

We need a method for computing x from y and Θ. Assume that input Θ is between 0 and π radians, and input d is between 0 and 1. To deal with numerical instabilities for Θ near $\pi/2$, we observe that x can be computed by either dividing y by $\tan(\Theta)$, or by multiplying y by $\tan(\pi/2\text{-}\Theta)$. The latter approach will be better for Θ between $\pi/4$ and $3{\cdot}\pi/4$:

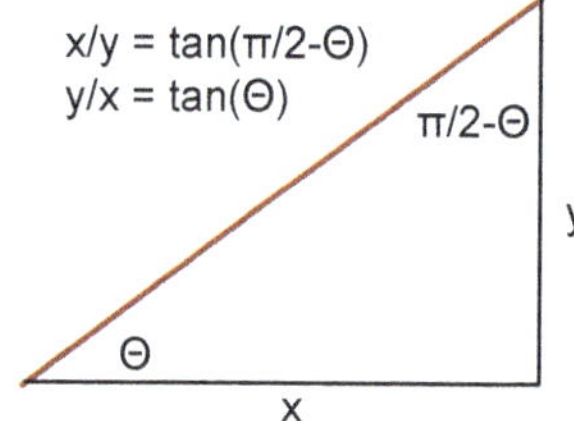


```
static double x(double y, double theta) {
   if ( theta<Math.PI/4 || theta>3*Math.PI/4 )
      return y/Math.tan(theta);
   else return y*Math.tan(Math.PI/2-theta);
   } /* x */
```

The whole solution is only about a dozen lines long!

Note that we have ignored the boundary condition that the bee-bee hits a corner of the box exactly, and another boundary condition that the bee-bee nicks the edge of a slit.

☞ **Flesh out corner cases that the problem statement omitted, or otherwise left unspecified.**

This is a lacuna in the solution for your further consideration.

We end with two intriguing, and possibly related, questions:

- Does our solution always terminate? Asked differently, is there a $0<d<1$, and $0<\Theta<\pi$ such that the bee-bee ricochets forever, and never emerges from the box?
- In analogy with the problem of Summing Integers from 1 to n, where iteration was unnecessary and there was a closed-form solution $n{\cdot}(n{+}1)/2$, might the Ricocheting Bee-Bee problem also have a closed form solution in terms of d and Θ?

Our analysis has greatly simplified the problem even if no closed-form solution can be found.

CHAPTER 17

Graphs and Depth-First Search

This chapter introduces graphs, an abstract mathematical structure, and Depth-First Search, an algorithm for enumerating the elements of a graph. Graphs and graph algorithms are a higher-level pattern of great utility. When problem analysis reveals that your problem can be framed as a graph algorithm, you have the opportunity to abstract away from the details of your problem, and apply one of the powerful, general-purpose methods that work on graphs.

We have advocated for use of everyday experience and intuition as a source of inspiration in programming, but have also advocated for analysis as an integral part of the process. Graphs and graph algorithms are an off-the-shelf analysis well worth knowing.

Relations

Let S and T be two sets. A *relation* between S and T is a set of ordered pairs, ⟨*s*,*t*⟩, where *s* is an element of S and *t* is an element of T. Set T need not be distinct from set S, i.e., we can have relations between a set and itself.

For example, let S={Adam, Eve, Cain, Abel}, where color is used only as a visual aid. The *has-child* relation between S and itself is:

{ ⟨Adam,Cain⟩, ⟨Adam,Abel⟩, ⟨Eve,Cain⟩, ⟨Eve,Abel⟩ }.

The pairs of a relation are ordered. For example, the relation:

{ ⟨Cain,Adam⟩, ⟨Abel,Adam⟩, ⟨Cain,Eve⟩, ⟨Abel,Eve⟩ }.

is not at all the same as the *has-child* relation; it is the *has-parent* relation.

Graphs

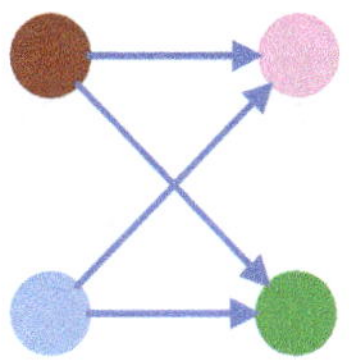

It is convenient to visualize a relation between a set S and itself as a collection of *nodes* and *edges*. The elements of S are nodes, and an edge from node *m* to node *n* represents the existence of the pair ⟨*m*,*n*⟩ in the relation. Such a visualization is known as a *graph.*

We can visualize the has-child relation as shown. A graph like this is called a *directed graph* because the edges have direction.

Some relations are *symmetric,* i.e., if ⟨*n*,*m*⟩ is in the relation, then ⟨*m*,*n*⟩ is also in the relation. For example, the relation *has-blood-relative* holds between Adam and his two children, and *vice versa.* It also holds between Eve and her two children, and *vice versa.* It does not hold between Adam and Eve, but it does hold between Cain and Abel, and *vice versa.*

A graph depicting a symmetric relation is called an *undirected* graph. Rather than depicting each directed (i.e., ordered) edge, we omit the arrowheads to signify that there are really two underlying ordered pairs for each edge. Thus, the has-blood-relative relation would be depicted as shown.

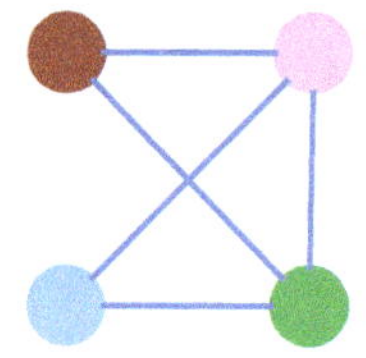

Elements of a set that are related to themselves would be depicted in the graph as nodes with self-edges. For the purpose of the example, we have not considered each person to be his/her own blood relative.

Depth-First Search

Depth-First Search is a process whereby we enumerate all nodes of a graph that are reachable from a given node n via a sequence of zero or more edges. It is defined in pseudo-code as:

```
/* If n was never visited, enumerate it and all its unvisited relatives. */
void DepthFirstSearch(node n) {
   if ( /* n has never been visited */ ) {
      /* Enumerate n. */
      for ( /* each edge ⟨n,m⟩ */ ) DepthFirstSearch(m);
      }
   } /* DepthFirstSearch */
```

The process is called "depth-first" because each visit to a neighbor m of a node n finishes all of the visits from m before n goes on to visit its other neighbors.

Let's apply Depth-First Search to the undirected has-blood-relative graph, above, starting with Adam. We signify that Adam has been visited by a black circle. He has two blood relatives: Cain and Abel.

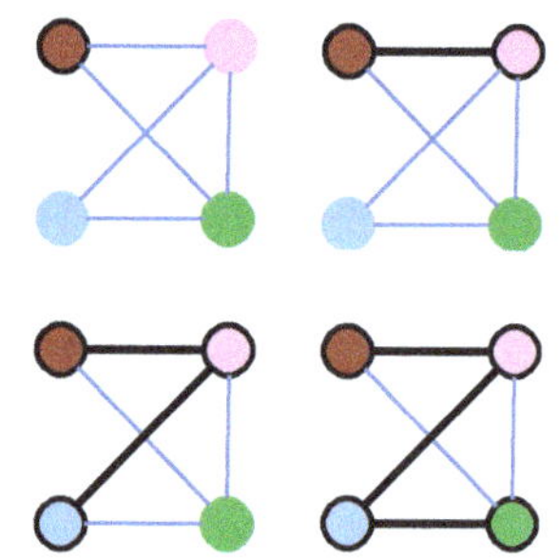

Adam visits Cain, and plans to visit Abel after Cain is done with his visits.

Similarly, Cain has three blood relatives: Eve, Adam, and Abel. Cain visits Eve, and plans to visit Adam and Abel when Eve is done with her visits.

Let's say that Eve visits Abel. Abel has three blood relatives: Adam, Eve, and Cain, but when he tries to visit them, he discovers that each has already been visited.[149] So, Abel is done and returns to Eve so that she can do the rest of her visits.

The situation at that point is that all her blood relatives have also been visited. Thus, Eve is done and returns to Cain, who is also done and returns to Adam, who is also done, and so, the enumeration completes. Note that as each person is done and returns (say, Abel to Eve), they are backing out of the edge that got them visited in the first place (shown in black).

What is Depth-First Search searching for? That depends on what you want. It is

149. The way we wrote the pseudo-code for Depth-First Search, we actually visit already-visited nodes, but they return immediately. Such code is equivalent to checking whether a node has already been visited before going there.

just an enumeration of all nodes reachable from a given node, and can therefore be used to find whether any specific node of interest is reachable. What you do when you find it is your business.

Running a Maze, Revisited

We have used the problem of simulating a rat in a maze throughout the text. In Chapter 1, it was used to introduce precepts and patterns; in Chapter 4, it provided an example of loop invariants and variants; in Chapter 15, it was a rich source of data-representation design issues. In the process, we learned much about precise programming, and some of its pitfalls. Armed now with the concept of graphs and Depth-First Search, we return to the maze problem, and use it to illustrate the power of that theory, and the value of abstraction, in general.

Each cell of a maze can be viewed as a node of an undirected graph, where nodes n and m have an edge between them precisely when they are adjacent cells of the maze with no wall between them.

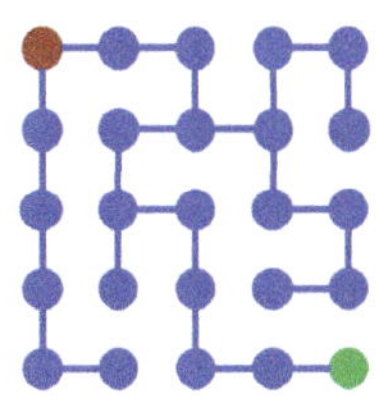

The rat seeks a path from the node for the upper-left cell (red) to the node for the lower-right cell (green). Depth-First Search can be used for exactly this purpose.

At any given moment, Depth-First Search is visiting some node n in its list of recursive instantiations. If n is a cul-de-sac, it just backs out of the recursion.

Loops, which caused so much consternation and were almost overlooked in Chapter 15, are standard fare for Depth-First Search, and are detected on attempting to visit an already visited node. Thus, Depth-First Search handles with aplomb the example:

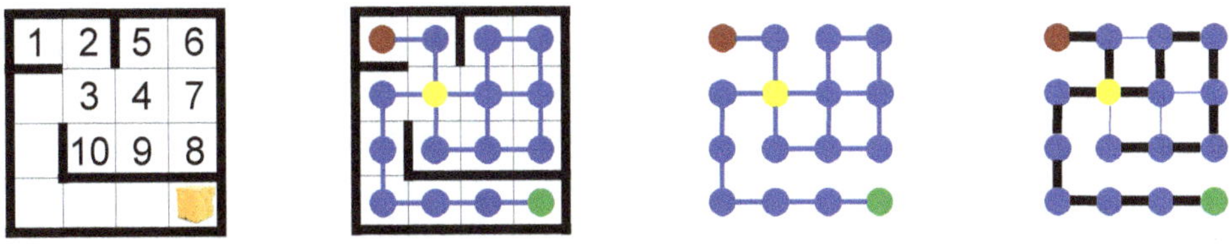

1	2	5	6
	3	4	7
	10	9	8

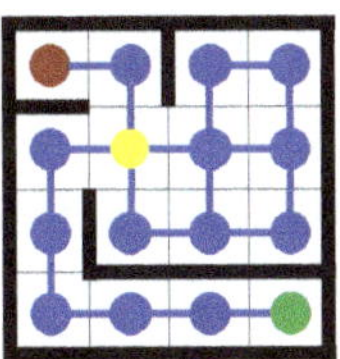
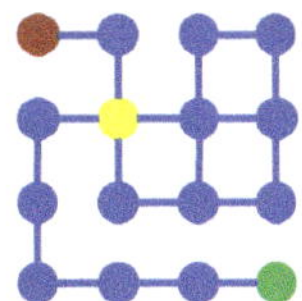
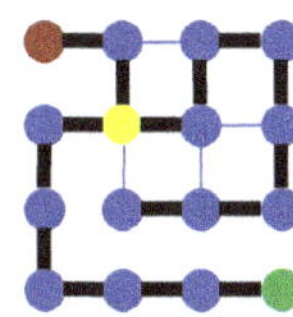

The rightmost image depicts a trace of the rat's path to each previously-unvisited cell, in black. The remaining thin blue edges are to cells discovered to have already been visited. The black edges form what is called a *spanning tree*. The spanning tree shown reflects the (arbitrary) order in which the rat chose to visit immediately-neighboring cells, e.g., it would have been different if the rat had selected a different path out of cell 4. However, for the given order chosen, the spanning tree provides a unique path from the upper-left cell to every reachable cell in the maze.

Depth-First Search is not bound to the outer wall (in all of its serpentine forms) because it performs a true exhaustive search, if necessary:

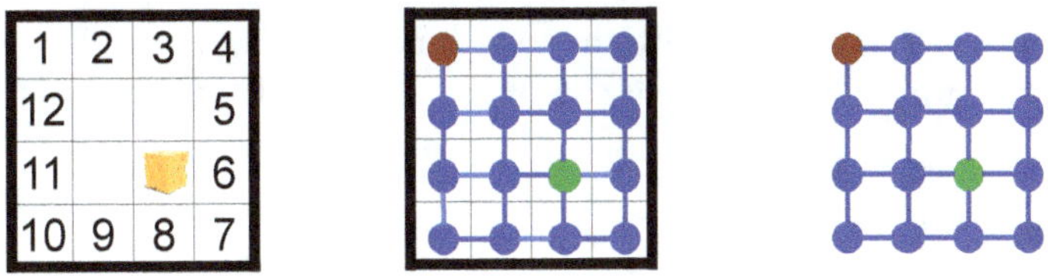

1	2	3	4
12			5
11			6
10	9	8	7

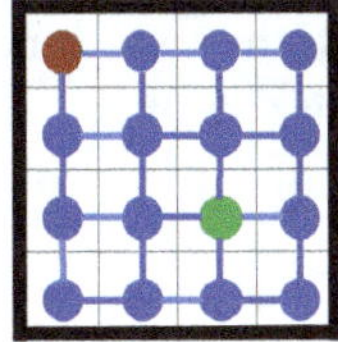
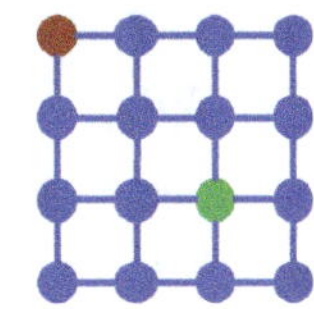

In a sense, you have been "led down the garden path" throughout the text because mazes are precisely the sort of problem for which the general framework of this chapter is intended, and we have been withholding.

One may legitimately wonder whether graphs and Depth-First Search are mere brute-force technology being applied to the problem, without relevance to rats. Is there a way to anthropomorphize the approach (if one can use that term for a rodent)? Sure: One must only imagine a rat with a pouch of breadcrumbs, and also a way to remember for each cell from where it came. The rat's algorithm at each cell is: If there is already a breadcrumb in the cell, immediately return to the cell from which it came. Otherwise, drop a breadcrumb in the cell, visit each neighbor, and then return to the cell from which it came, where it resumes visiting all of that cell's neighbors. A clever rat.

Representation. The graph representation of a maze completely abstracts away its two-dimensional spatial layout. The maze is just a collection of `N·N` nodes that are adjacent to certain other nodes. The fact that those nodes can be laid out in a 2-D grid called a maze is completely omitted and irrelevant. For all we care, the nodes could be rooms in a cave connected via secret passages of irregular geometry. Graphs represent pure connectivity.

Here is the representation invariant for a maze (as a graph), and a path (as an ordered list of graph nodes):

```
/* Maze, Rat, and Path (MRP) Representations. */                    1
class MRP {
   ...
   /* Maze. Maze cells are represented by N*N nodes of graph G, where G[n]
      is an edge list for node n, i.e., for 0≤e<G[n].length, G[n][e] is an
      adjacent node m, i.e., a cell m adjacent to n with intervening Wall.
      The upper-left cell is node 0. Cheese is at cheeseNode. */
      private static int G[][];              // Edge lists.
      private static int cheeseNode;         // Node containing cheese.
   /* Path. Array path[0..pathLength-1] is a list of adjacent nodes in
      G reaching from node 0 to some node path[pathlength-1]. */
      private static int path[];
      private static int pathLength;
      public static boolean isAtCheese()
         { return path[pathLength-1]==cheeseNode; }
   ...
   } /* MRP */
```

A graph is represented by nodes (integers, from 0 to N·N-1), and edges (a two-dimensional array `G[][]`). For each node `n`, `G[n]` is a one-dimensional array of the nodes `m` for which there is an edge ⟨n,m⟩. The order of nodes in each `G[n]` is irrelevant, but will influence the order in which Depth-First Search enumerates them.[150]

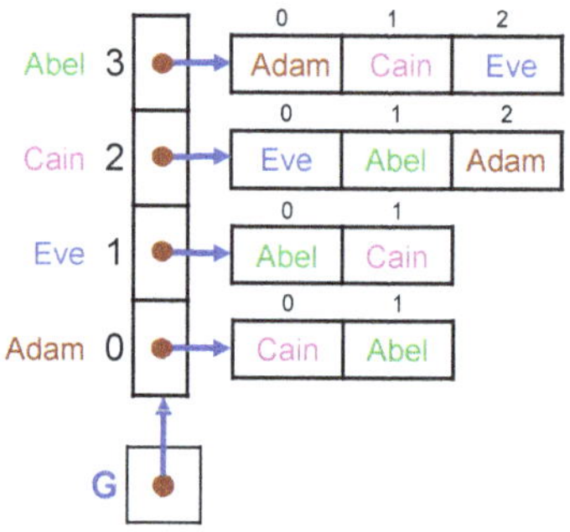

G		0	1	2
Abel	3	Adam	Cain	Eve
Cain	2	Eve	Abel	Adam
Eve	1	Abel	Cain	
Adam	0	Cain	Abel	

An encoding of our biblical example is shown in the right margin. The nodes in `path[0..pathLength-1]` will be a path from node 0, e.g., Adam.

Solve. To simplify the presentation, we assume that the `Input` and `Output` routines of Chapter 15 are retained, unchanged. Were we to have adopted the graph representation from the get-go, we might not have bothered with the two-dimensional-array representation `M[N][N]`; we might have gone straight to a graph. But

150. See the footnote on page 210 for a further discussion of the edge-list vs the adjacency-matrix representations of a graph in a two-dimensional array.

we now leverage that representation, as well as its `Input` and `Output` routines. We can jettison most of the paraphernalia of the interface that previously supported the algorithm, e.g., turning, stepping, and the saving and restoring of information about loop-head cells.

`Search` proceeds as follows:

- Convert the two-dimensional-array maze representation to a graph.
- Use Depth-First Search to determine a path to the cheese.
- Convert the path back to the two-dimensional-array path representation.

Depth-First Search (`DFS`) is written as a recursive method (red) that terminates as soon as it locates the cheese (blue), which it does by throwing an exception that is caught in `Search`.[151] We compute the direct path to the cheese in `path[0..pathLength-1]` as a side effect of `DFS` (green):

```
/* Maze, Rat, and Path (MRP) Representations. */                                2
class MRP {
   ...
   /* Convert representation M[N][N] to graph G, then perform DFS from
      upper-left, then convert computed path to representation M[N][N]. */
   public static void Search() {
      MakeGraphFromInput();
      try { DFS(0,0); } catch ( RuntimeException e ) {  }
      MakeOutputFromPath();
      } /* Search */
   ...
   } /* MRP */
```

`DFS` is given a node `n` from which to explore, and the depth `p` of the given exploration. It immediately returns if `n` has been visited before. Otherwise, it extends the path to `n`, and recurses on each node adjacent to `n` (unless `n` is the `cheeseNode`):

```
/* Maze, Rat, and Path (MRP) Representations. */                                3
class MRP {
   ...
   private static boolean mark[]; // mark[n] iff DFS reached node n.
   /* Depth First Search (DFS) of node n for cheeseNode at depth p. */
   private static void DFS(int n, int p) {
      if ( !mark[n] ) {          // Node n has not been visited before.
         mark[n] = true;         // Mark that n has been visited.
         path[p] = n;            // Extend the path to include n.
         if ( n==cheeseNode ) { // Terminate the search if cheese is found.
            pathLength = p+1;    // Length of path is one longer than p.
            throw new RuntimeException("found cheese");
            }
         for (int e=0; e<G[n].length; e++) DFS(G[n][e], p+1);
         }
      } /* DFS */
   } /* MRP */
```

The code for graphs and Depth-First Search has been placed in class `MRP` as a

151. We used Java's **`try-catch`** exception mechanism in Chapter 15 (p. 235) to localize the effect of an input failure due to malformed data. We now use Java's **`throw`** mechanism to terminate `DFS` (no matter how deep in the recursion) when the cheese is found.

short-term expedient, but we note that they really should be factored into a class of their own. We will not do that here.

`MRP.Search` is invoked as the implementation of `RunMaze.Solve`:

```
/* Rat running. See Chapter 15 and Chapter 17 of text. */          4
class RunMaze {
   ...
   /* Compute a direct path through the maze, if one exists. */
   private static void Solve() {
      MRP.Search();
      } /* Solve */
   ...
   } /* RunMaze */
```

This completes implementation of maze running as Depth-First Search in a graph. It is surprisingly simple. All that remains to implement is the mapping back and forth between the Chapter 15 representation of a maze and path, and the graph representation presented above.

Input and Output. The routines for converting from the two-dimensional array representation to the graph representation, and back again, are included here for completeness. They are a bit fussy, and are not of great intrinsic interest. High on the annoyance level is conversion back and forth between two-dimensional $\langle r,c \rangle$ coordinates, and one-dimensional node-number coordinates whereby the cells of a maze are numbered from `0..N*N-1` in row-major order. This would have been error-prone even were the two-dimensional system to have been N-by-N, but given our use of a (2·N+1)-by-(2·N+1) array `M`, it is triply so:

```
/* Maze, Rat, and Path (MRP) Representations. */          5
class MRP {
   ...
   /* Create undirected graph representation of maze and path. */
   private static void MakeGraphFromInput() {
      G = new int[N*N][];  // Edge lists.
      cheeseNode = N*N-1;  // Node containing cheese.
      path = new int[N*N]; // Path of rat from 0 to cheeseNode, if pos.
      mark = new boolean[N*N]; // mark[n] iff DFS has reached n.
      int n = 0; // Node number.
      for (int r=lo; r<=hi; r=r+2)
         for (int c=lo; c<=hi; c=c+2) {
            G[n] = new int[CountEdges(r, c)]; // Allocate edge list.
            int e = 0; // Edge number.
            for (int d=0; d<4; d++)
               if ( M[r+deltaR[d]][c+deltaC[d]]==NoWall ) {
                  G[n][e] = Node(r+2*deltaR[d], c+2*deltaC[d]);
                  e++;
                  }
            n++;
            }
      } /* MakeGraphFromInput */
   ...
   } /* MRP */
```

The auxiliary routines `CountEdges` and `Node` are:

6

```
/* Maze, Rat, and Path (MRP) Representations. */
class MRP {
   ...
   /* Return number of cells adjacent to ⟨r,c⟩ with no Wall between. */
   private static int CountEdges(int r, int c) {
      int e = 0; // Number of edges.
      for (int d=0; d<4; d++)
         if ( M[r+deltaR[d]][c+deltaC[d]]==NoWall ) e++;
      return e;
      } /* CountEdges */

   /* Return node number from ⟨r,c⟩ in M. */
   private static int Node(int r, int c) { return N*(r/2)+(c/2); }
   ...
   } /* MRP */
```

Copying the path discovered by DFS back into the two-dimensional array M is simple, but still involves getting the ⟨r,c⟩ coordinates of nodes right:

7

```
/* Maze, Rat, and Path (MRP) Representations. */
class MRP {
   ...
   /* Return ⟨r,c⟩ in M given node n. */
   private static int Row(int n) { return 2*(n/N)+1; }
   private static int Column(int n) { return 2*(n%N)+1; }

   /* Store path[0..pathLength-1] in M. */
   private static void MakeOutputFromPath() {
      for (int q=0; q<pathLength; q++)
         M[Row(path[q])][Column(path[q])] = q+1;
      } /* MakeOutputFromPath */
   ...
   } /* MRP */
```

Reflection. The consequence of recognizing that one's problem can be framed as a graph, and that Depth-First Search solves the problem, warrants reflection. In one fell swoop, all of the previous painstaking and detailed domain-specific analysis are obviated. We only had to establish that the problem at hand can be modeled as a relation, and that therefore one universal data-representation (graph) can be used. If an off-the-shelf algorithm, e.g., Depth-First Search, addresses your problem, you are done.

Depth-First Search imposes no rule on the order in which a node's neighbors are visited, and can be viewed as a framework within which such a discipline can be introduced. As written above, the order is baked in according to the order in which edges are listed for each node, but that need not be the case. As long as each neighbor is eventually visited, it is Depth-First Search. You are free to invent heuristics that may speed the search, including both generic ideas, and domain-specific approaches.

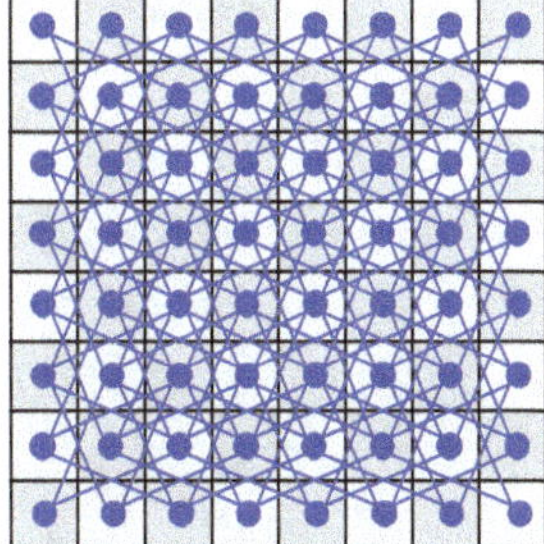

The Knight's Tour of Chapter 14 can be cast as a graph traversal problem, where there is an edge between every square of the board and the squares to which a knight could move from that square. In this case, however, the problem is not mere reachability from the upper-left node, as in the maze problem. Rather, it is what is called a *Hamiltonian Circuit*, which requires a traversal that visits every node of the graph exactly once. The problem of finding a Hamiltonian Circuit for an arbitrary graph is computationally very difficult.

CHAPTER 18

Classes and Objects

A *taxonomy* is a system of classification. The concept is fundamental, and is widely applicable. The natural world is partitioned into Animal, Vegetable, and Mineral. Geometry describes shapes: Polygon, Quadrilateral, Parallelogram, Rhombus, Square. Libraries organize their books according to the Dewey Decimal System, or Universal Decimal Classification, etc. Taxonomies are an essential mechanism for organizing subject matter.

Hierarchical taxonomies in which concepts are organized into tree structures are ubiquitous. In a hierarchy, the most general concept is placed at the root of the tree, and subordinate concepts branch out from there.

Taxonomies are not unique. For example, if the root of a hierarchy is Natural World, one naturalist may list three subordinate categories: Animal, Vegetable, and Mineral, while another may list two: Life and Non-Life, and within Life, list Protista, Plantae, and Animalia. We see that not only are the structures not the same, but the names assigned to the same groupings may differ.

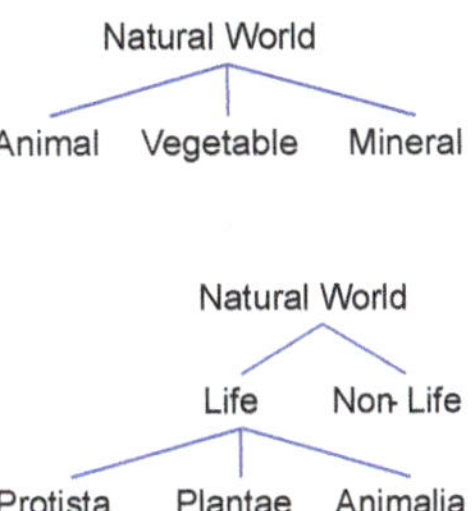

Each category is a set of individuals, i.e., instances of that category. As such, you can depict a taxonomy in a Venn diagram that consists of nested regions, with individuals denoted by dots:

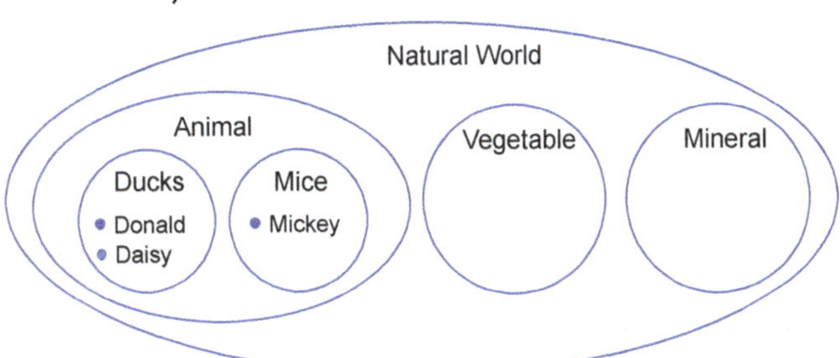

Individuals within the same region share common properties, e.g., Donald and Daisy share duck-like properties, and Donald, Daisy, and Mickey share animal-like properties. We say that each individual in a given category *inherits* the properties of all categories above them in the taxonomy, i.e., in the regions of the Venn diagram that enclose the individual, up to the root. The polygons of Geometry illustrate inheritance well: every Square is a Rhombus, which is a Parallelogram, which is a Quadrilateral, which is a Polygon.

An *object-oriented program* organizes a program's typed values into a hierarchy. Each category in the hierarchy is known as a *class*, and each individual of a category is known as an *object*. The root of the hierarchy is the class `Object`. Every object is an `Object`.[152]

We present the notions of class and object in this chapter using an earlier, unfinished problem as a motivating example: Enumeration of Rationals (p. 126). Recall that the problem was to list each rational number exactly once, e.g., after 1/2 has been listed, we must not subsequently list 2/4, 3/6, etc.

As a running example in this chapter, we will define classes `Pair`, `Fraction`, and `Rational` arranged in the inheritance hierarchy shown, and illustrate how each class can define properties specific to itself, while inheriting properties of the classes above it in the hierarchy. Thus, for example, a `Rational` is a `Fraction` that is reduced, i.e., one whose numerator and denominator have no common factors. A `Fraction` is a `Pair` of integers *n* and *d* that displays as *n*/*d*. A `Pair` is an `Object` consisting of two integers, *k* and *v*, that displays as <*k*, *v*>.

Object
|
Pair
|
Fraction
|
Rational

With the notion of `Rational` in hand, we will turn to the issue of eliminating duplicates from our enumeration of rationals. To record which values have already been output, we use the idea of a collection, as presented in Chapter 12. There, we had shown various ways to represent a collection of **`int`** values. Now that we can treat a rational as a value, we will see that collections of **`int`** can readily be generalized to collections of any type of object, e.g., values of type `Rational`.

Recall that one way to represent a collection of **`int`** values used an **`int`** array `A`, **`int`** variables `size` and `maxSize`, and satisfied the following representation invariant:

```
/* A[0..size-1] are the current items in A[0..maxSize-1], 0≤size≤maxSize. */
   int A[];      // receptacle for items in a list.
   int size;     // current # of elements in list, 0≤size≤maxSize.
   int maxSize;  // maximum # of elements storable in the list.
```

A limitation of Chapter 12 was that there was no way to group such variables, and treat them as one thing, i.e., a collection. The second half of this chapter implements class `ArrayList`, which binds up this representation, and the ways to manipulate it, all in one place. This packaging allows the whole collection to be treated as a value, i.e., as an object of type `ArrayList`. The example motivates the introduction of numerous additional technical details about classes and objects, and provides a mechanism for completing the Enumeration of Rationals problem.

Up until this point, the text has relied only on the universal programming- language features that are summarized in Chapter 2. We now introduce classes and objects, but do not attempt to cover the material in a comprehensive fashion. Rather, we present just enough to wrap up loose ends, give a taste of object-oriented programming, and provide a foundation for your further programming. Most importantly, you will learn enough about object-oriented programming to be able to read and understand a library specification, and use it.[153]

---

152. A more general version of object orientation organizes objects into a taxonomy that is not necessarily a hierarchy, i.e., the objects of a class may inherit properties from more than one parent class. Such a programming language, e.g., C++, is said to support *multiple inheritance.*
153. In contrast with the programming notation used in the book up until now, which is essentially universal, the specific syntax introduced in this chapter is unmistakably Java. Although the many object-oriented notions presented here are commonplace, and have their analogues in other languages, the notation and terminology used for these notions in other languages may differ.

Essential Notions

A *class* is a collection of variable declarations and method definitions. Until now, classes have only been used to aggregate such declarations and definitions, and to control code complexity: A class is a scope that can be used to restrict visibility of variables and methods, and to hide implementation details. As such, the concept of class has been used for abstraction, encapsulation, information hiding, and the division of code into clients and servers.

The essential aspect of a class that has been avoided until now is its use as a template for the dynamic creation of objects. By restricting examples to variables and values of type **int** and **boolean**, and arrays thereof, we have been able limit the conceptual prerequisites needed for the text, and have thereby been able to focus on programming principles rather than language features. Although arrays and `String`s are actually objects, we have limited our remarks related to that fact, but it is now time to confront the notion of object frontally.[154]

An *object* is a dynamic instantiation of the variables (and methods) of a class whose declarations (and definitions) are *not* prefixed by the modifier **static**. Such variables are known as *object fields* or *instance variables* (and such methods are known as *instance methods*).

Think of a class as a cookie cutter that can be used to make cookies (objects) of a given shape (non-**static** fields and methods). To stamp out a new cookie, we evaluate the expression "**new** *class-name*(...)".

In contrast with non-**static** variables and methods, those prefixed with **static** are associated with the class as a whole, and not with each object. Thus, there is precisely one instance of a **static** variable or method regardless of the number of objects of the class that exist.

If `C` is a class, a variable `v` of type `C` is obtained by executing the declaration:

```
C v;
```

The only difference between such a declaration and (say) "**int** `v;`" is the type of the variable so declared, and the default value that is used to initialize it. For an **int**, the default value is 0; for a variable whose type is a class, the default value is **null**, which is no object at all.

Suppose class `C` contains declarations for non-**static** variables $\texttt{field}_1$, $\texttt{field}_2$,... and definitions for non-**static** methods $\texttt{method}_1$, $\texttt{method}_2$,.... If variable `v` has been declared to have type `C`, and has been assigned a value of type `C`, then we depict the situation diagrammatically by the figure shown. The object itself is not shoehorned into variable `v` as its value. Rather, what is stored in `v` is a *reference* to the

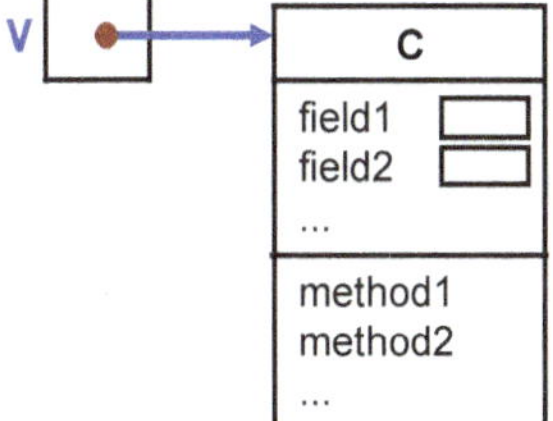

154. The appearances of objects in the text have been limited to these:
- In Chapter 2, we introduced, without comment, several locutions that involve objects:
  - Initialization of the variable `in` as a `Scanner` object, i.e.,
    ```
    Scanner in = new Scanner(System.in);
    ```
  - Use of methods of the `Scanner` object `in` for input, e.g.,
    ```
    int n = in.nextInt();
    ```
  - Creation of array objects, e.g.,
    ```
    int A[] = new int[10];
    ```
- In Chapter 7, Chapter 12, and Chapter 17, we used the `length` field of an array object.
- In Chapter 12, we revealed that an array is actually a reference to a sequence of variables in order to be able to replace that sequence with one twice as long. We also alluded to the need for collections of ⟨key,value⟩ pairs, and provided a forward reference to this chapter. Our depiction of hash tables foreshadowed objects, but without comment.
- In Chapter 14 and Chapter 15, we invoked a `String`'s `substring` method.

object, which itself is shown as freestanding. Each object is depicted in three parts: its type, its instance variables, and its instance methods. The reference to the object is depicted as a red dot (•), with an arrow emanating from it that points to the object. Think of the dot as the value itself, and the arrow as an explanation of what the value refers to.

The fields and methods of an object are not limited to ones that are declared or defined just in class `C`. Rather, they include the fields and methods of all classes from which class `C` inherits, i.e., the fields and methods of all classes in the class hierarchy along the path from `C` up to `Object`. This mechanism is how a more specific category of object accumulates all of the attributes of the more general categories that subsume it. However, inheritance is not only a matter of accretion; it allows for method specialization, as well. In particular, if the same method name appears in multiple classes in the inheritance hierarchy along the path from `C` up to `Object`, the definition *lowest* in the hierarchy prevails. The mechanism is called *method overriding*.[155]

The fields and methods of an object are accessed in code via a reference, where the reference-valued expression and field-or-method name are separated by a dot, e.g., `v.field`$_i$ or `v.method`$_i$`(...)`.

The distinguished value **`null`** is a reference to no object. If variable `v` contains the value **`null`**, evaluating the expression `v.field`$_i$ (or invoking `v.method`$_i$`(...)`) results in a runtime "null-pointer" exception, which terminates execution.

Pair

We wish to manipulate pairs of integers with the same ease as we do individual **`int`** values. We can do so by defining a class `Pair` that contains two **`int`** fields (`key` and `value`), two methods (`getKey` and `getValue`), and one constructor (`Pair`):[156]

```
class Pair {                                                            P1
   protected int key;
   protected int value;
   /* Constructor. */
      public Pair(int k, int v) { key = k; value = v; }
   /* Access. */
      public int getKey()   { return key; }
      public int getValue() { return value; }
   } /* Pair */
```

The fields and methods in this definition are not **`static`**, and therefore are instantiated for each and every individual instance of a `Pair`.[157]

155. In practice, we only list relevant fields and methods in an object depiction because there are too many to be exhaustive.

156. The names `key` and `value` could have been chosen to be anything, e.g., `first` and `second`, but are adopted here in alignment with a standard class of Java. The names `key` and `value` derive from use of `Pair` to represent items in a table that implements a function mapping keys to values.

157. Some occurrences of type **`int`** are colored blue in the text for future reference. Specifically, we plan to generalize `Pair` to be pairs of values of types other than **`int`**. It will be convenient to have color-coded these instances of **`int`** now so they can be easily identified later for replacement.

Object Creation

The keyword **new** in an *expression* indicates that we wish to create a new instance of an object of a given class. The class is signified by a *constructor*, which is a distinguished kind of method with the same name as the class name.

The constructor is automatically invoked on the newly-created object, and provides a way to reinitialize the object's fields. In general, a class can have multiple constructors, which allows for alternative ways in which to initialize the object. In the present case, we have defined only the obvious constructor for `Pair`, one that has two parameters, one for each of the two components of the pair.

Suppose we wish to create an object for ⟨2,3⟩, as shown at the right. We do this by evaluating the expression

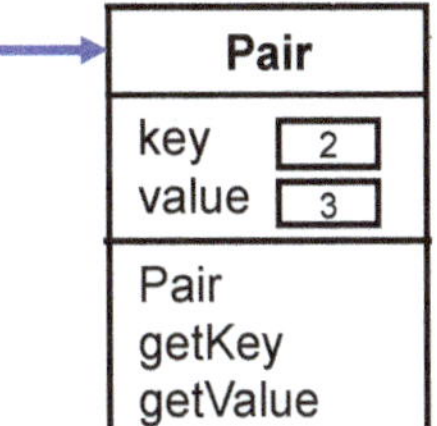


```
new Pair(2,3)
```

which:

- Dynamically creates a new object of type `Pair`. The object has two **`int`** fields, `key` and `value`, that are initialized with zero, the default value for type **`int`**.
- The constructor (method) of this newly-created object is then invoked with **`int`** arguments 2 and 3. The constructor assigns 2 and 3 into the respective `key` and `value` fields of the object on whose behalf it was invoked, overwriting the zeros.
- The value of the expression "**`new`** `Pair(2,3)`" is a reference to the object, i.e., the red dot.

What can one do with such a value? For starters, if you declare a variable to have type `Pair`, you can initialize it with that value, e.g.,

```
Pair v = new Pair(2,3);
```

Visibility and Modifiability

In support of information-hiding principles, a class can control its client's ability to see and modify the values of fields, and to invoke methods. It does so using field and method *modifiers*, and by providing access to certain methods, but not other methods.

You are already familiar with modifiers **`public`** and **`private`** from Chapter 15: A **`private`** field or method is invisible and inaccessible to clients, whereas a **`public`** field or method is visible and accessible. The modifier **`protected`** is a mixture of the two; it specifies **`public`**-like visibility in all classes that are subordinate to `Pair` in the class hierarchy, and **`private`**-like invisibility elsewhere. Thus, subordinate classes can be granted privileged access to implementation details of a class that is denied to general clients.

In `Pair`, we have declared the two component fields, `key` and `value`, to be `protected`. We have done this so that arbitrary clients will not have unconstrained access to the fields, but classes below `Pair` in the inheritance hierarchy (like `Fraction` and `Rational`, which we will soon define) do.

A *getter* is a method that returns the value of a field, and a *setter* is a method that changes the value of a field. Providing a getter, but not a setter, for a **`private`** or **`protected`** field renders the field *read only* for clients that are unable to see the field directly.

In `Pair`, we have defined **`public`** getters, `getKey` and `getValue`, but not setters. To extract the value of a component of `v`, you can evaluate the expression `v.getKey()` or `v.getValue()`. Methods `getKey` and `getValue` are executed in the context of the specific object on which they are invoked, e.g., in this case, the object representing ⟨2,3⟩ that is referred to by the reference contained in the variable named `v`. The code for `getKey` and `getValue` directly accesses fields `key` and `value`, respectively, without using a dot. Which fields? Those of the object on whose behalf the getter was invoked.

In `Pair`, we wish to provide read access to its fields, but not write access. Said another way, we want each `Pair` to seem *immutable* to clients of the class. We can motivate the immutability requirement by an analogy with **`int`** values. Consider the many variables of a program that might contain the number 3 at some given moment of execution. Now imagine how disconcerting it would be if your program could change all such 3s into 4s with a single assignment. Surely, we do not want to provide such a nonintuitive mechanism with which to shoot oneself in the foot. But indirect access to objects via references provides exactly such a mechanism. Specifically, imagine all the variables that might contain a reference to the pair ⟨2,3⟩ at a given moment of execution. Some of them may share the same object, and consider it to be an indivisible value. Were it not for immutability, a rogue actor (e.g., a careless programmer) might change the ⟨2,3⟩ that each such variable appears to contain into ⟨2,4⟩.

The notion of a getter can be used to implement a *virtual field*, i.e., a field that does not explicitly exist, but that can be computed from others. For example, you could define the class `Triangle`, and provide getters for three sides and three angles. Exactly which fields are actual and which are virtual would not be knowable.

Overriding Inherited Methods

We have simplified the earlier diagram by ignoring the fact that class `Pair` extends class `Object`, which defines many default methods for every object—in fact, too many to list. The two methods defined in class `Object` that are of immediate interest are `toString` and `equals`. Thus, a more accurate, but still approximate, depiction of an object instance of class `Pair` is as shown.

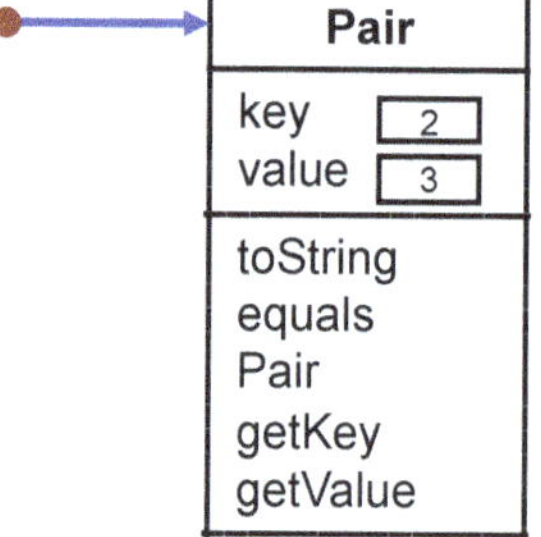

Representation as a String

Method `toString` creates a `String` representation of an object. The default definition of this method (in `Object`) is not particularly helpful because it just consists of the class name and a unique id number, e.g., "`Pair@20293791`". We can override this definition with a more-useful definition that is specific to `Pair`:

```
class Pair {
   ...
   /* String representation of this. */
   public String toString() { return "<" + key + "," + value + ">"; }
   } /* Pair */
```
P2

Given this so-called overriding definition of `toString`, the code:

```
Pair v = new Pair(2,3);
System.out.println( v );
```

would emit the line of text shown in the output (A), which is produced, as follows:

```
<2,3>
```
A

- `System.out.println` requires the `String` representation of its argument, which it obtains by invoking method `v.toString`.
- Since the value in variable `v` is an object of type `Pair`, its conversion to `String` invokes the overriding method for `toString` that is defined in class `Pair`.
- To compute the `String`, the `toString` method of `Pair` concatenates five `String` values: "<", the `String` representation of `key`, "`,`", the `String` representation of `value`, and ">".
- The `String` representation of an **`int`**, e.g., the value of the `key` or `value` field of the object on whose behalf `toString` was invoked, is its base-10 representation, as text.

Identity and Equality

Equality between one **`int`** and another, or between one **`boolean`** and another, is built into the programming language, and can be tested using the infix binary operators "==" and "!=". We have been using these operators all along. Similarly, equality of two references to objects is also built in, and can use those same operators. But in this case, "equal" is a misnomer because the operators really test the *identity* of two referenced objects, not their equality.

You may not be familiar with the distinction between *identical* and *equal*, but now is the time to understand it. Two things are identical when they are "one and the same thing"; two things are equal when (for whatever reason) we wish to treat them as being similar (in some respect). Thus, identity is an intrinsic notion that applies to any two things, but equality is a notion that can be defined to suit our convenience in any given context.

The difference between identity and equality is well-illustrated by remembering the distinction between a fraction and a rational number. The fractions 2/3 and 4/6 are manifestly not identical: They have different numerators, and they have different denominators. But as rational numbers, 2/3 and 4/6 are typically considered to be equal; we say that 2/3 and 4/6 are two different representations of one and the same rational number.

Let us see how the distinction between equal and identical plays out in a program. Specifically, consider the code:

```
Pair z1 = new Pair(2,3);
Pair z2 = new Pair(2,3);
Pair z3 = z1;
```

Notwithstanding the fact that `z1` and `z2` both refer to objects that represent the pair $\langle 2,3 \rangle$, the expression "`z1==z2`" would be **false** because they are two different objects, and are therefore two different references. In contrast, `z1` and `z3` both contain a reference to the same object (the one that was created when `z1` was created), and thus the expression "`z1==z3`" would be **true**. Despite the fact that `z1` and `z2` are distinct, nonidentical objects, we want them to be equal.

Equality between two objects is defined by method `equals`. However, as with `toString`, the default definition of `equals` given in `Object` is typically not what we want. Specifically, it defines two objects as equal only if they are identical objects, which is too strict a notion. We want two pairs $\langle p,q \rangle$ and $\langle p',q' \rangle$ to be equal if and only if p is equal to p', and q is equal to q'. Note that we are defining equality of pairs *qua* pairs, not as rationals.

Rather than taking two arguments, `equals` is a method of each object that takes a second object as its sole argument. Thus, to test whether objects o_1 and o_2 are equal, we invoke o_1`.equals(`o_2`)`, which returns either **true** or **false**. Alternatively, because `equals` should always obey the contract requirement that it be symmetric, one could invoke o_2`.equals(`o_1`)`.[158]

We define `equals` for `Pair` following a standard pattern for such code:

```
class Pair {
  ...
  /* Equality. */
    @Override
    public boolean equals(Object q) {
      if (q==null) return false;
      if (q==this) return true;
      if ( !(q instanceof Pair) ) return false;
      Pair qPair = (Pair)q;
      return (key == qPair.key) && (value == qPair.value);
      } /* equals */
  } /* Pair */
```
P3

@Override. This is an optional but recommended compiler directive that requests that the compiler issue an error warning if the following method definition does not override a definition of a method in a class higher up in the inheritance hierarchy, e.g., `Object.equals`. For example, if we had inadvertently declared parameter `q` to have type `Pair`, a not uncommon mistake, the compiler would warn that there is no such method to be overridden.

Argument checks. If the argument is the **`null`** pointer, it is clearly not equal to `this`, i.e., the object on whose behalf the `equals` method is running.[159] On the other hand, if the argument is a reference to `this`, then it is the very same object, so it should be equal.[160] Finally, we only wish two objects to be candidates for equality if they are both `Pair` objects, so we use `instanceof` to require (at runtime) that the argument be a `Pair`. Given that the argument `q` is indeed a `Pair`, we can assign it to a variable `qPair` of type `Pair`. The expression "`(Pair)q`" is called a *cast*, and is required to allow an `Object` `q` to be assigned to a `Pair` variable `qPair`. Were `q` not a `Pair`, the cast would cause a runtime exception, but this will not occur since we have been careful to rule out this possibility using `instanceof`. We then require that the respective `key` and `value` fields of the two pairs be equal.[161]

Keys and values. We require the `key` and `value` of the object on whose behalf equals has been invoked, to be equal to the `key` and `value` (respectively) of the object that has been provided as an argument to `equals`.[162]

---

158. Note that if o_1 is a variable containing **`null`**, i.e., o_1 doesn't refer to any object, then it is not permissible to invoke o_1`.equals(`o_2`)`.

159. **`null`** is not a reference to any object, but **`this`** is a reference to some object. In particular, **`this`** is a reference to the object on whose behalf `equals` was invoked, Nothing is not equal to something.

160. The standard contract for any implementation of `equals` requires that two identical objects be considered equal.

161. Your doppelganger on Kronos (a different class) may have all the same fields as you; nevertheless, we consider it to not be equal to you. In contrast, if two earthlings (objects from the same class) have all equal corresponding fields, then we consider the objects equal.

162. The uses of == here are colored blue because they will have to be replaced later when `Pair` is generalized to be pairs of arbitrary objects.

Fraction

A fraction is a pair of integers known as the *numerator* and *denominator*. Class `Fraction` can be defined by extending class `Pair`, which places it immediately below `Pair` in the inheritance hierarchy:

```
class Fraction extends Pair {                                              F1
   /* Constructor. */
      public Fraction(int numerator, int denominator) {
         super(numerator, denominator); // Apply the Pair constructor.
         assert denominator!=0: "0 denominator";
         }
   /* Access. */
      public int getNumerator()   { return key; }
      public int getDenominator() { return value; }
   } /* Fraction */
```

Class `Fraction` is called a *subclass* of `Pair`; conversely, `Pair` is called the *superclass* of `Fraction`. The term *subtype* is synonymous with the term subclass.

The constructor `Fraction` is implemented using the constructor of the immediate superclass of class `Fraction`, i.e., `Pair`. The abbreviation **`super`** for this class is convenient, but if used, must be the first statement in the body of the constructor for a subclass. Execution is terminated with an error message if a client ever attempts to construct a fraction with a zero denominator.

Evaluation of the expression "**`new`** `Fraction(2,3)`" creates an object that extends the fields declared for a `Pair` (there are two) with fields that are specific to a `Fraction` (there are none). Similarly, the methods of a `Fraction` extend those of `Pair` with those of `Fraction`, which includes getters `getNumerator` and `getDenominator`, and the constructor `Fraction`.

Access methods `getNumerator` and `getDenominator` are new getters appropriately named for `Fraction`. Although we could have implemented them using the getters of `Pair` (`getKey` and `getValue`), the field names `key` and `value` are directly visible in `Fraction` because they are **`protected`** components of the superclass `Pair`, so we just access the fields directly.

Since every Fraction is a `Pair`, the default `String` representation of a `Fraction` with numerator p and denominator q would be $<p,q>$, i.e., the representation of the `Fraction` as a `Pair`. However, we override this definition with one that is specific to a `Fraction`:

```
class Fraction extends Pair {                                              F2
   ...
   /* String representation of this. */
   public String toString() { return key + "/" + value; }
   } /* Fraction */
```

Given this definition of `toString`, the statement:

```
System.out.println( new Fraction(2,3) );
```

would output "`2/3`", not "`<2,3>`".

There is no need to override the definition of `equals` for `Fraction` because two fractions f and f' are equal if and only if they are equal when each is considered to be a `Pair`.

Rational

We implement Rational as an extension of Fraction. The central aspect that distinguishes a Rational from a Fraction is the notion of equality: Two fractions p/q and p'/q' represent the same rational if and only if $p{\cdot}q'$ and $p'{\cdot}q$ are equal.

One possibility would be to represent Rational values as unreduced Fraction values, but override the definition of equals in Rational to encode the above definition.

An alternative approach is called *canonicalization*, where each rational is given a unique representation as a fraction. We can do this by eliminating common factors in the numerator and denominator as part of the construction of a Rational value. If we do this, we do not need to override equals because two rationals will be equal precisely when their canonical representations as fractions are equal. We adopt this approach, and use the previously-presented Euclid's Algorithm for gcd (p. 80) to do so.

We do, however, override the definition of toString yet again so that a Rational value with a denominator of 1, i.e., an integer, is represented as such when converted to a String. If the denominator is not 1, we defer to the toString method of Fraction:

R1

```
class Rational extends Fraction {
   /* Constructor */
   public Rational(int numerator, int denominator) {
      super(numerator, denominator); // Apply the Fraction constructor.
      int g = gcd(numerator, denominator);
      key = numerator/g;
      value = denominator/g;
      }
   /* Euclid's Algorithm. */
   private static int gcd(int x, int y) {
      while ( x!=y )
         if ( x>y ) x = x-y;
         else y = y-x;
      return x;
      } /* gcd */
   /* String representation of this. */
   public String toString() {
      if ( value==1 ) return key + "";    // this as int
      else return super.toString();       // this as Fraction
      } /* toString */
   } /* Rational */
```

Subtype Polymorphism and Dynamic Method Dispatch

Recall that the general form of an initialized variable declaration is:

```
type name = expression;
```

which creates the named variable, associates it with the given *type*, and initializes it with the value of *expression*. Until now, the type of the value assigned to the variable has always been exactly *type*.

Introduction of the class hierarchy, and the notion of inheritance, allow us to now generalize the kinds of values that can be stored in a variable. Specifically, if the *type* of a variable is class *c*, then the variable is permitted to store a reference to any value whose type is exactly *c*, or whose type is a subclass of class *c*. This is known as *subtype polymorphism*.

We make this concrete with sample code. Recall the class hierarchy defined above: Every `Rational` is a `Fraction`, every `Fraction` is a `Pair`, and every `Pair` is an `Object`. The following code declares variable `o` of type `Object`, assigns values of various compatible types to that variable, and outputs each one.

In each case, the `String` representation of the contents of variable `o` is obtained by (implicitly) invoking `o.toString()`, but which specific method definition is invoked? The answer is that it depends on the type of the value referred to by `o` at the time of the invocation. This is known as *dynamic method dispatch*. Although each output statement is exactly same, the specific version of method `toString` that is invoked, and therefore the specific formatting, depends on the type of the *value*, not on the type of the *variable* `o`:

```
Object o;
o = new Pair(4,6);     System.out.println( o );
o = new Fraction(4,6); System.out.println( o );
o = new Rational(4,6); System.out.println( o );
o = new Rational(6,3); System.out.println( o );
```

The four lines of text emitted by the code are shown in the output (B). Polymorphic variables and dynamic method dispatch are powerful mechanisms that promote code succinctness and reuse.

B

```
<4,6>
4/6
2/3
2
```

This completes our implementation of rational numbers. We turn now to the implementation of collections of rationals.[163]

ArrayList

Consider a declaration that creates a one-dimensional array of `int` variables:

```
int A[] = new int[expression];
```

The length of the array is given by the value of the *expression* when the declaration is evaluated. The length is *dynamic* in the sense that each time the declaration is evaluated the length may be different, but is *fixed* in the sense that once the sequence of variables is allocated, that length cannot stretch or shrink.

Chapter 12 introduced the notion of a dynamic collection of values stored in an array. We distinguished there between the `size` of the collection (which may grow and shrink over the course of program execution) and the length of the array used to contain the collection.

To deal with the possibility that the size of a collection may grow to exceed the length of the array, we revealed that arrays are really references to objects, and then used that feature to double the length of the sequence of variables, when necessary.

We now package these ideas in a class called `ArrayList`. The correspondence between arrays and `ArrayList` values is summarized in this table:

---

163. The implementation of `Rational` is far from complete, but has served its purpose for this chapter. The exercises pursue further development: Implementation of the rational arithmetic operations, and replacement of `int` numerators and denominators with arbitrary-precision integers.

syntax	new int[0..size]	ArrayList
declaration	`int A[] = new int[`*expression*`];`	`arrayList A = new arrayList(`*expression*`);`
expression	`size`	`A.size()`
expression	`size==0`	`A.isEmpty()`
statement	`A[`$expression_1$`] =` $expression_2$`;`	`A.set(`$expression_1$, $expression_2$`)`
expression	`A[`*expression*`]`	`A.get(`*expression*`)`
expression	*Search*	`A.indexOf(`*expression*`)`
expression	*Membership*	`A.contains(`*expression*`)`
statement	*Insertion*	`A.add(`*expression*`);` `A.add(`*expression*, *expression*`);`
expression	*Deletion*	`A.remove(`*expression*`)`

An array has the benefit of a succinct bracket notation for subscripting, but this is abandoned for an `ArrayList`. Thus, rather than writing `A[k]`, we will have to write `A.get(k)`, and rather than writing "`A[k]=v`", we must write "`A.set(k,v)`". In return for this inconvenience, we gain the built-in notion that the capacity of an `ArrayList` doubles in size whenever necessary. We also gain the built-in notion of a list to which we can append values, e.g., "`A.add(v)`", insert values, e.g., `A.add(k,v)`, and within which we can remove values, e.g., `A.remove(k)`.

Here is the class definition, where item-by-item commentary appears in the text that follows the code. We continue the practice of coloring instances of **`int`** that we intend to subsequently replace in blue:

A1

```
class ArrayList {
   private int A[];      // ArrayList elements are in A[0..size-1].
   private int size;     // The default value is 0.
   /* Utility */
      private void checkBoundExclusive( int k ) {
         if (k>=size) throw new IndexOutOfBoundsException( "≥size" );
         }
      private void checkBoundInclusive( int k ) {
         if (k>size) throw new IndexOutOfBoundsException( ">size" );
         }
   /* Constructors. */
      public ArrayList( int m ) {
         if ( m<0 ) throw new IllegalArgumentException();
         A = new int[m];
         }
      public ArrayList() { this( 20 /* DEFAULT_SIZE */ );
  /* Capacity. */
      public void ensureCapacity( int minCapacity) {
         int currentLength = A.length;
         if ( minCapacity > currentLength ) {
            int B[] = new int[Math.max(2*currentLength, minCapacity)];
            for (int k=0; k<size; k++) B[k] = A[k];
            A = B;
            }
         }
```

```
/* Size. /
   public int size() { return size; }
   public boolean isEmpty() { return size==0; }
/* Access. */
   public int get(int k) {
      checkBoundExclusive(k);
      return A[k];
      }
   public int set(int k, int v) {
      checkBoundExclusive(k);
      int old = A[k];
      A[k] = v;
      return old;
      }
/* Insertion / Deletion. */
   public void add(int v) {
      if ( size==A.length ) ensureCapacity( size+1 );
      A[size] = v; size++;
      }
   public void add(int k, int v) {
      checkBoundInclusive(k);
      if ( size==A.length ) ensureCapacity( size+1 );
      for (int j=size; j>k; j--) A[j] = A[j-1];
      A[k] = v;
      size++;
      }
   public int remove(int k) {
      checkBoundExclusive(k);
      int old = A[k];
      size--;
      for (int j=k; j<size; j++) A[j] = A[j+1];
      return old;
      }
/* Membership. */
   public int indexOf(int v) {
      int k = 0; while ( (k<n) && (v!=A[k]) ) k++;
      if ( k==n ) return -1; else return k;
      }
   public boolean contains(int v) { return indexOf(v)!=-1; }
} /* ArrayList */
```

A1*

Fields. The fields A and `size` are **`private`**. The last thing we want is clients changing them directly. The representation invariant of the class is that the current values in an `ArrayList` are `A[0..size-1]`.

Utility. Indices for `ArrayList` values must be between 0 and `size-1`. The check for indices that are too big is performed by `checkBoundExclusive` and `checkBoundInclusive`; the check for negative indices is relegated to normal subscript bound checking. In the exclusive version of the test, element `A[size]` is not in the collection, and therefore an index of `size` is illegal. In the inclusive version of the test, element `A[size]` is about to become an element of the collection, and so, `size` is a legal index.

Constructors. Two constructors are provided. One has an integer parameter, and creates a new `ArrayList` with that initial capacity. The second has no parameter, and creates a new list with a default initial capacity. The whole point of the class is that the capacities are not fixed, and double as necessary, so these initial values are just a matter of efficiency for small lists. The constructor is said to be overloaded because it has two definitions. In general, when there is more than one method with a given name, the version invoked depends on the number and types of arguments at the invocation site. The keyword `this` in the definition of the second constructor invokes the 1-argument constructor on the same object.

Capacity. Method `ensureCapacity` allows clients to increase a list's capacity, at will. More importantly, it is used internally to double the capacity, when necessary.

Insertion / Deletion. Method `add` (with one argument) appends a value to the end of the list, method `add` (with two arguments) inserts a value at a given index, shifting values to the right to make room, and method `remove` deletes a value at a given index, shifting the following values left to fill the hole.

Membership. This is implemented with Sequential Search. Because the size of the list is not readily available to clients (without invoking a method), it is convenient to adopt the convention that a return value of -1 indicates that `indexOf` fails to find the value sought (rather than the size, which has been our wont for Sequential Search throughout the text).

Parametric Polymorphism and Generic Classes

Recall our partial implementation of code for enumerating rational numbers in Chapter 6 (p. 126). To prevent a given rational from being enumerated more than once, we proposed to maintain and consult a set of the reduced fractions that have already been output. However, we left the part in blue unimplemented because at that time we did not yet have a good mechanism for implementing rationals and sets of rationals:

```
/* Output reduced positive fractions, i.e., positive rationals. */     E2
   /* set reduced = { }; */
   int d = 0;
   while ( true ) {
      int r = d;
      for (int c=0; c<=d; c++) {
         /* Let z be the reduced form of the fraction (r+1)/(c+1). */
            int g = gcd(r+1, c+1);
            /* rational z = ⟨(r+1)/g, (c+1)/g⟩; */
         if ( /* z is not an element of reduced */ ) {
            System.out.println( /* z */ );
            /* reduced = reduced ∪ {z}; */
            }
         r--;
         }
      d++;
      }
```

Clearly, class `Rational` can be used to represent a reduced fraction, i.e.,

```
/* Let z be the reduced form of the fraction (r+1)/(c+1). */
```

can be implemented by

```
/* Let z be the reduced form of the fraction (r+1)/(c+1). */
   Rational z = new Rational(r+1, c+1);
```

ArrayList (as currently defined) can be used to represent a set of integers, but not a set of Rational values. It was a useful pedagogical step to first define ArrayList as a list of **int** values, but we must now generalize it.

One possibility would be to modify class ArrayList by replacing each occurrence of **int** by Rational.[164] Doing so would yield a version of ArrayList specialized for Rational values. But we really don't want to do such text editing for each new kind of ArrayList that ever arises. Rather, we want parametric code for ArrayList that can be used for any type of list element we may have in mind. What is needed is a *generic* class definition, which allows a class to be parametric in one or more types.

ArrayList<E>

We signify that class ArrayList is a generic class that is parametric in the *type parameter* E by writing:

```
class ArrayList<E> { ... } /* ArrayList */
```

We then abstract the body of the class definition with respect to the element type, i.e., uniformly replace **int** with the parameter E. The resulting class is said to be *parametrically polymorphic*, where the type parameter E stands for an arbitrary class, e.g., Pair, Rational, or whatever:

```
class ArrayList<E> {                                                          A2
   private E A[];          // ArrayList elements are in A[0..size-1].
   private int size;       // The default value is 0.
   /* Utility */
      private void checkBoundExclusive( int k ) {
         if (k>=size) throw new IndexOutOfBoundsException( "≥size" );
         }
      private void checkBoundInclusive( int k ) {
         if (k>size) throw new IndexOutOfBoundsException( ">size" );
         }
   /* Constructors. */
      public ArrayList( int m ) {
         if ( m<0 ) throw new IllegalArgumentException();
         A = (E[]) new Object[m];
         }
     public ArrayList() { this( 20 /* DEFAULT_SIZE */ ); }
   /* Capacity. */
      public void ensureCapacity( int minCapacity) {
         int currentLength = A.length;
         if ( minCapacity > currentLength ) {
            E B[] = (E[]) new Object[Math.max(2*currentLength, minCapacity)];
            for (int k=0; k<size; k++) B[k] = A[k];
            A = B;
            }
         }
```

164. As we shall see shortly, "A[k]==v" in indexOf also must be replaced.

```
/* Size. */
   public int size() { return size; }
   public boolean isEmpty() { return size==0; }
/* Access. */
   public E get(int k) {
      checkBoundExclusive(k);
      return A[k];
      }
   public E set(int k, E v) {
      checkBoundExclusive(k);
      E old = A[k];
      A[k] = v;
      return old;
      }
/* Insertion / Deletion. */
   public void add(E v) {
      if ( size==A.length ) ensureCapacity( size+1 );
      A[size] = v; size++;
      }
   public void add(int k, E v) {
      checkBoundInclusive(k);
      if ( size==A.length ) ensureCapacity( size+1 );
      for (int j=size; j>k; j--) A[j] = A[j-1];
      A[k] = v;
      size++;
      }
   public E remove(int k) {
      checkBoundExclusive(k);
      E old = A[k];
      size--;
      for (int j=k; j<size; j++) A[j] = A[j+1];
      A[size] = null; // Garbage-collection assist.
      return old;
      }
/* Membership. */
   public int indexOf(Object v) {
      int k = 0; while ( (k<n) && !v.equals(A[k]) ) k++;
      if ( k==n ) return -1; else return k;
      }
   public boolean contains(Object v) { return indexOf(v)!=-1; }
} /* ArrayList */
```

A2*

Type Parameter. Type parameter E is set off in angle brackets <> rather than parentheses ( ) to highlight the distinction between value and type parameters.

Constructors. Type parameter E may not be used as an array constructor, so the array is constructed as an `Object[]`, and is then cast to type `E[]` for assignment to A. The same approach is followed for the array construction in `ensureCapacity`.

Deletion. We have slipped "`A[size]=null;`" into the new version of `remove`. The motivation for this change is discussed in section Garbage Collection, below (p. 313).

Membership. To support testing membership of an arbitrary class of value v in an `ArrayList`, we have declared parameter v to have type `Object`, and have replaced "`v!=A[k]`" in method `indexOf` with "`!v.equals(A[k])`".

Instantiating a Generic Class

A variable declaration associates the variable with a particular type. For example, the declaration:

```
int k;
```

associates variable k with type **int**. Similarly, because classes are types, the declaration:

```
Rational r;
```

associates variable r with type Rational. However, because a generic class is *not* a type, and because ArrayList has now been turned into the generic class ArrayList<E>, the following is not a valid declaration:

```
ArrayList reduced;
```

Rather, one must obtain a specific type by *class instantiation*, i.e., by providing specific classes for class parameters:

```
ArrayList<Rational> reduced;
```

In the generic class ArrayList<E>, the declaration:

```
private E A[];
```

can be said to associate variable A with the type E[], i.e., a one-dimensional array of variables of type E. But this is just a manner of speaking because E is not a type *per se*; it is a type parameter that stands for whatever class will have been provided for the parameter in a class instantiation. Thus, in the class instantiation ArrayList<Rational>, the given declaration of A in the class associates A with the type Rational[], i.e., a one-dimensional array of variables of type Rational.

Enumeration of Rationals, continued

We now have enough to complete an implementation of code that enumerates positive rationals:

```
/* Output reduced positive fractions, i.e., positive rationals. */          E3
   ArrayList<Rational> reduced = new ArrayList();
   int d = 0;
   while ( true ) {
      int r = d;
      for (int c=0; c<=d; c++) {
         /* Let z be the reduced form of the fraction (r+1)/(c+1). */
            Rational z = new Rational(r+1, c+1);
         if ( !reduced.contains(z) ) {
            System.out.println( z );
            reduced.add(z);
            }
         r--;
         }
      d++;
      }
```

Declaration of reduced. Variable `reduced` is declared to have type `ArrayList<Rational>`, an instantiation of generic class `ArrayList<E>` with element type `Rational`, and is initialized with a newly instantiated `ArrayList<Rational>` object of default size. As a convenience, we are permitted to write the constructor invocation as `ArrayList()`, and the compiler infers that we intend the constructor invocation `ArrayList<Rational>()`.

Set insertion. Variable `reduced` is to be a *set* of reduced fractions, i.e., `Rational`. Accordingly, we only `add z` into `reduced` when it is not already a member of the list. We note that an `ArrayList`, in general, represents a multiset, and it is only by virtue our check for non-membership that `reduced` is a set, i.e., has no duplicate values.

Output. The program produces an unbounded enumeration of rationals, in diagonal order, as desired (C). The capacity of `reduced` doubles without bound, as necessary, while the program runs.

```
C
1
2
1/2
3
1/3      ← 2/2 omitted
4
3/2
2/3
1/4
5
1/5      ← 4/2, 3/3, and 2/4 omitted
6
5/2
4/3
3/4
2/5
1/6
7
5/3      ← 6/2 omitted
3/5      ← 4/4 omitted
1/7      ← 2/6 omitted
etc.
```

Uniformity

Some programming languages, e.g., Python, consider every value to be an object. In contrast, other languages, e.g., Java, distinguish between values of *primitive type* (like **`int`** and **`boolean`**) and objects. The advantage of considering every value to be an object is *uniformity*; the advantage of distinguishing between primitive-type values and objects is *efficiency*.

Uniformity confers conceptual economy, and avoids needless distinctions, but at the cost of efficiency. Whereas a primitive value like 3 fits neatly in the memory reserved for an **`int`** variable, there is extra overhead associated with objects, which must be accessed indirectly via references.

Java attempts to "have its cake and eat it too". As you have seen for most of this text, a subset of Java supports primitive types, with barely a mention of objects. But another subset of Java supports a uniform world of objects. In that part of the language, we wish to pair any two objects, not just any two **`int`** values. For example, you can imagine an application where you would wish to pair two values of type `ArrayList`. Accordingly, we now revise the definition of `Pair` to be a generic class.

Pair<K,V>

It is quite straightforward to give `Pair` two type parameters, `K` for the type of the `key` component, and `V` for the type of the `value` component:

```
class Pair<K, V> {                                              P4
   protected K key;
   protected V value;
   /* Constructor. */
      public Pair(K k, V v) { key = k; value = v; }
   /* Access. */
      public K getKey()   { return key; }
      public V getValue() { return value; }
   ...
   } /* Pair<K,V> */
```

Classes provided for `K` and `V` in instantiations of `Pair(K,V)` will have their own notions of `equals`, so the implementation of `equals` for a `Pair` must be upgraded to use their respective notions of `equals`:

P5

```
class Pair<K,V> {
   ...
   /* Equality. */
      @Override
      public boolean equals(Object q) {
         if (q==null) return false;
         if (q==this) return true;
         if ( !(q instanceof Pair) ) return false;
         Pair qPair = (Pair)q;
         return key.equals(qPair.key) && value.equals(qPair.value);
         } /* equals */
   } /* Pair<K,V> */
```

We are now in a position to have pairs of arbitrary objects.

But we have a new problem: Values of type **int**, e.g., the numerator and denominator of a fraction, are not objects. Now that Pair is a generic class, how can we use it to represent a Fraction or a Rational?

Boxed Primitive Values

In the part of Java in which we strive for object uniformity, we now need object versions of primitive values. In the case of integers, this is provided by the built-in class Integer. Objects of type Integer are known as *boxed* or *wrapped* integers. They are objects that have just one field of type **int** that contains the value. The Integer constructor has an **int** parameter, which it boxes as an Integer. There are similar boxed types for each primitive type, e.g., Boolean for boolean, Double for double, etc. This is how primitive values get to play in the uniform world of objects.

We were previously able to complete the program to enumerate rationals using the original version of class Rational, which extended class Fraction, which extended class Pair, which paired two **int** values. However, now that Pair has been turned into a generic class Pair<K,V>, the implementation of Fraction must be changed. Specifically, rather than the original:

```
class Fraction extends Pair {
   ...
   }
```

we must now write:

F3

```
class Fraction extends Pair<Integer,Integer> {
   ...
   } /* Fraction */
```

That is, we define Fraction to be a subclass of Pair<Integer,Integer>, which is an instantiation of the generic class Pair<K,V>. There is no need to update Rational similarly because it is defined as a subclass of Fraction.

Given the changed definition of Fraction, the object constructed by the expression **new** Rational(4,6) is as shown in the right margin. The key and value fields, which are inherited from Pair<Integer,Integer>, are each references to Integer objects, i.e., boxed integers. As before, the rational is stored as a reduced fraction., e.g., 2/3.

With this change, the program to enumerate rationals compiles and produces the same output as the previous version. The question an astute reader may ask is: Why? In particular, why aren't there type errors in all the places of the code where an `Integer` is now needed but an **`int`** value is provided, and *vice versa*? This question is discussed next.

Auto Boxing and Unboxing

Consider an initialized declaration:

```
Object o = new Pair(2,3);
```

Would it still work, or would it now have to be changed? In particular, must the arguments to the `Pair` constructor explicitly box the **`int`** values, as in the code:

```
Object o = new Pair(new Integer(2),new Integer(3));
```

This obligation would be unfortunate, but it would be even worse if the constructor `Pair` also had to be instantiated, as in:

```
Object o = new Pair<Integer,Integer>(new Integer(2),new Integer(3));
```

It is highly desirable that the distinction between boxed and unboxed values be minimized, and to that end, the compiler automatically boxes primitive values, as necessary.

In the construction `Pair(2,3)`, two **`int`** arguments are passed to a generic constructor `Pair<K,V>`, which expects two argument values of classes `K` and `V` (respectively). But the type of the first argument, 2, is **`int`**, not a class. Accordingly, the argument 2 is auto boxed to its object counterpart, i.e., the argument is implicitly treated as if it were "**`new`** `Integer(2)`", and the compiler infers that class parameter `K` is `Integer`. Similarly, the second argument, 3, is auto boxed, and the compiler infers that class parameter `V` is `Integer`. Happily, the compiler also infers that the generic constructor `Pair<K,V>` is a constructor of the class instance `Pair<Integer,Integer>`. Accordingly, the sample line of code works fine, as is.

Conversely, here is code that implicitly invokes unboxing:

```
Pair<Integer,Integer> p = new Pair(2,3);
int v = p.getValue();
System.out.println(v);
```

Variable `p` is declared to have the type `Pair<Integer,Integer>`, i.e., a specific instance of the generic class `Pair<K,V>`. Because the generic method `getValue` is known to return a value of type `V`, the compiler can infer that the expression `p.getValue()` has type `Integer`. But the assignment to `v` requires an **`int`**, so the compiler can also infer that the value returned by `getValue` must be auto unboxed. Accordingly, the sample code also works fine, as is.

In general, the rules for auto boxing and auto unboxing are subtle and persnickety. We just introduce the concepts here so that you will be aware that it is going on. The compiler is your friend, and will warn you when you mess up.

Polymorphism

Polymorphism is an essential notion in programming that supports code succinctness and reuse. Our code for Enumerating Rationals illustrates four distinct forms of polymorphism, which we recapitulate here:

Subtype polymorphism. We have seen that an object of a given class can also be viewed as an instance of each of its superclasses. For example, the object constructed by `Rational(2,3)` can be viewed as a `Rational`, a `Fraction`, a `Pair`, or an `Object`. Similarly, a variable declared to have a given class as its type may contain a value of that class, or of any of its subclasses. Dynamic dispatch supports the selection during program execution of the appropriate code for a method invocation. For example, the code that is executed for `toString` depends on the type of the object, e.g., `Rational`.

Parametric polymorphism. We have seen that a class definition can be abstracted with respect to one or more class parameters, resulting in a generic class. For example, `ArrayList<E>` and `Pair<K,V>`. Just as a class can be viewed as a cookie cutter that stamps out objects (i.e., class instances), a generic class can be viewed as a cookie cutter that stamps out classes (i.e., generic-class instances). This occurs during compilation, not during program execution. For example, the declaration of program variable `reduced` to have type `ArrayList<Rational>` illustrated generic-class instantiation.

Conversion. Every expression has a type, but the expression may occur in a context that expects an expression of a different type. A conversion changes the value *provided* from evaluating the expression into a corresponding value of the type *expected* by the context. Some conversions are implicit, e.g., the boxing of an **`int`**, and the unboxing of an `Integer`). Other conversions are explicit, e.g., the cast `(Pair)q` in the overriding definition of `equals` in class `Pair`. Another term for conversion is *coercion.*

Overloading. It is convenient to allow different methods to have the same name, and to distinguish between them based on usage. For example, `ArrayList<E>` has two constructors, one with no parameter, and the other with one parameter. It also has two `add` methods, one with one parameter, and the other with two parameters. Our client code for enumerating rationals used the `ArrayList` constructor with no parameter, and the `add` method with one parameter.

Precise usage rules associated with the different types of polymorphism are complicated, subtle, language dependent, and are best studied in the programming language's reference manual.

Garbage Collection

Each instantiated object consumes memory space, which is a limited computer resource. Any object that can no longer be accessed can be automatically deleted and the memory it consumes reclaimed. This process is called *garbage collection*, and happens beyond your control. The goal of garbage collection is to reduce gratuitous memory consumption.

Garbage collection is safe in the sense that any object your program can conceivably access will *not* be collected and deleted. As a consequence, any program variable that needlessly holds on to a reference to an object prevents a useless object from being reclaimed. While the memory of that one object may be of no great concern, the problem is that preserving it entails also preserving *all* objects that are accessible via its fields, and so on and so forth, all the way down.

To make garbage collection maximally effective, therefore, it is useful to follow a discipline whereby any unneeded object reference is relinquished rather being retained. Letting go of an object reference is done automatically when a variable containing such a reference goes out of scope. It can be done manually, if necessary, by assigning **null** to such variables, where **null** is a value that refers to no object.

When a collection is represented in a list data structure, the values in the array suffix A[size..A.length-1] are considered dead. If the list values have primitive type, there is no harm in leaving detritus in the suffix because the space is allocated anyway, i.e., there is no benefit in zeroing out those elements. But if the list items are references to objects, such references will inhibit garbage collection. This is the reason the implementation of the remove method in ArrayList (replicated below) contains a line for garbage-collection assist.

The code is a bit subtle, but it is instructive:

```
public E remove(int k) {
   checkBoundExclusive(k);
   E old = A[k];
   size--;
   for (int j=k; j<size; j++) A[j] = A[j+1];
   A[size] = null; // Garbage-collection assist.
   return old;
   } /* remove */
```

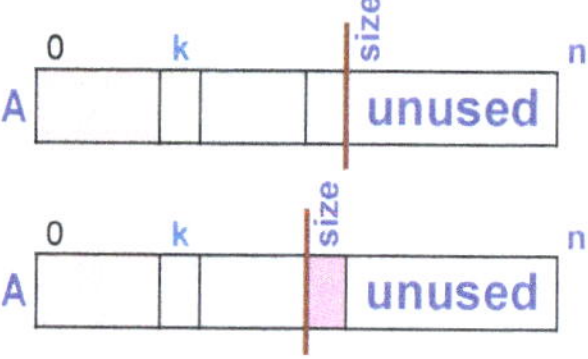

The left shift of (blue) values overwrites the (green) value that is being removed from the collection at A[k]. It was a reference to some object, and when no further references to that object remain anywhere in the program, it will be garbage collected. Thus, the value originally at A[k] is of no concern. Rather, it is the (violet) value that needs nullification. It was copied by the shift, but the original value remains in A[size]. Without nullification, that (violet) reference would prevent collection of the object it refers to—if and when the reference to the same object that is currently in A[size-1] is ever removed from the collection.

Libraries

A programming language consists of *core* features, and extensions provided by *libraries*. Some libraries are so central to a language that they are termed *standard*, and need not be explicitly requested; others are optional, and must be requested by name. A standard library is effectively a part of the programming language, and is packaged as a library merely as an implementation convenience.

The standard Java library is called java.lang, and contains numerous essential classes, including:

- Object, the root of the class hierarchy. All other classes are subclasses of this class, and inherit methods from it, which they are free to override.
- Math, a class that contains many built-in mathematical functions.
- String, the class for sequences of Unicode characters. A string constant, e.g., "Hello World", is a reference to a String object that contains the given sequence of characters.
- Integer, Boolean, etc., classes for boxed primitive values.

It would be good to browse this library; you now have the wherewithal to read the definitions of the classes it contains. The documentation is all online.

The library java.util contains many useful classes with which you should become familiar. The part of the inheritance hierarchy involving ArrayList<E> is as shown:

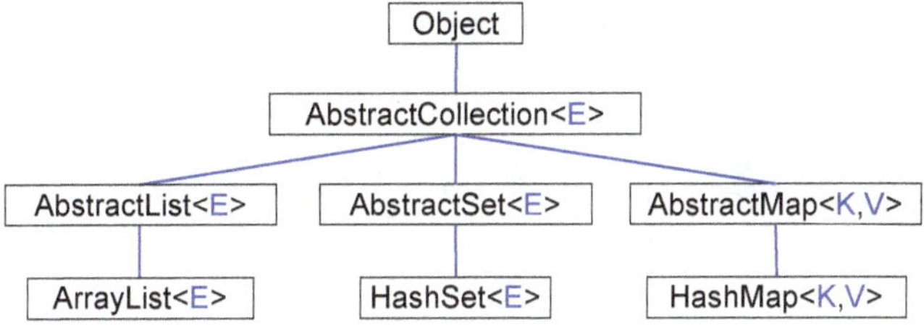

To access everything contained within this library, you must begin your code with the line:

```
import java.util.*;
```

The generic class ArrayList<E> in the library is largely as we have defined it in this chapter, but with many more methods. In other words, it was totally unnecessary for us to have implemented ArrayList. We did so just for pedagogy. The implementation in the library begins:

```
class ArrayList<E> extends AbstractList<E>
```

which states that ArrayList<E> is not a direct subclass of Object. Rather, it is a subclass of AbstractList<E>, which (if you were to look) would be found to be an abstract subclass of the abstract class AbstractCollection<E>, which is itself a direct subclass of Object.

An abstract class contains field declarations and method definitions that are inherited by its subclasses, but it is not permitted to be instantiated on its own, i.e., there are no objects of an abstract class, *per se*. Rather, its purpose is to factor declarations and definitions into groups that are then inherited by any of its non-abstract subclass instantiations (unless overridden).

The Java documentation provided by the Oracle corporation, which owns the copyright in Java, only provides a class's interface specification, and not its implementation [6]. As a client of a library class, the interface is all you really need to care about. However, you may wish to study the implementations of various library classes as a learning exercise. The Gnu Software Foundation has published open-source reference implementations of many classes [49].

If you intend to do any serious programming in Java (or any other language, for that matter), you should invest time browsing the language's libraries because you will see there many of the concepts you will otherwise find yourself programming. The next section walks you through a possible scenario in which you discover a library class, and use it to advantage.

HashSet

In reflecting on the program to enumerate rationals, you may feel queasy about the cost of using Sequential Search to look up each reduced fraction (using indexOf) to see whether it has already been output. As the set reduced grows, more and more time is spent in this lookup.

You recall from Chapter 12 that a collection can be implemented using a hash table, which offers vastly better performance than Sequential Search. You also notice

HashMap<K,V> and HashSet<E> in the class hierarchy. Given that we only want a *set* of fractions, not a mapping from keys to values, you select the documentation of HashSet<E> to peruse, and see that it fits the bill. You return to the code for enumerating rationals, and make a one-line change there:

```
/* Output reduced fractions, i.e., positive rationals; no repeats. */    E3
   HashSet<Rational> reduced = new HashSet();
   int d = 0;
   while ( true ) {
      int r = d;
      for (int c=0; c<=d; c++) {
         /* Let z be the reduced form of the fraction (r+1)/(c+1). */
            Rational z = new Rational(r+1, c+1);
         if ( !reduced.contains(z) ) {
            System.out.println( z );
            reduced.add(z);
            }
         r--;
         }
      d++;
      }
```

By virtue of their common inheritance from AbstractCollection<E>, classes ArrayList<E> and HashSet<E> both implement methods contains and add. Accordingly, those (blue) lines do not have to be changed in the code for enumerating rationals. Of course, the method definitions are completely different in the two classes, which is exactly the point of switching reduced from ArrayList to HashSet. But it is a great convenience that the two classes have a common interface because it allows us to readily try out alternative datatypes.

HashSet<E> uses whatever hash function is defined for its element type. As a rule, if a class has an overriding definition of method equals, it should also be given an overriding definition of method hashCode. Returning to class Pair<K,V>, we leverage the hashCode functions of types K and V, whatever they happened to be:

```
class Pair<K,V> {                                                         P6
   ...
   /* HashFunction. */
      @Override
      public int hashCode() {
         return key.hashCode() + value.hashCode();
         } /* hashCode */
   } /* Pair */
```

The benefit realized by use of HashSets is substantial. To measure and demonstrate the computational benefit, we comment out the line:

```
System.out.println( z );
```

whose timing would obscure the cost of maintaining the set reduced. We measure performance using the standard timing function System.currentTimeMillis, which returns time in milliseconds. We output the elapsed time after every 10,000 rationals are enumerated, up though the first 100,000 rationals:

E4

```
/* Output reduced fractions, i.e., positive rationals; no repeats. */
public static void timing() {
   HashSet<Rational> reduced = new HashSet();
   long startTime = System.currentTimeMillis();
   int rCount = 0; // # of rationals so far.
   int d = 0;
   while ( rCount<100000 ) {
      int r = d;
      for (int c=0; c<=d; c++) {
         /* Let z be the reduced form of the fraction (r+1)/(c+1). */
            Rational z = new Rational(r+1, c+1);
         if ( !reduced.contains(z) ) {
            /* System.out.println( z ); */
            reduced.add(z);
            rCount++;
            if ( rCount%10000==0 )
               System.out.println( System.currentTimeMillis()-startTime );
            }
         r--;
         }
      d++;
      }
   } /* timing */
```

After running this program and collecting the timing data for `HashSet` (D1), we change the type of `reduced` back to `ArrayList` and collect the timing data again for `ArrayList` (D2). The comparison reveals the stunning magnitude of the speedup.

This performance data rather dramatically illustrates the benefit of using hash tables. More generally, it demonstrates the potential payoff derived from just a little browsing in library documentation.

D1	D2
23	72
50	257
135	574
220	1035
308	1601
372	3206
463	5602
550	9236
644	14290
750	19711

Critique

Recall from Chapter 1 the story of Carl Friedrich Gauss, and how he outsmarted his teacher by following the precept:

> ☞ **Analyze first.**

Rather than adding the integers from 1 to 100, Carl took a hint from the precept:

> ☞ **Sometimes iteration is unnecessary because a closed-form solution is available.**

He derived the formula for the sum of the first `n` integers, `n·(n+1)/2`, plugged in 100 for `n`, and announced the answer: 5050.

We vowed to emulate Gauss.

For Running a Maze, we worked diligently in Chapter 4 to find a good loop invariant for the exploration, and in Chapter 15 were careful to choose good data representations for the maze and path, and to encapsulate them in a class. Many valuable principles were illustrated in the process. But in Chapter 17, all the problem's complexity miraculously disappeared when the notions of graphs and Depth-First

Search were introduced. It turned out that all we needed was to represent the maze as a graph, and then apply Depth-First Search. Abstraction and analysis are powerful.

Where was Gauss when we needed him?

The story for Enumerating Rationals has been similar. In Chapter 6, the need to list *all* fractions motivated diagonal-order enumeration. The requirement to list each rational only once led us to invent a data structure for maintaining the set of reduced fractions that have already been output. And the need to represent rationals as values motivated objects. Then, we learned that the Java library contains multiple ways to represent sets of objects, including `ArrayList` and `HashSet`. Finally, we demonstrated the dramatic speed advantage of `HashSet` over `ArrayList`. But our analysis fell short. Specifically, we (deliberately) overlooked the fact that a set was not needed at all because there is a closed-form way to test whether a fraction is reduced:

Fraction n/d, for $n \geq 0$ and $d > 0$, is reduced if and only if GCD(n, d) is 1.

Accordingly, we could have chosen to list a fraction only if it is a reduced fraction, using the above test for the purpose. Specifically, in the code of movie frame E4 (highlighted in blue), we can replace the set-membership test with the GCD test:

```
if ( Rational.gcd(r+1,c+1)==1 /* !reduced.contains(z) */ )
```

comment out the two lines that are specific to the `HashSet reduced`:

```
// HashSet<Rational> reduced = new HashSet();
```

and

```
// reduced.add(z);
```

and rerun the timing experiment. The results are decisive: 2, 5, 8, 11, 14, 16, 18, 20, 23, and 27 milliseconds. Although `HashSet` is much faster than `ArrayList`, computing GCD is much faster than maintaining a `HashSet`.[165]

Don't use brute force just because the computer is a brute:20

☞ **Analyze first.**

Iterators

In this chapter, we implemented many but not all the methods provided by the library version of `ArrayList`. We demonstrated the power of having a uniform interface to the different kinds of collection by showing how a one-line change to our solution

165. For completeness, there are two technical issues to mention. First, we use method `Rational.gcd`, but it was declared there as **`private`**; we assume this has been changed to **`public`**. Second, the new version is logically different from the first two versions. They displayed the reduced form of a fraction n/d when n/d first arises in the diagonal-order enumeration of fractions, and thereafter omit all fractions n'/d' that have that reduced form. In contrast, the new version lists a fraction n/d when it arises, but only if it is reduced. Whether the output is the same or not depends on the specifics of the order in which fractions are enumerated. We shall not further analyze this question, but note that the timings are comparable because they list the same number of rationals, regardless of the order.

of the Enumeration of Rationals problem could switch from one implementation of a collection (`ArrayList`) to another (`HashSet`), reaping an enormous benefit. However, we finessed one aspect of a collection that was described in Chapter 12, but not mentioned here: The enumeration of a collection's elements. Specifically, we left undiscussed how it is possible to write client code that iterates through the elements of a collection without introducing a dependence on the data structure used to implement the collection. Said another way, we now ask: How can we preserve information hiding, but still allow a client to enumerate the collection's elements?

The answer is provided by an *iterator* for the collection, i.e., an object `i` that provides these two methods:[166]

- `i.hasNext()`, which returns a **`boolean`** that says whether the iterator can be pumped for yet another element of the collection.
- `i.next()`, which returns a value of the collection. Provided `i.hasNext()` has just returned **true**, invoking `i.next()` returns the "next" element of the collection, where the order of enumeration is beyond your control.

Each generic form of collection, e.g., `ArrayList<E>` or `HashSet<E>`, must provide a method named `iterator` that constructs an iterator for a collection object.

More formally, let `C<E>` be a generic subclass of `AbstractCollection<E>`. Let `c` be an object of an instantiation of `C<E>` for some specific element type `EL`. Then `c` is a collection of `EL` items, where the collection implementation is defined by `C<E>`. The following code pattern can be used to pump collection `c` for elements until there are no more:

```
Iterator<EL> i = c.iterator();
while ( i.hasNext() ) {
   EL e = i.next();
   /* Process element e. */
   }
```

This client code is independent of the collection's implementation, and survives changes from one form of collection to another. Of course, the implementation of the iterator depends on the collection's data structure, but this difference is hidden from the client.

For a concrete example, suppose in method `timing`, above, after having enumerated 100,000 rationals and stored them in `reduced`, you wished to process each in some way. Then you could use the following code:

```
Iterator<Rational> i = reduced.iterator();
while ( i.hasNext() ) {
   Rational e = i.next();
   /* Process element e. */
   }
```

This same code would work for both the `ArrayList` and `HashSet` versions of the program.

166. Suppose the elements of the collection of interest have type `EL`. Then you can think of there being a generic class `Iterator<E>` that has an instantiation `Iterator<EL>`, and `i` is an object of that class. Although this is not technically accurate, it is close enough for our purposes.

CHAPTER 19

Debugging

To err is human, and despite our best efforts, problems inevitably arise. Rather than sweep this possibility under the rug, this chapter faces the issue frontally.

Authors distinguish between errors, mistakes, flaws, and defects, but we shall just call them all *bugs*. Some bugs are overt, and manifest with observable symptoms; other bugs are latent, and bite long after you think you have completed a correct program.

Bugs usually reveal themselves when the program is executed on some particular input, and there is an undesirable effect. Your first sign of the presence of the bug is the effect, and from that manifestation, you must *debug*, i.e., reason backwards to identify the cause. In the worst case, there is no effect, and you blithely assume that your code is bug-free. The purpose of *testing* is to make as many bugs apparent as possible.

The most glaring effect of a bug is when program execution doesn't terminate normally. It may "crash", i.e., stop prematurely with an error message, or it may fail to stop at all. Either way, you know immediately that something is wrong. In the first case, the error message usually provides a clue that can be used as a starting point for tracking down the problem. In the second case, you need to confirm that the program is indeed caught in an "infinite loop", and figure out why. Two reasons for false alarms are: (1) A "performance bug" that makes execution so slow that you falsely conclude that the code is stuck in a loop, and (2) the program is waiting for you to provide interactive input, which you didn't notice.

When program execution runs to completion, and produces reasonable looking output, it is up to you to confirm that the output is correct. Accordingly, you must:

☞ **Validate program output thoroughly.**

The symptom of a bug may be overt, e.g., the answer is dead wrong, or subtle, e.g., a numerical result seems reasonable, at first glance, but is also dead wrong. Many a research paper has been published based on incorrect calculations. Inspect your program's output, and convince yourself that it is correct.

The most overt evidence that your code's output is bad is that there is no output at all, or a whole section of output is missing. You may have forgotten to write the needed output statement, which will be immediately apparent on inspection of the part of the program you think should have produced the output. But, when the output statement is there, yet failed to produce output, there is a logical error in your code that prevents program execution from reaching the given output statement. You must figure out why.

Debugging is the backwards-reasoning process that seeks to identify the specific bug in your code that causes an observed, undesirable effect. Although this chapter endeavors to make debugging seem as pleasant as possible, you will notice that it is not very pleasant. This should reinforce the admonition first made in Chapter 1:

☞ **Avoid debugging like the plague.**

But, when the inevitable happens, you need to know how to proceed.

Example Bugs

We illustrate debugging by deliberately introducing bugs into the code of Appendix V Running a Maze. For each bug, we run the program on the input maze shown in the figure.

Each bug is presented in four sections:

- Mistake
- Observed effect
- Forward trace
- Debugging

A *mistake* made in the code results in an *observed effect*, which is explained with the aid of a *forward trace* of execution. This is Act 1 of the play, in which we introduce "dramatic irony", i.e., we learn about the mistake from the beginning, and see its consequences. In Act 2, we take on the role of detective: We don't know the mistake, haven't seen the forward trace, and are only aware of the observed effect of program execution. We then present how *debugging* starts from the effect, and discovers the offending mistake.

The fundamental approach is to selectively instrument code so that it emits increasingly useful, partial forward traces that eventually allow you to pinpoint the bug.

Bug A

This example illustrates code instrumentation in a simple setting.

Mistake. We have coded `isFacingWall` incorrectly, writing ">=" rather than "==":

```
public static boolean isFacingWall()
  { return M[r+deltaR[d]][c+deltaC[d]]>=Wall; }
```

Observed Effect. Execution completes normally after emitting the incorrect output "`Unreachable`".

Forward trace. Recall that `Wall` is -1 and `NoWall` is 0. Because the bug in `isFacingWall` causes it to always return **true**, the rat fails to find a way out of the upper-left cell. After three consecutive clockwise turns, it faces left (`d`=3), at which point `isAboutToRepeat` returns **true**, and `Solve` completes. The output routine calls `isAtCheese`, which returns **false**, so it prints "`Unreachable`".

Debugging. To start with, all we know is that the output is wrong. Our first thought is that `MRP.Input` may have failed to establish a correct maze representation in M. To confirm that it worked correctly, we insert a call to PrintMaze immediately after the maze is read in:

```
/* Input maze, or reject input as malformed. */
private static void Input() {
   MRP.Input();
   MRP.PrintMaze();
   } /* Input */
```

We run the program again, and see that input worked fine.

Since Solve emits no detailed output, we need to instrument it to obtain a forward trace of its actions. For this purpose, we write a general-purpose utility method, MRP.PrintState, which emits the parameter string s followed by the r, c, d, and move components of the MRP state:[167]

```
public static void PrintState(String s) {
   System.out.println(s+": "+r+" "+c+" "+d+" "+move);
   }
```

A convenient place to invoke PrintState is at the beginning of the loop in Solve because this will provide a top-level trace of the algorithm's execution as it proceeds through the maze:

```
8  /* Compute a direct path through the maze, if one exists. */
9  private static void Solve() {
10    while ( !MRP.isAtCheese() && !MRP.isAboutToRepeat() ) {
         MRP.PrintState("Solve");
11       if (MRP.isFacingWall()) MRP.TurnClockwise();
12       else if (!MRP.isUnvisited()) Retract();
13       else {
14          MRP.StepForward();
15          MRP.TurnCounterClockwise();
16          }
         }
17    } /* Solve */
```

We run the program again, and luck out because the output (A1) is very short. It is clear from this trace that line 11 of Solve is repeatedly invoking TurnClockwise, and that the rat never moves from the upper-left cell. This can only happen if isFacingWall is **true** in every direction. We have confirmed from the output of PrintMaze that there is no wall to the right of the upper-left cell, so the problem must be in isFacingWall. Inspection of its code reveals the bug.

A1

```
Solve: 1 1 0 1
Solve: 1 1 1 1
Solve: 1 1 2 1
Unreachable
```

This is about as easy as debugging gets: From the observed effect, i.e., the incorrect output, and from our first attempt at instrumentation, we were able to converge on the bug in short order.

167. This routine is in complete violation of the principle of information hiding, but it will only be used for debugging.

Bug B

This example illustrates that code instrumentation can produce vast amounts of diagnostic information, but that judicious search in that information may lead directly to information vital to pinpointing a bug.

Mistake. We have coded `isAtCheese` incorrectly, writing "`hi+1`" rather than "`hi`":

```
public static boolean isAtCheese()
   { return (r==hi+1)&&(c==hi+1); }
```

Observed Effect. Execution completes after emitting the incorrect output "`Unreachable`", the exact same output as in Bug A.

Forward trace. The rat exhaustively explores the maze, not stopping at the cheese in the lower-right cell because the bug in `isAtCheese` causes it to always return **false**. When the rat returns to the upper-left cell, and faces left (d=3), the exploration completes, and the output routine prints "`Unreachable`".

Debugging. The observed effect is exactly the same as in Bug A, so we proceed in the same manner. However, this time the diagnostic output (B1) reveals an exhaustive maze exploration that blows right by the cheese at ⟨`r`,`c`⟩ = ⟨9,9⟩. This is enough information to focus our attention on method `isAtCheese`, which inspection reveals why it returned **false** when the rat entered the lower-right cell.

B1

```
Solve: 1 1 0 1
Solve: 1 1 1 1
Solve: 1 3 0 2
Solve: 1 3 1 2
Solve: 1 5 0 3
...
Solve: 7 5 2 8
Solve: 9 5 1 9
Solve: 9 7 0 10
Solve: 9 7 1 10
Solve: 9 9 0 11
Solve: 9 9 1 11
Solve: 9 9 2 11
Solve: 9 9 3 11
Solve: 9 7 2 10
...
Solve: 3 1 3 2
Solve: 3 1 0 2
Unreachable
```

The example illustrates that instrumentation can easily produce vast amounts of diagnostic output. However, we need not study it in detail because the salient information is apparent from the sole fact that the rat reached the cheese at ⟨`r`,`c`⟩ = ⟨9,9⟩, and didn't stop.

Bug B was not much more difficult to diagnose than was Bug A.

Bug C

This example illustrates how deductive reasoning based on automatically-produced diagnostic error information can be used to find a bug.

Mistake. We have coded `TurnCounterClockwise` incorrectly, thinking that if increment-modulo-4 is `(d+1)%4`, then by analogy decrement-modulo-4 must be `(d-1)%4`:

```
public static void TurnCounterClockwise()
   { d = (d-1)%4; }
```

Observed Effect. Execution stops with a "subscript out-of-bounds" exception. The following diagnostic message is printed:

```
java.lang.ArrayIndexOutOfBoundsException: Index -1 out of bounds for length 4
   at MRP.isFacingWall(MRP.java:46)
   at RunMaze.Solve(RunMaze.java:11)
   at RunMaze.main(RunMaze.java:41)
```

The message states that an array of length 4 is being indexed with a subscript of -1. The next line states that the exception was triggered in method `isFacingWall`, at line 46 of class `MRP`:

```
45 public static boolean isFacingWall()
46    { return M[r+deltaR[d]][c+deltaC[d]]==Wall; }
```

The remaining lines are known as the *call stack*, and list (in reverse call order) the method invocations that have not yet returned, i.e., line 41 in `main` invoked `Solve`, which on line 11 invoked `isFacingWall`.

Forward trace. Because the (incorrect) expression `(d-1)%4` in `TurnCounterClockwise` correctly turns counterclockwise when `d` is greater than 0, the bug has no effect until the method is first invoked with direction `d` equal to 0, i.e., facing up. Accordingly, execution proceeds without incident until stepping forward into cell 6, whereupon it turns counterclockwise, which (incorrectly) sets `d` to -1. What happens next? The algorithm of `Solve` continues, and checks for the presence or absence of a wall by invoking `isFacingWall`. This is the moment when `d` is used to index array `deltaR`, and is out of bounds.

Debugging. How might a backward analysis proceed from the observed effect? The diagnostic output is sufficient to conclude that the proximal cause of the problem is likely that the value of `d` is -1. How so? Because the only arrays mentioned on the offending line of code that has been identified by the exception (`MRP.isFacingWall`:46) are `M[][]`, `deltaR[]`, and `deltaC[]`. Although it is conceivable that `M` has somehow been misallocated, and involves an array of length 4, it is far more likely that the array in question is either `deltaR[]` or `deltaC[]`, both of which have a declared length of 4. In both cases, the subscript expression is `d`.

How might `d` have gotten the value -1? Inspection of the code reveals five places where an assignment to `d` occurs:

> Initialization to 0 (at `MRP.Input`:109),
> increment-modulo-4 (at `MRP.TurnClockwise`:35),
> decrement-modulo-4 (at `MRP.TurnCounterClockwise`:38),
> locate the previous cell on the path (at `MRP.FacePrevious`:78-79)
> restore `d` to face the previous cell on the path (at `MPR.RestoreDirection`:69)

Considering these in turn, we can readily rule out the first two: The first sets `d` to 0, and the second adds to `d`. The third is plausible as a place where `d` might have been assigned -1. The code made sense when we wrote it, but we are now forced to reconsider it. Consulting online documentation for the modulus operator (%), we discover our misunderstanding. We are saved from having to consider the final two possibilities.

The diagnostic information provided by the runtime exception, together with systematic analysis, was sufficient to pinpoint the bug, even without instrumentation of the code.

Bug D

This example illustrates how debugging sometimes requires an iterative process.

Mistake. We have coded `isUnvisited` incorrectly, failing to scale the row offset by 2:

```
public static boolean isUnvisited()
   { return M[r+deltaR[d]][c+2*deltaC[d]]==Unvisited; }
```

Observed Effect. Execution stops with a "subscript out-of-bounds" exception. The following diagnostic message is printed:

```
java.lang.ArrayIndexOutOfBoundsException: Index 4 out of bounds for length 4
    at MRP.isFacingWall(MRP.java:46)
    at MRP.FacePrevious(MRP.java:79)
    at RunMaze.Retract(RunMaze.java:23)
    at RunMaze.Solve(RunMaze.java:12)
    at RunMaze.main(RunMaze.java:41)
```

The message states that an array of length 4 is being indexed with a subscript of 4. The offending line of code is the same code as for Bug C:

```
45 public static boolean isFacingWall()
46    { return M[r+deltaR[d]][c+deltaC[d]]==Wall; }
```

However, the call stack is different this time, and indicates that the error occurred in the course of retracting the path from a cul-de-sac.

Forward trace. Because the erroneous code for `isUnvisited` fails to scale the row offset by 2, the elements of `M` that it inspects do not always correspond to a cell of the physical maze. Rather, when `d` is 0 or 2, the code (erroneously) inspects an element of `M` that encodes the presence or absence of a wall of the current cell in the given direction. This causes program execution to go haywire.

As the rat proceeds in the forward direction, the algorithm in `Solve` steps forward into any cell that is not blocked by a wall, provided that cell is not on the current path, which it determines by invoking the (flawed) method `isUnvisited`. Such checks will work correctly when d=1 or d=3 because, in these cases, the (correct) row increment is zero, and therefore the missing scaling factor is irrelevant. However, when `d=0` or `d=2`, `isUnvisited` will always return **true**. Why? Because it will (erroneously) inspect the very same element of `M` that `isFacingWall` just inspected. Since there was no wall, `isUnvisited` will compare `NoWall` (which is 0) with `Unvisited` (which is 0), and return **true**.

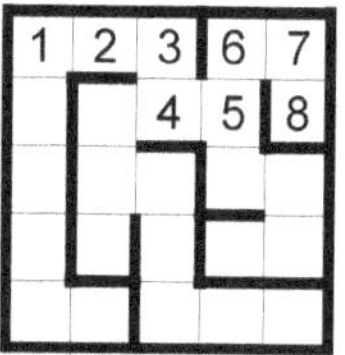

Thus, the rat makes it all the way to the end of the cul-de-sac at cell 8, at which point it (correctly) discovers walls in the right, down, and left directions, but no wall in the up direction. It is ready to step forward, but this is the precise moment when it is relying on correct execution of `isUnvisited` to detect the cul-de-sac. However, because `d=0`, the element of `M` that `isUnvisited` inspects is the one that encodes that there is no wall between cells 8 and 7, not the element that contains the 7. Accordingly, the rat blithely steps forward into the upper-right cell, overwriting 7 with 9, and then turns counterclockwise, facing left (`d=3`).

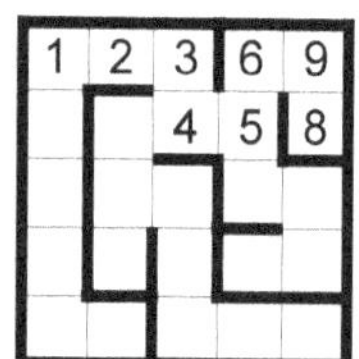

You may think that the rat will proceed forward, overwriting the existing path, but this is not what happens. Recall that `isUnvisited` works correctly when d=1 or d=3. Accordingly, the rat now (correctly)detects cell 6 as already visited, which stops its forward momentum. `Retract` is then invoked to back out of a (supposed) cul-de-sac at 9.

`Retract` invokes `FacePrevious`:

```
77 public static void FacePrevious() {
78    d = 0;
79    while ( isFacingWall() ||
              M[r+2*deltaR[d]][c+2*deltaC[d]]!=M[r][c]-1 ) d++;
80    }
```

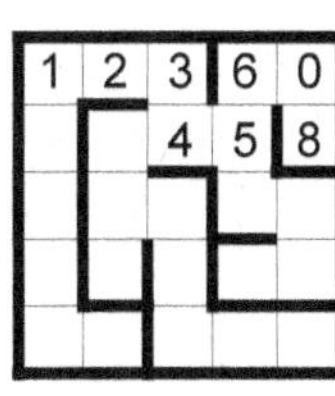

which (correctly) identifies cell 8 as the predecessor of cell 9, and orients the rat facing down. `Retract` then invokes `StepBackward`, which sets the upper-right cell to `Unvisited`, i.e., 0, and moves the rat back into cell 8.

Once again, `Retract` invokes `FacePrevious`, this time to search for the predecessor of cell 8, but none of its neighbors is numbered 7. This is a situation that is supposed to never arise. The search runs through all four legal values of `d`, and then invokes `isFacingWall` with (an illegal value of) `d=4`. This triggers the "subscript out-of-bounds" exception, with the call stack, as shown.

An important general-purpose takeaway from this forward trace is that once a bug upsets a carefully-crafted program design, it is possible for "all hell to break loose", at which point anything may happen.

Debugging. There is an old trope that "Ginger Rogers could do everything Fred Astaire could do, backwards ... and in heels". It is plenty difficult to understand the forward trace. We now have to find the bug by reasoning backwards without the benefit of having seen the trace in advance (heels optional).

As with Bug C, inspection of the code of `isFacingWall` leads us to conclude that the value of `d` is 4, which is improper for an array of length 4, i.e., `deltaR` or `deltaC`.

We identify the same five places in the code where `d` can (in principle) be assigned a value, but in this case, we know the culprit for sure. How so? The call stack shows that at the time of the exception, `isFacingWall` had been invoked by `FacePrevious`. Since that routine necessarily assigns a new value to `d`, the problem must be there. Its code searches for the direction to the cell from which the rat entered its present cell. The loop in `FacePrevious` invokes `isFacingWall` on each iteration to avoid looking outside the maze. We conclude that the search must have failed to find the cell from whence the rat came, which then resulted in `d` becoming 4. We ask: How can this be? Surely, the rat entered cell ⟨`r,c`⟩ from some cell that must have been numbered `M[r][c]-1`. There was no wall separating it from ⟨`r,c`⟩ when the rat came from there, and so the search in `FacePrevious` should have found it. We are befuddled.

Note that we are missing critical information: We don't know where the rat was at the moment the exception was raised, i.e., we don't know ⟨`r,c`⟩, and we don't know how the rat got there. The idea that the rat actually backed into 8 from 9 is beyond our wildest imagination.

In summary, we need to reason backward along the forward trace, but the program provided no such trace as it careened toward failure. In fact, it ran silently. What is needed now is a critical portion of the forward trace, i.e., a portion that is informative, and that points to the bug. In general, a complete forward trace from the beginning of execution is far too long and too detailed to be helpful. What is needed is a goal-directed process that selectively reveals relevant portions of the trace. The process is iterative: We intelligently interpret each trace to decide what new portion to reveal in the next trace.

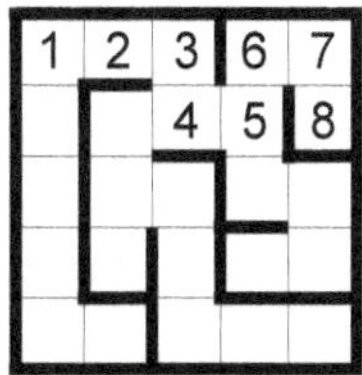

We can tell from the call stack that `Retract` has been invoked, and has not yet returned. However, because the maze has many cul-de-sacs, we don't know for sure whether this invocation of `Retract` is the first, or whether others may have come before. To answer this question, we can instrument `Retract`:

```
/* Unwind abortive exploration. */
private static void Retract() {
   System.out.println("Enter Retract");
   ...
   }
```

Running the program again reveals that the exception occurs within the very first invocation of `Retract`. We (incorrectly) suspect that this retraction starts from 8, and then backs out of 8, 7, and 6, but we don't know where along this sequence the exception occurs. To determine this, we instrument `FacePrevious`:

```
public static void FacePrevious() {
   PrintState("FacePrevious");
   ...
   }
```

and `StepBackward`:

```
public static void StepBackward() {
   PrintState("StepBackward");
   ...
   }
```

where `PrintState` is the same diagnostic method introduced in Bug A. Running the program again produces useful diagnostic output (D1) before the exception is thrown. This output can be paraphrased as:

D1

```
Enter Retract
FacePrevious: 1 9 3 9
StepBackward: 1 9 2 9
FacePrevious: 3 9 2 8
```

> `FacePrevious` was invoked with the rat in the upper-right cell (⟨r,c⟩=⟨1,9⟩).
> `StepBackward` was invoked from there with the rat facing down (d=2).
> `FacePrevious` was invoked again with the rat in the cell below the upper-right, i.e., ⟨3,9⟩.

This anomalous output reveals that the order of retraction is not as we had suspected. Rather than backing out of 8, the rat is backing *into* cell 8. At this point, there are two mysteries:

- Notwithstanding that we never should have been in the situation of backing *into* 8, we may ask why the program crashes?
- How did we get into this situation?

To answer the first question, we expand `PrintState` to include an invocation of `PrintMaze`:

```
public static void PrintState(String s) {
   System.out.println(s+": "+r+" "+c+" "+d+" "+move);
   PrintMaze();
   }
```

D2

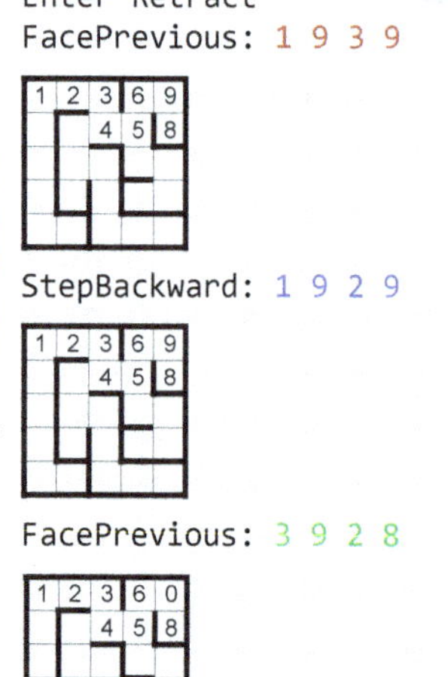

We then rerun the program, and obtain the output (D2), where we show a graphical rather than a textual version of the maze. How do we interpret this output?

- We can see that the rat reached the upper-right cell, and numbered it 9. We have no idea how it got there.
- We can see that the retraction started there, zeroed cell 9, and backed into cell 8. This makes sense, given where the retraction started.

- We can see that `FacePrevious` was invoked from cell 8, and must have been searching for a cell numbered 7. We can see that there is no such cell, which explains why `d` became 4, which is why `isFacingWall` triggered the "subscript out-of-bounds" exception.

So, now we understand the tail end of the trace, and why the program crashes. But we still have no idea how we got to cell 9, and why.

To get a picture of what happened leading up to the retraction, we decide to instrument `StepForward`. This could produce more output than we want, so to limit it, we condition the diagnostic on `move` being greater than 6:

```
public static void StepForward() {
   if (move>6) PrintState("StepForward");
   ...
   }
```

Rerunning the program, we obtain the more detailed output (D3).

How do we interpret this output?

- We can see in the path display that the rat's trajectory proceeded normally from 6 to 7, and then from 7 to 8. This is as it should be.
- We can see that the rat failed to stop at 8, and proceeded incorrectly to 9.

Why? Or more specifically, what code should have prevented the rat from doing so?

The program would have been executing the algorithm in `Solve`, proceeding along a forward trajectory:

D3

```
StepForward: 1 9 2 7
StepForward: 3 9 0 8
Enter Retract
FacePrevious: 1 9 3 9
StepBackward: 1 9 2 9
FacePrevious: 3 9 2 8
```

```
8  /* Compute a direct path through the maze, if one exists. */
9  private static void Solve() {
10    while ( !MRP.isAtCheese() && !MRP.isAboutToRepeat() )
11       if (MRP.isFacingWall()) MRP.TurnClockwise();
12       else if (!MRP.isUnvisited()) Retract();
13       else {
14          MRP.StepForward();
15          MRP.TurnCounterClockwise();
16          }
17    } /* Solve */
```

The rat would have been in cell 8 facing up (d=0). On seeing no wall (line 11), its next step was to detect whether it was about to enter a cell already on the path (line 12). Why did it fail to invoke `Retract`? Specifically, why was `isUnvisited` **true** when the upper-right cell so clearly contains 7? To answer this question, we turn to the code, and study it:

```
public static boolean isUnvisited()
   { return M[r+deltaR[d]][c+2*deltaC[d]]==Unvisited; }
```

Ideally, we would spot the problem as soon as we look at this code. But, if we don't, we can print out the values of the subexpressions, one-by-one:

```
public static boolean isUnvisited() {
   if (move==8) {
      int rr= r+deltaR[d];
      int cc= c+2*deltaC[d];
      int mm = M[r+deltaR[d]][c+2*deltaC[d]];
      System.out.println("M["+rr+"]["+cc+"] is "+mm);
      }
   return M[r+deltaR[d]][c+2*deltaC[d]]==Unvisited;
   }
```

Rerunning the program, this outputs the line:

```
M[2][9] is 0
```

which explains the expression returned by `isUnvisited` when `move`=8. Staring at this line, the row index "2" should jump out at us as wrong. Cells of the maze are indexed at odd row and column subscripts. What is that "2" doing there? Looking again at the code, we cannot fail to notice that the row subscript expression is "`r+deltaR[d]`" when it should have been "`r+2*deltaR[d]`".

Correcting this, we run the program one more time, and it works. All we have to do now is remove the diagnostic instrumentation, and we are done.

Bug E

This example illustrates looking for a pattern in diagnostic information that reveals the cause of an infinite loop.

Mistake. We have coded `deltaR` incorrectly in the down direction, entering the row offset as 0 instead of 1:

```
// Unit vectors in direction d =          0,     1,     2,     3
//                                       up, right,  down,  left
   private static final int deltaR[] = { -1,     0,     0,     0 };
   private static final int deltaC[] = {  0,     1,     0,    -1 };
```

Observed Effect. The program runs without producing any output, and without stopping.

Forward trace. If the rat faces down (d=2), both `deltaR[d]` and `deltaC[d]` will (incorrectly) be 0. Thus, access to `M[r+deltaR[d]][c+deltaC[d]]`, e.g., in `isFacingWall`, will really access `M[r][c]`. Likewise, access to `M[r+2*deltaR[d]][c+2*deltaC[d]]`, e.g., in `isUnvisited`, will also just access `M[r][c]`. The first time the rat faces down will be in cell 3.

The algorithm in `Solve` asks (on line 11) whether the rat is facing a wall by invoking `isFacingWall`:

```
public static boolean isFacingWall()
   { return M[r+deltaR[d]][c+deltaC[d]]==Wall; }
```

However, rather than inspecting the element of `M` that contains `NoWall`, method `isFacingWall`, in effect, inspects `M[r][c]`, which contains 3. Since `Wall` is encoded by -1, which is not equal to 3, `isFacingWall` returns **false**, which (serendipitously) is correct. Accordingly, the rat prepares to step forward into the cell below. But before doing so, `Solve` invokes `isUnvisited` to make sure the rat is not at a cul-de-sac, and about to step into a cell already on the path:

```
public static boolean isUnvisited()
   { return M[r+2*deltaR[d]][c+2*deltaC[d]]==Unvisited; }
```

However, rather than inspecting the value of the cell below, `isUnvisited`, in effect, inspects `M[r][c]`, which contains 3, not `Unvisited`. Accordingly, the rat (incorrectly) believes it would be entering a cell already on the path, and invokes `Retract` to back out of the apparent cul-de-sac:

```
/* Unwind abortive exploration. */
private static void Retract() {
   MRP.RecordNeighborAndDirection();
   while ( !MRP.isAtNeighbor() ) {
      MRP.FacePrevious();
      MRP.StepBackward();
      }
   MRP.RestoreDirection();
   MRP.TurnCounterClockwise();
   } /* Retract */
```

`Retract` first invokes `RecordNeighborAndDirection` to obtain and save the `neighborNumber` of the cell in direction `d`. But d=2, so "the cell in direction d" is (incorrectly) the very cell the rat is in, and `neighborNumber` is set to 3. Next, `Retract` invokes `isAtNeighbor` to see whether the unwinding is finished. But we are at cell 3, so the loop terminates immediately. Next, `Retract` invokes `RestoreDirection`, which sets `d` to 2, which it already was. Next, `Retract` invokes `TurnCounterClockwise`, which sets `d` to 1, i.e., once again facing a wall to the right. This completes execution of `Retract`, and control returns to `Solve`.

We have been in this state before: Method `Solve` calls `TurnClockwise`, which again turns the rat to face down, and the process repeats. We are caught in an unending loop.

Debugging. All we know at the beginning is that we are stuck in an infinite loop. The first thing we must do is to interrupt execution using whatever command our programming environment offers for this. The good news is that we can stop execution; the bad news is that we typically have no idea where in the program we stopped it.

As with Bug C and Bug D, we instrument the code to provide diagnostic information. This time, we choose to instrument (with calls to `MRP.PrintState`) the beginning of each time around the `Solve` loop, and entry to `Retract`. We quickly terminate execution (before too much output accumulates), and inspect the trace (E1).

E1

```
Solve: 1 1 0 1
Solve: 1 1 1 1
Solve: 1 3 0 2
Solve: 1 3 1 2
Solve: 1 5 0 3
Solve: 1 5 1 3
Solve: 1 5 2 3
Retract: 1 5 2 3
Solve: 1 5 1 3
Solve: 1 5 2 3
Retract: 1 5 2 3
Solve: 1 5 1 3
Solve: 1 5 2 3
Retract: 1 5 2 3
Etc.
```

The pattern in the output is clear: We are forever repeating the three lines shown in (E2), which we interpret as follows:

- We can see that the rat is in the cell that would be numbered 3, facing right (d=1).
- We can see that the rat turns clockwise so that it faces down (d=2).
- The rat must have seen no wall because it was prepared to step forward, but apparently it believed that would renter a cell already on the path, so it called `Retract`.
- The net effect of invoking Retract is to return the rat to facing right (d=1).

E2

```
Solve: 1 5 1 3
Solve: 1 5 2 3
Retract: 1 5 2 3
```

This is mysterious, but at least we now know the extent of the infinite loop. We instrument `isUnvisited` as we did in Bug D, but with output conditioned on `move==3` rather than `move==8`. Rerunning the program produces output (E3). The diagnostic output from `isUnvisited` is clearly problematic because it should be checking element `M[3][5]`, not element `M[1][5]`. Inspection of the code of `isUnvisited` shows nothing wrong. The only place to inspect is in the initialization of `deltaR`:

```
// Unit vectors in direction d =         0,     1,     2,     3
//                                      up, right, down, left
   private static final int deltaR[] = { -1,     0,     0,     0 };
```

```
Solve: 1 1 0 1
Solve: 1 1 1 1
M[1][3] is 0
Solve: 1 3 0 2
Solve: 1 3 1 2
M[1][5] is 0
Solve: 1 5 0 3
Solve: 1 5 1 3
Solve: 1 5 2 3
M[1][5] is 3
Retract: 1 5 2 3
Solve: 1 5 1 3
Solve: 1 5 2 3
M[1][5] is 3
Retract: 1 5 2 3
Solve: 1 5 1 3
Solve: 1 5 2 3
M[1][5] is 3 3
Retract: 1 5 2 3
Etc.
```
E3

There we spot the 0 instead of 1. Fixing the error, we rerun the program, and obtain the correct output.

Bug F

This example illustrates the difficulty of debugging when the effect of a bug is delayed until much later in program execution. It introduces the application of Binary Search (performed manually) to locate the bug.

Mistake. The mistake is contrived, but models a common occurrence: A rare event in obscure code causes damage that is often benign, but on occasion has disastrous effect. We concoct the example by inserting a nonsensical statement in `FacePrevious`:

```
public static void FacePrevious() {
   d = 0;
   while ( isFacingWall() ||
           M[r+2*deltaR[d]][c+2*deltaC[d]]!=M[r][c] 1 ) d++;
   if ( move==9 ) M[r-2][c-3] = Wall;
   }
```

If the rat is ever backing out of a cell when `move` is 9, a spurious wall will be inserted at a nearby place in the maze. The wall insertion may not be triggered for any test cases you devise. In those rare cases when it is, the new wall may not matter: It may not eliminate a solution, and even if it does, another solution may be found. The bug may never be noticed, but in this case, it is.

Observed Effect. The incorrect output "`Unreachable`" is printed.

Forward trace. The sample maze happens to have a cul-de-sac at move 9, so a spurious wall (shown in red) is introduced, which happens to eliminate the only available solution.

Debugging. The observed effect is exactly the same as in Bug A and Bug B, so we proceed in the same manner. In Bug A, the diagnostic trace immediately revealed that the rat was struck in the upper-left cell. In Bug B, it revealed that the rat reached the lower-right cell, but didn't stop. In this bug, the output shows that rat gets nowhere near the cheese. Unfortunately, the step where the rat is blocked by the offending wall is buried deep in the trace, and we are not likely to spot it. Furthermore, the offense of inserting a fictitious wall was committed at an obscure earlier moment. Making matters still worse, the encounter with the fictitious wall was perfectly ordinary, e.g., it didn't cause the program to crash, and execution continued for a long time thereafter. These are the bugs that try one's soul.

Devising an effective strategy is left as an exercise for the reader. We give one hint.

Suppose that by hard work, and some luck, you have spotted the fictitious wall. How might you discover how it got there? Answer: Use binary search along the timeline from the start of execution to moment when the wall's presence mattered. Repeatedly divide that interval (roughly) in half, checking on each probe for the presence or absence of the (spurious) wall, and choosing which half-interval of time to focus on next, accordingly. You will eventually converge on the moment when the wall was introduced. Lo and behold, it is a nonsensical line of code in `FacePrevious`. Who could have guessed?

Debuggers

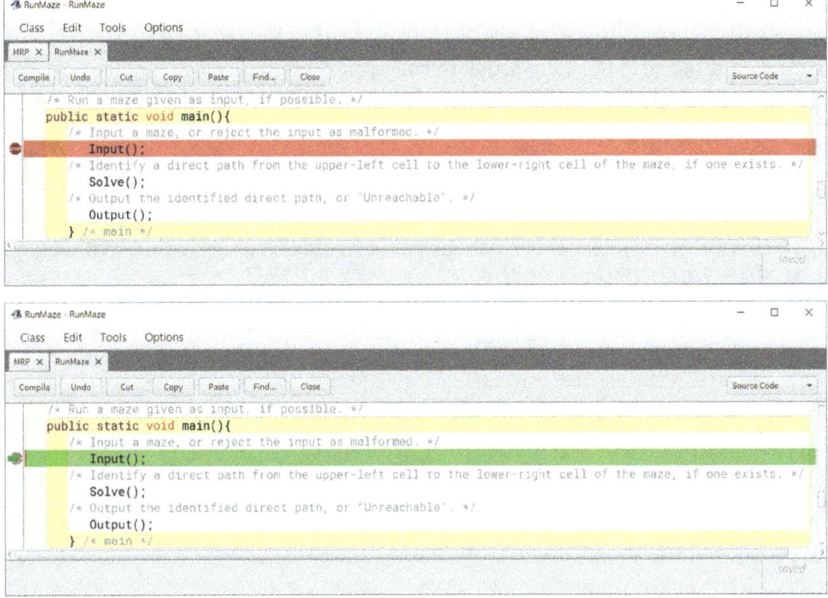

A *debugger* is a tool designed to assist in debugging. The fundamental debugging process is the same with a debugger, but the tool allows you to obtain diagnostic information without instrumenting the code. In this section, we illustrate use of the debugger that is built into the BlueJ programming environment [1].

The first step is to arrange to seize control of program execution from within the debugger. A *breakpoint* is a debugger directive to stop execution whenever control reaches a given line of code. We can set as many breakpoints in a program as we wish, and do so by clicking on the left column of the given line. To obtain control from the get-go, we set a breakpoint on the first executable line of method `main`. Now, when we rerun the program, it stops at that breakpoint. The debugger opens an additional window, which displays the call stack (referred to as the Call Sequence), the values of variables (there are none in class `RunMaze`), and various buttons for controlling execution.

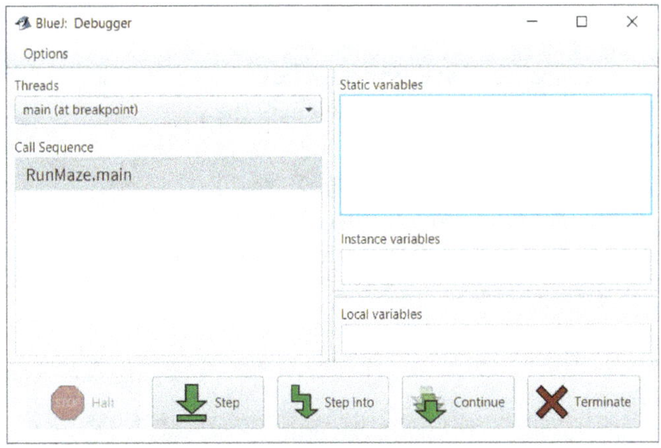

Step directs the debugger to execute the next line of code all in one step. This is known as *single-step execution*. The entire call to `Input` is performed, including its call to `MRP.Input`. Execution then stops at the next line, e.g., at the call to `Solve`.

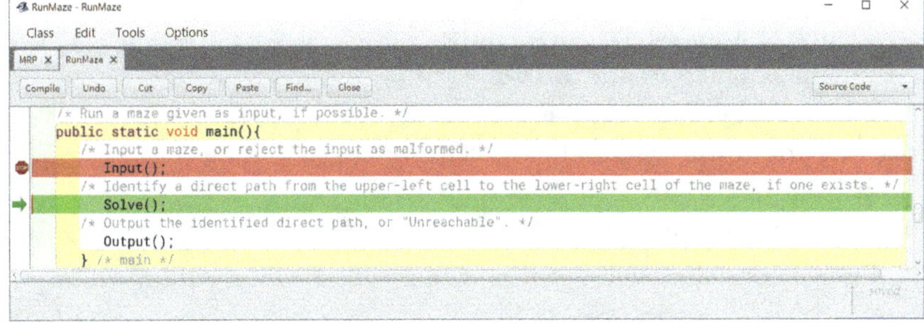

If we were to strike **Step** again, the entire invocation of `Solve` would be performed, all in one step. Instead, we strike **Step Into,** which directs the debugger to execute the current line, but to stop on the first line of any method that is invoked in the process. Thus, we step into method `Solve`, and stop at its first line, as shown.

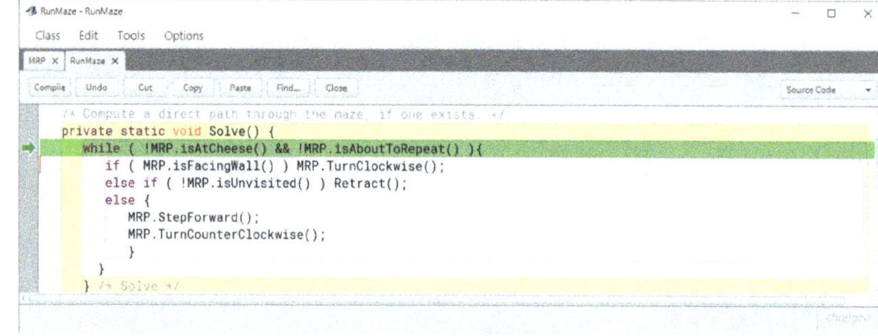

Let's assume that we are debugging Bug A. Recall that the mistake in Bug A causes the rat to never leave the upper-left cell. We can single-step execute `Solve` by repeatedly striking **Step**. The loop iterates just three times, calling `MRP.TurnClockwise` each time, and then terminates. This brings us to the last line of `Solve`, from which it is about to return. This is sufficient information to see that `isFacingWall` never returned **false**, and the rat is stuck in the upper-left cell. We can reason from this that the bug must be in `isFacingWall`. Once we inspect its code, we see the bug.

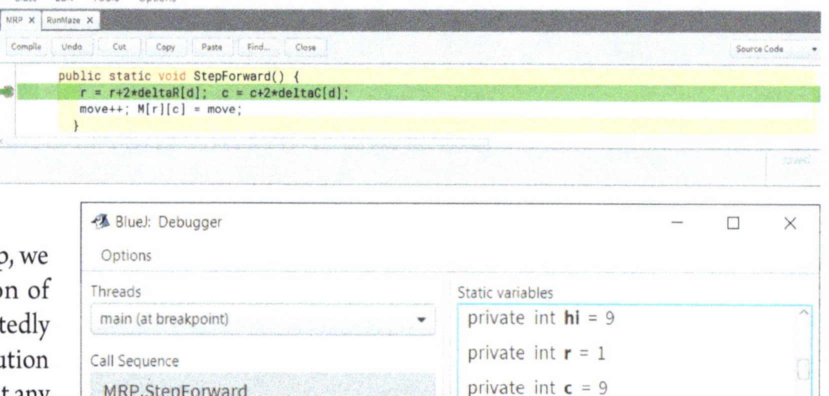

Now let's imagine that we were debugging Bug B rather than Bug A. Recall that the mistake in Bug B causes the rat to not stop when it reaches the lower-right cell. In this case, single-step execution of `Solve` gets tedious because the rat visits so many cells. To speed things up, we set a breakpoint on the invocation of `MRP.StepForward`. We then repeatedly strike **Continue**, which directs execution to proceed at full speed, but to stop at any breakpoint encountered, e.g., to stop at each invocation of `MRP.StepForward`.

Suppose we have continued enough times to suspect that the rat must be close to the lower-right cell. To see where the rat is, we strike **Step Into**, which brings us to the first line of `StepForward`, within class `MRP`. When execution suspends in class `MRP`, the debugger window provides access to its **`static`** variables. For example, the window might show that r=1, c=9, and d=2, so the rat is not there yet.

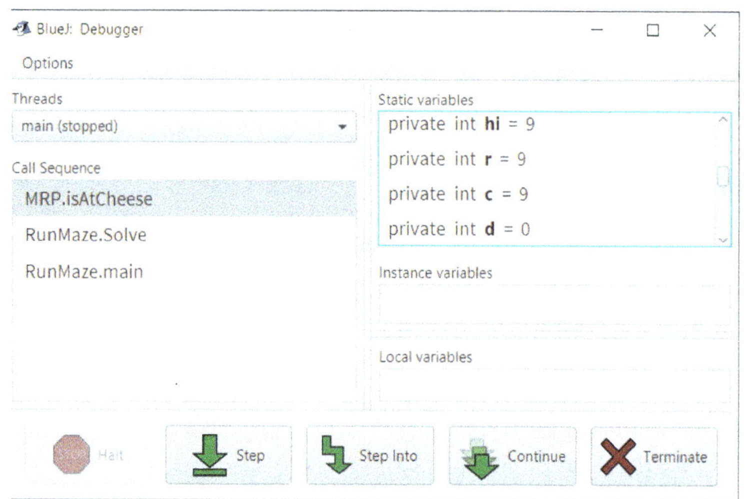

Repeatedly striking **Continue** from here resumes coarse-grained cycling around `Solve`. Whenever we wish, we can switch to **Step**, which gives a more fine-grained cycling around `Solve`.

When we believe that the rat has reached the lower-right cell, we can strike **Step Into** at the next invocation of `isAtCheese`, where we can confirm in the debug window that r=9 and c=9, i.e., the rat has indeed reached the cheese. Staring at `hi=9` in the debug window, and at the code of `isAtCheese` makes the bug obvious.

```
public static boolean isAtCheese()
   { return (r==hi+1)&&(c==hi+1); }
```

One more **Step** confirms that `isAtCheese` (incorrectly) returns **false**, and the loop fails to terminate, despite the rat's being at the cheese.

Recall that our first suspicion on encountering Bug A was that the maze `M` might not have been constructed correctly, and our first step was to invoke `PrintMaze` to check. Were we to have wished to inspect `M` directly in the debugger, we could have done so. In the image below, we have clicked on `M`'s value in the debug window (the small red box). Recall that an array is really a reference to an object. In the case of the 2-D array `M`, the object is a sequence of 11 variables (the rows), each of which is a reference to an object (a column). The image shows the row array (left), and the 0th column object, `M[0]`, an array of 11 **`int`** variables.

Although it is nice to be able to inspect values in this sort of gory detail, if necessary, the output provided by `PrintMaze` was more felicitous. Just because you have a debugger doesn't mean that you can't continue to use lower-tech techniques based on instrumenting code with print statements. A hybrid approach that uses both print statements and the debugger is probably best.

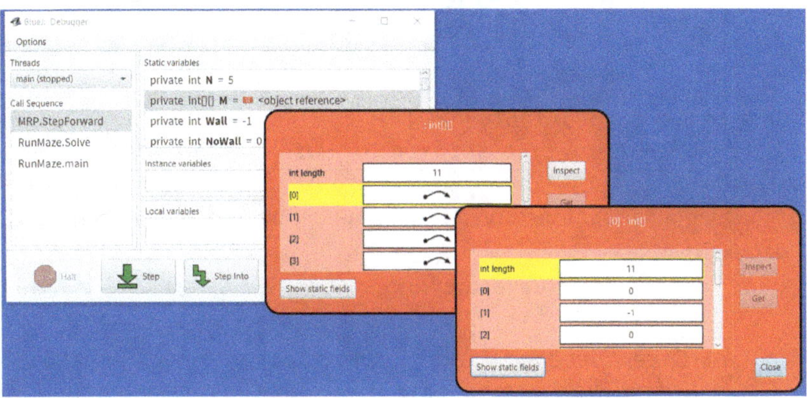

Defensive Programming

A program's code makes assumptions at various places without explicitly checking that they hold. The earliest manifestation of a bug is internal: An assumption is violated. However, such a violation is not immediately observable externally.

In some cases, the violation of an assumption is benign, e.g., a representation invariant gets broken, but program execution from that point on does not rely on the truth of the full invariant. In other cases, the program eventually throws a runtime exception, or gets caught in an infinite loop, or produces bad output.

Defensive programming aims to make the violation of assumptions manifest as early as possible during program execution. It does so by using **assert** statements. The main places in code at which assumptions can be checked are these:

- For an input statement, the code assumes that the input data will comply with its specified format.
- For a statement-level specification of the form:

```
/* Given precondition, establish postcondition. */
   Implementation
```

  the code assumes that the *precondition* is **true** before the first statement of the *implementation*, and the *postcondition* is **true** after the last statement of the *implementation*.

- For a declaration of the form:

```
declaration // representation invariant
```

or a declaration of the form:

```
/* Representation invariant. */
   declarations of related variables
```

the *representation invariant* is assumed to hold throughout the scope of the *variables,* except prior to initialization, and until completion of the code that seeks to reestablish the *invariant* after an update.

- For a loop of the form:

```
/* Loop invariant. */
   while ( condition ) statement
```

or of the form:

```
/* Loop invariant. */
   for ( init; condition; update ) statement
```

the *loop invariant* is assumed to be **true** before and after each execution of the *statement.*

- For a method definition of the form:

```
/* Given precondition on input parameters, establish
   postcondition on output parameters, and return value,
   if any. */
Method definition
```

the definition assumes that the *preconditions* of input parameters are **true** on entry to the body of the method, and the *postconditions* of output parameters (as well as of its return value, if any) are **true** just before returning from the method.

- For a method invocation of the form:

```
name( argument-list )
```

the code assumes that each input *argument* value satisfies the *precondition* of the corresponding input *parameter,* and that each output *argument* (as well as the return value, if any) satisfies the *postcondition* of the corresponding output *parameter* (or result).

We introduced **assert**-statements in Chapter 3 Specifications and Implementations (p. 49) during the initial discussion of preconditions. While it was logical to have done so, it was also premature in the sense that we didn't have a sufficiently complicated example in hand to have adequately motivated their use.

We illustrate the use of **assert** now in the program for Running a Maze. Specifically, we implement `isValid`, a **`boolean`** method that returns **false** if it discovers evidence that one of `MRP`'s representation invariants is not being correctly maintained.

Consider the rat's representation invariant in class `MRP`:

```
/* Rat. The rat is located in cell M[r][c] facing direction d, where a
   d of ⟨0,1,2,3⟩ represents the orientation ⟨up,right,down,left⟩,
   respectively. */
   private static int r, c, d;
```

We can write a utility method to confirm that this representation invariant holds:

```
/* Return false iff rat's representation invariant is violated. */
public static boolean isValidRat() {
   if ( r<0 || r>hi || c<0 || c>hi ) return false;
   else if ( d < 0 || d>3 ) return false;
   else if ( M[r][c]!=move ) return false;
   else return true;
   } /* isValidRat */
```

Similarly, consider the path's representation invariant in class MRP:

```
/* Path. When the rat has traveled to cell ⟨r,c⟩ via a given path through
   cells of the maze, the elements of M that correspond to those cells will
   be 1, 2, 3, etc., and all other elements of M that correspond to cells
   of the maze will be Unvisited. The number of the last step in the path
   is move. */
   private static final int Unvisited = 0;
   private static int move;
```

Routine `isValidPath` was introduced on page 271 to make our Running a Maze program self-checking, but it can be used now to validate maintenance of the path invariant.

We put these together in the definition of `isValid`:

```
/* Return false on evidence that a representation invariant is violated. */
public static boolean isValid() {
   return isValidRat() && isValidPath(r,c);
   } /* isValid */
```

We can then use this method in **assert**-statements in various places in the code where we wish to confirm that the invariant still holds, e.g., the first statement of the loop of `Solve`:

```
/* Compute a direct path through the maze, if one exists. */
private static void Solve() {
   while ( !MRP.isAtCheese() && !MRP.isAboutToRepeat() ) {
      assert MRP.isValid(): "Invalid MRP representation.";
      if (MRP.isFacingWall()) MRP.TurnClockwise();
      else if (!MRP.isUnvisited()) Retract();
      else {
         MRP.StepForward();
         MRP.TurnCounterClockwise();
         }
      }
   } /* Solve */
```

If we wish finer-grained validation, we can sprinkle more such assertions elsewhere, e.g., as the last statements of various state-altering methods of class `MRP` such as `StepForward`, `TurnClockwise`, and `TurnCounterClockwise`.

As long as there are no bugs, such assertions have no effect (except to slow down program execution). If there is a bug that breaks a representation invariant, we get an early warning with a helpful diagnostic message.

For example, if we had checked the representation invariant as shown:

```
public static void TurnCounterClockwise() {
   d = (d-1)%4;
   assert isValid(): "Invalid MRP representation.";
   }
```

then execution of Bug C would have immediately terminated as soon as `d` was set to -1, with the error message:

```
java.lang.AssertionError: Invalid MRP representation.
   at MRP.TurnCounterClockwise(MRP.java:39)
   at RunMaze.Solve(RunMaze.java:15)
   at RunMaze.main(RunMaze.java:41)
```

which would have been so much more helpful than:

```
java.lang.ArrayIndexOutOfBoundsException: Index -1 out of bounds for length 4
   at MRP.isFacingWall(MRP.java:46)
   at RunMaze.Solve(RunMaze.java:11)
   at RunMaze.main(RunMaze.java:41)
```

Use of **assert**-statements is fine while the program is still under development because your time is typically more important than the program's execution speed. Once program development is complete, you can eliminate the overhead of the runtime validation (in one fell swoop) by directing the compiler to ignore all **assert**-statements. Disabled **assert**-statements remain in your program text in case you need them in the future, but otherwise have no effect.[168]

168. Note that the default for some programming environments is that **assert**-statements are disabled, in which case you must explicitly enable them if you want them. Asserts are enabled in BlueJ by default.

About the Author

Tim Teitelbaum is an Emeritus Professor of Computer Science at Cornell University. He received his S.B. in Mathematics from M.I.T. in 1964, and his Ph.D. in Computer Science from Carnegie Mellon University in 1975. His early research focus was on Integrated Development Environments (IDEs), Syntax-Directed Editing, and Incremental Computation. His later work was on Automated Program Analysis for cybersecurity.

In 1988, Teitelbaum co-founded GrammaTech, Inc., a program analysis and cybersecurity firm. He retired from Cornell in 2011 to devote full time to the company, where he continued to pursue his research interests, and to transition that research to commercial products.

Teitelbaum's teaching focus at Cornell over many years was introducing beginners to programming, which he did for more than 9000 students, and for which he received numerous teaching awards from the College of Engineering. Upon retirement from GrammaTech in 2019, Teitelbaum returned to pedagogy, and wrote this book.

Acknowledgments

To thank Tom Reps for having reviewed chapters of this book would be a gross understatement. He has been my professional colleague, business partner, and friend since June, 1978 when we first met, and his influence on me has been immense. It has been a wonderful journey together for which I will always be grateful.

I assumed responsibility for Cornell's Introduction to Computer Programming course in 1975 from David Gries, who had authored the textbook and established the principles being taught. I am indebted to him for much of my point of view regarding the subject.

APPENDIX I

Precepts

	Precept	Issue	#
☞	Follow programming precepts.	Overarching	A01
☞	Ignore precepts, when appropriate.	Overarching	A02
☞	Resolve contradictory precepts with care.	Overarching	A03
☞	Code with deliberation. Be mindful.	Overarching	A04
☞	Be humble. Programming is hard and error prone. Respect it.	Overarching	A05
☞	Aspire to coding it right the first time. Do no harm. Avoid writing code that must be redone.	Overarching	A06
☞	Avoid debugging like the plague.	Overarching	A07
☞	Don't be wedded to code. Revise and rewrite when you discover a better way.	Overarching	A08
☞	Leverage features of the programming language and its compiler that protect you from mistakes.	Overarching	A09
☞	Make sure you understand the problem.	Overarching	A10
☞	Dovetail thinking about code and data.	Overarching	A11
☞	Confirm your understanding of a programming problem with concrete examples. Elaborate the expected input/output mapping explicitly.	Preliminaries	B01
☞	Flesh out corner cases that the problem statement omitted, or otherwise left unspecified.	Preliminaries	B02
☞	Seek algorithmic inspiration from experience. Hand-simulate an algorithm that is in your "wetware". Be introspective. Ask yourself: What am I doing?	Preliminaries	B03
☞	Consider the possibility that your manual approach may be suboptimal, and a different approach may be better.	Preliminaries	B04
☞	Analyze first. You don't (necessarily) have to use brute force just because the computer is a brute.	Preliminaries	B05
☞	Sometimes iteration is unnecessary because a closed-form solution is available.	Preliminaries	B06
☞	Consider problem transformation or problem reduction: Solve a different problem, and use that solution to solve the original problem.	Preliminaries	B07
☞	• An alternative problem may be intrinsically easier.	Preliminaries	B08
☞	• An alternative problem may be harder, but you happen to have the code available for it.	Preliminaries	B09
☞	Decide between an on-line vs off-line algorithm, e.g., processing data incrementally as it is input vs inputting all data, storing it in variables, and processing it thereafter.	Preliminaries	B10
☞	• Prefer on-line to off-line.	Preliminaries	B11

☞	• Anticipate possible future need for an off-line solution before you invest too much in an on-line solution.	Preliminaries	B12
☞	Invent (or learn) vocabulary for concepts that arise in a problem.	Preliminaries	B13
☞	Invent (or learn) diagrammatic ways to express concepts.	Preliminaries	B14
☞	Simple examples may be as good (or better) than complicated ones for guiding you toward a solution.	Preliminaries	B15
☞	Program top-down, outside-in.	Methodology	C01
☞	Use Stepwise Refinement. Write simple code immediately, otherwise refine the problem statement using: (a) Sequential Refinement, (b) Case Analysis, (c) Iterative Refinement, or (d) a known pattern.	Methodology	C02
☞	Start by writing a top-level decomposition of the solution.	Methodology	C03
☞	Specify how individual program steps will cooperate with one another.	Methodology	C04
☞	• Convey information between refinement steps using one or more variables.	Methodology	C05
☞	Use the constraints of Stepwise Refinement to guide creativity.	Methodology	C06
☞	When refining a *condition* placeholder, establish the operands first, then the relational operation.	Methodology	C07
☞	Refine specifications and placeholders in an order that makes sense for development, without regard to execution order.	Methodology	C08
☞	Use indentation under a statement comment to indicate "how" to accomplish "what" is demanded by the outdented statement comment above it.	Methodology	C09
☞	Beware of premature self-satisfaction.	Methodology	C10
☞	Consider Divide and Conquer when designing an algorithm.	Methodology	C11
☞	Consider recursion when designing an algorithm.	Methodology	C12
☞	Consider generalizing a problem when designing an algorithm.	Methodology	C13
☞	Write comments as an integral part of the coding process, not as afterthoughts.	Specification	D01
☞	The types of comments include: (a) statement-comments, (b) representation-invariants associated with declarations and loops, (c) header-comments associated with methods, (d) header-comments associated with classes, and I descriptions and asides. Rarely, (f) an expression comment when an expression is complicated.	Specification	D02
☞	(a1) Interpret a statement-comment as executable code. It says exactly **what** code must accomplish, not **how** it does so.	Specification	D03
☞	(a2) A statement-comment is written as a statement in a high-level language, i.e., English. As such, it is a specification for code not yet written.	Specification	D04
☞	(a4) A statement-comment is written in terms of program variables, and assumes the representation invariants of those variables.	Specification	D05
☞	(a5) A statement-comment often omits its assumed preconditions, and just states the postcondition to be achieved.	Specification	D06
☞	(a6) A statement-comment should not give any algorithmic details as to how the postcondition is achieved. Example: Set `y` such that `y*y==x`.	Specification	D07
☞	(a7) A statement-comment must include all essential details. It is a stand-in for the code not yet written, and must be complete so that you can hand-check the correctness of the rest of the program without that code having been written.	Specification	D08
☞	(a8) Consider including a brief summary prefix in a statement-comment.	Specification	D09
☞	(a9) To avoid information overload, statement-comments typically omit (i) performance requirements, and (ii) exceptions. But they are important: Many should be addressed somehow, while others are handled implicitly, or by global default.	Specification	D10
☞	• Performance requirements are often totally ignored.	Specification	D11
☞	• Integer arithmetic overflow is typically ignored.	Specification	D12
☞	• The out-of-memory exception is typically ignored.	Specification	D13
☞	• Ill formed input exceptions are sometimes addressed as part of "defensive coding".	Specification	D14

☞	(b1) A representation invariant describes the value(s) of one or more program variables, and their relationships to one another as the program runs. The invariant is typically written as a comment associated with the declaration(s) of the relevant variable(s).	Specification	D15
☞	• Write the representation invariant of a collection of related variables as a comment before the declarations of those variables.	Specification	D16
☞	• Write the representation invariant of an individual variable as an end-of-line comment.	Specification	D17
☞	(b2) A loop invariant is a local representation-invariant, and can be stated as a header comment to the loop.	Specification	D18
☞	(c1) A method header-comment specifies the effect of invoking it, and (if the method has non-**void** type) the value returned. If the method has parameters, the specification is written in terms of those parameters.	Specification	D19
☞	(d1) A class header-comment is descriptive, and omits the details of the methods and variables of the class. Reference available auxiliary documentation.	Specification	D20
☞	(e1) Descriptive comments and asides can be helpful, but should not supplant comments of types a-c.	Specification	D21
☞	(f1) Expression-comments may be useful placeholders during programming, but rarely survive refinement, e.g., In the heat of battle, you may write "if(/*n is even*/)..." and change it later to "if (n%2==0)...".	Specification	D22
☞	Repeatedly improve comments by relentless copy editing.	Specification	D23
☞	• Effort in perfecting comments is repaid later when code practically writes itself.	Specification	D24
☞	• Embrace succinct notations in comments, e.g., A[lo..hi] or A[lo:hi] for a range of array elements, ⟨p,q⟩ for pairs of values; etc. Your notation in comments doesn't have to be part of the programming language.	Specification	D25
☞	• For clarity, introduce variables in comments as pronouns. These may (or may not) correspond to program variables.	Specification	D26
☞	• Introduce defined terms, and use them for precision in comments.	Specification	D27
☞	• Omit specifications whose implementations are at least as brief and clear as the specification itself. Don't over-comment.	Specification	D28
☞	• Use article "the" for a unique instance; use articles "a" or "an" for an arbitrary instance.	Specification	D29
☞	• Specify only what is needed, and no more, e.g., if an arbitrary instance suffices, don't say which instance. Maximize flexibility for the implementation.	Specification	D30
☞	• Eliminate useless words. Make each word tell. Remove unneeded scaffolding.	Specification	D31
☞	• Adopt a standard vocabulary for comments, and use it consistently. Specify the return value of functions in header comments in a standard manner, e.g., "Return ...", or "== ...".	Specification	D32
☞	• Adopt standard abbreviations, and use them for succinctness, e.g., "wrt", "s.t.", "i.e.", "e.g.", etc.	Specification	D33
☞	• If in the course of refinement you realize that a specification was incomplete, revise the specification.	Specification	D34
☞	• If in, the course of refinement you realize that a specification can be simplified, revise the specification, and the refinement.	Specification	D35
☞	• Don't make postconditions any more specific than needed.	Specification	D36
☞	There is no shame in reasoning with concrete examples.	Reasoning	E01
☞	Alternate between concrete reasoning and abstract reasoning.	Reasoning	E02
☞	• Generate expressions, then test with concrete values.	Reasoning	E03
☞	• When generating an expression, get the positive and/or negative signs right first, then worry about the constants, e.g., the first element of A[0..n-1] is A[0], the k-th to last element is A[n-k], or is it A[n-1-k]? The k-th element of A[lo..hi] is A[lo+k], or is it A[lo+k-1]? Etc.	Reasoning	E04

☞	• Beware of off-by-one errors.	Reasoning	E05
☞	Be alert to high-risk coding steps associated with binary choices: "==" or "!=", "<" or "<=", "x" or "x-1", *condition* or !*condition*, positive or negative, 0-origin or 1-origin, "even integers are divisible by 2, but array segments of odd length have middle elements".	Reasoning	E06
☞	Reason about *conditions* using de Morgan's Law(s): **not** (P **and** Q) ≡ (**not** P) **or** (**not** Q) **not** (P **or** Q) ≡ (**not** P) **and** (**not** Q)	Reasoning	E07
☞	Never test two floating-point numbers for equality or inequality.	Reasoning	E08
☞	A program's internal data representation is central to the code; consider it early.	Representation	F01
☞	Design internal data representations based on internal computational needs, ignoring input and output conversion considerations.	Representation	F02
☞	Choose data representations that are uniform, if possible.	Representation	F03
☞	Choose representations that by design do not have nonsensical configurations.	Representation	F04
☞	Don't let the "perfect" be the enemy of the "good". Be prepared to compromise because there may be no perfect representation. Don't freeze.	Representation	F05
☞	Subproblems of a Sequential Refinement communicate via program state variables. In {S_1; S_2}, S_1 establishes by its postcondition the precondition for S_2, all as represented by program variables. Degenerate case: S_1 sets a variable, and S_2 uses that variable.	Representation	F06
☞	For each representation, state the "representation invariant" in a comment in terms of all the variables involved.	Representation	F07
☞	Introduce redundant variables in a representation to simplify code, or make it more efficient.	Representation	F08
☞	Use `row` (or `r`) and `col` (or `c`) to index a 2-D array, not `x` and `y`.	Representation	F09
☞	The touchstone of a data representation is its utility in performing the needed operations.	Representation	F10
☞	Aspire to making code self-documenting by choosing descriptive names.	Naming	G01
☞	Use single-letter variable names when it makes code more understandable.	Naming	G02
☞	Minimize use of literal numerals in code; define and use symbolic constants.	Naming	G03
☞	Declare variables with as small a scope as possible.	Naming	G04
☞	Avoid gratuitously different names for parameters and variables whose use is essentially the same. Practice conceptual economy.	Naming	G05
☞	Practice information hiding.	Naming	G06
☞	Procrastinate: Never code today what you can defer until tomorrow.	Coding	H01
☞	Defer challenging code for later; do the easy parts first.	Coding	H02
☞	Ignore fussy details for as long as possible.	Coding	H03
☞	Master stylized code patterns, and use them. (See separate list of templates.)	Coding	H04
☞	Beware of unnecessary Case Analysis; hope for code uniformity; avoid code bloat.	Coding	H05
☞	Introduce auxiliary data to allow code to be uniform.	Coding	H06
☞	Many short procedures are better than large blocks of code.	Coding	H07
☞	Maximize code reuse.	Coding	H08
☞	• Don't type if you can avoid it; clone. Cut and paste, then adapt.	Coding	H09
☞	• Abstract (a.k.a., factor) clones into appropriately parameterized procedures.	Coding	H10
☞	Avoid rigid code. Anticipate change. Parameterize.	Coding	H11
☞	• Aim for single-point-of-definition.	Coding	H12
☞	Learn and use algebraic laws that support code refactoring.	Coding	H13
☞	Consider reducing dimensionality by changing "coordinate systems", e.g., from 2-D ⟨r,c⟩ to 1-D ⟨k⟩.	Coding	H14

☞	Consider reducing dimensionality by transforming a 2-D problem into a 1-D problem whose solution gives you the solution to the 2-D problem.	Coding	H15
☞	Adopt a formatting style, and stick with it. Be tidy wrt that style.	Coding	H16
☞	Label the end of a long class or method definition with its name in a comment.	Coding	H17
☞	Don't optimize code prematurely.	Coding	H18
☞	Don't confuse a subscript value with the value of the array element with that subscript.	Coding	H19
☞	Avoid obscurity. Be as direct as possible.	Coding	H20
☞	Avoid index arithmetic, if possible and convenient.	Coding	H21
☞	Avoid gratuitous differences in code. Reuse code patterns, if possible.	Coding	H22
☞	If you "smell a loop", write it down.	Iteration	I01
☞	• Benefit from the fact that a **while**-loop divides a region of code into four subregions; a **for**-loop divides it into six.	Iteration	I02
☞	• Decide first whether an iteration is *indeterminate* (use a **while**) or *determinate* (use a **for**).	Iteration	I03
☞	• Beware of **for**-loop abuse; if in doubt, err in favor of **while**.	Iteration	I04
☞	Code iterations in the following order: (1) body, (2) termination, (3) initialization, (4) finalization, (5) boundary conditions.	Iteration	I05
☞	Body. Do 1st. Play "musical chairs" and "stop the music". Characterize the "program state" when the music stops, i.e., at the instant the loop-body is about to execute yet again. If you had stopped one iteration later, what would have looked the same (the "loop invariant"), and what would have changed (the "loop variant")?	Iteration	I06
☞	• In a **for**-statement, the control-variable update is effectively part of the body.	Iteration	I07
☞	• To get to `POST` iteratively, choose a weakened `POST` as an `INVARIANT`.	Iteration	I08
☞	• The "loop variant" is an integer-valued expression >= 0 that is reduced by at least 1 on each iteration. Its existence demonstrates termination.	Iteration	I09
☞	• Introduce program variables whose values describe "state".	Iteration	I10
☞	• If the problem lends itself to diagrammatic reasoning, draw diagrams that characterize the invariant, and label key boundaries with program variables.	Iteration	I11
☞	• Alternate between using a concrete example to guide you in characterizing "program state", and an abstract version that refers to all possible examples.	Iteration	I12
☞	• Write a comment that states succinctly, as an imperative, exactly what the loop body must accomplish each time it executes.	Iteration	I13
☞	• A Case Analysis in the loop body is often needed for characterizing different ways in which to decrease the loop variant while maintaining the loop invariant.	Iteration	I14
☞	• Use loop invariants to guide creativity.	Iteration	I15
☞	Termination. Do 2nd. Beware of confusion between *condition* for continuing and its negation, the *condition* for terminating. Beware off-by-one errors: stopping one iteration too soon, or one iteration too late. Prevent illegal references using "short-circuit mode" Boolean expressions.	Iteration	I16
☞	Initialization. Do 3rd. Initialize variables so that the loop invariant is established prior to the first iteration. Substitute those initial values into the invariant, and bench check the first iteration with respect to that initial instantiation of the invariant.	Iteration	I17
☞	Finalization. Do 4th, but don't forget. Leverage that the looping *condition* is **false**, the loop invariant remains **true**, and the loop variant is 0.	Iteration	I18
☞	Boundary conditions. Dead last, but don't forget them.	Iteration	I19
☞	• Find boundary conditions at extrema, and at singularities, e.g., biggest, smallest, 0, edges, etc.	Iteration	I20
☞	• Code the general case first. Then attempt to make the boundary case fit the general case, if possible, making as slight a change to the code as possible. Consider possible use of sentinels.	Iteration	I21
☞	Control complexity.	Testing	J01

☞	Develop programs with testability in mind.	Testing	J02
☞	• Consider conditional diagnostic output, e.g., "if (debug) …".	Testing	J03
☞	• Consider conditional assertions, e.g., "if (asserts) if (!assertion) …".	Testing	J04
☞	Write a test harness as an integral part of a class.	Testing	J05
☞	Never be (very) lost. Don't stray far from a correct (albeit, partial) program.	Testing	J06
☞	• Test programs incrementally.	Testing	J07
☞	• Write degenerate program stubs that allow partial programs to execute.	Testing	J08
☞	Test programs thoroughly.	Testing	J09
☞	• Test all corner cases.	Testing	J10
☞	• Consider generating test data programmatically.	Testing	J11
☞	Validate output thoroughly.	Testing	J12

APPENDIX II

Patterns

	Pattern	Name	#
☞	`/* Specification. */`	Specification	A01
☞	`/* Specification. */` `   Implementation`	Statement specification	A02
☞	`/* What. */` `   /* How. */`	Statement specification	A03
☞	`/* Given precondition, establish postcondition. */`	Statement specification	A04
☞	`type x; // Representation invariant of x.`	Declaration specification	A05
☞	`/* Representation Invariant. */` `   Declarations of related variables`	Declaration specification	A06
☞	`/* Specification. */` `Method definition`	Method specification	A07
☞	`/* Specification. */` `Class definition`	Class specification	A08

☞	/* Specification P. */
	   /* Specification P_1. */
	   /* Specification P_2. */
	   ...
	   /* Specification P_n. */
		Sequential Refinement	B01

☞	/* Specification P. */
	   if ($condition_1$) /* Specification P_1. */
	   else if ($condition_2$) /* Specification P_2. */
	   ...
	   else if ($condition_{n-1}$) /* Specification P_{n-1}. */
	   else /* Specification P_n. */
		Case Analysis	B02

☞	/* Specification P. */
	   /* Setup for P'. */
	   while (*condition*)
	      /* Specification P'. */
		Iterative Refinement	B03

☞	/* Specification *P*. */ **if** (*base case*) /* P_0. */ **else** /* Identify smaller instance(s) of *P* within *P* itself, apply this approach to each such instance, and combine the results. */	Recursive Refinement	B04
☞	/* Get from PRE to POST. */ /* Get from PRE to MID. */ /* Get from MID to POST. */	Sequential Refinement, w/ conditions	B05
☞	/* Get from PRE to POST. */ /* Get from A_1 to B_1. */ /* Get from A_2 to B_2. */ ... /* Get from A_n to B_n. */ where PRE implies A_1, B_k implies A_{k+1} (for 1≤k<n), and B_n implies POST.	Sequential Refinement, w/ conditions	B06
☞	/* Specification *P*: Get from PRE to POST. */ /* Get from PRE to A. */ /* Define problem *P′* based on PRE. */ /* Solve problem *P′*. */ /* Establish A from the solution to problem *P′*. */ /* Get from B to POST. */	Problem reduction, w/ conditions	B07
☞	/* Specification *P*: Get from PRE to POST. */ **if** (*condition*) /* Specification P_1: Get from PRE && *condition* to A_1. */ **else** /* Specification P_2: Get from PRE && !*condition* to A_2. */ where A_1 implies POST and A_2 implies POST.	Case Analysis, w/ conditions	B08

☞	/* Specification *P*: Get from PRE to POST. */
	/* Get from PRE to INVARIANT. */
	while (*condition*) {
	/* Get from *condition* && INVARIANT to INVARIANT. */
	}
	where !*condition* && INVARIANT entails POST.
		Iterative Refinement, w/ conditions	B09

☞	/* *Compute*. */ /* *Use*. */	Sequential refinement	C01
☞	/* *Search*. */ /* *Use the search result*. */	Sequential refinement	C02
☞	/* *Initialize*. */ /* *Compute*. */	Sequential refinement	C03
☞	/* *Initialize*. */ /* *Compute*. */ /* *Output*. */	Initialize, Compute, Output	C04
☞	/* *Input*. */ /* *Compute*. */ /* *Output*. */	Offline computation	C05

<table>
<tr><td>☞</td><td>/* Initialize. */
while (/* not finished */) {
   /* Compute. */
   /* Go on to next. */
   }</td><td>General iterative computation</td><td>C6</td></tr>
<tr><td>☞</td><td>for (initialize; condition; go-on-to-next) compute</td><td>General iterative computation</td><td>C7</td></tr>
<tr><td>☞</td><td>v = /* first input value */;
/* Initialize. */
while (v != /* stoppingValue */) {
   /* Process v. */
   v = /* next input value */;
   }
/* Finalize. */</td><td>Online computation</td><td>C08</td></tr>
<tr><td>☞</td><td>/* Swap x and y. */
   int temp = x; x = y; y = temp;</td><td>Exchange</td><td>C09</td></tr>
<tr><td>☞</td><td>/* Enumerate from start. */
   int k = start;
   while (condition) k++;</td><td>1-D Indeterminate enumeration</td><td>D01</td></tr>
<tr><td>☞</td><td>/* Search for or fail. */
   int k = 0;
   while (/* not passed the end? */ &&
           /* not at what seeking? */) k++;
if (k /* is passed end? */) /* fail */
else /* succeed */</td><td>1-D Indeterminate enumeration</td><td>D02</td></tr>
<tr><td>☞</td><td>/* Search for or fail, with sentinel. */
   /* Put example of what's sought one place passed
      the end.*/
   int k = 0;
   while (/* not at what seeking? */)
      k++;
if (k /* is passed end? */) /* fail, found sentinel */
else /* succeed */</td><td>1-D Indeterminate enumeration, w/ sentinel</td><td>D03</td></tr>
<tr><td>☞</td><td>/* Do whatever n times. */
   int k = 0;
   while (k<n) {
      /* whatever */
      k++;
      }</td><td>1-D Determinate enumeration</td><td>D04</td></tr>
<tr><td>☞</td><td>/* Do whatever n times. */
   for (int k=0; k<n; k++) /* whatever */
or
   for (int k=1; k<=n; k++) /* whatever */</td><td>1-D Determinate enumeration</td><td>D05</td></tr>
<tr><td>☞</td><td>/* Enumerate ⟨r,c⟩ in [0..height-1][0..width-1] in
   row-major order until condition. */
   int r = 0; int c = 0;
   while (r<height && !condition)
      if (c<width-1) c++;
      else { c = 0; r++; }
if (r==height) /* fail */ else /* succeed */</td><td>2-D Indeterminate enumeration, row-major order</td><td>D06</td></tr>
</table>

☞	/* Unbounded enumeration of ordered ⟨r,c⟩ until
	   condition. */
	   int d = 0;
	   while (!*condition*) {
	      int r = d;
	      for (**int** c=0; c<=d; c++) {
	         /* *whatever* */
	         r--;
	         }
	      d++;
	      }
		2-D Indeterminate enumeration, diagonal order	D07

☞	/* Enumerate ⟨r,c⟩ in [0..*height*-1][0..*width*-1] in
	   row-major order. */
	   for (**int** r=0; r<*height*; r++)
	      for (**int** c=0; c<*width*; c++)
	         /* *whatever* */
		2-D Determinate enumeration, row-major order (0-origin)	D08

☞	/* Enumerate ⟨r,c⟩ in [1..*height*][1..*width*] in row-major
	   order. */
	   for (**int** r=1; r<=*height*; r++)
	      for (**int** c=1; c<=*width*; c++)
	         /* *whatever* */
		2-D Determinate enumeration, row-major order (1-origin)	D09

☞	/* Enumerate ⟨r,c⟩ in [0..*height-1*][0..*width-1*] in
	   column-major order.*/
	   for (**int** c=0; c<*width*; c++)
	      for (**int** r=0; r<*height*; r++)
	         /* *whatever* */
		2-D Determinate enumeration, column-major order (0-origin)	D10

☞	/* Enumerate ⟨r,c⟩ in a closed lower-triangular region of
	   [0..*size*-1][0..*size*-1] in row-major order.*/
	   for (**int** r=0; r<*size*; r++)
	      for (**int** c=0; c<=r; c++)
	         /* *whatever* */
		2-D Determinate enumeration, closed triangular order	D11

☞	/* Enumerate ⟨r,c⟩ in a open lower-triangular region of
	   [0..*size*-1][0..*size*-1] in row-major order.*/
	   for (**int** r=0; r<*size*; r++)
	      for (**int** c=0; c<r; c++)
	         /* *whatever* */
		2-D Determinate enumeration, open triangular order	D12

☞	/* Let p be the location of what you are looking for,
	   or an indication that no such thing exists. */
	   p = *the-first-place-look*;
	   while (p *is-not-beyond-the-last-place-to-look* &&
	                p *is-not-what-you-are-looking-for*)
	      p = *the-next-place-to-look*;
	if (p *is-not-beyond-the-last-place-to-look*) /* Found. */
	else /* Not found. */
		Sequential Search (general case)	E01

☞	/* Given *P*(*x*), a **boolean**-valued expression parameterized
	   by x, with domain 0..n-1, let k be smallest int s.t.
	   P(*k*) is **true**, or n if there is no such k. */
	   int k = 0;
	   while (k<n && !*P*(*k*)) k++;
		Sequential Search (for integer with a property)	E02

☞	`/* Given int-valued function S(j) defined on non-empty`
	`   int domain first through last, let k in that domain`
	`   be s.t. S(k) is minimal. */`
	`   int k = first;`
	`   int minS = S(first);`
	`   for (int j=first+1; j<=last; j++) {`
	`      int s = S(j);`
	`      if ( s<minS ) { minS = s; k = j; }`
	`      }`
		Integer in domain of function S(j) for which S is minimal	E03

☞	`/* best = min value in A[0..n-1], n>=0. */`
	`   int best = /* +infinity */;  // min so far.`
	`   for (int k=0; k<n; k++)`
	`      best = Math.min(best, A[k]);`
		Minimal element in 1-D array	E04

☞	`/* Let k be s.t. A[k] is min value in A[0..n-1], n>0. */`
	`   int k = 0  // A[0] is min so far.`
	`   for (int j=1; j<n; j++)`
	`      if ( A[j]<A[k] ) k = j;`
		Index of minimal element in non-empty 1-D array	E05

☞	`/* Given array A[0..n-1], and 0≤k, shift elements of A`
	`   left k places. Values shifted off the left end of the`
	`   array are lost. Values not overwritten remain as they`
	`   were originally. */`
	`   if ( k>0 )`
	`      for (int j=0; j<n-k; j++) A[j] = A[j+k];`
		Left-Shift-k	F01

☞	`/* Rotate A[0..n-1] left 1. */`
	`   /* type */ temp = A[0];`
	`   /* Shift A[1..n-1] left. */`
	`   A[n-1] = temp;`
		Left-Rotate-1	F02

☞	`/* Reverse A[0..n-1] */`
	`   int lo = 0; int hi = n-1;`
	`   while ( lo<hi ) {`
	`      /* Swap A[lo] and A[hi]. */`
	`      lo++; hi--;`
	`      }`
		Reverse	F03

☞	`/* Rotate A[0..n-1] left k. */`
	`   /* Reverse(A,0,k-1); */`
	`   /* Reverse(A,k,n-1); */`
	`   /* Reverse(A,0,n-1); */`
		Left-Rotate-k	F04

☞	`/* A[0..size-1] are items in the collection, 0≤size≤n. */`
	`   int A[];  // receptacle for items in a list.`
	`   int size; // current # of elements in list, 0≤size≤n.`
	`   int n; // maximum # of elements storable in the list.`
		Data structure for a collection represented as a list	G01

☞	`/* Return k, a location of v in A, or return size if no`
	`   v in A. */`
	`static int indexOf(int v; int A[], int size) {`
	`   int k = 0;`
	`   while ( k<size && A[k]!=v ) k++;`
	`   return k;`
	`   }`
		Search utility for a collection represented as a list	G02

☞	`/* Add v to A. */`
	`/* Ensure that A has capacity for another element. */`
	`if ( size==n ) /* Make room, or sound an alarm. */`
	`A[size] = v;`
	`size++;`
		Add item to unordered collection represented as a list	G03

☞	`/* Remove v from A. */`
	`int k = indexOf(v, A, size);`
	`if ( k==size ) /* v is not in A. */`
	`else { size--; A[k] = A[size]; }`
		Remove item from unordered collection represented as a list	G04

☞	`/* Set b to true if v is in A, and false otherwise. */`
	`int k = indexOf(v, A, size);`
	`boolean b = (k<size);`
		Membership of item in collection represented as a list	G05

☞	`/* Set m to the multiplicity of v in A. */`
	`int m = 0;`
	`for (int k=0; k<size; k++) if ( A[k]==v ) m++;`
		Multiplicity of item in colletion represented as a list	G06

☞	`/* Enumerate elements of A. */`
	`for (int k=0; k<size; k++)`
	`/* Do whatever for A[k]. */`
		Enumeration of items in collection represented as a list	G07

☞	`/* Collection of items in range 0..maxValue, where`
	`multiplicity of v is H[v]. */`
	`int H[0..maxValue];`
		Data structure for a collection represented as a histogram	H01

☞	`/* Add v to H. */` `H[v]++;`	Add item to collection represented as a histogram	H02

☞	`/* Remove v from H. */`
	`if ( H[k]==0 ) /* Alarm: removal of value not in H. */`
	`else H[k]--;`
		Remove item from collection represented as a histogram	H03

☞	`/* b = true iff v is in H. */` `boolean b = (H[v]>0);`	Membership of item from collection represented as a histogram	H04
☞	`/* m = Multiplicity of v in A. */` `int m = H[v];`	Multiplicity of item in collection represented as a histogram	H05

☞	`/* Enumerate elements of H. */`
	`for (int k=0; k<=maxValue; k++)`
	`for (int j=1; j<=H[k]; j++)`
	`/* Enumerate k */`
		Enumeration of items in collection represented as a histogram	H06

APPENDIX III

Language Similarities

Think of a programming language as a variety of daisy, with a central "disk floret", and multiple "ray florets". The central disk is the set of universal features, and the rays are various specialized features that add to the language's appeal. There are many programming languages, but when you strip them down to their core (by plucking all their ray florets), they all look pretty much alike. The language of Chapter 2 is that core, and this Appendix describes it for Java [6], Python [7], C/C++ [52], and JavaScript [53]. You will be struck by the similarities, which is not to say that the differences are inconsequential; rather, it is just that at the level of this book, they are immaterial.[169]

Concepts

Typed vs Untyped Variables. In Java and C/C++, variables are declared with a specific types that remains the same throughout program execution, whereas in Python and JavaScript, variables are untyped, and can contain values of one type at one moment, and other types at other moments. There is, however, nothing to prevent you from following a self-discipline in which each variable is used for values of a single type.

Declared vs Undeclared Variables. Because Java and C/C++ provide types for variables, they are always declared. Variables in JavaScript are declared (albeit without a type), whereas variables in Python are not. Variables have scope (the textual region with a program where they matter), and the position of the declaration identifies that scope. In the absence of declarations, the scope of a variable is somewhat obscure, a detail that we omit.

Homogeneity vs Heterogeneity of Arrays. In Java and C/C++, each element of an array has the same type, whereas in Python and JavaScript each element of an array (known as a list), can be a value with a different type. The homogeneity of arrays in Java and C/C++ is ameliorated by the notions of subtype and class hierarchy, but these do not enter into the core language of Chapter 2.

Numerical Values. Java and C/C++ distinguish between integers and floating-point

169. For the purpose of this summary, we ignore languages for which the central cores are vastly different from the imperative programming languages listed. We also ignore the details of object orientation, i.e., the extended language of Chapter 18.

numbers, and between single precision (32 bits) and double precision (64 bits). Python treats all integers as arbitrary precision, whereas JavaScript treats all numbers as double-precision floating-point values.

Object Homogeneity. Some languages distinguish between primitive types, e.g., `int` and `boolean`, and object types, e.g., `Integer` and `Boolean`. This issue is not relevant to the core Chapter 2 language.

Type Compatibility. Some settings require only "compatible" types rather than identical types, e.g., interchangeability between different numeric types. The term "compatible" is used below without elaboration because we deem it a distracting detail.

Storage Management by Garbage Collection. Results of some operations (like string concatenation) draw on a shared pool of available memory. When a value is no longer needed, that memory is automatically returned to the pool by a process known as "garbage collection". Java, Python, and JavaScript have automatic garbage collection, but C/C++ does not. Because storage management is beyond the scope of the Chapter 2 language, string concatenation in C/C++ in omitted from the table below.

Insignificance vs Significance of Whitespace. Whitespace (e.g., spaces, newlines, and indentation) are totally ignored in Java, C/C++, and JavaScript (except within `String` constants) but are significant in Python for delimiting *statements*, and for indicating which *statements* are in a *block*.

Constructs

In the tables below, an item for a given language and syntactic category is *not* intended to be a comprehensive definition; rather it is provided as a near-equivalent of the Chapter 2 construct in the given language. For example, in JavaScript, a string constant can be signified by matched single or double quotation marks (to facilitate using the other kind of quote within the constant), but we only provide the double-quote variety (considering the question of quotation marks within string constants to be a detail not worth the distraction). Similarly, "⟨same as Java⟩" does not signify that the constructs are identical in the two languages; rather, it means only that for the purposes of this text, they are the same.

Statements

Assignment Statement

Java	`variable = expression;`	*Type* of *expression* must be compatible with the *type* of *variable*.
Python	`variable = expression`	*Variable* has no *type*, so a value of any *type* can be assigned to it. A *simple-statement*.
C/C++	⟨same as Java⟩	
JavaScript	`variable = expression;`	⟨same as Python⟩

Auto-Increment

Java	`variable++;`	
Python	`variable += 1`	A *simple-statement*.
C/C++	⟨same as Java⟩	
JavaScript	⟨same as Java⟩	

Auto-Decrement

Java	*variable*`--;`	
Python	*variable* `-= 1`	A *simple-statement.*
C/C++	⟨same as Java⟩	
JavaScript	⟨same as Java⟩	

Conditional (2-way)

Java	**if** (*condition*) *statement*$_1$ **else** *statement*$_2$	*Statement*$_1$ may not be a 1-way conditional statement.
Python	**if** *expression*: *block*$_1$ **else**: *block*$_2$	Separate lines for **if** and **else**. A *compound-statement.*
C/C++	⟨same as Java⟩	
JavaScript	⟨same as Java⟩	

Conditional (1-way)

Java	**if** (*condition*) *statement*	
Python	**if** *condition*: *block*	A *compound-statement.*
C/C++	⟨same as Java⟩	
JavaScript	⟨same as Java⟩	

Conditional (n-way)

Java	**if** (*condition*$_1$) *statement*$_1$ **else if** (*condition*$_2$) *statement*$_2$ ... **else if** (*condition*$_{n-1}$) *statement*$_{n-1}$ **else** *statement*$_n$	No *statement*$_i$ may be a 1-way conditional statement other than *statement*$_n$.
Python	**if** *condition*$_1$: *block*$_1$ **elif** *condition*$_2$: *block*$_2$ ... **elif** *condition*$_{n-1}$: *block*$_{n-1}$ **else**: *block*$_n$	Separate lines for each **if**, **elif**, and **else**. A *compound-statement.*
C/C++	⟨same as Java⟩	
JavaScript	⟨same as Java⟩	

Indeterminate Iteration

Java	**while** (*condition*) *statement*	
Python	**while** *expression*: *block*	A *compound-statement.*
C/C++	⟨same as Java⟩	
JavaScript	⟨same as Java⟩	

Determinate Iteration

Java	**for** (*init*; *condition*; *update*) *statement* <u>init</u> *type name* = *expression* *name* = *expression* <u>update</u> *name* = *expression* *name*++ *name*--	

Python	**for** *name* **in** *list-expression*: *block* list-expression range($expression_1$, $expression_2$)	A *compound-statement.*
C/C++	⟨same as Java⟩	
JavaScript	⟨same as Java⟩ but replace *type* by **var**.	

Output (with line completion)

Java	System.out.println(*expression*);	Use string concatenation (+) in *expression* to build line.
Python	print(*arguments*)	Use *arguments* to build line of space-separated values. A *simple-statement.*
C/C++	printf(*format-string, arguments*)	Use *format-string* to build the line, e.g., the format string "%i,%i\n" signifies two **int** values separated by a comma.
JavaScript	document.write(*expression* + " ");	JavaScript output can replace code that appears within <script>*code*</script> tags with text that is then interpreted as HTML for its formatting effect.

Output (without line completion)

Java	System.out.print(*expression*);	
Python	print(*arguments*, end="")	A *simple-statement.*
C/C++	printf(*format-string, arguments*)	See above for *format-string.*
JavaScript	document.write(*expression*);	See above for interpretation.

Output (line completion)

Java	System.out.println( );	
Python	print()	A *simple-statement.*
C/C++	printf("\n")	
JavaScript	document.write(" ");	See above for interpretation.

Method Invocation

Java	*name*(*arguments*);	Also known as a *procedure call.*
Python	*name*(*arguments*)	Also known as a *procedure call.* A *simple-statement.*
C/C++	⟨same as Java⟩	
JavaScript	⟨same as Java⟩	

Return (no return value)

Java	**return**;	Only in **void** method.
Python	**return**	A *simple-statement.*
C/C++	⟨same as Java⟩	Only in **void** method.
JavaScript	**return**;	Same as **return undefined**;

Return (with return value)

Java	**return** *expression*;	Only in non-**void** method.
Python	**return** *expression*	A *simple-statement.*
C/C++	⟨same as Java⟩	
JavaScript	⟨same as Java⟩	

Block instance

Java	*block*	Conditional clauses and loop bodies are *statement*, which is optionally *block*.
Python		Limited usage.
C/C++	*block*	Conditional clauses and loop bodies are *statement*, which is optionally *block*.
JavaScript	⟨same as Java⟩	

Block

Block statement

Java	{ *declarations-and-statements* }	*Declarations* and *statements* can be interleaved, provided *declaration* of a *variable* precedes its first use.
Python	*stmt-list* NEWLINE or NEWLINE INDENT *statements* DEDENT where *stmt-list* is a list of ";"-separated *simple-statements*, optionally followed by a ";", all on the same line and *statements* is a list of *stmt_list* NEWLINE or *compound-statement*	Individual *statement* forms are identified in the tables above as either *simple-statements* or *compound-statements.* See section Indentation in Python at the end of this chapter for a discussion on the syntactic role of indentation.
C/C++	{ *declarations statements* }	Optional *declarations* precede *statements.*
JavaScript	⟨same as Java⟩	

Variables

Scalar

Java	*name*	
Python	⟨same as Java⟩	
C/C++	⟨same as Java⟩	
JavaScript	⟨same as Java⟩	

Subscripted variable (one dimensional)

Java	*name*[*expression*]	
Python	⟨same as Java⟩	
C/C++	⟨same as Java⟩	
JavaScript	⟨same as Java⟩	

Subscripted variable (two dimensional)

Java	*name*[$expression_1$][$expression_2$]	
Python	⟨same as Java⟩	
C/C++	⟨same as Java⟩	However, see section Arguments and Parameters and section Array Parameters in C/C++.
JavaScript	⟨same as Java⟩	

Expressions

Constants

Integer

Java	`..., -2, -1, 0, 1, 2, ...`	*Type* **`int`**.
Python	⟨same as Java⟩	Integers are arbitrarily large.
C/C++	⟨same as Java⟩	
JavaScript	⟨same as Java⟩	All numerics are 64-bit floating point.

Floating-point (single precision)

Java	`3.14159f0, 6.0221409f+23,...`	*Type* **`float`**.
Python		Not supported.
C/C++	`0.0f, 3.14159f, 6.0221409e+23f,...`	
JavaScript		All numerics are 64-bit floating point.

Floating-point (double precision)

Java	`0.0, 3.14159, 6.0221409e+23,...`	*Type* **`double`**.
Python	⟨same as Java⟩	All floating point are 64-bit.
C/C++	⟨same as Java⟩	
JavaScript	⟨same as Java⟩	All numerics are 64-bit floating point.

Logical

Java	**`false`**, **`true`**	*Type* **`boolean`**.
Python	**`False`**, **`True`**	*Type* **`bool`**.
C/C++	`0`, ⟨any nonzero⟩	
JavaScript	⟨same as Java⟩	

Character

Java	`'a', 'b', 'c', ...`	*Type* **`char`**.
Python	`"a", "b", "c",...`	String of length 1.
C/C++	⟨same as Java⟩	
JavaScript	⟨same as Python⟩	

String

Java	`"`*`characters`*`"`	
Python	⟨same as Java⟩	
C/C++	⟨same as Java⟩	
JavaScript	⟨same as Java⟩	

Null reference

Java	**`null`**	
Python	**`None`**	
C/C++	`0`	
JavaScript	⟨same as Java⟩	

Primitives

Variable

Java	`variable`	
Python	⟨same as Java⟩	
C/C++	⟨same as Java⟩	
JavaScript	⟨same as Java⟩	

Integer input

Java	`in.nextInt()`	Provided `in` has been initialized by `new Scanner(System.in)`.
Python	`int(input())`	
C/C++	`scanf("%i", &variable );`	This is a *statement*, not an *expression*.
JavaScript	`(+prompt())`	Opens a popup dialog box for input, and returns a numeric.

Method invocation (of value-returning methods)

Java	`name( arguments )`	Also known as a *function call*.
Python	⟨same as Java⟩	
C/C++	⟨same as Java⟩	
JavaScript	⟨same as Java⟩	

One-dimensional array creation

Java	`new type[ expression ]`	Value of *expression* is length of array, initialized with elements that contain the default value of the given *type*, e.g., 0 for *type* `int`.
Python	`[ expressions ]`	Number of *expressions* is length of array whose elements are the values of the *expressions*.
C/C++	⟨possible, but without garbage collection⟩	Use *declaration*.
JavaScript	`new Array( expression )` `[ expressions ]`	Value of *expression* is length of array, initialized with undefined values. ⟨same as Python⟩

Two-dimensional array creation

Java	`new type[ expression1 ][ expression2 ]`	Value of $expression_1$ is length of a one-dimensional array, initialized with elements that are themselves one-dimensional arrays of length $expression_2$, initialized with elements that contain the default value of the given *type*, e.g., 0 for *type* `int`.
Python	`[ [ expressions ] ... [expressions] ]`	*Number of* "[*expressions*]" *is* height; each *expressions* determines values in column.
C/C++	⟨possible, but without garbage collection⟩	Use *declaration*.
JavaScript	⟨same as Python⟩	

Binary operations

`operand binary-operator operand`

where *operands* are *expressions*, and the *binary-operators* are as follows:

Arithmetic

Java	+, -, *, /, %	Result type integer if both operands integer, otherwise floating point.
Python	⟨same as Java⟩	
C/C++	⟨same as Java⟩	
JavaScript	⟨same as Java⟩	

Relational (arithmetic values)

Java	<, <=, >, >=, ==, !=	Result *type* **boolean**.
Python	⟨same as Java⟩	Result *type* **bool**.
C/C++	⟨same as Java⟩	Result *type* numerical.
JavaScript	⟨same as Java⟩	

Identity and equality (`String` *and* **array** *values)*

Java	==, !=	Identity. Result *type* **boolean**. See Chapters 12 and 18.
Python	⟨same as syntax as Java, but different meaning⟩	Equality. Result *type* **bool**.
C/C++	⟨same as Java⟩	Result *type* numerical
JavaScript	⟨subtle, and beyond the scope of this book⟩	

Logical

Java	&&, ||	Short-circuit mode **and** and **or**; result *type* **boolean**.
Python	⟨same as Java⟩	Short-circuit mode **and** and **or**; result *type* **bool**.
C/C++	⟨same as Java⟩	Short-circuit mode **and** and **or**; where nonzero operand is **true**, zero is **false**. Result is *type* **int** (0 or nonzero).
JavaScript	⟨same as Java⟩	Short-circuit mode **and** and **or**; result *type* **boolean**.

String concatenation

Java	+	If one operand has *type* `String`.
Python	+	If both operands have *type* `str`.
C/C++	⟨No exact analogue with garbage collection⟩	
JavaScript	⟨same as Java⟩	

Unary operations

`unary-operator operand`

where *operand* is and *expression*, and the *unary-operators* are as follows:

Negation (arithmetic)

Java	-	Result *type* same as operand *type*
Python	⟨same as Java⟩	Result *type* same as operand *type*.
C/C++	⟨same as Java⟩	
JavaScript	⟨same as Java⟩	

Negation (logical)

Java	!	Result *type* **boolean**.
Python	**not**	Result *type* **bool**.
C/C++	⟨same as Java⟩	

JavaScript	⟨same as Java⟩	

Grouping

Parentheses

Java	`( expression )`	
Python	⟨same as Java⟩	
C/C++	⟨same as Java⟩	
JavaScript	⟨same as Java⟩	

Types

Integer

Java	**`int`**, **`long`**	32-bit, 64-bit
Python		Values have unbounded range, i.e., they are not limited to 32 or 64 bits.
C/C++	⟨same as Java⟩	
JavaScript	**`Number`**	All numerics are 64-bit double-precision floating-point.

Floating point

Java	**`float`**, **`double`**	32-bit, 64-bit.
Python	**`float`**	All floating point are 64-bit.
C/C++	⟨same as Java⟩	
JavaScript	**`Number`**	All numerics are 64-bit double-precision floating-point.

Logical

Java	**`boolean`**	
Python	**`bool`**	
C/C++	**`int`**	
JavaScript	⟨same as Java⟩	

Character

Java	**`char`**	
Python		Just a string of length 1.
C/C++	⟨same as Java⟩	
JavaScript		Just a string of length 1.

String

Java	`String`	
Python	**`str`**	
C/C++	**`char*`**	
JavaScript	⟨same as Java⟩	

No value

Java	**`void`**	*Type* of method that doesn't return a value.
Python	⟨same as Java⟩	
C/C++	⟨same as Java⟩	

JavaScript	⟨same as Java⟩	

Array (one dimensional)

Java	`type[]`	
Python	`list`	
C/C++	⟨same as Java⟩	
JavaScript	`array`	

Array (two dimensional)

Java	`type[][]`	array (of arrays)
Python	`list`	list (of lists)
C/C++	⟨same as Java⟩	
JavaScript	`array`	array (of arrays)

Declarations

Scalar variable (with default initialization)

Java	`type name;`	*Variables* are declared with *types*. Scope is determined by the innermost "{}" in which the *variable* is declared.
Python		*Variables* are not declared. Values have *type* but *variables* do not. Scope is subtle, and is not discussed here.
C/C++	⟨same as Java⟩	
JavaScript	`var name;`	*Variables* are declared, but without *types*. Values have *type* but variables do not. Scope is ⟨same as Java⟩.

Scalar variable (with initialization by specific value)

Java	`type name = expression;`	
Python		*Variables* are not declared.
C/C++	⟨same as Java⟩	
JavaScript	`var name = expression;`	*Variables* are not declared with *types*.

One-dimensional array of type elements (with initialization as array of given length)

Java	`type name[] = new type[expression1];`	*Expression* is length of array that is initialized with default values for *type*.
Python		*Variables* are not declared.
C/C++	`type name[expression];`	*Expression* is length of array that is initialized with undefined values.
JavaScript	`var name = new Array(expression);`	*Variables* are not declared with *types*. *Expression* is length of array that is initialized with undefined values.

Two-dimensional array of type elements (with initialization as array of given height and width)

Java	`type name[][] =` `new type[expression1] [expression2]`	*Expression*$_1$ and *expression*$_2$ are height and width of array. Array is initialized with default values for *type*.
Python	`name = [[0 for i in range(expression2)]` `for j in range(expression1)]`	*Variables* are not declared.

C/C++	`type name[expression1][expression2];`	*Expression*$_1$ and *expression*$_2$ are height and width of array that is initialized with undefined values.

JavaScript	`let name = Array(expression1);`
	`for (var i = 0; i<expression1; i++) {`
	`   name[i] = new Array(expression2);`
	`   }`
		Variables are not declared with *types*. The array is initialized with undefined values.

One-dimensional array of elements(with initialization by list of specific values)

Java	`type name[] = { expressions } ;`	*Expressions* are comma separated. Each expression value has the same *type*.
Python	`name = [ expressions ]`	*Variables* are not declared, but you can just write this assignment *statement*.
C/C++	⟨same as Java⟩	*Expressions* are comma separated. Each *expression* value has the same *type*.
JavaScript	`var name = [ expressions ];`	*Variables* are not declared with *types*.

Definitions

Method

Java	`type name( parameters ) block`	
Python	`def name( parameters ): block`	
C/C++	⟨same as Java⟩	
JavaScript	`function name ( parameters ) block`	

Class

Java	`class name block`	
Python	`classdef name: block`	Top-level *statements* of a program do not need to be in a class.
C/C++		Not needed for the language of Chapter 2 because separate files can be used for modularity.
JavaScript	⟨same as Java⟩	

Arguments and Parameters

Arguments

Java	An ordered, comma-separated list of `expressions`.	
Python	⟨same as Java⟩	
C/C++	⟨same as Java⟩	
JavaScript	⟨same as Java⟩	

Parameters

Java	An ordered, comma-separated list of `type-name` pairs.	
Python	An ordered, comma-separated list of `names`.	
C/C++	Each `parameter` is: `t name` ⟨if `name` is scalar of type `t`⟩ `t name[]` ⟨if `name` is 1-D array of `type` `t` elements⟩ `void *name` ⟨if `name` is 2-D array of `type` `t` elements⟩	See section Array Parameters in C/C++ at the end of this chapter.
JavaScript	⟨same as Python⟩	

Comments

Block comment (can cross lines)

Java	`/* any-text */`	
Python		Not supported.
C/C++	⟨same as Java⟩	
JavaScript	⟨same as Java⟩	

Comment (to end of line)

Java	`// any-text-to-end-of-line`	
Python	`# any-text-to-end-of-line`	
C/C++	⟨same as Java⟩	
JavaScript	⟨same as Java⟩	

Indentation in Python

Specifications written in comments play an important role in our methodology, so clear rules for mapping them into Python are important. Python only supports comments that begin with a hash mark (#) and extend to the end of the line. Comments with matched left (/*) and right (*/) delimiters are not supported.

Consider the Sequential Refinement:

```
/* Specification P. */
   /* Specification P1. */
   /* Specification P2. */
   ...
   /* Specification Pn. */
```

where any /* Specification P_i */ can be a code-level *statement* rather than a comment.

We can map the given specification and its refinement to Python, as follows:

```
# Specification P.
   # Specification P1.
   # Specification P2.
   ...
   # Specification Pn.
```

but how are we to know when one multi-line sub-specification P_i ends and the next sub-specification P_{i+1} begins? We suggest that when a specification continues on subsequent lines, indent those lines within the comment:

```
# Specification P.
#   <continuation of P.>
   # Specification P1.
   #   <continuation of P1.>
   # Specification P2.
   #   <continuation of P2.>
   ...
   # Specification Pn.
   #   <continuation of Pn.>
```

A second and more important complication for mapping our notation into Python is a consequence of Python's use of indentation (rather than matched braces) to indicate a *block*. Thus, for example, the Java code:

```
if ( condition ) {
   declarations-and-statements
   }
else {
   declarations-and-statements
   }
```

would be written in Python as:[170]

```
if condition:
   list-of-statements
else:
   list-of-statements
```

The rationale for this feature is that since you will indent the *list-of-statements* anyway, why not let the indentation determine the *block*, spare the programmer having to type matched braces, and save lines.

An adverse aspect of the feature is that all top-level *statements* in the *block* are required to be indented the same amount, regardless of where they happen to fall in a refinement hierarchy used to organize them within the *block*.

For example, consider the following method definition from Chapter 1: Each *statement* is indented relative to its encompassing specification by a fixed amount, e.g., three spaces:

```
static void main() {
   /* Output the Integer Square Root of an integer input. */
      /* Obtain an integer n≥0 from the user. */
         int n = in.nextInt();
      /* Given n≥0, output the Integer Square Root of n. */
         /* Let r be the integer part of the square root of n≥0. */
            int r = 0;
            while ( (r+1)*(r+1) <= n )
               r++;
         System.out.println( r );
   } /* main */
```

The following direct transcription of `main` into Python is *incorrect* because the four red top-level *statements* must be identically indented in the body of `main`:

```
def main():
   # Output the Integer Square Root of an integer input.
      # Obtain an integer n≥0 from the user.
         n = int(input())
      # Given n≥0, output the Integer Square Root of n.
         # Let r be the integer part of the square root of n≥0.
            r = 0
            while (r+1)*(r+1) <= n :
               r += 1
         print( r )
   # main
```

170. We write *list-of-statements* as a simplification of the actual syntax.

A *correct* transcription aligns those top-level *statements*:

```
def main():
   # Output the Integer Square Root of an integer input.
      # Obtain an integer n≥0 from the user.
            n = int(input())
      # Given n≥0, output the Integer Square Root of n.
         # Let r be the integer part of the square root of n≥0.
            r = 0
            while (r+1)*(r+1) <= n :
               r += 1
         #
            print( r )
   # main
```

In this transcription, we have abandoned the individualized indentation of each *statement* relative to the specific specification that *it* implements in order to have the required uniform alignment of *all* of the *block*'s top-level *statements* in the same column (to the right of *all* of their respective encompassing specifications).

The example illustrates two other fine points of the mapping:

- The green hash mark (#) is inserted and aligned below the green specification as a way to signal that `print(r)` is its sibling in the refinement of the violet specification that they collectively implement.
- The blue *statement* "`r+=1`" can be indented any amount (to the right of the red *statements*) because it is in its own nested *block*.

Array Parameters in C/C++

Array arguments in C/C++ are provided to a procedure "by reference", which means that the base address in memory of the elements of the array is provided as the argument value.

In the case of a one-dimensional array, the base address of the array, and the number of bytes of each element, are sufficient to compute the byte address of an arbitrary array element, e.g., the kth element:

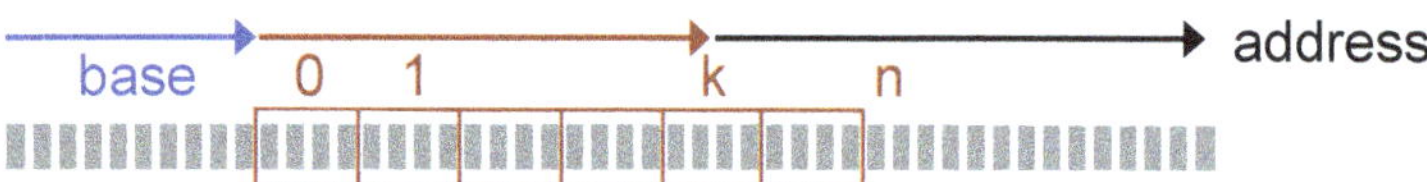

However, in the case of a two-dimensional array, extra work is required because in C/C++ the array elements are laid out in row major order in contiguous memory locations. Thus, for example, to compute the byte address of an element in row `r` and column `c` of a 3-by-2 `int` array requires knowing the width of each row (in bytes), i.e., 2·m, where m is the number of bytes in each element:

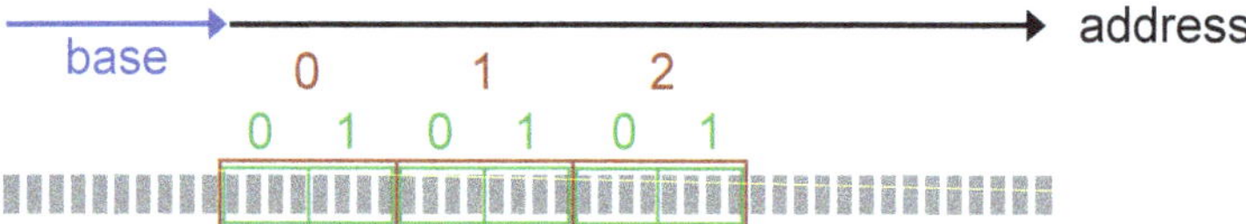

We illustrate how to deal in C/C++ with parameters that are two-dimensional arrays by showing how the following Java method would be implemented:

```
/* Display the elements of a two-dimensional int array
   A[0..height-1][0..width-1] in row major order. */
void Display(int A[][], int height, int width) {
   for (int r=0; r<height; r++) {
      for (int c=0; c<width; c++) System.out.println( A[r][c]+" " );
      System.out.println();
      }
   }
```

A client who has declared a particular array, say, B, by:

```
int B[][] = new int[3][2];
```

can print it without difficulty in Java by invoking:

```
Display( B, 3, 2);
```

But in C/C++, it is not permissible to subscript an array parameter such as A because the width of an arbitrary argument such as B must be associated with A *explicitly* rather than just *implicitly* by virtue of another parameter of `Display`. The corresponding method in C/C++ would be:

```
/* Display the elements of a two-dimensional int array
   A[0..height-1][0..width-1] in row major order. */
void Display(void *A, int height, int width) {
   int (*p_A)[height][width] = (int (*)[height][width]) A;
   for (int r=0; r<height; r++) {
      for (int c=0; c<width; c++) System.out.println( (*p_A)[r][c]+" " );
      System.out.println();
      }
   }
```

where `int` parameter A is defined as "`void *A`", a generic reference to anything. Variable "`p_A`" is then declared to have type "reference to a `height`-by-`width` `int` array", and is initialized to the value provided as an argument for A. An array element on row r and column c of the referenced argument array B can then be accessed in the body of `Display` using "`(*p_A)[r][c]`".

APPENDIX IV

Knight's Tour

```
/* Knight's Tour. See problem statement in Chapter 14. */
import java.util.*;
class KnightsTour {
   /* Chess board B is an N-by-N int array, for N==8. Unvisited squares
      are BLANK, and row and column indices range from lo to hi. */
      static final int N = 8;                // Size of B.
      static int [][] B = new int[N+4][N+4]; // Chess board, initially 0s.
      static final int BLANK = 0;            // Vacant square in board.
      static final int lo = 0+2;             // First row or column index.
      static final int hi = lo+N-1;          // Last row or column index.

   /* A Tour of length move is given by elements of B numbered 1
      to move. Squares numbered consecutively go from ⟨0,0⟩ to
      ⟨r,c⟩, and correspond to legal moves for a Knight. */
      static int move;       // Length of Tour.
      static int r, c;       // Position of Knight.

   /* Neighbor coordinate system. */
      static final int CUL_DE_SAC = 8;    // Not a neighbor.
      /* Row and column offsets for eight neighbors. */
         //                            0   1   2   3   4   5   6   7
         static final int deltaR[] = {-1, -2, -2, -1,  1,  2,  2,  1};
         static final int deltaC[] = { 2,  1, -1, -2, -2, -1,  1,  2};

   static Random rand = new Random();  // Random number generator.

   /* Establish invariant for a tour of length 1. */
   static void Initialize() {
      /* Set B to N-by-N board of BLANKs in 2-cell ring of non-BLANK. */
         for (int r = lo-2; r<=hi+2; r++)
            for (int c = lo-2; c<=hi+2; c++)
               B[r][c] = BLANK+1;
         for (int r = lo; r<=hi; r++)
            for (int c = lo; c<=hi; c++)
               B[r][c] = BLANK;
      r = lo; c = lo;
      move = 1; B[r][c] = move;
```

```
      } /* Initialize */

   /* Return # of unvisited neighbors of ⟨r,c⟩. */
   static int score(int r, int c) {
      int count = 0;
      for (int k=0; k<8; k++)
         if ( B[r+deltaR[k]][c+deltaC[k]]==BLANK ) count++;
      return count;
      }

   /* Extend the tour, if possible. */
   static void Solve() {
      int k = CUL_DE_SAC-1;
      while ( k!=CUL_DE_SAC ) {
         /* Let k = # of an unvisited neighbor, or CUL_DE_SAC if no such. */
            /* Let bestK be neighbor with best score. */
               int bestK = CUL_DE_SAC;
               int bestScore = 8;
               for (k = 0; k<8; k++) {
                  if ( B[r+deltaR[k]][c+deltaC[k]]==BLANK ) {
                     int s = score(r+deltaR[k], c+deltaC[k]);
                     if (s<bestScore) {bestScore = s; bestK = k; }
                     }
                  }
            k = bestK;
         if ( k!=CUL_DE_SAC ) {
            r = r+deltaR[k]; c = c+deltaC[k]; move++; B[r][c]=move;
            }
         }
      } /* Solve */

   /* Output: Print tour as numbered cells in N-by-N grid of 0s. */
   static void Display() {
      for (int r = lo; r<=hi; r++) {
         for (int c = lo; c<=hi; c++)
            System.out.print( (B[r][c]+"    ").substring(0,3) );
         System.out.println();
         }
      } /* Display */

   /* Output a (possibly partial) Knight's Tour. */
   static void main() {
      /* Initialize: Establish invariant for a tour of length 1. */
         Initialize();
      /* Compute: Extend the tour, if possible. */
         Solve();
      /* Output: Print tour as numbered cells in N-by-N grid of 0s. */
         Display();
      } /* main */

   /* Compute: Extend the tour, if possible, making random moves. */
   static void RandomSolve() {
      int k = 0;  // Neighbor number.
      while ( k != CUL_DE_SAC ) {
         /* Let unvisited[0:count-1] be neighbor numbers of the count
```

```
         unvisited neighbors of ⟨r,c⟩. */
         int unvisited[] = new int[8];
         int count = 0;  // # unvisited neighbors
         for (k = 0; k<8; k++)
            if ( B[r+deltaR[k]][c+deltaC[k]]==Blank ) {
               unvisited[count]=k; count++;
               }
      if ( count==0 ) k = CUL_DE_SAC;
      else {
         k = unvisited[rand.nextInt(count)];
         /* Extend the tour to neighbor k. */
            move++; r = r+deltaR[k]; c = c+deltaC[k];  B[r][c]=move;
         }
      }
   } /* RandomSolve */

/* Perform random Knight's Tours until finding a solution. */
static void MonteCarlo() {
   int freq[] = new int[N*N+1]; // Histogram of Tour lengths.
   while (move != 64 ) {
      /* Initialize: Establish invariant for a tour of length 1. */
         Initialize();
      /* Compute: Extend the tour, if possible. */
         RandomSolve();
      /* Bin the path length. */
         freq[move]++;
      }
   /* Output: Print tour as numbered cells in N-by-N grid. */
      Display();
   /* Output the histogram freq[1:64]. */
      for (int j=1; j<=64; j++) System.out.println( j+" "+freq[j] );
   } /* MonteCarlo */
} /* KnightsTour */
```

APPENDIX V

Running a Maze

```
/* Abstract datatype for Maze, Rat, and Path. */
import java.util.Scanner;
class MRP {
   /* Maze. Cells of an N by N maze are represented by elements of array
      M[2*N+1][2*N+1]. Maze cell  ⟨r,c⟩ is represented by array element
      M[2*r+1][2*c+1]. The possible walls ⟨top,right,bottom,left⟩ of the
      maze cell corresponding to ⟨r,c⟩ are represented by Wall or NoWall
      in ⟨M[r 1][c], M[r][c+1], M[r+1][c], M[r][c 1]⟩. The remaining
      elements of M are unused. Lo is 1, and hi is 2*N 1. */
      private static int N;      // Size of maze. */
      private static int M[][];  // Maze, walls, and path.
      private static final int Wall = -1;
      private static final int NoWall = 0;
      private static int lo, hi; // Left/top and right/bottom maze indices.

   /* Rat. The rat is located in cell M[r][c] facing direction d, where a
      d of ⟨0,1,2,3⟩ represents the orientation ⟨up,right,down,left⟩,
      respectively. */
      private static int r, c, d;

   /* Path. When the rat has traveled to cell ⟨r,c⟩ via a given path through
      cells of the maze, the elements of M that correspond to those cells will
      be 1, 2, 3, etc., and all other elements of M that correspond to cells
      of the maze will be Unvisited. The number of the last step in the path
      is move. */
      private static final int Unvisited = 0;
      private static int move;

   // Unit vectors in direction d =          0,     1,     2,     3
   //                                       up, right, down,  left
      private static final int deltaR[] = {  1,     0,     1,     0 };
      private static final int deltaC[] = {  0,     1,     0,     1 };

   public static void TurnClockwise()
      { d = (d+1)%4; }

   public static void TurnCounterClockwise()
```

```
      { d = (d+3)%4; }

   public static void StepForward() {
      r = r+2*deltaR[d]; c = c+2*deltaC[d];
      move++; M[r][c] = move;
      }

   public static boolean isFacingWall()
      { return M[r+deltaR[d]][c+deltaC[d]]==Wall; }

   public static boolean isUnvisited()
      { return M[r+2*deltaR[d]][c+2*deltaC[d]]==Unvisited; }

   public static boolean isAtCheese()
      { return (r==hi)&&(c==hi); }

   public static boolean isAboutToRepeat()
      { return (r==lo&&c==lo)&&(d==3); }

   private static int neighborNumber;    // Recorded visit #.
   private static int neighborDirection; // Direction at time of recording.

   public static void RecordNeighborAndDirection () {
      neighborNumber = M[r+2*deltaR[d]][c+2*deltaC[d]];
      neighborDirection = d;
      }

   public static boolean isAtNeighbor()
      { return M[r][c]==neighborNumber; }

   public static void RestoreDirection()
      { d = neighborDirection; }

   public static void StepBackward() {
      M[r][c] = Unvisited;
      move  ;
      r = r+2*deltaR[d]; c = c+2*deltaC[d];
      }

   public static void FacePrevious() {
      d = 0;
      while ( isFacingWall()||M[r+2*deltaR[d]][c+2*deltaC[d]]!=M[r][c]) d++;
      }

   /* Input N, and (2N+1) by (2N+1) values; non BLANKs are walls. */
   public static void Input() {
      /* Maze. As per representation invariant. */
         Scanner in = new Scanner(System.in);
         try {
            N = in.nextInt(); in.nextLine();
            M = new int[2*N+1][2*N+1];
            lo = 1; hi = 2*N-1;
            for (int r=lo 1; r<=hi+1; r++) {
               String line = in.nextLine();
               for (int c=lo 1; c <= hi+1; c++)
```

```
                  if ((r%2==1) && (c%2==1)) M[r][c] = Unvisited;
                  else if (line.substring(c,c+1).equals(" "))
                     M[r][c] = NoWall;
                  else M[r][c] = Wall;
               }
            /* Insert any missing walls. */
               for (int k=lo; k<=hi; k=k+2) {
                  M[lo 1][k] = Wall; M[hi+1][k] = Wall; // top; bottom
                  M[k][lo 1] = Wall; M[k][hi+1] = Wall; // left; right
                  }
            }
         catch (Exception e) {
            System.out.println("Malformed Input");
            System.exit(1);
            }
      /* Rat. Set the rat in the upper left cell facing up. Facing up. */
         r = lo; c = lo; d = 0;
      /* Path. Establish the rat in the upper left cell. */
         move = 1; M[r][c] = move;
      } /* Input */

   /* Output N by N maze, with walls and path. */
   public static void PrintMaze() {
      for (int r = lo; r<=hi+1; r++) {
         for (int c = lo; c<=hi+1; c++) {
            String s;
               if ( M[r][c]==Wall ) s = "#";
               else if (M[r][c]==NoWall || M[r][c]==Unvisited) s = " ";
               else s = M[r][c]+"";
               System.out.print((s+"    ").substring(0,3));
            }
         System.out.println();
         }
      } /* PrintMaze */

   public static void PrintState(String s) {
      System.out.println(s+": "+r+" "+c+" "+d+" "+move);
      PrintMaze();
      }

   /* Return false iff rat's representation invariant is violated. */
   public static boolean isValidRat() {
     if ( r<0 || r>hi || c<0 || c>hi ) return false;
     else if ( d < 0 || d>3 ) return false;
     else if ( M[r][c]!=move ) return false;
     else return true;
     } /* isValidRat */

  /* Return false iff rat reached lower-right cell via an invalid path.*/
  public static boolean isSolution() { return isValidPath(hi,hi); }

  /* Return false iff rat reached cell ⟨p,q⟩ via an invalid path.*/
  public static boolean isValidPath(int r, int c) {
     if ( M[r][c]==Unvisited ) return true; // No claim if Unvisited.
     else {
```

```
      while ( !((r==lo)&&(c==lo)) ) {
         /* Go to any valid predecessor; return false if there is none. */
            int d = 0;
            while ( d<4 && (M[r+deltaR[d]][c+deltaC[d]]==Wall ||
                    M[r+2*deltaR[d]][c+2*deltaC[d]] != M[r][c]-1) ) d++;
               if (d==4) return false;
            r = r+2*deltaR[d]; c = c+2*deltaC[d];
            }
      return true;
      }
   } /* isValidPath */

   /* Create an N by N maze with walls given by the bits of w. */
   public static void GenerateInput(int N, int w) {
      /* Maze. */
         M = new int[2*N+1][2*N+1];
         lo = 1; hi = 2*N 1;
         /* Set boundary walls. */
            for (int i=0; i<=hi+1; i++)
               M[lo 1][i] = M[hi+1][i] = M[i][lo 1] = M[i][hi+1] = Wall;
         /* Set 2*n*(n 1) interior walls to the corresponding bits of w. */
            for (int r=lo; r<=hi; r++)
               for (int c=lo; c<=hi; c++)
                  if ( (r%2==0 && c%2==1)||(r%2==1 && c%2==0) ) {
                     if ( w%2==1) M[r][c] = Wall; else M[r][c] = NoWall;
                     w = w/2;
                     }
      /* Rat. */
         r = lo; c = lo; d = 0;
      /* Path. */
         move = 1; M[r][c] = move;
         } /* GenerateInput */

   } /* MRP */
```

```
/* Rat Running Algorithm. */
class RunMaze {
   /* Input maze, or reject input as malformed. */
   private static void Input() {
      MRP.Input();
      } /* Input */

   /* Compute a direct path through the maze, if one exists. */
   private static void Solve() {
      while ( !MRP.isAtCheese() && !MRP.isAboutToRepeat() )
         if (MRP.isFacingWall()) MRP.TurnClockwise();
         else if (!MRP.isUnvisited()) Retract();
         else {
            MRP.StepForward();
            MRP.TurnCounterClockwise();
            }
      } /* Solve */

   /* Unwind abortive exploration. */
   private static void Retract() {
```

```
      MRP.RecordNeighborAndDirection();
      while ( !MRP.isAtNeighbor() ) {
         MRP.FacePrevious();
         MRP.StepBackward();
         }
      MRP.RestoreDirection();
      MRP.TurnCounterClockwise();
      } /* Retract */

   /* Output the direct path found, or “unreachable” if there is none. */
   private static void Output() {
      if ( !MRP.isAtCheese() ) System.out.println("Unreachable");
      else MRP.PrintMaze();
      } /* Output */

   /* Run a maze given as input, if possible. */
   public static void main() {
      /* Input a maze, or reject the input as malformed. */
         Input();
      /* Compute a direct path through the maze, if one exists. */
         Solve();
      /* Output the direct path found, or “unreachable” if there is none. */
         Output();
      } /* main */

   /* Generate and solve all mazes of size N, and validate paths found. */
   public static void test() {
      int N = 3;
      for (int i=0; i<Math.pow(2,2*N*(N-1)); i++) {
         MRP.GenerateInput(N,i);
         Solve();
         assert MRP.isValidPath(): "internal program error";
         }
      System.out.println( "passed" );
      } /* test */

   } /* RunMaze */
```

APPENDIX VI

Enumerating Rationals

```
/* Pairs. */
class Pair<K,V> {
   protected K key;
   protected V value;
   /* Constructor. */
      public Pair(K k, V v) { key = k; value = v; }
   /* Access. */
      public K getKey()   { return key; }
      public V getValue() { return value; }
  /* Equality. */
      @Override
      public boolean equals(Object q) {
         if (q==null) return false;
         if (q==this) return true;
         if ( !(q instanceof Pair) ) return false;
         Pair qPair = (Pair)q;
         return key.equals(qPair.key) && value.equals(qPair.value);
         }
   /* String representation of this. */
   public String toString() { return "<" + key + "," + value + ">"; }
   } /* Pair<K,V> */
```

```
/* Fractions. */
class Fraction extends Pair<Integer,Integer> {
   /* Constructor */
   public Fraction(int numerator, int denominator) {
      super(numerator, denominator); // Apply the Pair constructor.
      assert denominator!=0: "0 denominator";
      }
   /* Access. */
      public int getNumerator()   { return key; }
      public int getDenominator() { return value; }
   /* String representation of this. */
      @Override
      public String toString() { return key + "/" + value; }
   } /* Fraction */
```

```
/* Rationals. */
class Rational extends Fraction {
   /* Constructor */
   public Rational(int numerator, int denominator) {
      super(numerator, denominator); // Apply the Fraction constructor.
      int g = gcd(numerator,denominator);
      key = numerator/g;
      value = denominator/g;
      }
   /* Euclid's Algorithm. */
      private static int gcd(int x, int y){
      while ( x!=y )
         if ( x>y ) x = x-y;
         else y = y-x;
      return x;
      } /* gcd */
   /* String representation of this. */
   @Override
   public String toString() {
      if ( value==1 ) return key + "";   // this as int
      else return super.toString();      // this as Fraction
      }
   } /* Rationals */
```

```
/* ArrayLists. */
class ArrayList<E> {
   private E A[];     // ArrayList elements are in A[0..size-1].
   private int size;  // The default value is 0.
   /* Utility */
      private void checkBoundExclusive( int k ) {
         if (k>=size) throw new IndexOutOfBoundsException( "≥size" );
         }
      private void checkBoundInclusive( int k ) {
         if (k>size) throw new IndexOutOfBoundsException( ">size" );
         }
   /* Constructors. */
      public ArrayList( int m ) {
         if ( m<0 ) throw new IllegalArgumentException();
         A = (E[]) new Object[m];
         }
      public ArrayList() { this( 20 /* DEFAULT_SIZE */ ); }
   /* Capacity. */
      public void ensureCapacity( int minCapacity) {
         int currentLength = A.length;
         if ( minCapacity > currentLength ) {
            E[] B = (E[]) new Object[Math.max(2*currentLength, minCapacity)];
            for ( int k=0; k<size; k++ ) B[k] = A[k];
            A = B;
            }
         }
   /* Size. */
      public int size() { return size; }
```

```
      public boolean isEmpty() { return size==0; }
   /* Access. */
      public E get(int k) { checkBoundExclusive(k); return A[k]; }
      public E set(int k, E v) {
         checkBoundExclusive(k);
         E old = A[k];
         A[k] = v;
         return old;
         }
   /* Insertion / Deletion. */
      public void add(E v) {
           if ( size==A.length ) ensureCapacity( size+1 );
         A[size] = v; size++;
         }
      public void add(int k, E v) {
         checkBoundInclusive(k);
         if ( size==A.length ) ensureCapacity( size+1 );
         for (int j=size; j>k; j--) A[j] = A[j-1];
         A[k] = v;
         size++;
         }
      public E remove(int k) {
         checkBoundExclusive(k);
         E old = A[k];
         size--;
         for ( int j=0; j<size; j++ ) A[j] = A[j+1];
         return old;
         }
   /* Membership. */
      public int indexOf(Object v) {
         int k = 0;
         while ( (k<size) && !v.equals(A[k]) ) k++;
         if ( k==size ) return -1; else return k;
         }
      public boolean contains(Object v) { return indexOf(v)!=-1; }
   } /* ArrayList */
```

```
/* Unbounded enumeration of positive rationals. */
import java.util.*;
class EumerateRationals {
   /* Output reduced fractions, i.e., unique positive rationals.*/
   public static void main() {
      ArrayList<Rational>  reduced = new ArrayList();
      /* Can substitute: HashSet<Rational> reduced = new HashSet(); */
      int d = 0;
      while ( true ){
         int r = d;
         for ( int c=0; c<d; c++ ) {
            /* Let z be the reduced form of the fraction r/(c+1). */
               Rational z = new Rational(r, (c+1));
            if ( !reduced.contains(z) ) {
               System.out.println( z );
               reduced.add(z);
               }
```

```
         r--;
         }
      d++;
      }
   } /* main */
/* Time the enumeration of 100,000 rationals */
public static void timing() {
   ArrayList<Rational>  reduced = new ArrayList();
   /* Can substitute: HashSet<Rational> reduced = new HashSet(); */
   long startTime = System.currentTimeMillis();
   int rCount = 0; // # of rationals so far.
   int d = 0;
   while ( rCount<100000 ){
      int r = d;
      for ( int c=0; c<d; c++ ) {
         /* Let z be the reduced form of the fraction r/(c+1). */
            Rational z = new Rational(r, c+1);
         if ( !reduced.contains(z) ) {
            /* System.out.println( z ); */
            reduced.add(z);
            rCount++;
            if ( rCount%10000==0 )
               System.out.println(
                  System.currentTimeMillis()-startTime
                  );
            }
         r--;
         }
      d++;
      }
   } /* timing */
} /* EnumerateRationals */
```

APPENDIX VII
Exercises

Exercises reveal your ability to apply the techniques presented in the text, and help you build skills.

Some of the following exercises ask you to compare running times of alternative codes on a computer. Use the standard Java timing function `System.currentTimeMillis` to get the time in milliseconds before and after execution of code:

```
long startTime = System.currentTimeMillis();
   ⟨Code to be timed⟩
long elapsed Time = System.currentTimeMillis()-startTime;
```

Introduction

Exercise 1. Describe the difference between a skilled crafts-person's use of tools, and a novice's use of tools. Draw an analogy with programming, and the facility you hope to acquire.

Exercise 2. What are similarities and differences between the notions of adage, admonition, aphorism, diktat, edict, maxim, moral, motto, precept, principle, rule, saying, and suggestion? Is "precept" the best term for the list in Appendix I?

Exercise 3. What are similarities and differences between the notions of motif, pattern, plan, and template? Is "pattern" the best term for the list in Appendix II?

Exercise 4. The text illustrates asking probing questions about the Running a Maze problem in order to thoroughly understand it before coding. Do likewise for the Ricocheting Bee-Bee problem.

Exercise 5. Forward reasoning and backward reasoning are two approaches to problem solving. Forward reasoning starts at an initial state, and attempts to reach a goal state; backward reasoning starts at the goal state, and attempts to see how one might have gotten there from the initial state. Does backward reasoning offer any advantage for running a maze (even if it does not correspond to what a rat would do)? Geometric symmetry is the property whereby a rigid transformation of a shape leaves it unchanged. List the ways in which a maze is symmetric. Use symmetry to argue that backward reasoning cannot offer any advantage over forward reasoning for solving a maze.

Exercise 6. The text argues for a highly-controlled and methodical style of coding, and advocates for an approach to coding in which you aspire to never take a misstep, and never write code that must be redone. Is this goal realistic, or is it a pompous conceit? Can you make a case for trial-and-error coding, and its possible advantages?

Exercise 7. Can problem analysis be systematic, or is it necessarily a chaotic exploration? One is reminded of the somewhat clawing aphorism: "Tidy desk, tidy mind", to which Einstein apocryphally said [29]: "If a cluttered desk is a sign of a cluttered mind, of what, then, is an empty desk a sign?" What does this suggest about creative exploration?

Exercise 8. Let `n` be an **`int`** variable that contains a positive integer. Implement the following specification:

```
/* Output the sum of the first n odd integers. */
```

For example, if `n` is 1 output 1, if `n` is 2 output 1+3, which is 4, etc. Be sure to analyze the problem before writing the code.

Exercise 9. The text's approach to the Integer Square Root problem involved a key decision: Iterate through the integers, one by one, in sequence:

```
/* Let r be the integer part of the square root of n≥0. */
   int r = 0;
   while ( condition ) r++;
```

Explicitly modeling the code on the expression `Math.floor(Math.sqrt(n))` would have been an alternative approach:

```
/* Let r be the integer part of the square root of n. */
   /* Let float variable root be the square root of n≥0. */
   int r = (int)root; // Let r be the integer part of root.
```

Review the literature on computing square roots, e.g., the Babylonian method [30], and discuss the relative merits of alternative approaches. How does this example inform you about the care you should take on each coding decision?

Prerequisites

Exercise 10. Define each of the concepts and constructs in Chapter 2 in your own words, being as precise and succinct as you can, i.e., treat the chapter's contents as a set of flashcards, and convince yourself that you can define each term.

Exercise 11. Clearly, a good vocabulary is important for communications, but what is the role of vocabulary in thought itself [32]? Is a good vocabulary ever a hindrance?

Exercise 12. Is the following a *syntactically* correct English sentence?

> Colorless green ideas sleep furiously [33].

Each word has a well-defined meaning, but is the whole utterance a *semantically* correct English sentence? Write a program fragment that is similar to the given sentence in terms of its syntactic correctness, and its semantic incoherence.

Exercise 13. Is 2021 even or odd? How did you decide? Which of the following two algorithms did you use?

A: Divide by two and if the remainder is zero, it's even, and otherwise it's odd.
B: If the last digit is 0, 2, 4, 6, or 8, it's even, and otherwise it's odd.

Suppose a value is provided as input data to a computer program. Which algorithm should the program use to determine whether the value is even or odd? Why?

Exercise 14. In Mathematics, a function *f* is a single-valued mapping from a domain Dom to a range Ran. Symbolically, we write *f*: Dom→Ran. A function *f* is applied to *x*, a value in Dom, to produce *f*(*x*), a value in Ran. For example, the square function *sq*:Z→N maps integers in Z to natural numbers in N, e.g., *sq*(2) is 4, and *sq*(-3) is 9.

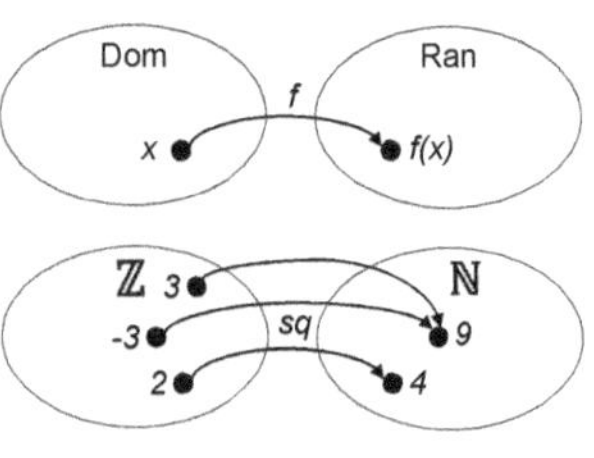

The *graph* of a function *f*: Dom→Ran is the set of ordered pairs:

{ ⟨*d*,*r*⟩ | *d* in Dom and *r* is the unique element in Ran such that *f*(*d*)=*r* }

The graph of a function is called the function *in extension*. If the graph of a function is finite, it can be defined in extension by an explicit enumeration of pairs, e.g., one can define a function by:

{ ⟨0,0 ⟩, ⟨1,1⟩, ⟨2,4⟩, ⟨3,9⟩ }

If the graph of the function is not finite, we may resort to ellipses, e.g., the function *sq* is

{ …, ⟨-3,9⟩, ⟨-2,4⟩, ⟨-1,1⟩, ⟨0,0⟩, ⟨1,1⟩, ⟨2,4⟩, ⟨3,9⟩, … }

but the ellipses are really an appeal to an unstated rule; ellipses say "You know what I mean; apply the rule".

A function that is defined by a *rule* is known as a function *in intension*. For example, the rule $sq(z)=z\times z$ is an intentional definition of the square function. Such a definition is a recipe for how to compute the mapping *sq* applied to a value *z* in ℤ: Multiply *z* times itself.

In Mathematics, the right side of an intentional function definition (the *definiens*) is a closed-form expression, i.e., a finite composition of known operations like +, −, ×, ÷, and exponentiation with rational powers. The language of expressions that are allowed in the definiens is established by convention and context, e.g., algebraic expressions, although the exact set of operations is often implicit.

In Computer Science, functions are defined intentionally using a programming language, e.g., Java or Intel x86 machine code. We use boldface to distinguish between the mathematical function, *f*, and a program that defines the function intentionally, ***f***.

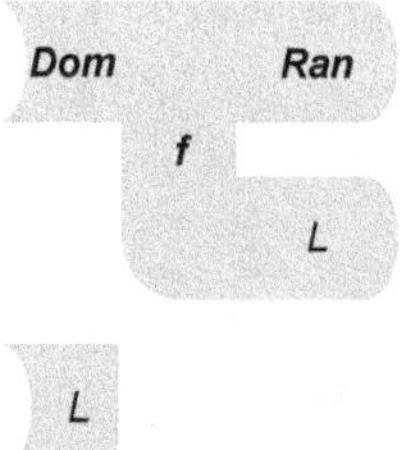

In diagrams [34], we depict three aspects of the program ***f***: its input domain ***Dom***, its output range ***Ran***, and the language in which the program is implemented, *L*, as shown.

In diagrams, we depict a computer that is capable of executing a program implemented in language *L* as a lens-like box whose concave left edge matches the convex lower-right edge of a program implemented in language *L*, as shown.

Execution of program ***f*** by an *L* computer in an environment where the input data is x, and that produces output data $f(x)$ is depicted by composing the diagrams for those entities, as shown:

For a concrete example, let **sq** be the following Java program that squares a numerical input:

```
/* Output the square of input z. */
static void sq() {
   int z = in.nextInt();
   System.out.println(z*z);
   }
```

We depict **sq** running on a Java computer, given input 2, and producing output 4, in the diagram, as shown.[171]

PCs don't understand Java; rather, they understand Intel x86 machine code. Accordingly, our Java program must first be translated to Intel x86 before it can be applied to input 2 on a PC. The program that performs the translation is known as a *compiler*. Paraphrase the diagram shown to the right in your own words.

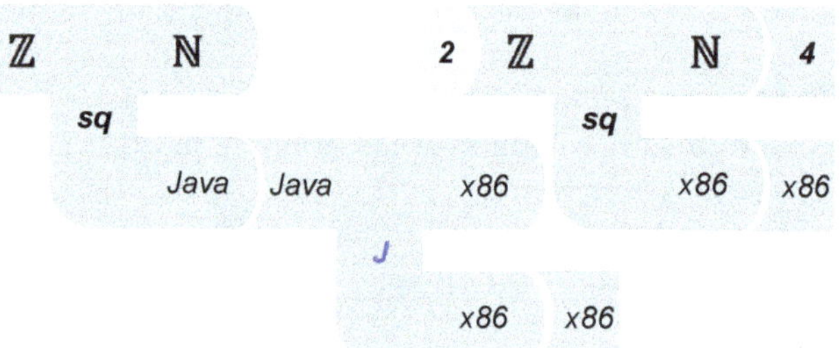

Typically, compilers are written in high-level programming languages, not machine code. Where then did compiler J (that can be executed by an x86 computer) come from? Extend the diagram above to explain your hypothesis.

Exercise 15. Exercise 14 simplifies the story of what a Java compiler really does. Specifically, rather than translating a Java program to machine code (like Intel x86), a Java compiler actually translates to so-called byte codes for a fictitious computer called the Java Virtual Machine (JVM). How then does a program written in JVM byte code get executed on an x86 computer? A byte-code program is "executed" on a real computer by a program called an *interpreter*, which is a program that (while running on an L computer) acts like an L′ computer. An interpreter is said to emulate one computer on another. In the following diagram, the interpreter I is the component that is colored pink.

Paraphrase the following diagram in your own words. Because of its vital role in efficiently executing Java programs (as translated to JVM), the interpreter I is likely to have been implemented in the C programming language. Extend the diagram above to show the lineage of interpreter I (depicted in pink) that runs on an x86 computer.

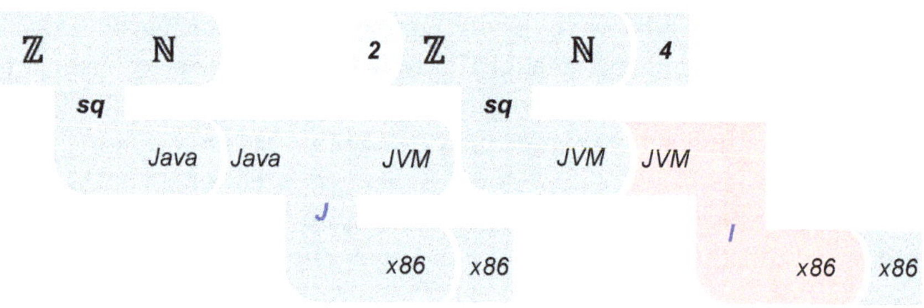

171. We have simplified the discussion by omitting the distinction between mathematical integers and natural numbers (symbolized by ℤ and ℕ), and decimal numerals that may be input into a Java program, converted to 32-bit two's complement binary integers, stored in an **int** variable, squared, and output as a decimal numeral. How do the diagrams change if you make this distinction?

Specifications and Implementations

Exercise 16. What is the difference between the following two specifications?

```
/* Rearrange values of A[0..n-1] into non-decreasing order. */
/* Set A[0..n-1] so that its values are in non-decreasing order. */
```

Write trivial code that implements the second specification literally, but that subverts its obvious intent.

Exercise 17. For each of the following descriptions, write a precise specification:

- Assume that 2-D arrays A and B have the same size. Set the variable `same` to **true**, and then run over A and B in row-major order, and if any ⟨r,c⟩ pair is found such that `A[r][c]!=B[r][c]`, set `same` to **false**, and stop the iteration.
- Are two lines given in slope-intercept form perpendicular?
- Reduce a fraction.
- Factor a number.
- Factor a polynomial of degree 2.

Exercise 18. The United States has a bicameral Congress consisting of a Senate and a House of Representatives. Each of the fifty states has two Senators; thus, there are a hundred Senators, in all. The House consists 435 Representatives apportioned to the states "fairly" based on their respective populations. The following specification is clearly too vague, and is therefore deficient:

```
/* Apportion 435 Representative seats to 50 states fairly. */
```

The following improvement clarifies input-output requirements, but is still deficient because the notion of "fair" remains too vague:

```
/* Given state[0..49], where state[s] is the population of state s, set
   reps[0..49] fairly, where reps[s] is the number of seats apportioned to
   state s. */
```

If fractional politicians were allowed, a precise specification would be simple:

```
/* Given float array state[0..49], where state[s] is the population of state
   s, set float array reps[0..49] s.t. reps[s]==435*state[s]/N, for each
   state s, where N is the total population of the country. */
```

Alas, we are not allowed to dismember politicians. Reflect on fairness in apportionment, and write a specification that corresponds to your notion. See the Internet for notions of fairness that have been used historically [35].

Stepwise Refinement

Exercise 19. Stepwise Refinement is intrinsically associated with top-down programming, i.e., repeatedly refining a specification given "at the top" until no further specifications remain unrefined. What are the strongest arguments you can make for bottom-up, as opposed to top-down, programming, i.e., repeatedly combining program fragments given "at the bottom" until code for the complete problem is obtained?

Exercise 20. In Algebra, you learn to factor expressions using the laws:

$(a^*c)+(b^*c) \Rightarrow (a+b)^*c$ (right Distributive Law)
$(c^*a)+(c^*b) \Rightarrow c^*(a+b)$ (left Distributive Law)

In words, we say: Multiplication distributes over addition. Analogously, in programming, we say: Sequential execution distributes over conditional execution.

State the right and left Distributive Laws for programming. Hint: Think of sequential and conditional execution as expressed by binary operators "`;`" and "**if** *condition* **else**", where given statements S_1 and S_2, statement "S_1 ; S_2" performs one statement after the other, and "S_1 **if** *condition* **else** S_2" performs one statement or the other. In Algebra, both right and left Distributive Laws hold for all *a*, *b*, and *c*. In contrast, in programming, the left Distributive Law has a side condition that restricts its applicability. What is it? Describe the analogue in programming of factoring, and describe how you might use it effectively in the course of Stepwise Refinement?

Exercise 21. "Pump priming" is often required for a hand pump to work: Before you start to pump, you pour a little water into the pump to tighten its seal. What about an Iterative Refinement is analogous to pump priming?

Exercise 22. Chapter 1 developed this code fragment:

```
/* Given n≥0, output the integer part of the square root of n. */
   /* Let r be the integer part of the square root of n≥0. */
      int r = 0;
      while ( (r+1)*(r+1) <= n ) r++;
   System.out.println( r );
```

What are the invariant and variant for its indeterminate-enumeration loop? Chapter 3 (p. 49) introduced **assert**-statements as a way to check that certain required conditions hold during program execution. Define **boolean** method `invariantHolds(r,n)` to complete this modified code:

```
/* Given n≥0, output the integer part of the square root of n. */
   /* Let r be the integer part of the square root of n≥0. */
      int r = 0;
      while ( (r+1)*(r+1) <= n ) {
         assert invariantHolds(r,n): "invariant failure";
         r++;
         }
   assert invariantHolds(r,n): "invariant failure";
   System.out.println( r );
```

Exercise 23. An approach to driving from LA to NYC would travel from capital to capital of adjoining states:

```
/* Drive from LA to NYC. */
   /* Drive from LA to Sacramento. */
   while ( /* not in Albany */ ) {
      /* Let c be the capital of a suitably-chosen adjoining state. */
      /* Drive to c. */
      }
   /* Drive from Albany to NYC. */
```

Define "suitably-chosen" so that the algorithm works. Given your definition, what are the invariant and variant of the loop?

Exercise 24. Consider the following Iterative Refinement:

```
/* Get from Tokyo to NYC. */
   /* Establish INVARIANT: In USA. */
      /* Fly from Tokyo to LA. */
   while ( not in NYC )
      /* Drive one mile closer to Manhattan. */
```

and ponder:

- Does the loop body preserve the INVARIANT?
- Does the loop body necessarily reduce a loop variant on each iteration, or must it be modified to do so?
- What is the set of endpoints in NYC that this algorithm cannot reach?
- What is the effect of under-specification in this code? For example, (a) we don't say exactly where in LA we land; and (b) we don't say how the loop body breaks ties, or whether we must stay on roads.

The answers depend on the specific shape of the USA, but we suggest that you not try to answer accurately. Rather, consider hypothetical USA geographies that illustrate possible answers you are considering.

Exercise 25. The text defines a recursive method:

```
/* Count down from n, and say "BLASTOFF" at zero. */
static void countdown(int n) {
   if ( n==0 ) System.out.println( "BLASTOFF" );
   else { System.out.println( n ); countdown(n-1); }
   }
```

What is the effect on the output of reversing the order of the two statements:

```
{ System.out.println(n); countdown(n-1); }
```

Exercise 26. The Fibonacci sequence is defined to start with two 1s, and thereafter each number in the sequence is the sum of the two previous numbers, e.g., 1, 1, 2, 3, 5, 8, 13, ... The following recursive function hews closely to the definition:

```
/* Return the kth Fibonacci number. */
static int fib( int k ) {
   if ( k<=1 ) return 1;
   else return fib(k-2)+fib(k-1);
   }
```

How many times will the function `fib` be invoked to compute `fib(n)`? Implement `fib` using iteration rather than recursion.

Exercise 27. Euclid's Algorithm sometimes performs multiple consecutive subtractions of the same smaller value from the larger value. Nicomachus observed that these consecutive subtractions can be replaced by computing the remainder (%) of the larger divided by the smaller. Write code for the Nicomachus `gcd` algorithm, and measure its performance advantage over Euclid's Algorithm by comparing their running times for a range of different arguments.

Exercise 28. Write a program that reads input integer n, and tests the correctness of the Collatz Conjecture for all values between 1 and n. The program should be self-protective in the sense that if the test for some integer k would encounter an arithmetic overflow, a warning message is emitted stating that the test is incomplete for k.

Exercise 29. The text states that whether a loop terminates may be not merely unknown, but may be unknowable [13]. Here we consider a related claim: There is no program P that can inspect an arbitrary program s given as input, and determine whether s would terminate or not when given a copy of itself as input text. The proof of this statement is by contradiction, i.e., we show that the existence of program P would lead to logical nonsense.

Suppose there were such a program P. Without loss of generality, it could have this form:

```
static void P( ) {
   Scanner in = new Scanner(System.in);
   String s = in.nextLine();
   /* Let boolean h be true iff s halts when given input s. */
   if ( h ) System.out.println("halts");
   else System.out.println("runs forever");
   }
```

where P assumes that the text of the program s that is to be tested has been placed all on one line in the input data. If P exists, then program P′ (a simple modification of P) would also have to exist:

```
static void P'( ) {
   Scanner in = new Scanner(System.in);
   String s = in.nextLine();
   /* Let boolean h be true iff s halts when given input s. */
   if ( h ) while (true);
   else System.out.println("runs forever");
   }
```

where "**while**(**true**);" is an infinite loop.

Now run program P′ on a copy of itself as input data. What happens? Specifically, does it halt (after printing "runs forever"), or does it run forever, and never print anything?

Exercise 30. In discussing the design of loop variants and invariants, the text discusses the benefits of micro-operations (p. 91). There is an interesting historical parallel in the field of computer design. Recall that a machine-code program iteratively fetches and executes *instructions* from memory (p. 21). In an early period of computers, it was thought that complex instructions were better than simple instructions because this would allow the processor to get more done each time around the fetch-execute loop [36]. Such a computer is termed CISC (Complex Instruction Set Computer). A later innovation took the opposite point of view that less complex instructions are better because this greatly simplifies the hardware that implements instructions [37]. Such a computer is termed RISC (Reduced Instruction Set Computer). Read the history of RISC vs CISC. What do you learn about the design of loops from this analogy?

Online Algorithms

Exercise 31. The Cutting Stock problem is introduced in Exercise 71, where the possibility of distinct online and offline solutions is mentioned. Devise sample input data to illustrate that an offline algorithm may be able to fit more pieces from a given stock than an online algorithm, i.e., that being greedy is sometimes suboptimal.

Exercise 32. The text develops an online algorithm for run encoding whereby `n` occurrences of a repeated value `r` are represented by the pair of values ⟨`r`,`n`⟩. Discuss generalizations of this idea that would find more complicated patterns of repeated occurrences, and represent them compactly. Google "data compression", read articles found, and implement some of the ideas described.

Enumeration Patterns

Exercise 33. Write a program that demonstrates that the largest positive **`int`** value is 2^{31}-1, and that incrementing that number yields -2^{31}.

Exercise 34. Write a program that discovers the largest positive **`int`** value that can be represented (as if you didn't know that it is 2^{31}-1).

Exercise 35. Write a program that inputs two positive integers, each no larger than 2^{31}-1, and outputs their average. Demonstrate that your program works correctly for inputs 2,147,483,645 and 2,147,483,647. These are the third largest positive **`int`** (i.e., 2^{31}-3) and the largest **`int`** (i.e., 2^{31}-1), and their average should be 2,147,483,646.

Exercise 36. Write a program that enumerates all **`int`** values in increasing order, starting at the most negative value.

Exercise 37. Write a program that enumerates all **`int`** values in decreasing order, starting at the most positive value.

Exercise 38. Write a program that inputs positive integer `N`, and outputs a table of `(j-1)%N` and `(j+n-1)%N`, for `j` ranging from `-2*N` to `+2*N`.

Exercise 39. Write a program that inputs a positive integer `N`, and outputs the individual decimal digits of `N` in the reverse order, e.g., given input `12345`, the program outputs `54321`. Hint: This exercise can be thought of as an application of the equation that is central to Horner's Method for polynomial evaluation:

$$a_0+a_1 \cdot x^1+a_2 \cdot x^2+ a_3 \cdot x^3+ \ldots +a^n \cdot x^n = a_0+x \cdot (a_1+x \cdot (a_2+x \cdot (a_3+ \ldots +x \cdot (a_{(n-1)}+x \cdot a_n)\ldots)))$$

You may wonder: What does this have to do with the digits of a decimal numeral? Recall that the meaning of decimal numeral is given by (either side of) the equation above when x is 10. Accordingly, you can code the exercise using integer division ("`/`") and modulus ("`%`").

Exercise 40. Write a program that inputs a positive integer `N`, and outputs the individual decimal digits of `N` in the same order separated by spaces, e.g., given input `12345`, the program outputs the digits: `1 2 3 4 5`. Hint: This is similar to the previous exercise, but the digits must be printed in the same order, not the reverse order. Ironically, this is harder because the individual digits naturally "peel off" from right to left. This is a good opportunity for a recursive procedure, which can be used to reverse orders as execution emerges from recursion.

Exercise 41. A perfect number is a positive integer that is equal to the sum of its divisors, e.g., 6 is perfect because it is equal to 1+2+3. Write a program that inputs a number and outputs whether or not the number is perfect.

Exercise 42. Each stanza (other than the first) of the cumulative song *The Twelve Days of Christmas* builds on the previous stanza [38]:

On the first day of Christmas, my true love sent to me
A partridge in a pear tree.
On the second day of Christmas my true love sent to me
Two turtle doves, and a partridge in a pear tree.
On the third day of Christmas, my true love sent to me
Three French hens, two turtle doves, and a partridge in a pear tree.
Etc.

Write a short program that interprets data provided in arrays, and outputs the song. You may find it useful to know that the code:

```
String[] S = { "first", "second", "third" };
```

declares S to be an array of length 3 containing the text "first", "second", and "third".

Exercise 43. Mathematician Gregor Cantor introduced the notion of the size of an infinite set, defining a *countable set* to be one whose elements can be itemized on numbered lines, i.e., 0, 1, 2, ... All countable sets are said to have the same size. What does the Enumeration of Rationals problem illustrate about the size of $\mathbb{Q}$, the set of rationals?

Exercise 44. Let Σ be a finite alphabet, e.g., $\Sigma = \{a,b,\ldots,z,A,B,\ldots,Z,0,1,\ldots,9\}$. Write a program that enumerates Σ^*, which is defined to be the infinite set of all finite sequences of symbols in Σ. Think of Σ^* as all sequences of length 0, e.g., "", followed by all sequences of length 1, e.g., "a", "b", ..., "9", followed by all sequences of length 2, e.g., "aa", "ab", ..., "a9", "ba", "bb", ..., "b9", ..., "9a", "9b", ..., "99", etc.

Exercise 45. Gregor Cantor proved in 1891 that the size of the set of all mathematical functions f: $\mathbb{N}\rightarrow\mathbb{N}$ is not countable, i.e., that the set of functions that map $\mathbb{N}$ to $\mathbb{N}$ is a fundamentally larger set than the set $\mathbb{N}$ itself [39]. Let Σ be the finite alphabet of symbols that can appear in the text of Java code, and consider **JF**, the subset of Σ^* consisting of all programs of the form:

```
/* Compute f: ℕ→ℕ */
static int F(int x) {
      int y;
      ⟨Program text that assigns f(x) to y.⟩
      return y;
      }
```

Is set **JF** countable? What does this observation say about the ability to compute any possible mathematical function f: $\mathbb{N}\rightarrow\mathbb{N}$? (To dispel any concern about the restriction of `int` variables to 32-bit integers, imagine replacing `int` in the above code template with `BigInteger`, Java's implementation of unboundedly-large integers.)

Sequential Search

Exercise 46. Write a program that uses a library timing function to compare the worst-case efficiency of sequential search with and without sentinels, i.e., study the performance of

```
/* Let k be an index in A[0..n-1] containing v, or n if no v in A. */
   int k = 0; while ( k<n && A[k]!=v ) k++;
```

versus:

```
/* Let k be an index in A[0..n-1] containing v, or n if no v in A. */
   int temp = A[n]; A[n] = v;
   int k = 0; while ( A[k]!=v ) k++;
   A[n] = temp;
   if ( k==n-1 && A[k]!=v ) k=n;
```

Exercise 47. A popular way to write Sequential Search is

```
for (int k=0; k<n; k++) if ( A[k]==v ) break;
```

where the construct **break** terminates execution of the **for**-loop and continues at the next sequential statement thereafter. Add this style of writing Sequential Search into the timing analysis of the previous exercise. How does it compare with the forms studied there?

Exercise 48. The performance of Sequential Search can be improved by moving frequently-sought values earlier in the array. One way to do this is by moving found values earlier, e.g.,

```
/* Given array A[0..n-1], n≥0, and value v, let k be smallest non-
   negative integer s.t. A[k]==v, or let k==n if there are no
   occurrences of v in A. As a side-effect of the search, move a value
   that has been found to be one earlier in array A. */
   int k = 0;
   while ( k<n && A[k]!=v ) k++;
   if ( k<n && k!=0 ) {
      /* Swap A[k-1] and A[k]. */
         int temp = A[k-1]; A[k-1] = A[k]; A[k] = temp;
      k--;
      }
```

Use a library timing function to study the effectiveness of this self-organizing technique. You will have to generate various distributions of search arguments for your study.

Exercise 49. The text implements primality testing for an individual integer p using Sequential Search for the smallest divisor of p greater than 1 (p. 130). The text also implements the Sieve of Eratosthenes, which computes all primes up to n (p. 119). Suppose you know, in advance, the number of individual primality tests that will be executed. Under what circumstance is it advantageous to precompute the Sieve of Eratosthenes, and then replace individual primality tests with table lookups?

Exercise 50. The *mode* of a collection of values is a most-frequent value in the collection. Chapter 5 illustrated various ways to process a collection of grades in the range 0 to 100: print, count, average, max, and frequency distribution. Implement an additional statistic for that application: Mode.

Exercise 51. A *nonempty closed integer interval* is a set of consecutive integers from *lo* to *hi* (inclusive), where *lo*≤*hi*. Call *hi-lo*+1 the *width* of the interval, and generalize the notion of mode (for a finite collection of integers), as follows: A *peak of width w* is the closed integer interval of width *w* that contains the most elements of the collection. Generalize your solution for Exercise 49 so that it outputs the peak grade interval of width *w*, where *w* is provided as a defined constant of the program.

Binary Search

Exercise 52. Chapter 1 used Sequential Search for the Integer Square Root problem (p. 12). Use Binary Search instead.

Exercise 53. The implementation of binary search in the text doesn't bother to check whether the midpoint value is exactly equal to `v`, in which case the iteration could stop. Would this be a worthwhile addition to the code, or not?

Exercise 54. Dictionaries often have a thumb index, i.e., notches along the fore edge of the book labeled A-Z that provide for direct access to the words that begin with the given letter. Would a thumb index associated with an ordered array be a useful innovation, or would it be of little value?

One-Dimensional Array Rearrangements

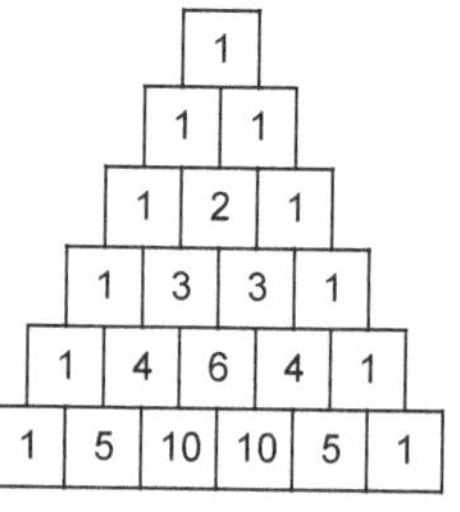

Exercise 55. *Pascal's Triangle* has 1s down the left and right sides, and values in the interior that are the sum of the two values that are diagonally above-left and above-right, e.g., 3 is 1+2. Output `n` rows of Pascal's Triangle using only a one-dimensional array `A`, and updating it *in situ*. Assume `n>0`.

Exercise 56. A *perfect shuffle* of two ordered lists of `n` values alternately interleaves their values. Write a program segment that given `int` arrays `A[0..n-1]` and `B[0..n-1]`, creates `int` array `C[0..2*n-1]` containing the perfect shuffle of `A` and `B`. Performing a perfect shuffle of the left and right halves of a single array `A[0..2*n-1]` *in situ* is far more difficult.

Median

Exercise 57. Implement the worst-case linear-time median algorithm, as described in the text, starting from `QuickSelect`. Specifically, replace the line:

```
int p = /* value of pivot */ ;
```

with code to (a) rearrange values in `A[L..R]` so that the medians of each group of 5 elements are moved to contiguous locations in `A`, and (b) recursively call `QuickSelect` on those medians to find the median of medians, and assign it to `p`. To facilitate the recursive call, you will find it useful to restore `L` and `R` to be parameters of `QuickSelect` rather than as local variables of its body.

Exercise 58. Let $T(n)$ be the running time of the worst-case linear-time median finding algorithm. Show that $T(n)$ is bounded by $c{\cdot}n$, for some constant c, i.e., that the algorithm's running time is really linear in n. Start from the observation that $T(n)$

$\leq$T(n/5)+T(n·7/10)+k·n, for some constant k. In this formula, the term T(n/5) refers to the time to compute the median of medians, the term T(n·7/10) refers to the computation time on the reduced region, and term k·n refers to the time to partition an array of n items [40].

Sorting

Exercise 59. The schematic diagrams for QuickSort and MergeSort presented in Chapter 11 do not show "loop invariants"; in fact, there are no loops in sight. What are the analogues of loop invariants in these methods, and where exactly in the code do they hold? Said another way, if you were to insert **assert**-statements into the code, where would you place them, and what exactly would they assert?

Exercise 60. Write code that given integer `n` initializes array `A[0..n-1]` with a sequence of `n` values that are pessimal for the running time of `QuickSelect` when its pivots are computed as suggested in the text, i.e., as `(A[L]+A[R])/2`.

Exercise 61. Write code that given two arrays, `A[0..n-1]` and `A'[0..n'-1]`, each in non-decreasing order, determines the median of the collection of the `n+n'` values in the two arrays.

Exercise 62. A popular but elementary way to sort an array `A[0..n-1]` is called Bubble Sort:

```
/* Rearrange values of A[0..n-1] into non-decreasing order. */
   boolean done = false;
   while ( !done ) {
      done = true;
      for (int k=0; k<n; k++)
         if ( A[k]>A[k+1] ) {
            done = false;
            /* Swap A[k] and A[k+1] */
               int temp = A[k]; A[k] = A[k+1]; A[k+1] = temp;
            }
      }
```

What are the invariants and variants of its outer and inner loops? What is the worst-case running time of Bubble Sort?

Exercise 63. For which of the sorting algorithms presented in the text (QuickSort, MergeSort, Selection Sort, and Insertion Sort) and in Exercise 62 (Bubble Sort) is the running time linear in `n` when the array `A[0..n-1]` is already in non-decreasing order? Of course, one could always add a special case to any of them; the question is: Which ones don't need a special case to have linear running time when the array is already ordered?

Exercise 64. In section Running time and space (p. 187), the text suggests tail-recursion as a way to limit the depth of recursion in QuickSort. Start with the code for QuickSort given in the text, and implement the suggested tail-recursion.

Exercise 65. In preparation for coding MergeSort in the next exercise, revise Collation (p. 173) following the modified specification:

```
/* Given sections of an array A[j..m-1] and A[m..k-1], each ordered
   separately, create an ordered section of array C[j..k-1] consisting of
   those values. */
```

Exercise 66. Code MergeSort using its description (p. 188) and the previous exercise. You may find it helpful to wait until reading Chapter 12 Collections, where a useful fact about arrays is revealed.

Collections

Exercise 67. The Josephus Problem concerns where to stand in a circle of n people if every k^{th} person will be brutally murdered (and removed from the circle) until there is only one survivor. Write a program to compute where to stand if you want to survive, i.e.,

```
/* Given n people numbered 0 through n-1 and arranged in a circle, and 0<k,
   let s be the number of the survivor after the Josephus procedure. */
```

Might there be a closed-form solution that is parametric in n and k?

Exercise 68. Recall Exercise 28, which tests all integers between 1 and n for the validity of the Collatz Conjecture. Observe that all Collatz sequences that reach the same integer k share a common suffix from that point on. Use this observation, and a bit vector, to speed up the code for Exercise 28.

Exercise 69. In ranked-choice voting, each of v voters rank their preferences for 1 or more of c candidates. The winner is the candidate who first obtains a majority of first-choice votes after repeated elimination from the election of the candidate with the fewest first-choice votes. Design an input format for votes, and implement a program that selects the election winner.

Cellular Automata

Exercise 70. Given an M-by-N **int** array, **int** h, and **int** w, find the upper-leftmost h-by-w rectangle of zeros in A. Restate the requirement if you consider it to be ill-defined.

Exercise 71. A discrete and rectilinear version of the *Cutting Stock* problem is as follows: Given an M-by-N piece of material (the stock), and a list of integer pairs denoting the heights and widths of desired pieces, arrange the pieces so that they can be cut from the stock. It is your choice as to whether to allow 90-degree rotations or not. Read M, N, and the desired heights and widths of pieces from the input, and output the solution as an M-by-N array of piece numbers, and a list of piece numbers for which no placement was found. A greedy (online) algorithm will process the pieces first-come-first-served. An offline algorithm will attempt to do better, perhaps using some heuristic.

Exercise 72. The straightforward implementation of the Game of Life requires M*N steps to update an M-by-N Universe on each generation, regardless of the number of live cells. What if, in addition to the two-dimensional arrays for the Universe, you were to maintain the ⟨row,column⟩ of each live cell in lists `row[0..numberLive-1]` and `column[0..numberLive-1]`? Rewrite method `NextGeneration` so that it requires only `numberLive` steps to update the Universe. Note that if you do this, the running time of the program will be dominated by method `Display`, so the effort will only be worthwhile if you refresh the output occasionally rather than every generation, or if you can similarly speed up `Display`.[172]

Knight's Tour

Exercise 73. The 15-Puzzle arranges numbered tiles in a 4-by-4 grid, with one open space. The goal of the puzzle is to slide tiles one at a time within the confines of the 4-by-4 frame to transform the initial configuration (left) into the final configuration (right). Design a succinct way to represent a proposed solution given as input data. Then, write a program that inputs a proposed solution, and prints whether or not it is correct.

1	2	3	4
5	6	7	8
9	10	11	12
13	14	15	

1	5	9	13
2	6	10	14
3	7	11	15
4	8	12	

Historical Note: Prominent puzzle specialist Sam Loyd claimed (inaccurately) in 1891 to have invented the 15-Puzzle, and was responsible for puzzle mania when he offered $1000 prizes for solutions to various alternative final configurations, which he presumably knew to be impossible [41]. Only half the conceivable final configurations are possible.

Exercise 74. (Hard) You probably can solve the 15-Puzzle (see Exercise 73), which means you know an algorithm to do so, but what exactly is it? Write a program that solves the 15-Puzzle, i.e., that transforms a 4-by-4 array given in the initial configuration into the final configuration by moving tiles one at a time to fill the blank space.

Exercise 75. In the Knight's Tour code, tables `deltaR` and `deltaC` provide a measure of variability that might permit the code to be readily generalized for the other kinds of chess piece. What are the limitations of `deltaR` and `deltaC` for characterizing chess moves, and what additional parameterization(s) would be required to encode the moves of the other kinds of pieces? Why, other than as a mental exercise in data representation, is the idea of generalizing the code for other pieces a fundamentally stupid idea?

Exercise 76. Chapter 15 Running a Maze introduces the technique whereby code that is specific to a particular data representation is encapsulated within a class that provides only abstract data-representation-independent services to its clients. This strategy allows a representation to be changed without affecting the client's code. Restructure the code of `KnightsTour` given in Appendix IV Knight's Tour to employ this technique.

Exercise 77. What fraction of the area of a square is covered by an inscribed circle? Write a program that uses this observation and the Monte Carlo method to compute π, e.g., 3.14159, etc. You may think of this as throwing random darts at such a dartboard, and counting the fraction that land within the bullseye. The text illustrates (p. 231) how to obtain a Java random number generator `rand` by writing:

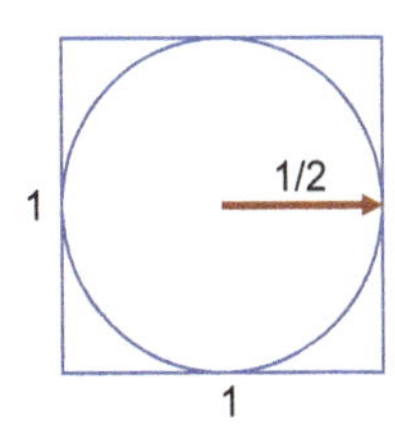


```
Random rand = new Random();
```

after which a sequence of `float` values between 0.0 and 1.0 can be obtained by repeatedly invoking "`rand.nextFloat()`". By the way, this is not a particularly good way to compute π. Compare it to computing π using the formula:

$$\frac{\pi}{4} = 1 - \frac{1}{3} + \frac{1}{5} - \frac{1}{7} + \frac{1}{9} - \frac{1}{11} + \cdots$$

172. The output statements provided in our simple programming language are insufficient for this because they do not provide a mechanism to selectively update characters on the screen.

Running a Maze

Exercise 78. Starting with the code from Chapter 15 for Running a Maze, implement an alternative data representation, and evaluate it compared with the one chosen in the text.

Exercise 79. The self-checking method `isValidPath` presented on page 272 doesn't check for detritus in cells off a valid path. Complete the implementation so that it returns **false** if there are any such "noise" cells in the purported solution.

Exercise 80. Write a program that inputs a positive integer N, and outputs the integers from 1 to N^2 in a two-dimensional clockwise spiral of increasing size that starts centrally, as shown in the diagrams. Thinking of the output as an `N`-by-`N` array `A[0..N-1][0..N-1]`, start with 1 in `A[(N-1)/2][(N-1)/2]`, and first move horizontally. Primes have gray backgrounds in the figures, in support of Exercise 81.

7	8	9	10
6	1	2	11
5	4	3	12
16	15	14	13

21	22	23	24	25
20	7	8	9	10
19	6	1	2	11
18	5	4	3	12
17	16	15	14	13

Exercise 81. It has been observed that if integers are written in a rectangular spiral, then the prime numbers often seem to align along rays emanating from the center. The pattern is approximate, and is not visible in small examples. Combine Exercise 80 and Exercise 48 to demonstrate this effect.

Creative Representations

Exercise 82. The presentation of Tic Tac Toe in the text provides an efficient test for a win by "X" in 1-4 moves. Devise a similar efficient test for a win by "X" in 5 moves, or say why it seems too difficult to do so.

Exercise 83. The solution to the Ricocheting Bee-Bee problem in the text does not address boundary conditions. Modify the code to address them, if necessary.

Exercise 84. (Hard) The text asks: Might there be a closed-form solution to the Ricocheting Bee-Bee problem, i.e., some way to compute the total distance traveled by the bee-bee that does not require iteration? Specifically, is there some way to compute the distance δ by which the bee-bee misses the nearest slit for y=2, and then leverage the regularity of the problem to compute the smallest `y` such that the bee-bee goes through a slit in terms of δ?

Exercise 85. (Hard) Does the Ricocheting Bee-Bee always emerge from the box, or might it go in but never leave? What if the diameter of the bee-bee is zero, and the slit width and gun angle are infinite-precision real numbers?

Exercise 86. Complete the Eight Queens Problem by implementing:

```
/* Given array A[], a permutation of 0, 1, ..., A.length-1, update A to be the
   next permutation in lexicographic order. */
static void NextPermutation(int A[]) { ... }
```

Hint. Let `n` be `A.length`. If `A[j+1..n-1]` is the longest descending suffix of `A[0..n-1]`, and `A[k]` is the smallest value in `A[j+1..n-1]` that is greater than `A[j]`, then the next permutation in lexicographic order can be obtained by swapping `A[j]` and `A[k]`, and then reversing `A[j+1..n-1]`. Don't forget the boundary condition that `j` turns out to be -1.

Exercise 87. (Hard) An interesting aspect of Exercise 86 is that the state of the process whereby permutations are enumerated is characterized entirely by the most recent permutation. This allows `NextPermutation` to be "pumped", i.e., to pick up at that point, and proceed to the next.

Suppose you have a procedure that enumerates all permutations (say, printing them in sequence), but that is not organized for "pumping", e.g., it has extensive state saved in method variables, and outputs the permutations deep within control statements and local-variable scopes (signified here by `...`):

```
/* Print all n! permutations of 0..n-1. */
static void ListAllPermutations(int n) {
   ...
      ...
      /* Print next permutation. */
      ...
   ...
   }
```

How, in general, can you turn such a procedure into one that can be "pumped" for the next permutation in a one-at-a-time fashion?

Graphs and Depth-First Search

Exercise 88. Compare and contrast the solution for Running a Maze in Chapter 15, and the solution given in Chapter 17.

Exercise 89. Write a program that inputs an `N`-by-`N` maze, and outputs the shortest path from the upper-left corner to the lower-right corner, or "Unreachable" if there is no path. Borrow heavily from Chapter 15 and Chapter 17.

Classes and Objects

Exercise 90. Design and implement a class `Rational` that provides arithmetic operations on rational numbers akin to those built into Java for **`int`** values.

Exercise 91. Develop a *unit test* for class `Rational`, i.e., a method named `test` that exercises the class's methods, and demonstrates their correct working behavior. The individual checks are boring; the challenge is to devise a comprehensive collection; typically, only failures are reported. For example:[173]

```
public void test() {
   Rational zero = new Rational(0,1);
   Rational one = new Rational(1,1);
   Rational two = new Rational(2,1);
   if ( !isZero(zero) ) System.out.println( "Test1 fails" );
   if ( !one.equals(add(zero,one)) System.out.println( "Test2 fails" );
   if ( !one.equals(add(one,zero)) System.out.println( "Test3 fails" );
   if ( !two.equals(add(one,one)) System.out.println( "Test4 fails" );
   ...
   } /* test */
```

Testing can only reveal the presence of bugs; it cannot confirm the absence of all bugs.

Unit testing can be *black box*, *gray box*, or *white box*. In black box testing, you know the specification of each of the class's **public** methods, and the representation

173. If `test` is packaged within the class, names do not have to be qualified by `Rational`; if written as client code, then they must be qualified, e.g. `Rational.isZero(...)`.

invariant of each of its **public** variables, but have no knowledge of how the implementation works. Such a test can be written as a client with no access to the class's code. The test is adversarial, and attempts to break the underlying implementation using any of the class's legitimate operations. In gray box testing, you leverage knowledge of the implementation to tailor checks that stress its points of vulnerability, albeit as a client without programmatic access to the internals. A white-box test can inspect and validate the class's **private** data structures.

Exercise 92. Type `Rational`, as defined in Chapter 18, has only a finite number of values because numerators and denominators are type **`int`**. Replace those types with `BigInteger`, Java's arbitrary-precision integers. Consult online Java documentation, as needed [50].

Exercise 93. Implement a class `Polynomial` whose objects are polynomials in one variable (call it `x`) with rational coefficients. Implement appropriate methods for `Polynomial`, e.g., `add`, `sub`, `mult`, `div`, `mod`, as well as operations like `toString`, evaluation at a given value of x, and differentiation.

Exercise 94. Recall the unfortunate explosion of method calls when the kth Fibonacci number is computed using recursion (Exercise 26). *Memoizing* is a general purpose technique whereby, in principle, it is unnecessary to evaluate a function *f* more than once on any given argument. Rather, whenever *f* is computed for an argument x, the pair $\langle x, f(x)\rangle$ is stored in a **static** table for possible reuse. On being called, the method for *f* first looks in the table to see if it has been computed before for the given argument, and if so, the value from the table is returned rather than recomputing it.

Memoizing only works for *pure functions*, i.e., methods that are guaranteed to (a) always return the same value for every invocation on the same argument, and (b) that have no side effects, either on variables outside the function, or on the input/output. The first requirement guarantees that function evaluation only uses the argument(s) provided, and does not depend in any way on the program state at the time the method is invoked. The second requirement is necessary because finding the function value in the table and returning it bypasses any side effects of the original method definition.

Exercise 14 explained the difference between a function *in extension* and a function *in intention*. You can think of memoizing as building an extensional definition of a function (in the table) incrementally as a side effect of demands to evaluate the function on given arguments using its intensional definition, i.e., its code.

Study online documentation for the library datatype `HashMap` [51], and use it to implement a memoized version of function `fib`.

Exercise 95. A limitation of the implementation suggested in the previous exercise is that the `HashMap` will grow without bound. Google for "hashmap as bounded cache", and use what you find to bound the amount of extra memory that *memoizing* uses. (This is really an exercise in learning how to use the Internet to help you program.)

Debugging

Exercise 96. Deliberately introduce a mistake into a program, and contemplate how you would debug the erroneous code from the observed effect. Repeat.

Bibliography

[1] BlueJ, https://www.bluej.org.

[2] Merriam Webster, “Precept”, https://www.merriam-webster.com/dictionary/precept.

[3] R. W. Emerson, “Self-Reliance”, https://www.goodreads.com/quotes/353571-a-foolish-consistency-is-the-hobgoblin-of-little-minds-adored.

[4] B. Hayes, “Gauss’s Day of Reckoning”, https://www.americanscientist.org/article/gausss-day-of-reckoning.

[5] “Arc length”, https://en.wikipedia.org/wiki/Arc_length.

[6] J. Gosling, B. Joy, G. Steele, G. Bracha and A. and Buckley, “The Java Language Specification; Java SE 8 Edition”, 13 02 2015, https://docs.oracle.com/javase/specs/jls/se8/html/index.html.

[7] Python Software Foundation, “The Python Language Reference”, https://docs.python.org/3/reference.

[8] Unicode, https://home.unicode.org.

[9] A. De Morgan, “Siphonaptera”, https://en.wikipedia.org/wiki/Siphonaptera_(poem).

[10] “Division algorithm”, https://en.wikipedia.org/wiki/Division_algorithm.

[11] “Euclidean Algorithm”, https://en.wikipedia.org/wiki/Euclidean_algorithm.

[12] “Collatz Conjecture”, https://en.wikipedia.org/wiki/Collatz_conjecture.

[13] “Halting Problem”, https://en.wikipedia.org/wiki/Halting_problem.

[14] “Sieve of Eratosthenes”, https://en.wikipedia.org/wiki/Sieve_of_Eratosthenes.

[15] “1729 (number)”, https://en.wikipedia.org/wiki/1729_(number).

[16] C.-K. Shene, “An Analysis of Two In-Place Array Rotation Algorithms”, September 1997. https://www.researchgate.net/publication/220458460_An_Analysis_of_Two_In-Place_Array_Rotation_Algorithms.

[17] K. Schwarz, “Randomized Algorithms”, https://web.stanford.edu/class/archive/cs/cs161/cs161.1138/lectures/09/Small09.pdf.

[18] A. Alexandrescu, “Fast Deterministic Selection”, *16th International Symposium on Experimental Algorithms (SEA 2017)*, vol. 24, p. 24:1–24:18, 2017.

[19] Küküllőmenti legényes, “Quick-sort with Hungarian (Küküllőmenti legényes) folk dance”. https://www.youtube.com/watch?v=ywWBy6J5gz8.

[20] AlgoRythmics, “Merge-sort with Transylvanian-saxon (German) folk dance”, https://www.youtube.com/watch?v=XaqR3G_NVoo.

[21] AlgoRythmics, “Select-sort with Gypsy folk dance”, https://www.youtube.com/watch?v=N-s4TPTC8whw.

[22] AlgoRythmics, “Insert-sort with Romanian folk dance”, https://www.youtube.com/watch?v=ROal-U379l3U.

[23] “Cellular Automaton”, https://en.wikipedia.org/wiki/Cellular_automaton.

[24] S. Wolfram, “A New Kind of Science”, https://www.wolframscience.com/nks.

[25] “von Neumann Universal Constructor”, https://en.wikipedia.org/wiki/Von_Neumann_universal_constructor.

[26] “Conway's Game of Life”, https://en.wikipedia.org/wiki/Conway%27s_Game_of_Life.

[27] "Arthur Samuel", https://en.wikipedia.org/wiki/Arthur_Samuel.

[28] "Wheat and the Chessboard Problem", https://en.wikipedia.org/wiki/Wheat_and_chessboard_problem.

[29] Quote Investigator, "If a Cluttered Desk Is a Sign of a Cluttered Mind, We Can't Help Wondering What an Empty Desk Indicates", https://quoteinvestigator.com/2017/09/02/clutter.

[30] "Methods of computing square roots", https://en.wikipedia.org/wiki/Methods_of_computing_square_roots.

[31] "Integer square root", https://en.wikipedia.org/wiki/Integer_square_root.

[32] "Language and Thought", https://en.wikipedia.org/wiki/Language_and_thought.

[33] "Colorless green ideas sleep furiously", https://en.wikipedia.org/wiki/Colorless_green_ideas_sleep_furiously.

[34] J. a. B. P. Wickerson, "Diagrams for Composing Compilers", 21 May 2020, https://johnwickerson.wordpress.com/2020/05/21/diagrams-for-composing-compilers.

[35] US Census Bureau, "About Congressional Apportionment", https://www.census.gov/topics/public-sector/congressional-apportionment/about.html.

[36] "Complex instruction set computer", https://en.wikipedia.org/wiki/Complex_instruction_set_computer.

[37] "Reduced instruction set computer", https://en.wikipedia.org/wiki/Reduced_instruction_set_computer.

[38] "The Twelve Days of Christmas (song)", https://en.wikipedia.org/wiki/The_Twelve_Days_of_Christmas_(song).

[39] "Cantor's diagonal argument", https://en.wikipedia.org/wiki/Cantor%27s_diagonal_argument.

[40] "Median of medians", https://en.wikipedia.org/wiki/Median_of_medians.

[41] "Sam Loyd", https://en.wikipedia.org/wiki/Sam_Loyd.

[42] "P. Erdős", https://en.wikipedia.org/wiki/Collatz_conjecture.

[43] "Geometric Series", https://en.wikipedia.org/wiki/Geometric_series.

[44] "George Bool", https://en.wikipedia.org/wiki/George_Boole.

[45] "John_von_Neumann", https://en.wikipedia.org/wiki/John_von_Neumann.

[46] "Turtles all the way down", https://en.wikipedia.org/wiki/Turtles_all_the_way_down.

[47] "Venus", https://en.wikipedia.org/wiki/Venus.

[48] "von Neumann Architecture", https://en.wikipedia.org/wiki/Von_Neumann_architecture.

[49] "GNU Classpath 0.95", https://developer.classpath.org/doc/.

[50] "BigInteger", https://docs.oracle.com/javase/8/docs/api/java/math/BigInteger.html.

[51] "HashMap", https://docs.oracle.com/javase/8/docs/api/java/util/HashMap.html.

[52] "C/C++", https://learn.microsoft.com/en-us/cpp/c-language/.

[53] "JavaScript", https://developer.mozilla.org/en-US/docs/Web/JavaScript.

Index

Symbols

A

J

K

L

M

N

O

Q

R

S

www.ingramcontent.com/pod-product-compliance
Lightning Source LLC
LaVergne TN
LVHW081656050326
832903LV00026B/1778